The Short Oxford History of the Modern World

General Editor: J. M. Roberts

The Short Oxford History of the Modern World
General Editor: J. M. Roberts

The Crisis of Parliaments: English History 1509–1660
Conrad Russell

The Old European Order 1600–1800
Second Edition
William Doyle

Endurance and Endeavour: Russian History 1812–1992
Fourth Edition
J. N. Westwood

The Limits of Liberty: American History 1607–1980
Maldwyn A. Jones

The British Empire 1558–1995
Second Edition
T. O. Lloyd

Modern India: The Origins of an Asian Democracy
Judith M. Brown

Barricades and Borders: Europe 1800–1914
Robert Gildea

Rebellions and Revolutions: China from the 1800s to the 1980s
Jack Gray

British History 1815–1906
Norman McCord

The European Dynastic States 1494–1660
Richard Bonney

Empire, Welfare State, Europe

His
19

Fifth

T.

Prof
Univ

OXFORD
UNIVERSITY PRESS

OXFORD
UNIVERSITY PRESS

Great Clarendon Street, Oxford OX2 6DP

Oxford University Press is a department of the University of Oxford.
It furthers the University's objective of excellence in research, scholarship,
and education by publishing worldwide in

Oxford New York

Auckland Cape Town Dar es Salaam Hong Kong Karachi Kuala Lumpur
Madrid Melbourne Mexico City Nairobi New Delhi Shanghai Taipei Toronto

With offices in

Argentina Austria Brazil Chile Czech Republic France Greece
Guatemala Hungary Italy Japan South Korea Poland Portugal
Singapore Switzerland Thailand Turkey Ukraine Vietnam

Oxford is a registered trade mark of Oxford University Press
in the UK and in certain other countries

Published in the United States
by Oxford University Press Inc., New York

© Oxford University Press 2002

The moral rights of the author have been asserted

Database right Oxford University Press (maker)

First edition 1970
Second edition 1979
Third edition 1986
Fourth edition 1993
Fifth edition 2002

British Library Cataloguing in Publication Data
Data available

Library of Congress Cataloging in Publication Data
Data available

ISBN 0-19-870067-9   978-0-19-870067-9

3 5 7 9 10 8 6 4 2

Typeset in Minion and Congress Sans
by RefineCatch Limited, Bungay, Suffolk
Printed in Great Britain
on acid-free paper by
Biddles Ltd., King's Lynn, Norfolk

Author's preface

'The age of chivalry is gone. That of sophists, economists and calculators has succeeded, and the glory of [England] is extinguished forever.' Thus Burke, with only one
word changed, might have described the history of the United Kingdom in the twentieth century. It stood in 1900 as the envy of 'less happy breeds', and its inhabitants
were very conscious of this. History could be told as the history of great men, whether
of leading politicians like Gladstone or empire-builders like Cecil Rhodes who, when
asked by Queen Victoria what he had been doing since she last saw him, could reply
quite truthfully: 'I have added 12,000 miles of territories to your dominions.'

Individual heroes can no longer achieve such feats. In the First World War Lloyd
George may have been 'the man who won the war', but in the Second World War
Churchill was the man who saved England from losing the war after a crippling defeat—
the best that the hero could do was to hold back the forces of history and stop their
onward march until better times. And those forces more and more take material form:
millions of tons of steel, billions of pounds in the balance of payments, hundreds of
thousands of soldiers. For a time it was thought that Margaret Thatcher might be a hero
in this mould; historians would now like to take a longer view of her period in office.

These changes, which rob history of the colour and glamour of kings and queens
and heroic charges in battle, are only the reverse of the growth of democracy and of a
greater concern for ordinary people; perhaps it should be added that it is the result of a
greater capacity to make concern for ordinary people into an effective political force.
Building an empire was much easier in the past, when new subjects could be acquired
without much resistance. Lord Rosebery once said that if all the Indians in India spat
at us, we should drown; and in a way this was what happened. The British Empire was
dissolved in a fairly amiable way, without any disastrous wars to try to preserve it,
which showed that its rulers realized that the weight of numbers made it impossible to
continue with the old system.

And the same sort of change has taken place inside the country. The dominance of
the statesman as an example of Carlyle's hero, which was the way that people saw the
late nineteenth-century struggles between Gladstone and Disraeli, has been replaced
by the idea that politicians are servants of the people, required to give the people what
they want. And what do the people want? The simple answer is 'More'. There are signs
that this may not be enough, but even in the simple terms of maximizing the gross
national product the politicians of today are asked to take on a rather harder job than
Gladstone or Disraeli had to face. How can we tell when politicians have done their
job? We can try measuring it, and in the age of economists and calculators the evidence
is available to do so. Statistics can be misleading and tables of figures (including those
at the end of this book) give an appearance of accuracy and certainty that is never
completely justified, but they do provide new sources of information.

In fact there are great masses of evidence for almost everything. Perhaps it is a little
harder to find out about the people at the very top; in the past they used to negotiate
by writing notes to each other, but now that they can talk on the telephone, the
historian finds the evidence is gone. Fortunately the intrigues of politicians seem a

little less important than in the past, they still matter, and they still deserve attention, if only because the actions of the government have so great an effect on the lives of its subjects. As late as 1900 the voters could treat politics as a form of drama in which the politicians put on a variety of plays which were watched and admired or condemned. By 1906 things were already a little different; politicians were trying to send up the price of food (for good and reasonable purposes). And throughout the century the government has been ready to take on new roles, fighting wars on a larger scale than ever before, providing more education, looking after people's health, trying to disentangle the problems of industry.

All these activities of government are documented. And private activity is documented as well. Newspapers tell more than they used to; television tells things that were never told before. The Inland Revenue and the Companies Act find out more about the rich than in the past; sociologists and market researchers find out more by sample surveys about the poor. The brilliant descriptive phrase or the moment of insight can be as important as ever, but in the past historians had to rely on such evidence because there was nothing else. It is still pleasanter (for the writer and for the reader) if the evidence comes in this attractive form, but if the worst comes to the worst the historian can always sit down with an adding machine and work out how much the country imported, or how many people vote Conservative because they think the upper class should rule the country.

This does not mean that historians writing about the twentieth century have a harder job than anyone writing about an earlier period, but it does mean that they have a different job. Historians writing about earlier periods have to search for evidence, and they usually have to work at piecing together an imperfect record to make up a coherent story. The historians of the twentieth century have to make sure that they have found the right materials, but they never run short of things to read; telling a coherent story is just as hard as it is for any other century, because the twentieth-century material comes in large enough quantities to support two or three different and contradictory stories.

The economists and calculators could not flourish in the past; there was no material to support them. And chivalry is an ideal that was always confined to a few people who could afford to have ideals that were denied to the great mass of the population. It would be silly to pretend that the twentieth century is in every way better than those that have gone before, but anyone who has too many regrets for the world we have lost should remember Tom Paine's comment that Burke had pitied the plumage and forgotten the dying bird. The statesman as hero has less freedom of action, both at home and abroad, than he had at the beginning of the century; ordinary people in Britain have distinctly more freedom, political and economic, than they had eighty years ago.

I should like to acknowledge the help of the University of Toronto, who gave me a year's leave of absence in which much of the work for this book was completed. I should like to thank Sheila Hill and Nicholas Faith for their help with the first edition, and to thank Nicholas Faith and my brother Ifan for their comments on Chapter 15, and Dr Hartwell, who kindly allowed me to use in my tables statistical material he had compiled for another book. I should also like to thank John Roberts, the editor of this series, who read the later drafts and carried out the work of editing with tolerance and imagination.

And lastly I should like to dedicate this book to my parents, from whom I have learned a good deal of what I know about the last century.

Contents

1

Time of hope

1906–1911

The Liberals come to power

Sir Henry Campbell-Bannerman, the leader of the Liberal Party, sat waiting at home in his long frock coat and black trousers. Unexpectedly a journalist came in to try and smooth relations between Campbell-Bannerman and Lord Rosebery, the last Liberal leader but one. Sir Henry listened with a curious and characteristic twinkle in his eye, and brushed it aside. 'Within two hours from now I expect to have accepted the King's commission to form a government.'[1]

The royal summons of 4 December 1905 was the end of twenty years of frustration for the Liberal Party, even though the invitation came only because the government was collapsing from internal disagreements. A twenty-year period in which the country had been willing to accept political change had been ended decisively when Gladstone's attempt to pacify Ireland by giving her 'Home Rule'—control over her domestic affairs—had been defeated in 1886. Some Liberals had joined the Conservatives and the combined Unionist forces had held a majority in the Commons for seventeen of the next twenty years. In the general election of 1900 they had a majority of about 130, and though they had lost some by-elections they still had about 100 seats more than the Liberals and their Irish allies in 1905. Campbell-Bannerman's tenure of office might be short-lived, and he would obviously have to hold a general election if he was to win effective power.

He might reasonably have accepted the premiership in the spirit of Lord Melbourne, who was encouraged to take the post seventy years earlier by a friend who said, 'such a position was never held by any Greek or Roman and if it lasts only three months it will be worth while to have been Prime Minister of England'.[2] The Prime Minister had a position worthy of an emperor, for England was the country that other nations wanted to imitate.

They picked out many different aspects for imitation: American plutocrats

---

1. J. A. Spender, *Life, Literature and Politics* (1927), i. 127.
2. Lord David Cecil, *Lord M* (1954), 111.

imitated London society; American reformers wanted their political systems to move towards the British pattern; autocratic rulers in Russia and Turkey found they could not avoid giving their subjects some form of parliamentary institutions; team games like cricket were spreading all over the world from England; Anglo-German relations were made more complicated by Kaiser William II's mixed feelings of love and annoyance about England. The diffusion of British influence throughout the world was owing partly to the fact that Britain had been the first country to become industrialized so that she had more experience of modern conditions, partly to her position of economic and political power all through the nineteenth century, and partly to the stability of her society, which had been free from revolutions and invasions for well over a century.

The British government held the gorgeous East in fee; hundreds of millions of people in India were ruled by a handful of British soldiers and civil servants. The far-flung colonies settled by immigrants from the United Kingdom had control over their internal affairs, but were not seriously considered in the formation of the foreign policy of the British Empire. British territory in Africa had expanded dramatically in the last twenty years of the nineteenth century, placing almost another 100 million subjects under British rule. The latest acquisition, the two Afrikaner republics in South Africa, had been made only after the Boer War (1899–1902) had gone on too long and cost too much, but nobody felt it was to be the last time Britain fought to gain more territory.

Britain was the world's major financial power; the international short-term money market depended on a steady flow of credit based on the pound sterling, and most long-term loans for development in countries outside Europe and the United States were made in London. The country was not the commanding commercial power that it had been fifty years earlier; the United States was already the world's leading industrial nation, and in some ways Germany was ahead of Britain. Industrialists had not been as ready as the Americans and Germans to take an interest in the new developments in steel, chemicals, and electricity.[3] Early in the nineteenth century almost half the world's trade was with Britain; by 1913 the figure had fallen to one-sixth (by the 1970s it had fallen to about 7 per cent). The Royal Navy dominated the seas, but the German army held an equally commanding position on land.

3. Output in 1900 was as follows (m. tons):

	United States	United Kingdom	Germany
steel	13.5	6	8
pig-iron	16.0	8	6

Source: A. J. P. Taylor and J. M. Roberts (eds.), *History of the Twentieth Century* (1968–70), 5, 35.

Even in the 1890s some politicians were worried by the possibility that the United Kingdom would soon be overshadowed by Russia and the United States.

Some of them thought the danger could be met by developing the Empire, though imperial enthusiasm was frothy rather than deep-seated. Oscar Wilde could make his joke about the spendthrift having to choose between 'this world, the next world, and Australia' at a time when imperial sentiment was at its highest pitch.[4] One very attractive feature about empire-building had been that it cost so little; when the Boer War began to cost substantial sums, enthusiasm declined; and the counter-insurgency tactics used in the war, which Campbell-Bannerman had called 'methods of barbarism' because they led to discomfort and death for many women and children, had made imperial expansion look less attractive.

Lord Salisbury, who had been Prime Minister ever since 1885, with two Liberal interludes, was fading from the scene, and on 11 July 1902 he resigned and was succeeded by his nephew Arthur Balfour. New ideas were endangering the unity of the Conservative Party: in three years they destroyed the government and led to Campbell-Bannerman's summons to office. Balfour's own first step was in the field of education. The courts had declared that School Boards were not entitled to run the technical and 'advanced' departments which they had opened to provide something more than the elementary teaching intended by the 1870 Education Act. Balfour's 1902 Education Act dissolved the School Boards and required the county councils to take over their powers and in addition to organize a system of secondary schools.

The county councils took the private grammar schools as the model for their secondary schools, charging relatively high fees (with scholarships for a very talented minority), laying heavy emphasis on Latin and Greek, and rejecting the interest in technical and scientific subjects shown by the 'advanced' departments of the School Boards. The Education Act also dealt with the position of the voluntary schools run by the Churches. The county councils had to levy an education rate and transfer part of it to Church of England and Roman Catholic schools, which enraged Free Church Protestants. Some of them refused to pay their rates as a result, a form of passive resistance, particularly strong in Wales, which showed that something more than ordinary political feelings had been aroused.

Joseph Chamberlain, a Unitarian who had left the Liberals over Home Rule in 1886, was unhappy about the Education Act. However, as Colonial Secretary he was more concerned about the Empire. At Imperial Conferences in 1897 and 1902 the Prime Ministers of the self-governing colonies had argued in favour of Imperial Preference, a system of lower tariffs for goods from other parts of the Empire than from the rest of the world; Britain had got rid of

4. Cecily Cardew in Act II of *The Importance of Being Earnest*, first performed in 1895.

practically all protective tariffs in the 1840s and was devoted to Free Trade, but Chamberlain was not to be held back by old-established arrangements. If Imperial Preference would bring the Empire closer together, and perhaps encourage the self-governing colonies to provide military support for an imperial foreign policy, he would take up Preference.

In September 1903 he resigned from the Cabinet to campaign for 'Tariff Reform', as the Imperial Preference scheme became known. At the same time Balfour squeezed some of the more determined Free Traders out of the Cabinet and committed his party to using tariffs when they would help push foreign countries into giving trading concessions to Britain. Chamberlain's programme aroused a good deal of enthusiasm among convinced Protectionists and believers in the Empire, but did not win new support; Balfour's programme was not easy to understand, and did not hold the party together. The response to the two schemes reflected the personality of the two leaders. Balfour was an aristocrat of immense charm—people often felt after a conversation with him that they had talked unusually brilliantly. Underneath, he was very resolute, and unshakeable once he had decided on a policy. His trouble was that he had little capacity for arousing public enthusiasm, so that his well-balanced policies did not attract followers. Chamberlain was equally resolute, but in his other qualities very different. He could awaken great loyalty, but he could not negotiate with people inclined to be hostile to him and win them to his side—he could only lead his own followers out to the fight.

Chamberlain was trying to deal with genuine problems. Unemployment was nothing new, but it was just beginning to be regarded as an important issue, and the campaign used the slogan 'Tariff Reform means Work for All'. Industries were not reorganizing to face new developments, apparently as a result of inefficiency and lack of enterprise among the industrialists. The government had very few ways of helping the economy, and perhaps a tariff was the best method at its disposal. The Tariff Reformers said that the country's balance of payments was disastrously weak because visible exports amounted to little more than two-thirds the value of visible imports; in 1906, a typical year, it imported £147 million more merchandise than it exported. But this gap was more than covered by what were coming to be known as 'invisible' exports: fees and commissions from shipping, banking, and insurance provided an inflow of £130 million, and dividends from foreign investments made in the past a further £134 million. So there was a surplus of £117 million available for bankers to lend overseas.[5] Some of them made long-term investments, notably in building railways all over the world; others made short-term loans, which meant that if interest rates went up in London they could bring their money back to help borrowers there. Dependence on 'invisible' exports was an unusual way to run an economy, and might be vulnerable

---

5. A. H. Imlah, *Economic Elements in the Pax Britannica* (1958), 75.

in wartime; foreign investment might encourage manufacturers to stick to traditional products because favourable financial terms made it easy for them to find export markets; and London bankers assumed that a surplus for foreign investment would always be available, even when this was no longer the case.

Tariff Reform was an attempt to deal with problems that troubled the country for a long time to come, but the policy was not immediately attractive. Restrictions on trade might hinder the free flow of invisible exports. Almost every British industry imported raw materials, worked them up, and sold the finished product. Chamberlain said that raw materials would come in free of charge under Tariff Reform, but he never managed to define a raw material: sugar refined abroad was dangerous competition for British refiners but refined sugar was raw material for jam manufacturers, and steel plates from overseas were a threat to the steel masters but valuable raw material for shipbuilders. There were supporters of Tariff Reform in some sections of these trades; there were practically none in the cotton textile trade. This industry exported more than any other, and still held the mid-nineteenth-century position of world dominance that other trades were losing. It depended on cheap imports of cotton and upon cheap food to make sure that wage rates were not driven up too far. Most of Lancashire depended for its prosperity on the cotton trade, and although the county was Conservative from Church of England and anti-Irish feeling, it was most unlikely to support a Protectionist Conservative Party.

All over the country Tariff Reformers were handicapped by the fact that the self-governing colonies were exporters of food and could be given worthwhile preferences in the United Kingdom only if imports of food from other countries were taxed. This aroused memories of the Corn Laws; the Liberals issued posters showing the 'big loaf', or standard loaf of the time, and the 'little loaf' of the 1840s, which they said would return to British shops if duties were imposed on foreign wheat to help the self-governing colonies. Many Conservatives were worried by these arguments; Winston Churchill, a Conservative MP since 1900, left his party and joined the Liberals. Less impulsive Conservatives organized for action inside the party.

The Liberals amused themselves by putting down resolutions in favour of Free Trade for debate in the Commons. Balfour avoided the issue with great, almost perverse skill, even leading his entire party out of the House to avoid one division which would have shown how strong the Unionist Free Traders were. He was determined to hold on to office, partly because he hoped the split might heal, but also because he did not want to leave the important issues of the day to another government. To reduce the problems of drunkenness he produced a Licensing Act which gave some compensation to the owners of pubs that were closed down; without compensation, he claimed, no magistrates would be so heartless as to deprive an owner of his livelihood, even if his pub was clearly a centre of disturbance and rowdiness. But the idea of compensation for a licence annoyed temperance supporters, who wanted forfeiture to be imposed as a penalty and did not want to have to pay compensation for all licences if they were able to establish Prohibition.

Balfour's government ended the twenty years of strained relations with France that had begun in 1882 when Britain became the dominant power in Egypt, and had almost boiled over into war when the imperial ambitions of the two countries clashed at Fashoda on the Nile in 1898. In the 1890s the British attitude to Europe had been described as 'splendid isolation'; the first signs of emergence came with the Anglo-Japanese Agreement of 1902, which was designed to protect British interests in eastern Asia. As war between Japan and Russia was likely, the new alliance might easily lead to a war with Russia's ally France. To avoid this danger, Britain and France patched up their relations: France accepted the established position in Egypt in return for British recognition of its claims in Morocco. Apart from this change of policy, the Conservatives wanted to improve the army, which had emerged badly from the Boer War. They did not succeed in this, but Balfour did establish the Committee of Imperial Defence to work out the principles of British grand strategy.

A new political force opposed to the government had been growing in strength since 1900. In 1893 a small group of socialists led by Keir Hardie, a Scottish miner who had been elected in 1892 as an independent labour MP, set up the Independent Labour Party (ILP). Hardie was a good leader for a small missionary group, energetic, always ready to address meetings, and tirelessly devoted to the cause. He was not a good organizer, and fresh talent would be needed for the ILP to grow into a national force. The new party set about trying to persuade the trade union movement to take an interest in its political aspirations. Several union leaders were socialists, but many others were enthusiastic Liberals and a few were Conservatives. The Trades Union Congress (TUC) would probably not have gone into politics to support a socialist programme, but because Liberal constituency organizations very rarely selected working-class candidates except in coal-mining areas, many trade unionists wanted to arrange an effective way to get their point of view heard in Parliament. The Labour Representation Committee (LRC) was set up in 1900 with no commitment more ideological than to secure an increased number of Labour representatives, though its executive committee of seven trade unionists and five representatives of socialist groups like the ILP, the Social Democratic Federation, and the Fabian Society was clearly going to lean strongly to the left. The ILP continued to act as a pressure group, trying to pull the LRC to a more distinctly socialist position.

At first the trade unions took little interest in the body they had helped to launch. But the final appeal in a case over the 'Taff Vale railway' strike led to a verdict in 1902 which, especially when taken with other recent decisions, indicated that a trade union could be obliged to pay out of its funds for all the financial loss caused by a strike. Previously it had been fairly generally believed that union funds were not liable in this sort of case. A large number of unions enrolled in the LRC to get the *Taff Vale* decision reversed. Herbert Gladstone, the Liberal Chief Whip, was alarmed at the thought of a flood of LRC candidates who might draw off working-class votes that would otherwise go to the Liberals. He discussed the question with Ramsay MacDonald, the secretary of the LRC, and they worked out a list of seats in which the Liberals would support LRC candidates. Because the Conservatives had done so well in 1900, this was more a matter of sharing out the seats the allies hoped to gain than of giving up Liberal seats to working-class representatives. Only about two-thirds of the adult male population had the vote, so manual workers were not a dominant section of the electorate and the LRC could not expect many seats. It did not hope to form a government, and was in this way rather like the Home Rule Party, which returned about eighty Members from Ireland to press for greater autonomy.

Taff Vale and the LRC provided a political organization for the working class, but 'Chinese slavery' did the government at least as much harm among ordinary workers who were not very interested in politics. Milner, the talented but politically insensitive High Commissioner in South Africa, believed that the quickest way to get the gold mines of the Witwatersrand running again after the Boer War was to bring in Chinese workers on long-term contracts. The contracts were not slavery, but the Chinese workers were pitied by benevolent Liberals and were disliked by the working class, who thought they were the early stages of a flood of cheap and non-unionized labour.[6] When Jews fled from pogroms in eastern Europe at the beginning of the century, working-class pressure forced the government to pass an Aliens Act reducing the previous freedom of access to the country. The Tariff Reformers claimed that protecting labour by limiting immigration was just the same as protecting industry with a tariff; on the whole the working class was against immigration and was also against tariffs. Some Liberals entered into the spirit of the working-class objections; Lloyd George, who had gained a reputation by his oratory in opposition to the Boer War, asked if they were to have slavery on the hills of Wales. J. A. Hobson in his wide-ranging and influential book *Imperialism* (1902) suggested that British capitalists would intensify their foreign investments in China in order to obtain more cheap labour, which would weaken the economy and increase the risk of imperialist wars.

None of these developments improved the prospects for the Conservatives, and the quarrels inside the party were getting worse. Balfour thought he saw signs that the Liberals were about to disagree among themselves over Home

---

6. Graham Wallas, *Human Nature in Politics* (1908), has a comment on 'Chinese slavery' on pages 107–8.

Rule, and gave his resignation to the King. And so Sir Henry Campbell-Bannerman found himself awaiting his summons to the Palace. Because an election would have to be held immediately, the Liberals were under heavy pressure to present a united front; Asquith, Grey, and Haldane, three active Liberal imperialists, had intended to refuse to serve under Campbell-Bannerman unless he went to the Lords and made Asquith leader in the Commons, but they could not abandon the cause of Liberalism and Free Trade on the eve of an election.

Campbell-Bannerman's Cabinet soon became legendary for its talent. Its social composition was distinctly different from previous Cabinets, which had consisted almost entirely of landowners. The new Cabinet contained a large number of men who had earned their living from the law (Asquith, Haldane, Lloyd George, and later Simon and Isaacs) or from the higher ranks of journalism (Morley, Birrell, Bryce, and later Churchill, and, for a few months, Masterman). It contained Whig aristocrats like Grey and Lord Crewe, and its most striking innovation was that it included a man from the working class, John Burns. The ministers who dominated the government for the next ten years had highly trained intellects; the jobs they held before joining the government had given them relatively little experience of administration, but they showed considerable administrative capacity in office.

This government carried out great changes, but it owed its initial strength to its willingness to stand by old-established Liberal principles. Campbell-Bannerman personified the spirit of improvement to be seen in Gladstone's 1868–74 government, which provided the basic principles of the government of 1906. The position of the unmoving, unyielding Liberals who had stood by the cause in the defeats of 1895 and 1900 was put by Bernard Shaw in his play *John Bull's Other Island*.

BROADBENT. Of course there are some questions which touch the very foundations of morals; and on these I grant you even the closest relationship cannot excuse any compromise or laxity. For example—
DOYLE. [*impatiently*]. For instance, Home Rule, South Africa, Free Trade and putting the Church schools on the Education Rate.[7]

Campbell-Bannerman was a sound party man on the last three issues and was ready to press for the Liberal position to be applied at once. Home Rule, he made it clear, would come on a step-by-step basis, which meant it would not come in the lifetime of the Parliament about to be elected. This reassured Liberal Unionists that they could vote Liberal against Protection without any immediate fear of Home Rule.

The Liberal majority was overwhelming. The government had to decide what to do with its success. The Liberals in 1906 had not asked for a

7. Act I of *John Bull's Other Island*, first performed in 1904.

clear statement of public support for a single proposal like Gladstone's Disestablishment of the Irish Church in 1868.

	Votes	Seats	% of all votes cast
Conservative	2,451,454	157	43.6
Liberal	2,757,883	400	49.0
Labour	329,748	30	5.9
Irish Home Rule	35,031	83	0.6[a]

Sources: [a] These figures, and the figures for subsequent general elections, are from David Butler and Gareth Butler, *British Political Facts 1900–2000* (2000), 233–9, supplemented by *The Times House of Commons*, produced after each election. Irish Home Rule candidates were usually returned unopposed.

External problems

In foreign policy the government had begun to take up a position before the election. The German government had been bullying the French over Moroccan issues in the Algeciras Conference; the settlement of colonial issues between Britain and France had developed into a revival of the *entente cordiale* of the 1850s, but this meant the country would be to some extent committed to France's side against Germany. Grey, who had just been appointed Foreign Secretary, promised support to France, and by initiating military talks he brought the two countries closer than before. He told Campbell-Bannerman, Asquith, and Haldane about this, but did not tell the rest of the Cabinet when it reassembled after the election. According to Lloyd George, foreign policy was not discussed in the Cabinet, and Grey and Asquith waved diplomatic problems aside as though they were too delicate for so large a body.[8] The picture of Lloyd George, soon joined in the Cabinet by Churchill, being silenced in this way is pleasant, but not convincing. Members of the Cabinet were told some technical details of war preparation, but may have forgotten them simply because they were technical. A full-dress discussion of the topic might have been uncomfortable, because ministers would be to some extent committed by it; if they left the subject alone, they might never have to face it.

The enemies of secret diplomacy were not entirely justified in saying, after 1918, that Grey had deceived the Cabinet or deliberately left it in ignorance of his intentions. Haldane, the Secretary of State for War, had reorganized the army in a way that showed quite clearly the direction in which British foreign

8. D. Lloyd George, *War Memoirs* (1933), 46–51.

policy was moving. His predecessors had tried to reform the army without knowing what sort of war it would be required to take part in. All that they knew was that Cardwell's army, which had proved satisfactory in small-scale colonial wars, had not met the needs of the Boer War. Haldane was certain that the country needed an army that could cross the Channel and take part in a European war. Granted this assumption, all the rest followed: there were to be six divisions ready to go overseas and a second line of defence, the Territorials, to defend the country against any troops that might be put on shore by an enemy that had managed to evade the Navy. Haldane's objective was clear-cut: 'We should have an expeditionary force sufficient in size and also in rapidity of mobilising power to be able to go to the assistance of the French Army in the event of an attack on the Northern or North-Eastern parts of France.'[9] He reorganized the army accordingly, a step which implied a clearly defined attitude to foreign affairs. It is not clear why the Cabinet never examined his assumptions.

The other serious overseas problem facing the government was South Africa. The Treaty of Vereeniging, which brought the Boer War to an end in June 1902, had laid down that the Dutch republics would become self-governing colonies in due course, and that the native population would not be enfranchised before self-government. The British found the Boers hard to defeat and were in no position to insist on enfranchisement. As only 65 per cent of adult males had the vote in the United Kingdom, the South African system that enfranchised only 25 per cent did not look so bad, though the British no doubt expected that twentieth-century South Africa would undertake the gradual extension of the franchise that had taken place in the United Kingdom in the nineteenth century. The Conservatives had set up a constitution of the type that had existed in Canada in 1839 when Lord Durham wrote his Report pointing out the disadvantages of having elected representatives but leaving control of the executive in the hands of the Colonial Office; Campbell-Bannerman saw no point in delaying self-government as it was coming in any case and no great changes could be made before it arrived. He had probably decided to act before he saw Smuts, the representative of the Transvaal Afrikaners, but in any case it was after their interview that he announced that the ex-republics would become self-governing as soon as could be arranged. In terms of the next thirty or forty years, this was a very successful move: the Afrikaners were a majority of the white, politically effective population of South Africa and they remained a majority despite the efforts of men like Milner to bring out British settlers, and the policy of Kitchener at Vereeniging and Campbell-Bannerman in 1907 attached a section of the Afrikaners, led by Botha and Smuts, to British

---

9. R. B. Haldane, *An Autobiography* (1929), 187.

interests long enough to commit South Africa to Britain's side in the two world wars.[10]

In 1907 the Liberals faced a conference in London of the Prime Ministers of the self-governing colonies—Canada, Australia, New Zealand, Newfoundland, and the four provinces that were soon to be united in the Union of South Africa. In his enthusiasm for imperial union Chamberlain had wanted to find out what sort of connection would be acceptable, and had gone on to advocate the colonies' idea of the way the Empire should be linked together. Voters in Britain had shown their opinion of the idea in 1906, but the Liberals had to explain their attitude to the colonial premiers, who were unanimous for Imperial Preference. As a gesture of recognition, the self-governing colonies were to be called Dominions, but nothing was done in response to the suggestion of Deakin of Australia that institutions should be set up that might lead towards the creation of an imperial federation.

British interest in imperial expansion had been replaced by a feeling of uneasiness about German policy. In 1898 the German government had begun to build a navy which, while not as large as the British, nevertheless looked like being big enough to be embarrassing. The essential diplomatic point was put, in an undiplomatic way, by Churchill some years later: a fleet was for Germany something of a luxury and for Britain a necessity.[11] Germany would suffer no immediate harm without a powerful navy, but Britain depended on imports so much that her whole international position would change if she ceased to be dominant at sea. German shipbuilding made Britain build as well, and made the British worry about Germany. Haldane's estimate that the army ought to be ready to resist a German invasion of France was a calculation of strategic probabilities, but officials at the Foreign Office and the Admiralty, such as Eyre Crowe and Admiral Fisher, came much closer to emotional anti-Germanism. The sentiment was quite understandable, and it did not show itself in so obvious and vulgar a form as German anti-English feeling, but in the years before 1914 the British did come to feel that, while war was not inevitable, any war that came would be against Germany.

Liberal legislation and the people's budget

Many of the newly elected Liberal Members were less interested in the naval race than in poverty and unemployment. The surveys on the conditions of the poor drawn up by Booth and Rowntree had awakened interest, and in books

10. Left-wing Liberals and members of the Labour Party protested at the flimsy guarantees for African rights contained in the South African Act of Union of 1910 but, unless it was willing to fight another war in which British and Afrikaner settlers would have fought together against British intervention, there was nothing the government could have done.

11. The word 'luxury' (translated *Luxus*, which has a pejorative meaning) was taken as an insult in Germany (W. S. Churchill, *The World Crisis* (1923), i. 101).

like *The Heart of the Empire*[12] young Liberals had argued that people should worry about social conditions in Britain as well as the problems of Empire. The Liberals had wanted to amend the *Taff Vale* decision by making some complicated changes in the law of agency that would have given trade unions some protection, but Campbell-Bannerman decided to accept the proposals put forward by the Labour Party (as the LRC chose to be called after the election) for reversing the *Taff Vale* decision by freeing trade unions from practically all risk of legal action. This simplified the legislation, and kept the Labour Party closely linked to the Liberals. Balfour thought it unwise to oppose the Trade Disputes Bill, and the House of Lords, made up almost entirely of hereditary peers with a few judges and bishops, was much more concerned with questions about land than industrial matters, so it passed into law easily.

If Labour deserved its reward, so did the Free Churches. The 1906 Education Bill was exclusively concerned with the religious organization of schools: all schools that received any help from the rates were put under the county councils, who were to provide facilities for religious education and, to make sure that teachers were appointed on the basis of teaching ability rather than their religious affiliation, no full-time teachers were to give religious education. In the Lords the Bill was amended out of recognition, and was then laid aside, so Balfour could claim some success for his assertion that 'the great Unionist party should still control, whether in power or opposition, the destinies of this great Empire'.[13] The Liberals seemed to have no idea what to do next; in 1907 no substantial legislation was put forward and, for the last time but one, Parliament had no autumn session. The great Liberal majority had been elected for better things than this, and Campbell-Bannerman spoke of coming to a conflict with the Lords. Before this could happen he retired, on 5 April 1908, and died a fortnight later. He had held his party together at a very difficult time during the Boer War; his two immediate successors in the Liberal leadership, Asquith and Lloyd George, were abler and certainly more brilliant men, but after a quarter-century of their leadership the party was shattered beyond repair.

Asquith's emergence as Prime Minister in 1908 was inevitable. He was a fine if rather formal speaker and, while he was a quick-witted debater, he also had the ability to see the long-term implications of a policy. He was not very original in his thinking, and in fact he seems not to have enjoyed thinking about politics any more than was strictly necessary, but this presented no problem as long as he could find ministers with original minds for his Cabinet. And in this he was well provided for; he brought forward two radical Little Englanders, making Lloyd George Chancellor of the Exchequer and

12. G. P. Gooch, G. M. Trevelyan, *et al.*, *The Heart of the Empire* (1901).
13. Randolph Churchill, *Winston S. Churchill* (1967), ii. 316.

putting Churchill in the Cabinet as President of the Board of Trade. They were young and active, and were looking for ways to distinguish themselves: the government soon began to find that social reform provided the positive reason for existence which had almost disappeared.

The Liberals still had to pay off their obligations to their Free Church supporters and an Education Bill and a Bill revising Balfour's 1904 Licensing Act were brought forward in 1908. Both Bills were killed in the Lords. Clearly these defeats were serious. Defeatism among Liberals who saw themselves helpless before the Lords was said to have caused the government's losses in by-elections in 1908. The voters were probably affected by the depression of trade, and a recovery of trade might have restored the government's position, but at the time the morale of its supporters was low. There had, however, been some hints of the social legislation which was to establish the fame of the government, even before the period of intense activity that began with the budget of 1909.

Asquith had already begun to use the budget as an instrument of social change. At that time income tax was paid by the most prosperous 10 per cent of the population, who earned over £160 a year. His 1907 budget drew a distinction between earned and unearned incomes, and cut the tax from 5 per cent to 3.75 per cent on earned incomes below £2,000 a year. The vast majority of income taxpayers would benefit from the cut, and probably the very rich and the receivers of unearned income from rent, interest, and dividends were Conservatives while relatively prosperous people working for a living were Liberals.

Although he had just become Prime Minister, Asquith introduced the 1908 budget himself, as it contained the proposals for old-age pensions that he had been working out. Pensions of 5s. a week (25p in present-day money),[14] starting at 70, were given as a right to old people, who were freed from the fear of being made to go into the workhouse.[15] After it had been introduced, Lloyd George took charge of the budget and administered the pension scheme. Some of its popularity rubbed off on him. ' "God bless that Lord George (for [the pensioners] could not believe that one so powerful and munificent could be a plain 'Mr.') and God bless *you*, miss!" and there were flowers from their gardens and apples from their trees for the girl who merely handed them the money.'[16]

Another, smaller but still significant piece of legislation in 1908 established an eight-hour working day for miners. This was the first time Parliament had

14. See Note on Statistical Evidence on pp. 499–500, which explains about currency changes and cost-of-living figures.

15. The 1834 Poor Law required all people who needed government assistance to go into a workhouse to receive it, and required workhouse conditions to be 'less eligible' (i.e. more unpleasant) than an unskilled labourer's standard of living.

16. Flora Thompson, *Lark Rise* (1939), 100, quoted in E. H. Phelps Brown, *The Growth of British Industrial Relations* (1959), 305.

been ready to limit the working hours of adult males. Nineteenth-century factory Acts had in theory limited the working day for women and children, on the grounds that they were weak and needed more protection than men, though of course in practice the Acts limited men's working hours as well. Because the 1842 Act had kept women and children out of the mines, miners' hours had been unregulated. If the government was going to legislate for adult men, where would it stop? When Churchill was asked why the government had confined itself to legislating for the mines, he said he saw no reason for not going further. The tide of social reform was beginning to flow.

The Boer War had encouraged the rising interest in social reform by convincing people that an unhealthy and poverty-afflicted nation was militarily weak. People were more concerned about the unemployed in the slowing-down of trade that helped launch the Tariff Reform movement than in previous recessions: the slogan 'Tariff Reform means Work for All' had shown that some politicians had gone beyond thinking that the unemployed were idle fellows who could find a job if they set their minds to it, and had realized that men out of work were suffering from the effects of the 'free play of the market'.

On his last day in office Balfour set up a Royal Commission on the Poor Law, under the chairmanship of Lord George Hamilton, with Beatrice Webb as one of the members. The Poor Law was in theory still the legislation of 1834, designed to be unpleasant enough to stop anybody asking for help who was not on the verge of starvation, and the privately run Charity Organization Society—which appears to have taken 'cold as charity' as its motto—still supported the principles of 1834. The Local Government Board, the government department which tried to coordinate the policy of the municipal authorities, was more merciful; for instance, in 1900 it issued instructions that people who wanted help simply because they were too old to work should be given grants on which they could live at home rather than being forced to come into workhouses. The more humane municipalities already took this approach, and the Board was only extending the practice to the whole country.

Because the old-age pensions of 1908 were granted as a right, rather than as something for which the elderly poor had to make a special request, many more people applied for them than had asked for poor relief previously. The reputation of the Poor Law had kept people away and stopped them asking for help. John Burns, the President of the Local Government Board from 1906 to 1914, is often said to have missed a great chance to take the lead in social reform. Undoubtedly his attitude was surprisingly conservative for a man who had been a radical trade union leader in the 1890s, and the officials of his department did nothing to make him more active, but the Local Government Board was not a good place from which to launch great changes. From the first very rudimentary social legislation of the sixteenth century onwards, responsibility had always lain with local authorities: parishes, Poor Law Unions, municipalities. However, changes had always been in the direction of greater centralization, and almost all twentieth-century social legislation has involved transferring services to the central government.

The establishment in 1908 of labour exchanges, where men looking for work and employers looking for men could register their requirements to get in touch with each other, was almost inevitably a matter for the central government. Making the labour force better informed could not have upset the most laissez-faire of Liberals; in fact the leading negotiator in labour disputes of the day, G. R. Askwith, later complained that the exchanges made it too easy for employers to return to the nineteenth-century notion of a reserve army of unemployed. At the time, however, they were accepted as a useful innovation. Trade Boards, set up the next year as official bodies to investigate the 'sweated industries' and lay down minimum wages, were more of a departure from laissez-faire; apart from the simple humanitarian arguments, it was pointed out that in these industries the workers were so downtrodden that they could not form trade unions to defend themselves, and employers who wanted to pay a decent wage would be undercut if the Boards were not set up.

In 1909 the Commission on the Poor Law presented a Majority and a Minority Report. Both Reports said that the system of Boards of Guardians to run the Poor Law should end; the majority wanted the duties of the Guardians handed to the municipal and county councils but the minority wanted 'the break-up of the Poor Law', by which they meant that the different categories of people asking for help—old, ill, unemployed, widowed, orphaned—would be assisted by separate and specialized agencies.

Over the next fifty years one function after another was transferred from the Guardians to municipal and county councils, but this turned out to be only a transition to direction by the central government. It took over one section of the welfare services after another, usually in schemes financed to some extent by insurance payments, though in some cases it left day-to-day administration to local councils. In this piecemeal way most of the programme suggested by the Minority Report was turned into law. By the time of her death in 1944 Beatrice Webb, who had done a great deal of the work on the Minority Report, had triumphed over the principles of 1834 and of the Majority Report, though she would have been disappointed at how little of the training and rehabilitation for which she had hoped was carried out in practice.

Asquith's budgets had depended to some extent on economies at the War Office and the Admiralty. By 1908 the period of easy budgeting was coming to an end. The trade depression reduced revenue, and early in 1909 the Admiralty claimed that it needed another six battleships to be sure of retaining command of the sea. The Lloyd George–Churchill wing of the Cabinet said the Exchequer could only provide four, and eventually the Cabinet reached an apparently acceptable compromise by agreeing to build four immediately, with a commitment to build another four in the very near future. However, the Admiralty was equal to the situation. Fisher, the First Sea Lord, provided the Conservative journalist Garvin with all the information needed to launch a strong campaign in favour of eight ships immediately—hence the slogan 'We want eight and we won't wait'. Garvin's success was fatal to his party; he had pressed for higher naval expenditure in the belief that it could not be paid for except by tariffs, and he gained such prestige in the naval agitation that he was allowed to lead the party into extreme courses that did it no good. His success on the naval issue pushed the Liberals into producing a bold budget in 1909 that revived the fortunes of the government; the Conservative reaction to this budget was so ill judged that it forfeited the powers of the House of Lords in 1911, and in their attempt to save the House of Lords the Opposition announced that they would not introduce tariffs until they had been approved by a referendum, which was a polite way of saying 'Never'.

Lloyd George's budget was intended to increase the government's revenue by about 8 per cent—from £148 million to £160 million—and to provide the basis for future increases. The income tax, which had previously been graduated only by remissions for incomes between £160 and £700, was now graduated at the top by means of a supertax, so that incomes above £2,000 paid more. The tobacco duties were increased. So were the alcohol duties, which gratified the temperance Liberals, who had been frustrated by the Lords' rejection of the Licensing Bill, but annoyed the Irish, who voted against the budget as a result. Motor vehicles were taxed, and the receipts were reserved for a Road Fund. In addition, taxes were imposed on landowners, with the tactical advantage that an attack on landowners was a good way to hold together an alliance of employers and employees, as Joseph Chamberlain had shown in 1885. The main tax on land was a form of capital gains tax, levied on resale at 20 per cent and on new leases at 10 per cent. Like any other capital gains tax it was expected to take some years to become fully productive. There was also a tax on land that was lying idle and not being used for farming or building or mining. The form-filling caused by this tax was an extra irritant to landlords.

The budget itself was sweeping and even provocative, though there is no evidence that it was intended to sting the Lords into rejection. Lloyd George's budget speech was long and uncharacteristically dull, and in the months of parliamentary debate that followed, running from the end of April until early November with only a week or two of recess, he was polite and businesslike. In the Commons his job was to get the budget through; in public speeches he had to rouse the Liberals by showing that their cause was righteous and would prevail. He did both jobs well, and if his speeches annoyed the House of Lords, that was an additional advantage. His speech at Limehouse on 30 July was regarded as very fierce, though in fact it was all in the normal language of party speeches from the platform. Most of it was concerned with the sharp increases in land prices; the section that was considered most inflammatory dealt with the Duke of Westminster's renewal of the lease to Gorringe's Stores, which was built on his land. The terms included a £50,000 fine on renewal and gave the Duke a veto on any building put up on the land leased; Lloyd George said 'it is not business, it is blackmail'. This was not polite, and Lloyd George did not really understand the leasehold system, but the Lords responded far too violently for their own good. If they were going to attack the budget, they would have been prudent to keep cool, but they were not accustomed to being attacked, much less to being laughed at. So the Duke of Beaufort said he wanted to see Lloyd George and Churchill in the middle of 'twenty couple of doghounds', and the Duke of Buccleuch announced he was going to save a guinea by giving up his subscription to the local football club. The Dukes seemed eager to prove Lloyd George was right in calling them 'a class that declined to do the duty that it was called on to perform'.

The budget passed the Commons at the beginning of November. The Lords could not amend the budget but in theory they could reject it. Constitutional experts did not agree whether theory could legitimately be translated into practice,[17] but the Lords had tasted blood; ignoring the fact that rejections of previous legislation had been successful only because they had picked out unpopular Bills, or perhaps assuming—entirely incorrectly—that the budget was unpopular, they prepared to defeat it. Lord Milner told them to reject the budget and damn the consequences; they followed him all too enthusiastically. Lloyd George, Churchill, and their closest allies would have welcomed rejection, but they did nothing to provoke it by teasing Balfour or taunting the Lords with their helplessness, perhaps because they knew how little their Cabinet colleagues would like such a step.

By November the official Conservative leaders, Balfour and Lord Lansdowne, would have had great difficulty restraining their followers even if they had tried. The budget was thrown out in the Lords. Lloyd George, as if aware that the time had come for a more solemn approach, withdrew to devise new measures of social welfare and left the work of constitutional rebuke to Asquith. On 2 December the Prime Minister moved a resolution which declared that the Lords had no right to touch a Bill concerned with taxation, and announced that there would be a general election.

The two elections of 1910 and the House of Lords

The resolution had of course no legal effect. It was part of the Liberal election programme, along with the controversial budget itself. The Lords had forced the government to dissolve Parliament, if only because no taxes had been

17. Erskine May (cont. F. Holland), *Constitutional History of England* (1912), iii. 358, on the constitutional experts.

voted, and if the government won the election and simply passed the budget into law it would be conceding the Lords' claim to force an election any time they chose. By the time of the first election Asquith knew he would have to win a second general election before he could expect a royal promise to create the additional peers that might be needed to reduce the power of the House of Lords. Asquith was a very far-sighted political tactician and acted very skilfully between late 1909 and the summer of 1911; he had probably seen just how far he would have to go, and could concentrate on advancing along the line he had chosen.

He had first to win his election in January 1910. The Conservatives said the result simply meant that the budget had been approved. The Liberal and Labour Parties said it also meant that the Lords should lose their power to reject legislation. The Irish said it meant the Lords should lose their powers and a Home Rule Bill should be passed. Asquith knew his Labour allies would stand by him, though the decision in the *Osborne* case, in December 1909, that trade unions were not entitled to spend their funds on political activity, made it necessary to amend trade union law again.

The Irish had voted against the budget because they disliked the taxes on spirits. Their hope of getting Home Rule through parliamentary success depended on finding an occasion when the two large parties were equally balanced; it was partly because they had not been equally balanced since 1895 that the measure had almost dropped out of sight. Now it revived, and its prospects seemed better than before because the Liberals were about to destroy the Lords' power to reject a Home Rule Bill.

	Votes	Seats	% of all votes cast
Conservative	3,127,887	273	46.9
Liberal	2,880,581	275	43.2
Labour	511,392	40	7.7
Irish Home Rule	124,586	82	1.9

Redmond, the Irish leader, was so eager to break the Lords' veto that he wanted Asquith to amend their powers before reintroducing and passing the 1909 budget; Asquith was determined to pass the budget first, and was ready to resign if Redmond insisted on the point. Further enquiry showed that Redmond really only wanted to be sure that Asquith was in earnest about attacking the Lords. Asquith had no doubts on the issue; some people played about with schemes to change the membership of the Upper House, but he defined his position on 21 March in three resolutions which in brief declared that:

The Lords were not allowed to touch a Bill if the Speaker said it was a Money Bill.

A Bill passed by the Commons in three successive Sessions would pass into law whether the Lords consented or not.

The length of a Parliament should be shortened from seven years to five.

The debates on these resolutions convinced the Irish that Asquith was in earnest, and after this the Liberal majority was safe. The 1909 budget was put quickly through the Commons, and was accepted by the Lords. It remained to be seen whether the Parliament Bill, enacting the three resolutions, would go through with anything like the same ease.

The Lords, who had been sure they could judge which legislation should be returned to the electorate, showed signs of self-doubt and debated possible reforms of their membership. The party leaders began to be afraid that things were slipping out of control, and when Edward VII died unexpectedly on 6 May 1910 they decided to try to reach a peaceful compromise. For six months the whole issue was left in the hands of a committee of four Liberal and four Conservative leaders. Home Rule was the real point of division; the Liberals seem to have conceded that the first time the Lords rejected it there should be a general election, but they wanted the Commons to be able to pass it eventually. The Conservatives wanted the Lords to be able to demand a referendum on legislation affecting the Constitution, which would include Home Rule. It was also suggested that a joint sitting of the Commons and a section of a modified House of Lords should decide on disputed legislation, which probably meant that a Liberal government would not be able to pass its Bills if its majority in the Commons was under fifty.

Lloyd George, who was always happiest when he could make agreements and get something done, suggested a coalition government that could reach a compromise on Ireland and on other issues as well. On Ireland the compromise was bound to move towards the Liberal policy, but on issues like tariffs or compulsory military training any compromise involved a change in the direction favoured by the Conservatives. Several of the party leaders in the committee and outside were interested in the proposals, but Conservative backbench opinion was distinctly hostile. The parties returned to the open battlefield.

When the Constitutional Conference broke down, Asquith asked the King to promise that if the government gained an adequate majority in the election that was clearly imminent, peers would be created. The King understandably disliked being asked to commit himself in advance and, less reasonably, thought it unfair that this pledge was to be kept secret. He gave his word, though it seems he might have been rash enough to refuse if he had known that Balfour, contemplating just such a situation, had said he would form a government to save the King from having to give an assurance in advance. By this time the Conservatives' attitude to the constitution was becoming a little cavalier. Balfour's apparent willingness to replace Asquith suggests either that he thought the King had the right to dismiss a Prime Minister who held a majority in the Commons or that he believed the King's natural personal reluctance to create peers had some constitutional validity.[18] When the Parliament Bill reached the Lords, the Conservatives again asked for legislation of fundamental importance to be subject to a referendum.

The Conservative view that each important item of legislation should be acceptable to the public meant that a government elected to carry out a popular programme which depended on some unpopular measures might find the whole programme destroyed. In the circumstances of 1910 it meant that the government might be re-elected with every intention of carrying Home Rule for Ireland and then find that it could not pass the measure in a referendum.

When the second 1910 election was held, in December, the Conservatives pressed for the referendum and warned the voters that if the Liberals won they would bring in Home Rule as well as passing the Parliament Bill. Balfour was generally considered to have done well by promising that Tariff Reform would also be submitted to a referendum, which was expected to bring the Unionist Free Traders back to the party. The results show little sign of this; the number of contests dropped, the number of votes cast dropped even further, a fairly large number of seats changed hands, but after the election the parties were exactly where they had been at the beginning of the campaign. As nobody could contemplate a third general election, the issue had now to be settled in a way that would satisfy Asquith and his parliamentary majority.

	Votes	Seats	% of all votes cast
Conservative	2,424,566	272	46.3
Liberal	2,293,868	272	43.8
Labour	376,581	42	7.2
Irish Home Rule	131,721	84	2.5

The Conservatives did not admit defeat. As the Parliament Bill passed through the Commons, the Lords prepared schemes for altering the composition of their House. Asquith made it clear that the limitations on the Lords' right of rejection would apply to any Upper House, no matter what its membership. Despite this, the Conservative peers convinced themselves that the government was only bluffing. The more unrealistic of them decided to

18. F. W. Maitland, *Constitutional History of England* (Cambridge, 1908), 397: 'The king is bound to act on the advice of his ministers; he must choose his ministers, or rather his first minister, in accordance with the will of the House of Commons.'

throw out the Parliament Bill and see if Asquith would then dare to create peers to override their decision. As it became clearer and clearer that he would, the resistance grew increasingly frantic. When he announced at the end of July that he had in November obtained the King's promise to create peers, he was shouted down in the Commons by the Conservatives. This did nothing to take the knife from the Lords' throat; the Liberal ministers were not men to be hurried into a false step. On 9 and 10 August the Lords debated the Bill. The 'Diehards' (or 'Ditchers', ready to die in the last ditch by rejecting the Bill and bringing about an immense creation of new peers) outnumbered the tiny Liberal group in the Lords; the only way to avoid a creation of peers was to find enough Conservatives to vote for the Bill, and against their own inclinations. The reality of the choice was made clear; Lord Morley read a message that the King would assent 'to a creation of peers sufficient in number to guard against any possible combination of the different Parties in Opposition by which the Parliament Bill might again be exposed a second time to defeat',[19] or, in numerical terms, 500 Liberal peers would be created to pass the Bill, a Home Rule Bill, and any other proposals that the government might put forward. Enough Conservative moderates were found for the Parliament Bill to pass, 131 to 114.

Social and class structure

The list of proposed peers found among Asquith's papers, containing names like Bertrand Russell, Thomas Hardy, and Ian Hamilton, suggests that a large addition would have added to the personal distinction of the House of Lords.[20] But it would still have left the old British upper class greatly weakened. The struggle over the Lords, and perhaps the death of Edward VII the previous year, mark a distinct step in the crumbling of its position. The First World War did not change the way things were moving, even if it accelerated the process.

Lansdowne picked out the central feature of the upper class when he said that he hoped the members of a revised House selected from among the existing peers would be 'familiar with country life, familiar with landed property'.[21] The upper class consisted of men whose ownership of land and influence over their tenants gave them some political power, if only at the local level. The ownership of land was ceasing to give this sort of power, and it was becoming impossible for people to reach positions of political importance without earning them by a record of achievement.

Lloyd George said in 1911 that paying income tax was the dividing line

---

19. R. Jenkins, *Mr. Balfour's Poodle* (1954), 179.
20. J. A. Spender and C. Asquith, *Life of Asquith* (1932), 329–31, give a list of 249 potential peers Asquith had picked out.
21. Jenkins, *Mr. Balfour's Poodle*, 126.

between gentility and subsistence; 1,150,000 paid income tax, and most of them belonged to the middle class. Above them was the richest 1 per cent of the population, which owned about 66 per cent of all property. When Marx studied the country's social structure in the 1860s the country could be divided into property owners, who had land or business interests, and the rest. The professional class was small and the salaried professional class almost non-existent. By 1910 the salaried professional class had become an important part of the middle class, and because it managed a good deal of industrial and financial property the ownership of property did not have the same decisive effect as it had fifty years earlier.

Most of the middle class was dominated by the desire for respectability, and the ideal of a sober, thrifty, churchgoing family life was accepted by a large part of the population. It was of the essence of respectability that everybody had someone a very little lower in the scale to look down on, so respectable society was intersected by 20 or 30 million graduations which between them contrived that a member of respectable society never saw an equal. Though the ideal first took root in the middle class, it spread upwards and downwards. Members of the upper class who wanted effective political power had to behave, at least in public, in a middle-class way.

Naturally some members of the upper class behaved in a more traditional manner; as Edward VII was one of them, the jolly and slightly vulgar way of life of the members of the upper class who did not think it was their business to go round setting a good example became known as Edwardian. Upper-class life, strict or relaxed, of the Edwardian period has since then become the subject of laments for the splendour that has been lost. The general level of prosperity increased greatly in the next eighty or ninety years, but the richest salaried and professional people in 2000 are still in some ways less well off than people in equivalent positions before 1914. It is not clear whether property owners have lost ground to the same extent, because the desire to escape from taxation has led the rich to hold their property in increasingly complicated ways during the century.[22] The rich clearly continue to exist, but they are less noticeable than at the beginning of the century, partly because other types of celebrity command attention, and partly because it is harder to spend money in a way that produces so much outward show. The number of servants has conspicuously declined in the last sixty years and, less conspicuously, the increase in real wages has led to a sharp increase in the price of things made by individual labour unassisted by machinery.

Edwardian shooting-parties, in which enormous flights of carefully reared

22. Guy Routh, *Occupation and Pay in Great Britain 1906–60* (1965), 55, shows that the real post-tax income of employees rose on the average by 80 per cent between 1906 and 1960, but the income of the top millile fell by 22 per cent. Pages 62–5 show that the highest-paid professional people lost even more ground. R. M. Titmuss, *Income Distribution and Social Change* (1962) shows how hard it is to draw firm conclusions from statistics on the ownership of property.

birds were driven by armies of beaters over a line of men armed with splendidly designed hand-made guns, were practicable only when servants and craftsmen got low wages; as wages went up, strictly upper-class entertainment became harder and harder to afford. About 800,000 families, which would include almost all of the middle and upper classes, employed servants in 1911; 60 per cent of them had only one, 20 per cent had two, and the remaining 20 per cent had more than two.[23] The style of life based on battalions of servants has disappeared, perhaps mainly because of the increase in wages, but also because a good deal of the work servants used to do, such as carrying hot water to bedrooms and lighting fires, is now performed more efficiently and for a much larger proportion of the population by hot water systems and central heating.

The middle-class ideal of respectability spread downwards into the working class. The dividing lines of occupation and of income did not correspond precisely; people who worked with their hands were probably considered members of the working class and people below the income tax line were probably not well enough off to be established members of the middle class, but obviously no line could be drawn which left no anomalies and exceptions. Just as the dividing line between the middle class and the working class was real but hard to draw, there was a dividing line within the working class, between the poor and the relatively comfortable, that was equally real but hard to draw. Relatively comfortable men would in most cases have a vote, would often be union members or skilled craftsmen working on their own account, and could aspire to some aspects of respectability if they chose to. About 30 per cent of the population were below the poverty line indicated in Charles Booth's survey of London and Seebohm Rowntree's survey of York; they rarely had the vote, they had difficulty becoming unionized, and only with a great effort could they live respectably. The municipal and central governments were just beginning to consider doing something about the housing conditions of the poor, though the problem turned out to be very intractable. One reason was that wages made up a large part of the total cost of housing and so, unlike almost everything else except upper-class luxury goods, the cost of housing went up about as fast as real wages for most of the century.

The ideas of the Edwardians

This emphasis on the gradations of society and on respectability may seem peculiarly Victorian. Perhaps it was more marked during the Queen's reign than in the dozen years before 1914, and certainly the literary climate of the years before the war was more relaxed than in the nineteenth century. This

---

23. D. Lloyd George, 16 Nov. 1911, *Commons Debates*, xxxi. 541.

relaxation must not be overstated, though the pattern of life indicated by writers in the 1900s spread and became accepted as the normal way of life for the middle class. The social material of novels remained unchanged; authors wrote about tension between society and the individual, with problems of love and sex taken as the issues that most often brought them into conflict. To a considerable extent readers were worried by bold new literary departures, whether novels or plays or poetry, because they were worried about the solidarity of society; the Lord Chamberlain intervened to forbid performance of plays such as Bernard Shaw's *Mrs. Warren's Profession*. In the course of the century readers grew less worried about the possibility that society might collapse as the result of some novel or play.

The writers and thinkers who dominated intellectual circles in the 1900s wanted to be reasonable, wanted to be modern, and felt a fairly strong tendency to puritanism, which expressed itself in disapproval of the upper classes. Bernard Shaw illustrated this very well. A good deal of his best work had been done before 1906, and even in the years before 1914 there was a slight falling-off in the flow of his writing. In the 1890s and the early years of the new century he wrote about a play a year, including *Candida, The Doctor's Dilemma*, and *Man and Superman*. By 1912 he had written another half-dozen substantial plays and had progressed from being a playwright of considerable prestige to being a commercial success. Years previously he had said that managers who cared about being up to date made a point of putting on plays by newcomers who became fashionable fifteen years later; Shaw's allotted fifteen years had elapsed and he had arrived. There were still a few important plays, such as *Heartbreak House* and *St. Joan*, to come, but the bulk of his work was done by the time Edward VII died. Shaw and the other writers of the pre-First World War years shaped an audience for themselves, and in some ways they came into their own after the war. Of course, they could not change society by themselves. They flourished at a time when the old dominance of the upper class was crumbling under blows like the Parliament Act and the much heavier impact of the First World War. The post-war world was not completely satisfactory to pre-war writers like Wells and Shaw and Forster, but it was a world that had moved in the direction that they had pointed in the years before the war.

The literary climate of the Edwardian years did not have much in common with the Modern movement. Sometime around 1908, when Ezra Pound arrived in England, or 1911, when the Diaghilev Ballet first came to London, a new spirit appeared that was quite different from the measured rational approach of the liberal reforming writers. The exhibition of Post-Impressionist painting which Roger Fry organized in 1910 revealed an even wider gulf in popular understanding: people who had learned to accept the liberal reforming writers rushed forward in denunciation, like Sargent, the fashionable portrait painter, who said: 'I am absolutely sceptical as to their having any claim whatsoever to being works of art.'[24] Painting in Britain tended to follow the style fashionable in Paris, but at an interval of several years, and it was still taken for granted that people looking at pictures did not need to make any great effort to accept the particular point of view of the artist; as acceptance of the point of view of the artist became increasingly important for comprehension, the opportunities for misunderstanding and denunciation grew larger and larger. The success of the Diaghilev Ballet at first owed something to the support of aristocratic society, which felt that it was an upper-class form of entertainment. This opened the gates a little to the modern artists who designed the stage settings, and to modern composers like Stravinsky. English music of the period was by general European standards not very distinguished, and Elgar, the leading composer, was at least on the surface rather too inclined to accept some of the complacencies of Edwardianism.

The writers of the 1900s had a good deal in common with the philosophers of the time. British philosophy had become an amalgam of Hegel and nineteenth-century Liberal thought, in which Hegel's admiration for the state and for the gradual combination of disparate parts into a whole was found in surprising but apparently harmonious combination with the Utilitarian concern for the maximization of the happiness of the free individual. Karl Marx represented one version of this combination, but much the most fashionable version was that of T. H. Green, who, as a tutor at Balliol and a writer on political philosophy, had been a strong influence on several members of the Cabinet. Bosanquet and F. H. Bradley continued the tradition of Hegelian thought at the universities; in the Cabinet, Haldane was something of a Hegelian scholar.

Two distinct but related lines of attack on modified Hegelianism were appearing at Cambridge in the last years of the nineteenth century. The mathematical philosophers Russell and Whitehead set out to show that a basis for mathematics could be found in logical propositions. Their *Principia Mathematica* (1910) reduced and harmonized the assumptions to be made; its approach was so elegant and attractive that the same principles were applied, by them and by later writers, to philosophy in general, with results that were disastrous to Hegelianism in England, though not in Scotland. Their mathematical work had cut the ground from under the feet of philosophers who had tried to show, by devising paradoxes, that mathematics was not logical and that therefore the visible world was illogical and not real. Whitehead later tried to reintroduce quasi-Platonic. Ideals into the world that he and Russell had been stripping of such things, but the main stream of English philosophy followed the line of Russell's axiom that all meaningful statements are either

---

24. *The Annual Register of World Events for 1910*, pt. 2, p. 100. He made a partial exception for Gauguin.

assertions about sense-data, which could in some circumstances be tested, or else are tautologies that extract logical conclusions from assumptions, in the same way as mathematical equations. Most of the successors of Russell and Whitehead lacked the mathematical technique of their leaders, and were ready to believe that the logical problems concerned with mathematics had been finally resolved. English philosophers turned their attention to problems of language and tried to resolve its problems in the same way. This line of approach, expressed most briskly in A. J. Ayer's *Language, Truth and Logic* (1937), had a considerable impact in the English-speaking world, and very little outside it; although one of the most respected of the linguistic philosophers was the Austrian Wittgenstein, who settled at Cambridge, the interest in European philosophy which had been noticeable in the nineteenth century diminished. In a way the withdrawal from ambitious problems about the nature of things to smaller—though equally intractable—problems about the nature of statements about things was a return to the relatively unambitious approach of the English empirical philosophers, with a strong addition of the scepticism of David Hume thrown in. This sort of reasoning was not likely to produce a 'philosophy of life' in the old sense of a set of beliefs which told people how they ought to act.

A philosophy of life could be found in the work of G. E. Moore, a Cambridge philosopher who wrote a few years earlier than Russell and Whitehead. His ethical system went on from fairly austere foundations about men's duty to do what was good to an assertion that the really important things in life are personal relationships and artistic experiences, and that other things are valuable only as means to these ends.[25] Moore enjoyed a great reputation for the rigour of his logic, and his friends remembered long afterwards the incisiveness with which he asked, 'Now exactly what do you mean by that?', a question that was later a great favourite among the linguistic philosophers. Moore's philosophy of life provided a blend of puritanism and hedonism which was what his admirers were trying to find, and was what suited a larger and larger number of people in the new century.

One of the most important ways in which Moore's philosophy found its way to a wider audience was through the attitudes of the people who came to be known as Bloomsbury; they were not professional philosophers, but they were strongly affected by Moore's teaching. Bloomsbury, as a gathering of writers, artists, and art critics, was less concerned with the rights and wrongs of society than were Galsworthy or Arnold Bennett, or D. H. Lawrence; people like Fry and Duncan Grant and Clive Bell were not particularly worried about the general state of the world, and Virginia Woolf's concern about problems of society was not clearly revealed in her novels. Lytton Strachey was

25. G. E. Moore, *Principia Ethica* (Cambridge, 1903), 25. His statement on page 188 about 'the most valuable things which we know or can imagine' puts his view concisely though in language that is now out of date.

concerned with these problems in the rather special sense that he devoted a fair amount of his writing, and owed a great deal of his reputation, to his attack on the constrictions of Victorian respectability: his *Eminent Victorians* (1918) and even his *Queen Victoria* (1921), though not intended as an unqualified attack on the dead Queen, were among the weapons with which people of the 1920s developed their attack on the conventions of society. But two other distinguished members of Bloomsbury, Leonard Woolf and John Maynard Keynes, deeply influenced by the hedonistic aspects of Moore, also reflected the other side of his principles and were ready to take part in politics to help other people. Woolf in the Labour Party and Keynes in the Liberal Party were close enough together to show why, even after 1918, some people could think of the Labour Party and the Liberal Party as two parties of the left, with much more in common with each other than either had with the Conservative Party. E. M. Forster seemed almost ready to say in books like *A Passage to India* (1924) that all political problems are a matter of proper personal relationships, but he could not quite bring himself to say that this approach would solve the problems of economics or of war.

In *Howards End* (1911) he looked at the question 'Does [England] belong to those who have moulded her and made her feared by other lands, or to those who have added nothing to her power, but have somehow seen her, seen the whole island at once, lying as a jewel in a silver sea, sailing as a ship of souls, with all the brave world's fleet accompanying her towards eternity?'[26] The book, as might be expected from this passage, comes down on the side of the seers.

In his attractive account of the beginnings of Bloomsbury, Leonard Woolf explained how he came back in 1911 from seven years in Ceylon and found that in the circle of his friends, who were advanced and liberal in thought, some of the stiffness and formality of life had eased while he was overseas. He also wrote that anyone who doubted his account of the stiffness of life had no idea what Victorianism was all about. 'Clearly that revolt which Shaw and his generation began and my generation helped to extend was so effective that our successors are not even aware how and why, while we were born in chains, they are comparatively free.'[27]

Some of these chains were undoubtedly the special manacles of the middle class, forged by a concern about respectability. Aldous Huxley described, in *Eyeless in Gaza*, the way a young intellectual at Oxford in 1912 saw the freedom from inhibition of the upper-class undergraduates. 'By the mere force of social and economic circumstances these ignorant barbarians found themselves quite naturally behaving as he did not dare to behave even after

---

26. E. M. Forster, *Howards End* (1911), 172.
27. L. Woolf, *Beginning Again* (1964), 34.

reading all Nietzsche had said about the Superman, or Casanova about women.'[28]

Oxford and Bloomsbury had little immediate impact on ordinary members of the middle class. One great liberating influence for many of them was H. G. Wells. In the first few years of the century he was turning from the science fiction, in which he had first earned his reputation, and was becoming a novelist of the conventional type. At this time science was entering a period of development which made it harder for the amateur to understand it; Lord Salisbury could take an active amateur interest in science when he first became Prime Minister in 1885 but this would have been much harder by the end of his tenure of office. The Michelson Morley experiments on the speed of light had shown that the universe was not built in quite the way common sense had suggested and had led (just before Campbell-Bannerman became Prime Minister) to Einstein's Special Theory of Relativity. Radioactive elements had been purified and Rutherford was beginning his study of the particles they threw off and the possible disintegration of matter. Two other Cambridge scientists, Soddy and J. J. Thomson, were demonstrating that atoms in an element which were chemically identical might have different atomic weights and different radioactive properties. Developments like this were making physics into the dominant science of the new century, but they were also making it much less intelligible to anyone with no specialist training in the subject. Wells had received a scientific education and had a good journalistic understanding of what was going on—he referred to an 'atomic bomb' in 1913—and might have become a very good guide to these developments if he had not turned to writing novels of the traditional type.

In the years before 1914 it was probably on the subject of women and women's rights that he wrote most and had most influence. One of his first non-science-fiction novels, *The Wheels of Chance* (1896), was based on the enthusiasm for bicycling in the last years of the nineteenth century and the emancipating effect it had on young men and women. *The New Machiavelli* (1911), if it is mentioned at all today, is remembered because it satirizes the work habits, the meagre hospitality, and the relentless string-pulling of those determined social reformers Sidney and Beatrice Webb. But when it was written, Wells was disagreeing with the Webbs on a serious issue of social policy: they thought the next step in social reform should be to destroy the old Poor Law of 1834, as they had indicated in the Minority Report on the Poor Law, and he thought the next step should be to pay all mothers a living wage to enable them to bring up their children in decent conditions. Wells's proposal would have struck a blow at all the many aspects of poverty related to large families and, by enabling a mother to bring up her family without being financially dependent on the father, it would have altered the institution of

28. A. Huxley, *Eyeless in Gaza* (1938), 91.

marriage. His *Ann Veronica* (1909), seen as 'daring' (and somewhat auto-biographical) because the heroine went to live with a married man, argued like *The New Machiavelli* that women were unable to make free choices in work or marriage and needed to be liberated from the forces of convention which restricted them. The social planners saw this as one of the factors to be considered when extending welfare services; the women themselves responded by going into revolt.

Wells was not as good a writer as Shaw; he lacked the clarity of argument which, while not essential for writing novels, is a great help for writing novels with a social purpose, and he had none of Shaw's wit or readiness to explore the impossible side of a paradox. But he was always up to date with the problems that everybody was interested in, and he had a considerable stock of material to work on: his own early life in the lower middle class, working behind a shop counter, was useful, in *Kipps* (1907), when shopworkers' hours were being discussed in Parliament. He took it for granted that his readers did not have religious beliefs. He did not offer solutions to the problem of loss of belief; he simply accepted that it caused difficulties, which suggested that he understood his audience better than either the writers who thought a deter-mined effort to believe would solve the problem of belief or the writers who thought loss of faith was already an easy and natural matter.

It was not the dominant intellectual problem that it had been a little earlier. On the whole the philosophies of Mill or of Moore, sometimes diluted with an attitude of respect to the Deity, satisfied the highly educated, and a blend of puritanism and hedonism spread more and more widely during the twentieth century, sometimes in a theistical form but more usually in an unaggressively non-theistic form. In the middle of the nineteenth century it had been esti-mated that half the adult population went to church. By the end of the century the figure was probably rather lower. The Protestant Churches were never successful at getting in touch with the urban poor; the Roman Catholic Church did hold its own among the poor, helped by the fact that almost all Catholics were Irish immigrants who were subject to the pressures of anti-Irish feeling. But once poor people from elsewhere in the United Kingdom had reached a big city, they were very likely to lose touch with any Christian Church. The Salvation Army had been started in the 1880s to deal with just this problem, and it had had some success. The attitude of derision, and sometimes of active hostility, that other Christian organizations took to its efforts shows the way that church going and respectability were linked, and suggests that the unrespectable were not welcome inside the church.

Respectable people went to church about as regularly under Edward as in the later years of Victoria; perhaps there was a slight falling-off, but it was nothing to the decline in church attendance in the years between the two world wars and the even sharper drop after 1945. But enthusiasm about religion was already less than in the late nineteenth century,

Anglo-Catholicism provided opportunities for a few would-be martyrs and a few would-be heresy-hunters, and some clergymen took part in the growing concentration of attention on social reform, but religion was no longer a central issue. From the 1840s to the 1880s the conflict between the assertions of religion and the theories of science had occupied the attention of many of the cleverest men in the country—Gladstone took this to an extreme when he published an article on the theological problems of the Gadarene swine just before forming his Home Rule government in 1886, but many other laymen felt deeply concerned about these religious arguments. The laity showed much less interest in the next great struggle in the Church, over Modernism and the extent to which the Church ought to adapt to a changing world. The Churches followed the views of the vehemently patriotic majority during the First World War with a lack of restraint that probably did them no good in the long run, but the decline in their position made the Churches even less likely to resist the opinions of men in authority than they had been in previous decades. And it was among men of authority that the churches were losing ground; apart from the drift among the highly educated, there was a shift of opinion among politicians, even though their followers had not yet noticed the change. The Free Churchmen followed Lloyd George in the years before the war, just as they had followed Gladstone a generation earlier; but Lloyd George's attitude to life and to politics was not permeated by religious feeling in the way that Gladstone's had been. Victorianism appeared to stand relatively unshaken; in fact its foundations were crumbling.

2

Heedless of their fate

1911–1914

Social reform and other legislation

Lloyd George emerged from the inconspicuous position he had adopted during the struggle over the Parliament Bill to present his National Insurance Bill, in which he offered, as he put it, ninepence for fourpence (i.e. 3.75p of weekly benefits for 1.66p of insurance payments). Part I of the Bill covered most people who worked for a living against ill health by requiring workers with earnings too low to pay income tax to contribute their 1.66p a week while their employers paid 1.25p. A government payment of 0.83p made up the 3.75p; and people earning less than 12.5p a day were exempted from paying. An insured worker received 50p a week in sick pay (falling to 25p in cases of prolonged illness) and could call on the services of the doctors who had enrolled on the insurance panels. Any trade union, insurance company, or Friendly Society which had previously been insuring people against the expenses of ill health could be an 'approved society' and go on acting as an insuring agent. This increased the number of trade unionists, increased the profits of the insurance companies, and saved from bankruptcy a number of Friendly Societies, which had been too optimistic in their rates of benefit.

The doctors were less easy to conciliate. Some of their claims were simple requests for more money: Lloyd George, always ready to oblige, increased the capitation fee paid to a doctor for each patient on his list. The demand that coverage should be given only to people with under £2 a week, which would have excluded the more prosperous members of the working class, came closer to destroying the principle of the Act, and was rejected. The British Medical Association, an organization that has always been bellicose in defending the interests of its members, threatened not to take part in the scheme, but found by 1912 that so many of its members were ready to take part that resistance was impracticable. The scheme was nevertheless not immediately popular; employers and employees disliked paying for the stamps needed for the insurance premiums, the only direct tax that the employees paid, and probably a lot of contributors felt that the whole thing was a nuisance. A mass meeting of servants and their mistresses who all said that they would never lick the insurance stamps was thought to be a little silly, but the Liberals' losses in a number of by-elections about this time were attributed to the unpopularity of the Insurance Act. On the other hand, Law, the new Conservative leader, was taken to have blundered when he said he would repeal the Insurance Act. Not many people were very enthusiastic about the Act, and a number of people were determinedly opposed to it, but a solid majority accepted the Act and wanted to keep it.

Part II of the Act, which aroused much less controversy, provided insurance against unemployment for workers in the building and engineering trades, in which the demand for labour fluctuated particularly sharply. This part, enlarged in 1920, became grimly relevant in the inter-war years, but until then attracted little attention. Churchill had pushed it forward as a natural part of the labour exchange scheme; a man went to the exchange seeking work, but if he could not find it he had proved his good intentions and should receive benefit.

The two parts of the Act were run by two different ministries, and almost the only thing that united them was the principle of insurance, based on a flat-rate per capita charge and paying a flat rate of benefit. Labour MPs who were consciously socialist objected to the flat-rate charge and said the whole cost should be paid out of general taxation like old-age pensions. Labour MPs who were more conscious of being trade unionists accepted the charges, on the grounds that they strengthened workers' claims to receive benefit as a matter of right. The entire Act was a considerable departure in British social legislation, though so much of Part I was borrowed from German experience that it had no great claims to originality.

Lloyd George did not neglect the traditional duties of his office, including the struggle to keep down the defence estimates, and at the same time showed his gift for getting things done by setting up an administrative system that might have been a full-time job for a normal departmental minister. His 1911 budget gave MPs a salary of £400 a year. This led to complaints that it opened the doors to professional politicians and adventurers, a way of saying that poor men might go into politics for the money. Someone from the working classes, unlikely to have been making as much as £150 a year, could go into the Commons and, despite increased living expenses, emerge no worse off. A salaried member of the middle class would suffer a considerable drop in his standard of living, and would probably have to pay heavily to maintain a constituency organization. The change meant that members of the unionized working class could join the landowners, large-scale industrialists, rentiers, lawyers, and financiers who made up almost the whole of the Commons; the dominance of the middle and lower-middle class in the electorate was not reflected in the House.

Payment of Members was almost the last Liberal measure of any importance that actually passed into law, but their legislative activity went on. The Lords were determined to use the delaying power allowed by the Parliament Act to hold up the three substantial pieces of legislation which the government wanted to pass. The Home Rule Bill was the most important, but the Lords also rejected the Welsh Disestablishment Bill and the Plural Voters Bill. The Bills were put forward again in 1913 and 1914; but none of them had passed into law under the Parliament Act when war broke out.

Conservative opposition to the Liberal programme became more dogged and tenacious, though perhaps less skilful, after Balfour was forced to retire in November 1911 by his followers' anger that they had done so badly during the nine years of his leadership. Two men had obvious claims to lead the Conservatives in the Commons: Joseph Chamberlain's son Austen, who was supported by the Liberal Unionists, most of the Tariff Reformers, and most of the urban Conservatives including the growing business interest; and Walter Long, who was supported by the landed interest and by Conservatives of the traditional sort. Their forces were evenly balanced, and in a curious mood of self-denial both of them withdrew in favour of Bonar Law, a Glasgow business man who originally came from Canada. Law's initial support came from a small section of the more extreme Tariff Reformers, but he represented the mood of the whole party very well; he was a bitter and determined debater who believed, correctly, that he was not Asquith's equal in parliamentary warfare. Ulster and Tariff Reform were the two political issues that interested him, though the latter broke in his hand. He stated that the party no longer felt bound to submit Tariff Reform to a referendum, apparently without realizing that the offer of a referendum was what held the party together in Scotland and the north of England. Pressure from the north forced Law to say that a Conservative government would not impose taxes on imports of food until after a general election on the issue. Foodstuffs were so large a part of the exports of the Dominions that this pledge destroyed most of the proposals for Imperial Preference. For the next ten years the Conservatives' policy on tariffs could never really be pinned down, though they continued to recommend Protection as a solution to problems.

The Opposition tried to reunite itself by opposing every measure put forward. For thirty years Scotland and Wales had been as strongly committed to the Liberal Party as Ireland was to the Home Rule Party. Scottish Liberals saw the advantages of being able to settle distinctively Scottish issues at Edinburgh and brought forward Bills proposing Home Rule for Scotland. In 1913 one of these Bills passed its second reading, but the Liberal leadership did not want to commit itself on the issue and it made no further progress. For Welsh Liberals the great symbolic issue was Disestablishment of the Church of England in Wales: they saw the Church of England as one Protestant Church among many, and disliked its privileged position and its connection with the English landowning class. The government proposed that, as had happened when the

Church of England in Ireland was disestablished, part of the Anglican endowment would be taken over for education and other national purposes in Wales, and understandably there was heated argument about the scale of disendowment. The unconciliatory attitude of the Conservatives to the Welsh can be seen from Law's statement: 'If it be true that [the Church of England] can make no appeal to the Welsh temperament, I think that it is a condemnation not of the Church but of the Welsh temperament.'[1]

The Plural Voting Bill was resisted in much the same spirit. The Bill was designed to establish 'one elector, one vote', which would undoubtedly have helped the Liberals because most men with several votes from widely distributed property, sometimes reinforced with an extra vote for a university seat, were Conservatives. The Opposition claimed that this should be accompanied by a redistribution of constituencies, but redistribution would have been hard to carry out at the point the Irish question had then reached. Ireland was conspicuously over-represented because the number of seats had been fixed by the 1800 Act of Union before the population was reduced by the Famine of the 1840s and the subsequent emigration. The Home Rule Bill that was about to be introduced would cut Irish representation, and it was hard to work out redistribution for the United Kingdom before the fate of the Bill was known.

Threats to stability: unions and suffragettes

Historians have argued about the condition of the country in the two or three years before the outbreak of war in 1914. Some writers see it as a period of golden tranquillity, and others dismiss this picture as the fantasy of classes whose financial and social position suffered during the war. The sober and responsible Halevy spoke of boredom and anarchy; the less restrained Dangerfield foresaw revolution in every direction. The decade before 1914 was certainly not as peaceful as is suggested by reminiscences about the Oxford of Raymond Asquith and the Cambridge of Rupert Brooke or the pleasant and untroubled existence of the established upper-middle class. Apart from the large problem of Ireland, people were worried by trade union militancy and by the agitation carried on by women who wanted the right to vote. Trade unions were undoubtedly more active just before the war than they had been for at least two decades, but there were economic reasons for militancy which had nothing to do with anarchy and revolution.

From the early 1870s to the middle of the 1890s trade in Britain had been dull: interest rates were low but this did not stimulate much new investment, unemployment rates were higher than had been normal in the 1850s and 1860s, prices fell, and so did money wages, though as they fell more slowly the level of real wages rose. This was not a depression like the 1930s, but it was not

---

1. 21 Apr. 1914, *Commons Debates*, lxi. 868.

a period in which people were conscious of new opportunities opening up. British businessmen neglected new areas of enterprise and stuck to well-tried old favourites, such as railways and textiles, at a time when Germans and Americans were taking more interest in steel, chemicals, and the uses of electricity.

The twenty years before 1914 were rather different. Investment abroad, which had in fact been dropping for some years before Hobson's denunciation of it in *Imperialism* in 1902, rose steadily for the next twelve years; from 1906 to 1913 it was always higher than domestic investment, and by 1913 it had reached 9 per cent of the national income. Most of this overseas investment involved a certain amount of export credit and so helped British trade. There was a smaller, but perceptible, increase in government spending on armaments, which helped the coal and steel trades and, in particular, shipbuilding. Trade was also stimulated by the increase in the world gold supply as more and more was discovered in South Africa. The economy became more active, unemployment diminished, and prices went up. Wages went up more slowly; real wages did not rise above the 1900 level and sometimes dropped below it.[2] The population increased and the national income was larger, but individuals were not in general better off. The population increase was directly linked to a decline in infant mortality, so the labour force was not increasing so quickly. The people of the years before the war did not realize that per capita income was stationary, and might have found it hard to reconcile with all the visible signs of economic activity and of a high level of conspicuous consumption that went with it. In these circumstances disturbed labour relations were only to be expected. The slight recessions of 1904, which helped the Tariff Reform movement win its initial successes, and of 1908, which temporarily weakened the position of the Liberal government, were only minor incidents in a period of steady full employment.

With their position strengthened by the ready availability of jobs, the unions set out to improve real wages. Dangerfield's *Strange Death of Liberal England*, one of the most excitingly written of the books arguing that Britain stood on the verge of social catastrophe in 1914, relies (even more than is apparent from the footnotes) upon G. R. Askwith's memoirs of the period, and it is particularly relevant to look at Askwith's own analysis. He performed prodigies in bringing together employers and employees in the negotiations of the period, and saw more disputes from closer quarters than anyone else at the time. He wrote (in a passage not quoted by Dangerfield): 'What is to be said about these disputes? My own strong opinion is that they were economic. . . . Prices had been rising, but no sufficient increase of wages, and certainly no general increase, had followed the rise.' He gave second place to a desire for union recognition, and added that he thought workers overestimated the

---

2. A. L. Bowley, *Wages and Incomes in the United Kingdom since 1880* (1937), 94.

value of getting formal recognition from their employers. Very much in third place he mentioned the existence of what he called 'irritation' strikes.[3] This account gives a convincing explanation of what happened in industrial relations between 1910 and 1914, without any need for apocalyptic assertions that the fabric of society was crumbling.

Askwith thought ministers' eagerness to be seen dealing with strikes had an unsettling effect. They had done so at times in the past twenty years, and a Liberal government was especially likely to intervene because its own electoral position depended on an alliance of employers and employees. At first it seemed that the alliance could stand a considerable amount of strain and that the government had no need to worry about the political effect of strikes. The nine-month strike in the South Wales coalfields, which ran from October 1910 to June 1911, had begun well before the December 1910 election but did not affect the position of the Liberals. In the wave of strikes in the summer of 1911 people were most immediately affected by dockers' strikes, first at Hull and Manchester and then at London. Part of the obstinacy of the two sides was attributed to the great heat of the summer, which also weakened the bargaining position of the employers by making perishable goods rot faster. Within a week the economy was affected by an even more disruptive strike by the railway workers; Lloyd George did a lot to end this by appealing to the two sides to remember that the international situation was uneasy and that the government needed industrial peace for the sake of its diplomacy. During these strikes there was some fear of danger to law and order, and the Home Secretary had to see that there were enough police to keep the peace and to provide troops in support of the police if necessary. Troops were provided in the South Wales coal strike, and during the railway strike preparations were made to run the railways on a military basis if the European situation deteriorated. Soldiers were also used to protect trains running the limited service that the companies provided; near Llanelly soldiers opened fire and killed two men. The working-class memory of the story was that Churchill, as Home Secretary, was the minister responsible for two miners being killed at Tonypandy. The confusion with the miners' strike of the previous winter was inaccurate, but the general impression was not unjust: introducing soldiers with loaded rifles into an industrial dispute was asking for trouble. Cabinet ministers, except for John Burns, had no idea what a strike was like, and they were at once too easily alarmed and too ready to assume that a display of force would settle things peacefully.

The situation looked all the more alarming because some strikers adopted syndicalist slogans. The syndicalist theory that workers should take over and run the industries in which they worked gave dissatisfied militants a principle to oppose to the insistence of union leaders that negotiations should be

3. G. R. Askwith, *Industrial Problems and Disputes* (1920), 175, 350, and 353.

confined to wages and working conditions, and that workers should strike only when the leaders thought it appropriate. The leaders had learned their business in the difficult days of dull trade in the 1880s and 1890s, and may well have been too cautious for the times. Syndicalism also provided a basis for opposition to the Labour alliance with the Liberal government, and if hostility to the government rested more on dislike for the Insurance Act than on admiration for the theories of G. D. H. Cole and of Orage, the editor of *New Age* magazine, its effects were still serious. In its strictly theoretical form syndicalism was one of the few attempts to apply an anarchist version of socialism in Britain, and yet even when it seemed most successful its effect was generally to push the government into becoming more interventionist.

The coal strike of 1912 underlined the point. The government set out to bring coal miners and coal owners together, and found it had undertaken a remarkably difficult task. In most strikes both sides, like people outside the dispute, expected a fairly quick decision; the effect of a rail strike or a dock strike was felt too quickly to be allowed to last long. In coal strikes from the 1870s to the 1980s a struggle of months was regarded as nothing abnormal. When the government intervened in 1912, it did not understand how slowly things would move, and once it had become involved it felt it had to settle the dispute quickly. The government's Minimum Wage Act set up Boards to grant minimum wages, on a district basis, to miners when they were handicapped by working in difficult seams. The miners would have liked minimum daily rates set by law, 25p for a man and 10p for a boy, and would have preferred national rates to district rates, but although they did not get their own way on these details they had induced the government to take a long step away from laissez-faire: workers in the 'sweated industries' might need state help because they could not set up unions of their own, but the miners had a very effective union and they had used it to obtain more state intervention.

Membership of the TUC increased fairly sharply during the years before 1914, rising from 1,648,000 in 1910 to 2,232,000 by 1913. As trade unions were among the 'approved societies' with which people could insure under the Insurance Act of 1911, Charles Masterman, the Financial Secretary to the Treasury, could declare in 1913 that this was the real reason for the increase in membership.[4] No doubt the Insurance Act did a great deal for union membership, but Masterman's explanation was incomplete because he did not refer to the industrial disputes of these years and the way that successful strikes often provided an opportunity for recruiting new members in a partially unionized labour force. Probably he ignored the disputes because he thought they were a natural result of negotiation at a time of full employment; the decade from 1910 to 1920 was the only long period of full employment in the British economy between 1874 and 1939, and nobody had acquired much practice in

4. Lucy Masterman, *Charles Masterman* (1939), app. 3, esp. p. 387.

dealing with this unusual phenomenon. In Dublin James Larkin, a union leader more skilled in oratory than in negotiation, did say alarming things, but Ireland was not urbanized enough for industrial workers to become a dominant factor in the economy. In Britain the foundations were being laid for the Triple Alliance of mineworkers, railway workers, and transport workers.

Even if trade union activity did not mean that syndicalists could hope for a revolution, the conduct of women's agitation for the vote and the activities of the more militant defenders of the Union with Ireland do suggest that respect for the letter of the law was declining. The number of women in paid employment had increased sharply between 1891 and 1911, and many of the new working women held responsible jobs in offices, teaching, or nursing. The House of Commons had voted for the principle of women's suffrage in two Parliaments before 1906, but had allotted no time for further debate. Just before the 1906 election there were signs that women intended to attract attention to their cause by demonstrations; Ann Kenney and Christabel Pankhurst were fined (and went to prison rather than pay) for disorderly conduct at a meeting at which Churchill and Sir Edward Grey were speaking. It was a curious foretaste of future suffragette tactics that they chose to interrupt two supporters of women's suffrage.

The 1906 House of Commons contained a large majority in favour of women's suffrage, but the government still saw no need to provide time for a Bill and supporters of an extension of the franchise saw no reason for immediate action: Liberals wanted a Bill giving the vote to the one-third of adult males who had not been enfranchised by the 1884 Act, and also to a less clearly defined part of the female population, and such an extension of the franchise would normally be followed fairly quickly by a general election. From 1906 onwards militant supporters of women's right to vote broke the law and were arrested in a steady succession of protests. They tried to force their way into the House of Commons, refused to move when asked by the police to leave, and used a range of methods of civil disobedience. The question of civil disobedience divided women who were struggling for the vote: the law-abiding National Union of Women's Suffrage Societies (suffragists) and the Women's Social and Political Union (WSPU, the suffragettes), which was dominated by Christabel Pankhurst and her mother, Emmeline, could not agree about the means to their common goal. The process of demonstration followed by imprisonment went on into 1909, when women prisoners went on hunger strike and the authorities retaliated by feeding them forcibly.

By this stage two distinct struggles were developing. The suffragists would have been satisfied to get a Bill through Parliament, and they realized that considerations of party tactics made this harder than it looked. The suffragettes were beginning to see the issue as a contest between men and women in which women would not be treated fairly unless the eventual solution accepted women's right to vote as a paramount principle. They were not interested in a compromise, or in any scheme to combine some female enfranchisement with the extension of male suffrage. As this mood developed, it became less a question of politics and more a matter of asserting that women had to be taken seriously. Many legal restrictions on women, which had prevented them from owning property, being admitted to universities, or entering professions, had been removed in the late nineteenth century, but this had not altered the fact that women were not treated equally. The vote seemed to be the last formal issue on which there could be a struggle and the suffragettes wanted to use it as a battleground on which to assert the general principle of equality or, it sometimes seemed in the more passionate outpourings of the Pankhursts, the principle that in everything except brute strength women were men's superiors.[5] In its more extreme manifestations women's struggle for the vote became an unpolitical movement. The cause attracted supporters who were rebelling against the trammels of family life or against inequalities imposed on women that had nothing to do with the law. In all previous agitations to extend the right to vote, the lead had been taken by politicians who were already enfranchised and thought that other people should be brought into the electorate. In the struggle for votes for women the great bulk of the work of agitation was carried on by women, though a few men were useful auxiliaries: Pethick-Lawrence was perhaps the most helpful and George Lansbury, who resigned his seat in Parliament and fought unsuccessfully in the subsequent by-election as a Women's Suffrage candidate, was the most quixotic.

In 1910 a Conciliation Bill was introduced; it was designed to enfranchise a small enough number of women to convince opponents of women's suffrage that there was nothing dangerous about it. The vote was to be given to slightly over a million women who owned property in their own right which would have allowed them to vote if they had been men. This formula would have given the vote to a relatively wealthy and relatively elderly section of the female population, so it would have benefited the Conservative Party. Churchill spoke for those Liberals who wanted women to have the vote but did not like confining the vote to this particular group of women. The Bill was killed by being sent to a committee of the whole House, but it continued to attract the suffragettes because it was a measure for women only.

A less pro-Conservative version of the Conciliation Bill got a second reading, but was again killed, in 1911. In the intervening election the government had promised to give all men over 21 the right to vote and had declared that opportunities for women's suffrage amendments would be provided. It repeated these pledges after the 1911 derailment of the Conciliation Bill. The suffragettes saw tacking women's suffrage on to men's suffrage in this way as intolerable. Civil disobedience had been going on, with occasional truces,

5. See C. Pankhurst, *The Great Scourge* (1913).

since 1906 and had helped to establish the question in the public eye: meetings had been interrupted and speakers had been attacked, and the suffragettes had accepted the principle of using violence to advocate their cause. From the beginning of 1912 violence became more organized and deliberate: Mrs Pankhurst advised her followers to break windows, and they broke windows. They broke them all the more enthusiastically when the Speaker ruled on 27 January 1913 that amendments turning a Bill based on manhood suffrage into one based on adult suffrage were far too drastic for the rules of parliamentary procedure, and the government dropped the Bill altogether. The constitutional supporters of women's suffrage were left with nothing to do but bring forward another Bill moved by Dickinson, a Liberal backbencher. The suffragettes moved on to arson and other violent methods; Emily Davison threw herself in front of the horses at the Derby and was trampled to death.

Extreme militancy did not help the cause of women's suffrage. Opinion in the House of Commons moved against it. In 1911 the House had accepted the principle by giving a Second Reading to the Conciliation Bill; in 1913 a private member's Bill was defeated. In the same year the government felt strong enough to arm itself against hunger strikers by passing an Act allowing it to release hunger strikers and then rearrest them as soon as they were well enough to serve their sentences. The Act, nicknamed the 'Cat and Mouse' Act, probably helped the women's cause; the public seems to have accepted that civil disobedience was a reasonable method by which women could show that they were in earnest, though 'militancy'—the use of violence and the destruction of property—was not accepted in the same way. The political struggle seemed less hopeful in late 1913 than for some years, perhaps because of militancy, or a desire to keep the parliamentary timetable clear for Home Rule, or a calculation that women's suffrage would help the Conservatives, or irritation at the way the WSPU attacked the Liberal and Labour Parties, most of whose members supported women's suffrage. The defeat of the private member's Bill meant that the government no longer felt it had to provide time for another Bill, so the cause was blocked indefinitely unless the Prime Minister took a hand. And as Asquith had all along been the most eminent of the opponents of women's suffrage, it seemed unlikely that he would do anything.

He left the door slightly ajar. On 20 June 1914 he received a delegation of working-class women from the East End of London, organized by Sylvia Pankhurst, Christabel's sister. At the meeting he seems to have accepted that working-class women did want the vote; these women he saw were so poor that nothing short of an adult suffrage Act would enfranchise them, and he acknowledged that such an Act might be needed. The suffragettes responded with a new and more violent outburst of destruction; the Act would not be a measure for women only, and in any case Mrs Pankhurst and her daughter Christabel had moved a long way from the family's original socialism, to which Sylvia Pankhurst was still loyal.

Threats to stability: Ireland

While the suffragettes caused alarm and confusion for some years, they could not overthrow the government or bring about a collapse of law and order. Things were different in Ireland; when Asquith had his relatively conciliatory meeting on the suffrage question, he was keenly aware that two private armies had formed in Ireland, and that his government was about to pass legislation that might launch the armies at one another's throats.

The Home Rule Bill set up a Parliament for the whole island of Ireland and gave it roughly the powers enjoyed by the parliament of Northern Ireland between 1920 and 1972, though the financial provisions were less generous than the eventual settlement for Northern Ireland because they assumed that Ireland would some day cease receiving money from the British taxpayer. In 1903 the Conservatives had set up a government-financed scheme to buy out the Irish landlords, so they were no longer so directly affected by Home Rule. The Protestants of Ulster were as worried as ever, and their objections were encouraged by the British Conservatives. Opponents of the Bill produced a number of unsubstantial grounds for saying that it was not constitutional. They said that, because the Parliament Act declared in its preamble that the membership of the Lords ought to be revised, the Lords ought to retain their veto until the revision took place. They said that on this subject Irish votes ought not to count. A Conservative Home Ruler like W. S. Blunt could say with some logic, 'though with a majority of 126, Asquith is really in an English minority of fourteen', but other Conservatives came fairly close to saying that the Irish were not to have a parliament of their own but at the same time their votes at Westminster were not to be counted.[6]

The Home Rule Bill would take two to three years to pass into law under the Parliament Act, which gave its opponents time to prepare to resist it by force. Before it was even introduced into the House of Commons the Ulster Protestants had begun to hold large demonstrations, had entrusted Carson with the leadership of their movement, and had spoken of setting up a provisional government if it were passed. The Bill was introduced for the first time in April 1912, and Ulster preparations became more organized. Orangemen drilled, which they were legally entitled to do after obtaining the permission of two magistrates; Law declared that he 'could imagine no length of resistance to which [Protestant Ulstermen] might go in which they would not be supported by the overwhelming majority of the British people'.[7] It would be hard to go much further in the direction of incitement to rebellion without giving direct orders to break the law.

At the end of September the Ulstermen produced their Covenant, on the

6. W. S. Blunt, *My Diaries* (1920), ii. 347.
7. Robert Blake, *The Unknown Prime Minister* (1953), 130.

lines of the Covenant which the Scots had signed before resisting the government of Charles I. Hundreds of thousands of people took an oath to stand together against any government that tried to impose Home Rule. Some of them signed in blood; all of them were clearly moving towards rebellion. Equally steadily the government took the Home Rule Bill through the House of Commons in 1912, resisting suggestions of a special status for Ulster. After the Lords rejected it, the government brought the Bill forward again in 1913. At this point the Cabinet considered proposing a special status for the Protestants of Ulster, but they knew that their parliamentary majority, which depended on the Home Rulers, would not survive a precipitate move towards compromise. Meanwhile the Conservatives protested that Asquith had only pressed on with Home Rule because he had made a corrupt bargain to get the Irish to vote for the budget and the Parliament Bill, and that Home Rule had never been before the electorate. Why it should be corrupt for Asquith to promise to do something which had been part of the Liberal programme for twenty-five years was not explained, and Home Rule had been before the people in the election of December 1910, for the Conservatives had referred to it frequently. The Lords had not dominated the contest to the exclusion of all other issues; Home Rule Free Traders and Protectionist Unionists had put their arguments forward, and outside Ireland the electorate had voted against Protection and the Lords without showing much concern about Home Rule.

The Conservative Party in Great Britain in this period behaved as though it was above the constitution. It was entirely reasonable for the Ulster Protestants to hold demonstrations to show fully their deep detestation of the idea of being ruled from Dublin. It may have been defensible for them to make plans to set up a provisional government. It was not reasonable for them to say that, because the Protestant section of Ulster wanted to remain part of the United Kingdom and at the same time was opposed to partition, no part of Ireland should have Home Rule. Redmond opposed partition in a way that dented the rights of a minority in Ireland; Carson opposed partition in a way that denied the rights of a majority in Ireland. But if Carson's attitude was undemocratic, that of the British Unionists who secretly collected money to finance a rebellion was worse, and that of Sir Henry Wilson, who used his position at the War Office to undermine the government's control of the army, was much more disreputable.

By the beginning of 1914 the government admitted that the Ulster Protestants were entitled to some sort of special treatment. An Amending Bill was drafted, to be introduced when the Home Rule Bill set off on its third and final trip round the parliamentary course. The nine counties of Ulster would be allowed to hold plebiscites, which would allow the four indisputably Protestant counties of Antrim, Armagh, Down, and Londonderry, and perhaps the two evenly divided counties of Fermanagh and Tyrone, to opt out of the new Ireland ruled from Dublin: everybody accepted that the three Catholic counties in Ulster would opt in. The Bill provided that counties which opted out would be united with the rest of Ireland at the end of six years. This curious arrangement meant that, if the Conservatives won either of the two general elections that would be held in these six years, they could amend the Home Rule Act to let the counties opt out for ever. Redmond accepted this; many of his followers preferred to go off and join the Nationalist Volunteers, who were drilling and preparing like the Ulstermen.

The government had abstained from any action so far; in March it prepared to send troops north to Ulster to secure points of strategic value, but when it tried to do this it was confronted with what has been called, rather misleadingly, the Mutiny at the Curragh. In 1912 Keir Hardie had asked Haldane's successor at the War Office, Colonel Seely, if it would be possible for recruits to declare in advance whether they were willing to take part in action against strikers, and Seely had said the idea was fantastic. There was a good reason for his answer: a soldier who simply obeys legal orders does not need to approve of the policy implied by the orders, but a soldier who has to choose whether to obey certain orders has to decide whether to approve of the policy. Seely saw the difficulties of asking soldiers whether they were willing to shoot strikers or not, but he failed to make it clear that this applied to Ireland as well. When steps to secure the strategic points were being planned, General Paget, who was in command at the Curragh camp to the west of Dublin, asked Seely to show consideration for the feelings of officers from Ulster; Seely said that officers from Ulster could 'disappear' for the duration of the operation. When Paget told his officers of the plans, they formed the impression that resistance to the advance into Ulster was expected, and that officers from Ulster were being allowed to 'disappear' and return later, while other officers were being asked to resign their commissions if they did not choose to go forward against Ulster. Almost all the officers at the Curragh resigned; they thought they had been asked to commit themselves to the policy of Home Rule and to agree to shoot civilians if that was necessary to carry the policy out. Seely tried to repair the damage by issuing a statement of policy drawn up by the Cabinet, but he only made matters worse when he added extra paragraphs promising that the army would not be used to impose Home Rule on Ulster. This was too much, and Seely's resignation was accepted. The episode left the Opposition confident that the government had disarmed itself and that it was now impossible to impose Home Rule.

Carson's provisional government-in-waiting became bolder; it allowed people to know that arms had been imported and that Ulster was beginning to feel a strong attachment to Germany. As the rest of Ireland drilled to prevent Ulster's secession, the situation grew more tense. Redmond became afraid that he had been too concerned with parliamentary affairs, and forced the Nationalist Volunteers to accept him as their leader. Their organization was two years behind that of Ulster, and they did not have Mr Astor, the Duke of Bedford, and other rich men to finance purchases of arms, but of course both these paramilitary organizations carried out a good deal of parading to show weight of numbers and opinion rather than actually to fight.[8] Even so, Home Rule could not have been set up in Ireland without settling the Ulster question because a provisional government in Belfast, fully supported by Protestant Ulster, would have been proclaimed as soon as Home Rule was established. The Unionists in Britain who were ready for civil war did not command widespread support for their violent approach even within their own party. The Conservatives had been saying, ever since the introduction of the Home Rule Bill, that there ought to be a general election on the issue; however, when intransigent Unionists suggested privately that the House of Lords should use its remaining powers and reject the annual Army Act in order to force an election, the moderates refused to hear of such a thing, partly because they did not think it would be very sensible to disband the army and partly because they thought an election on the issue of the Army Act would be a Liberal landslide.

The Amending Bill to the Home Rule Bill was introduced into the Lords and was altered out of recognition. As a result the government could foresee a situation in which the Home Rule Bill would have passed the Commons the requisite three times and there would be no Amending Act to hand. George V apparently had doubts—which the Conservatives anxiously encouraged—whether he should sign the Home Rule Bill if it came to him without an Amending Bill. He was afraid that he would be denounced by half his subjects whether he signed or did not sign; he seems not to have noticed that this apparent dilemma could arise on any controversial legislation as soon as he departed from the safe course of accepting his Prime Minister's advice as binding. But his uneasiness made him eager to bring together the leaders of the Liberal and Conservative Parties and of the Ulster and Home Rule organizations to work out an agreed settlement. A conference was held at his suggestion; it started on 21 July, but as it could not agree on the boundaries of Protestant Ulster, which ran somewhere through the counties of Fermanagh and Tyrone, it broke up on the 24th. The next day brought another reminder of the seriousness of the position; the Irish Volunteers had arranged to bring in 1,500 rifles at Howth, which might be thought to be only a fair exchange for the 30,000 that the Orangemen had brought ashore at Larne in April. But there was a difference; after Larne it had been established that importing arms was illegal, which was not clear previously. The Dublin authorities sent troops to intercept the rifles, but were unsuccessful; the Dublin mob threw stones at the soldiers as they marched back to barracks, and in Bachelor's Walk the soldiers' discipline broke down; they opened fire without orders and killed three people. The Nationalist Volunteers became more bellicose than before.

8. A. M. Gollin, *Proconsul in Politics* (1964), 188.

The calm of the government in the face of these events was alarming, but not incomprehensible. General Macready, in command in Northern Ireland, must have reported to Asquith along the lines indicated in his autobiography:

I have often been asked what would have happened in Ulster if the [First World] war had not intervened. I do not know. When going about the country outside Belfast during the summer of 1914 it would seem from the reports of the police and soldiers that the state of feeling between Catholics and Protestants was improving. . . . In the North, Belfast was the centre of all trouble, and in travelling through the country one noticed the change of feeling directly that city was out of sight . . . the troops looked on with amused indifference at the warlike preparations of the Ulstermen, and I had no more fear that the soldiers would be the aggressors in any conflict than that they would not carry out their duty if called upon. . . . The policy I did advocate was 'Govern or get out,' and that is exactly what in 1914 Mr. Asquith would not do.[9]

Asquith might reasonably have replied that he was trying to get out (of Ireland) as fast as the Lords would let him. He could not do much while he was waiting for the Bill. Carson had probably committed sedition or even treason, but neither conviction nor acquittal in a state trial would have carried much weight because it was almost impossible to find a politically unbiased jury. In the negotiations the Ulstermen declined to accept the result even if another general election were held specifically on Home Rule: the government was left to conclude that any concessions on Ulster would only encourage pressure for further concessions on other points. The government decided to wait and see what the final Ulster position was, and meanwhile relied on Macready's troops and the fact that the general public, if things came to civil war, would tend to be against the people who fired the first shots.

Future prospects: tension in politics and art

From the government's point of view Ireland was only one of a cluster of problems that surrounded the future of the Liberal Party, its allies in the House of Commons, and the next stage in the development of its policy. The Home Rulers would stick by the government, despite their uneasiness about the Cabinet's evident willingness to compromise over Ulster, as long as a substantial measure of Home Rule went through. Satisfying Liberal and Labour supporters in Britain was a little harder. One energetic social reformer, Churchill, had left the field; he had moved to the Admiralty in October 1911 and thrown himself into his new work, insisting on more money for bigger ships and becoming correspondingly less ready to see money spent on domestic welfare. The success of the 1909 budget, with its attack on the landed interest, convinced Lloyd George that the electorate was eager for a programme that would open the way to a great many other reforms by changing

---

9. C. F. N. Macready, *Annals of an Active Life* (1924), i. 196–8.

the structure of land ownership. The first and most fully developed part of his programme would have broken up the great estates and created a Ministry of Land to finance development by tenant farmers, encourage smallholdings, and enforce a minimum wage for farm labourers. It seems unlikely that this programme would have been electorally very attractive or that it could have had much effect on the land. The flow of population from country to town was very hard to stop, let alone reverse, which was what Lloyd George's plan called for. Farmers may have been slightly underfinanced, but they were competing with North American farmers, who, even when less well financed, could undersell them because of the scale of operations on the open prairies. Nothing short of tariffs or subsidies, neither of them acceptable to the party of Free Trade, could have enabled farmers in the United Kingdom to compete with the 'last, best West' in Canada which was at this time being heavily settled for the first time. The immense British capital exports of the time, a large part of which went to build the Canadian Northern Railway, showed that London financial opinion thought Canadian wheat was unlikely to be displaced by Lloyd George's programme.

The urban part of the programme probably held out better prospects for the Liberal Party. Urban landlords have never held the positions of honour and respect attained by the best rural landlords, and have often been very unpopular. The urban programme linked the ownership of land with the removal of slums and the improvement of housing; governments had been hovering on the edge of taking some responsibility for housing for three decades, and it would have helped the Liberals a great deal if Lloyd George convinced the electorate that they would really do something.

The land programme was held up when Lloyd George's career suffered a sharp temporary check in 1913. Early in 1912 the government gave the English Marconi Company a contract to build stations for wireless radio communication round the Empire. Shortly after, rumours were heard that ministers had been making money for themselves by buying Marconi shares at a time when they knew the company was going to benefit from this contract. The rumour was made public by the anti-Semitic Chestertons, who thought the Postmaster-General, Herbert Samuel, had given the contract to Godfrey Isaacs, managing director of Marconi and brother of Rufus Isaacs, the Attorney-General, as part of a Jewish conspiracy. The award of the contract was entirely proper; however, Godfrey Isaacs had persuaded Rufus to take up shares in the American Marconi Company, and Rufus Isaacs had not only taken up the shares but had passed some on to Lloyd George and some to the Liberal Party funds. Perhaps this was a natural thing to happen inside a family, and in any case American Marconi gained nothing from the English Marconi contract. But when the issue came up in Parliament in October, Rufus Isaacs and Lloyd George showed that they knew their behaviour would be hard to justify; they avoided mentioning American Marconi when they denied buying

English Marconi shares. A Select Committee of the House of Commons was set up to investigate the rumours; inevitably the purchases of American Marconi shares came out, and equally inevitably the failure to mention them in October made the whole transaction look even worse than it had been. In June 1913 the Committee presented two reports. The Liberal majority said the purchasers had no stain on their honour, though the Liberal chairman had wanted to say the purchase was ill advised. The Conservative minority said the purchase was a grave indiscretion. The reports were debated, and the House divided on the normal party lines. There is no sign that Lloyd George felt any lasting gratitude to Asquith for keeping him in the government when dismissing him would have reduced political tension, or felt any lasting resentment against the Conservatives who had wanted to crush him. In 1914 he showed all his old ability to take on two jobs at once; apart from running the land campaign he produced another complicated budget which increased taxes, though it did not impose any new ones, and provided much larger grants from the central government to local authorities to cover increased spending on social welfare. The budget turned out to be too time-consuming for a parliamentary timetable crowded with Irish business, so the grants had to wait until the next year, but the proposal did show that the government had not run short of new schemes for the future.

The Opposition was happily placed; for purposes of criticism they could simultaneously ask for increased spending and denounce the high level of the existing taxes, and justify this by saying that Tariff Reform would provide the extra money needed. On the whole they wasted their opportunity by concentrating on asking for more expenditure on armaments, a request that probably gained few votes. The government had its problems. but was not directly troubled by the strength of the Opposition in 1914. In the days before opinion polls people measured the government's standing from the by-election results. The government and their Labour allies lost fifteen seats in elections between 1910 and 1914, a normal enough setback, but the pattern of seats lost was more significant. Apart from Lansbury's seat lost on Women's Suffrage, in three of the eight seats lost before the end of 1912 Liberal and Labour candidates had opposed one another and between them polled a majority of the votes cast, and this also happened in five of the seven seats lost in the next nineteen months. If this pattern of results had continued, the fate of the next election would have depended on the course of relations between the Liberal and Labour Parties. MacDonald and his supporters in the Labour Party were quite willing to continue to operate the division of seats originally arranged for the 1906 election, and if they had been able to hold back the enthusiasts who wanted an all-out attack on the Liberal Party and confine three-cornered contests to by-elections, the Liberal and Labour Parties could have benefited from the Plural Voting Bill, which was due to pass into law in 1914, and from an Adult Suffrage Bill if it could be passed. Despite Ireland, the government was reasonably well placed politically as long as it could restore good relations with the Labour Party.

One obstacle to good relations between the Liberal and Labour Parties was the creation of the Triple Alliance, an agreement to cooperate reached by the railway workers, coalminers, and transport workers, who were mainly dockers and carters in the days before commercial motor transport. There were relatively few labour disputes in the early months of 1914, but it was generally accepted that this was only the lull before the storm; a combined strike by the Triple Alliance was thought to be very likely, and their command over transport would have made it into something very like a general strike. In economic terms probably the situation would have produced nothing worse than the 'strenuous time' which Askwith predicted for the autumn,[10] but in political terms a general strike would have made it hard to restore the Liberal–Labour alliance. The slight slackening of trade noticed in 1914 made a strike less likely, but it could have damaged the government's political prospects in other ways.

While Britain was not on the verge of plunging into disorder and chaos in 1914, people were uneasy about what was going on. Something of this state of tension can be seen in the division to be found among poets at the time. The writers who flourished during the reign of Edward VII had very little in common with the Modern movement, but in the years before the war writers were emerging who were very different from the rational prophets of progress who had dominated the literary scene. This development was not so clear at the time: in the first years of the reign of George V the most obvious change in the literary scene was the appearance of a new group of poets who were published in *Georgian Poetry*, which was launched at the beginning of the new reign. Today they may be dismissed as the last thin squeezings from the great flow of Romantic poetry that had begun with Wordsworth, but at the time they were seen as something altogether more lively, and at times Georgian poets like Rupert Brooke even shocked the critics by the frankness with which they wrote about such things as seasickness.

There is not much sign that the Georgians knew about any poetic tradition except the Wordsworthian; Kipling could have told them that there had been quite a number of new ideas about poetry in France since the death of Wordsworth. The approach to poetry of the Symbolists was arriving in Britain during these years before the war, but this poetic wave of the future received relatively little attention. Because he was seen as a war poet of the early, optimistic part of the struggle and because of his death at the Dardanelles in 1915, Brooke gained much more attention than, poetically speaking, he deserved; later on he was picked out as one of the pre-war writers to be attacked by supporters of the Modern school. His contemporary T. S. Eliot

---

10. Askwith, *Industrial Problems and Disputes*, 356.

(born in 1888, a year after Brooke) went to England just after the war had begun, and in a few years had set English poetry down its new path. But it is not possible to look backwards and pass judgement on what would have happened if the war had not come: writers like Pound and Lewis were winning some acceptance for the approach of the Symbolists before Eliot arrived, but it was the war itself that encouraged among thoughtful and artistic people a pessimistic feeling that welcomed *The Waste Land* and the general attitude of Eliot. Just as nobody can say whether the Georgian poets would have developed, in a happier world, into a dominant and effective school of writers, on the wider stage nobody can say whether the peaceful and tranquil England that they represented would have survived the problems that confronted it in mid-1914 if the war had not come.

The outbreak of war

In July 1914 the government had its difficulties; the suffragettes, Ireland, the possibility of widespread strikes in the autumn, and perhaps the question of relations with the Labour Party were problems without obvious solutions, but it seems that not even Grey had realized that the murder of the Archduke Franz Ferdinand at Sarajevo on 28 June could lead to disaster. This was a curious oversight, for Grey had done a lot in 1913 to make sure that conflict in the Balkans did not spread in a way that involved the Great Powers. The international situation looked better in 1914 than for some time; for a few years after 1908 Germany had been building battleships at a rate which seemed to be threatening Britain's maritime supremacy, and there had been some tense weeks in 1911 after the German government had sent a warship, the *Panther*, to Agadir to demonstrate the seriousness of German claims to a position of influence in Morocco. But after the tension of 1909 Britain had settled down to building two battleships a year more than Germany, and by 1914 the naval race was attracting less attention. Relations between France and Germany had also grown less strained. The British would not have been totally surprised by a war with Germany over naval or colonial issues, and probably many of them were willing to fight to stop Germany obtaining mastery in Europe, but the idea of taking part in a war over a country in the Balkans would have struck them as very odd. Grey's own leisurely approach is easy to understand: during the three weeks between the assassination and his proposal of a conference, very little seemed to be happening. The Austrian government was screwing up its courage to make use of the imprudently wide-ranging promise of support given to it by the German government, but its ultimatum of 24 July, which gave the Serbian government forty-eight hours to accept terms which left little of the sovereignty of Serbia intact, was unexpected and was out of keeping with the pace of previous developments. It was delivered on the day of the breakdown of the King's conference on

Ireland, when politicians in the United Kingdom were understandably pre-occupied; Churchill wrote that 'a strange light began immediately, but by perceptible gradations, to fall and grow upon the map of Europe',[11] and some of his colleagues did not see the first of these gradations of light. Churchill himself agreed with the First Sea Lord's decision that the naval squadrons, which had been concentrated at Portsmouth for exercises, should not be dispersed, and Grey again attempted to arrange a conference. The Austrian government refused to be placed on a footing of equality with Serbia, for the whole object of its diplomacy was to demonstrate its superiority; accordingly, on the 28th it declared war on Serbia, which had accepted most of the ultimatum of the 24th but had appealed to its ally Russia for defence against the more humiliating terms.

Presumably the German government had realized that one effect of the ultimatum was to test Russia's ability to protect Serbia. Failure to protect an ally would be as humiliating as Austria's annexation of Bosnia and Hercegovina in 1908 over Russian protests, and the French might begin to doubt the value of the Russian alliance. By the end of July the British government understood what might happen: the fleet was moved to its battle station at Scapa Flow, and Grey advised the German ambassador that if the war spread Britain might not remain neutral. Austrian troops had marched into Serbia on the 29th; when Russia ordered mobilization on the 31st, the Germans told the Russians to stop mobilizing and told the French not to start.

Russia might have allowed Serbia to be bullied without intervening on her behalf, but Russia and France could hardly let Germany dictate their mobilization arrangements. On the other hand, a fully mobilized Russia would be a threat to Germany. A war on the Continent was probably inevitable by this stage. The French ambassador, Cambon, asked Grey on 31 July if the United Kingdom would enter the war; Grey pointed out perfectly accurately that his country had no treaty commitments to France and said that they would have to wait. Grey might have been able, at this point, to ensure that Britain did not enter the war immediately, though probably it would have been drawn in to preserve the balance of power when it was seen that France was losing. Instead he asked France and Germany for promises that they would not invade Belgium. France gave the required promise, but Germany declined. Next day the German ambassador asked if this promise would by itself be enough to keep Britain out of the war, but Grey declined to answer. Grey had probably decided that, if there was a major war, he would try to bring the country in to support France as soon as he could, but he did not want to make this clear to the French because they might become more eager to fight if they knew they could reckon on British help. Later writers have suggested that Grey should have said unequivocally that Britain would fight and thus deter Germany as

11. W. S. Churchill, *The World Crisis* (1923), i. 193.

much as possible, but a statement of this sort might easily have made France more bellicose. In any case his diplomacy was almost paralysed because he was not certain that he could speak for a united government. If he had taken ministers into his confidence earlier, he might have been able to intervene more effectively. Lloyd George seemed ready to place himself at the head of the peace party on 31 July, and this would have meant that the country would not enter the war united. Lloyd George was ready to fight on 1 August; on the 2nd he was at the head of three other opponents of British entry in the Cabinet. The discussion went on, two of the opponents resigned, but two, of whom Lloyd George was one, stayed in the government.

German command of the Channel took up a good deal of the attention of the Cabinet: during discussions between French and British military men, the British had encouraged the French to move their fleet to the Mediterranean, and the Cabinet was not prepared to let the Germans dominate the Channel as a result of this decision. By the time the German government announced on 3 August that it was willing to treat the Channel as a neutral zone if the United Kingdom stayed out of the war it was too late. After the Cabinet had gone home on the 2nd, the German government issued an ultimatum demanding to be allowed to send troops through Belgium to attack France.

What is now known of the rigid plans of the German High Command makes it hard to see why war had been delayed even this long. German arrangements for mobilization were laid down in the Schlieffen Plan, which took it for granted that in any war Germany would have to fight France and Russia simultaneously. The plan provided for a holding operation against Russia in the east while the bulk of the German army marched, not against the difficult terrain of the Franco-German frontier, but round the north through Belgium, outflanking and eventually surrounding the French army as it had been surrounded at Sedan in 1870. The German High Command had not prepared any alternative plan; this was why it insisted on forcing France into the war, by the ultimatum of 31 July, and it was completely unconcerned about the possibility that invading Belgium would lead the British government to declare war. No doubt the High Command would have preferred it to remain neutral, and Kaiser William was undoubtedly very disturbed to hear that Britain might enter the war. But the High Command certainly did not think that the risk of British involvement should deter them from marching through Belgium, and the Kaiser did not think that risk would justify him in opposing the strategy of the High Command. Because no other plans had been pre-pared, Germany would have had great difficulty in fighting at all without invading Belgium; the British response was not thought important enough to affect the issue. Even if the German ambassador had reported on the 1st that the United Kingdom would remain neutral if Belgium were not invaded, it would have been too late to devise a new plan of campaign.

Grey's diplomacy was often criticized after 1914. German apologists said in essence said that their country would have respected the neutrality of Belgium if it had known how seriously Britain was concerned about it. But one difficulty about negotiating with Germany about Belgian neutrality was that the German government had already undertaken to respect it in the 1839 Treaty of London; if Germany had based its strategy on ignoring that treaty, it would have been hard to rely on any subsequent German undertakings. Grey was also criticized by the British left. They wanted the country's policy to be peace-loving and upright, and they were determined to make their government live up to these ideals. But they had two distinct objectives which were hard to reconcile: they wanted Belgium to be protected, and they did not want Britain to go to war. They overestimated their country's place in the world: it was not at all certain that a British threat of war would have saved Belgium from invasion, and in any case Grey could deliver such a threat convincingly only if he took a bellicose attitude that the left would have found very objectionable. There is an irritating philosophic calm about Grey's remark that 'the lights are going out all over Europe', but probably there was nothing that he could have done about it.

The invasion of Belgium made it relatively easy for Grey to rally the House of Commons behind the government on 3 August. The Conservatives had already made it clear that they would support war; Grey needed to appeal to his own backbenchers and the opinion of the neutral world. He was greatly helped in both tasks when Redmond said that the violent agitation for Home Rule would be called off and the Volunteers would place themselves at the disposal of the government. But the voice of the Gladstonian approach to foreign policy was not completely silent; one speaker did say that this was not a war for Belgium but a war that would upset the whole balance of Europe. It was not a good omen for the Liberal Party that the speaker was the leader of the Labour Party, Ramsay MacDonald. Next day the government called on Germany to pledge itself to respect Belgian neutrality. German troops had already crossed the frontier; at 11 p.m. Britain entered the war.

3

'Blow out, you bugles, over the rich dead'[1]

1914–1918

Grand strategy

Haldane once said he wanted a Hegelian army; and certainly the 1914–18 war was a Hegelian war, drawing more of the nation's resources into the hands of government, giving more power to the State, and making national survival more dependent on wise decisions by its rulers than ever before in British history. All this was even more true in the Second World War, but the difference between the First World War and the Second was a matter of degree. The First World War was different in kind from any previous war in which Britain had fought.

A sketch of the grand strategy of the war will set the activities of the British people and its government in context. In August and September 1914 the German army tried to follow the Schlieffen Plan, swept through Belgium, and forced its way almost to Paris. It was checked by a counter-attack on the Marne and forced to fall back, but it continued to occupy almost all of Belgium and a large slice of north-east France. German attention was distracted by an attack on its eastern frontier by the Russian army, which proved more mobile than Schlieffen had expected, but the Russian attack was defeated. The German High Command reversed the strategy of the Schlieffen Plan, staying on the defensive in the west (with one big exception) until 1918, and devoting its offensive efforts to the east. In 1915 the French and, to a lesser extent, the British attacked the German defensive lines. British interest, though not the bulk of British resources, concentrated on trying to force a way through the Dardanelles, hold the Bosporus, and open a line of communication to Russia where most of the materials needed for modern war were already running short. In 1916 the Germans launched an unsuccessful attempt to capture Verdun, their only serious offensive in the west between 1914 and

1. This is the first line of Rupert Brooke's third war sonnet, 'The Dead'.

1918, and later in 1916 the newly recruited British armies made their first full-scale attack on the German defensive position. This was also unsuccessful, and although British command of the sea, on which her tight blockade of Germany depended, was not broken at the Battle of Jutland, a German counter-blockade by submarine became a more serious threat. In the east Romania entered the war against Germany and Austria-Hungary and was quickly crushed by them, and the Russian military and political structure began to disintegrate. Early in 1917 the United States entered the war as an 'associate' of the United Kingdom and France, and a revolution swept away the tsarist government of Russia. The submarine blockade became increasingly dangerous until the adoption of convoy tactics defeated the threat to British supplies. The German defensive line was attacked by the French in the first half of 1917 and by the British in the second half of the year. The Germans held their positions and completed the work of destroying Russia as an effective force; by the end of the year a Bolshevik government was in power with little choice but to make peace immediately, and the German High Command could bring its troops back to the west. By 1918 the Germans had to take the initiative; the blockade was slowing down their whole economy, and the United Kingdom and France could afford to wait until American support reached them. From March to July the Germans launched five great offensives upon the British and French, forcing their enemies back in almost every case without ever gaining a decisive victory. By the end of July their forces were overstrained and their reserves used up. The Western powers had held on successfully; in the summer and autumn of 1918 they once more attacked the German line and this time broke it. Weighing the factors that caused the sudden collapse is difficult; however, within four months of the last German offensive the generalissimo of the Western powers granted an armistice to the leaders of the German army and saw the old constitution founded on the hegemony of Prussia and the rule of the house of Hohenzollern swept away.

The volunteers' war

In August 1914 the War Book, which listed all the instructions to be sent out to British forces when war began, was in good order. The Fleet was in position. The British Expeditionary Force crossed the Channel, and moved forward into Belgium. When it reached Mons, it came into contact with the weight of the German advance. The retreat from Mons that inevitably followed was conducted quite skilfully, but it was already clear that the French and British High Commands had not worked out how to coordinate their operations. The German armies, which might conceivably have fulfilled Schlieffen's ambitious plan if they had marched south-west from Belgium towards Paris, slipped into marching due south. As a result they lost their chance of outflanking the French and British armies, and opened their own left wing to an attack by the troops of the garrison of Paris; half of one division was hurried to the front by taxicab. The German army, which had reached the River Marne, fell back about forty miles in late September to the River Aisne. At this stage there were no forces worth mentioning north or west of the exposed German left wing, but both sides quickly extended their lines. The Germans hoped to capture the Channel ports to cut Britain's communications with France; the French and British were correspondingly determined to save the ports. The German advance was held up for a few days by a makeshift force put together and sent to Antwerp by Churchill, who offered to leave the Cabinet to become an army commander. But the days for imaginative expedients were coming to an end, though Churchill had two other ideas to offer later. The German outflanking attempts were checked at the first battle of Ypres, where the pounding tactics which dominated most of the war were already to be seen. By the end of November the Channel ports were safe, and the line ran north from the German position on the Aisne to the sea. The armies dug their trenches deeper and deeper, and prepared for the next season's campaign.

By the end of 1914 the Navy had swept the oceans clear of the German ships which had been at sea when war began; most of them had been sunk, but two German ships, the *Goeben* and the *Breslau*, had slipped through the Mediterranean at the very beginning of the war, and helped to persuade Turkey to enter the war on the German side. The destruction of a German squadron at the Falkland Islands, after its initial success at Coronel, meant that British trade was safe from attack until the submarine offensive began. The blockade of Germany was already effective, though it could have been made even more complete if the Foreign Office had not been obliged, by constant American protests, to remind the Admiralty that the United States was a neutral power and that her shipping had to be treated with some respect. For the first three years of the war the belligerent governments had to woo 'neutral' opinion, which really meant the opinion of the United States. The British and French understood the importance of the United States, though sometimes they assumed too readily that the Anglophiles and Francophiles of the east coast, led by ex-President Theodore Roosevelt, were typical of all American opinion. Although the United States always leaned in the direction of Britain and France, so that there was no likelihood that she would enter the war against them, which would have led almost immediately to their defeat, most Americans hoped to remain at peace. Immensely exaggerated accounts of German atrocities in Belgium encouraged anti-German feeling in the United States, as well as building up enthusiasm for the war in Britain and France, but the Germans were quite wrong to think that the United States was committed against them, or to imagine that its views were of no importance. Wilson was re-elected President in 1916 as the man who kept the United States out of the war; if he had not been provoked by the remarkably foolish and (by the standards of the day) barbarous policy of submarine warfare, he would probably have continued to keep her out.

The German forces in German East Africa (later Tanganyika) avoided capture until the end of the war, but Samoa was captured in 1914, German South West Africa in 1915, and the Cameroons early in 1916. All the Dominions took it for granted in 1914 that when Britain was at war they were at war, and raised volunteer armies in a mood of imperial enthusiasm and unity. Before the campaign in South West Africa the South African government of Botha and Smuts, which was completely committed to support of the British Empire, dispersed some rebels who wanted to take the opportunity to reverse the verdict of the Boer War.

In Britain Lloyd George's first wartime budget increased taxation rather lightly and set the pattern of paying for the war by loans; this was maintained to the end, and only in 1918 did income tax reach 30p in the pound. The rich and the middle classes found the money to finance the war, but as a good deal of their contribution came as loans at rising rates of interest, those who had money to invest were repaid later. Many rich people responded to war by cutting down spending, companies found themselves unable to carry on their old lines of trade, so unemployment rose initially; price levels went up sharply while 'business as usual' (a slogan partly intended to help people put out of work during the first few months of the war) went on into the winter of 1914, and wage rates lagged behind. Although wage rates did not catch up with prices while the war was on, few workers suffered a decline in living standards, because employment was much more continuous once the first dislocation was over, and a great many people had moved to better-paid jobs.

Thinking about the war in a more imaginative way than most people, the First Lord of the Admiralty produced two suggestions during the winter. Several other people around the same time thought of building an armoured vehicle running on caterpillar tracks which could crawl over a line of trenches, an idea which had effects for decades to come. It was not immediately made effective, but Churchill's other suggestion, that the British should force the Dardanelles, knock Turkey out of the war, and open supply lines to Russia, dominated the government's approach to the war for most of 1915. At first he thought the older battleships not needed for watching the German High Seas Fleet could do the job. As most authorities then and later (though not Lord Fisher, once more First Sea Lord) agreed, his plan must have had some substance to it, even though taking forts with ships is a difficult operation. The naval attack took place on 25 March, but was held up by uncharted mines, which sank three battleships and reduced the Admiralty's faith in the operation. Although persistence would have brought success, the naval attack was not likely to be resumed. However, the government had decided just after the naval attack to allot a division to the operation; on 25 April troops landed at Gallipoli and established themselves on the shore but could not press forward.

In France the Germans stood on the defensive most of the time; the French attacked fiercely but with no noticeable success. The British regular army was too small to absorb losses of the size suffered by all armies in 1914, and if it had been free to choose, the British government might have spent the year training and equipping its new volunteer army. The demands of the alliance made this impossible. The second battle of Ypres was the most important British battle in France in 1915. It began with an ill-organized German attack, preceded by the first use of poison gas, at just about the same time as the British landing at Gallipoli. The struggle was kept going by a series of British counter-attacks to pin down German troops while the French prepared their offensive. As the battle went on, it became clear that British forces were paralysed by a shortage of shells for their guns because the pre-war supply department of the War Office had not foreseen the large-scale bombardments which now proved necessary.

In mid-May the Liberal government found itself obliged to take the Conservatives into a coalition. MPs knew about the shell shortage and blamed the government; suddenly they heard that Fisher had resigned from the Admiralty because he disapproved of the Gallipoli operations. The Conservatives were ready to oppose the policy of the government openly: Asquith hurriedly put together a coalition to prevent this, partly to avoid revealing any weaknesses at just the moment Grey was persuading Italy to enter the war on the British side, but mainly because the political position of the Liberals was not strong enough for them to resist. The old ministers dominated Asquith's Coalition; Asquith and Grey remained unchanged, Kitchener gave up the War Office supply responsibilities to Lloyd George, who became Minister of Munitions, McKenna replaced Lloyd George at the Exchequer, and the only Conservative who gained a position of central importance was Balfour, who replaced Churchill at the Admiralty. Although Haldane was dropped and Churchill relegated to the Chancellorship of the Duchy of Lancaster, the allocation of jobs suggests that the Liberals still controlled the situation. This may have encouraged the Conservatives not to feel any great loyalty to Asquith's Coalition.

Reinforcements were sent to Gallipoli in August. Another opportunity to press forward was presented, and again it was not taken. After this the Turks and Germans brought up more troops, and the Cabinet slowly realized that the position was too exposed for winter operations. By January 1916 the force had been withdrawn tidily and bloodlessly. Gallipoli remains one of the great question marks over the war. German and Turkish sources indicate that on two or three occasions a little extra speed or resolution would have carried the advance forward to the European side of the Bosporus. Supporters of the expedition said that such an advance would have led to Turkey's collapse. Supplies would have reached Russia, the 1917 revolutions could have been averted, and Germany would have been crushed between two well-armed opponents. The British High Command believed that the only essential area was the western front; they, and their later supporters, argued that even if Turkey had been defeated there was no real surplus of arms to give to Russia and that conducting a campaign in the Balkans was too difficult. The second point was illustrated a little later: Britain and France set up a large army at Salonika in northern Greece, but while this force ensured that Greece did not follow the pro-German inclinations of her King, it was not able to march north into the Balkans.

While the preparations for evacuation were being made at Gallipoli, the British army in France was launching another attack on the German defensive line. Sir John French, the British commander in France, mismanaged the battle of Loos and was soon replaced by Haig, but it seems unlikely that more skilful handling would have led to a breakthrough.

This failure added force to the pressure for conscription in Britain. When the war began, people had talked about it being 'all over by Christmas'; their ideas of war were clearly drawn from the wars in Europe in 1866 and 1870, which ended quickly, rather than from the long-drawn-out American Civil War of 1861–5, in which the power of the defence and the importance of industrial preparation were made clear. The government believed in 1914 that while the small, highly trained professional army would be sent to France as planned, the main British contribution would be naval, financial, and industrial, supplying materials for France and Russia. When the war began, Kitchener, an immense figure, a hero from the wars of colonial expansion in the 1880s and 1890s with a commanding presence that few people would argue with, had been made Secretary of State for War. In one of his moments of deep insight he saw that it would be a long war—he estimated three years. This justified raising and training a large army; if the war was to be over by Christmas, the volunteers who had rushed forward at the outbreak of war could not have played any effective part in the fighting. Whether Kitchener saw the other consequences of a long war will not be known; he did not say enough about how he intended to equip the new army, and what strategy he meant it to follow, to win the support of his ministerial colleagues for his policy.

Voluntary recruiting was easy at first. Men came forward in the spirit of Rupert Brooke's poem 'Now God be thanked who has matched us with His hour', and while this may not have been great poetry, it was not rashly ignorant of danger. All five of Brooke's very popular war poems are permeated with the thought of the 'best enemy and friend', death. People were ready not only to accept but to welcome war; the idea that war meant that 'nobility had returned to the earth' would not have been accepted after the early months of fighting and casualty lists. Grey was, by the standards of the diplomats of his time, rather unwilling to consider war as a normal instrument of policy, but most of the people of the United Kingdom were as willing to accept it as people elsewhere.

If this simply meant that armies could be raised by voluntary methods, the administrative inconvenience might have been justified by the moral benefits. But volunteering was not a simple matter of individual choice; enthusiasm had to be stimulated and social pressure applied to possible recruits. Demagogues like Horatio Bottomley took to the platform to stir young men to come forward, and attracted recruits by exploiting the wild anti-German feeling that had broken out. Because Germany was at war with Britain, people broke the windows of shopkeepers with German names, denounced owners of dachshunds as unpatriotic, and suggested that the music of Beethoven and Bach was worthless. The sharp decline from Brooke the romantic poet to Bottomley, a company promoter who took large fees for his recruiting speeches and was twice expelled from the House of Commons for financial misconduct, showed the strain imposed by the need to keep up the flow of volunteers.

This hysteria did not help the war effort. Battenberg, the First Sea Lord, who had taken the initial decision to mobilize the fleet and was married to a granddaughter of Queen Victoria, was obliged to give up his post because of his name (which he changed to Mountbatten at about the same time as the royal family declared its name to be Windsor). Women took to giving white feathers to men they thought should be in uniform; when they picked on soldiers on leave this was merely offensive, but when they picked on skilled munitions workers they were—to use their own language—doing the Kaiser's work. Voluntary recruitment made good sense when a small army had to double in size, and the government assumed that increasing the army to ten or fifteen times its original size was much the same thing. It behaved as though war was a matter of running a budget and getting troops over to France, without thinking about prices, production, and the rational use of manpower.

Asquith's last year

When the Asquith Coalition had been formed, Lloyd George found the War Office's attempts to reorganize its supply department had left a great deal to be done in his new Ministry of Munitions. He turned his energies to everything: he set up state factories despite the traditional laissez-faire view that these things were done best by private firms; he brought businessmen in to help run his ministry; he negotiated with trade unions, and persuaded the engineering unions to relax their rules of job demarcation and let unskilled workers do work that had previously been reserved for skilled craftsmen. At the same time he became convinced of the strength of the case for conscription and began to press for it in Cabinet. His views came closer to those of the Conservatives, who also wanted conscription, though acquaintance with the Liberal ministers renewed Conservative suspicions of Lloyd George's methods and made them more ready to see the virtues of McKenna, the leading exponent of the case against conscription.

The advocates of conscription had a variety of policies in mind: the Army Council wanted to get more troops, the Conservatives shared this view and in addition thought the war economy would run better under 'industrial conscription' which made everybody work where he was told, and Lloyd George found it very hard to manufacture munitions when many skilled men had already volunteered and more were doing so. He set about getting skilled men back from the front and making sure that no others went. The attitude of the military men was the least reasonable: they spoke, throughout the war, as though they could have an unlimited supply of men and at the same time have an unlimited supply of munitions. The Conservative attitude had a harsh logic about it when taken to an extreme, as it was by F. S. Oliver, who was in favour of 'beating that dog [organized labour] to a jelly'.[2] If this could have been done without breaking civilian morale, it would no doubt have provided a flexible labour force; without such a preliminary process, 'industrial conscription' was bound to lead to an even more bitter struggle than military conscription. Supporters of 'industrial conscription' seemed unable to see the difference between conscripting men to go and fight—this was unpopular with the trade unions but would be accepted—and conscripting men to go and work for somebody else's profit. If employers knew the government would supply employees who could not defend themselves by strike action, their handling of labour relations was likely to become more insensitive. Lloyd George's approach to conscription was more moderate; he wanted to keep skilled workers out of the trenches, and to do this he had to provide other people to go and fight.

Kitchener had been ready, and even flattered, to serve as recruiting sergeant to the Empire, and as long as he accepted this role and declared that the voluntary system was adequate it was hard for anyone to stand against him and say that conscription was necessary. By late 1915 his authority was beginning to weaken. Asquith held back the pressure for a few more months by getting Lord Derby to lead a last great campaign of voluntary recruiting, in which all men of service age were asked to say that they would serve when called upon, on the understanding that unmarried men would be called upon first. After this recruiting campaign clearly had not brought forward the required number of men, it was relatively easy for Asquith to bring in the first Conscription Bill in January 1916. It called up unmarried men, on the grounds that it would be unfair to make married men go to the front, as a result of their pledge under the Derby scheme, while unmarried men remained in Britain. Asquith's Bill passed with little opposition: the libertarian Liberals, the trade unions, and the economists who did not believe that Britain's

2. A. M. Gollin, *Proconsul in Politics* (1964), 540.

resources could stand conscription were able to muster only thirty-one votes in the Commons. The main upholders of the economic argument in the Cabinet were Runciman and McKenna, and Asquith, Balfour, and Kitchener were impressed by what they said. However, Lloyd George, the newspapers of Lord Northcliffe, the majority of the Conservative Party, and the national feeling that everybody ought to do his share of the work were on the side of conscription. The Act of January 1916 was not enough; another Act, covering all men of military age, was passed in April.

Conscription kept the British armies in France at a steady level of about a million men; two and a half million troops were raised on a volunteer basis by early 1916, and almost as many were raised by conscription during the rest of the war. Sir Auckland Geddes, the Minister of National Service, later wrote: 'With perhaps more knowledge than most of the working of conscription in this country ... I hold the fully matured opinion that, on balance, the imposition of military conscription added little if anything to the effectiveness of our war effort.'[3] Conscription enabled the government to regulate the flow of men; if it had been accompanied by a sensible classification of jobs, and a level of taxation that convinced factory workers that the owners were not profiting immoderately from the war, it could have been used to coordinate the various sections of the war effort. The simplest way for the government to control the economy was by regulating something vital that was in short supply, and the supply of labour could have been used for the purpose. The opportunity was missed, mainly because Asquith had been in office too long; his urge to get things done, never very strong, had been worn away. Coordination of effort had to wait until the shortage of shipping early in 1917.

The supporters of all-out warfare, most of whom believed that all Britain's efforts should be concentrated in France, gained another success in December 1915. Kitchener had been in effect, though not in name, Chief of the Imperial General Staff (CIGS) as well as Secretary for War, initiating strategy as well as directing the War Office. The results had not been satisfactory, and he was pressed to appoint an effective CIGS. The choice fell on Sir William Robertson, who laid down detailed rules for his position which excluded the Secretary for War, and as a result the Cabinet, from the formation of strategy. Though no outstanding leaders emerged during the war, Allenby, Haig, Plumer, and Wilson were not completely lacking in imagination, but Robertson behaved at times as though having ideas was a symptom of pro-German tendencies. The new commander in France, Douglas Haig, had a more open mind; like Robertson he was committed to the policy of unremitting concentration on the western front, but it was his job to win in France, while it was Robertson's duty as CIGS to think about the war as a whole. Haig was quite ready to look at new suggestions like the tank and to consider rearrangement

3. Geddes's views are discussed in B. H. Liddell Hart, *Memoirs* (1965), ii. 532.

of forces in the west, and to accept civilian experts like Sir Eric Geddes, who was made a major-general so that he could organize transport more effectively. Although Haig was not enthusiastic about unity of command (which naturally meant a French commander-in-chief because the French army was larger), he was distinctly less opposed to it than Robertson.

The triumph of the conscriptionists, and the changes in command, came at a time when the war was beginning to have a considerable effect on British society. During the first year of the war the position of women did not change very much; during the next twelve months the shortage of men led to the appearance of women in all sorts of work that had been done by men. Women making munitions, land girls working on farms, and bus conductresses seem to have been the most obvious signs of a changed world. The decline in the number of domestic servants is sometimes overestimated. Their numbers fell by only 25 per cent during the war. Some women munition workers had worked in mills or factories before the war, but many of the new women workers had not previously had jobs—they came from the classes in which women who worked were not thought respectable, and it was these women whose position was changed more deeply by the war.

Trade unionists were ready to accept women workers under the rules negotiated with Lloyd George for 'dilution'—allowing unskilled workers to do work that had previously been reserved for skilled men—but they had no intention of losing the rights built up before the war and they wanted to make sure that wages kept pace with the rapidly rising cost of living. The fiercer conscriptionists said that the soldiers in the trenches had no use for trade unionists quarrelling over who should do what, but soldiers sometimes wrote back from the trenches to tell their brother unionists not to give up the Rule Book; they were fighting to preserve liberty, and for them the Rule Book was a substantial part of liberty. In forming his 1915 Coalition Asquith brought in Henderson, the leader of the Labour Party. Asquith disliked creating new ministries, so at first Henderson was nominally President of the Board of Education, but it was understood that he would act as Minister of Labour.

The government preferred to place contracts with people who employed union labour, partly to show that the government was treating labour fairly and partly because it realized that union labour would strike less often and could be negotiated with more easily than non-union labour. The Ministry of Munitions was particularly insistent that its contractors should employ union labour, in order to deal with problems before they led to a strike. Lloyd George was not himself a very good negotiator in labour disputes, except in the sense that he was prepared to be rather generous with the employers' money for the sake of harmony,[4] but the conduct of his ministry did change the pattern of

---

4. G. R. Askwith, *Industrial Problems and Disputes* (1920), 394–5, on his settlement of the South Wales coal strike in 1915.

labour relations for most of the country. Union membership rose steadily throughout the war, and trade union leaders were accepted as men who could make a serious and statesmanlike contribution to the war effort.

The war led to enormous profits for manufacturers in any way connected with military supply. If the government was not going to control the economy and was going to rely on private manufacturers, the manufacturers were bound to make profits. They also made enemies, as can be seen from the complaints of the comfortable classes about the nouveaux riches, and the suggestions that there was something immoral about becoming rich during a war, which were heard so often for a dozen years after 1914. The response of the unions was more straightforward. They had no special status that was menaced by the success of the munition millionaires, but they wanted some of the money. When the traditional union leaders were too committed to the war effort, new leaders emerged. The shop stewards, unpaid organizers in factories, took over some of the responsibility for wage negotiations of the regular union officials. Their position was particularly strong on the Clydeside, where discontent was increased by the housing conditions, bad enough at the best of times and made much worse by the influx of new workers.

In Britain the government interfered with personal liberty much less than in other countries in the war. However, the Defence of the Realm Act entitled it to do a great many things by Order in Council, including imprisoning people for hindering the war effort. Relatively few people were worried by this and probably more people were annoyed by the government's persistent policy of diluting beer than by infringements of the more textbook forms of liberty. Ordinary members of the working class felt that light beer and steps towards industrial conscription meant the war was not really being fought for them at all, and some liberal and socialist intellectuals supported them in this. The government deported a few shop stewards to other parts of the country and also imprisoned conscientious objectors. Neither group of 'prison graduates' rose as high in politics as their Irish contemporaries, but they were not without influence after the war and they were likely to oppose any idea that the Labour Party could treat the Liberal Party of Asquith and Lloyd George (the two Prime Ministers who had interfered with their liberty) as a party of the left.

Pacifists only became a legal problem with conscription. Some people had opposed British foreign policy, such as MacDonald and the left-wing fringe of the Liberal Party, who formed the Union for Democratic Control (that is, control of foreign policy). Some people thought it wrong to fight in the war, because they thought shedding blood was wrong or because they thought the war was wicked. When conscription came, the government set up tribunals to investigate the sincerity of the 'conscientious objectors'. The tribunals were more sympathetic to objections based on long-standing religious principles than to any others, and they had relatively little difficulty in finding non-combatant duties for anyone who was simply concerned to avoid killing his fellow men. Agricultural work could be accepted as work of national importance, and many conscientious objectors spent the war digging. The position of the most rigorous objectors, who believed the entire war to be wicked, was harder. If they were lucky they were sentenced to two years' imprisonment, with the prospect of further imprisonment if they refused to join the army on release. If they were less lucky they were put into the army, which inevitably led to field punishments for refusing to obey orders, and a number of objectors did not survive this process.

Once conscription had been enacted, the generals could plan to attack in France. The initiative was not entirely in their hands. The only important German attack in France between 1914 and 1918 was the 1916 onslaught on the fortress of Verdun. It was chosen for attack because the French were in so unfavourable a position, with artillery massed on three sides of the town, that they were likely to suffer more than the attackers, but could not afford to give it up. Verdun held out, but the French army was cruelly punished and its commanders became more and more insistent that the British should attack elsewhere to relieve the pressure.

The government had problems closer to home. The willingness of the Home Rule Party to support the war had alienated the more determined nationalists, and a few of them prepared to fight for independence under the leadership of Patrick Pearse and James Connolly. At Easter 1916 a rebellion broke out in Dublin, and Pearse was proclaimed President of the Irish Republic. The rising was suppressed after a few days of bitter fighting. Most of the surviving rebel leaders were tried by court martial and shot, which inflamed hostility to Britain in the United States, where Irish opinion was of some importance—Eamonn de Valera, one of the leaders of the rising, was saved from execution because he was an American citizen. After the rebellion Lloyd George managed to get the Ulstermen and the Home Rulers to agree on a scheme for Home Rule for most of Ireland, but the landed interest in the Cabinet, led by Lansdowne and Long, declined to accept the scheme, and the last chance to settle the Irish question peacefully was lost. Yeats wrote that in Easter 1916 a terrible beauty was born; there was also born an Irish determination to settle the question without bothering about parliamentary methods.

At the end of May the German High Seas Fleet steamed out into the North Sea. On 31 May it met the British Grand Fleet in the Battle of Jutland. The fast, easily manoeuvrable battlecruisers of the two fleets were the first to meet; the German battlecruisers drew the British on until they were almost in contact with the entire German fleet. The German fleet pursued the battlecruisers until, early in the evening, the German fleet found itself immediately to the south of the British fleet. The British had not planned this, and had suffered losses in reaching this position; nevertheless, the immense and unquestioned power of the British battle line meant that the German fleet was on the brink of destruction. It turned away, on a course that took it to the west so that it was cut off from its base. When it tried to steam east, its move had been anticipated and the British line of battle was waiting for it. The Germans turned away to the west again, and by this time it was too dark for the British to be sure of keeping in touch. Because of this, and because some intercepted German radio messages were not sent on to the British commander, the German fleet was able to slip past the British in the night. In terms of ships sunk, Jutland was a German success; however, the battle demonstrated that the German fleet could not stand and fight, and so British command of the sea was secure. A decisive British victory would have had effects on the morale of both countries, but it could not have affected the strategy of the war very much.

A few days later British morale was affected more sharply than by the failure to win decisively at Jutland. Kitchener, the Secretary for War, was shipwrecked and drowned on his way to Russia. His reputation among his colleagues was by this time low, but he was still greatly admired outside the circle of the men at the top. After a short tussle Lloyd George took his place. Asquith had wanted to take the War Office himself, which would have solved the problems of keeping the government in touch with the military administration. The Conservative leaders objected, and in view of Asquith's lack of driving force, they were probably right. But Lloyd George's emergence as Secretary for War, with Tory support, led Mrs Asquith to fear that her family's days in Downing Street were numbered.

Once installed at the War Office, Lloyd George tried to regain some of the control over strategy that Kitchener had surrendered to Robertson. Before he could make any progress in this direction the Battle of the Somme had begun, and for the rest of the year the British army was committed to the struggle. The desire to relieve the strain on Verdun, the feeling that the new armies raised since the beginning of the war were ready to advance, and the belief that the war could be won only by a direct attack on the Germans all combined to make the battle a natural part of British policy. There was a less satisfactory reason for joining battle: in 1915 the idea had grown up, initially at Joffre's headquarters, that as the populations of Britain and France exceeded that of Germany, victory could be won by a process of attrition which would leave a surplus on the Anglo-French side; this surplus would emerge even if the Anglo-French losses were up to 25 per cent higher than those of the Germans. The Somme began disastrously. After an enormous and remarkably ineffective bombardment, vast, well-disciplined masses of troops marched forward, some of them in rigid lines, and they fell before the German machine guns or were caught on the barbed wire. Nearly 60,000 men (about 1 per cent of the entire male population aged between 20 and 40) were killed or wounded on 1 July 1916, the first day of the battle. The battle lasted for four and a half months, and though the casualties were not at the same high rate they remained damaging enough. The British losses were over 400,000, the French perhaps 200,000. Argument about the German losses still goes on; though the official history places them at 680,000, it seems unlikely that the defenders would lose more men than the attackers, who neither broke nor outflanked their lines, and later criticism suggests that the official estimate was 30 per cent too high. Certainly the battle on the Somme did not tie down German military strength; while it went on, the German armies in the east forced Romania to make peace.

At this moment, as Lord Beaverbrook (then Sir Max Aitken) put it, 'a strange figure sprang into the arena to do battle. It was clad in a jewelled breastplate set in a vesture of rags and tatters. It faltered in its walk and yet sprang with a wonderful swiftness. The sword looked as fragile as a rapier and yet smote with the impact of a battleaxe.'[5] Lloyd George was indeed a most improbable war leader. Like Churchill in the Second World War he had been a partisan and controversial figure in pre-war politics; unlike Churchill his physical courage was not beyond question. And, again unlike Churchill, he had not advocated rearmament before the war; his main concern had been with social reform, and his chief supporters took a pacific attitude to foreign policy. He was a great orator, but not an orator whose phrases will be remembered: whether dealing with one man or with a crowd he could gauge exactly what his listeners were thinking, and could adapt his arguments so that their interests and his interests always seemed to be the same. When he roused people to enthusiasm, it was more by the way that he seemed to express their own best instincts than by an eloquent statement of new ideals.

The Somme convinced him that the generals had no idea how to handle the western front. He had three ideas for strategy: unity of command, switching troops to Italy, and switching troops to the east end of the Mediterranean. To make any one of them effective he had to regain control over strategy. In the struggle to change the system of government in 1916 his determination to fight an all-out war gained him allies who agreed neither with his views on strategy nor with his ideas about the relationship between generals and politicians.

When President Wilson hinted at a negotiated peace, Lloyd George stepped forward and, ignoring the existence of the Foreign Secretary, said in a press interview on 29 September that Britain and France would end the war by a 'knock-out blow'. He had accepted the logic of conscription to the full: Britain could keep up an almost infinitely protracted war under the voluntary system, but a large army raised by conscription could be maintained for only a limited period of time. The enormous industrial effort brought this limit all the closer. German generals at the Somme had been worried by British superiority in supplying shells and other munitions, but this immensely expensive type of fighting could not go on for ever; apart from the strain on industry, the need

5. Lord Beaverbrook, *Men and Power* (1956), 344.

to import material from the United States imposed a heavy strain on foreign exchange and foreign credit. Credit was by no means exhausted at the end of 1916, but it would not last for ever.

Lloyd George's talk of a 'knock-out blow' upset his Liberal colleagues, and it encouraged the section of the Conservative Party which thought that the country should make an unlimited effort. A Commons debate on 8 November about the sale of German property in Nigeria was taken to symbolize the desire to wage war more vigorously. So many Conservatives voted against the government that Law felt he had to come to terms with Carson, the leader of the rebels. Carson, Law, and Lloyd George were brought together by a Conservative backbencher, Sir Max Aitken, and at the end of November they proposed to Asquith that he should appoint the three of them as an executive committee to run the war. Asquith accepted a weakened version of the scheme; Lloyd George sent Asquith's proposal on to Law with a brief note: 'The life of the country depends on resolute action by you now.'[6] In an interview with Law, Asquith gained the impression that the Conservative leaders would resign unless he accepted the original proposal, and he agreed to set up the committee on condition he could attend its meetings whenever he chose. He then discovered that, except for Law, the Conservative leaders were not committed to the scheme; on the whole they opposed Lloyd George, but what they really wanted was to get the conflict settled one way or the other. Heartened by this, Asquith withdrew his acceptance. Lloyd George then resigned, and it became clear that Asquith could not reconstruct his government and replace his War Minister. Accordingly he in turn resigned.

There is a controversy about Asquith's motives and hopes at the time he resigned. Some historians have suggested, apparently following Beaverbrook's account, that Asquith intended his resignation as a tactical move to show that he was the only man who could form a government. However, Beaverbrook made it quite clear that by the end Asquith had to resign.[7] He had a good prospect of returning to power because almost all his Liberal colleagues would not serve under anyone else, and four of the more important Conservative Cabinet ministers had also pledged their support. Asquith declined to serve under anyone. Lloyd George first gained the support of Balfour, Milner, the majority of the Labour Party, and about 126 Liberal MPs (more or less half of the backbenchers) before he could win over the Conservative ministers who had been on Asquith's side. But when they joined him, any hopes Asquith may have had that he would return to office as the indispensable Prime Minister were dashed.

6. Lord Beaverbrook, *Politicians and the War* (1960), 406.   7. Ibid. 452.

Lloyd George's first year

Asquith had run the war by allocating responsibility for new problems to ministerial committees, of which the War Committee was the most important, and he relied on the Cabinet to coordinate their decisions. But the committees could not meet often enough and the Cabinet moved too slowly to be able to control them. Lloyd George set up a number of new ministries, and he established his executive committee as a War Cabinet of five: Law, as Leader of the Commons, a post previously held by the Prime Minister unless he sat in the Lords, Curzon and Milner, who as imperial pro-consuls in India and South Africa respectively were accustomed to taking decisions, Henderson as the representative of labour, and himself. The Cabinet in its previous form disappeared; the new Cabinet was the direct descendant of Asquith's War Committee, freed from the need to refer things back to any larger authority. The War Cabinet continued and extended the War Committee's practice of calling experts, civil servants, and ministers who were not members; the CIGS and the First Sea Lord had been at many meetings of the War Committee and continued to attend the new War Cabinet. The War Cabinet, like the War Committee, kept minutes, and it inherited the Committee's invaluable Secretary, Hankey, who had done much to make Lloyd George think the War Committee was the model to follow. As the new Cabinet ministers, except for Law, had no departmental duties, they could meet every day, which the War Committee had not been able to do.

On the whole the new ministries were successful, but Lord Devonport, the first Minister of Food, was a conspicuous exception. This threatened the whole British war effort, because food was beginning to run short by the beginning of 1917. The Minister of Agriculture increased grain production by paying guaranteed prices to encourage farmers to plough up grazing land. But Devonport was convinced that rationing was undesirable and merely issued statements indicating how much people ought to eat. His suggestions were ignored. He had to be replaced by Lord Rhondda, a man of considerable political experience, who first imposed fixed prices and moved towards rationing when this understandably left demand unchecked. Early in 1918 cards were issued which entitled the holder to a fixed amount of meat, and as the year went on the scheme was extended. In July booklets were issued that contained coupons to buy a fixed amount of meat, sugar, butter, margarine, and cooking fat. Prudently, the booklets included additional sheets, to cover the possibility that other food would have to be sold in limited quantities.

In other new ministries Sir Joseph Maclay was very successful in organizing shipping, and Lord Beaverbrook was equally successful in organizing propaganda at the Ministry of Information. Despite his later doubts about its worth, Geddes ran the National Service system efficiently, Northcliffe had a triumphant period in the United States coordinating British and American war production, and Lord Cowdray did reasonably well at the Air Board. By bringing these businessmen into the new departments Lloyd George brought them closer to the political community; before the war businessmen would not be considered for political positions unless they had retired from all commercial connections, but in 1916 they provided a new supply of talent, with experience of running larger concerns than civil servants had handled. The long-term results cannot have pleased Lloyd George, for they became convinced that no more reforms were needed once they were established in politics; before the war 'a businessmen's government' was a radical cry, but after the war it became a reactionary slogan.

While most of the new posts went to businessmen, the Ministry of Labour and the Ministry of Pensions went to Labour MPs. Once the Liberal Party was divided, the Labour Party could not simply follow the Liberals and had to devise a policy for itself. The appointment to office of Labour MPs reminded people that Labour was an important part of the economy and had to be treated seriously. In 1917 prices ran further ahead of wages than ever, and the effect of a once-for-all shift into better jobs was wearing off for most workers. As the government was not sufficiently in control of the economy to stabilize prices, it had to allow wages to go up, with all the dislocation that wage negotiations involve. This economic discontent began to make trade unionists wonder whether the war was as unquestionably justified as they had previously believed. Until 1917 the objections to the war of the liberal and socialist intellectuals had gained very little support; Galsworthy's memories of the Boer War had led him to suggest, in *The Mob* (produced in March 1914), that an anti-war speaker might get lynched and, although this never happened, meetings were broken up and opponents of the war were beaten up. MacDonald had to resign the leadership of the Labour Party in 1914 because he opposed British entry to the war; whatever his views of Grey's diplomacy, he did not say that the war was wicked, but he insisted so strenuously that Britain should take any chance to secure a negotiated peace that he was regarded as an ally of the people who said the war was wicked.

Henderson became leader of the party in the House of Commons but insisted that there was to be no proscription of MacDonald, who remained Treasurer of the party, or of the pacifists. Henderson's restraint may seem natural and prudent, but it was not easy at the time. Parties of the left were invited to cooperate with their governments in all the countries at war, and in France, Germany, and Italy they went on to purge their ranks of their anti-war colleagues. When war-weariness swept over the working class in 1917, the old parties of the left could do very little about it. Their expelled colleagues could appeal to the example of Russia, which in February had overthrown the Tsar; the pacific left in Europe was pro-Russian before Lenin and the Bolsheviks seized power on a platform of 'peace, bread, and land' in the November Revolution and set up a Soviet government, and it became all the more pro-Russian when it saw that Lenin was actually doing something to stop the war.

The British working class felt no need to look to Russia in this way. Because there had been no expulsions, MacDonald and the pacifists could put their case at party conferences, and by 1917 they were getting some response. Henderson knew desire for a negotiated peace was growing, and felt a good deal of sympathy with it. A proposed meeting at Stockholm of socialist leaders from all belligerent countries led to a crisis in the government: Henderson wanted to go; Lloyd George wanted him not to go, and also wanted to keep him in the Cabinet. If Lloyd George had accepted Henderson's resignation when it was first offered, they might have parted company amicably instead of quarrelling in the House of Commons about where Henderson had had to wait while the Cabinet tried to decide whether to accept his resignation, but the principle was clear: Henderson and a large proportion of the Labour Party wanted a negotiated peace, and were quite ready to act separately from either section of the Liberal Party. George Barnes took Henderson's place in the War Cabinet, but he sat as an ambassador from labour, not as the leader of the Labour Party.

Lloyd George had no desire for a negotiated peace and was not free to ask for one. He had been placed in power by critics who thought Asquith was not getting on with the war; his policy had to be (as Clemenceau put it) 'Je fais la guerre'. Lloyd George's energy and determination, and his readiness to sweep away any obstacle to making war, were invaluable, and no other politician could make people feel that the government knew what it was doing and that the efforts of everyone in the country would not go wasted and unappreciated. A great leader has to be a fountain of ideas and of inspiration: Lloyd George always had new ideas, was always ready to listen to other people's ideas, and was always able to make almost everyone believe that things were going well and could go even better.

His colleagues in the War Cabinet were also open to new ideas; his followers in the Commons, including some ministers, were much more ready to accept the dominance of the experts, just as Asquith had done. The most obvious example, and the one most nearly fatal to the country, was Carson. As First Lord of the Admiralty he had complete and not always justified faith in his Sea Lords; in normal times this might have done no harm but the Admiralty had a crisis to deal with. At about the same time as Lloyd George was overthrowing Asquith the German government was also going through an upheaval in which the men determined to wage all-out war were successful. The significant difference in Germany was that these men were unable to resist the military High Command. Submarine warfare was the vital issue: naval calculations suggested that if submarines set about torpedoing without warning any ships they saw, then Britain would be cut off from imports and unable to carry on after August. The Germans realized this policy would probably bring the

United States into the war but they knew the United States could not do anything before August.

Unrestricted submarine warfare began; American ships were sunk and American lives were lost (the British blockade was distasteful to the United States, but nobody had been killed). On 6 April 1917 the United States entered the war. Britain and France were now bound to win if they could hold out until the United States could take an effective role in the war. If there had been no submarine warfare, and no American entry to the war, British financial credit might easily have broken down, and the British and French might have found themselves with neither equipment nor men to resist the German attacks of early 1918. But so many ships were sunk that the German calculations seemed justified. The rate of losses rose from 1.1 million tons in 1915 and 1.5 million tons in 1916 to about 2.5 million tons in the first half of 1917. Despite efforts to economize on shipping and the first steps towards the rationing of food, it was estimated that the United Kingdom would have to ask for peace. The Admiralty wrung its hands and said everything possible was being done but that it was impossible to protect all of the 2,500 ships a week coming into British ports. Carson remained immobile in his support of his naval subordinates, who had nothing to offer.

Lloyd George made his enquiries, consulting junior officers secretly and in defiance of custom. He learned that 2,400 of the 2,500 ships were in the coasting trade; only 100 ships a week had to be protected against attacks on the high seas. The Admiralty had insisted that merchant seamen were incapable of the precise navigation needed for sailing in convoy; Lloyd George showed that they were already sailing the Channel in convoy. Late in April the War Cabinet made it known that the convoy system was going to be imposed on the Admiralty and on 30 April Lloyd George and Curzon took the Admiralty over for the day, made sure that convoys would be organized, and arranged for the creation of a naval general staff. As the admirals had been given two or three days' notice of what was coming, Lloyd George did not officially dictate naval policy during his visit, but this was one of the decisive interventions of the war and it made Lloyd George even less respectful about expert opinion than before. Convoys did not solve the problem immediately; about 0.5 million tons of shipping was sunk while travelling in convoy. Nevertheless, the crisis was over.

Lloyd George had schemes for winning the war on land as well as for saving it at sea. His proposal that troops should be sent to Italy was unsound in principle because, as the military staff told him, the Germans could move troops to meet any British or French troops that were moved to the Italian front and would be able to move faster because they had better rail communication. His proposal that there should be a unified command in France made much better sense but, instead of winning support for it by argument in the War Cabinet and presenting it to Robertson as official policy, he slipped it

through the Cabinet and brought it forward without preparation at a conference with the French about transport. Nivelle, the French commander, was
accepted by the British generals as commander for the duration of the coming
offensive, but they felt less inclined than ever to trust Lloyd George after this,
and the abrupt manner of command which Nivelle revealed on one or two
occasions made matters worse. There were several weak points in the German
front at the beginning of 1917; Hindenburg and Ludendorff, who had been
given control of the entire German army in August 1916 and had then asserted
their control over the politicians as well, were still intent on operations in the
east, so in the west they withdrew to the well-prepared defences of the
Hindenburg line and Nivelle was left aiming a blow into empty space. He
hastily reorganized his attack and in April threw his army against the German
line of the Chemin des Dames. His attack was more successful than those of
Joffre in 1915 and of Haig in 1916, but his army had expected a decisive victory.
The French soldiers suffered heavy losses and they refused to go forward
again, though they defended their own lines; Pétain coaxed them back to some
semblance of fighting spirit by the end of the year, but any further full-scale
attack in 1917 would have to be by the British.

Haig's offensive east from Ypres is one of the hardest things to explain in
the whole war.[8] Fairly certainly he did not attack to take pressure off the
French; it appears that he did not know how completely the French were
paralysed by the mutinies. Jellicoe, the First Sea Lord, thought the submarine
offensive was mainly based on Belgian ports and could be defeated only if
these ports were captured, and Haig did his best to help. He was also led on by
his belief, which was just as incorrect, that the morale of the German army was
breaking down. He attacked in what had become the established manner: an
enormously heavy artillery barrage, followed by an infantry advance. The
approach rested on an immense overestimate of the effectiveness of shells;
only a very small proportion of shells fired ever killed or even wounded
anyone.[9] Staff calculations spoke of a barrage 'which no man could live
through'; in pursuit of this elusive goal they put a larger and larger quantity of
high explosive into the area they wanted to occupy. This was, apart from being
a fairly clear guide to the German command where to put its reserves, a rash
gamble with the weather. August, when Haig began his attack from Ypres,
was wetter than usual; the barrage broke up the drainage system and condemned the troops to advance into a morass. September was a month of
drought, with a rainfall under a quarter of the normal amount, and the

---

8. J. A. Terraine, *Haig* (1963), 298; B. H. Liddell Hart, 'Basic Truths of Passchendaele' *Royal United Services Institution Journal* (Nov. 1959).

9. In the first five months of fighting at Verdun 37m. shells were fired, and there were about 500,000 casualties, of whom a great number were killed or wounded by bullets, bayonets, gas, hand grenades, shovels, and bare hands (A. Horne, *The Price of Glory: Verdun 1916* (1962), 300).

artillery bombardments were more successful.[10] A series of three neat and small advances were made, but October was again wet; the British army forced its way through the last few thousand yards of mud to the village of Passchendaele in November.

Liddell Hart tells the story of the staff officer who was driven up towards the front line. When he entered the great bog he said: 'Good God, did we send men to fight in that?' 'It gets worse further on' was the answer, and around the battle line the mud was so deep that a man who left the well-defined paths— which were under shellfire—could sink in it and, encumbered by his service equipment, drown.[11] Passchendaele was one of the extreme horrors of the war, but anyone who considers the general conditions under which men fought in France and Belgium will be astonished that so few people broke down under the strain of the constant presence of death, the absence of any prospect of a swift and successful offensive, and the natural discomforts of mud, lice, cold, and isolation. Soldiers in other wars have had the consolations of inspired leadership, or the hope of loot, or the thought that it would soon be over. In the First World War the generals were not in the front line, the war was fought in a narrow strip of devastated and desolated land which became more and more like the craters of the moon, and there was no sign that the remorseless grinding process would come to an end as long as there were men alive on both sides. The men who did break down under the strain met little mercy. Soldiers who would in later wars have been treated for shell-shock were court-martialled and shot.

The sacrifices of Passchendaele brought very little strategic advantage. The Germans were able to hold their line in the west and at the same time complete the destruction of Russia as an effective military force. Later in November a tank attack at Cambrai, where the land was unbroken by shellfire, gained in a couple of days about as much ground as the long slaughter of Passchendaele. The British commanders were convinced the German army was almost broken by the Passchendaele fighting, and did not prepare to resist a counter-attack which came at the end of the month and recaptured almost all the ground won by the tanks.

1918

Lloyd George had to put up with the generals because his own political position depended on Conservative votes and was never strong enough to allow him freedom of action. By the end of 1917 his colleagues in the War Cabinet agreed with his low opinion of the generals and their constant passion for the offensive, but the House of Commons was another matter and Lloyd George

---

10. D. Lloyd George, *War Memoirs* (1938), 1306; (this edition contains letters from people who fought at Passchendaele).
11. B. H. Liddell Hart, *The Real War* (1930), 367.

did not feel confident of his position there. He thought it might be possible to control the generals either by returning to the policy of unity of command, or by restricting the number of men supplied to them. Unity of command became involved all too closely with the attempt to circumvent the power of Robertson as CIGS. In February 1918 an Executive War Board was set up by the American, British, French, and Italian governments to control the military reserves; Lloyd George nominated Sir Henry Wilson as British representative, and made it clear that the CIGS would not have any authority over him. Robertson resigned rather than accept this division of power, and after failing to persuade Plumer to take his place, the War Cabinet gave it to Wilson, who worked better with the politicians as CIGS, though he was no more prepared than Robertson to share power with a general at Versailles.

Unity of command seemed to have been dealt a final blow when Haig declined to contribute any troops to the proposed central reserve because he had worked out an arrangement for exchanging reserves with Pétain, although Wilson warned him that he might find Pétain's charity very cold. The British government did not press the point, because it did not intend to provide any fresh troops; its faith in Haig's estimates of future needs had fallen very low because of his 'constant depreciation of the Germans when he wanted to attack'.[12] There were many other demands on any available manpower: ships and munitions had to be provided, people were sent back to the land to grow more food, and the Navy and the Royal Flying Corps (renamed the Royal Air Force in April) had to be expanded.

On 21 March the German armies attacked the British line just south of Arras, broke it, and within a couple of weeks came very close to capturing Amiens and paralysing railway communication between the British and French. The attack showed that the trench line could be broken, and suggested that surprise was the best way to do it. A short bombardment to destroy communications rather than kill the defenders, an early morning attack to make use of any fog there might be, and small groups who pressed forward rather than neatly aligned waves of troops seemed to be the answer. Using these new tactics—or, rather, applying traditional tactics to a new situation— Ludendorff seemed able to break the British or French line at will. Five attacks between March and July met with varying degrees of success, but all of them gained more ground than the British advance towards Cambrai which had caused so much exultation the previous November. Under this pressure a Supreme Commander was at last appointed; Foch was accepted as generalis-simo over the British, French, and American armies, though his powers were never as great as they sounded. His staff was small and the reserve at his disposal was never intact because of the calls made on the troops which might have been allotted to it before the 1918 battles began. His tactics were fairly

12. M. P. A. Hankey, *The Supreme Command 1914–1918* (1961), ii. 803.

simple, he encouraged the generals under his command to attack as soon as they could, and he tried to build up a strategic reserve to make this possible. But the German attacks went on, and the British and French were visibly not doing much more than holding on until American troops or German exhaustion saved them.

In London Lloyd George had passed through a period of difficulty. When Lord Lansdowne in November 1917 argued that the government should try to get a negotiated peace, an Asquith–Lansdowne ministry was thought possible. The desire to know what peace terms would be given to Germany was a sign that people were growing tired of the war, though not that they were ready to end it. Anti-German feeling was no longer enough to keep up morale, and in early 1918 President Wilson made his war aims explicit in his Fourteen Points. Lloyd George put roughly the same policy, though with a little less emphasis on self-determination, to the TUC, which was accepted as the leading respectable body supporting a negotiated peace. The aims of Wilson, Lloyd George, and the people who listened to them approvingly were not a real basis for a negotiated peace; no German government would accept the Fourteen Points except after military defeat. The statement of war aims was more an exercise in domestic public relations than in diplomacy, but it did show that the government had to take popular feeling seriously even in foreign policy. The Soviet publication of some of the secret treaties reduced people's willingness to let their governments carry on diplomacy in secret.

Lloyd George's government realized that it needed to show people what the country was fighting for. A Ministry of Reconstruction had been set up in 1917. A large measure of electoral reform was passed in 1918: it tripled the electorate by giving the vote to all men over 21, instead of confining it to householders, and also to women over 30—the age difference was introduced to make sure that men should remain a majority in the electorate. Plural voting was reduced to one extra vote for a university degree or for business premises. The granting of votes to women attracted people's attention but it had no immediately visible political effect. To some extent women had wanted the vote to assert their right to greater equality, and other changes were doing something to bring this about. Votes for women may have brought new issues into the political arena; it is possible that housing and the non-religious aspects of education became important after the war because they were likely to interest women. The vote may also have had defensive uses: although the number of women in the labour force had fallen back to the 1911 level, by 1921 attempts to stop them working in the years of high post-war unemployment might have been more intense if they had not had votes.

Giving the vote to the one-third of adult males who had not previously been enfranchised may have had more far-reaching effects. Most of these new voters would probably have supported the Liberal Party if enfranchisement had come before the war because it had a nationwide organization and had a wider appeal among the poor than the Conservatives. But in 1918 the Liberal Party was divided, and it had a rival for the votes of unskilled workers. Trade unions had two or three times as many members at the end of the war as at the beginning, and could try to persuade new members to vote Labour. The Labour Party had to consider becoming a party of government, if only because it could no longer trust the Liberal Party to follow a Gladstonian policy and wanted a foreign policy of its own. After Henderson had left the Cabinet on an issue of foreign policy he was all the more willing to undertake the work of changing the party. MacDonald's prestige within the party rose as a negotiated peace became more acceptable, and the great expert on collectivism, Sidney Webb, was drawn into the inner circles of the party because the obvious domestic effect of the war had been an increase in collectivist activity.

By 1918 Lloyd George had demonstrated that the State could take over most of the economy and run it effectively enough to maintain 5 million men under arms and keep most of the population no worse off than they had been before the war. The old Independent Labour Party (ILP) point seemed proved; if people were to be treated reasonably in the economic sphere, the first step was to nationalize industry. Clause IV of the new constitution adopted by the Labour Party in 1918 included a commitment to nationalization; the founders of the ILP had achieved their objective of setting up a party based on organized labour which would accept the policy of nationalization. The Labour Party now set up constituency branches, which ran side by side with the old ILP branches. This was meant to attract more people to the party by enabling them to join it without having to join a socialist group like the ILP though, as the Labour Party itself was now socialist, the distinction was hard to see. One effect of setting up Labour Party branches on a separate basis was to lead the old ILP branches to see themselves as the conscience of the party, and it might have led to a quieter life for everybody if they had to serve as the basis of the Labour Party's constituency organization.

The German offensive of March 1918 had political effects in Britain. It helped the Labour Party by making reunion harder for the Liberals. In February Asquith had supported Robertson's efforts to remain as CIGS with unrestricted authority; this made life no easier for Lloyd George, whose hold on office was weakened by the issue. When the March offensive broke the British front, swift action to repair the damage was needed; a more skilful deployment of troops might have made the line harder to break, but once the attack had come it was too late to worry about such things. The government sent troops to France and once again diverted people from making munitions into the ranks of the army. Hankey commented that 'The withdrawal of a few thousand engineers to the Army . . . caused the tank programme to fall by half,' which illustrated why it was not possible both to keep the army at the strength the generals wanted and to provide the weapons they wanted.[13]

When he explained the situation to the House of Commons, Lloyd George said British troops in France in 1918 were at their 1917 level. The Director of Military Operations, General Maurice, published a letter in *The Times* on 7 May saying that the Prime Minister was not telling the truth. For the only time in the war Asquith made an attack on the Prime Minister which he carried to the extent of voting against the government; he was careful not to say that Maurice's figures were correct, but he insisted that there should be a committee of inquiry. During the debate Asquith's case was destroyed; Lloyd George gave figures which, he stated, had been sent by General Maurice's own office. Apparently the original figures Lloyd George had used included British troops in Italy. Maurice had corrected them, and his figures in *The Times* were accurate though it is not clear Lloyd George knew this. In any case Maurice's letter was bound to look like an attempt to use confidential information to embarrass Lloyd George and benefit Asquith and the generals. The debate on Maurice's charges and the division, which the government won 293–106, relieved Lloyd George from the fear that he might lose control of the House of Commons. Two secretaries say that Maurice's corrected figures were later found in an unopened dispatch box, but that Lloyd George never saw this second version.[14]

By July the German army had committed almost all its reserves to the battle and, although it had broken the trench line in several places and created very large salients, it had not been able to use these advantages to turn the flank of either the British or the French armies. The German attacks lost momentum, and when the counter-attack began at the end of July, the German position was very ill placed for resisting it. The salients created by the great offensive meant that the line was longer than it would otherwise have been, and because the reserves had been used up in attacks the German generals had lost almost all power to decide how they should defend themselves. The arrival of tanks in adequate numbers made their position worse; on 8 August a very successful British tank attack destroyed the last German chances of concentrating troops for a counter-attack.[15] On 29 September Ludendorff's self-control broke down and he declared that peace must be made at once; German diplomats might have been able to get better terms for an armistice if they had not been hustled into the preliminary negotiations in this way. But by October it was quite clear that no effective resistance could be offered by the Germans on French soil. Their best hope was to carry out a very considerable retreat and then try to

---

13. Hankey, *The Supreme Command*, ii. 829.

14. Lord Beaverbrook, *Men and Power*, 262–3; John Gooch, 'The Maurice Debate', *Journal of Contemporary History*, 3 (1968), 4.

15. 'Ludendorff in the most frequently quoted passage of his Memoirs described 8 August as "the black day of the German army"' (C. R. M. Cruttwell, *A History of the Great War* (1934), 550).

defend the Rhineland, but it was doubtful that the authority of the German High Command would have survived such a step.

Lloyd George's domestic position was accordingly eased, and he could look to the future. By mid-1918 people in Britain were showing signs of exhaustion, though not of any loss of determination. An influenza epidemic whose victims were comparable in number to the entire war casualty list struck Europe in the later months of 1918. The anti-German hysteria of the early stages of the war reappeared and this led to an Act against naturalized enemy aliens—that is to say, Germans who had moved to Britain, taken out British citizenship, and settled down. Earlier attacks on people of German origin could be rationalized by saying that after all they might be spies; by 1918 it was altogether more obvious that they were being persecuted because of their former nationality. Lloyd George summed up the feeling very well in a speech on 10 December when he said that he stood for 'Britain for the British'.

By that time he was involved in a general election. An election would probably have been held late in 1918 whether the war was over or not, and Lloyd George had to prepare for it. In September he unofficially invited Asquith to join the government as Lord Chancellor and take part in drawing up the Peace Treaties. Asquith said he would help with the Peace Treaties but would not join the government. Lloyd George did not want Asquith (or Lord Northcliffe) at the peace conference untrammelled by ministerial responsibility. If Asquith would not join it, the Coalition would have to go on unchanged, and in October the Whips of the Conservatives and the pro-Lloyd George Liberals completed an agreement by which the Conservatives left 150 seats uncontested, which would give Lloyd George at least as many Liberal followers after an election as he had in the existing House.

By November the war had drawn towards an end. The events of the last weeks did not provide decisive evidence to show what grand strategy should have been adopted in the war. The pressure was kept up in the west and the German army was driven back, but on the other hand Germany's three allies, Turkey, Bulgaria, and Austria-Hungary all collapsed shortly before the eventual plea for an armistice. Italy had ceased to be much of a danger to Austria after the battle of Caporetto in October 1917. Turkey had first been driven out of Arabia and then defeated in Palestine and Syria, but while the campaigns of Allenby and the guerrilla warfare of T. E. Lawrence had been interesting and imaginative, they were never a danger to vital German interests. On the other hand, Germany had been obliged to divert resources to help her allies. The fiercely committed Lloyd George, supported by the somewhat more impartial Hankey, argued that the collapse of her allies left Germany helpless; the supporters of the claims of the western front pointed out that all through the war far more men were fighting in France than in any of the areas that distracted Lloyd George's attention, so that if the Germans had won in France they could have mopped up all the other theatres of war at their leisure; and supporters of the blockade stressed the industrial and domestic weakness which deprived Germany of the means to continue the war.

One historian of the war, unable to determine what was decisive, concluded: 'The simple truth is that Germany ended the war because she had come to the end of her endurance, and it is doubtful whether any other country would have endured so long.' The tribute to what Liddell Hart called 'an epic of military and human achievement' is not undeserved; because of the blockade, and because the generals took too many people from the farms for the army, the Germans were at an immense disadvantage, and the German and Austrian urban populations suffered worse than anybody except those directly involved in the fighting.[16] German strategy would have been hard to improve at any level except the highest; in the realm where strategy joins hands with diplomacy it was disastrous, because it made Britain's entry certain when she might have stayed out, and it provoked the entry of the United States quite unnecessarily. But, apart perhaps from the shifting of the weight of force away from the original pattern of the Schlieffen Plan, it is very hard to see any way in which the German generals could have handled better the problem of being outnumbered and forced to fight on two fronts that they had created for themselves.

However deserved the tributes to the Germans, the countries opposed to them showed no less capacity for endurance. An American who had seen the last stages wrote: 'This western front business couldn't be done again, not for a long time. The young men think they could do it but they couldn't. . . . This took religion and years of plenty and tremendous sureties and the exact relation that existed between the classes. . . . You had to have a whole-souled sentimental equipment going back further than you could remember.'[17] The British writers who had begun the war in a mood of nobility untouched by reality became silent. What was going on in the trenches could only be described in words that suggested that no long-term benefits promised by politicians could justify the suffering. The most immediate impact was that of Sassoon, whose *Counter-Attack* (1918) was published while the war was on, though the posthumous anti-war poems of Owen (1920) and Rosenberg (1922) have influenced subsequent writing rather more. When the war came to an end at 11 a.m. on 11 November 1918 the feeling of triumph and the desire for vengeance was uppermost in almost everybody's mind. This mood did not last, and one reason why it came to an end was that people began to realize more fully than they had allowed themselves to do while the war was on what it had been like to spend months and years in the trenches.

16. Ibid. 597; Liddell Hart, *Memoirs*, 508.
17. F. Scott Fitzgerald, *Tender is the Night* (1934), 75.

4

'Rooted in nothing' [1]

1918–1922

The peace settlement of 1919

The day after the Armistice was announced, Lloyd George told a gathering of about 150 of his Liberal followers that he was going to have an election. The Asquithian Liberals complained loudly, but it was a natural time to have an election. Parliament had been sitting for eight years and had just tripled the electorate. The Asquithians never explained what else Lloyd George could have done: Asquith would not join the government, Lloyd George was not likely to step down from the premiership and ask to be accepted as second-in-command of the Asquith party, and it was hard to tell the electorate to do without an election until the two Liberal leaders had sorted out their relationship.

On the other hand, if the government could unite the 'Lloyd George vote' and the Conservative vote (and the rather small vote of the pro-Coalition Liberals), it could look forward to an enormous majority. If the Liberals had been united, and had had the prestige of Lloyd George on their side, they would very possibly still have lost the election, but they would probably have emerged as an Opposition of a respectable size, in no danger of being overtaken by the Labour Party. But if Lloyd George and the Conservatives were on the same side, there was very little hope for any Liberal candidate unless he had a guarantee of respectability from Lloyd George and Bonar Law. The guarantee of respectability—the letter, signed by Lloyd George and Law, saying that a candidate was a good and loyal servant of the Coalition—was the point that the Liberals fastened on; Asquith called it 'the coupon' (i.e. a ration coupon), and 'the coupon election' it has remained. But, if Lloyd George's influence was going to be thrown against his old party, the coupon was the only way to preserve a Liberal remnant.

While the distribution of the 'coupons' under the agreement made in

---

1. 'Mr. Lloyd George is rooted in nothing' (J. M. Keynes, *Essays in Biography* (1933), 37). The phrase was originally in his *Economic Consequences of the Peace* (1919) but was omitted in a not wholly successful attempt to make the book mild and conciliatory.

October was natural enough, the course of the election ran steadily downhill. Lloyd George told his Liberal supporters on 12 November that he would take a line that Liberals would have no difficulty in following. During the campaign he never fully committed himself to the policy of hanging the Kaiser and making Germany pay which the ordinary run of pro-government candidates put forward, but his reservations were not very explicit: they might have been understood in the House of Commons, but meant rather less to voters. Ordinary people were glad to hear that Germany was going to have to pay for the war, though this was more as a punishment than out of any idea that the social expenditure summed up in the slogan 'a fit country for heroes' would be paid for by Germany and provided without any extra taxation. Lloyd George did not use his position and prestige to warn the electorate that things might not be so easy. Unless he really did think that making Germany pay was simply a matter of making a German Minister of Finance sign a large cheque, he should have warned the electorate about the problems. An election is a great opportunity for political education, and a party which is likely to win a big victory has a particular responsibility to warn public opinion and avoid being swept along by uninformed popular feeling.

Any educating of the public in 1918 would have had to begin among the Coalition's own candidates, who clearly shared the feelings of the electorate. Neither the Asquithian Liberals nor the Labour Party were immune from anti-German feeling and a belief in making Germany pay, though in both parties there were groups who urged restraint. Polling day came, with all constituencies voting on the same day for the first time, and the Coalition won an enormous majority. The results were in one way even more devastating for the

	Votes	Seats	% of all votes cast
Coalition parties	5,121,259	478	47.6
Other Conservatives	663,097	48	6.1
Liberal	1,298,808	28	12.1
Labour	2,385,472	63	22.2
Sinn Fein[a]	486,867	73	4.9

[a] Sinn Fein ran only 102 candidates, of whom twenty-five were returned unopposed.

parties in opposition than the figures show. Not a single Liberal ex-minister was re-elected, and the most talented Labour leaders, MacDonald, Snowden, and Henderson, were also defeated; Adamson, the Scottish miner who had been made chairman of the Parliamentary Labour Party, was leader of the largest party sitting in opposition. The Labour Party had put forward many more candidates than before the war, and had laid the foundations for a nationwide effort, but the Labour Members elected in 1918 were trade unionists of the pre-war type. In the previous Parliament twenty-five of them had served as solid backbenchers; they had done no harm then, but their presence in the new Parliament showed that the Opposition was weak in talent as well as in numbers. There were practically no Home Rulers in the new House. The Irish electorate had lost patience with the delays of the parliamentary system and returned Sinn Fein Members who declared themselves to be the Parliament of Ireland and did not come to Westminster.

These years immediately after 1918 are immensely crowded with events that have little connection with one another. In the first half of 1919 Lloyd George was watching over demobilization, restraining his War Minister Churchill from sending the army to Russia to overthrow Lenin and the Bolshevik revolution, facing a series of strikes most of which were simple economic disputes but a few of which—like that of the miners with their demand for nationalization—had political implications that could not be neglected. And at the same time he was negotiating the Treaty of Versailles. He was accused of taking too much on himself. This may have been so, but his experiences with Churchill did not encourage him to delegate power very widely, and in any case President Wilson and Clemenceau were at the Versailles negotiations so he had to be there.

Germany had asked for an armistice that would lead to a Peace Treaty which embodied Wilson's Fourteen Points. Roughly, very roughly, the treaty did embody the Points but it fell away from them on a number of issues, always in the direction contrary to German interests. Lloyd George had to consider the situation at three distinct levels: the climate of opinion which had been encouraged at the general election meant he could not assent to a treaty that could be denounced for being too soft to the Germans; his country wanted to secure a great number of relatively secondary points at the diplomatic level; and he was aware that completely destroying Germany would not really be a long-term national advantage. Lloyd George had no difficulty in being moderate about frontiers in Europe, because they were not seen as vitally important. Apart from the integrity of Belgium, the United Kingdom was concerned with naval strength, colonies, and reparations. The Armistice had put the German navy in British hands and, just before the treaty was signed, its officers cleared the stage by scuttling their ships. Colonies were out of fashion, but the British Empire spread wider yet by taking over new territories as 'mandates', a term devised by General Smuts. Germany forfeited her colonies in Africa and the Pacific: small slices in Africa went to France and Belgium, but the bulk of them went to Britain and the Dominions: Tanganyika was entrusted to Britain, South West Africa to South Africa, New Guinea to Australia, and Samoa to New Zealand.

These transfers had symbolic importance for the Empire or, as it now began to be called, the Commonwealth. The Dominions had acted as sovereign states by organizing their own war efforts, and they now undertook another, almost anachronistic function by acquiring new territory at the end of a successful war; Wilson found the Australians a little too outspoken about this for his taste. Undoubtedly the position of the Dominions had altered, though the direction in which the Commonwealth was moving was not yet decided. The leading Dominion Prime Ministers of the war years, Botha of South Africa, Borden of Canada, and Hughes of Australia, were good nationalists, and at the same time were strongly in favour of the British connection. They were self-confident men, with no fears that close contact would be bound to make their policies subordinate to Britain's. In 1917 Lloyd George had held an Imperial Conference which was more detailed in its discussions and more willing to take decisions than previous conferences had been, and it was referred to as the Imperial War Cabinet; it was united in its policy of beating Germany, and needed only to agree on ways of carrying out that policy. The Prime Ministers hoped that after the war they could continue on the same basis, with a common policy worked out in discussion and applied by a united Empire. In the past the countries in the Empire had been committed by British policy, in the sense that if Britain was at war all the Dominions were legally in a state of war, but they had not been obliged to do anything about it. The British government could put pressure on them to help, in the way Joseph Chamberlain had pressed the governments of the self-governing colonies to help in the Boer War. But in the Empire that Lloyd George envisaged the Dominions would be politically committed to help, because they would have taken part in forming policy. Whether this was practicable remained to be seen, but at Versailles the Commonwealth acted as a unit though the autonomy of its members was recognized when they signed the treaty as individual countries; at first it was suggested that the Dominions were only pawns in the hands of the British government, but this went down very badly with the Dominion representatives, who pointed out that they had done as much in the war as any of the countries at Versailles except the United Kingdom and France.

While the treatment of the German colonies prompted questions about imperial relations, the division of Turkey-in-Asia was mainly an Anglo-French problem. The negotiators accepted the Sykes–Picot Agreement of 1916 which meant that most of these territories were to be partitioned between Britain and France; they also accepted that the British government had special commitments because of the Balfour Declaration of 1917, which said that a National Home for the Jewish people would be set up in Palestine. It was clear that any promises to the Arabs, made in the course of persuading them to rebel against Turkish rule, would be ignored if they did not fit in with the Sykes–Picot and Balfour policies. The French were given a mandate for Syria (which contained what is now Lebanon), Britain got mandates for Iraq and Palestine, which was subdivided into Palestine and Transjordan a few years later. The Arabs were left with Arabia and a sense of grievance. When the Arab leader Faisal was eventually turned out of Damascus to make way for the

French, he was compensated by being made ruler of Iraq, where the British mandate would clearly run for only a short time. Palestine, into which dedicated and industrious Jewish immigrants began to flow, was obviously going to be a harder problem; the Arabs who lived there lacked the skill and capital to compete with the newcomers, and regarded them with fear and resentment.

Reparations came closer to the heart of the treaty. Lloyd George's first concern was to make sure that Britain got some share of whatever the Germans were made to pay. On a straightforward reading of Wilson's Fourteen Points and the accompanying correspondence, the terms of the Armistice committed the Germans to paying for all the civilian property destroyed in the war. Apart from merchant ships torpedoed, only a small amount of British civilian property had been damaged by bombing, and on this interpretation of the terms, Lloyd George's boasts about making Germany pay looked impossible to fulfil. The British government argued successfully that all war pensions should be included in the total bill, and it was really as a result of this decision that reparations took the form so brilliantly and effectively attacked by Keynes in *The Economic Consequences of the Peace*. Keynes's argument was that civilian damage would amount to £2 billion, and that this was just about the amount that Germany could pay; pensions would raise the cost to £7 billion or £8 billion, a debt which could never be paid and would cripple Germany. The implication was that France had agreed to expand the debt to an unreasonable size in order to make German economic recovery impossible, and that this policy (which he called the 'Carthaginian Peace') would benefit nobody. His argument was applauded at the time, and was soon accepted by the conflicting countries: the Versailles Conference could not agree on the level of reparation, and referred the issue to a committee, which fixed a nominal total of £6,600 million to be paid, but fairly clearly did not expect to obtain much more than £2,500 million; this reduced figure was formally accepted in the Dawes Plan for payments worked out in 1924. The introduction of war pensions at Versailles had merely transferred to Britain an increased share in the payments, without having much effect on the total. Germany proved more or less able to keep up the payments until the international system broke down at the end of the 1920s. Historians have argued whether Keynes's calculations were correct or not, often without noticing that the Dawes Plan accepted them.

Keynes's book made it intellectually fashionable to condemn the treaty, and people may have been too ready to follow the fashion. Even if there had been no argument over reparations, Germany was unlikely to obey the treaty willingly. She had been disarmed, but the other nations showed relatively little desire to adopt corresponding programmes of disarmament. Self-determination was supposed to be the guiding principle of the treaty, but while there were good economic reasons for giving Danzig to Poland, good strategic and economic reasons for giving the Sudetenland to Czechoslovakia, and good balance-of-power reasons for not allowing Austria to join Germany, each of these decisions ignored the principle of self-determination. French politicians justified the treaty by arguing that Germany was so dangerous that all Europe should devote its energies to holding her down, but when they pressed for harsher terms, they might have asked themselves how they could get support for this policy; they might feel sure that their country would always be hostile to Germany, but it was rash of them to commit France to a policy which depended on perpetual British support. A 'Carthaginian Peace' assumed that Britain would remain hostile to Germany, but this would only be the case if the British thought Germany was unreasonable and France was reasonable, so the policy would only work if France gave Britain a veto over her foreign policy. What Keynes did in his book was to convince British and American opinion that the Germans of the Weimar Republic were no worse than any other European statesmen—a fair if unexacting standard—and it was irrelevant that he showed this by analysing the reparations settlement which was rapidly corrected, when the provisions which 'laid the foundations of a just and durable war' were concerned with armaments and frontiers. These clauses were not seriously changed until Neville Chamberlain and Hitler got to work in the 1930s.

Wilson devoted an unnecessary amount of his energy at Versailles to making sure that Britain and France joined the League of Nations and it would have been useful if he had spent some time establishing what it was to do. In Britain the League was seen as something like Gladstone's Concert of Europe, and Gladstonians like Bryce, Ramsay MacDonald, and General Smuts had done a good deal to develop the idea of the League. The Liberal and Labour Parties welcomed it, though the Conservatives were more divided on the issue and some of them complained that Article 16 committed Britain to fight to resist aggression in a quarrel that did not concern her directly. France saw the League as something much more like an enforcement agency for the treaty. By the end of the negotiations British interest was declining. Parliament had pushed Lloyd George in a 'Carthaginian' direction early in the negotiations, but later on he had felt he could safely urge Wilson and Clemenceau to take a more moderate approach.

People with a long historical perspective could see after the war that 'America was thus clearly top nation, and History came to a .'[2]—a comment which brought out the British feeling that nothing was worth while if they were not superior to other countries. However, the United States and the Soviet Union kept off the centre of the world's stage for two more decades, and so Europe remained the part of the globe most likely to influence other countries. The United Kingdom emerged as the least devastated European country, with

2. W. C. Sellar and R. J. Yeatman, *1066 and All That* (1930), 115.

some claims to world dominance by default. England had an additional claim on the attention of the world as the chief seedbed of new ideas for about two centuries. The world that fought from 1914 to 1918 was the world of Locke, Newton, Mill, and Darwin, the Industrial Revolution, and the opening-up of the world by maritime exploration. The line had not come to an end: one important intellectual descendant of these men, J. M. Keynes, was just embarking on work that was seen as displacing the old economics of Adam Smith and Ricardo. He was a reasonable, logical man, with perhaps a greater gift for intellectual debate than any of them had possessed; Russell, probably the most distinguished English philosopher of the century, said of him: 'Obviously a nice man, but I did not enjoy his company. He made me feel a fool.'[3] People less concerned about their own intellectual standing found him charming and kind, except in debate. During the 1920s he was laying the foundations of his serious work, and incidentally acquiring a fortune on the Stock Exchange; during the 1930s he published the books which convinced most people that it is not enough to run a government's finances like those of a household, making sure that there is a bit left over at the end of the year.

The post-war mood

For much of the rest of the twentieth century men from the German Jewish community took on the intellectual role that had been played by the British a little earlier. The Russian Revolution, and the difficulties of the capitalist system, inspired renewed interest in Marx's writings. Freud's ideas were breaking through to general acceptance; he was of course invoked to justify a somewhat overdue relaxation of the idea that sex, though widespread, was not respectable,[4] but the more serious implication of his work was that people were dominated by their unconscious minds, over which they had very little control.

An eclipse of the sun, about a month before the treaty was signed at Versailles, provided empirical evidence to support Einstein's General Theory of Relativity. The theory asserted that the speed of light was a limiting factor, because nothing could move faster; that it is not possible to say which of two unrelated events took place first; and that the difference in time between the two events varies when they are seen from different points in space. People on this earth may think that the battle of Hastings took place 900 years ago and that a new star has just exploded into prominence, but from some point in space the events will appear simultaneous.

3. H. Nicolson, *Diaries* (1966–8), iii. 202.
4. The enormous sales, and considerable scandal, of Marie Stopes's quite harmless *Married Love* (1918) show how overdue the change was.

Einstein's earlier equations linking energy and mass suggested that matter could be disintegrated with explosive effect. Laymen amused themselves with the thought of 'splitting the atom' and blowing up the world. Rutherford, already a dominant figure in the study of radioactivity, made a reassuring statement that this was impossible. Einstein's theory was widely discussed, partly because of a mere play on words: people thought from the name of the theory that it justified a relativist attitude to philosophical and moral questions. This was not a simple matter of ignorance. A major speech in the last act of Shaw's play *Too True to be Good* (1928) expresses the puzzlement that atheists of the Herbert Spencer school felt as a result of the overthrow of the simple and easily calculable Newtonian laws of motion. Thinkers in the previous period had assumed that a reasonable man could stand outside the system he was analysing and impose order upon it. Marx, Freud, and Einstein had a common tendency to deny the possibility of taking a detached and unbiased attitude.

The distaste for Victorianism which had been spreading before the war found expression in Strachey's *Eminent Victorians* (1918), a set of satirical lives of four honoured and respected Victorian figures. It was the first public triumph of Bloomsbury and the tendency to frankness and open analysis of motive which the disciples of G. E. Moore had been practising for some years. This attitude was not universal: most of the substantial biographies of late Victorian political figures were published in the 1920s, and they were written with all the adulation and lack of analysis that Strachey had tried to combat, but the fashion of the decade was to look at Victorian prudery with disgust, at Victorian literature with amusement, and at Victorian architecture as little as possible.

Eliot's *The Waste Land* (1922) finally forced English poets to recognize the work of the French Symbolist writers and stop trying to squeeze out a few more drops from the Romantic heritage. Almost all the poets already writing were cut off from the people who started writing after *The Waste Land*. Transformations like that of Yeats, who turned himself into a Symbolist, were rare. *Georgian Poetry* survived until 1922 and the style of its writers changed very little. Apart from its effect on poetic style *The Waste Land* expressed a feeling, widespread among people who thought about such questions, that the world had suffered a mortal blow during the war. Until 1914 it was taken for granted that visible economic progress implied progress in every other direction as well. There was some justification for this view: European countries were more kind-hearted and more tolerant in 1914 than they had been in 1815. But the war came, and demonstrated that human beings still had a great capacity for causing suffering. Economic progress went on after the war, but it was less easy to be certain that other sorts of progress continued. The war ended in the mood of 'the world's great age begins anew', but the problems of reorganizing society were large enough to make people soon ask,

'What are the roots that clutch, what branches grow I Out of this stony rubbish?'[5]

Lloyd George once described the House of Commons elected in 1918 as 'the Trade Union Congress on the opposition benches and the Chamber of Commerce on the government side'. Neither this, nor Keynes's more one-sided comment that 'they are a lot of hard-faced men who look as if they had done very well out of the war', was accurate: there were about twenty trade unionists and about eighty businessmen more than in 1910, and they did not between them make up a majority of the House.[6] But Lloyd George's comment brought out two social changes that followed the war. At the time people talked mainly about the increased political strength of the working class and the possibility of 'Bolshevism', by which they meant anything from Leninist revolution to a narrowing of the social and economic gap that separated the working class from the upper and middle classes. The proportion of the national income that went to the working class did increase between 1914 and 1920, but this did not last long.[7] Some social legislation was passed, and trade unions retained some of the position in industrial relations they had gained during the war. But none of this altered the relationship of the working class to their 'betters' nearly as much as the war altered relationships within the more comfortable classes.

If the people from the working class were better off by the end of the war than at the beginning, and if manufacturers inevitably became much better off, it might reasonably be asked who paid for the war. First, of course, all those who went off and fought did very badly economically as well as in other ways. Apart from them, the professional classes and the landowning classes did badly. They were caught by six years of inflation and rising taxes, and could do relatively little to raise their incomes to meet these changes. The most obvious sign of the times was the great land sales of 1918–21, which produced a transfer of land on a scale 'probably not equalled since the

5. Lord Curzon quoted the line of Shelley in moving the Address to the Throne to celebrate the end of the war (18 Nov. 1918, *Lords Debates*, xxxii. 165); the second quotation is from *The Waste Land*, lines 19 and 20.

6. J. M. McEwen, 'The Coupon Election of 1918 and the Unionist Members of Parliament', *Journal of Modern History*, 34 (1962), 294–306.

7. From S. Pollard, *Development of the British Economy 1914–1950* (1962), 289–90, it appears that some of the disproportion developed because more of the population was of working age.

	Net income per head	Real wages
1920	100.0	100
1938	118.5	113

Norman Conquest'.[8] The sales were said to have been caused by the impact of death duties upon noble and gallant families in which a number of owners were killed one after another, with duties to pay each time. This interpretation was too romantic: the Death Duties (Killed in War) Act reduced death duties for the first owner who was killed and remitted all duties for subsequent deaths in action. In any case, it was not the owners who were killed; Curzon told the Lords early in 1917 that six peers and sixty-two heirs had been killed,[9] and the death of an heir who had an infant son or a younger brother would delay the incidence of death duties. Part of the reason for the break-up of estates was a move away from the practice of leaving all the landed property to the eldest son, formalized in the 1922 Law of Property Act which established a legal preference for equal division among children. Before 1914 there had been an upper class in the United Kingdom, in the sense that landowners had a recognized claim on the personal and political loyalty of their tenants; this class had been losing its power before the war and it lost more power during the war. While Lord Derby continued to dominate Lancashire politics, it could not be said that the old upper class had gone, but his position was exceptional enough to illustrate by contrast what had happened to the political power of other landowners. They may have given up their rural land because income tax at 30 per cent was too much for them, or because they decided that accepting the low economic return yielded by land made no sense as it was no longer a source of power. They kept their urban land, which eventually restored the fortunes of those who held on long enough, they kept up a large number of the smaller country houses, and they kept their unsaleable shooting estates in Scotland, but for the rest they sold out to their tenants or to manufacturers who wanted a place in the country.

A minor political issue of the period shows the changes that were taking place within the ruling class. Lloyd George brought businessmen into the government in 1916. In a wider sense he was ready to establish them as members of the ruling class, and they were ready to encourage him to do so. The easy way to recognition was through the granting of honours: the Prime Minister could advise the King to make businessmen into peers, baronets, knights, or lesser notabilities for their contributions to the war effort. Lloyd George gave honours lavishly to businessmen, which could have been a sensible acceptance of the country's changing social structure. People who disliked having to face the changes that were taking place would have objected in any case, but enemies of change who liked neither Lloyd George nor businessmen were able to protest much more plausibly because it was clear that these honours were being sold for cash contributions to Lloyd George's political treasure chest. This was nothing new; honours had been sold previously, and

---

8. F. M. L. Thompson, *English Landed Society in the Nineteenth Century* (1963), 332–3.
9. Feb. 1917, *Lords Debates*, xxiv. 21.

everybody knew about it. But the scale of Lloyd George's operations, and the sort of people to whom he sold them, strengthened the position of those who thought the existing class structure ought not to be disturbed. Estimates of the amount raised by the sale of honours range from £1 million to £6 million; even the lower figure, at the rates quoted of £10,000 for a knighthood and more for higher honours, disturbed the decent order of things, and also cast a doubt on honours that had been obtained in more acceptable ways.

People who had done badly out of the war naturally complained, and were joined by people who had been doing badly in any case and could now blame the war, while those who had done well out of the war remained discreetly quiet. After a short burst of enthusiasm for reconstruction, strong pressure for getting back to 'before the war' developed. 'Diehards' dreamed of the impossible and hoped to get back to pre-war levels of government expenditure, pre-war patterns of trade, and pre-war social relationships between manufacturers and their betters. The manufacturers whom Lloyd George had brought into close relations with the Conservative Party tended to settle down there; businessmen were not unknown in the pre-war Conservative Party, but they had been much less important. They were not yet fully convinced of the desirability of Protection, but they were being drawn in that direction.

Tariffs were brought in to provide ' "safeguarding duties" in any case in which an industry proved it was suffering from unfair competition. In this way we could build up a chain of cases which proved that protection was right.'[10] Any chain of cases would probably be intended to save one of the traditional industries of the country, often faced with competition from countries with lower wages, from having to contract. New industries would find it hard to establish a right to be protected while the chain of proof was being built. A protectionist policy could not help traditional industries like cotton and coal which had to export in order to return to their pre-war levels, but throughout the 1920s the desire to get back to 1913 inhibited attempts to get people out of the declining industries and into those with a future.

The brief attempt at reconstruction in 1919 and 1920 had not faced this problem. After five or six months of transition, during which 70 per cent of the demobilization of the army was carried out, the country set off on a frantic boom. The great land sales took place, manufacturers who felt it was time to retire were able to sell their factories at very high prices, and war gratuities, rising wages, easy credit, and the relaxation of government controls over industry all encouraged a brief period of full employment and hope for the future. Before 1914 Britain had been able to rely on old and tested branches of industry that were already showing signs of becoming out of date. Investment in prosperous but capital-hungry countries like Canada and Australia provided these industries with some of their export opportunities. During the

10. Lord Swinton, *Sixty Years of Power* (1966), 78.

war all the traditional industries like mining, textiles, and shipbuilding had been vital, and nobody doubted that this would continue to be the case. But so many overseas investments had been sold during the war that Britain no longer had a large favourable balance of current payments to finance new foreign investment. Former customers for British goods had built up their own industries, and British industry could not rely on old-established markets any longer. The reconstruction boom was only a matter of catching up on depreciation that had been neglected, and there was not much modernization in industry. In any case the monetary policy that the Bank of England and the Conservative backbenchers were determined to follow would have broken even a more soundly based expansion of trade. By 1921 the economy was in a slump which, measured by the number of people out of work, was as bad as any in the records.

The Bank of England contributed to some of the unbalance of the year of boom by allowing the pound sterling to slip from the exchange rate of $4.76, at which it had been held during the war, and the subsequent depreciation encouraged prices to go up. The Bank's policy also provided fairly liberal credit for reconstruction, and for the considerable purchases of land and of businesses that took place in 1919 and early 1920. But the Bank's long-term goal was to restore the pound to its pre-war gold value; as the American Treasury was committed to a policy of buying gold at $20.67 the ounce, the rate of exchange with the dollar became the main consideration for the Bank, which was determined to get back to the 1914 rate, when a pound had been worth $4.86. The decisive step was taken in April 1920, when the bank rate was raised to 7 per cent and kept there for almost a year. The boom would not have gone on indefinitely even if the bank rate had remained at a lower level, but the slump that followed need not have been so severe, nor need the recovery have been so incomplete. Throughout the 1920s Montagu Norman, the Governor of the Bank of England, was determined to return to 1914, and to achieve this he was prepared to handicap British industry very severely. Successive Chancellors of the Exchequer from 1920 to 1931 accepted his policy without any real dispute. Getting back to 1914 was even harder than the Bank realized. Everybody spoke as if it would be enough to bring British prices down to the same relationship to American prices as in 1914 and, at the cost of keeping British interest rates well above American interest rates and keeping British industry much less fully employed than American industry, something like this equality of price levels was reached by the late 1920s. What could not be restored so easily was London's assured dominance of the short-term money market. Before the war the London money market had not only undertaken large foreign investments but had also been able to make large short-term loans to bankers working in other money markets—the difficulty in August 1914 had been that bankers in other financial centres had found it almost impossible to repay their London debts, and their London creditors had been embarrassed accordingly. But after the war London had no such easy dominance; people with short-term money to lend either were Americans or wanted to send their money to America. This increased the pressure on the Bank of England to keep its interest rates above the American level, which made it all the harder to adapt British industry to new conditions.

The businessmen elected in 1918 may have been Liberal or they may have been Conservative, but most of them agreed about the importance of 'anti-waste' or, in the language of an earlier generation, 'retrenchment'. Austen Chamberlain, the Chancellor of the Exchequer, budgeted for a large surplus at a high level of expenditure, which would deflate the economy. This did not satisfy the opponents of government spending, who wanted a large surplus at a lower level of overall expenditure, which would be even more deflationary. On the Opposition benches the Asquithian Liberals had to decide how they would interpret the old Liberal slogan of 'Peace, Retrenchment, and Reform' in the post-war world. A peaceful and conciliatory foreign policy naturally appealed to them, and on this point they found themselves in agreement with the Labour Party. But 'Reform' in the twentieth century had come to mean heavy government spending on social welfare, and was not easy to reconcile with 'Retrenchment'. The Asquithians preferred 'Retrenchment' and called on the government to practise economy. Perhaps this suited the temperament of the older generation of Asquithians, because Lloyd George was bound to do better than Asquith in any contest about who could spend money faster. But it did mean that, in a period in which willingness to spend money was taken to be one of the signs of a left-wing party, the Liberals were placing themselves firmly on the right. The Labour Party naturally favoured high expenditure, to be devoted to social services. The government had no desire for this sort of support when struggling with its backbenchers, and felt little sympathy for the Labour Party's enthusiasm for a capital levy which would take money from all rich men and help the poor. The Asquithian Liberals also proposed a capital levy, to be based on war gains by taxing the difference between taxpayers' 1914 and 1918 wealth. This might attract owners of established wealth who wanted to penalize the nouveaux riches, but people like this were normally Conservative. People who were enthusiastic about taking money from the rich would probably prefer the Labour Party's more sweeping approach, and the nouveaux riches themselves, many of whom were pre-war Liberals, felt they might be safer if they stuck to the Conservative Party to which Lloyd George had introduced them.

Lloyd George's followers in Parliament were not prepared to make the Coalition permanent by joining the Conservatives as the Liberal Unionists had done. The political leaders among them, Churchill, Addison, Mond, and Montagu, had been on the left of the party before the war, and the Liberal manufacturers distrusted the enthusiasm their Coalition partners always showed for Protection. Churchill was drawn towards the Conservatives by his fear of Bolshevism, his belief that the Labour Party was riddled with it, and his desire to crush the Communist government in Russia, but his suggestion that Liberals and Conservatives should join to form a centre party underlined the difficulties of the situation. A centre party meant resistance not only to the Labour Party but also to the more right-wing of the Conservative back-benchers. At the time people looked at the National Party under its leader, General Sir Henry Page Croft, who had campaigned on a programme of 'No sale of honours', the 'anti-waste MPs', loosely led by the notoriously extravagant Horatio Bottomley, who had to leave the Commons for the second time in May 1922, and opponents of negotiations in Ireland like Lord Carson, and lumped them all together as Diehards. They had relatively little in common except right-wing opposition to the government. Whether the Conservatives in office were willing to be divided from these Diehards remained to be seen.

During the post-war boom industrial relations deteriorated; Labour Party supporters felt that the election had been held in such a hurry that they had not had a fair chance to state their case, and that this justified strike action to get the political changes they wanted. 'Direct action', as this approach was called, was used by the coal miners, who threatened to strike in February 1919 to obtain an increase in wages and the nationalization of the coal mines. The government bent before this pressure and appointed a Royal Commission, with six members sympathetic to the coal miners, six sympathetic to the owners, and an impartial chairman, Mr Justice Sankey. Quite possibly the government was ready to accept a Report that favoured nationalization when it set up the Commission; a Transport Bill which pointed towards nationalization of the railways and an Electricity Bill which gave much wider powers to the central government were being introduced into the House of Commons at just about the same time. However, the Conservative backbenchers who now made up a majority of the House—which they had not done during the 1916–18 period of Lloyd George's Coalition—forced the government to promise that it would not use this legislation to nationalize either industry. When Sankey came down on the side of nationalizing the coal mines (and the other Commission members divided as might be expected) the Report was rejected on the grounds that the government was not pledged to accept a Report which was so far from being unanimous. The government granted the miners' other demands, including legislation for a seven-hour day, and, as the miners were not ready to go on strike for nationalization when no immediate issues were at stake, they accepted the government's decision.

The seven-hour day for miners was part of a much wider move to a shorter working week. Before the war the average working week had been about fifty-four hours (miners, with heavier work, had a shorter week), and in the course of 1919 and 1920 it was reduced to about forty-eight hours. This increase in leisure was probably the most substantial gain made by the working classes in the post-war settlement; it narrowed the gap between them and the middle classes and made it profitable to provide week-day entertainment all over the country. The cinema, greyhound racing, and dirt track (motorbike) racing all depended on working-class audiences with more time, as well as more money, than before 1914.

Legislation and economics

The working classes expected more from Parliament after 1918 than they got. The post-war legislation settled, in a hasty, unidealistic sort of way, most of the burning issues that had kept the Liberal Party alive for generations; by the time Lloyd George fell from power in 1922 the party needed new ideas and issues because most of its old ones had been passed into law—not always in a very edifying way, but none the less conclusively. When the wartime restrictions on pubs were made permanent, which cut the drinking day down to about six hours, supporters of stricter regulation asked for more limitations and some people even wanted complete Prohibition, but the shorter hours took the fire out of the campaign, which never recaptured its nineteenth-century fervour.

Fisher's 1918 Education Act had begun the work of social legislation before the war ended. It raised the school-leaving age to 14 and, while it kept the 1902 division between free elementary education and fee-paying secondary education, it increased the number of scholarships. Larger grants were given to local authorities to make substantial increases in teachers' salaries possible. The Act also required local authorities to provide part-time education up to the age of 18 for children who left school at 14, although this provision had little effect because of the pressure for government economy that soon developed. British politics between the wars were marked by considerable hostility to education: some people opposed it on the grounds that it made children less willing to work and intensified the servant problem, and others thought that if the poor were educated they would no longer be content to work hard at boring jobs. When R. A. Butler was introducing the next important Education Bill in 1944 he felt it necessary to say: 'To the question "Who will do the work if everybody is educated?" we reply that education itself will oil the wheels of industry and bring a new efficiency, the fruit of modern knowledge, to aid the ancient skill of field and farm.'[11]

Other people realized that education has very few harmful effects, but believed that the country could not afford it, because it might produce unemployable intellectuals, fit only to teach, and unwilling to undertake more directly productive labour. This was short-sighted: it is sometimes said the unemployment of the 1920s and 1930s made the working class resist change, but the economy had been inflexible for some time before the period of high

11. 9 Jan. 1944, *Commons Debates*, ccclxxxxvi. 215.

unemployment, and lack of education, which was not something that appeared for the first time in the 1920s and 1930s, probably caused some of the inflexibility.

Lloyd George's government had several pre-war problems to settle. It was pledged to carry out the Home Rule and Welsh Disestablishment Bills left in suspense at the outbreak of war, and to do something about housing. Welsh Disestablishment went through without difficulty: the heart had gone out of the struggle and the Church of England no longer hoped for a position of monopoly. A Ministry of Health was set up under Christopher Addison in June 1919, with a commitment to improve housing. The principle of government responsibility towards which the pre-war Liberals had been moving in Lloyd George's urban land programme was now accepted. Before 1914, according to Professor Bowley,

builders were free to vary the quality and size of working-class houses according to what they judged to be the demand, that is, according to the willingness and ability of people to pay for them. Since the Great War a different attitude has been taken, rightly or wrongly. A much higher minimum standard for new houses has been established, partly by law and partly by public opinion.

This public opinion required more money to be spent on housing, for the sake of the children or of the neighbourhood, than poor people wanted (or could afford) to pay: and the slums of Glasgow or Whitechapel showed clearly enough why this was so. The Ministry of Health required local authorities to show what they were going to provide for the people who could not afford decent housing, and this pushed the local authorities into building during the last and most frantic stages of the sudden and short-lived post-war boom. Naturally the houses that were built were very expensive, and this led to a reaction against government intervention in housing. If the commitment to government intervention had come after the boom had broken, it might have had a stimulating effect on the economy, but people in the 1920s did not believe in stimulating the economy during a slump. Before the war the government spent so small a proportion of the national income that even a relatively large budget deficit would not have done much for the economy. The politicians of the 1920s ignored wartime experience which showed that a large budget deficit could produce an active and adaptable economy, and remained convinced that the way to deal with a slump was to cut government expenditure. If Addison had not committed the government to taking some interest in housing by his instructions to the local authorities, the problem might have been ignored for a good many years to come.[12]

Unemployment Insurance was extended during the boom in much the

12. M. Bowley, *Housing and the State 1919–44* (1945), 209. This book has a sympathetic account of the Addison housing programme (pp. 26–8).

same spirit; it seemed safe to extend Part II of the 1911 Insurance Act to all industrial workers and to promise additional 'uncovenanted benefit' beyond the amount covered by insurance. Only if they remained unemployed for a long time could workers lose their (nationally organized) insurance rights and be forced back on the (locally organized) Poor Law system which would keep them from starvation. Unemployed workers preferred the insurance system to the Poor Law system, partly because the Poor Law almost always gave less than the insurance system. Poplar Borough Council, one of the first London boroughs to vote Labour, gave benefits in 1921 at about the same rate as the insurance scheme, but the municipal finances headed towards bankruptcy and the councillors were ordered to pay for their generosity out of their own pockets and were imprisoned when they failed to do so. People who were free from the fear of unemployment called the whole system 'the dole' and were contemptuous about its organization. Conservatives and Liberals wanted to run the system of relief as cheaply as possible; the Labour Party wanted to raise the level of unemployment benefit to what they called 'work or maintenance'—maintenance at a level as close as possible to the normal trade union rate of pay.

Economic expansion came to an end soon after the unemployment insurance system had been extended. Prices reached a peak in the summer of 1920; wages continued to rise until the beginning of 1921. Forcing down wages was not easy. Trade unions had become powerful during the war and maintained their position in the two years after the war. In 1919 'direct action' had compelled the government to set up the Sankey Commission, and it enjoyed something of a triumph the following year. The government seemed to be drifting towards intervening on Poland's side against Russia; in May the London dockers refused to load arms for Poland onto the *Jolly George*, and the issue sank out of sight for a few weeks. During the summer intervention again seemed possible; trade unions formed councils of action and made it clear that intervention would be followed by strikes. Lloyd George drew back; probably he realized that fighting for Poland would be unpopular, and allowed the trade unions to push him in the direction he wanted to go, but the episode must have helped to convince the unions of their political strength.

As a result they were very unwilling to allow any reductions in wages. The miners were the centre of resistance. Their wages had been high before the war, and they had a tradition of long and inflexible strikes. They wanted to return to 1914, to rebuild the Triple Alliance and join the railwaymen and the transport workers in a struggle against any reduction in wages. Before the war the miners had been looked up to as a very powerful union, and the two other unions had been very glad to combine with them, even though the tactics of a transport strike and a coal strike were quite different—an effective transport strike would either be settled in a few days, or else would force the government to step in, and, if it did, the less skilled workers might find themselves replaced. Miners were not so easy to replace. Ernest Bevin and Jimmy Thomas, the post-war leaders of the transport and the railway unions, were in any case not men who wanted to strike for the sheer pleasure in combat that sometimes carried the miners away.

When the mines were returned to full private control in March 1921, the owners clearly wanted to reduce wages and conduct future wage negotiations on a 'district' not a national basis. The miners preferred a national basis because they wanted the costs of mining 'pooled' so that good mines would pay for poor mines and wages would not be driven down to the level that just kept the worst mines going. A strike over this seemed inevitable, and the Triple Alliance would, a little unenthusiastically, have supported the miners. But on 15 April the secretary of the Miners' Federation said that negotiations on a district basis might be acceptable; the railwaymen and transport workers were immensely relieved and said the strike was off. But this was not so. The miners went on with their strike, and denounced their allies for deserting them. 'Black Friday' passed into labour legend as the day when the miners were betrayed. It might more reasonably have been seen as the day when the more astute trade unionists saw that the day of the miners' supremacy was over. For thirty or forty years the miners had been the most aggressive union, and miners' wages had risen faster than those of any other large industrial group. But coal-mining was overextended, many more miners wanted jobs than before the war, and for the next two decades they did very badly.[13] In a period in which unemployment was generally high, it was particularly high in mining, and in hours of work and wages earned the miners were less able to hold their position than almost any other industrial group.

Post-war nationalism: Ireland, India, and Chanak

The sale of honours and even the level of government expenditure caused less trouble than the development in Ireland. In 1918 Lloyd George had said Ireland could have whatever status it wanted if it stayed in the Empire and allowed Northern Ireland to choose its own status. Sinn Fein asked for national independence for the whole of Ireland, and won almost three-quarters of the Irish seats. It sent representatives to Versailles, although they were not received there, and began to emerge as the effective government in most of Ireland, helped by the fact that some relaxation of British rule was inevitable, which made policemen and other officials unwilling to show themselves as pro-British. It owed most of its strength to the fact that Irishmen were tired of waiting for the Westminster parliamentary machine and had been inspired by the enthusiasm for small nationalities which had often been heard in war propaganda; the British might have wished this enthusiasm to

13. 980,000 in 1912, 1,197,000 in 1924 (A. J. Youngson, *The British Economy 1920–57* (1960), 40).

confine itself to Belgians, Serbs, and subjects of the Austro-Hungarian Empire, but it did not. In 1919 Ireland was moving towards a system of dual government, with legal rule by Dublin Castle and effective rule by Sinn Fein.

In February 1920 the long-delayed Home Rule Bill was passed. The Coalition wanted to give Northern Ireland a Home Rule Bill, so the 1920 legislation offered Sinn Fein only the bare and meagre provisions that Redmond was struggling to avoid accepting in 1914. And in Northern Ireland it remained in force for fifty years; from the battles that raged around Gladstone, Parnell, and Redmond, it might have been thought that Home Rule was a wild and reckless piece of legislation, but in fact it offered Irishmen no more than the limited and revocable powers enjoyed by the Parliament of Northern Ireland. Successive British governments behaved as if they had given Northern Ireland a great deal of autonomy, and did not intervene when the new Parliament at Stormont legislated on the basis that Catholics were disloyal and wanted to unite with the Irish Free State and Protestants should be treated as the only true citizens of Ulster.

Law and order broke down in the twenty-six counties and the British government began trying to restore its authority by force of arms. Fighting began in 1919, went on in 1920, and reached new levels of brutality in the first half of 1921. The Sinn Fein forces were not strong enough to fight pitched battles against the British army, but they could ambush patrols, shoot soldiers in the streets of the towns they occupied, and punish Irishmen who obeyed the British government. Warfare in which one side does not wear uniform is bound to be confused and vindictive, and it is worse when both sides claim to be the legitimate government; if the British took their claims to their logical conclusion, all Irishmen who took up arms could be hanged as traitors, and if Sinn Fein took its claims seriously all Irishmen who cooperated with the foreigner were traitors. To strengthen the police the British government raised special forces, the 'Black and Tans' and the 'auxis' (auxiliaries). These irregulars were recruited from demobilized soldiers, like the Freikorps in Germany, who beat up political opponents and conducted guerrilla warfare on the Polish frontier; and they behaved rather more like the Freikorps than the government cared to recognize. The practice of 'reprisals', which became official policy in January 1921, meant burning down houses, destroying the farming economy, and shooting prisoners who were constantly 'trying to escape'; it was popular in Britain at first, but it could not be continued for long. By the early months of 1921 Lloyd George was wondering whether he could make peace in Ireland. The Conservative backbenchers did not trust him, and his position became no easier when ill health forced Bonar Law to retire in March 1921. Lloyd George's system of government needed a devoted second-in-command to serve as leader of the Conservative Party. Law was not only devoted and loyal, but he was also recognized as a man who would look after the interests of Ulster. His successor as Conservative leader, Austen

Chamberlain, was no less loyal to the Prime Minister, but had no particular claim to speak for Ulster.

If Lloyd George could have negotiated an Irish settlement that Law was ready to support, it would have been accepted without too much difficulty. But there were four months of civil strife in Ireland before Sinn Fein responded to some friendly words (inserted by Smuts) in George V's speech opening the Northern Ireland Parliament. The IRA had almost been fought to a standstill by the time the truce began in July, but the British government realized that nothing better than the peace of exhaustion could be expected in Ireland unless Sinn Fein was substantially satisfied by the negotiations. De Valera, the President of the Irish Republic, did not go to London to negotiate; his representatives were slightly less intransigent than he would have been. It was accepted that Ireland would at the very least have the same status as the Dominions. The argument over that question had come when Lloyd George had won over Birkenhead and Churchill to support his policy in the spring. But the position of Ulster was not settled, and it was not clear that Ireland was going to stay inside the British Empire.

Lloyd George got his way on both points, on the first by trickery and on the second by a threat of renewing the war. He promised the Irish representatives that a Boundary Commission would revise the 1920 frontier and reduce Northern Ireland to a small and unviable area; it was unlikely that the boundary revision would ever take place, but the assurance met the needs of the Irish negotiators. They were also required to demand republican status for Ireland; as this was not compatible with being part of the Empire as it then stood, it would turn Ireland into a completely independent country with certain treaty obligations to Britain. Lloyd George reckoned that Dominion status was the most he could persuade his supporters to accept, and he said the war would begin again if the Irish negotiators did not immediately agree that their country should become the Irish Free State, with the same status as Canada and a commitment to provide harbour facilities for the Royal Navy at half a dozen ports. The Irish negotiators accepted this without referring it back to de Valera. So on 6 December 1921 the treaty was signed. De Valera denounced it, and Ireland disintegrated into a new civil war between pro-treaty and anti-treaty parties. As the pro-treaty party won, the civil war made no real difference to the United Kingdom, but it gave Unionists who thought the treaty ought never to have been made an opening to complain that the fighting in Ireland showed how wrong Lloyd George had been to imagine the Irish could run their own affairs.

By 1922 Lloyd George needed a success somewhere. He wondered whether he could fight another election under the Coalition banner. The boom had been broken altogether too thoroughly, and the supporters of economy forced him to set up a committee, under Sir Eric Geddes, to reduce government expenditure. Its report, presented in February 1922, suggested economies on the army and Navy, and on education; the government managed to avoid some of the cuts proposed in education, though the idea of compulsory part-time education after 14 disappeared. A low level of spending on arms was accepted, and even welcomed as a gesture to the League of Nations, and no coherent opposition to it could be mounted in Parliament. But, when Britain suggested disarmament during the inter-war years, the nations of Europe were unimpressed, because they knew that it had already disarmed, and had done so for budgetary reasons. The Coalition backbenchers, who would have preferred to see the full range of the Geddes reductions in education expenditure carried out, were not satisfied.

Lloyd George was artful and deceptive when negotiating over relatively small matters, and was at least as attached to his principles as any normal Prime Minister when dealing with large issues. This meant that the Conservatives in the Coalition got very little that they wanted. Cabinet ministers, who knew that there would have to be changes after the war, trusted Lloyd George to make sure that these changes were not too sweeping, but the Conservative backbenchers simply felt that all they valued was being betrayed. To some extent they blamed the Coalition Liberal ministers: Addison, as minister in charge of housing, and Fisher were responsible for increased expenditure on social welfare, and Montagu, the Secretary of State for India, was blamed for giving way to Indian demands for independence.

This was not reasonable; the Indian nationalist movement had been growing for some time, and the British government could not resist all of its demands. Undoubtedly independence for India was not going to attract much support in Britain. Apart from the sentimental appeal of owning a vast Empire—whenever people talked about the numbers of people within the British Empire, rather than its vast area, they were really talking about the population of India, which made up about two-thirds of the population of the entire Empire—India was of substantial importance to a good many people in the United Kingdom. The Lancashire cotton industry was still a dominant force in the export markets of the world, but India was its largest single market. There were so many millions of people in India that, though most of them were very poor, they could between them buy a great deal of cloth.

India had once had a cotton industry of its own, and was trying to revive it. The Congress Party, the main political instrument of the Indian nationalists, was a curious mixture of saintly leaders like Gandhi, who believed in a revival of handicrafts and village spinning of cotton, and manufacturers who wanted India to be free to impose a tariff on Lancashire cotton. Independence for India would clearly do the British cotton trade no good. In the years after 1918, when India was still a long way from independence, the government of India did acquire the right to impose tariffs to promote Indian industry without intervention from London, and it used this right to protect the Indian cotton industry.

The cotton trade was important but it was not the only substantial British interest in India. A small number of people from Britain ruled India; the Indian Civil Service, recruited by examination and inspired by high and austere ideals, contained only a few thousand men, but these men—the 'heaven-born', or, as Lloyd George put it, 'the steel-frame which holds India together'—were a relatively small part of the British community in India. Engineers and doctors went to India to find work; merchants settled in Bombay and Calcutta and at first formed the majority of the municipal electorates in the big trading cities. The Indian army was as large as all the rest of British military strength before 1914; during the rapid expansion of the Empire in Africa soldiers with Indian experience, like Baring in Egypt and Roberts in the Boer War, played leading roles, and poor but hard-working officers often went to India while officers who joined the army for social reasons stayed in the United Kingdom. Particularly after the Indian Mutiny of 1857 the government of India took care to have regiments of British soldiers available in India, but the Indian forces were a powerful instrument in their own right, guarding imperial interests all round the Indian Ocean, and Indian regiments took part in the First World War; some of them went to France, which was too cold and wet for them, but others fought more successfully in the war in the Middle East against Turkey.

The pre-war Liberal government had considered India's constitutional position, and Morley, the Secretary of State, and Minto, the Viceroy, had worked out proposals for allowing Indians a little more control over provincial and municipal affairs. Morley spoke as if this represented the limit of change, which did not help to satisfy the Indian nationalists. But before the Congress Party could fully organize itself to take account of the new situation, the war had begun.

The wartime propaganda of the British government and its allies laid considerable stress on the principle of self-determination. Congress became more militant, and in 1917 the British government announced that in the fullness of time India would have 'responsible government', which meant that a government responsible to an Indian electorate would control domestic issues, as in the Dominions. In the event, some issues handled by provincial governors were entrusted to ministers responsible to Indian provincial assemblies and a representative assembly, without much power, was set up at Delhi. These Montagu–Chelmsford reforms took some little time to come into effect, and it was in the months of agitation immediately after the war that Gandhi, the great apostle of non-violent civil disobedience, rose to his position of power in Congress. Under his influence it became more militant; his methods provided a new way to agitate, and his ascetic life convinced thousands of Indian peasants previously not interested in politics that he was a saint whose political leadership should be followed.

In 1919 General Dyer, in command at Amritsar, found his authority challenged by the mob. Normally the challenge would have been faced and put down by the usual methods of crowd dispersal, but Dyer used machine guns. It was officially reported that 379 people were killed. The massacre was unnecessary, for British control over India had not been shaken so much that it had to depend on armed force. Dyer was dismissed, a step which helped to reassure Indian opinion, and the post-war agitation died down. The Indians were divided; some of them were ready to take office in provincial governments, and to sit in the central representative assembly; Congress declared that as the central government was not in any way responsible to the assembly it was all just a sham. The Diehards at Westminster took a simpler view: they were convinced that Dyer's methods were right, and they felt that Indian nationalism was all Montagu's fault.

They also complained about the Egyptian settlement of 1922. At the beginning of the war Britain had annexed Egypt, which she had been occupying on a temporary basis for the previous thirty-two years. The Egyptians, who had been independent in practice before 1882, expected to be allowed self-determination after the war, and the British government realized that no formula could fit Egypt into the British Empire. In any case Allenby as High Commissioner realized that no government would be willing to hold down Egypt for long, and he offered his resignation rather than undertake a policy of repression. The government set about trying to re-create the pre-war situation: Turkey's theoretical sovereignty over Egypt which had been ended in 1914 was not to be revived, but Egypt's independence was to be limited. A British officer was to be commander-in-chief of the Egyptian army, and he, rather than the Minister for War, was to direct military expenditure. With control of the army thus kept out of Egyptian hands, it could be expected that advice from the British High Commissioner in Cairo would be taken almost as seriously as advice from the British agent-general had been taken before 1914. Even this slight concession to 'Egypt for the Egyptians' increased the backbenchers' dissatisfaction with Lloyd George.

The international scene offered no brighter prospects. At the Genoa Conference the government hoped to settle reparations, persuade the European powers to start paying their war debts to Britain at a rate that would cover the British repayments to the United States, and at the same time reconcile France and Germany. But it was so complete a failure that it buried the conference system to which the European countries had turned, as they always had done after wars. Russia made an agreement, at Rapallo, with Germany, but nobody gained anything at the official Genoa negotiations.

Further east the last part of the post-war settlement had still to be made effective. By the Treaty of Sèvres Turkey had given up not only her Balkan and Arab territories, but also parts of Asia Minor, which were handed to Greece. After a revolt in Turkey the treaty was repudiated and the Greeks were defeated and driven out of their new acquisitions; those who failed to get on to the boats leaving Smyrna were slaughtered. This undoubtedly encouraged Lloyd George in his natural Gladstonian feeling of friendship for the Greeks. He had encouraged them to go into Asia Minor, and he wanted to help them now they had been thrown out. But the Turkish army swept on towards the Dardanelles, where a small British force at Chanak was guarding the area of the Straits, which had been neutralized under the Sèvres Treaty. The British and the Turks glared at each other, while Lloyd George prompted his Cabinet to prepare to fight for the Straits. Churchill, as Secretary for the Colonies, went further and summoned the Dominions to send any help that might be needed. This ignored all the changes in Commonwealth relations in the previous half-dozen years. If Britain needed assistance, the Dominions had to be told what was going on and why. The claim for automatic, unexplained support had never been made before; in 1914 the Dominions had given immediate support without being asked, and in the Boer War there had been discussion before help was sent. Churchill made matters worse by publishing his message in the press before the Dominion Prime Ministers had received it. Mackenzie King, the Canadian Prime Minister, was not in favour of close cooperation, and he welcomed an opportunity to repudiate the whole system on an occasion when it had not been put into effect properly.

The Turkish government did not insist on its point at Chanak. It knew a new treaty would have to be negotiated, and it could be fairly certain that it would regain the Straits by waiting patiently. The British government assumed that by checking Turkey it had raised its own prestige. But this was not the case. The Conservative backbenchers were on the whole pro-Turkish, and all the natural anti-Turks in British politics were against the idea of going to war at all, even against the Turks. Law, whose health had temporarily improved, appealed to the feelings of both groups when he declared that the British Empire could not be the policeman of the world. Nevertheless, Lloyd George was now determined to force an election before the Conservative backbenchers could overthrow the Coalition, and Austen Chamberlain agreed to call a meeting of ministers and MPs at the Carlton Club at which he would try to win their support for an election under Lloyd George's leadership.

Supporters of the Coalition had to admit that the government had not solved the problems of Europe and had not passed the legislation the Conservatives wanted, but it had steered the country through its post-war difficulties and provided enough social welfare legislation to calm people down. Their argument for continuing the Coalition was that the growing power of the Labour Party was so menacing that the forces of Bolshevism would sweep over the country unless all men of good will stood together, which they would only do under Lloyd George's leadership. Even this argument lost some of its weight when, just before the meeting at the Carlton Club, an anti-Coalition Conservative defeated a Coalition and a Labour candidate in a by-election.

The Conservatives met on 19 October. Partly because of his own desire for a peaceful foreign policy and partly because Beaverbrook had persuaded him that the time was ripe for a tariff policy, Law was there: the backbenchers had an alternative Prime Minister who could replace Lloyd George. His speech, and the even more effective speech of Stanley Baldwin, the President of the Board of Trade, answered the question raised by all discussion of a 'centre party'. They said that the Conservative Party should not allow itself to be divided, and should not let Lloyd George drag one section of the party behind him while leaving the Diehard section isolated and embittered. This argument prevailed. The pro-Lloyd George Cabinet Ministers were rejected by 187 votes to 87; Law, Baldwin, and the backbenchers entered on their inheritance.

5

From the Carlton Club to the General Strike

1922–1926

The 1922 Parliament

When Lloyd George had resigned, Law had to form a government without being able to call on the ministers who had supported the Coalition and he had to fight a general election. There had been no purely Conservative government for sixteen years, and the men chosen in 1922 dominated British Cabinets for the next eighteen. Neville Chamberlain, Edward Wood (better known as Lord Halifax), Lloyd Graeme (later Lord Swinton), and Sir Samuel Hoare were first brought into the Cabinet by Law; by the critical period of the later 1930s they had already been in office almost continuously for over a dozen years, struggling with problems like unemployment to which none of them knew the answer. Apart from these men of the future the Cabinet contained a number of peers who helped give it strength and respectability among the Diehards.

On 23 October Law was elected leader of the Conservative Party and then accepted the position of Prime Minister. The electoral prospects for the new government were quite good: the Liberal Party was still divided; the Labour Party was not considered as an alternative government; Lloyd George depended on his command over the loyalty of his Coalition colleagues and behaved more like a minister pushed out of office by members of his own party than the leader of another party. Law would have to reconstruct his Cabinet to include the Coalitionists unless he won a clear majority, and new government kept this possibility open by not opposing the Coalitionists. Beaverbrook, who was not included in the government, had no liking for this half-hearted warfare; he encouraged more candidates to stand, in order to keep the breach open.

For perhaps twenty years, ever since Joseph Chamberlain raised the issue of Tariff Reform, political life had been in turmoil: Dreadnoughts, the budget, the Lords, Ireland, the war, the peace, Ireland again, and then the risk of war in the Near East had left people exhausted. At the Carlton Club meeting Baldwin had made a considerable impression when he called Lloyd George 'a dynamic force' and had reminded his listeners that a dynamic force could be very dangerous. Law gained a very favourable response from voters when he said the time had come for 'tranquillity'. No further commitments abroad and rigid economy at home appealed to the feelings of a solid majority of the people. From time to time during the next few years efforts were made to break out of this lethargy, but the mood to which Law was appealing had very deep roots. The clearest example of his unwillingness to disturb things was to be seen in his promise that he would not change the Free Trade system before the next general election, despite his own Tariff Reform views.

Apart from this, he was probably helped by the petulance of the Coalition-ists. Birkenhead said the new Cabinet was made up of second-class brains, exposing himself to Lord Robert Cecil's reply that second-class brains were better than second-class characters; and Lloyd George called Law honest to the verge of simplicity, though he was unwise to raise the issue of honesty at all.[1] The new government won its clear majority, free from any dependence on the National Liberals. Many Liberals who had voted for a Conservative for the first time in 1918 seem to have stayed with the Conservatives after the Coalition ended. Perhaps thirty Coalition Unionists followed Austen Chamberlain, but they were unlikely to vote against Law. The government had the only political organization which was intact and able to fight on a nationwide scale, and its success was not really surprising.

	Votes	Seats	% of all votes cast
Conservative	5,500,382	345	38.2
National Liberal	1,673,240	62	11.6
Liberal	2,516,287	54	17.5
Labour	4,241,383	142	29.5

The other significant result of the election was the advance made by the Labour Party. It won eighty seats more than in 1918 and it remained the largest party in opposition. The Asquithian Liberals doubled their numbers, Lloyd George's National Liberals were halved, so that even if Asquith and Lloyd George could have patched up their differences the Liberals would have been the smallest party. The two Liberal groups naturally obtained a larger aggregate of voters than the Asquithian Liberals in 1918, but even so they polled fewer votes than the Labour Party. Probably the Liberal vote increased

1. R. Blake, *The Unknown Prime Minister* (1955), 465; Lord Swinton, *Sixty Years of Power* (1966), 68.

because some Coalition voters returned to the party; the increased Labour vote seems to have come from people who had not voted when they were first enfranchised. In 1918 the Labour Party had retained its strength in areas where it had been strong before the war, but had not done well in places like Glasgow and East London; in 1922 the total vote cast, and the Labour vote, went up considerably in such places. The Liberal and Conservative vote taken together had not increased; the result could have been caused by elaborate switching of votes, but the simple explanation is that the newly enfranchised were just beginning to use their power.

Because Labour strength had increased, the leadership of the party was more important and Ramsay MacDonald, re-elected to Parliament after his defeat in 1918, challenged the incumbent J. R. Clynes for the post. The new Labour members from Glasgow and the Clydeside wanted a strongly socialist programme at home and abroad. Some of them had been imprisoned for their organizing activities during the war: confronted with a choice between confirming Clynes, who had held office during the war, in his position as leader or turning to MacDonald, who had suffered for his beliefs as they had, it was natural for them to choose the latter and assume that he was strongly socialist in all his views. MacDonald defeated Clynes by a narrow margin; he clearly received support from more moderate men as well as the Clydesiders, and this was perfectly reasonable: he was probably the best man the Labour Party could have chosen to get a Labour government elected to office quickly. He seemed born to rule; Emanuel Shinwell said that 'he was a prince among men'; some years later, when MacDonald and the Independent Labour Party were at daggers drawn, Jimmy Maxton, the sea-green incorruptible leader of the Clydesiders, cried as he listened to MacDonald speaking, though he retained enough self-control to mutter 'the bastard' through his tears; and Beatrice Webb called him 'a magnificent substitute for a leader'. Mrs Webb regarded her neat, precise, fussy, and omniscient husband Sidney as perfection, and was a little inclined to judge everybody else by the same standards, but there was some substance in her comment. MacDonald's views on foreign policy were the natural product of Gladstonian Liberalism, and did not imply any very determined impatience for socialism. He had joined the Labour Party when socialism did not necessarily mean much more than a heartfelt commitment to social reform, with no special implications about the policy to be used. Throughout his political life he clearly wanted social reform—in a way he knew more about it than any other Prime Minister, for he was the illegitimate son of Scottish peasants, and had at times gone hungry while he was working his way forward. This was no guarantee that he had any policy for reducing poverty, and the sting in Beatrice Webb's remark was that he did not know in what direction he should lead his party.

He possessed the great gift of making his words seem to mean more than they said, which enabled him to arouse the enthusiasm of his followers without committing himself to extreme policies that might alarm moderate opinion. By the end of his career people had realized that his skill in avoiding a commitment to hasty action was accompanied by some incapacity to take action at all, but this had yet to be seen. He had stood up for his beliefs during the war, and by 1922 people felt he had been ill treated for his devotion to his ideals. He was a fine platform speaker, in his prime he was a master of the House of Commons, and, until he formed his National government in 1931, he had no difficulty in dominating the Labour Party.

The two Liberal leaders, Asquith and Lloyd George, were too well matched for one to dominate the other and too dissimilar for one to serve the other without reservations. Reunion in the near future seemed unlikely, nor did it look as though Law could easily fit the Conservative Coalitionists into his ministry. They drifted away from Lloyd George, but for a time it seemed that there would simply be two Conservative and two Liberal Parties feuding in Parliament.

In accordance with his election pledges Law did very little once he was in power. Baldwin, the Chancellor of the Exchequer, went to Washington in January 1923 to arrange terms for the repayment of the British war debt. The United States wanted the $4,000 million outstanding to be repaid by sixty-one annual payments of $187 millon including interest at 3.5 per cent. Baldwin hoped to reduce this to fifty annual payments of $140 million, with interest at 2.5 per cent. But his bargaining position was weak: Keynes's comment on the situation, 'It is the debtor who has the last word in these cases', applied only if the debtor was ready to consider repudiation, and Baldwin came much closer to accepting Coolidge's 'Well, they hired the money, didn't they?' He agreed to ten payments of $161 million and fifty-two of $184 million and returned to Britain to recommend these terms to the Cabinet.

When he disembarked at Southampton, he rashly told reporters that American opinion would not consider a settlement that offered anything less. After this statement the Cabinet could hardly ask for new negotiations, and opponents of the terms had to consider the alternative of repudiation. Law was prepared to do so, and the Chancellor of the Exchequer and almost all his colleagues found themselves ranged against the Prime Minister. Law's willingness to stand alone made the Duke of Devonshire think: 'It practically meant that there was not a Cabinet but a Dictator, the one thing we had complained about with regard to the last government.'[2] But Law was not Lloyd George; he gave way and relieved his feelings by writing an anonymous letter of protest to *The Times*.

Tranquillity was not enough to please everybody. Three by-election defeats quickly showed that people wanted the government to do something about housing conditions. Neville Chamberlain brought in a Bill to give grants to be

2. R. Churchill, *Lord Derby* (1959), 495.

administered by the municipalities; for each house built a subsidy of £6 a year would be paid for twenty years. Private building was preferred, but municipalities could make contracts with private firms or employ direct labour on their own account. Only houses with a surface area of no more than 850 square feet qualified for a grant, and this turned out to be the controversial part of the Bill. Chamberlain wanted as many small houses as possible, and did not intend to subsidize houses large enough to satisfy people who could afford to pay a market price. The Labour Party objected that his houses would be too small; the issue was made tangible for ordinary people by the question 'Should working-class houses have a parlour?'

Chamberlain argued that one big room (perhaps a combined kitchen and parlour) made good sense and that if there were a parlour it would be left unused. The Labour Party replied that courting couples, children doing their homework, and many other people would use the parlour. Chamberlain was probably correct in thinking that people really wanted a parlour to be kept tidy and unused as a sign of respectability, but he gave way and allowed houses with a surface area of 950 square feet to qualify for the grant.[3]

Baldwin's reputation continued to rise. His colleagues thought he had taken an honest and straightforward approach to the war debt question, his budget was regarded as sound, and he was widely praised for a speech in which he declared: 'Four words, of one syllable each . . . contain salvation for this country and the whole world, and they are Faith, Hope, Love and Work.'[4]

When Law resigned in the middle of May, a victim of cancer of the throat, Lord Curzon was the obvious candidate for the succession. As ex-Viceroy of India and as Foreign Secretary, he had strong claims, and he had taken the chair when Law had been absent from meetings. There were disadvantages, as Balfour told the King, about appointing a Prime Minister in the Lords when the official Opposition was not represented there. Furthermore, the King was given to understand, in an informal but well-considered memorandum, that Baldwin would be Law's choice.[5] Baldwin had a reputation for amiability and honesty, Curzon a reputation for arrogance combined with a great talent, demonstrated in 1916 and in 1922, for deserting sinking ships.

Even so, the choice of Baldwin was a surprise, though one that was quickly accepted. Law in his post-war mood of calm had been surrounded by an air of mild melancholy. Baldwin gave the same impression that he would not undertake any unnecessary activity, but he seemed altogether more cheerful. He could obtain people's respect without standing on his dignity, he was always determined to be conciliatory, and nobody believed he would attempt to deceive his followers or even his political opponents: these qualities were the foundations on which a great Prime Minister could have stood.

3. 24 Apr. 1923, *Commons Debates*, clxiii. 303–419.
4. G. M. Young, *Stanley Baldwin* (1952), 47.
5. Thomas Jones, *Whitehall Diary* (1969), i. 235–6.

During the early months of his premiership attention was fixed on Poincaré's attempt to extract France's reparations from Germany by occupying the Ruhr. The British correctly thought this would get nowhere. The occupation placed a great strain on Anglo-French relations, but a bold British step, of the type Lloyd George's Coalition might have taken, would have attracted very little support. Baldwin would not concentrate on foreign problems when there were questions at home to hold his attention, and by this time the question of unemployment was causing concern in Britain.

Social issues in politics

When unemployment increased suddenly in 1921, it looked like one of the crises that was a normal part of pre-1914 trade cycles. By 1923 unemployment seemed to be taking an altogether different form; the number of men out of work continued to be high, running for most of the 1920s at over 1 million. Exact comparisons with the pre-1914 world, or, to take another period of depression, with the years of slack trade between 1874 and 1896, are difficult to draw, because the pre-1914 statistics cover principally the relatively prosperous workers who were in trade unions. In the 1880s unemployment among trade unionists was reported to be just over 5 per cent and in the years just before 1914 it was 4.5 per cent, which probably meant that 6 or 7 per cent of all workers were unemployed and others were underemployed. These figures contrast very sharply with conditions in the 1920s. Clapham concluded that in an average month 12 per cent of the population who were insured against unemployment (which by then meant more or less the whole wage-earning labour force) was out of work. And as a result of the 1918 Act, almost all the unemployed had votes.

The really conspicuous unemployment was in jobs which had been seen as the 'aristocracy of labour' in the nineteenth century. Coal miners and ship-builders were men with a well-established way of life that had been destroyed by changes in the economy. As skilled workers they would have felt they were stepping down if they had taken new jobs in other industries, even if new jobs had been available; in transport jobs clearly did change rather than disappear, because the number of men employed on the railways dropped by over 120,000 in the 1920s but the number of people engaged in motor transport rose by 220,000.[6]

A few of the most resilient of the unemployed no doubt found some compensations. As an unemployed coal miner the youthful Aneurin Bevan could further his education, but obviously the great majority of the unemployed found their situation incomprehensible in a way that robbed them of the

---

6. Sir John Clapham, *Economic History of Modern Britain* (1950–2), iii. 532 and 541, on transport and unemployment.

desire to do anything. Because of what Engels once called the 'damned want-lessness' of the proletariat, unemployment never looked like leading to revolution, and the unemployed sank deeper into a passive detachment about what was happening to them. To some extent it was this deadness of the men out of work which D. H. Lawrence was talking about when he suggested that

If only they were educated to *live* instead of earn and spend, they could manage very happily on twenty-five shillings [£1.25 a week]. If the men wore scarlet trousers as I said, they wouldn't think so much of money: if they could dance and hop and skip, and sing and swagger and be handsome, they could do with very little cash.[7]

This path of renunciation was unlikely to win many followers. As Lawrence knew and deplored, young miners wanted motorbikes and jazz and cinemas, and wanted money to pay for them. Lawrence might be resigned to a two-and-a-half-day week for the mines, but the country could not run satisfactorily on half-time. In the early 1920s three approaches to the problem of unemployment held the field. They were not mutually exclusive: people could believe all three of them, and certainly several politicians believed in more than one.

One approach was to revive international trade by acknowledging and paying debts, such as the US war loans, and try to get back to the pre-1914 pattern of trading by steps like returning to basing the currency upon gold. The Labour Party preferred the capital levy; nationalization was also a Labour proposal, and speakers did claim that it would reduce unemployment, but the capital levy was the really controversial plank in the Labour platform. Apart from advancing socialist ideals by reducing inequalities in the possession of wealth, it would lighten the load of debt and make sure that less money went to rentiers who drew interest without taking any risks. The Protectionist approach, designed to defend the home market, was the one to which Baldwin turned when he tried to work out a policy for dealing with unemployment during the later months of 1923. It could be argued that Protectionism was not relevant to the specific areas of unemployment. As exporting trades which depended on keeping their costs of production as low as possible, coal, ship-building, and cotton could not be protected. Agriculture might benefit if it was protected by tariffs, but the Protectionists of the early 1920s were afraid that stomach taxes—tariffs on food—would take them right back to 1906. Protectionism was by no means certain to be popular. The Conservative Party was not united behind it, and the depressed industries were likely to be hostile to it.

Baldwin had always believed that Tariff Reform was the best policy. As an ironmaster he had had experience of a branch of British industry in danger of being overwhelmed by American and German products, and he saw tariffs as

7. D. H. Lawrence, *Lady Chatterley's Lover* (first complete British text 1960), 315.

the way to keep them out. Nevertheless, it would divide his party and it would force him to consider holding another general election. He felt bound by Law's 1922 pledge not to introduce tariffs before another general election had been held, and this meant that he needed an election to free his hands.

Tariff Reform had some tactical advantages, as well as providing a possible answer to unemployment. Many of the Tories who had followed Austen Chamberlain when he remained loyal to Lloyd George were Protectionists. If Baldwin declared himself in favour of tariffs, they would find it relatively easy to accept him as the leader of the party, which might make up for any loss of Free Trade support. Lloyd George was said to be thinking of coming out in favour of tariffs, which would strengthen his links with the Coalition Conservatives and might attract some of the Tariff Reformers who had followed Law and Baldwin.

Adopting a new policy is not easy for a party in office. The Prime Minister has to show that he has taken the initiative rather than having it forced upon him, but he cannot force a policy upon his colleagues without a considerable period of preparation. Baldwin could rely on the support of Neville Chamberlain and several other Cabinet ministers, but Lord Derby, who had led the Tories who opposed Tariff Reform before the war, Lord Curzon, and Lord Salisbury had still to be faced. Baldwin avoided rather than solved this problem by taking the issue at the gallop, and left Lord Derby complaining (privately) of 'a policy which was only disclosed in brief to the Cabinet forty-eight hours before it was launched on the public'.[8] Baldwin first said on 25 October 1923 that he wanted a free hand to impose tariffs, and the general election was held on 6 December. This was not long enough to give the government a reasonable chance of convincing the electorate that it ought to accept a change of policy.

The failure of the Liberals to emerge as the leading party of the left in this election probably decided their fate for years to come; Free Trade was their special issue, on which they could hope to attract Free Traders who normally voted Conservative and to hold a good deal of their working-class support on the issue of dear bread. While these factors improved the Liberals' prospects, the Labour Party also gained ground and remained the larger of the two left-wing parties. The Liberal Party had very little to offer that was not in the Labour programme; the Liberal Party might have done well as a rallying-point for people who did not want to move right to Protection or left to nationalization, but apparently the electorate contained relatively few middle-of-the-road voters of this sort. Such a position would have had few attractions for the politically active people who make up the base of party strength for electoral organization, and the Labour Party certainly had a very enthusiastic, if not always efficient, volunteer organization.

8. Churchill, *Lord Derby*, 537.

The Labour Party did not really expect to do well in the election, and seems not to have thought in terms of becoming a party of government. MacDonald himself probably looked forward to forming a government at some time in the future, and one of his services to his party was to think in these terms. But probably in 1923 he was quite satisfied to hear the chairman say, at one of his meetings: 'It would be a great loss to public life if Mr. Ramsay MacDonald did not lead the next Opposition.'[9]

Presumably some people who voted for 'tranquillity' in 1922 were opposed to any change; Baldwin's support for Protection made him into an innovator, and the Liberal Free Traders became the defenders of the status quo. The issue reunited the Liberals: Lloyd George laid aside any Protectionist leanings he might have had and Churchill buckled on his Free Trade armour once more. The image of the lion lying down with the lamb was brought into several Liberal speeches celebrating reunion; Asquith's daughter Lady Violet Bonham Carter tried to put life into the phrase by saying she had 'never seen Mr. Lloyd George look less voracious or my father more uneatable'.[10] Her father may have wondered if it was necessary to cast Lloyd George as the lion of the partnership.

	Votes	Seats	% of all votes cast
Conservative	5,538,824	258	38.1
Liberal	4,311,147	159	29.6
Labour	4,438,508	191	30.5

The first Labour government (1924)

No party had a majority, and although the Conservatives had more seats than anyone else the case for a Labour government was quite good: Baldwin had said he could not govern without a tariff and, as he was not going to get a tariff, he had to resign; the Leader of the Opposition had to be sent for, and could probably form a government with some assurances of Liberal support. Many Conservatives feared that the Labour government would take office, present a popular budget including pension benefits and a capital levy, and then dissolve when the budget was defeated. As the election would be fought on the Labour Party's proposals it would have a good chance of winning. Conservative alarmists concluded that the two anti-socialist parties should immediately form a government of national unity. Mussolini had just come to

9. The speaker was the ex-Liberal Addison (*The Times*, 5 Dec. 1923).
10. R. Jenkins, *Asquith* (1964), 499.

power in Italy at the head of a Fascist government, set up to keep the Socialists out. His readiness to suspend democracy in the face of an emergency seems to have inspired the proposal that a government of national trustees should be set up to hold power for a fixed period of two years.

The left wing of the Labour Party argued, as the Conservatives feared, for forming a minority government and using the ministerial front bench as a platform to state the socialist programme. MacDonald had no intention of behaving in such a way; he did not believe the electorate knew which way it wanted to go, and he believed that putting forward a programme simply to be defeated would convince people that the Labour Party was irresponsible. He believed it would suffer if it gave the impression that it was not interested in governing, and that it could gain ground by showing that it possessed the administrative skill to do the job. When he knew that Baldwin was not going to resign until defeated in the Commons, and that some of the Conservatives were thinking of overthrowing their leader to set up a Conservative–Liberal coalition, he denounced attempts to 'wangle the constitution' to keep the Labour Party out.[11]

Baldwin's decision to face the Commons forced the Liberals to decide which of the larger parties should govern. Asquith cut through the confusion by announcing on 17 December that he 'would not lift a finger to keep the Conservative government in office'. He probably wanted to make sure that nobody thought the Labour Party was being treated unfairly or conspired against, and he knew that the Liberals who had opposed Lloyd George's government distrusted any idea of a coalition. A more subtle argument was that if Liberals and Conservatives had to form a single party to keep Labour out, they only made it the more certain that Labour would eventually get in with a clear majority. And, as Asquith reflected, 'if a Labour government is ever to be tried in this country, as it will be sooner or later, it could hardly be tried under safer conditions.[12]

Apart from this, the decision reflected the problems of the Liberal struggle to survive. The Liberal Party was most unlikely to coalesce with the Labour Party to the extent of being absorbed into it. The individual Liberal politicians who joined the Labour Party attracted more attention than those who joined the Conservative Party, though there were several of the latter. Haldane, the only man who had reached the first rank as a Liberal and later joined the Labour Party, was balanced by Churchill, who by 1923 was a Conservative on everything except Free Trade. Men like Hamar Greenwood and Mond could be set against the less important Liberal 'recruits to Labour'. But these individual changes did not affect the roots of the situation; the Liberal Party could expect to survive any alliance with the Labour Party, but alliance with the Conservative Party might easily turn into fusion. If this happened, some

11. *The Times*, 24 Dec. 1923.   12. Jenkins, *Asquith*, 500.

Liberals would probably turn into Conservatives, as happened after the Coalition.

The decision to support a Labour government in 1924 and again in 1929 was an attempt to escape the attractions of fusion and to hold in check the Liberals whose reaction to a move towards the Conservatives would be to join the Labour Party. People at the time thought the Liberal Party was closer to the Conservatives than to the Labour Party—there were complaints that the Liberals were betraying the country by letting the Labour Party in, and the Labour Party always said that there was no real difference between the capitalist parties.

Anxiety about keeping the Labour Party out was based on a quite unreasoning fear. Proposals for some nationalization and for a capital levy had been put forward by people outside as well as inside the party, and neither policy could be carried out by a minority government. The Labour Party was prepared to accept the logic of gradualism; MacDonald was applauded at the party's victory celebration when he said, 'one step enough for me? Yes, as long as it leads on to the next step,' a remark which reflected a realization of the limits of manoeuvre.[13] Not all the party thought that the immediate object of holding power was to nationalize the means of production, distribution, and exchange.

The Labour Representation Committee had originally been launched to improve the political position of the working class. That spirit can be seen in Clynes's comment on his own moment of apotheosis:

As we stood waiting for His Majesty amid the gold and crimson magnificence of the Palace, I could not help marvelling at the strange turn of Fortune's wheel which had brought MacDonald the starveling clerk, Thomas the engine-driver, Henderson the foundry-labourer, and Clynes the mill-hand, to this pinnacle beside the man whose forebears had been kings for so many splendid generations.[14]

Shortly after the government had been formed, a dispute broke out over the question whether ministers should wear court dress for formal ceremonies. MacDonald, who wanted to convince another 15 or 20 per cent of the electorate that the Labour Party was mild-mannered enough to be trusted with power, was in favour—his enemies suggested that he thought he looked particularly impressive in court dress. More implacable fighters of the class war said that court dress showed that Labour had sold out to the aristocratic embrace. MacDonald got his way: the Labour government was not going to start with any departures from tradition.

Parliament reassembled, the government was duly defeated, and MacDonald was asked to form a Cabinet. The leading men were those Clynes mentioned, together with Snowden, and they provided a firm working-class foundation. Eleven Cabinet ministers came from the working class, most of

13. *The Times*, 9 Jan. 1924.   14. J. R. Clynes, *Memoirs* (1937), i. 343.

whom—though not MacDonald, Snowden, and Wheatley—had worked in the trade union movement. Three Cabinet ministers had been left-wing Liberal Members of Parliament before 1914. Sidney Webb was also an ex-Liberal. The claims of Labour had not been neglected among the fifteen commoners, but MacDonald had a little difficulty finding people to conduct business in the Upper House. His five peers did their work satisfactorily, but except for the veteran Fabian Olivier they had no real connections with the Labour movement.

The whole nine months of the first Labour government's existence was devoted to proving that Labour was fit to govern. Examining what legislation was passed is relatively unimportant; relatively few governments pass important legislation in their first few months, and what mattered in 1924 was that the new men showed that administration did not dissolve into chaos in their hands. After that, a large section of the working class would go on voting Labour whatever happened, and this meant the Liberal Party could not find any foundation on which to rebuild itself as the party of the left.

The Labour government did a little more than establish its reputation for competence. Snowden as Chancellor of the Exchequer recognized that he could not have a capital levy; instead he had a Free Trade budget which partially reconciled the Liberals to the informal alliance. The McKenna Duties were abolished and the 'free breakfast-table' (i.e. free from custom duties) was almost established with the reduction of tariffs on sugar, cocoa, tea, and coffee. These reductions may have encouraged private spending, and the breakfast-table changes certainly helped the poorer classes, but they left little money over for public works to combat unemployment. Snowden at the Exchequer would forbid anything that might produce a budget deficit, and public works would be expected to pay for themselves. The Labour government did not have any proposals in mind which would reduce unemployment, though its supporters continued to believe that it cared more deeply about the problem than the other parties. This was reasonable enough; unemployment benefits were increased, and benefits not covered by insurance payments were declared to be a right, not a grant payable at the discretion of the minister, which in practice meant that officials at the Labour Exchange interrogated applicants and decided whether to give them anything. The change made a difference; in the 1924 election Walter Elliot noticed that little boys shouted at him 'Vote Labour—and be treated like a gentleman at the burroo' (meaning bureau, or Labour Exchange).[15]

Wheatley's Housing Act might have done something to reduce unemployment in the long run. In the short run it brought building contractors and trade unions together and, helped by an increase in the subsidy to £9 a year for forty years, they guaranteed a higher rate of production without an increase in

15. C. Coote, *A Companion of Honour: The Story of Walter Elliot* (1965), 86.

prices. The Act placed a heavy emphasis on municipal building for renting and the ground area remained the same as in the final version of the Chamberlain Act, which suggested that the minister saw that subsidies for larger houses would waste scarce resources.

While the government's legislative progress was slow and prosaic, its performance in foreign affairs produced swift and impressive results. Diplomacy was made less secret by providing that all treaties must be submitted to the House of Commons for approval. MacDonald took the Foreign Office himself, and was fortunate enough to do so at a time when his Gladstonian principles of peaceful reasonableness suited the situation, and also helped to reassure the Liberals that they had acted wisely in putting him in office.

France was beginning to realize that the occupation of the Ruhr was producing no positive effects; Germany was beginning to realize that inflation and passive resistance would destroy German society before they had much effect elsewhere. This made it easier for MacDonald to act as the pacifier of Europe.

Mr. MacDonald wished to re-establish relations of confidence and cooperation with France and Italy; to break the deadlock over reparations; to secure a French evacuation of the Rhineland; and to reintroduce Germany into the community of nations. He wished to further the cause of general disarmament by strengthening the machinery of international arbitration; and to bridge the gulf that, both politically and financially, sundered Great Britain from Soviet Russia. Within the space of eight months he was able either to attain or promote all these seven objects.[16]

Some of the work was done before Poincaré lost the May 1924 election, but the formation of a centre-left government under Herriot made the restoration of contact easier. Restoration of contact did not restore the *entente cordiale*; from the French occupation of the Ruhr until Hitler's accession to power Britain stood uncommitted between France and Germany, and to some extent this attitude persisted even after 1933. In the 1920s it had advantages; neither the Geneva Protocol (the Labour sketch of a return to the Concert of Europe on the basis of League arbitration) nor the Locarno Treaty (the completed Conservative pattern for restoration, running on more traditional lines) would have been possible if Britain had appeared to be committed to France against Germany.

Before MacDonald could turn France's withdrawal from the Ruhr and Germany's acceptance of the Dawes Plan for reparations into anything more permanent, his government ran into trouble over relations with Russia. It had recognized the Soviet government very soon after taking office and had then begun the complicated task of negotiating a trade treaty and of defending the interests of English owners of tsarist bonds. Eventually two treaties were drawn up: a trade treaty, which opened up the possibility that new jobs would

16. H. Nicolson, *George V* (1952), 393.

be created, and a treaty providing among other things that long-term trade credits could be negotiated for Russia once the question of the bondholders had been settled. The Commons could reject the treaties, and soon it was clear that neither consideration for the bondholders, nor memories of their previous complaints about the difficulties of negotiating treaties with the United States which could be repudiated by the Senate, would persuade Liberals or Conservatives to approve of long-term credits which looked like throwing good money after bad.

A much more trivial incident brought the government down before the treaties were debated. The *Workers' Weekly*, a Communist magazine, published an article calling on soldiers not to shoot their working-class comrades during military or industrial warfare. The Director of Public Prosecutions decided to prosecute the editor for sedition; the Attorney-General decided to withdraw the prosecution. Campbell, the editor, had been crippled during the war, and the prosecution looked a little like an interference with the right of free speech; on the other hand, the withdrawal was said to have been forced on the government by Labour backbenchers. The Conservatives accepted the latter point and moved a vote of censure; the Liberals offered a way out by suggesting a House of Commons committee of inquiry and tried to avoid clashing with the government by offering to surrender their places on the committee to the Labour Party. MacDonald declined to let the decisions of ministers be referred to committees of the House, and when the Liberal amendment was carried he asked for a dissolution. George V consulted the Liberal and Conservative leaders but found no way to avoid granting it.[17]

The election presented the question 'Should the Labour government go on or not?' In this context the Liberals were irrelevant; Baldwin had been at some pains to lay aside the proposal of Protection and so the tariff issue no longer made it difficult for Liberals to vote Conservative. The election campaign found the electorate returning to a two-party system. In 1923 and in 1924 Selfridges asked every twentieth voter to return a postcard. Selfridges' shoppers would not be an adequate sample of the electorate, but they might show how opinion moved between the parties. By the last week of the campaign this poll showed the Liberals doing distinctly less well than in 1923, with every sign that the Conservatives would benefit more than the Labour Party from this change.

At this point the Foreign Office published a letter apparently from the Comintern, signed by Zinovieff—whose name was promptly given to the letter—calling on British Communists to take steps to overthrow the bourgeois Labour government. The letter's authenticity could not be properly tested: MacDonald was uncertain about it but, disregarding his instructions,

17. Nicolson, *George V*, 400.

the Foreign Office published it, with a crisp expression of disapproval, to forestall publication in the *Daily Mail* while he was away campaigning.

It now seems clear that the letter had been forged by Polish anti-Communists, and that because the Conservative Party knew about the letter, it was able to alarm the Foreign Office. What could be seen at the time was that the Foreign Office had published the letter, with disapproving comments. Publication implied that the letter was genuine and, if the letter was genuine, the Labour government had been unwise to negotiate with people who had so low an opinion of it. At a less logical level, the letter may have had the effect of confirming some people in the belief that all socialists were dangerous and all anti-socialists should rally round the stronger of the two parties in opposition.

The shift of votes between the parties was rather larger than the fairly primitive Selfridges poll had suggested before the Zinovieff letter was published, so it may have made some difference.[18] The Labour party felt it had been defeated by a trick. The Conservative vote went up by a great deal and, mainly because more candidates came forward but partly also because of increased support in constituencies already contested, the Labour vote went up as well. The Liberals got far fewer votes than in 1923, with most of them moving to the Conservative Party, and their representation in Parliament fell to a level where they ceased to be taken very seriously.

	Votes	Seats	% of all votes cast
Conservative	8,039,598	419	48.3
Liberal	2,928,747	40	17.6
Labour	5,498,077	151	33.0

18. Selfridges' advertisement in *The Times*, 29 Oct. 1924, based on 411,000 replies.

	Selfridges' 1923 poll	Actual vote	Selfridges' 1924 poll	Actual vote
Conservative	50.74	38.1	55.94	48.1
Liberal	21.26	29.6	15.50	17.6
Labour	27.57	30.5	28.39	33.0

In 1923 the Conservatives did 12 per cent better at Selfridges than in the actual vote, which was natural enough. If they had got 12 per cent less than the Selfridges' poll in 1924 they would have got 43 per cent of the actual vote. On this basis five per cent of the total vote moved to the Conservatives in the last week of the campaign, six per cent moved away from the Liberals and two per cent moved to the Labour Party.

On the Liberal vote, see D. E. Butler, *The Electoral System in Britain since 1918* (1963), 175–9.

Baldwin back in office

The period of quick-changing Prime Ministers was over. Evelyn Waugh's *Vile Bodies* (1930) is set, politically speaking, against the background of the twenty-four months in which the prime ministership changed hands four times and, like his *Decline and Fall* (1928), is in other ways a product of the middle 1920s. The Bright Young Things, who first achieved public notice in 1924, had begun to fade from the scene before Waugh began chronicling their exploits; and public notice was one of the ways in which they differed from their predecessors. The notorious young men and women of the upper classes probably drank no harder than Lady Diana Manners's 'Corrupt Coterie' had done just before the war, and their sexual behaviour was probably no more relaxed than had become normal during the war. The laws about drugs had become much stricter during and just after the war, and were sometimes broken by a small minority who wanted to show that they were really wicked.[19]

The enthusiasm of the Bright Young Things for being talked about matched the journalistic discovery that their mildly outrageous activities made good copy. In a perverse way, they reduced class differences or, more precisely, newspaper publicity reduced inter-class ignorance. To the newspapers could be added the influence of the cinema and the radio telling people what was going on, and the change in clothes—more particularly, women's clothes—must have helped this development. Before the war women's clothes demonstrated very clearly who worked and who had servants. After the war upper-class clothes were simpler and working-class clothes were more attractive, which diminished the gap. An industrial advance which encouraged this was the introduction of rayon or artificial silk. Under the latter name it was taxed in the 1925 budget on the same principles as real silk; although this implied that it was a luxury with no very wide appeal, it continued to be sold in increasing quantities and to make life easier, socially and physically, for working-class girls.

Literature no doubt presented life in strong colours, but always took some time to catch it up. While *Vile Bodies* came out half a dozen years after the period in which it was set, the book that was advertised extensively in 1924 was E. F. Benson's *David of King's*, which radiated a wholesomeness of moral tone not always associated with the 1920s. Galsworthy's second set of three Forsyte novels, *A Modern Comedy*, shows how well pre-war values had survived into the 1920s. Only in the mid-1920 did *Ulysses* and *The Waste Land* begin to be heard of in Britain. Organization followed inspiration; *The Adelphi* and *The Criterion* were rapidly becoming accepted as the leading literary magazines. But the country had not become more sensitive artistically than before;

---

19. R. Graves and A. Hodges, *The Long Week-End* (1940), 125; Lady Diana Cooper, *The Rainbow Comes and Goes* (1958), 82.

hearties and aesthetes continued to grate on one another's nerve ends at the universities, and Epstein's statues served as red rags to the bull-headed. It was in 1924 that Mary Webb published *Precious Bane*, the novel of the Marches which attracted praise from Baldwin that set her on the road to posthumous and understandably transient fame.

Baldwin had other things to worry about at the time. His new government was designed to reconcile all Conservatives. Austen Chamberlain went to the Foreign Office, which showed that the Coalitionists had returned to the party; other sections of opinion were probably reassured by the appointment of the ex-Liberal Free Trader Churchill to the Exchequer. The inclusiveness of the Cabinet, and the size of the majority, did suggest that Baldwin might have some difficulty in taking positive action in any direction. But his government demonstrated its competence as effectively as the previous government had done and, with more time at its disposal and a secure majority behind it, dealt with several problems in a way that MacDonald and his followers could not really object to. It also showed the same inability as its predecessor to do anything about unemployment.

In one important way it probably increased unemployment. Conservatives believed that, if Protection was ruled out, re-establishing the position of the pound as a currency based on gold would restore prosperity by getting back to pre-1914 world trading conditions. Practically everybody took it for granted that this meant returning the pound to its pre-war value of $4.86, and the exchange value of the pound had been quoted as a discount from $4.86 during the eleven years in which gold exports were suspended.

In 1924 the pound seemed to be settling at about $4.40. Then it began to climb, without any noticeable changes in the British or American domestic price levels, by about 10 per cent. Churchill announced in his 1925 budget that the Bank of England was to be enabled to anchor the $4.86 exchange rate permanently by dealing in gold bars weighing 400 troy ounces (a little over 15 kilograms) which would show anyone trading with Britain that it was always possible to exchange sterling for gold. Churchill did not explain that, as gold coins were not returning to circulation, it would be easy to abandon this gold support for the pound overseas without altering the currency used domestically. Oswald Mosley denounced 'an unnaturally high rate of exchange artificially maintained in the chimerical pursuit of the dollar', and Keynes expanded the point in articles which were later published as *The Economic Consequences of Mr. Churchill* (1925). The title was neat but perhaps unfair; economic orthodoxy insisted that establishing a fixed gold value for the pound would cure international trade difficulties and Churchill did not really know enough about the subject to contradict this argument. The Labour motion of disapproval did not suggest that the link between gold and the pound would be inflexible or that the value chosen for the pound was too high. The rest of the budget was unspectacular: it restored the McKenna

Duties and imposed duties on silk, but for popular appeal it relied on its forecasts of Neville Chamberlain's proposals for increased welfare benefits.

The increase in the value of sterling meant that British exports cost more unless producers deliberately cut their prices. Coal-mining was the trade most deeply affected by revaluation; labour was so large a part of the costs of production that reducing wages was the only immediate way to cut prices. Neither mine owners nor miners had changed their positions since 1921. The miners still wanted a seven-hour day and wage rates determined by a national settlement; the owners still wanted district settlements and an eight-hour day.

The miners had not digested the lessons of Black Friday sufficiently to set the Triple Alliance on a more effective basis. It remained an uncoordinated entente in which the miners relied on the transport workers and railwaymen to take the first shock of a nation-wide dispute. In 1925 this alliance was successful; on 31 July, 'Red Friday', the government gave way before the threat of a general embargo on all transport of coal, appointed a Royal Commission under Sir Herbert Samuel to report on the industry, and granted a subsidy to keep wages unchanged for nine months.

The government also set about improving its emergency scheme for saving the community from the worst inconveniences of a general strike by arranging road transport services, some supply of electricity, and a very limited scheme for dock work. Baldwin certainly wanted to avoid industrial strife. In March 1925 he had resisted proposals by his backbenchers to make trade unions change from 'contracting out' to 'contracting in' when collecting political subscriptions by asking his followers not to use their parliamentary majority to drive their opponents to extremes, and he ended with the petition of the Prayer Book 'Give peace in our time, O Lord'.[20]

In foreign affairs some progress was made towards this objective. The Labour government had considered adopting the Geneva Protocol, which provided for compulsory arbitration among signatories by the League of Nations. The Conservative government laid it aside, but Austen Chamberlain needed something in its place to satisfy public opinion. He set to work to bring France and Germany together. The Locarno Treaty of 1925 confirmed the Versailles frontiers in western Europe and committed the signatories to defend them against any infractions. The Dominions stayed out of the treaty system, and its guarantees did not apply to eastern Europe, though Chamberlain denied that Germany had been given a free hand in the east. Locarno was the formal expression of the readiness of the countries of western Europe to live peacefully together, and, if they returned to their former bellicosity, it could provide the basis for signatory nations to work together in a system of mutual defence.

The major constructive work of the government at home was inspired by

---

20. 6 Mar. 1925, *Commons Debates*, clxxi. 840.

Neville Chamberlain, who used the Ministry of Health as the base for an extension of social services that would have gladdened the heart of his father. In 1925 old-age pensions were set up on a contributory basis, starting at 65 instead of 70 and accompanied by pensions for widows and orphans. By setting up this scheme the central government took another step forward into the welfare problems that had previously been handled by local government. Chamberlain had followed his father's footsteps into Birmingham municipal government, but greater activity in social services inevitably meant that only the central government could find the money for these reforms. Chamberlain's Rating and Valuation Act showed that the central government was ready to intervene in municipal affairs by cutting down the number of local authorities which could impose municipal taxes on property and establishing a new and more up-to-date pattern of valuation for these property taxes. Other steps would clearly follow.

The BBC

In July 1925 the government set up the Crawford Committee to investigate the position of the British Broadcasting Company, and eighteen months later it took the company over and renamed it the British Broadcasting Corporation. The chairman of the company's board of directors wrote in the *Radio Times* just before the change of authority: 'The Directors of the British Broadcasting Company have had the stewardship of a great public service for only four years, during which time broadcasting has emerged from nothing to the position it occupies today—an accepted essential part of the machinery of civilization . . .'[21]

Wireless transmission had begun partly as a product of military and transport needs, partly as a matter of amateurs putting sets together for the fun of the thing. Broadcasting had not been designed to send out messages or programmes for a large audience to pick up; government contracts for communication services seemed to be the only commercial use for the invention, which was why the Marconi Company had been in such close contact with the Cabinet in 1911. Even after the war broadcasting for entertainment was the American rather than the British approach; in Britain technically minded people put together their sets and 'listened in' to weather reports and other messages intended for other listeners. They bought radio parts, and the manufacturers realized that they might widen their market if they put out regular programmes. At the end of 1922 there were about 35,000 licence holders.

Trial programmes, providing 'listeners-in' with something to pick up on their sets, had been running for some months when the manufacturers came together to discuss prospects for a broadcasting company. Partly because the

---

21. *Radio Times,* 24 Dec. 1926.

Marconi Company held so many patents concerned with transmitting, partly because the Post Office encouraged them, the large manufacturers of radio parts formed a single company to put out broadcasts to 'listeners': on its first night it broadcast the results of the general election of 1922.

The broadcasting company was limited to a dividend of 7.5 per cent, and the manufacturers expected to make their profits by selling radios. The Post Office, which granted the licence to transmit, could not let a company earn large profits from broadcasting. The armed services, which were much more influential in Britain than in the United States in the 1920s, opposed almost any expansion of broadcasting, on the ground that they wanted all the radio-length waves for themselves. The press was alarmed at the thought of competition and was much better placed to get its own way than a few decades later, in the early days of television.

Reith, the Managing Director of the Company and later the Director-General of the Corporation, was exactly the man to deal with these pressures. He showed all the best qualities found in the Indian Civil Service: his immense administrative capacity required for taking an entirely novel development and introducing it into the lives of people who had never met it before, his ability to hold together a rapidly growing organization, and his determination to use the organization to improve and elevate the people it served were all marks of 'the heaven-born'.

Even if he had wanted to run a system devoted to entertainment, he would have encountered too much suspicion among entertainers to achieve very much. The Company had transmitted for only five or six hours a day, of which over half was music. Reith was determined that it should be good music, and between the wars the BBC produced a wide audience that was much more interested in music, and much better educated about it, than before. The BBC also made it slightly easier for performing musicians to find work. A good deal of the rest of broadcasting time was devoted to talks, organized at first by the Education Department. Reith had a great respect for education, and was ready to extend it into topics which other theories of broadcasting might not have touched.

He was much more willing to allow controversial discussion than his masters on the Board of Directors or in the Post Office. His basic principles of life may have been narrow, but the width of the field in which he thought they should be applied made him into one of the forces opening people's minds in the 1920s. 'BBC English' probably helped to reduce the strain of an accent-divided society, because it meant that everybody who could afford a radio—it cost a few weeks' wages—could learn what a socially acceptable accent sounded like; the division had of course existed previously and had been made worse by ignorance. The other mass medium of the day, the popular press, did not always treat its readers as responsible people; the BBC never forgot that it was speaking to responsible people.

Reith has sometimes been judged by the standards of later decades and made to look like a son of the manse out of his depth; insisting that announcers should wear dinner jackets looked old-fashioned even in the 1930s. But this could be said about so much of the 1920s: even witty Mr Huxley's *Antic Hay* (published in the first full year of Company broadcasting) seems a bit tame eighty years later. At the time, handling a mass medium under public licence, Reith probably did as much as he could. He suggested that political speeches should be broadcast in the 1923 election. The Post Office turned the idea down, but in 1924 one speech by each party leader was allowed. As might have been expected Baldwin did very well on the radio, partly because he took the trouble to adjust to talking to an audience of people listening at home.

Nobody objected when the Crawford Committee reported in favour of public ownership of the broadcasting system; the manufacturers were quite happy to go on selling radios, and the press saw the radio as a rival but not as another medium to be brought into the orbit of the newspaper chains. Reith's blend of caution, rectitude, imagination, and good taste reassured men in high places and convinced them that he could go on running the Corporation under government ownership perfectly satisfactorily. By the end of 1926 there were over 2 million licence holders.[22]

Baldwin's government had no doctrinaire fear of public enterprise. Electricity had not been developed in Britain as effectively as in other countries, partly because the generating stations—whether privately or municipally owned—were too small and served too narrow an area. In 1926 a Central Electricity Board was set up to construct a nationwide power grid. The pylons of the system did the rural landscape no good, but they enabled efficient power stations, running on the standard frequency, to supply power which the grid could distribute round the country. The local producers continued to operate, but the central authority had taken a considerable step towards becoming the effective controller of the system.

The General Strike of 1926

The strengthening of central authority, which could be seen in the foundation of the BBC and the Central Electricity Board and was a part of Chamberlain's reform of local government, was also a part of the struggle over coal. The miners thought nationalization would make coal cheap and saleable and at the same time keep wages high by 'pooling' all the coal from good pits and bad and selling it at a price which let the good pits subsidize the bad. In March 1926 the Samuel Commission presented a Report which showed some sympathy with this argument. It asked for nationalization of the mineral rights and for steps towards amalgamating the producers. The miners would still

22. A. Briggs, *The Birth of Broadcasting* (1961), 18.

work for competing private employers, but not for private landlords and not under a system of hundreds of competing collieries. The Commission advised against longer hours and in favour of a national wages agreement; it suggested that current wages, agreed when the coal supply was dislocated by the French occupation of the Ruhr, were too high and should be reduced at least during the period of reorganization. And it advised against continuing the subsidy.

The miners' stand was not flexible: 'not a minute on the day, not a penny off the pay.'[23] Nor were the owners more helpful: district agreements, longer hours, and lower wages was their answer. The government showed no readiness to impose the Samuel recommendations, and yet everybody could see that they would not be accepted voluntarily by the two sides. The owners declared that at the end of April, when the subsidy ran out, they would establish new pay scales which took the principle of district settlements for granted by imposing much sharper cuts in some areas than in others.

The miners assumed that the Triple Alliance would step forward as effectively and as unquestioningly as in 1925; Bevin of the Transport and General Workers' Union had no desire to see his union placed unsupported in the front line, and asked for the General Council, of the TUC to be given powers by its component unions to conduct a general strike on behalf of the miners and to decide when satisfactory terms had been gained for them. The final decision was a little ambiguous; undoubtedly the great majority of unions thought they had delegated their power of strike action to the General Council but the miners believed that the other unions had, with an unusual lack of regard for union autonomy, undertaken to stay on strike until the Miners' Federation was satisfied.

The owners withdrew the demand for district agreements but insisted on cutting wages and increasing hours from seven to eight, and did not accept the Samuel recommendations for reorganization. The TUC and the Cabinet continued to negotiate; the miners and the owners held aloof with the sulky determination which led Birkenhead to say he could assert the miners' leaders were the stupidest men in the country if he had not had the misfortune to meet the owners. The Cabinet broke off negotiations on the night of 2–3 May, because it thought a strike at the *Daily Mail* was the beginning of the General Strike. In fact the *Daily Mail* dispute was an isolated incident, but the negotiators were so far apart at this point that the strike was inevitable.

The organization on both sides proved entirely adequate. The unions had not done much advance planning, but union solidarity led to a prompt and almost complete response to the General Council's instructions that transport workers and railwaymen, electrical workers, and some industrial workers should strike. On the government side food and milk supplies were kept moving and some passenger transport services were provided. No official

23. A. Bullock, *Life of Ernest Bevin* (1960), i. 328.

efforts were made to keep private industry running. The government simply wanted to prevent the community from being so seriously inconvenienced that a settlement had to be reached.

Obviously the General Strike was designed to put pressure on the government. The government said that this was unconstitutional, but the TUC denied that it was putting unconstitutional pressure on the government. 'In a challenge to the constitution, God help us unless the government won,' as Jimmy Thomas said.[24] At the time many people thought that if the trade unions proposed to force their will upon the government, they must be ready to take the place of the government. The organizers of the General Strike certainly did not want a revolution; peaceful demonstrations often try to push the government in one direction or another without wanting to overthrow it, and organizations sometimes try—not always unsuccessfully—to impose their will on the government, as the British Medical Association attempted in 1911 and 1947, but this is not usually considered to be a revolutionary act.

Once they had decided not to let themselves be compelled to give a subsidy or pass legislation to help the coal miners, ministers argued among themselves about the right way to handle the strike. Baldwin got his own way, and made sure that there was no brusque policy of repression. But a group of ministers was consistently in favour of stronger action, and of these men Churchill was perhaps the most irresponsible. When he suggested escorting a food convoy through the streets of London with troops carrying loaded rifles, Sir John Anderson asked the Chancellor of the Exchequer to stop talking nonsense. Churchill spent most of his time during the strike editing the *British Gazette*, a newspaper put out by the government during the strike which showed some disregard for the facts when it asserted 'The owners have agreed to nearly everything recommended by the Commission. . . . The miners' leaders have not however made the slightest advance towards an acceptance.'[25]

Its attitude was in sharp contrast to the BBC approach. Reith and Baldwin took practically similar views of the strike; they regarded it as an attempt to coerce the government and were determined to prevent this from happening, but they wanted to avoid alienating the strikers from the rest of the community. If the transmitting stations had been 'commandeered', as was legally quite possible, they might have been deployed like the *Gazette*. The BBC gave the strikers no encouragement and it refused to broadcast an appeal for a compromise settlement by the Archbishop of Canterbury, but unlike the *Gazette* it did not put out anti-strike propaganda nor did it compromise its reputation for accuracy by publishing false reports of a return to work.

By telling people what was going on it probably contributed to the general air of calm. With the passage of time this calm has been exaggerated to

---

24. G. Blaxland, *J. H. Thomas* (1964), 194.
25. J. W. Wheeler-Bennett, *John Anderson* (1961), 106; *British Gazette*, 5 May 1926.

legendary proportions; there were some struggles between police and strikers, and probably there would have been more bitterness if the strike had begun to inflict hardship on the general public. Treating the whole thing as a game may have been possible only because nothing very serious seemed to be happening. But when all allowances have been made for this, the observers, British and foreign, who expressed awed admiration at the peaceful way in which the struggle was conducted were still passing a sensible judgement on a civilized conflict.

The TUC leaders did not want the strike to go on indefinitely. A prolonged strike cost money and might lead public opinion to support Churchill's type of sternly anti-union policy. They began to look round for a line of retreat, and Samuel provided one. He presented a Memorandum for settling the coal-mining dispute which seemed satisfactory to the TUC. But the miners did not agree, because it included acceptance of a wage cut, and the alliance began to break up. The process was accelerated by a speech of Sir John Simon, in which he said that a general strike was illegal and could lead to the forfeiture of union funds. This opinion had no solid foundation; the Act passed the following year, which declared general strikes illegal, was not considered to be merely a declaratory measure; at the time, however, Simon's view helped to weaken the morale of the TUC leaders.

By 12 May they were convinced the strike should be ended and, after a final attempt to persuade the miners to accept the Samuel Memorandum, they informed the Prime Minister of their decision. The retreat was not well planned; there were a number of struggles over reinstatement, but in general the trade union movement survived as well as it had any right to expect. The miners stayed out for months, but eventually they obtained neither the recommendations of the Samuel Commission nor those of the Samuel Memorandum.

A whole cycle of working-class militancy, beginning about 1910, had come to an end, though the spectacular closing act had come in an economic situation much less favourable to strike action than the 1910–20 period. The General Strike, for all the reluctance of its leaders, was at least an attempt to make something happen. The forces of change, which had been at work during the war and immediately after, were now exhausted. For the next five years immobility reigned triumphant and almost unchallenged.

6

The years of inaction

1926–1931

The new way of living

The failure of the General Strike, and the long-drawn-out defeat of the coal strike, ushered in a period of industrial calm.[1] Employers felt that attempts to cut wages drastically might be unwise, and the trade unions took care not to avoid large and ill-prepared adventures. The miners, who spent eight times as many days on strike as the average trade unionist, had been the centre of intransigence; their weakness was made obvious when the Act that had reduced their working hours from eight to seven was repealed. Power in the trade union movement passed from the miners' leaders to Bevin and Thomas. The new mood led to the Mond–Turner talks, begun in 1928, between employers and trade unionists: Turner was chairman of the General Council of the TUC and Mond was a progressive Liberal-turned-Conservative who played an important part in creating Imperial Chemical Industries. They had no effective proposals for restoring the economy, but at least they could talk to each other more politely than employers and employed had been able to do since 1910.

The Trade Disputes Act of 1927 did not destroy this relative harmony in industry. For just over a century Parliament had preferred trade unions to have as few legal rights and duties as possible, and it had reversed a number of legal decisions in which the courts had tried to treat the unions like companies. No political party wanted to adopt the North American system of giving unions legal claims on employers and legal responsibilities, and as nobody was prepared to eliminate unions altogether, their industrial role was left untouched. The Act made general strikes illegal, and laid down that civil

---

1. Days lost through strikes:

1919–25	194,107,000
1926	162,233,000
1927–32	28,719,000
1933–9	11,918,000

David Butler and Gareth Butler, *British Political Facts 1900–2000* (2000), 399–400.

servants were not to belong to trade unions. These measures guarded against an unreal danger that the trade unions might try to take over the government of the country by syndicalist methods, but they did not affect the normal process of collective bargaining. The only really important change made by the Act was that, when a trade union had voted to contribute to a political party, money could be collected only from union members who had specific-ally permitted the deduction; previously money had been collected from everybody who had not signed a form asking to be exempted. This change was inspired partly by a belief that really only a small minority of the working class wanted to support the Labour Party, and partly by a belief that political parties ought to be financed by individual donations. Most of the Conservative Party's money came from a relatively few large contributions from wealthy individuals, and other ways of raising money were thought improper. But while the attitude of Conservative Members was understandable, it was not the way to establish political peace and harmony. The Act looked as though the General Strike was being used to damage the political prospects of the Labour Party, and the proportion of trade unionists subscribing to the unions' political funds fell steadily from 58 per cent in 1928 to 48 per cent in 1945, the last year before the Act was repealed.[2] The right wing of the Conservative Party was also pleased when the police raided Arcos, the Soviet trade mission in London, which was suspected of being a centre for spies. The British government then broke off diplomatic relations though no real proof of spying had been found.

Baldwin could not convert his backbenchers to his own philosophical acceptance of the post-war world, but he could stop them putting the clock back. An attempt to restore the power of the House of Lords to roughly what it had been in 1910 was defeated. The vote was given, almost absent-mindedly and without any agitation, to the women between 21 and 30 who had been left out in 1918. While he presented himself as the embodiment of English common sense Baldwin found opportunities at the same time to suggest that he had particular affinities with the Scots and the Welsh, and yet new parties emerged during his premiership that in later decades transformed the question of countries within the United Kingdom. The launching in 1925 of Plaid Cymru, and in 1928 of the National Party of Scotland (which became the Scottish Nationalist Party in 1934), had little immediate effect but it showed how the situation had changed. Before 1914 nationalists could hope for some moderate sympathy from the Liberal Party, and more active support from the small Labour Party. The two parties of the left had responded in this way to developments in Ireland under Lloyd George. But the Labour Party took a more centralizing approach to the problems of Scotland and Wales; it believed that only a strong government could impose public ownership upon the heavy

---

2. M. Harrison, *Trade Unions and the Labour Party since 1945* (1960), 32–3.

industries of south-east Wales and the Glasgow area and that, if this was not possible, it made better sense to mobilize all the resources of the United Kingdom to help the unemployed than to encourage Scotland and Wales to become more independent and try to deal with it from their own limited resources. As a result the nationalist parties of the 1920s were cut off from the most densely populated parts of their countries, which were also the centres of immediate discontent. Plaid Cymru represented a rural linguistic minority; the Scottish Nationalist Party advertised its opposition to the modern world by leaning towards Jacobitism. The two parties were asking for Dominion status rather than complete separation, but even this would cut them off from England's economic resources. Baldwin could be forgiven for thinking that very little would come of these two backward-looking movements.

One opportunity of modernizing the country came in 1926, when the Hadow Committee submitted a Report on the education of adolescents that shaped the pattern of British education for the next forty years. It declared that everybody should stay at school until 15, and should receive 'secondary' education for the closing years of school life. 'Secondary' education had previously meant the teaching given to the 7 or 8 per cent of the population that went to grammar schools. The Committee decided to retain the existing examination, taken at 11 plus, for free places at grammar schools, but it did ask whether the schools for everybody else, which it wanted to call 'modern' schools, could be made equal to the grammar schools. On the whole it argued for spending as much money on 'modern' schools as on grammar schools, a view that did not appeal to the Conservative Party, which saw little use in educating the working classes. Most supporters of the Labour Party welcomed the Report because it opened opportunities to talented working-class children, and kept less talented children in school and out of the labour market. However, the Catholic supporters of the Labour Party felt uneasy because the Report meant they would have to provide a decidedly larger amount of money for secondary education than was needed for their elementary schools and, if the government had acted on the Report, it might have faced similar protests from supporters of Church of England schools.

The most exciting moments in the 1924–9 Parliament had nothing to do with the government's legislative programme. The Anglo-Catholic section of the Church of England had been gaining ground, and a new Prayer Book had been prepared which moved in a High Church direction. Changing the Prayer Book required an amendment to the Act of Uniformity of 1662, which had defined the position of the Established Church after the Restoration. When the change was proposed in 1927, eloquent speeches were made in favour and eloquent and bitter speeches, denouncing the tendency to adopt Roman Catholic practices in ritual, were made against the change. The proposal was defeated, and defeated for a second time in 1928. Supporters of the change pointed out how odd it was that MPs who might be Free Churchmen, Jews, or atheists had a power of veto over the Church of England. But the Established Church, with its special place in the life of the country, was bound to concern everyone in the country; England had always been an anticlerical country in the sense that there was a strong lay dislike for clerical power, and much of the objection to the leanings towards Roman Catholic practices detected in the new Prayer Book came from a fear that clergymen wanted to acquire the power over their parishioners that Roman Catholic priests were understood to possess.

The fierceness of the debates on the Prayer Book showed that politicians still saw England as a Christian country. Most of the urban working class had never taken much interest in religion and, at least since 1914, the Churches had been losing their influence in other classes, though church attendance remained about as high as ever until at least the 1930s. The Church of England tried, without much success, to win more urban support. Previously its members had enjoyed a virtual monopoly of high offices such as the premiership, but because high office in the twentieth century was no longer confined to the landed upper class Free Churchmen were no longer excluded. This did not mean that the influence of the Free Churches had increased; they had always worked through the Liberal Party, and the decline of the Liberal Party was accompanied by a decline in their authority. The Labour Party never felt as deep an attachment to any religious group as the Liberals, though many of its leaders were in their rhetoric and imagery children of the chapel.

The influence of the Churches was still strong on issues like divorce and birth control where it reinforced the opposition to change. Before the war divorce was very infrequent; after the war it became more common, though the law on the subject changed very little until 1937. People blamed the war and the hasty marriages of wartime, they blamed the influence of the United States, and they blamed the wickedness and depravity of the younger generation. The Churches did not condone the change, and George V made his disapproval clear. All the same, MacDonald's first Cabinet included Josiah Wedgwood, who had been divorced.

Christian and traditional influences were also ranged against the spreading of information about methods of birth control. The birth rate had been declining since the 1870s although, because people lived longer, the population continued to increase. The decline was seen first in the middle classes; in 1905 the Fabian Society surveyed its membership to discover the reasons but, although Fabians were not the most reticent section of the middle class, the survey revealed only that they had chosen deliberately to limit their families and said nothing about the means they used.[3] During the First World War British troops were issued with condoms to reduce the wastage of troops from venereal disease, and this meant that a section of the male population

---

3. E. R. Pease, *History of the Fabian Society* (1918), 161–2.

indirectly learned something about birth control. After the war it became quite clear that middle-class families were being limited, but working-class families continued to be large. Reformers set out to explain to the poor how they could plan their families, but the subject was still regarded as unsuitable for open discussion. A little illogically, some of the opponents of change most enthusiastic about suppressing the spread of knowledge about birth control also deplored the fact that the working class had more children than the middle class. The Church of England was changing its position, and in 1930 a majority of the bishops declared that using contraception to limit a family was justified in 'exceptional circumstances'.

The Victorian family, at least in theory, had looked after its members: old-age pensions, and widows' and orphans' pensions, were part of a general recognition that the family would no longer carry out all the welfare responsibilities expected of it. The family unit had never been as effective or as respectable in practice as in theory: during the war the government had had to change the regulations to allow married women's allowances to be paid to 'unmarried wives' of soldiers. If divorce had been cheaper and easier to obtain, presumably many people in this position could have divorced and remarried.

Upholders of Victorian attitudes could take some satisfaction from the decline in drinking. Especially when allowance is made for the reduction in the alcohol content of beer, the amount drunk by the average adult went down steadily during the first half of the twentieth century. Smoking, on the other hand, increased steadily. Nicotine and alcohol were accepted and taken for granted as ordinary commodities which were widely consumed, and yielded a gratifyingly large amount of revenue. The 1920 Dangerous Drugs Act made exotic and powerful drugs, such as cocaine and heroin, illegal; consumption had not been high, and many more people must have been affected as opium-based patent medicines were removed from circulation in the 1920s and 1930s. The mild pressure for Prohibition on the American pattern during the 1920s had no force behind it: drunkenness was no longer the danger to home life and to peace and quiet that it had been in the nineteenth century, and not enough people had motor cars to make it a menace on the roads.

Baldwin's Home Secretary, Joynson-Hicks, was determined to restore moral standards to the high level he believed had existed before the war. This involved the police force in a good deal of raiding of night-clubs suspected of serving alcohol at illegal hours, investigation of parks after dark, and prosecutions for obscenity. Imposing a moral code that did not suit the period put some strain on policemen; they took bribes from owners of night-clubs who wanted to know when police raids might be expected, and gave perjured evidence against men and women accused of 'undue familiarity' in the parks.

The struggle between writers and the authorities entered a new phase. The Lord Chamberlain continued to uphold traditional standards in the theatre, but this was no longer the main area of struggle. Some of the most distinguished novelists of the period were now pressing into new fields. D. H. Lawrence had been recognized shortly before the war as a leading writer in the movement away from the highly rational authors and playwrights who had dominated the scene in the early years of the century. In the 1920s he became increasingly committed to approval of untamed nature and the irrational, and he wrote more explicitly about sex than before. *The Rainbow* had been prosecuted in 1915, and *Lady Chatterley's Lover* (1928) could not be published in Britain without expurgation for over thirty years. James Joyce's *Ulysses* (1922) was kept out of the country for the same reason.

Writers like Eliot and Virginia Woolf did not have trouble with the authorities, but their readiness to explore new stylistic techniques affected their public position as authors. Nineteenth-century authors like Tennyson and Dickens had been accepted as good writers and had also sold to wide audiences. In the twentieth century fewer and fewer of the writers who were admired in literary circles were popular with the general reading public. The great creative outburst, stretching over about a dozen years, in which modern writers came to grips with symbols, the unconscious mind, and the apparent need to extend the boundaries of language in an attempt to express the complexity of the world was also a period in which the gap between writers and ordinary readers grew wider. The dominant school of writers of the period was not directly concerned with the problems of man and society; works like Shaw's *St. Joan* and Forster's *Passage to India*, both of which appeared in 1924, were by authors of the pre-war generation.

By the end of the 1920s writers were returning to social and political problems. One of the earliest signs of this was the appearance of books about the war; a few, such as A. P. Herbert's *The Secret Battle* (1919), had been published shortly after the war, but they were not popular until about 1928, when Blunden's *Undertones of War*, Graves's *Goodbye to All That*, the immense success of R. C. Sherriff's play *Journey's End*, and the popularity of Remarque's *All Quiet on the Western Front* (translated from German) showed a revival of concern about political questions. Any honest account of war in the trenches made people feel that this must never be allowed to happen again, and this was reinforced by a belief that the next war would be much worse. Aerial manoeuvres in 1927 suggested that, if an enemy country decided to attack London, as much as 200 tons of high explosive might be dropped in an air raid. This prospect was frightening; nobody realized how little harm 200 tons would do. When the general public thought about war in the 1920s and 1930s it thought about aerial bombing, though this uneasiness about war did not have any immediate effects, The pacifist movement did not really gain strength until the early 1930s, but on the other hand there was no increase in military spending.

Economic attitudes and issues in the late 1920s

Churchill, as Chancellor of the Exchequer, was as enthusiastic about keeping spending low as he had been about high expenditure at the Admiralty before 1914. He induced the service ministers to accept, as a rule to be changed only by a Cabinet decision, that their estimates for each year should be based on the assumption that there would be no major war for ten years to come. Even with this rule, the purists were never satisfied that his budgets balanced properly. By the late 1920s the budget had settled down at just over £800 million a year: interest on war debt at somewhat over £300 million was much the largest single item, ordinary expenditure was just under £400 million, and the surplus for the Sinking Fund to reduce the debt was expected to be £40 million a year. Against this repayment of debt could be set some minor borrowing by the Unemployment Insurance Fund, of about £5 million a year.

The budget debates between Churchill and Snowden were among the most entertaining moments of the parliamentary year. On the whole Snowden seems to have been the victor, because he left everybody feeling the purists were right in thinking that the budget did not really balance. In any normal terms the budget showed a surplus because the debt was reduced every year, even if it was not reduced by the full £40 million required by the provisions for the Sinking Fund. Churchill needed some financial expedients that were too ingenious to be convincing: in 1926 a tax on betting was tried, but it turned out to be administratively impracticable; taxes were collected earlier than usual; money from the Road Fund, which was supposed to be devoted exclusively to road-building, was used for the general budget. Churchill's budgets were less deflationary than firmly balanced budgets would have been, though businessmen's confidence may have been reduced by the apparent deficits. The balance of payments, which attracted much less attention than the budget, caused more trouble. Imports at £1,100 million were met by visible exports of £700 million and invisible exports (consisting mainly of interest and dividends) of £450 million, leaving an average annual current surplus of something over £50 million. The City of London went on lending heavily overseas as it had done before 1914 and, because the current surplus was so small, this put the country's international position under some strain. The only defence was to hold interest rates at a relatively high level. Export industries were still doing badly; they were helped by the American boom in 1927 and 1928, but they had not recovered from the problems of the early 1920s.

Neville Chamberlain's comprehensive reform of local government offered some help to industry. In the nineteenth century new organizations had been set up to deal with each new local government problem, such as education or poor relief, when it became serious. Chamberlain's Act, like Balfour's 1902 Education Act, moved towards transferring the duties of the separate organizations to county councils and borough councils. The Boards of Guardians for poor relief disappeared, as the Minority Report of the Poor Law Commission had suggested in 1909. Parish councils were relieved of their road-making duties, which were becoming a heavy burden as motor transport became more important. Local rates on industrial plant were reduced to a quarter of the previous level, and agriculture was freed from rates altogether. To make up the revenue lost by this 'derating', councils were given grants from the Exchequer on the basis of factors like the number of children they had to educate.

Derating gave depressed industries some help; because of their heavy bills for unemployment relief, rates in the depressed areas were higher than average. Industries made some attempts to solve their problems by amalgamation. In cases like the launching of Imperial Chemical Industries this was a merger of firms into a single unit which could then expand; some 'rationalization' involved merging firms that were resigned to the inevitable contraction of industries like cotton textiles. Amalgamation did not cause as much unemployment as bankruptcy would have done, but it did not provide many new jobs. A new Unemployment Insurance Act passed in 1927, which gave unlimited cover instead of the previous twenty-six weeks of payments to anybody employed fifteen weeks in a year, was based on the assumption that about 6 per cent of the working population would be unemployed. This was a distinctly optimistic assessment of the position in the late 1920s.

Orthodox politicians had accepted the restoration of the link between gold and the pound, and the mild deflation and relatively high interest rates that followed. No politician could face even higher levels of unemployment if that was the only way to secure the exchange value of the pound. Politics became more and more concerned with unemployment as it became clear that there was no other issue of comparable importance. In 1926 the Liberals looked as if they might fade away from the political scene. However, during the General Strike Lloyd George refused to associate himself with the Liberal 'shadow Cabinet's' disapproval of the strike; when Asquith rebuked him for this, it became clear that party opinion was on Lloyd George's side and Asquith had to give up the Liberal leadership. Lloyd George took over the post and began trying to put life into the party.

He showed, as he had done before 1914, some interest in schemes for reviving agriculture, but the main proposal in his programme was that the government should issue a large loan to be spent on national development, mainly by a great scheme of road-building. His party accepted the programme, set out in *We Can Conquer Unemployment*, but more because he was the leader and his followers were tired of quarrels than because they understood it or believed in it. As recently as 1927 Lloyd George had himself been in favour of 'economy', by which he meant lower government spending on armaments. He had to take risks to save his party from fading away, but no reputable politician could campaign on a platform of budgeting for a deficit. Raising a loan was more acceptable, but it would have been easier to convince people if some pillar of financial respectability had declared that a loan was justified. Lloyd George's reputation did nothing to help him. He had made a number of promises in the past, and was blamed because they had not been fulfilled. In any case, he did not have long enough to explain the economics behind his proposal: his programme appeared only two or three months before the 1929 election, which turned out to be the final Liberal struggle to challenge the Labour Party's position as the Conservatives' main opponents.

At the same time as Lloyd George was moving his party to the left, Mac-Donald and Henderson were moving their party to the right. The Labour programme put forward in 1928, *Labour Faces the Nation*, was concerned with immediate reforms rather than the proclamation of distant visions. The move to a moderate policy must not be overestimated: Snowden, in a later and hostile mood, said that the welfare proposals in *Labour Faces the Nation* would have increased government spending by £1,000 million a year. The left wing of the party did not feel it was being ignored completely though it had its own programme to propose. The Independent Labour Party wanted legislation fixing a 'living wage' at a level that inefficient firms could not meet, so they would have to hand the business over to the State, which would then run the firm and continue to employ the workers, which amounted to nationalization, inefficient firm by inefficient firm, and implied a large budget deficit. Very shortly after the return to gold Mosley and Strachey argued that the government should set up central planning boards and inflate the currency by setting minimum wage levels and making more money available so that firms could pay the new rates. Neither the ILP nor the Mosley–Strachey proposals were accepted by the Labour Party; they were too novel and did not fit in with the Gladstonian views of Snowden, the party's financial expert.

Both proposals, like the Lloyd George scheme, would have produced budget deficits and reduced the number of unemployed, but this does not mean that the people putting the proposals forward had understood why they would work. The Mosley–Strachey proposals were inspired by J. A. Hobson's theory that people invest too much and as a result cannot consume all that is produced. Lloyd George had been advised by Keynes about his plans, but Keynes's position at that time was far from clear. In his *Treatise on Money* (1931) he showed that he was in favour of an increase in prices, but did not lay the responsibility for this on the government. Even in his *General Theory of Employment, Interest and Capital* (1936) the main argument was that the beneficial effect of a loan to increase public expenditure would be to provide more investment rather than simply to produce a budget deficit. Chapter 10, 'The Marginal Propensity to Consume', became the basis of the way most governments ran their affairs in the second half of the twentieth century, but it was in the footnotes rather than the text that Keynes said a budget deficit would cure unemployment no matter how it is produced. After this version of Keynes's thought had gained general acceptance, 'the enormous condescension of posterity' sometimes led historians to step forward to show how much better they could have run things, without looking at the views about economics available to politicians at the time.[4]

In the 1929 election neither the Conservative nor the Labour Party were prepared to take any risks. Socialism and Protection, the electoral bogeymen of the 1920s, were kept out of sight. Baldwin's position as leader was no easier than MacDonald's. His followers were resigned to the fact that they could not break the trade unions and force down wage rates; most of them believed that Protection was the only real answer, but they had to admit that it had not been a satisfactory issue in previous elections. Instead they went forward with the new road traffic slogan 'Safety First'. This was less attractive than promises to conquer unemployment, but people were far from sure that they wanted a change of government and the results were inconclusive.

	Votes	Seats	% of all votes cast
Conservative	8,656,473	260	38.2
Liberal	5,308,510	59	23.4
Labour	8,389,512	288	37.1

The second Labour government (1929)

For over a hundred years effective changes of government have required an incubation period of about four years, in which there may be a steady fall in government popularity leading to electoral disaster, as in 1992–7, or a government with an uneasy majority like the Labour government of 1974–9. Both of the Labour governments in the years between the wars found that the electorate was flirting with the idea of an effective Labour government, but then decided the prospect was unattractive. The uncertain tenure of the Labour government was shown by the way people, then and later, spoke of 'giving Labour a second chance'. If this meant anything at all, it implied that after an unsatisfactory Labour government the Liberals would be reinstated as the major party opposed to the Conservatives. But both Labour governments were followed by elections in which the major transfer of votes was away from the Liberals and towards the Conservatives. The Liberal leaders knew this might happen, because most of their followers felt more at home with the Conservatives' general attitude, but agreed with the Labour Party about particular issues. On foreign and imperial policy, and on the great domestic issue

---

4. For example: 'The Ministers should have propounded radical schemes for disciplining the economy, for marshalling the unused industrial resources and for increasing purchasing power' (C. Cross, *Philip Snowden* (1966), 257).

of Free Trade, the Liberal Party and the Labour Party could work together without difficulty. This cooperation did not look like leading to unification; on the other hand, when Liberals and Conservatives came together they formed coalitions, and when the coalitions ended a large number of Liberals stayed with the Conservatives.

The second Labour government was sufficiently like the first not to cause surprise. MacDonald reluctantly allowed Henderson to become Foreign Secretary; Henderson was a little more ready than MacDonald to see that, if the problem arose, Britain would have to support France to prevent Germany from dominating Europe. The French thought MacDonald was pro-German, and they came to think the same about Snowden; he believed that in the long run Reparations should be abolished, and in the short run at The Hague in 1929 he resisted any suggestion that France should be allowed a larger share of Reparations at Britain's expense. Henderson served to balance this appearance of anti-French feeling. He began preparations for a World Disarmament Conference, to be held in 1932. MacDonald went to the United States to see whether steps could be taken towards naval disarmament, which he kept in his own hands. Not much was done, but MacDonald seems to have been the first British Prime Minister to see that entering into closer relations with the United States was the change of foreign policy that involved least realignment. He was welcomed in America, but he did not imagine that he had done much to reduce the American desire to keep out of European problems. Henderson resumed diplomatic relations with Russia, though more slowly than the left wing of the party had hoped. In Egypt he dismissed Lord Lloyd, the High Commissioner, for taking altogether too autocratic a view of his position. Lloyd had gone too far for Austen Chamberlain, and much too far for the Egyptians, who were showing signs of irritation.

A Commission under Sir John Simon had been set up in 1927 to investigate the government of India. No Indians were appointed to the Commission, probably to avoid annoying the British authorities in India, though the government said that including any Indian leaders would irritate those who had to be left out. The result was that no Indians of importance appeared before the Commission to give evidence, and Indian nationalist feelings were strengthened. After consultations with MacDonald's government, which bore the ultimate responsibility, the Viceroy, Lord Irwin, declared in October 1929 that Dominion status was the natural conclusion for India's constitutional development. Baldwin, as leader of the Opposition, did not deny that Dominion status was inevitable, but he did say that he wished Irwin had not made the statement. It caused considerable trouble inside his party and it also cut some of the ground from under the feet of the Simon Commission. The Commission's Report, which appeared in June 1930, recommended responsible government in the provinces. Power over important questions, such as defence and foreign policy, should remain in the hands of the Viceroy at Delhi, though an additional conference to discuss these powers was suggested. The proposals were discussed at Round Table conferences at which the Indians who had refused to appear before the Commission were represented. But a wave of civil disobedience had begun in April, when Gandhi led a 200-mile march to the sea and then gathered salt in defiance of the government monopoly. During the year 54,000 people were convicted on civil disobedience charges, and over 23,000 of them were in prison at the end of the year.

In a more peaceful area of imperial relations the government drew up legislation to make the Balfour Declaration of 1926 legally effective. The Statute of Westminster made it clear that Dominions could have as much freedom to legislate as they wanted. This did not worry the British government, which had tended to assume that they already had this freedom. By 1931 Britain was concerned only to try to persuade them to follow a single foreign policy; in 1930 the British government rejected Dominion suggestions, of the sort that had been made for thirty years, that a system of imperial customs preferences should be set up.

The disagreements in Britain about these imperial questions were fought out inside the Conservative Party. Baldwin's position was weak immediately after the election. He was blamed for defeat, just as in 1923, and for not using the majority gained in 1924 to get back to the days before the war. He was also attacked because of his position on Protection and on India. Some Conservatives were attracted by the idea of a tariff system for the whole Empire in which all the members, including Britain, taxed imports from outside but accepted each other's products free of duty. The policy of Empire Free Trade was probably never practicable, because the Dominions had no intention of exposing their newly launched industries to competition from Britain. But the scheme had the support of the great newspaper owners Lord Beaverbrook and Lord Rothermere, and had to be taken seriously by any Conservative leader.

The political influence of their papers was less than people imagined; the *Daily Express* and the *Daily Mail* attracted large readerships, but they were readers who did not take politics seriously enough to worry about the details of a particular issue. In his struggle with Beaverbrook and Rothermere, Baldwin said that their newspapers relied on tendentious and selective reporting. Some of the compressed and emotionally loaded reporting of these newspapers was an attempt to make politics palatable to people who had not previously read a daily newspaper. There were disadvantages about the newspapers with which Baldwin was implicitly comparing the *Express* and the *Mail*; Spender (of the *Westminster Gazette*) in his *Autobiography* and Hammond's *Life of C. P. Scott* (of the *Manchester Guardian*) show how close these respected editors came to running party bulletins. They suppressed news, they wrote editorials designed to influence policy which were deliberately made incomprehensible to anyone who did not know how discussions were going in the Cabinet, and Spender took it for granted that his paper ought to be subsidized by a small group of wealthy Liberals. The mass circulation papers probably did their job of giving the uninterested a vague outline of what was going on rather better than the 'quality' newspapers set about enabling people interested in politics to find out what they needed to know in order to consider problems properly. But the owners of the mass circulation papers could not marshal their readers to support a particular policy.

Protection was popular enough in the Conservative Party to make their challenge dangerous. Baldwin met the challenge by declaring his support for Imperial Preference, which had from time to time been part of the Conservative programme. This gave him a short breathing space, but by October 1930 he had to defend himself at a meeting of Conservative MPs, peers, and candidates. He won by 462 votes to 116, a majority large enough for survival but not for comfort. The question of India was beginning to be felt; Baldwin was pressed not to go beyond the Report of the Simon Commission by expressing sympathy for Dominion status. In January 1931 Churchill left the 'shadow Cabinet' because he wanted to be free to oppose any move towards it; in the long run this step meant that he was outside the government during the 1930s, and for most of the decade was regarded as dangerously right-wing. But in the short run it made Baldwin's position even weaker. He had placed Neville Chamberlain at the head of the party organization, a risky step because Chamberlain, who was much more acceptable to the Protectionists, was now his natural successor. In February the Chief Agent suggested that it would help the party if Baldwin retired, and for a few days he thought of doing so. *The Times* had prepared its editorial on the subject, Baldwin had told Chamberlain that he was going, and it is said he had written his letter of resignation. But he decided to stay and fight. In the Commons he made a successful speech in which he refused to commit his party against Dominion status as the final goal of policy in India.

Beaverbrook and Rothermere had intensified the conflict by running Empire Free Trade candidates against official Conservatives in a number of by-elections, with some success. A by-election was coming up in the very safe Conservative seat of St George's, Westminster. At first Baldwin thought he might stand himself, partly because nobody else seemed to be willing to defend the policy of the party leadership. When Duff Cooper, who had lost his seat in the 1929 election, came forward to resist the Empire Free Traders, Baldwin made a speech in his support in which he denounced Beaverbrook and Rothermere for seeking power without responsibility, 'the prerogative of the harlot throughout the ages'. This was hardly fair to the press lords, who had conducted one of the most open attacks on a party leader to be seen in the century. By attacking Baldwin at by-elections, on a genuine issue of economic policy, Beaverbrook and Rothermere were giving him a chance to defend his programme and to test public opinion; other party leaders have been driven out by secret discussions ending in a sudden 'failure of health'. It is a measure of Baldwin's political skill and of his readiness to avoid issues of policy that he could defeat the assault by concentrating on the personal failings of his opponents and retain a reputation as a purifying influence in politics. His success was not decisive; Duff Cooper was elected in St George's, but the Empire Free Trade candidate was not disgraced, and the assault would have been resumed in the autumn.

Baldwin survived these attacks better than might have been expected. The other parties had their problems. The Liberals had rallied behind Lloyd George in the two or three years before the election, and had allowed him to write his own policy and control the party machinery. In return for this they expected success. They may have done less well than they hoped in 1929 because Lloyd George launched his unemployment programme too close to the election to have time to convince people of its merits, or because he committed the party to an economic programme which it did not really believe in, or because no section of society felt the Liberals were wholeheartedly devoted to its interests. In any case they had done badly; Lloyd George was blamed, and he found it hard to get all his followers to vote together in the Commons.

Tension was at its highest in the first few months of the new government. The Liberals spoke as if they would vote on each measure strictly on its merits and turn the government out if it brought forward any proposals they disliked, and the government was no more conciliatory. But when the Liberals and the government contemplated the disadvantages of having another general election, they became less intransigent. The government was taking up the process of rationalization, which until then had been a matter for private enterprise; as the Commons would reject nationalization of the coal mines it introduced a Mines Bill early in 1930 which reduced working hours to seven and a half and set up a Reorganization Committee with some legal powers to encourage rationalization. The Liberals decided to support the Bill; it was a step away from Free Trade, but Free Trade had unexpected disadvantages for declining industries. Other industries were rationalizing, or forming themselves into cartels, without government intervention: in 1929 the Millers' Mutual Association was launched; in shipbuilding, National Shipbuilders Security Ltd had been set up to buy shipyards and keep them idle so that they would not force prices down still further in an attempt to obtain contracts, and in cotton-spinning Spindles Ltd was formed for the same purpose. Probably these steps helped the declining industries to contract, but as the new industries were not growing fast enough to take on so many workers the old industries were blamed for reducing their labour force and increasing unemployment.

The slight improvement in British industry in the later years of Baldwin's ministry was coming to an end. It had always depended to a considerable extent on the much more flourishing expansion in the United States, and by the time of the 1929 election the American boom was already slowing down. In the autumn prices fell spectacularly on the New York Stock Exchange, but this only confirmed a decline in production that began some months earlier. The result of the international decline in trade spread to Britain, and unemployment began to rise.

From economic paralysis to economic crisis

The government had set up a committee to reduce unemployment under J. H. Thomas. In some ways he was a good choice; he was a genial and ebullient man who could get on well with businessmen, and he would have been ideally suited for jollying a boom along. But Thomas was not the man to fight rising unemployment. Snowden at the Exchequer insisted on balancing the budget and declined to provide money for public works programmes to relieve unemployment unless they were productive, in the sense that they would produce a profit, and Thomas accepted this point of view. Road-building, the form of public works that came most readily to everybody's mind, had to be strictly limited.

The other members of Thomas's committee, Lansbury, Johnston, and Mosley, could not do much against the resistance of the Treasury. Mosley felt confident that he possessed an answer to the problem of unemployment, along the lines that the Labour Party in Birmingham had been considering for some years. What he wanted was an attempt to shut Britain off from the mounting crisis abroad by a tariff wall and run her industries with a managed currency that would if necessary be devalued. This programme, formulated in the Mosley Memorandum, was put to the Cabinet. Thomas felt offended because he appeared to have been ignored, and Snowden refused to have anything to do with the idea.

Mosley resigned, and continued the battle from the backbenches. He explained his programme to a meeting of the Parliamentary Labour Party, at which his speech was well received, and then pressed the matter to a vote; loyalty to the leadership triumphed over doubt, and Mosley was heavily defeated. By forcing a vote he had driven MacDonald and Snowden together; MacDonald knew very little about economics, and was not very interested, but left to himself he might have given Mosley some encouragement—he was not a convinced Free Trader and he certainly had no friendship for Snowden. Mosley's open support in the parliamentary party came largely from the left wing of the ILP. This section of the ILP in effect claimed to be a separate party working in alliance with the Labour Party but entitled to vote against it if they chose. The Labour Party was not tightly disciplined—over a hundred Members voted against the party Whip on one occasion or another during this Parliament—but the ILP was going too far. The Clydeside group that controlled the ILP drove out all the Members of Parliament who were first and foremost Labour Party supporters and belonged to the ILP much as they might have belonged to the Fabian Society; after this supporters of the ILP followed its policy even when it conflicted with Labour Party policy, though for the time being they remained members of the Labour Party.

When people were in this mood, Mosley could expect a good deal of support. He put forward his policy at the party conference in October 1930; it received 1,046,000 votes against the 1,251,000 votes cast in support of the party leadership. If he had kept up the pressure after doing so well, the Prime Minister might have felt it was wise to encourage Snowden to become more flexible. The breadth of his support was too much for Mosley's self-restraint, his combination of planning, tariffs, and national spirit was attractive to Conservatives as well as to socialists, and this made him think he could set up a party of his own. In February 1931 he launched the New Party to put the case for his economic policy, and although it won no seats in the 1931 general election, the Conservatives kept a watchful eye on it for two or three years and wondered whether they wanted Mosley back; he was believed to represent youth in politics and his policy was very like that of the Conservatives after 1931. But his movement drifted towards Fascism, and took up anti-Semitism in October 1934, after which he was politically untouchable.

The government passed very little important legislation apart from its Mines Act, but in the 1930–1 session it submitted three Bills that caused some controversy. Trevelyan brought forward his Education Bill, which had been crowded out in 1930, and it was given plenty of legislative time. The most important clause provided that children had to stay at school until 15, which would be expensive but was almost essential if they were to go to secondary schools at 11 plus, as proposed in the Hadow Report; if they could leave at 14 they would attend their new schools for only two years. The original Bill provided very little money for Roman Catholic schools, and the Catholic section of the Labour Party, made up mainly of Members with a sizeable number of voters who were Irish by descent, moved an amendment to give a grant of the order of £1 million. The government opposed the amendment, but it was carried with Conservative support. When the government accepted the amendment, the Conservatives, whose support for the amendment was inspired partly by their success in by-elections, said it was being spineless. The Bill was defeated in the Lords on the grounds that it would cost too much. The government showed no desire to renew a struggle in which they were bound to annoy either their Catholic or their Nonconformist supporters. Trevelyan did not accept this as a good reason for abandoning the issue, and resigned when it was obvious that nothing more was going to be done.

The Trade Union Bill and the Electoral Reform Bill look like a bargain by which the Liberals would vote for the repeal of the Trade Disputes Act to please the trade unions, and the government would establish the alternative vote to repay the Liberals. The alternative vote would let voters indicate a second preference at elections and the Liberals could reasonably hope that both Labour and Conservative voters would pick them as a second choice, while the Labour Party had no real reason to expect to benefit more than the Conservatives from Liberal second choices. On the other hand, the Trade Union Bill did not really extend the powers of the unions, and did not allow general strikes for political purposes. By restoring 'contracting out' of the political levy, it would have made Labour Party finances somewhat more secure, but the 1929 election results had shown that 'contracting in' was not a complete barrier to success. In February the Liberals turned on the Trade Union Bill and mangled it so much that it was dropped. The government went on with the Electoral Reform Bill, presumably in the belief that cooperation in the Commons might lead on to cooperation in elections, for which the alternative vote might be useful.

By this stage the government had realized that legislation could not solve the three interlinked problems that really mattered: reducing unemployment, balancing the budget, and maintaining the external value of the pound. In 1929 Snowden had appointed a Commission under Lord Macmillan to investigate the working of the financial system and its effect on the economy; the British economy then seemed in some way exceptional, because other countries were enjoying prosperity and full employment, and were free from serious unemployment. But while the Commission was sitting, American production was declining and world trade was contracting. By the time the Macmillan Report appeared[5] in May 1931, the hardest-hit countries were Germany and the United States.

The collapse in world trade, which fell to about half its 1929 cash value by 1932, reinforced the idea that Britain's position was exceptional. The world-wide depression was marked by a fall in investment, a fall in the price of raw materials, and a decline in employment. British investment had been sluggish in the late 1920s, but maintained this low level without any prolonged drop in the early 1930s. Almost everybody in the country benefited when low prices for raw materials meant that exports would buy more than before. The volume of exports dropped rather sharply, but their cash value did not decline so fast.

In its Report the Macmillan Commission asked for international cooperation in raising price levels, as a way of escaping from the great increase in the real burden of debt caused by the steady fall in prices in the 1920s. It also recommended adoption of a managed currency instead of allowing the supply of money to be affected by the amount of gold available. Its terms of reference did not allow it to ask whether the Bank of England ought to keep the pound at a fixed rate in terms of gold (known as 'remaining on the Gold Standard'), but it did consider one question which tended to be ignored: if the pound had

5. *Parliamentary Papers*, Cmd. 3897.

been overvalued in 1925 and was still overvalued, ought it to be devalued? The Bank could quite easily retain a fixed gold value for the pound at a lower rate of exchange, such as $4 to the pound, by increasing the sterling price at which it bought and sold gold bars. The Commission rejected the idea of devaluation, on the grounds that it would be a shock to international confidence. But once international confidence was introduced into the discussion, whatever the Report said was bound to be harmful. Saying that the pound was overvalued made people less willing to hold sterling, and the suggestion that prices should be driven upwards was also discouraging; soon after the Report appeared money began to leave London.

All the fourteen members of the Commission except the chairman submitted addenda or reservations to the Report, which was bound to make investors uneasy about leaving their money in London. The most important reservation was signed by six members including Keynes and McKenna, the Chairman of the Midland Bank—a man radical only by the standards of other chairmen of banks. They asked for a tariff and a subsidy on exports, which meant a virtual devaluation, and they suggested a general agreement to reduce wages and prices simultaneously. They wanted the government to run a managed currency inside the country and at the same time maintain a stable currency unit for international trade; this dual policy was more or less accepted by governments in the 1940s, and they hoped to achieve this objective through the international financial institutions set up at the end of the Second World War. Two members of this group of six, Ernest Bevin and Sir Thomas Allen of the Co-operative Movement, went as close as they could to saying there ought to be a devaluation, adding that the Bank might be forced off gold if it would not devalue, and they recommended a large loan to be spent on projects that would stimulate the economy. His newspaper and magazine articles at this time suggest that Keynes agreed with this view, but presumably he held back to consolidate support for the Keynes–McKenna reservation.

Arguments of this sort became the orthodoxy of the future. But when Keynes questioned Sir Richard Hopkins, who was putting the Treasury's point of view and argued that investment by the government would stimulate the economy, Hopkins replied that government borrowing would force interest rates up, thus making life harder for other borrowers and making marginal borrowers give up projects they had in mind. Thus, government intervention might change the nature of the investment carried out, but could not increase the total amount of investment. In one of the more important moments in the Commission discussions Lord Macmillan described the argument between the two men as a drawn battle.[6]

It would be hard for a government to change its policy on the basis of an indecisive encounter. Politicians could have had ideas of their own without

6. R. Harrod, *The Life of John Maynard Keynes* (1951), 422.

waiting for academic economists to produce them, even if 'soon or late, it is ideas, not vested interests, that are dangerous for good or evil',[7] but Snowden's reasons for opposing the deficit-producing schemes were understandable; Keynesian economic policies would at first reduce real wages, in order to provide more employment and a more buoyant economy in which wages would regain their former purchasing power. In 1929 Snowden had claimed that the Labour Party would balance the budget as well as conquering unemployment, thus avoiding the initial fall in real wages. He was not irrevocably opposed to new ideas: in a Cabinet memorandum in 1930 he said he did not accept Hopkins's rigid version of the Treasury point of view on loans,[8] and a few years later when the collapse had come and he had lost everything for which he had fought, Gold Standard, Free Trade, and his own honoured position in the Labour Party, he declared that a large government loan could stimulate development. He argued that in 1929 there had been unemployed people; in 1934 there were not only unemployed people but also unemployed capital, and it was the business of the government to bring them together. This was just another way of saying that the pound had been overvalued in 1929, though Snowden seems not to have seen the connection. During the half-dozen years from 1925 that the pound was linked to gold, there was a steady flow of gold out of the country, mainly to France because the franc was distinctly undervalued. Any proposal that would increase the budget deficit would only have encouraged the loss of gold and made it harder to maintain the exchange value of the pound.

Public works provided employment for a few people, but at a cost which was producing a budget deficit. The general financial position of the government was made worse by the steady deficit of the Unemployment Insurance Fund. Insurance contributions to the Fund were supposed to balance benefits paid out, though the complaints of the financial purists did suggest that the Fund was meant to make a profit. Rising unemployment after 1929 forced the Fund to borrow to pay benefits, and this borrowing was seen as one of the causes of financial weakness. Snowden had forced the Commons to accept his 1930 budget, which raised income tax to 22.5p in the pound, but pushing another budget through with a minority seemed almost impossible even though everyone agreed a firm policy was needed. In February 1931 he accepted a Liberal suggestion and set up a committee to look into ways of carrying out economies. Sir George May, the chairman, had been secretary of the Prudential Insurance and was assumed to be without party allegiance; MacDonald, Lloyd George, and Baldwin each nominated two representatives. The Committee was to find out the facts about the government's financial position and if necessary make suggestions about what should be done. Until

7. J. M. Keynes, *The General Theory of Employment, Interest and Money* (1936), 384.
8. PRO, Cab. 24 C.P. 392 (30), 86.

it reported Snowden made no financial changes, perhaps because he thought the report would provide all-party support for the policies that he believed to be necessary.

By July 1931 there was definite uneasiness in Paris and New York about the financial soundness of the City of London. The Macmillan Commission made it clear that, despite rumours to the contrary, British investors had not been borrowing money for short periods in order to make long-term loans elsewhere. But London was less able to attract short-term money than before 1914, and some short-term money had been lent to German firms that either had gone bankrupt or were not allowed to remit money out of the country, and in this way the short-term loans became loans of indefinite length. London was not well placed to deal with withdrawals of short-term money. As part of a programme of cheap money undertaken by central banks in an effort to stimulate trade, the Bank of England had brought its rate down to 2.5 per cent. In July it recognized that this would no longer work, and raised the bank rate to 4.5 per cent, a level at which it remained for seven weeks. The Governor of the Bank, Montagu Norman, had been working hard to help deal with the crisis facing the German banks; he possessed the charm and temperament of the artist at a time when physical stamina or deep originality of thought were the qualities required of the Governor, and at this point he had to take a long holiday.

Just after the second increase in the bank rate the May Committee presented its report.[9] The Liberal and Conservative representatives and May himself declared that the British government was rushing to ruin. They announced that there would be a budget deficit of £120 million, and they made their suggestions for dealing with it. Their figures showed a deficit of £70 million in the normal meaning of the word; they raised it to £120 million by laying down that £50 million of debt should be repaid and arguing—much as Snowden had done with Churchill—that the government had a deficit of £20 million if only £30 million were repaid. The report examined several government departments in great detail, and made suggestions for cutting their spending by £9 million. Apart from these small sums it suggested more drastic cuts of £13 million from education, £7 million from road-building, and £66 million from the expenditure of the Unemployment Insurance Fund. As the committee itself estimated that the Fund would, at the current rates, need to borrow only £40 million, this amounted to saying that in a year of heavy unemployment the Fund should provide a surplus of £26 million. Presumably the committee intended the Fund to provide a steady annual contribution to general revenue. MacDonald may have reflected how wise he had been to refuse to have a committee on the Campbell case in 1924; the government had meant the May Committee to make recommendations on technical issues but

9. *Parliamentary Papers*, Cmd. 3920.

it had instead taken a long step into the field of policy, for the report was simply a collection of small proposals thrown together around the central assertion that unemployment benefit ought to be cut. Keynes had suggested in January: 'The best guess I can make is that whenever you save five shillings, you put a man out of work for a day.'[10] At this rate a deficit of £120 million would have cured unemployment, though it would fairly certainly have forced the government to reduce the value of the pound in terms of gold.

The two Labour members of the Committee drew up a minority report. Like the majority they could find very few examples of waste. They did not regard it as their business to propose changes of policy, and in any case they had no desire for cuts in education, road-building, and unemployment benefit. Paragraphs 38–43 of their Report are a good statement in non-technical language of the case for high government expenditure in time of depression and paragraph 131 puts what became the accepted view of the situation: 'The present financial difficulties of the country and industry do not arise from any pursuit of wasteful public expenditure or lack of responsible control of such but are much more closely related to the policy of deflation followed since the war and confirmed by the return to the gold standard.' The position of the Liberals on the Committee was odd. If they had taken seriously the programme on which Lloyd George had fought the 1929 election, they would have signed the Minority Report, thus making it into a Majority Report.

The establishment of the National government in 1931

From the end of July onward the story grows more fascinating but harder to follow. Politicians refought the August struggles when the House reassembled, providing many more versions of the events than is usual in Cabinet disagreements. Disagreement, then and later, came at different levels: there are arguments about what was done, and even more about what was said: arguments about the constitutional propriety of the behaviour of the King and the Prime Minister; arguments about the extent to which a politician has a duty to his party and to his election pledges when they conflict with what he believes ought to be done in a crisis; arguments about whether the government's economic policy was justified; and arguments about whether it could have been expected to have found a better policy. It is still hard to say anything about the crisis that will be universally accepted.

The outflow of foreign exchange which had caused the July increases in the bank rate became faster after the publication of the May Report. There the figure was in print: a budget deficit of £120 million. The bankers in London now declared that it was all the government's fault, that no financial measures other than a balanced budget would set things right, and that the government

10. *The Listener*, 14 Jan. 1931; repr. in J. M. Keynes, *Essays in Persuasion* (1931), 152.

should do something to save the City of London. On 12 August the Economy Committee of the Cabinet met to consider the May Report. Snowden accepted the May Committee's view that the budget was only balanced when ample provision had been made for paying off the National Debt, and added that the deficit would be £170 million, rather than £120 million. For reasons that are not quite clear, this figure was accepted for the next four months. Snowden suggested about £70 million or £80 million of new taxation. The Committee then worked out general reductions in expenditure along the lines suggested by the May Committee. The government needed a majority in the Commons to pass economy measures, so the proposals had to satisfy at least one of the parties in opposition and, if measures were to be passed quickly, the support of both would be required. As a result, MacDonald and Snowden had to have frequent discussions with Baldwin, Neville Chamberlain, and Hoare, and with Samuel, who was acting as Liberal leader while Lloyd George was recovering from a prostate operation.

On 19 August the Economy Committee put its proposals to the Cabinet: £30 million of saving on general expenditure and £48 million of saving on payments to the unemployed. After a long meeting the Cabinet accepted £56 million of the cuts, but it rejected the proposal to reduce 'transitional payments' to unemployed people who had exhausted their rights under the insurance system, which was expected to bring in about £20 million. These cuts did not include reducing the standard rate of unemployment benefit paid to unemployed workers under the insurance scheme. Next day the Cabinet representatives met the opposition leaders again, and appear to have given them the impression that the Cabinet had accepted the full £78 million of cuts proposed in the Economy Committee. Chamberlain said it would be best to make all of the £96 million of cuts suggested by the May Committee, which involved reducing the standard rate of unemployment benefit. Later in the day the Economy Committee met the National Executive Committee of the Labour Party and the General Council of the TUC, and at this meeting Snowden said that while various cuts were to be made, the Cabinet had not decided to cut the standard rate of unemployment benefit.

The General Council refused to have anything to do with the government's proposals. In the next few days the Council played an increasingly important role, mainly because some of its members had a coherent idea of what to do. Its proposals—increase direct taxation, especially on unearned income, suspend the Sinking Fund, and perhaps impose a tariff for revenue—came much closer to the orthodoxy of later decades than anything else heard during the crisis. The TUC's deputation, which included Bevin from the Macmillan Commission and Pugh from the May Committee minority, put these suggestions to the Cabinet, but they were rejected. Sidney Webb said, after hearing the proposals, 'The General Council are pigs'; however, as he said later that nobody told the Cabinet that it could give up linking the pound to gold, he cannot have understood much of what was going on.

On 21 August the Cabinet discussed the idea of a tariff: fifteen of them were in favour of a 10 per cent duty on manufactured goods, but they did not insist that Snowden and the minority should accept the suggestion. On the other hand, the Cabinet refused to impose any cuts beyond the £56 million agreed previously. As a result, when MacDonald and Snowden met Chamberlain and Samuel, the opposition leaders learned that the cuts would in fact be less than they had been told on the 20th. They protested and asked for more. Snowden and MacDonald told the Cabinet on the 22nd that the Liberals and Conservatives wanted further cuts, including some reduction of unemployment benefits. Snowden spoke of 'reducing the standard of living of the workmen by 50 per cent, which would be the effect of departing from the Gold Standard'.[11] The Cabinet was not impressed by this alarmism. MacDonald then proposed reducing spending by £20 million, £12.25 million to come from a 10 per cent cut in the standard rate of unemployment benefit, and £7.75 million from economies in other departments. The Cabinet refused to accept MacDonald's scheme; Snowden and Thomas were so annoyed by the refusal that they asked that their dissent should be recorded, which meant that they were considering resignation. Perhaps because of this the Cabinet then allowed MacDonald and Snowden to find out from Baldwin and Samuel whether the new programme, amounting to £76 million, including the 10 per cent reduction, would be sufficient for the government to put to Parliament. There would clearly be trouble if Baldwin and Samuel accepted the programme and the Cabinet continued to reject it.

By this time another problem had arisen. The Bank of England was still paying out gold to meet a stream of withdrawals, and was coming to the end of its resources. Additional money, in gold or in foreign exchange, could be found only by a short-term loan arranged by the government, which would have to be raised from New York commercial banks because the Federal Reserve Bank of New York was not allowed to lend to foreign governments. So, the government had to find out whether £76 million of cuts would satisfy the New York commercial banks that a loan was safe if the Bank of England was to be helped to maintain the exchange value of the pound.

On 23 August MacDonald saw the King and warned him that the Cabinet might not survive. The King, with MacDonald's permission, then saw Samuel and, later in the day, Baldwin. Samuel put to the King the arguments in favour of a coalition (though of course no Liberal could use this word because it awoke memories of Lloyd George's 1916–22 government) under MacDonald, if the Labour government could not agree on a policy. Baldwin, at his audience, agreed to serve under MacDonald in a coalition if the question arose.

---

11. PRO, Cab. 23/67, 22 Aug. 1931.

That evening the Cabinet met again to learn the response of the New York banks to the request for a loan. The New York banks passed the question back to London by saying they would provide the loan if the Bank of England considered the programme of cuts was adequate. As the loan was designed to save the Bank of England from disaster, this reliance on its advice was a tribute to its reputation for integrity, though New York could depend on men like Montagu Norman, who, at one stage in the German negotiations that led to his breakdown, had noted with some satisfaction that German workers were ashamed to be on the dole. He clearly felt that British workers ought also to be ashamed of it. Norman's economics and his national psychology were wrong: even if German workers had been ashamed of their position it would have done nothing to reduce unemployment, and in any case the German workers seem to have been bitterly angry rather than ashamed. It was in Britain that the unemployed were corroded by shame at their idleness.

After the request for a loan had been referred back from New York to London, the money would come only if the government accepted the reductions of £76 million, including the cut in the standard unemployment benefit. This sort of programme would always have been hard to steer through the Cabinet and by 23 August the opponents of reductions were gaining strength. Accepting a policy because the bankers required it was in itself distasteful. MacDonald said that the programme could be passed only if nobody resigned, but Henderson and seven or eight others said they could not remain in a government that imposed the £76 million of cuts. MacDonald told the King that the government was about to break up, and returned to tell the Cabinet that he would meet Baldwin, Samuel, and the King next morning, and would then see the Cabinet again. The King asked him to lead a National government and, though he declined that evening, he accepted at the morning meeting with Baldwin, Samuel, and the King. He went to the Cabinet meeting, told the ministers that they were out of office, and asked Snowden, Thomas, and Sankey to join his new Cabinet, which they did. Baldwin, Neville Chamberlain, Cunliffe-Lister, and Hoare from the Conservative Party, and Samuel and Lord Reading from the Liberals also joined the National Cabinet.

The Labour Party claimed that this transformation scene had been brought about by treachery and that the King, the bankers, and MacDonald had plotted to turn the Labour government out. The King's position was quite simple: the duty of a constitutional monarch is to name the head of the strongest government that can be found, which normally means appointing a Prime Minister with a party majority in the Commons though the advantages of a coalition must at times be in the monarch's mind. The government that MacDonald formed in August 1931 was undeniably strong, and the King behaved reasonably in asking him to form it although if he meant to be taken seriously when he said, a few weeks later, that he would refuse to accept

MacDonald's resignation he was behaving a little like George III with Lord North.[12]

The behaviour of the New York banks also seems reasonable; they were being asked to lend money, and wanted to know if it was a sound risk. The Labour complaints that there had been a 'bankers' ramp' presumably meant that the banks had departed from normal commercial practice in order to embarrass the Labour government. But lending to London was not free from danger, because the general fear of devaluation might easily lead to such rapid withdrawals of gold that the New York banks could not be repaid for some time to come, and the bankers were entitled to protect themselves against this. The Bank of England's desire to avoid devaluation probably harmed the nation's economy, but this does not mean it was plotting against the government.

MacDonald's behaviour has come under suspicion: it was said he had been plotting to set up a coalition for months previously, but this is hard to pin down because the parliamentary situation had made several people think about a coalition in the previous two years. It was unusual for him to arrange to meet Baldwin and Samuel at Buckingham Palace at the time of his pro-posed resignation on 24 August; and it is not clear why he did this. The Labour leaders in the new Cabinet were also criticized on less easily tangible grounds: they had been elected on one programme and had now become convinced that a radically different programme was necessary. As MacDonald put it to his Cabinet, 'the proposals as a whole represented the negation of everything the Labour Party stood for, and yet he was absolutely satisfied that it was necessary, in the national interest, to implement them if the country was to be secured'.[13] The harsh rules for statesmen in this predicament have been laid down by two great Conservatives in speeches denouncing their leaders. Churchill in the 1930s argued that, mandate or no mandate, the gov-ernment had a duty to do what it thought was right and rearm the country. On the other hand, Disraeli fought his way to the head of the party by his denunciation of Peel for abandoning the Corn Laws to which his party was pledged.

The National government

MacDonald was the most convenient leader for a government that included both Baldwin and Samuel. He did not attempt to persuade the Labour Party to make his new government all-inclusive by joining it. He might have pointed out that only a National government could impose Snowden's programme of taxation on the rich, and only a National government with Labour support could maintain Free Trade. Instead he discouraged Labour junior ministers

12. H. Nicolson, *George V* (1952),   13. PRO, Cab. 23/67, 23 Aug. 1931.493.

from joining his government and neither he nor Snowden went to the meeting of the Parliamentary Labour Party on 28 August to explain their policy to their ex-followers. Both of them had been finding the criticism of the Labour backbenchers increasingly irritating and seem to have been thinking of retiring from politics very soon. This would explain why they said on 25 August that the new government would exist only for the duration of the crisis. When they disagreed with the main body of the party in the First World War, they had kept in touch with the party, but they made no attempt to remain in touch in 1931.

Snowden's budget of 10 September was deflationary and egalitarian. It imposed £80 million of new taxes, including an increase in the standard rate of income tax from 22.5p to 25p and a 10 per cent increase in surtax. Next day MacDonald presented the Economy Bill, which reduced government spending by £70 million. This included the 10 per cent cut in the standard rate of unemployment benefit, which was defended on the ground that the cost of living had fallen by more than 10 per cent. During the debates the Labour leaders in opposition came round to the programme suggested by the TUC and repudiated the cuts. At times they spoke as though they had never agreed to any of them and could not approve of anything like cuts in teachers' salaries.

The formation of the National government did a certain amount to reassure foreign lenders. Although money continued to leave the country, the Economy Bill and the budget might have succeeded in their aims if all their victims had accepted them. On 15 September sailors in the Royal Navy at Invergordon went on strike over the reductions in pay. During the week the Bank of England lost £50 million in gold, and by the 19th it was defeated: on the 21st it suspended sales of gold and the pound was no longer linked to gold. The general policy of the Bank was surprising: it had left the bank rate unchanged throughout the crisis, and the 4.5 per cent rate maintained in August and September was in fact lower than the average annual rate for practically every year since Norman became Governor in 1920. Even if it was going to abandon the high-interest policy of the 1920s, the Bank took a very drastic step when it gave up supporting a fixed value for the pound; it might have been less unsettling for world trade to adopt and defend a lower exchange rate than $4.86. Until 1939 the Bank ran a 'managed float' of the pound, and as it initially fell to $3.20 its fluctuations were uncomfortably large.

Abandonment of the link with gold ignored a major—though completely unreal—fear that had been dominating policy for some weeks: almost the only economic event mentioned in the September debates was the collapse of the mark in 1923, and retention of the link with gold at a different rate of exchange would have helped to make sure that the pound would not go the same way. *The Times* did say, 'a suspension of gold payments by a Socialist government would have been one thing. But a suspension by a National government committed to retrenchment and reform is another.'[14] Presumably the Bank shared this feeling that the National government could be trusted.

Certainly the people trusted the National government. The budget was received with enthusiasm. People stinted themselves of old-age pensions, cancelled their War Loan bonds, and paid their income tax early. It was a great moral vindication of democracy: for years it had been said—and it was soon to be said again—that a democracy would not follow the path of sacrifice. The events of 1931 showed that ordinary people were ready to accept a stern policy applied by a man with faith in himself. Unfortunately, this self-denial only made things worse and deepened the depression, but the fine spirit that inspired it should not be forgotten.

The National government held together over ending the link with gold, and afterwards there was no obvious occasion for it to break up. The Conservatives, who provided most of the votes for the government in the Commons, wanted an election followed by a policy of Protection. The Labour Party was still the largest party in the House, and would be in a strong position if Lloyd George recovered his health and led the left wing of the Liberals away from the National government. Everybody expected that eventually the cuts and the increases in taxation would be unpopular; the Labour Party believed that this would destroy MacDonald and his government.

Tariffs were the main cause of division in the government. Snowden and the Liberal ministers were Free Traders. The Conservatives believed tariffs were the only cure for the country's economic problems. After some discussion the government decided to ask for a 'doctor's mandate'; as MacDonald put it in his election manifesto, 'the government must be free to consider every proposal likely to help, such as tariffs'.[15]

The dissolution of Parliament seemed to have settled whether the Liberal Party belonged to the left or the right: in the moment of decision it was coming down on the Conservative side. Samuel asked Lloyd George to support the National government in the election, and Lloyd George replied that if he had to die fighting he would prefer to die fighting on the left. But this had no effect; Samuel had no difficulty in taking over the Liberal leadership, because the Liberals reckoned that if they joined MacDonald's government they would not have to die after all. National government candidates could expect to poll the combined Conservative and Liberal strength, and this by itself would be enough to lead to a great victory.

The Labour Party fought as a Free Trade party, saying that a tariff which might have been useful while the pound had a fixed value was no longer necessary if it was to be on a floating rate. It advocated the other measures of planning and of deficit finance that had been discussed privately in the

14. *The Times*, 21 Sept. 1931.   15. R. Bassett, *1931* (1958), 284.

previous two or three years. But, just like Lloyd George in 1929, it was offering these proposals to the electorate with far too little preparation. Snowden's broadcast talk of 17 October, in which he said that the policy of the bulk of the Labour Party was not socialism but bolshevism run mad, and his encouragement of the idea that people's savings in the Post Office would not be safe if the Labour Party was re-elected, were heavy blows to his former party.

	Votes	Seats	% of all votes cast
Conservative and National	13,129,417	521	60.5
Samuel Liberal	1,403,102	33	6.5
Labour	6,649,630	52	30.6

By-elections before the crisis had shown that the Labour Party was losing ground, and its conduct during the crisis could not have encouraged the electorate to think it had a clear policy and knew what to do next. It suffered for being in office at the time of the slump: no government, left or right, had much chance of surviving the slump in any democratic country. In any case, the Labour Party revived; it was the ideals of laissez-faire and the free play of the market which really suffered a mortal blow in 1931, for there was nobody left to defend them for years to come.

7

The National government

1931–1939

Domestic record of the National government

The election result made it hard to hold an open-minded inquiry into the virtues of tariffs. The overwhelming majority of the Commons were Conservatives, who were convinced that tariffs were needed, and they were unlikely to change their views now they were in power. A tariff seemed so certain that a great flood of imports poured in to anticipate it. The government's first step towards Protection was the Abnormal Importations Act, designed to defend the balance of payments from these imports. More permanent legislation followed; on 4 February 1932 Neville Chamberlain introduced a tariff that, while moderate by the standards of the period, was a decisive step away from Free Trade. He included an assurance that the tariff could be reduced in favour of countries of the Empire with which preferential trading agreements could be made, and he ended his speech by reminding his listeners of his father's work for Protection. The Liberal ministers who were committed to Free Trade and Snowden (who had become a peer) wanted to resign over Chamberlain's tariff, but he was able to persuade them to remain on the rather unusual condition that they were at liberty to attack his Bill from the government front bench. Their opposition had no effect, and the tariff was established.

The Tariff Reform movement had always wanted closer links with the Empire. The Commonwealth Prime Ministers had kept up their pressure for Imperial Preference in 1930, and now the National government was ready to cooperate with them. The Ottawa Conference in 1932 showed what Free Traders who said that setting up a system of Imperial Preference would lead to quarrels had been talking about. Commonwealth countries did set up a network of bilateral agreements, but at the cost of a good deal of irritation during the negotiations; the British representatives had expected a rapturous welcome for the prodigal mother country come home, and were a little taken aback by the sharpness of the bargaining. Nevertheless, agreements were reached, and in the 1930s Commonwealth trade increased rather more than world trade. Acceptance of the agreements, which were to run for five years in the first instance, forced the Free Traders in the Cabinet to recognize that the government was unchangeably Protectionist. In September the orthodox Liberals under Samuel left the government, accompanied by Snowden. Apart from the great central body of Conservatives, MacDonald was left with a tiny group of National Labour supporters, among whom J. H. Thomas was the only person of political importance, and a larger group of National Liberals who accepted Protectionism under the leadership of Sir John Simon.

The difficulties of MacDonald's position ought not to be exaggerated. His relationship with Baldwin was stable and satisfactory and, after the 1931 crisis, Baldwin could resist the critics inside his own party much more easily. Mac-Donald had become a socialist before it was regarded as synonymous with nationalization; when he thought about economic problems at all, he hoped for a gradual increase of state influence that would reconcile the two sides of industry. The interest in planning shown during the 1930s suited his ideas. The Import Duties Advisory Committee, which was set up to recommend tariff rates to the Treasury, was bound to carry out some of the tasks of planning the economy. In agriculture there was a Milk Marketing Board and a Bacon Marketing Board, there were import duties for fruit and vegetables, and there were subsidies for farmers growing corn. Coordinating agencies tried to lay down a policy for firms inside some industries which had benefited from tariffs. Iron and steel was the most obviously planned industry in the 1930s; hostile observers might even say that it had been turned into a cartel with the assistance of a tariff. In reality planning was mainly an attempt at orderly withdrawal from the ageing industries whose position, bad enough in the 1920s, was if anything worse in the 1930s. In the 1920s the government had ignored their position and had not helped their efforts to contract through rationalization, but in the 1930s it did provide some help for them. The industries that flourished and expanded in the 1930s were not planned, though the tariff certainly helped them to build up their position in the domestic market.

This policy was not too far from MacDonald's notion of socialism; and the National government's foreign policy and Indian policy were reasonably close to his own Gladstonian Liberalism. The government's Indian policy was more acceptable to the Labour Party than to the right wing of the Conservative Party. The Simon Report had said that a parliamentary government of the British type could not be set up at Delhi to rule India, partly because of its fear that the Hindu majority would not treat the Muslim minority fairly. It did not explicitly rule out the possibility of establishing an Indian government independent of the British Secretary of State for India, which was the essence of Dominion status, but it would, if accepted, have made constitutional development more complicated. The National government accepted the objective of Dominion status, but it faced difficulties inside the Conservative Party. Not until 1934 did it produce a White Paper on the Indian constitution, in which it suggested that the elected provincial governments should take over all remaining provincial affairs, and that ministerial responsibility for some central government affairs should also be given to elected representatives while the Viceroy kept others (particularly defence and foreign policy) in his own hands. The Indian government would then have reached roughly the position suggested for Canada by Lord Durham in his Report, which had assumed that foreign policy and a few other issues should be retained in the hands of the British government while the inhabitants of the country ran their domestic affairs. The Congress Party was determined that India should be as free to run its own foreign policy as the Dominions had been since 1918, and at times asked for independence and departure from the Commonwealth. Other Indians opposed the dominance of the Congress Party, but did not seriously oppose the idea of independence.

Churchill, Lord Wolmer, and Sir Henry Page-Croft fought the government's policy at debates in the National Union of Conservative Associations and in the Central Council of the Conservative Party in 1933 and 1934, and gained substantial support though not enough to make the government change its mind. In late 1934 the Government of India Bill came before Parliament and was again resisted by the Conservative right wing; it was also criticized by the Labour Party, for not going far enough. The right-wing opposition, though unsuccessful, made life harder for the government; it also convinced the Labour Party and the majority of the Conservative Party that Churchill was a dangerous reactionary. The Act itself worked as well as could be expected; the Congress Party won the Indian elections held under its provisions, and the only organized party that could make any headway against Congress was the Muslim League, which stood on an explicitly religious basis.[1] As independence became a possibility, mutual suspicion between Hindus and Muslims increased: the Indians said this was the result of a covert British policy of 'divide and rule', and the British said it was the unfortunate but natural result of the Indian realization that when they had power in their own hands they would have to work out a policy on religious issues. The leaders of Congress were tolerant in religious questions. Gandhi of course had strong religious convictions of his own and the Nehrus, father and son, did not, but all three of them believed that religious differences could be kept out of politics. On the other hand, their work in turning the Congress Party into a mass movement had brought in many people for whom religion was inextricably linked to politics. Congress used non-violence and civil disobedience to publicize its case, and these methods belonged to the Hindu tradition rather than the Muslim. The great evangelists of the Congress Party came from a Hindu background. Inevitably, the mass membership of Congress was

---

1. In the jargon of constitution-makers, 'communal' was used as a euphemism for 'religious', as in 'communal rioting'.

overwhelmingly Hindu. The Muslims made it clear that they expected the British to protect them and British officials tended to be pro-Muslim, because of a feeling that the Muslims were closer in spirit to the British: non-violence was not a part of the tradition of the Muslims or of the rulers of India. They thought Muslims deserved support because their demands for independence were less strident, and because the minority's wish for protection seemed reasonable. Congress regarded this pro-Muslim attitude as the most obvious aspect of the policy of 'divide and rule'.

Congress gained majorities in several provinces in the 1937 elections and took office after some debate. It did not take any part in running the central government in Delhi in case this should impede its agitation for independence. Most of the provincial governments worked well, and this may have shown some pessimists in Britain that Indians were not as incapable of looking after their own affairs as had been thought. But the creation of Indian provincial governments at a time when there was continued British rule at the centre did not make it easier for Indians to see their country as a unity in which all interests had to be looked after.

During the struggle over the Government of India Bill the National government could present itself as a middle-of-the-road body fighting off wild men to the left and right. The Labour Party moved somewhat to the left in the early 1930s. It adopted policy statements that committed it to wide measures of nationalization; the Labour government of 1945, which had very deep roots in the 1930s, carried out most of these commitments. The habit of quarrelling with the left wing continued to be noticeable in the party. Most of the argument in the 1920s had been over the issue of keeping the Communist Party out, but there had also been a good deal of discussion of the position of the ILP. In the months just after the fall of the Labour government the ILP was expelled from the Labour Party, and after this step, which involved a considerable amount of distress in the party, it was ready to discipline other sections of its non-Communist left wing. Organizations like the Socialist League were discouraged, and the party leaders did not always remember that, if they were going to cut off the flow of ideas from dissidents, they would have to do some thinking for themselves. The idea of nationalization was a legacy from the ILP and Lansbury, who became party leader because he was the only Cabinet minister to survive the 1931 election, was a man of the left.

The deep gloom of the economy was bound to drive opinion to the left. Unemployment in the 1920s, running above 1,100,000, had been bad enough; in the 1930s unemployment never fell below 1,400,000, and usually was distinctly higher. Areas that relied on cotton did badly, and areas that relied on coal or shipbuilding did worse: in some towns dependent on these trades the unemployment rate went up to over 60 per cent of the working population.[2]

2. Jarrow 67.8 per cent; Merthyr Tydfil 61.9 per cent (C. L. Mowat, *Britain between the Wars* (1956), 465).

These industries produced for export, and tariffs on imports did nothing to help them. Other countries were increasing their tariffs in order to keep out imports, which reduced the advantages British exporters could gain from the devaluation of the pound, and several countries devalued in order to remain competitive with British products. The World Economic Conference, held in London in 1933, came to no conclusions, but it did illustrate the diversity of answers offered to the problems of the slump. The cooperation of the United States was essential if world problems were to be solved, and President Franklin Roosevelt had told MacDonald beforehand that he believed price levels ought to be pushed upwards. At the conference people spoke of the need for stability; Roosevelt decided that the United States had to solve its domestic problems first and that it could do this better if it withdrew from any active part in the conference. The politicians at the conference were not sorry to be able to blame Roosevelt for their failure, but even if the United States had undertaken to accept whatever solution was reached by the other countries, they could not have agreed among themselves on a policy apart from repudiating their debts to the United States, which they did in any case. The American departure from a fixed value for gold for some months in 1933, and an eventual stabilization at $35 to the ounce instead of $20, meant that the dollar sank to roughly the 1925 (or pre-1914) parity with the pound, and the Exchange Equalization Board tried to maintain this level. This did not wipe out all the benefits of making the pound independent of gold; the British government no longer had to worry about defending any specific value for the pound and, as the franc remained at its previous level, France suffered all the disadvantages of an overvalued currency.

In the 1920s Britain was almost the only country to suffer a prolonged depression, and its problems were fairly directly linked to the high exchange rate and high interest rates. In the 1930s British financial policy was much more sensible, though the economy could not prosper when world trade was collapsing. All the Free Trade arguments made much less sense in conditions of high unemployment. The balance of payments became less satisfactory, partly because the terms of trade moved in Britain's favour, making exports even harder to sell and imports even more attractive to buy, and partly because the foreign interest and dividends that provided invisible exports were not being paid.

While the export industries did so badly, industries that produced for the home market were more prosperous than in the 1920s. The largest contribution to a revival of investment was made by house-building:[3] Private contractors could finance their operations more easily because of the low interest rates. In England they were building for owner-occupiers rather than for landlords to let, and cheap money, combined with the readiness of building

3. Reasons for the building boom are discussed in M. Bowley, *Housing and the State, 1919–1944* (1945), 81–2.

societies to lend for longer repayment periods than before, made it easier for people to buy the houses once they had been built. In Scotland most house-building was undertaken by municipal councils for rent, but this was also easier when loans were inexpensive. The central government withdrew from most of the housing market and concentrated on slum clearance. Builders who ran thin fingers of 'ribbon development' out into the countryside pro-voked criticism, but the new houses were in many ways much better than anything previously available for anybody below the upper-middle class. They were built in such numbers that by the end of the 1930s there were almost as many houses as there were people looking for houses. Housing needs had not all been met: areas of declining population had empty houses and areas of growing population suffered from shortages; there were still slums; and economic insecurity may have made people cautious about spending money on housing. But the supply of houses was more adequate than before or for twenty-five years to come.

	Housing (£m.)	Manufacturing, gas, water, and electricity (£m.)	All other investment (all sectors declined) (£m.)	Total (£m.)	Consumption (£m.)
1930	122	120	195	435	4,206
1934	188	134	145	467	4,482[a]

Source: [a]This table is extracted from a table in H. W. Richardson, *Economic Recovery in Britain, 1932–39* (1967), 126. Non-housing investment did not do much more than cover depreciation.

At the same time new industries were beginning to flourish, making motor cars, radios, chemicals, synthetic fabrics, and electrical appliances such as vacuum cleaners. Most of the new development took place in the south of England. For about two hundred years the country had been sharply divided into a relatively hilly section in the north and west that was industrialized, and a reasonably flat section in the south and east that looked like a garden suburb supplied with money from the industrialized area and from foreign invest-ment. In the 1920s and 1930s the south and east section began to develop new industries of its own. Electric power, which became readily available in the years after the setting-up of the national grid, freed industry from its depend-ence on coalfields, and as the new industries were making comparatively light products they did not have to be near the iron-smelting plants.

This deprived the depressed areas of one way of escape from their plight. The government would have liked new industries to establish themselves in places where they could provide jobs for the unemployed of the depressed areas, but it was not willing to offer any large subsidies and obviously could not take the risk of discouraging new factories that opened in areas of lower unemployment. The new industrialists could get workers wherever they set up their factories, and were not attracted to the depressed north and west. Coventry, Oxford, Slough, and London were closer to the markets in which they hoped to sell their products, and were less encumbered by declining industries. The prosperity of the Midlands and south-east was a relative matter; in 1937, the best year of the 1930s, its unemployment figure of 7 per cent of the working population compared very well with 15 per cent in the rest of the country, but was too high to encourage a really large movement of people out of the depressed areas—even if they moved to more prosperous areas they ran the risk of being unable to find work. The expanding trades attracted workers, who came forward faster than the new industries could grow, so levels of unemployment in expanding trades were in many cases higher in 1937 than in 1929. Despite a perceptible movement of population from areas of high unemployment to areas of relatively low unemployment, a dominant feature in the industrial scene was still the unemployed army of over a million people in the old and decaying industrial areas. Scotland, Wales, Lancashire, and the north-east of England were weighed down by the old industries that had done so well in the early stages of industrialization, and now needed new industries. The government produced schemes for helping people to become smallholders, and private organizations tried to provide adult education for some of the unemployed, but activities like this had an effect on only a few thousand of the men out of work. The long-term results of unemployment were overdramatized; at the time people spoke as though men over 40 out of work would never get jobs again and had in any case been corroded by unemployment so that they would not be capable of returning to work if the opportunity arose. But when the war came they fitted back into the economy without noticeable difficulty.

British production recovered fairly quickly from the worst of the slump, and real wages improved. 'The figures for rate of growth of *per capita* income are not quite so favourable as those of late Victorian times, but they indicate that the slow progress at the beginning of the twentieth century was again being surpassed.'[4] Some of this improvement must be due to the change in the age structure of the population, which at the same time made it harder to generate enough new jobs to prevent mass unemployment: 'between 1921 and 1938 the labour force increased from 45.3 per cent to 47.3 per cent of the population, and the number of persons in work from 41.3 per cent to 43.4 per cent'. Over a longer period it could be said: 'Between 1891 and 1947 the number of people aged 15–64 per consumer has risen from 0.60 to 0.68. Thus if we still had the 19th century age distribution the national income per head would be . . . about one-eighth lower than it actually is.'[5]

4. W. Ashworth, *Economic History of England, 1870–1939* (1960), 415.

5. Ibid. 417; 1949 Royal Commission on Population, quoted in S. Pollard, *Development of the British Economy 1914–50* (1962), 291.

Aggregate demand in the economy was too weak to enable all of these people to find work; people did not starve in the 1930s—a family on unemployment benefit in the 1930s was about as well off as a family before the First World War where the father was in normal work—but a great opportunity was lost. The human resources represented by these additional men and women of working age were wasted.

The failure of the National government to end unemployment did not reduce its popularity much. The great demonstrations in which unemployed workers marched to London to try to convince Parliament of the sufferings of South Wales or of Jarrow had relatively little effect. The government appeared resigned to high unemployment and to the decline of the traditional industries; its choice of tariffs and easy money as the way to fight the slump helped exporting industries less than the home market. Coal-mining and shipbuilding constituencies were likely to vote Labour in any case, and to some extent this was true of all the areas affected by the outburst of feeling over unemployment benefit early in 1935.

Chamberlain as Chancellor of the Exchequer followed a reasonably orthodox policy of administrative reform. The bank rate, which had been raised to 6 per cent when people imagined that cutting the link with gold would cause inflation, was brought down to 2 per cent. Apart from the general economic benefits of this step it helped to make it possible to convert £2,000 million of War Loan from an interest rate of 5 per cent to one of 3.5 per cent. In 1934 he put through Parliament an Unemployment Insurance Act that gave the central government ultimate responsibility for looking after the unemployed through a centrally financed Unemployment Assistance Board. This was a further and almost a final step towards 'breaking up' the Poor Law and taking welfare services out of the hands of local authorities. The old system could not survive the pressure of unemployment; towns impoverished by high unemployment were pushed down further by the burden of the local taxes needed for poor relief. At the same time the insurance provisions of the Act rested on the assumption that 15 per cent of the working population would be out of work, which shows the despair with which the government faced the unemployment figures.

The Act had important long-term administrative implications, but the explosive part lay in its regulations for deciding how to provide relief. Workers who had used up all the unemployment benefit due under the insurance scheme had to apply for additional benefit and were then required to undergo a means test to make sure that they did not have savings or other resources to draw on instead of receiving public assistance. However it was applied, the inquisition into personal resources was likely to discourage thrift. As it was applied to the whole family, by testing the means of the entire household, it tended to break the family up. The earnings of sons and daughters living at home were included in the total resources and the assistance given was restricted accordingly, which encouraged young men and women earning wages to move away from home. On the whole the Conservatives were the party most ready to praise the nineteenth-century virtues of thrift and home life, but their policies operated rather differently.

The new Insurance Act altered the basis of the means test and made it uniform for the whole country. In many places the financial position of the unemployed was improved; in many others it became worse. There were demonstrations in Glasgow, Sheffield, South Wales, and elsewhere, and there was an angry debate in the House of Commons at the end of January. The government had believed that a great many Public Assistance Committees were giving unemployment benefit on a more generous scale than it intended. The swift reaction when the new Board tried to apply its uniform nationwide scale showed how hard it would be to reduce benefits. The unemployed had not agitated in great numbers for the right to work; they did believe they had a right to the existing levels of benefit. The government gave way and withdrew the provisions making benefit uniform for the whole country. Benefit was improved in areas where it had been low, but was not reduced anywhere at this time. The issue then died away quickly and seems to have had little effect on the general election later in the year.

Two incidental factors helped to keep the number of the unemployed high. The failure to raise the age at which children could leave school, which was constantly discussed and constantly deferred, meant that employers could take on a steady stream of cheap workers when they left school at 14 and dismiss them when they began to ask for adult wages. School leavers were blamed for going into 'dead-end jobs' but, considering the state of the labour market, it was hard to expect them or the employers to act any differently. At the same time one outlet for surplus population was drying up. For over a hundred years people had been emigrating to the rest of the English-speaking world. This movement of population was considered normal and even desirable. In the 1930s the flow was reversed: emigrants no longer went out, and recent emigrants came back, because employment was even harder to find in other English-speaking countries. Later in the 1930s the population increased because of the troubled state of Europe. Many people, mostly though not exclusively Jewish, moved to Britain to escape from the spread of Nazism. The drop in emigration meant that more people of working age stayed in the country. Immigration from Europe undoubtedly improved the quality of British scientific and intellectual life, but it also led to some tenseness about the position of Jews in Britain. A large number of people held a view concisely and honestly stated by Harold Nicolson, 'Although I loathe anti-semitism, I do dislike Jews', which meant that persecuting Jews and depriving them of their rights was detestable, but that Jews were not socially welcome.[6] This

6. H. Nicolson, *Diaries* (1967), ii. 469.

feeling in the 1930s seemed to follow the general pattern that increased immigration into Britain leads to increased hostility to newcomers.

With a relatively slight amount of help from the recent immigrants, British scientists achieved a great deal in the 1930s. The Cavendish laboratory at Cambridge was one of the world's great centres for inquiry into subatomic physics, and in 1932, the laboratory's greatest year, Chadwick established some of the properties of the neutron, and Cockcroft and Walton disintegrated atoms by bombarding them with protons: in this way they reduced lithium to helium. The British discoveries in the 1930s seem, if measured by the number of Nobel prizes awarded, to have been less impressive than British advances in chemistry in the 1950s and 1960s, but they happened to lie in an area which came, rapidly and spectacularly, to be of vital importance. The phrase 'splitting the atom' had been used at least since the public excitement over Einstein's Theory of Relativity. Rutherford decided that he might have been mistaken in his public statement in the early 1920s that the atom could not be split in a way that would be useful for military purposes; he told Hankey, the Secretary to the Cabinet, that an atomic bomb might be possible. The old ideal of supranational science, in which knowledge was open to all, was dying away and he did not make public his change of mind. By the outbreak of war all the scientific work that underlay the manufacture of the atomic bomb had been carried out. Considering how little support was given to scientific research, money would probably not have provided for the technological work needed for further development, peaceful or warlike, if the war had not come.

Foreign policy under MacDonald and Baldwin

The National government was confronted with problems of foreign policy almost as soon as it was formed. While it was going through the crisis about gold, Japan was launching an invasion of Manchuria, often seen as the first step in the destruction of the League of Nations. In Britain the most fully committed supporters of the League of Nations were people who believed that foreign policy should rest on principles of morality, and they talked as though conditions in China were as peaceful as in Europe and as though the Japanese invasion was as aggressive and unprovoked as a German invasion of Poland would have been. But Manchuria was not a quiet and settled area; when the Japanese invaded it, they were only moving into a troublesome border region like so many imperialists ever since the Romans. The Lytton Commission set up by the League of Nations reported that the Japanese had been badly treated in Manchuria but that they did not have a legal right to take the territory over. The British Foreign Secretary, Sir John Simon, probably leaned too far towards believing that the Japanese were ambassadors of progress, but Britain was not strong enough in the Far East to oppose Japan, and no other country in the League could do much about it. The United States was not willing to recognize that Japan had acquired Manchuria, and to ignore the puppet government of Manchukuo, but this was not an adequate basis for a policy in the Far East. Throughout the 1930s the British government tried to look after British interests, and protect British traders there, with forces that were too weak. In ports like Shanghai the Japanese had the advantage of possessing a powerful force on the spot, and they were determined to use that advantage to squeeze out British commercial interests.

Britain's inability to intervene over Manchuria could be taken as a sign that she had disarmed too much, and the rule that the armed forces should not budget for a war within the next ten years was relaxed. But as the long-awaited Disarmament Conference was beginning, 1932 was no time to rearm. There had not been enough preparation for the conference, but by the normal standards of such meetings it began quite harmoniously. As was to be expected, the countries at the conference began by putting forward schemes that would enable them to keep all their own weapons while their neighbours disarmed—thus Britain, fearful of aerial attack because so large a proportion of her population lived in one large city, put forward proposals for aerial disarmament but asked to keep some aeroplanes to bomb rebellious tribesmen on the boundaries of empire. If countries had taken more time to discuss each other's proposals, they might have found areas for compromise, but because they had not had much experience of disarmament negotiations, they too often took proposals at face value instead of trying to whittle them down to reasonable dimensions. In any case the situation inside Germany was deteriorating while the conference sat. Economic disintegration and the breakdown of law and order because of fierce party clashes were leading to a crisis which was resolved early in 1933 when the Nazi leader Adolf Hitler became Chancellor on a nationalist programme that included the destruction of the Versailles treaties. Patient negotiation became impossible; Hitler was even more determined to gain military equality for Germany than his predecessors, and as France and its east European allies resisted his demands, Germany withdrew from the conference in October. By this stage the warnings of the pessimists were beginning to be justified; governments were on the point of rearming if they could not reach an agreement on disarmament, and the breakdown of the conference made rearmament very hard to avoid.

There had been considerable effort in Britain to arouse support for disarmament; Baldwin, the second-in-command of the government, had said in November 1932 that if attempts at disarmament failed it would be because young men were too enthusiastic about retaining aeroplanes, and that they should not blame the old men if the policy of disarmament was not successful. The young men at Oxford accepted this view: they were not certain whether the cause of peace should be defended by pure pacifism or by adherence to the League of Nations, but supporters of these two approaches voted together in

February 1933 to pass a resolution at the Oxford Union (the university debating society) that 'this House would not fight for King and Country'. There was probably a considerable amount of pacifist feeling behind this vote, for opposition to all war was still strong. But in the next few years this feeling turned into support for the League of Nations.

When the Beaverbrook and Rothermere newspapers began arguing that public opinion had no use for the League of Nations, a great survey of opinion was organized by the League of Nations Union, a non-party group which contained a large number of Liberals, many people from the right wing and centre of the Labour Party, and some pro-League Conservatives like Lord Robert Cecil. Just over 11 million sets of answers were collected: responses to the first four questions in the survey showed that opinion was overwhelmingly in favour of the League and of disarmament. Question 5 asked 'Do you consider that, if one nation insists on attacking another, the other nations should combine to compel it to stop by (a) economic and non-military measures (b) if necessary, military measures?' About 10 million people voted in favour of economic sanctions; 6,784,368 people voted in favour of combined military measures to restrain an aggressor, and 2,351,981 voted against. Historians have argued what the answer to question 5b proved; on the whole people anxious to justify the policy of the British government have written as though the minority opposed to military sanctions was too large to be ignored, and people anxious to condemn the policy of the British government have pointed out that over 70 per cent of the people answering were in favour of military sanctions. The problem is insoluble, because nobody knows in what spirit the minority voted against sanctions; a very small group recorded that they were Christian pacifists, but perhaps most of the minority were people who were ready to fight when Britain's interests were involved. The government showed during the crisis over Abyssinia (present-day Ethiopia), later in 1935, that it was ready for economic sanctions but would not fight for the League unless it thought British interests were directly involved.

In June 1935 MacDonald retired from the premiership, in which he was becoming more and more a figurehead, and was succeeded by Baldwin, and Sir Samuel Hoare replaced Simon at the Foreign Office. The rearranged government seemed to have a choice between two foreign policies. In April 1935 British, French, and Italian leaders had met at Stresa and agreed on a policy of resisting German expansionism in the way Mussolini had forced Hitler to draw back from his attempt to absorb Austria into Germany in 1934. The other approach was to rely on the League of Nations and use it as an alliance that would crush any attempt to use force to change the existing political situation. The two policies were not reconcilable because Mussolini made it clear that his price for acting as a stabilizing force in Europe was that he should be allowed to take over Abyssinia. Public opinion, as shown by the survey by the League of Nations Union, supported the

League; in September Hoare made a speech at Geneva, which was well received in Britain, in which he committed the country to support collective action by the League. This did not mean that the country was ready to act as a solitary policeman on behalf of the League, but it did mean that it had abandoned the Stresa Front policy of cooperation between France, Italy, and Britain.

When Italy did invade Abyssinia the immediate effect on British politics was to disrupt the Labour Party. The government, with the support of most of the Labour Party, imposed economic sanctions against the aggressor by placing partial restrictions on Italian trade. George Lansbury, the leader of the Labour Party, disapproved of this policy because it could easily lead to war and he believed all wars to be wrong. He tried, perhaps with insufficient determination, to resign but his followers would not let him go. Lansbury was one of the kindest men in politics and had led his small band of supporters in the House of Commons with considerable skill and great determination; the party's attachment to him was no more than his due. But at the 1935 Labour Party conference Bevin set out to make sure that a resolution was passed in favour of sanctions and also that it was passed in circumstances which made it clear that Lansbury had got to go. Bevin possessed the talents and the inclination for this work of destruction and humiliation but, stripped of insults, Lansbury had to be told that 'It is placing the movement in an absolutely false position, to be taking your conscience round from body to body asking what you ought to do with it.'[7]

Lansbury was replaced as leader by Attlee, a quiet and modest man who, along with some less obvious talents, possessed the qualification of being the antithesis of MacDonald. He was the first of the men who had fought in the First World War—apart from Churchill, who had spent a few months in the front line—to achieve a leading position in politics; young men like Eden and Duff Cooper were making their way forward on the Conservative side, but the men who gained power when Lloyd George fell in 1922 still led the party. It was not certain that Attlee would remain leader of his party after the election; his position and Baldwin's unassertive manner meant that party leaders dominated the scene less when Parliament was dissolved in 1935 than in any other post-1832 election. The National government was never in any serious political danger. It still held most of the votes that used to go to the Liberals; as the Labour Party's share of the total vote continued to fluctuate between 30 per cent and 37 per cent, only a strong Liberal challenge could draw off enough votes to endanger the Conservative position. At the time people did not realize the stability of the Labour vote that was so marked a feature of elections between the wars. Governments and politicians expected

7. Bevin may have said 'trailing' or 'hawking' your conscience (A. Bullock, *Life of Ernest Bevin* (1960), i. 568).

swift reversals of fortune, and the one-sided 1931 election result made them more apprehensive than usual.

This mood of uneasiness had a considerable effect on foreign policy and rearmament. The Labour Party clearly intended to benefit from pro-League feeling; the government, by steps like Hoare's speech at Geneva, had made sure that it could not be outflanked. An election in which both sides concentrated on claiming to be heartily in favour of the League was not likely to clarify policy much. The Labour Party put forward its proposals for nationalization in more detail than before, but they did not attract much attention; the high unemployment of the past four years did not arouse much enthusiasm for the government. The Labour Party gained a slightly larger proportion of the popular vote than in 1929, its best previous performance, but the Conservatives held on to enough of the Liberals who had joined them in 1931 to secure a large majority. The Liberal Party faded further from sight in a world in which everybody professed Gladstonian principles in foreign policy and nobody wanted Free Trade. Lloyd George formed Councils of Action, which urged candidates to support Keynesian economics and the League, but there is no sign that the Councils had more effect than any other pressure group at election time.

	Votes	Seats	% of all votes cast
Conservative	11,810,158	432	53.7
Liberal	1,422,116	20	6.4
Labour	8,325,491	154	37.9

After the election Hoare went to Switzerland for a holiday. On the way he was ill advised enough to meet Laval, the French Prime Minister (and also Foreign Minister), in Paris and discuss a plan for ending the Abyssinian war by giving Italy a large slice of territory and compensating Abyssinia by giving her a small slice of Somaliland. This plan was hard to reconcile with a pro-League attitude but it made good sense to the French, who wanted to get back to the policy of the Stresa Front. The proposal leaked out in Paris before the details had been completely arranged; the House of Commons and the public were furious when they learned what had been planned. Hoare continued to think that it offered the best way out of the Abyssinian problem, and for a short time the government agreed. But as the storm grew it became clear that Hoare could not be supported, and his resignation was accepted. In the debate on the proposal Attlee, who had been re-elected as leader, said that Baldwin had been acting dishonourably during the election when he declared his support for the League. The dissident Conservatives decided that this was going too far and gave up any idea of voting against the government.

Sanctions were maintained for a time, not entirely without hope of success; Italy might not have been able to go on if the Abyssinian war had stretched into a second campaign. The League did not prevent oil from going through the Suez Canal to the Italian armies because the British government was afraid Mussolini would be driven to war by such a step and the Admiralty was not confident that it could hold the Mediterranean against him. As supplies were unimpeded, Italy went quickly forward to a brutal victory, and the British government had to disentangle itself from the policy of sanctions. The failure of collective action had undermined faith in the League, and it was hard to find any other British foreign policy which could command united support in the country. The result of the Peace Ballot suggested that a policy based on the national interest, which would appeal to people on the right who were not ready to fight a League of Nations war, would have to be combined with support for the League to satisfy the large body of opinion that was ready to fight for the League. Abyssinia might have provided an opportunity for uniting the two strands of British opinion behind a firm policy; the next incidents in the deterioration of the international situation divided British opinion so sharply that a firm policy was not likely to be found.

The left had always thought that the Treaty of Versailles was too harsh, and in the 1930s the progressive wing of the Conservative Party had accepted this view. In 1935 an Anglo-German naval agreement released Germany from some of the restrictions of the treaty, and in particular allowed her to build as many submarines as Britain. In March 1936 Hitler removed another of Germany's grievances in the simplest possible way; his armies marched into the Rhineland, which had been demilitarized by the treaty. France was alarmed but would not do anything without British support. British opinion believed that keeping the Rhineland demilitarized was a futile and unjustified interference with German sovereignty. Perhaps this was reasonable, but the fact that he was able to take this step unilaterally was bound to encourage Hitler to break other, more defensible parts of the treaty. The British attitude also reduced French faith in the effectiveness of the entente.

In July a revolt broke out in Spain. Most of the army mutinied against the recently elected government. To enlist outside support propagandists called the army Fascist and called the government Communist; but the civil war was less a struggle between Fascists and Communists, and much more a struggle between clericals and anticlericals, than people outside Spain realized. The Communists were not members of the government, and the Spanish Fascists were only a small part of the coalition gathered together behind General Franco. The rule of international law was that helping the established government was legal and helping the rebels was illegal, but both the British and the French governments knew that it would cause them trouble at home if they accepted this wholeheartedly. They proposed a policy of non-intervention, which meant that no country would help either side in the struggle. Holding Germany and Italy back from helping the rebels had its attractions, and the French Socialist Prime Minister, Léon Blum, was able to persuade the Labour Party to approve of non-intervention on this ground. Germany and Italy signed the Non-Intervention Agreement but soon showed they were not going to be restrained by it. When they saw that Franco was not going to sweep through to an easy victory, they began to organize volunteers to assist him and sent supplies and weapons to help him. By the time of its 1936 annual conference the Labour Party was already beginning to regret its acceptance of non-intervention, and it asked the government to increase pressure on Germany and Italy to keep the agreement.

Life in the late 1930s

The government had problems at home to worry it. Its control over the House of Commons was not secure because many of its backbenchers distrusted it. The Chief Whip, Captain Margesson, has been blamed for taking an authoritarian approach, but he was no harsher than other Whips. The unusual thing was not that Margesson tried to keep the party in order but that the party was so determined not to be kept in order. In April the government lost a division in the Commons and in the summer there were rumours that Baldwin was going to retire. His position became even weaker when he told the House, during a debate on rearmament in November, that the government had been convinced of the need for rearmament ever since 1933 but that since it saw no prospect of winning an election on rearmament at that time it had waited until 1935. This announcement was received with what the *Annual Register* called 'raised eyebrows' and it has continued to be regarded as controversial ever since.[8]

Some critics spoke as though Baldwin had said he could not win an election on rearmament in 1935 and as a result had kept the issue out of the campaign. This misunderstanding was reasonable enough, because rearmament had not been discussed much in 1935 and the election had not been used as an opportunity to warn people why it was necessary. But all that Baldwin said to the Commons was that an election on rearmament in 1933 would have led to a Conservative defeat, which he quite reasonably felt would have done nothing to help rearmament. For a man with a mandate—and a mandate that he had acquired two years later than he thought it was needed—Baldwin did not move very quickly towards rearmament, perhaps because he was exhausted by a long term of office, and because he was not certain whether he really had a mandate at all. It has been suggested that one reason for the slowness of rearmament in the 1930s was fear of the Labour and Liberal opposition; the government would not have been worried by this opposition if it had really

---

8. *The Annual Register of World Events for 1936*, 93.

believed that it had put the case for rearmament to the voters and convinced them in 1935.

Baldwin redeemed his personal position a few weeks later. George V died early in 1936; his Victorian virtues, his desire to do his best, and his anxiety that everybody should have fair play had represented one aspect of life in the first third of the century very well. His son Edward VIII did not possess the conscientiousness, the stamina, and the willingness to endure boredom that are so necessary for a constitutional monarch. In any case he was in love with Wallis Simpson, who was American and was married. She could get a divorce easily enough, but marriage to a divorced American woman was a serious matter for a British monarch. The situation was known all over the United States, and in London society; the newspapers thought it best that the public should not learn about this distressing problem. So it was for many people a complete surprise to learn that Edward and his ministers were discussing what should happen to the King. The issue came into the open on 3 December; a little support for the King appeared, but when Members of Parliament went and talked to their constituents they thought better of it. Neither Baldwin nor any other conceivable Prime Minister would serve under Edward if he married Mrs Simpson after she had obtained her divorce, and Edward had no intention of parting from her.

On 10 December Baldwin presented Edward's abdication to the House of Commons and gave his account of the way he had tried to persuade the King not to follow this course. Everyone agreed that Baldwin had behaved very well; the Church, the Dominions, and the Opposition all supported him, and the King's few supporters in public life, such as Mosley, Beaverbrook, and Churchill, were regarded as irresponsible. This was unimportant in the case of Mosley and Beaverbrook, but the position of Churchill was more important. Once the Government of India Act had been passed, there was no obvious reason why he should not be taken into the government, but there were still doubts about his reliability. He had been rebuilding his position in 1936; at one moment it had looked as though he might slip into support for Franco in Spain, but by November he had come to believe that a victory for the allies of Italy and Germany would harm British interests and should be resisted. In the organization Arms and the Covenant in late 1936 he worked with members of the Liberal and Labour Parties, putting the argument that the Covenant of the League of Nations must be supported by force. This did not appeal to the government, and it may not have been sorry that Churchill's attitude over Edward VIII's abdication reduced his political authority.

On Abyssinia and on the Rhineland people had at least been able to agree that aggressive unilateral action had been wrong, though they could not agree whether Britain ought to do anything to stop it. Over the Spanish Civil War a division of opinion in Britain matched the division in Spain: most Conservatives thought Franco was doing a useful job; some Conservatives and almost all the Liberal Party and Labour Party were convinced that the Spanish Republic had become the first line of defence for democracy. The policy of non-intervention enabled the government to stand between the two opinions, and probably most people who were not interested in politics would not have been willing to see the country take part on one side or the other. Those who were interested in politics found that the Civil War was the moment of choice for the decade, and also that 'the 1930s saw the last of the idea that the individual, accepting his responsibilities, could alter the history of the time. From now on, the individual could only conform to or protest against events which were outside his control.'[9] Spender may have overestimated the number of fortunate individuals who could affect the course of history, but certainly many people felt it was their duty to go out to Spain and fight. The left, organized in the International Brigade, attracted many more recruits from Britain than the right. On the whole the people who went to fight on the side of the Spanish government were committed to a Marxist point of view, though this did not necessarily mean that they were members of the Communist Party. The war reduced the appeal of pacifism; as Fenner Brockway asked: 'How could I regard myself as a pacifist when I desired so passionately that the workers should win the civil war?'[10] Another effect was to provide a well-defined cause for a number of writers of the period who accepted the desirability of political commitment.

Most of the authors who emerged between 1910 and 1930 were not interested in politics and tended either to support traditional values or to be opposed to the zeal for rationality found among writers at the beginning of the century. Most of those who appeared in the 1930s were affected by the slump and the rise of Fascism and Nazism; they were interested in politics and accepted a socialist point of view. A political framework of thought need not have done them any harm, but men like Spender and Auden were temperamentally better suited for an anarchist approach to socialism than for the Marxism that they adopted. Orwell, who spent more time fighting in Spain than most of the writers, decided that he preferred the Spanish anarchists to Communists. His contemporaries might have benefited if they had taken a little longer sampling the diversity of left-wing opinions available in Spain; all that they really knew was that the Labour Party was not wholeheartedly committed in the way they wanted. Early in 1937 the question arose of a United Front, to combine the Communist Party, the Labour Party, and the ILP. Sir Stafford Cripps and his supporters in the Socialist League were warned that if they continued to act as a pressure group for a United Front they would be expelled from the Labour Party. This was probably sensible for a party which had to appeal to an electorate which was not very interested in Spain, but it

9. S. Spender, *World within World* (1951), 290. He went on to mention 'specifically, the cause of Spanish democracy'.
10. F. Brockway, *Inside the Left* (1942), 338.

helps to explain why writers who were enthusiastic about politics felt that the Communist Party was the genuine party of the left. Writers like this, and their readers, found Victor Gollancz's Left Book Club, with a socialist book to read every month, ideally suited to their intellectual needs.

By 1937 the pace of rearmament had become fast enough to affect national finance. Chamberlain had been doubtful that the country could afford a large armament programme, but as the government had committed itself to a £1,500 million programme, the money had to be found. His proposal for a £400 million defence loan was criticized on the grounds that defence spending in peacetime had always been met out of taxation. He replied that this defence spending was a long-term investment to make up the omissions of the past and to provide for the safety of the next generation. He also imposed a tax on increased profits, arguing that firms had done a good deal better in the last few years because of government spending; he proposed that they should be taxed on the amount that their profits had gone up from the 1933–5 level. Businessmen argued that this would penalize the active firms which were making a contribution to the economy and would favour firms that were doing less. Chamberlain gave way, and substituted a direct tax on all profits.

The Labour Party reconsidered its position on defence, and decided to stop voting against the financial Estimates that allowed the government to undertake a rearmament programme. Previously it had thought that its disapproval of the government's foreign policy meant it should not vote for the defence expenditure that followed from it. The Labour Party was no happier about foreign policy in 1937 but it acknowledged that a vote against the Estimates looked like opposition to all defence preparations, which would worry the electorate and encourage Germany and Italy.

In May 1937 Baldwin retired. Perhaps he was the most successful of all the politicians of the century in achieving the objectives he had set himself: the standard of personal integrity in politics had been maintained; the Labour Party had been absorbed into the general framework of politics and the danger of class war had been warded off; the possibility that politics would be dominated by men of talent concerned with getting things done rather than men of rigid principle had been averted, so that Churchill, Lloyd George, Beaverbrook, and Birkenhead had been kept out of power. Probably he overestimated the dangers from unprincipled men and from class war—he behaved as if he thought any sudden change must be bad and should be resisted. When he made mistakes it was out of a desire to keep in step with most of the people of the country. Low, the famous left-wing cartoonist of Beaverbrook's *Evening Standard*, drew a picture of Baldwin springing his rearmament policy on an unprepared population and saying 'If I hadn't promised not to lead you here, you wouldn't have come.'[11] But rearmament

11. David Low, *The Years of Wrath* (1949), 40; originally pub. 14 Nov. 1936.

was not proceeding at unexpected speed when he retired, and subsequent criticism has always suggested that Baldwin's mistakes were the result of too little rather than too much activity.

Most people had become decidedly better off during the fifteen years since he first took office as Prime Minister, though it would be hard to show that his policies had done much to bring this about, and at the time commentators found it hard to discover that improvements had taken place. Social surveys showed that there was still a good deal of poverty in Britain in the 1930s. Seebohm Rowntree went back to York and repeated an investigation of living standards and the poverty line that he had first carried out in 1899. By the standards used in the first survey he found that just under 4 per cent of the population fell into the lowest category, which had included just under 10 per cent of the population in 1899. About 17.5 per cent of the population fell below the line if a new definition of poverty was adopted, to allow for the fact that standards in general had improved. The reasons for falling into poverty were not surprising: unemployment, old age, bad health, and large families brought up on low wages. The results of poverty were studied, about the same time, by Boyd Orr. His *Food, Health and Income* (1936) showed that at least half the population was ill fed, and this half included more than half the nation's children. Some of this malnutrition was the result of ignorance, which led to deficiencies in minerals such as calcium. But the poorest 30 per cent of the population were suffering from a great many shortages, and even with the greatest care they would have found it almost impossible to afford a proper diet. These people were better off than the bottom 30 per cent at the beginning of the century; life at the bottom of Edwardian society was grimmer than people realized and it was only in the years between the wars that people began to know enough about the social structure of the country to be able to think about it as one united and interconnected nation.

A fair amount of the increased prosperity took the form of a wider distribution of things that had previously been available only to a small, comfortably prosperous class. The rich had in the past spent their money on quite different things from the rest of the community; there was no substantial diminution of inequality of incomes between the wars, but the rich bought the same things as everybody else, in larger quantities or in better quality. Seen from on top, this meant that some of the best things in life were disappearing. Subsidized and highly literate evening newspapers like the *Westminster Gazette* did not survive the 1920s. In the 1930s the total sales of newspapers increased, as the result of a fierce struggle for circulation between the *Express*, the *Mail*, and the *Herald*. The goal of the contest was to be able to offer advertisers a guaranteed circulation of 2 million; this did mean that more people saw newspapers than before, and while the quality of news and comment provided by the mass circulation press was not high, the years of the circulation war were also the years when *The Times*, following the tradition of Scott and Spender, was toning down or suppressing news from Germany in order to avoid embarrassing British foreign policy. The *Express* prophesied peace until the very eve of war, because Lord Beaverbrook believed that people ought to be kept happy, but it did print unedited accounts of what was happening in Germany under Hitler.

The *Express* stood apart from one of the changes in the newspaper business between the wars. Beaverbrook did not try to build up provincial chains of papers in the way that the Rothermere or Berry companies acquired local papers and ran them as parts of a newspaper empire. He dominated his three newspapers in London, though it was unreasonable for people to complain that he gave his editors too little freedom—he was the best editor available for the sort of papers he wanted to produce, and he knew it. He had no printing interests outside his newspapers. The *Herald*, on the other hand, was always being pushed forward by the printing interests of Odhams Press under J. S. Elias, which influenced its activity as much as the control that the TUC had over editorial policy. Pressure from Odhams intensified the circulation war and in particular encouraged the practice of giving premiums such as books by Dickens, travelling clocks, and insurance policies to new readers. This undoubtedly induced people to take newspapers who had not previously done so, though readers of this sort were not the informed students of public affairs who were understood to read the quality papers.

In 1936 an Act was passed which required children to stay at school until 15 after September 1939. The change was prevented by the war, but it was a part of the pattern of widened distribution. The same process could be seen in things like holidays and motor cars. Before 1914 and even into the 1920s, motor cars had been treated as though they were just the same as the carriages kept by prosperous people in the nineteenth century. But horse-drawn carriages would have led to traffic chaos much sooner than an equal number of motor cars. In the 1920s lorries replaced most of the horse-drawn vans, and at the same time challenged the place of railways in long-distance transport. The railway workers found that lorry drivers were rising into the aristocracy of labour; the railway companies found it hard to pay dividends. Private cars became less expensive, and were owned by a wider and wider section of the middle class. At least until the First World War the motor car was a rich man's toy; as the cheapest models cost as much in money terms before 1914 as in the 1960s, they were far beyond the means of the ordinary man and must have cost as much to keep up as a carriage. In 1915 there were 277,000 current car licences. The new, widely distributed cars made by Morris Motors and by the Ford Motor Company's British subsidiary after the war were fairly cheap; the 'baby Austin' was in no sense meant for the comfortable classes. By 1938 there were 2,400,000 current car licences.

The internal combustion engine provided for a few people the excitements of motor racing and of air racing; at the end of the 1920s Britain won the world air racing championship, the Schneider Trophy, three times running, and a good deal of public attention was paid to events like Amy Johnson's flight to Australia—the first solo flight over so long a distance by a woman. But these were special occasions, picked out by the newspapers because they provided headlines, rather than part of the everyday world of sport. The division of sporting interest remained much as it had been before 1914: the upper class killed animals, though no longer with Edwardian profusion, the middle class watched and played cricket and rugby football, and the working class watched association football all over the country and rugby football in Wales. Cricket and rugger were for amateurs; soccer had become a game for professionals in the last years of the old century, when the Saturday afternoon holiday had spread enough for a wide demand for entertainment to exist. Somewhat later a professional, speeded-up version of rugger, Rugby League, gained ground in the north of England.

One distinct change took place in the nation's betting habits after the war. Previously the great medium for gambling had been horse racing; it was a fairly popular sport in its own right, with an aristocratic class owning the horses and a working-class audience to watch the races. Apart from the Derby, the crowds were not large by comparison with football crowds but there was a much larger gambling interest, and thousands of men who never watched a race put their money on horses. This was legal for the upper classes, and usually illegal for the working class, because the law said that all betting must be on credit, except on the racecourse itself. It was taken for granted that the working class could not bet on credit, but there was notoriously a very large weekly turnover of cash betting through the hands of illegal bookmakers.

In the 1920s football pools rose quite quickly to become a major outlet for gambling. People paid for one week's bet when sending in a forecast for the next matches in the following week so this was betting on credit, which was legal, and acceptable to many people who did not bet on horses. The nature of the winnings was different; football pools offered people an admittedly very small chance of winning an amount of money that would transform their whole lives, which was never possible with the relatively short odds offered in horse racing—the Irish government made use of its freedom to set up a sweepstake with very large prizes, but football pools offered similar opportunities every week. Another attraction of the pools was that they were honest; horse racing was no longer nearly as crooked as it had been in the Victorian period, but betting was still a matter of inside information, whispers about what the stable boy had said, and the risk that a bookmaker would disappear if he lost too heavily. Footballers provided a more straightforward sort of betting; the success of the pools showed that the country was no longer divided as sharply into respectable people and unrespectable people as it had been at the beginning of the century.

Other divisions were narrowing at the same time. Before 1914 the middle class took it for granted that they went away for holidays, and people in the working class who were lucky enough to have holidays never went far from home. In the 1930s holidays by charabanc became popular, and naturally the people who had grown used to substantial holidays before 1914 looked down on them. In the mid-1930s holidays with pay became much more widespread. In April 1937, 4 million manual workers had at least one week of holiday with pay; by June 1939 the number had risen to 11 million. To some extent this was just another type of wage increase, but more people went away, mainly to the seaside, than before.

Before 1914 London had been a great city for public display, but it was display provided mainly by private people. After the war the great houses began to turn into hotels or company offices. The activities of the Bright Young Things were not an adequate substitute for pre-war displays like society weddings, but probably the post-war working class lived less dull lives and did not need the upper class to entertain them. The demolition and rebuilding of the period, which included assaults on the public taste like the destruction of the Quadrant of Regent Street, showed that private artistic taste would not satisfy London's needs any longer.

The enthusiasm for such small steps as Lansbury's opening of the Lido at the Serpentine showed how much people wanted public entertainment. As Minister of Transport between 1929 and 1931 Herbert Morrison introduced a Bill for nationalizing and coordinating the bus, tram, and underground electric train system in London; the scheme made such good sense that the National government took it up and passed it into law after August 1931. The London Passenger Transport Board managed to deal with London's traffic problems and at the same time its architecture and furnishing made the capital more attractive than before. Morrison lost his seat in the 1931 election, and devoted his attention to improving the London Labour Party; in 1934 it gained control of the London County Council and retained its position until after the LCC was turned into the Greater London Council in 1964. Labour's electoral success in London owed a good deal to the steady emigration of the middle class to Surrey and to 'Metroland'—the area of Middlesex and Hertfordshire served by the Metropolitan railway. The policy of the new administration was symbolized by the handsome new Waterloo Bridge that it built despite the government's refusal to help to pay for anything except a reconstruction of the old bridge.

Compared with the other municipal governments in the country the LCC was a distinguished patron of the arts, though the absence of crippling unemployment in London during the slump and also the pressure concentrating so much of the cultural life of the country in London made its work easier. The BBC had a centralizing effect, and the rapid expansion of cinemas in the 1920s drove theatres out of business in almost all towns outside London. This seemed to the prosperous classes another example of the way that standards were being driven down to the level of the lower-middle class though, as the English drama was slipping back from the level of Shaw and falling under the dominance of writers of the technical competence and triviality of Noel Coward and Frederick Lonsdale, perhaps the theatre was no longer a centre of intellectual and artistic activity. On the other hand, the films that did well were American; attempts to build a British industry by making cinemas show a quota of British films merely led to the production of 'quota quickies'. Well-made and relatively inexpensive documentary films were produced by John Grierson, but this approach did not really come to fruition until the development of television after the war. The magazine *Picture Post*, which flourished in the late 1930s, had a distinguished staff, but they were people who would have done at least as well on television. In 1936 the BBC did begin television broadcasts, though the audience was small and the programmes sometimes makeshift, but when war broke out they were brought to an end. The non-literary arts showed signs of promise for the future during the 1930s. Composers like Vaughan Williams made good use of medieval and folk music models, and there were the first signs of the emergence of Benjamin Britten. English sculptors like Henry Moore and Barbara Hepworth and painters such as Sutherland were laying the foundations of their fame in the 1930s.

The poets, with their concern about Spain and their fear that another general war was going to break out, best expressed public feeling about politics when Neville Chamberlain became Prime Minister. Of the men in politics who wanted to get things done, he was the only one who came up to the standard of integrity set by Baldwin. He was not an amiable man: Halifax, whom he made Foreign Secretary and in 1940 wanted to make Prime Minister, said: 'Chamberlain's great fault was that he sneered at people. He sneered at the Labour Members and they never forgave him.'[12] He did not come to power at a happy time. The recovery from the depression of the early 1930s was beginning to taper off. The economy was so sluggish, and had such difficulty finding jobs for the growing population of working age, that, even though demand was helped by rearmament, the proportion of the working population out of work was higher at the top of the 1937 trade cycle than at the unimpressive 1929 peak in the trade cycle. Chamberlain as Chancellor of the Exchequer had not done much to help. He had been the most powerful personality in the Cabinet since 1931; he was devoted to orthodox economics and (except in 1932) had kept his budgets balanced. This had not stimulated demand, but it had kept the confidence of businessmen relatively high. In the United States large and persistent budget deficits weakened business confidence; government spending by itself was not enough, though Chamberlain may have overestimated the British fear of budget deficits.

He would have preferred to concentrate on domestic problems as Prime

---

12. Nicolson, *Diaries*, iii. 260.

Minister. Even in quieter times he might not have found any way to deal with the rising unemployment and falling production of 1938, but the legislation of the period shows he was not inhibited by doctrinaire views about the virtues of laissez-faire. In 1938 a Coal Mines Act continued the cartelization of the industry begun by the 1930 Act; the Commissioners for the industry were given the power to compel collieries to amalgamate, and the government nationalized the coal royalties by buying out the landlords who owned the coal under the ground. The colliery owners, who undertook the work of digging it up, were no longer held back by arguments about the ownership of a seam at a particular point under ground, though the Labour Party insisted that nationalizing the entire industry would provide the same benefits and make it easier to amalgamate collieries. In 1939 the government bought out the two overseas airlines which it had been subsidizing for some time. Imperial Airways had to fly routes that linked the countries of the Empire, and it was very hard to do this profitably. British Airways flew a more manageable set of routes to Europe but, despite its subsidy, was not making a profit. Long-distance aeroplanes were intended to compete with ocean liners in comfort, and airlines expected that all their passengers would be rich, which was probably a reasonable assumption in the 1930s. After nationalization British Overseas Airways Corporation was set up to combine the two lines. The new organization did not have much freedom to change policy because by this time most of the resources of the aircraft industry were devoted to rearmament.

Reorganization of the army went ahead under the new government. Hore-Belisha, the Secretary of State for War, was a thoroughly modern-minded man. He made life more comfortable for private soldiers, he hastened the leisurely pace of the conversion from cavalry to tanks, and he retired a number of generals: all these steps were necessary preparations for war, but they were bitterly resisted by army officers. Shortly after war began, Hore-Belisha was squeezed out of office, partly out of anti-Semitism, partly because he neglected administrative routine, but mainly because he and the generals could not work together.

Foreign policy under Chamberlain

Chamberlain was by nature an active and even an interfering Prime Minister; he had said in 1932: 'It amuses me to find a new policy for each of my colleagues in turn.'[13] In the late 1930s his attention was inevitably drawn to foreign affairs, and he showed great willingness to find a policy for the Foreign Office. The Foreign Secretary, Anthony Eden, resented this. He distrusted Chamberlain's lack of experience in the field, and in addition disagreed about

13. Macleod, *Neville Chamberlain* (1961), 164.

specific points of policy. Chamberlain accepted the view, which had been widely held in Britain ever since the Treaty of Versailles, that Germany had some just causes of complaint. He believed that discontent in Europe was a serious matter and should be dealt with, though his ideas were not precise.

In the absence of any powerful ally, and until our armaments are completed, we must adjust our foreign policy to our circumstances, and even bear with patience and good humour actions which we would like to treat in very different fashion. . . . I am about to enter upon a fresh attempt to reach a reasonable understanding with Germany and Italy, and I am by no means unhopeful of getting results.[14]

This ambiguity of approach could be dangerous. If he thought the dictators were prepared for a 'reasonable understanding', it made sense to satisfy them as soon as possible. If he thought that Britain needed to buy time to rearm, it was more prudent to give way slowly, obtaining as much time for each concession as could be managed. Chamberlain showed a tendency to force the pace in negotiation that suggests that buying time was not dominant in his mind.

The Spanish Civil War was still the major international problem at the time he became Prime Minister. Eden combined a strong commitment to the policy of non-intervention with a considerable contempt for Italy. The government seemed to have accepted this approach when it let him take a firm line at the Nyon Conference and insist that Germany and Italy should take their commitment to non-intervention seriously, but Chamberlain was not convinced. He felt that Eden's policy showed too little consideration for Italy, and he set out to conciliate Mussolini. This meant accepting Italy's victory in Abyssinia and reducing British involvement in Spanish affairs to nothing. As Chamberlain could not convince Eden of the virtues of this policy, and would not give it up, the government moved towards a dual policy. Eden's temper was not improved when Chamberlain waved aside a suggestion by Roosevelt for a conference to discuss tensions in Europe. Eden hoped that, although Roosevelt could not commit his country to anything, the conference might begin the process of bringing the United States into European affairs, but Chamberlain wanted to pursue private discussions with Hitler and Mussolini uninterrupted by the United States or anybody else.

Eventually the dual policy went too far. Chamberlain and Eden had a conversation with Grandi, the Italian ambassador in London, which became in effect an argument between the two British ministers in which Chamberlain put the case that would normally have been put by Grandi. Eden resigned on 20 February at this sign that the Prime Minister had lost confidence in him, and was replaced by Lord Halifax, who was much more willing to let Chamberlain run foreign affairs. A good deal of influence passed from the Foreign Office to Sir Horace Wilson, a distinguished civil servant who was trusted by

14. K. Feiling, *Neville Chamberlain* (1946), 324.

Chamberlain but had little experience outside labour and economic issues. The policy of appeasement could now be followed without opposition inside the government.

A settlement with Italy did not necessarily involve appeasing Germany. The Stresa Front had rested on the idea of cooperation with Italy and firmness to Germany. *The Times* advocated conciliatory measures in each diplomatic conflict with Italy and Germany, but did not put forward a coherent long-term policy. Chamberlain fairly certainly had a single unified policy that he wanted to apply in European affairs, and the attitude of the government was deeply affected by estimates given to it in 1937 that the next war might begin with sixty days of German bombing, which would cause 600,000 deaths. This assumed that the Germans could drop more than 600 tons every twenty-four hours, and that every ton of explosive dropped would kill sixteen people. The German air force was not designed for flying from Germany to England, and even when it had acquired bases in France it was never able to attack in such force; and on average each ton of high explosive in the Second World War killed one person. But if Chamberlain believed the figures, which seem to have been put together in the mood that once led Baldwin to prophesy that the bomber would always get through, it was natural for him to think in terms of gaining time.

How much time his policy gained is another question. If Chamberlain intended to make friends with Hitler this objective was not pursued seriously. When Hitler seized Austria in March 1938, the British government might have tried to conciliate him by approving of the move, which was not impossible to justify on grounds of ethnic identity, or might have tried to rally opponents of German expansion by denouncing the seizure, but Chamberlain took an attitude of ungracious acceptance that was not likely to do anything except convince Hitler that Britain disliked his policy but was too weak to resist it.

Once Austria had been absorbed, the western end of Czechoslovakia was enclosed in German territory. Hitler could turn his attention to the next provision of the Versailles Treaty that he wanted to overthrow. The Sudetenland had been included in Czechoslovakia in 1919 partly to give the new country a defensible strategic frontier and partly because of the skill with which the Czech case was presented. A large number of Germans had been placed under Czech rule, which could not be justified on principles of self-determination. The claim that the Sudetenland ought to be given to Germany had some validity, and a Sudeten German movement, led by Henlein and secretly financed from Berlin, began agitating in favour of the transfer. In May a flurry of rumours suggested that Germany was about to attack Czechoslovakia: the Czech and the British and French governments took a firm attitude and protested at the idea of changing the frontier settlement by force. Hitler had in fact not intended to attack at that time, and he was not pleased when advocates of resistance to German expansion said that he had been driven back by the firmness of the British and French.

The Sudeten agitation went on, and Chamberlain became convinced that it was a threat to the peace of Europe. In August he sent Runciman to investigate the situation; the Czech government did not want him to come, because it implied that there was some doubt about their position in the Sudetenland, but Chamberlain said that if the investigation could not be carried out Britain could not take much interest in Czechoslovakia's problems. Runciman's mission became a form of pressure on the Czech government to make concessions to the German population; this would have been reasonable if the Sudeten Germans had been negotiating in good faith, but as Hitler constantly encouraged them to raise their demands they could not be satisfied. By the time Runciman returned to London at the beginning of September, the claims of the Sudeten Germans had risen so high that it was hard to see how they could be met by anything short of a 'transfer of territory' to Germany. When *The Times* said so, on 7 September, it seemed to be only the logical outcome of British policy. Chamberlain had not yet accepted this; he wanted to visit Germany and discuss the issues with Hitler in person.

On 15 September he flew to Berchtesgaden to meet Hitler. He conceded the principle that Czech territory should be transferred to Germany. He returned to London, and then set about convincing the French government that the only thing to be done with the Czechs was to persuade them to give up the German areas of the Sudetenland with as little fuss as possible. Britain's only diplomatic obligation to Czechoslovakia was a general commitment to the Versailles Treaty; France had a treaty with Czechoslovakia, but the French government was willing to be argued out of taking it seriously. French diplomacy rested on a series of alliances with the new states in eastern Europe created at Versailles, but French strategy had become committed to a defensive position behind the heavily fortified Maginot line, which meant that France made no preparations for helping her allies.

Chamberlain went to Godesberg to meet Hitler on 22 and 23 September. The detailed German proposals meant that Czechoslovakia would lose parts of the Sudetenland in which the population was mainly Czech, and the inhabitants of the areas to be transferred would be given no choice between staying or leaving. Chamberlain rejected these proposals. When he went back to London it seemed possible that the British government would stand firm, would encourage the French government to honour its treaty obligations to Czechoslovakia, and would support the Czechs if they resisted. On 28 September the Fleet was mobilized, and when Parliament was called together Chamberlain explained the course of the negotiations in a way that seemed to point inexorably to war. But as he reached the last stage of his speech a message was passed to him; he read it out; he announced that he would be flying once more to discuss the question with Hitler. His supporters burst into applause.

At Munich on 30 September the British and French were interested only in finding some way of softening the blow that was to be dealt to Czechoslovakia. They accepted the German claims in principle, even though the fact that the meeting was being held at all showed that Hitler knew his position was not impregnable. Some of his generals were so convinced that it would not be possible to carry out a successful invasion of Czechoslovakia against opposition that they were apparently ready to overthrow Hitler if he went further on the path to war. Stories like this are always a little hard to evaluate, but it is true that the Czechs had built a powerful defensive system in the hills of the Sudetenland which German tanks would have found hard to penetrate. However, the British and French leaders gave way and only asked for plebiscites in the most obviously Czech areas. They allowed the Germans to take over a wide belt of territory almost immediately, which meant that the Czechs lost their defensive system without being able to remove much of their equipment, and the population had very little time to leave the ceded area. The Czech representatives did not take part in the conference; they were told by the British and French representatives what terms had been arranged, and they received the terms in the spirit of Masaryk's earlier comment: 'If you have sacrificed my nation to preserve the peace of the world, I will be the first to applaud you, but if not, gentleman, God help your souls.'[15] The Czechs accepted their fate because their allies would not fight but, even so, if they had resisted a German invasion, Britain and France might have found it hard to stay out of war.

The Munich settlement has not been regarded kindly by posterity. The name has been applied—even by Germans—to policies thought to err in the direction of softness and compliance, and 'appeasement' has remained a term of abuse. Historians are more ready to see something to be said for Chamberlain. He could reasonably argue that if a war had started in 1938 the English-speaking world would not have been ready to join in; the British Empire would have been divided, because men like Hertzog in South Africa and Mackenzie King in Canada would not have gone to war over the Sudetenland, and the United States would have felt less sympathy for Britain and France than it did a year later. Against this support from outside Europe must be set the fact that Czechoslovakia had a better-equipped army than any other eastern European country and a strong defensive position; if Britain and France were to fight for any of the states created at Versailles, Czechoslovakia was the best ally they could have had.

Other defenders of the Munich settlement have pointed out that the Royal Air Force improved its strength so much between 1939 and 1940 that it was eventually able to win the Battle of Britain and retain control of the air over

15. J. W. Wheeler Bennett, *Munich, Prologue to Tragedy* (1966), 171.

England. This argument seems to assume that, whenever war broke out, France was going to be defeated nine months later, so that if war had begun in 1938 the Battle of Britain would have been fought in the summer of 1939. Opponents of the Munich settlement say this was not bound to happen: if Britain and France had helped Czechoslovakia, Germany might not have been able to fight a war on two fronts and Hitler would have been defeated without bringing the United States and Russia into the middle of European affairs. In any case, Britain did not make full use of the extra time gained at Munich; for instance, the decision to increase the British wartime contribution to the Anglo-French alliance from five divisions to thirty-two was not taken until March 1939.

Whatever effect the different rates of growth of military strength had on the situation, the British government had done no good at all by taking an ill-conceived interest in the Sudeten question. If Czechoslovakia was indefensible, then it had to be abandoned, but in that case the British government only made things worse by taking part in the operation. Chamberlain seems to have thought Hitler was a reasonable man who could be persuaded to accept less than he really wanted. Hitler was not a reasonable man; he wanted to get his own way and, while he did not at this stage want war for its own sake, he did not care whether his diplomacy led to war or not. If Chamberlain could do nothing to stop him, it would have been more sensible to keep away and not expose the country's weakness. Chamberlain's diplomacy encouraged Hitler to think Britain would not resist him, and it provoked taunts like the story that Haile Selassie of Abyssinia had written to Benes: 'I hear you are receiving the support of the British government. You have my profound sympathy.'[16]

Munich was the culmination of appeasement. After negotiating the Czechoslovakian agreement, Chamberlain and Hitler signed a separate declaration that their two countries would never go to war with each other. Chamberlain's policy of pacifying Hitler seemed to have reached a successful conclusion. There were scenes of wild enthusiasm when he got back to London, and he was so overcome by his reception that he said that he had brought back 'peace with honour', just as Disraeli had in 1878. But this reaction from the immediate danger of war did not last long. The First Lord of the Admiralty, Duff Cooper, resigned from the government over the agreement. A number of Tory rebels abstained in the vote expressing approval of the Munich negotiations. Members of the Liberal and Labour Parties began to work together. The leaders of the Labour Party, who had discouraged the United Front in the mid-1930s, opposed Liberal and Labour cooperation in a Popular Front in late 1938. Despite this, Popular Front and independent candidates did well at by-elections in the last three months of the year.

16. F. L. Lucas, *Journal under the Terror* (1939), 287. The title is misleading; the author felt shame, as well as terror, at living under a government led by Neville Chamberlain.

Chamberlain was not convinced that the settlement had really ensured the peace of Europe and went on with rearmament. Aircraft factories were not stretched to their full capacity but, although 1.5 million workers were unemployed, the rearmament programme was running into shortages of skilled labour. The unemployed might be available for jobs, but one result of the high level of unemployment was that little attention had been paid to training them for skilled work. The government wanted to draw up a national service register, so that people in jobs that were vital for a wartime economy would not leave them and join the forces as in 1914. Trade unions were persuaded to cooperate with this scheme, partly by a government promise, repeated as late as March 1939, that there would be no conscription in peacetime.

In the New Year some of the shock of Munich began to wear off. On 10 March Sir Samuel Hoare hoped that a new era of peace and prosperity was about to begin. Hitler, who seems never to have been in the least affected by anything done to appease him, seized what was left of Czechoslovakia five days later. He had applied the Munich Agreement in such a way that he had gained almost everything he had asked for at Godesberg; he now swept away the defenceless remnants. At Munich Britain and France had promised the Czech representatives that they would defend what was left of Czechoslovakia; after Hitler's coup they said, perhaps a little pedantically, that they could not carry out guarantees to a state that no longer existed. Chamberlain seems to have taken a day or two to realize how completely he had been hoodwinked, but at Birmingham on the 17th he came forward with a forceful denunciation of what Germany had done, and this led on to a reversal of British policy.

To guard against further German aggression, a guarantee was given to Poland on 31 March, and Romania and Greece were given guarantees in April. The question of making the guarantees effective was not considered until too late. An alliance with the Soviet Union was the natural way to defend the countries guaranteed, but none of them were on good terms with the Soviet Union and the purge trials of 1936–8 suggested that the Soviet system had serious weaknesses. France had made an agreement with Russia in 1935, but this did not guarantee the 'little entente' of post-Versailles states that France had built up. Communist Russia and Nazi Germany were deeply hostile to each other, but this did not mean it was easy to arrange a collective system of alliances in eastern Europe.

To add strength to the guarantee that had been given to Poland, Chamberlain introduced on 26 April measures to provide six months of compulsory military training for men aged 20 and 21. Conscription was never likely to be popular with the parties of the left; as it was brought forward without consultation with the opposition leaders and only a month after the government had said conscription would not be imposed in peacetime, it was bound to be opposed. Chamberlain said in the debate, 'Nobody can pretend that this is peacetime in any sense in which the term could fairly be used,' but the situation had not changed since he gave his assurance against conscription in peacetime. Conscription was no doubt necessary, but it was introduced in a way that increased the feeling that the government was not concerned about the unity of the country. In foreign policy, and now in defence policy, the government had taken for granted the correctness of its own approach; the parties in opposition remained sceptical and the country was divided.

Negotiations with Russia proceeded slowly. The Soviet Union claimed a very extensive right to resist 'indirect aggression', which probably meant that it would intervene in any country that set up a pro-German government. The British clearly felt that there was plenty of time for discussing the issues, but they found the Russians becoming increasingly dilatory. Partly because his army had been weakened by the great purges, partly because Munich had left him doubtful about the willingness of the Western powers to fight, Stalin was turning away from the policy of resisting the other dictators. If he had been offered recognition as the natural dominant power in eastern Europe, he might have been persuaded into an agreement, but as the British had already made an alliance with Poland, they did not have a free hand. At her most powerful, when she was ready to intervene almost anywhere in the world, Britain had left eastern Europe to Germany, Russia, and Austria-Hungary. She had now undertaken responsibilities in eastern Europe, and overestimated her ability to fulfil these obligations without assistance.

Russia was not without diplomatic resources. German complaints and protests and threats made it clear that Poland was the next target. The inhabitants of Danzig were German; why, Hitler demanded, were they not part of his Reich? East Prussia was cut off from the rest of Germany by the Polish Corridor; was not this a part of the Versailles *Diktat* that ought to be overthrown? In fact the Polish Corridor was inhabited mainly by Poles, and Danzig had been set up as a free city at Versailles so that Poland could have one port that was not ruled by Germany. Even if Hitler's demands had been in themselves reasonable, they clearly implied that Poland was to become a satellite of Germany. This was a direct threat to Russia, and as the Russian government became increasingly convinced that Britain and France would not accept its claim to dominance in eastern Europe its thoughts turned to a fourth partition of Poland. So, in the last ten days of August, 'the scum of the earth' and 'the bloody assassin of the workers' came together:[17] they announced that they had signed a non-aggression pact, and this treaty contained secret clauses for a partition of Poland. Germany could now intensify the pressure on Poland, and Hitler did so in language that made it clear that the risk of war would not stop his efforts to get his own way. He had not accepted the arguments of the Fascist visionaries who thought war was in itself better than peace; he

---

17. Low, *The Years of Wrath*, 90; originally pub. 20 Aug. 1939.

intended to have Danzig and to turn Poland into his puppet, but probably he thought Britain and France would not fight on this issue. As the Poles certainly would not give way, German diplomacy in the last few days of August concentrated on suggestions for a conference to work out terms for handing over Danzig and the Corridor. Then, if the Poles refused to put up with the terms, Britain and France would announce that their guarantees would lapse. This pattern was probably far too like Munich to have worked, and on 1 September Germany invaded Poland. Negotiations went on; Hitler was still ready to get his own way by a Polish Munich rather than war, if Britain and France would agree.

He had in fact pressed them too far. The revolt inside the Conservative Party was on the verge of boiling over. When the House of Commons debated the issue, Chamberlain made a dull and non-committal speech; one Conservative MP, clearly dissatisfied with it, shouted 'Speak for England' across the floor to Greenwood, the acting leader of the Labour Party, as he began to speak.[18] Greenwood expressed the general discontent when he asked why it was that, thirty-eight hours after the attack on Poland, England was still at peace. But the government already felt itself committed to war; Chamberlain later explained that he had been making sure that France came into the war at the same time as Britain, a discreet way of saying that the friends of appeasement had been more powerful in Paris than in London, during the last hours of peace.

18. Who said 'Speak for England'? Amery, according to L. S. Amery, *My Political Life* (1953–5), iii. 324; Boothby, according to Nicolson, *Diaries*, i. 419.

8

The military side of the war

1939–1945

The first year

Even when the United Kingdom and France had made up their minds to enter the war, they could not do anything for Poland; the French army had not prepared for a swift forward movement, so it could not take advantage of the fact that only about one-third of the German army was in the west. The Polish campaign was soon over, with the Polish cavalry overwhelmed by tanks and aeroplanes. The country was partitioned between Russia and Germany, and the German army moved to the western front. No more fighting was possible before the winter, and a period of calm followed. From the point of view of imperial relations, Britain may have been fortunate that the war came when it did: despite the 1936 treaty, Egypt was not in a position to stay effectively neutral, in India Congress had not tried to take up the powers of government and the Viceroy could commit the country to war on his own authority, in South Africa Smuts was able to overthrow the Prime Minister, Hertzog, who wanted to stay out of the war, and in Canada MacKenzie King knew that national sentiment would not allow him to listen to his isolationist advisers in the Department of External Affairs. In a few years' time the bonds of Empire might have frayed a little more in all these places. In 1939 Ireland was the only Commonwealth country to stay out of the war, and many men from Ireland joined the British army.

The British and French hoped the blockade would make Hitler fade away. A few naval actions took place; the defeat of the pocket battleship *Graf Spee* by three British cruisers was a sign that British command of the sea had been established, and Winston Churchill, brought back to the position of First Lord of the Admiralty that he had held in 1914, was soon seen to be the active man of the government. British confidence rose so much that when Russia attacked Finland in November some people suggested helping Finland and fighting both dictators at once. The Finns resisted the Russians bravely, but were defeated before anything could come of this idea.

As Britain and France became more fully mobilized for war, Chamberlain went so far as to say that Hitler had 'missed the bus'. In April a sudden German attack took Denmark over before any resistance could be offered and captured most of the strategic points in Norway; it was hard to find a port to land supplies, hard to fight against German aerial superiority, and hard to resist German mechanized units. The British had to withdraw and abandon Norway. This defeat led to the replacement of Chamberlain by Churchill, who became Prime Minister on the day of the next German piece of aggression.[1] On 10 May an attack by tanks, bombers, and paratroops struck at Belgium, the Netherlands, and Luxembourg. The three countries had been careful about maintaining their neutrality and had declined to have staff talks with Britain and France, although it was so impossible to abandon them if they were invaded that some plans for assisting them had been prepared. On paper the British, French, Dutch, and Belgians had about the same number of divisions and the same number of tanks as the Germans, but they were not coordinated, the tanks were dispersed instead of being kept together as a concentrated force, and the morale of the French army was not good. It expected to stay in its Maginot line and wait for German attacks to break against its impregnable defences which would make up for the great disparity of numbers until eventually the French could go forward to the attack. The population of Britain and France put together was larger than that of Germany, but the allocation of duties, by which France provided a defensive line while Britain built up an army and looked after the sea, air, and industrial production, had left France with the uncomfortable basic tasks of war and opened the way to the German taunt that Britain would fight to the last Frenchman.

Hitler was determined to avoid a long-drawn-out war. He had been in the trenches; to save the Germans from suffering as they had done in the First World War, he did his best to shield them from shortages and hardships, and he tried to win the war by a few decisive victories. The blitzkrieg (lightning war) was meant to be won by tactical skill rather than hard pounding and immense loss of life, and the invasion of the Netherlands and Belgium showed exactly what he had in mind. Once French and British forces were moving into Belgium, the real attack burst through the Ardennes and broke the front just above the north end of the Maginot line. There was no recovery from this blow; within a fortnight the forces that had gone into Belgium were cut off from the main body of the French army. Britain's first concern was to get as many troops back across the Channel as possible. Almost all the trained soldiers had gone to France, and defeat might easily be followed by the disappearance of any possibility of further resistance. Hitler held his tanks back from what could have been a decisive blow against the troops on the Dunkirk beaches, probably to avoid blunting their force before the final attack on the

---

1. The replacement of Chamberlain by Churchill, which was one of the turning points of the war, is covered in detail on pp. 218–19 below.

French, and on the other side of the Channel the Royal Navy, assisted by an amateur armada of small boats, began the work of evacuation. The beaches were bare of cover, RAF fighters had to fly a long way to give protection, and the German air force was committed to preventing the embarkation and pinning down the troops assembled for departure. The losses among the British and French were heavy, but Operation Dynamo was far more successful than anyone in Britain had dared to hope; by 2 June about 335,000 men had been brought back to provide the nucleus of an army to continue the war.

Dunkirk was part of a great defeat, but it kept Britain in the war; the damage had been done long before the men were taken off the beaches, and the relief that the country felt when the troops were saved was justified. Added to relief was an unquenchably optimistic feeling that things could not get any worse, and therefore were bound to improve. This showed little feeling for the position of the French as the blitzkrieg rolled on; Churchill flew several times to France to try to inspire the government with some of the hope and determination that he was giving to Britain, but the military situation was hopeless. The sustained German attack was a model of organization, in which tactical air support broke up defensive positions without permanently destroying the lines of communication, tanks forced their way ahead and arrived long before the French expected them, and motorized infantry followed up the attack and consolidated the gains.

Churchill offered France an Act of Union, to turn the two nations into one. But he had a short time earlier refused—on sensible strategic grounds—to commit the country's last reserves of fighter planes to the air struggle over France; the Act of Union must have looked like an attempt to ensure that when France was overrun her fleet, her colonies, and her other assets remained in British hands. French politicians were already wondering how to make the best peace they could, and they needed bargaining counters for this. When the Third Republic collapsed, and Marshal Pétain signed an armistice on 22 June, the most the British could hope for was that the French would be able to arrange for their overseas possessions to remain neutral. Hitler agreed to this, probably because he thought Britain would soon follow France's example.

1940: alone

During the Dunkirk evacuation Halifax as Foreign Secretary thought it might be prudent to investigate what peace terms could be obtained, but Churchill knew how hard it would be to break off negotiations once they had begun and kept his government away from this dangerous course. Its strategic analysis held out little realistic prospect of victory: it hoped that blockade, heavy bombing, and an eventual rebellion in the countries Hitler had conquered would leave Germany too shattered to resist an invasion of the Continent. On the other side of the Channel the Germans hoped that bombing, and the conviction that resistance was hopeless, would undermine British morale and lead to a request for peace, to save them the difficult task of mounting an invasion. A force might have been rushed across the Channel just after Dunkirk and established at some port like Dover, but by the time Germany had completed the pursuit of the French and had made peace with them, the worst of the shock was over and the British had stabilized their position. The Germans assembled an invasion army and collected a fleet of barges between mid-July and mid-August, but by then it was clear that an assault would meet serious opposition, so a large force would have to be moved across and supplied in southern England, which meant that Germany needed control of the Channel, which was much better defended than the seas between Germany and Norway. A successful invasion of England was impossible unless Germany gained command of the air and bombed the Royal Navy out of the Channel before the barges sailed.

German bombing did make life difficult for British shipping in the Channel, but the German air force could gain command of the sky only by defeating the British air force. The Germans had considerably more aeroplanes, and their bases in northern France were close to the struggle. Because the fighting took place over England, some RAF planes that had been shot down could be restored to service, and pilots who got safely to the ground could fly again, but the pilots were few and the reserves of aeroplanes were limited. Although the odds against them were less overwhelming than was thought at the time, the men of Fighter Command fully deserved Churchill's eulogy: 'Never in the field of human conflict was so much owed by so many to so few.' If the fighters had been defeated, German command of the Channel would have made possible an invasion which would almost certainly have been successful. Once unchallenged in western Europe, Hitler could have turned his full forces to the east, and Russia's chances of surviving such an assault would have been slight.

For some weeks in August and September the RAF was in some danger of finding all its limited resources committed to the battle, so that it could not protect its aeroplanes from being bombed while they were on the ground refuelling. In August the attack shifted from the ships in the Channel to the airfields and communication systems of Fighter Command. This attack might have broken Fighter Command; the British depended on radar warnings that an attack was coming, followed by prompt radio-telephone instructions to airfields about to be attacked, to offset German numerical superiority, and if the Germans had destroyed the communication system the weight of numbers would have told much more than before. Early in September the Germans threw away their chance of winning the Battle of Britain by changing to direct attack on London. This made much less sense; the attacking planes had to fly further to reach their target and the defensive communication system could operate effectively. The British fighter pilots, who had been pressed almost to the limit, now gained aerial superiority, and the Germans gave up the idea of invasion. London was attacked because it was thought that bombing would destroy civilian morale and industrial production, but the German bombers suffered so heavily in daylight raids that they had to switch to night-time bombing. In Britain this period became known, inaccurately enough, as the Blitz—blitzkrieg meant a quick end to the war, and night-time bombing offered no hope of a quick end. From October until April German planes attacked towns all over the country, from Plymouth to Glasgow, but concentrating mainly on London. It was hard to ward off these attacks; radar provided some help and, as the nights grew shorter, the raids died away.

In the course of the attack the Germans had dropped something like the 36,000 tons of high explosive which it had been expected, before the war, would fall in the first two months of fighting. This bombing had nothing like the destructive effect that had been expected; in reporting on the attack Churchill said that statistics showed that at their current rate of progress the Germans would take ten years to knock down half of London, after which the rate of destruction would grow less because they would be bombing areas that had already been devastated, and that one ton of high explosive killed about three-quarters of a person.[2] The German air attack, and its failure, greatly strengthened Britain's diplomatic position. In July 1940 neutral opinion, which meant primarily United States opinion, inclined to think Germany would win. The daytime air fighting over England modified this opinion; Hitler had demonstrably fought and lost a battle. Americans who wanted Britain to win could see some hope of success; Americans such as Joseph Kennedy, the US ambassador, who would not have been disappointed by a British defeat, found it harder to say that it was inevitable. The night-time bombing of London reinforced these attitudes. Bombing had been expected to destroy cities and to frighten civilians so much that they would surrender at once. The British people showed no signs of being frightened and went on with their work without being too disturbed by bombs. The exaggerated pre-war idea of the effectiveness of bombing had been accepted so widely that it looked as if the English—the Londoners were reported in greatest detail—were doing something that nobody else could have done. Later events have shown that all ordinarily patriotic people stand up to bombing about equally well, but nobody knew this in late 1940. The Blitz convinced many Americans that St Paul's Cathedral was a vital and defensible outpost of their own country.

Around the close of the year a series of British victories helped to show that

---

2. Churchill's broadcast of 8 Oct. 1940 (P. Fleming, *Invasion 1940* (1957), 142). The idea of the Germans wasting their bombs on buildings that had already been destroyed was at the time thought very amusing.

the war was by no means over. Italy had rushed to help the victor in June, and had then overrun British Somaliland and nibbled at the frontiers of Egypt and Sudan. In December the British struck back in Egypt, and by the end of February the Italians had been driven out of Cyrenaica, the eastern province of their colony of Libya, losing 130,000 prisoners in the course of their flight. In January attacks from Kenya and Sudan were launched on the Italian position in East Africa, and by May the main Italian armies had surrendered, though a few groups held on until November.[3] The Italians clearly had neither the equipment nor the determination needed for fighting. Their weakness had already been exposed when they attacked Greece, from their newly acquired possession of Albania, in October 1940; the Greeks had resisted, and then had begun to push the Italians back towards the Adriatic. Italy's failures reduced the prestige of the Axis, and this made Churchill's assertion directed to the American people 'Give us the tools and we shall finish the job' seem realistic.[4] By this time Americans were ready to pay for Britain to fight, though they would not willingly send men to be killed, and Churchill was assuring them that they would not be asked to provide troops.

The need for imports of food, raw materials, and weapons was forcing Britain to spend its gold and sell off its foreign investments, and they were running out fairly quickly. In March 1941 the US Congress passed the Lend-Lease Act allowing the President to supply arms to other countries on any terms he chose. Lend-Lease did not end economic difficulty, but it freed British production from the fear that imports would be cut off by bankruptcy. Britain could make full use of her access to the world outside Europe, and could realistically hope that Germany would run short of materials first. A great deal of Lend-Lease material went into making aeroplanes, which absorbed about half the total British production of war material, and most of this was devoted to the bombing offensive against Germany. Before the war the Air Ministry had concentrated, just in time, on radar and on producing the newest types of fighter plane; this had been a wise and well-rewarded choice, but the subsequent concentration on bombing is harder to justify. The early bombing attacks were useful; when Churchill was asked how he proposed to win the war, he could tell the Americans that he would do it by bombing Germany. There were diplomatic advantages in bombing Berlin when Molotov, the Russian Foreign Minister, visited his German allies; he was able to fend off Ribbentrop's assertion 'England is finished' by asking 'Then why are we in this air raid shelter?'[5] But for anything more than propaganda a

---

3. F. S. Playfair, *The Mediterranean and Middle East* (1954), 362 and 447: the Italian army in East Africa numbered 350,000 men but many of them were natives of the region who disappeared without being captured.

4. Churchill's broadcast of 9 Feb. 1941 (Winston S. Churchill, *The Second World War* (1948–54), iii. 111).

5. Ibid.. ii. 518.

much larger effort would have to be made. During the air battles of the summer of 1940 Lord Beaverbrook had performed wonders in getting new planes produced and in having planes that had been shot down repaired and returned to service or cannibalized to provide spare parts for planes less badly damaged. After the Battle of Britain his talents turned to producing a mighty fleet of bombers that would destroy Germany without a shot being fired on the ground.

The air force had always believed that an independent aerial offensive could destroy an enemy. In the opening months of the war a few important strategic targets had been bombed by daylight, but as Germany was too far away for fighter support to be provided, the losses soon became insupportable. No deliberate attacks on towns and civilians were made, partly because such attacks might lead the Germans to strike back equally devastatingly. In the event the Germans made the first deliberate attacks on civilians, when attacking Warsaw and Rotterdam in order to help their advancing armies, but in the British mood of 1940 it did not matter much that it was the Germans who started it. The object was to hit the enemy, and when France collapsed it looked as if bombing was the only way to hit the enemy, so the government felt it had to adopt the air force policy. As daylight bombing was not practicable, bombers could only attack at night, just as the Germans had done in the winter of 1940. These attacks were directed against important points inside towns, and the leaders of Bomber Command were sure they could bomb accurately enough at night to hit selected targets, although incidental and unintended harm might be caused to civilians as well.

Before this new approach could be properly tested, a set of defeats was followed by a new cause for hope. The Germans had been establishing their position in the Balkans by the methods of peaceful penetration that they had used before the war. Hungary, Romania, and Bulgaria passed into their control without much trouble, but an anti-German revolt broke out in Yugoslavia. Hitler had to help Mussolini in any case: he sent troops to Libya, and on 6 April he attacked Yugoslavia and Greece. British forces were moved from the Middle East to help Greece, with the result that the forces left in Libya were forced back almost to where they started from, though they retained Tobruk as a stronghold behind the enemy line which could be supplied by sea. Sending troops to Greece did not make much strategic sense, though for political purposes Britain probably had to show it would support any country that would fight against Germany. The small British army at the end of a long sea route was soon driven out of Greece by large German forces with overland communications and took up new positions on the island of Crete, which looked much easier to defend. But the Germans established command of the air, and on 20 May launched a paratroop attack, rapidly followed by more troops in transport aircraft. The Navy suffered heavy losses from the air—as many sailors were killed trying to hold the sea as soldiers fighting on land—and within ten days all was over: almost half the British force had to surrender. Hitler had made himself master of the Balkans and seemed to be well on the way to making himself master of North Africa. Wavell, the British commander-in-chief in the Middle East, was dismissed; he may have lost his usefulness because he had been worn down by defeat and by Churchill's constant urging to attack, but the generals who succeeded him would probably have done no better if they had had to cope with the lack of men and shortages of materials that handicapped him.

The German attack on Russia

Hitler was not concerned about North Africa, and regarded the Balkans as a tiresome diversion from his major enterprise, an attack on Russia. War with Russia had probably always been his final objective, and he may have thought the 1940 operations against Britain and France were only a prelude to the real struggle. The historian of the British blockade of Germany does suggest that fear of future shortages of wheat and oil encouraged Hitler to make his attack,[6] but it had certainly been in his mind since the time of the Hossbach Memorandum in November 1937 and, in vaguer form, since the writing of *Mein Kampf.* The British knew the attack was coming, and tried to warn Stalin. Not entirely unnaturally he regarded this as an attempt to stir up trouble between Germany and Russia. The invasion, on 22 June 1941, came as an almost complete surprise, and German forces moved briskly eastwards, capturing large numbers of prisoners. In Ukraine they were welcomed as liberators from the tyranny of Moscow but they disabused the Ukrainians of this idea very quickly, killing them off and confiscating their grain as brutally as Stalin had ever done; a good deal of Hitler's policy was aimed at providing living space (*Lebensraum*) for Germans in the east, and this involved clearing the Slav population out. Partly for this reason the war in the east was much more ferocious than elsewhere. The less Nordic the civilian populations under German rule could claim to be, the more severely they suffered. Norway and Denmark were not too badly treated. France was partitioned; the Pétain government retained most of south-east France, which it ruled from Vichy. The Free French government set up by General de Gaulle after his flight to London in June 1940 acted as a counter-magnet to Vichy. The area of France not left to Vichy was under German rule, and suffered more than Norway and Denmark, but the Slav lands were far worse off: no east European intellectual could have written as relatively calmly about the Occupation as de Beauvoir in *The Prime of Life,* and the armies in the east could hardly have adopted an enemy song in the way that the British troops in the North African desert accepted 'Lili

6. W. N. Medlicott, *The Economic Blockade* (1959), ii. 646.

Marlene', or felt the respect for an opposing commander that the British felt for Rommel.

The war in the east involved more troops and resources than the whole of the rest of the war. From 1941 onwards over half the German divisions were at all times committed to the eastern front, and as these divisions were engaged in combat they had to be above the average in quality. From 1940 to 1944 the divisions kept in France were a reserve army that included a number of units recovering from the strain of fighting in Russia. The Russians were assisted with equipment; as soon as he heard of the German attack, Churchill expressed support for Russia (in accordance with his privately expressed readiness to make a favourable reference to the Devil in the House of Commons if Hitler invaded Hell) and began sending out material. Roosevelt soon extended Lend-Lease to assistance for Russia as well as Britain; by this stage the American government was not much concerned about the legal niceties of neutrality, and it provided several opportunities for Hitler to declare war on it if he chose; the 'shoot on sight' instruction, which allowed American ships to attack German submarines in the Atlantic, was a very broad interpretation of the rights of neutrals to free passage over the seas. Shipping supplies to Russia was even harder than bringing supplies across the Atlantic to Britain. Convoys sailed to Murmansk and Archangel throughout the war, draining shipping resources in conditions of cold and bad weather far worse than the British met anywhere else in the war. The Russians never expressed as much gratitude for this equipment as the British and Americans thought they should have done, nor did they cooperate effectively in running the convoys. They had overwhelming problems of their own. The Germans by December 1941 had forced their way almost to the suburbs of Moscow. There they were held up by a desperate defence. As winter settled round them, a Russian counter-attack began, and for the first time a German army was compelled to retreat.

A world war

By this time Churchill felt confident that the war, which had suddenly spread to cover the whole world, would be won. Japan in the 1930s had gone on from involvement in Manchuria to war with China. The United States tried to restrain Japanese expansion by cutting off supplies of oil, and by 1941 Japan had to consider whether to withdraw from its Chinese involvement or seize territory to the south, from which it could get raw materials to go on fighting. It chose the latter, and prepared to do this by striking a paralysing first blow at the American Pacific fleet at Pearl Harbor in Hawaii. On 7 December an air attack on the fleet was almost completely successful, and Japan could move forward on a career of expansion in South-East Asia and the Pacific.

Hitler honoured the Tripartite Treaty that linked him to Japan (and also Italy) by declaring war on the United States when he heard of the attack on

Pearl Harbor. This was as crucial as his earlier decision to attack Russia, and as little likely to do him good. He may have thought that once the United States was at war she would soon turn on Germany, or he may have felt the strain of the American moves away from neutrality, or he may simply have felt that treaties with allies should be taken seriously—his loyalty to Mussolini in later years shows that in some things he was a man of his word. If he had not taken this step the United States might have had to concentrate on the war in the Pacific. Staff discussions in 1941 about what to do if the United States found itself at war with both Germany and Japan had indicated that the war with Germany should come first, and landing a force on the shores of Europe would certainly have been much harder if Germany had already conquered Russia, but the American public might have refused to accept this line of reasoning if Germany had not declared war.

While Britain could feel tolerably sure of success with both Russia and the United States as allies, it was still hard to find a way to attack Germany. Photographic surveys in the summer of 1941 showed that night bombing was far less accurate than anyone had thought. Attacking squadrons sometimes bombed the wrong town, and even when they got to the right place their chances of hitting anything important seemed very slight. The British High Command stuck to the independent air offensive, but it now became something quite different from what had been originally intended. A policy of 'area' bombing, which meant trying to knock down German cities, was undertaken. This involved some questionable judgements: the air commanders believed that German morale was less good than British, so that an attack like the bombing of London would destroy the German will to fight, and that the German economy was already under such heavy strain that it would be probably collapse if extra burdens were placed upon it, whether the additional demand was for consumer goods and houses to replace those destroyed or for fresh supplies of weapons.

Churchill's approach to bombing was shown when he heard about the possibility of making an atomic bomb. The decisive step from studying radioactivity to making a bomb came on the British side when it was worked out in February 1940 that if all the atoms of atomic weight 235 (U235 isotopes) were separated from the U238 isotopes in a piece of uranium, the U235 uranium would be much more fissile than ordinary uranium.[7] In a lump of U235 uranium above a certain critical size, the number of internal collisions would so far exceed the loss of energy escaping at the surface of the metal that it would explode. This part of the process was easy enough to work out; it was possible to calculate—though computers, whose development was encouraged by the war, had hardly come into use—that it could be carried in an aeroplane. When Churchill was told about these possibilities he said,

7. See above, p. 28.

'Although personally I am quite content with the existing explosives, I feel that we must not stand in the path of improvement.'[8] The atomic bomb turned out to be far more expensive than had been realized: to separate the U235 isotopes, of which there were seven or so in every thousand U238 isotopes, the uranium had to be turned into a gas and forced through a series of very fine membranes, sifting away a few U238 isotopes at each membrane. The gas itself, uranium hexafloride, was very hard to handle; the membrane was hard to manufacture; the electricity required for the operation would have serviced a large town. The British had taken the Americans into their confidence, entrusting them with a number of British scientific secrets such as the development of radar, and among other information in the 'black box' delivered in the United States in the autumn of 1940 were notes on the development of an atomic bomb. The Americans were greatly impressed, and in 1941 the British might have been able to persuade them to establish a consortium which would have done the work of making a bomb on a basis of equality. But the opportunity was missed and once the Americans were aware that an atomic bomb was a possibility they could devote far more resources to the project; by mid-1942 the British wanted to set up a consortium to handle the entire operation and found the Americans unwilling to consider the suggestion.

Churchill may not have been serious when he said he was satisfied with the existing explosives, an issue of great importance to the bomber offensive. In the First World War high explosive turned out to be less destructive than expected when it was used to shell enemy trenches. High-explosive bombs were never as deadly as strategists expected, and it took a great deal of time and labour to get the bombs to the target. Churchill's scientific adviser Lord Cherwell worked out his calculations for area bombing on the basis that an average aeroplane would drop about 40 tons of bombs before it was shot down, but in the whole argument about the bomber offensive the question of what other uses could be made of the material for building the bombers, the skilled airmen in the aircrews, and the aviation spirit for flying to Germany was not considered seriously. Cherwell and many other people seem to have overestimated the damage that bombing would do to Germany, but when Sir Arthur Harris was appointed head of Bomber Command in February 1942, the 'area' offensive became accepted as part of British strategy.[9]

The Japanese plan for expansion in Asia which had begun with Pearl Harbor included a swift attack on British possessions east of India. Hong Kong was captured after a week, but it was known to be indefensible. A far worse shock came when air attacks sank the *Repulse* and the *Prince of Wales*, the two British capital ships sent to guard sea communications in the region. The pattern of the whole naval war with Japan had been set; the heaviest ships

8. Churchill, *The Second World War*, iii. 730.
9. Lord Birkenhead, *The Prof in Two Worlds* (1961), 249.

were at the mercy of aeroplanes, and victory would go to the side which could bring up its aircraft carriers and deploy a crushing aerial attack. On land the Japanese advanced down the Malayan peninsula against troops much less well trained for jungle warfare and much too heavily equipped to respond to the speed of the Japanese assault. By 31 January the whole of Malaya was conquered, and only Singapore remained. It was primarily a naval base, never intended to resist an attack from the land because no one had imagined that an invading army would be able to sweep through Malaya. Singapore held out for about a week of siege and a week of assault. The garrison then had to surrender because their water supply had been destroyed. The British were then driven out of Burma, and by early 1942 the whole of South-East Asia was under Japanese control.

The loss of Singapore was the blow that did most damage to Britain's imperial position in the whole war. Her power depended on prestige, on the idea that one Englishman could defeat ten Asians and rule a province single-handed. The fall of Singapore showed that an Asian army could defeat the British. The direct consequence in India was that Congress opposition to British rule, which had been entirely passive, became more visible; the loss of Singapore marked a decisive change for the Empire in India, and also for relations with Australia. In the years between the wars Australia and New Zealand had been readier than Canada or South Africa to think in terms of a closely united Empire, partly because their populations had been almost entirely of British descent but also because they saw Singapore as a pledge that the Japanese fleet would never be allowed to endanger them. When Singapore fell, the complaints of the Australians sounded a little as though they considered Britain had betrayed them by allowing the base to be taken. These reproaches were not very reasonable, but it was natural that after this they saw the United States as their chief defence against Japan. Whatever the strategic arguments for giving priority to the war against Germany, it was not possible to ignore the Japanese threat to India and Australia.

Difficulties for Britain and for her allies multiplied in 1942. Auchinleck, who had replaced Wavell in North Africa, was able to advance from his position on the old Libyan-Egyptian frontier and relieve Tobruk, but could do no more, and as long as the Germans still had a foothold in North Africa advancing in the desert merely increased difficulties of supply. The little island of Malta, which was vital for restricting German control of the Mediterranean, held out against very severe bombing and was in constant danger of running out of food or munitions. The vital March convoy to the island was escorted only by a force of light cruisers, which held off a battleship and two heavy cruisers. As the Mediterranean was virtually closed, supplies for Egypt had to go round the Cape of Good Hope or across the Indian Ocean from the United States, and any advance from the Suez Canal area added to the distance that supplies had to travel. Despite inferior numbers, Rommel forced the British to withdraw and on 21 June Tobruk fell. It had gained symbolic significance because of the earlier successful defence, and the loss seemed particularly serious. The British armies retired in more or less good order to El Alamein, closer to Cairo than they had ever retreated previously. The position was strong and could be regarded as the equivalent of the lines of Torres Vedras, Wellington's final defensive position in the Peninsular War. The British had already, in February, installed a reliable Egyptian government, by threatening to depose King Farouk if he did not accept their nominees. The Germans were now at the end of long supply lines, their control of the Mediterranean was uncertain, their harbour facilities were not good, and Hitler was not interested in the North African campaign.

For the Germans the serious fighting was in Russia, and an offensive was launched in south Russia to gain control of the Caucasian oilfields, which turned into a deep but slender salient which almost reached the Volga at Stalingrad. From July until November the Russian and German armies were locked in a struggle over the ruins of the city. If the Germans could reach the Volga, the Russian line of north–south communication would be cut; and the attack on Stalingrad also protected the northern flank of the German armies advancing on the Caucasus. In November the Russian counter-attack began and the flanks of the salient were crushed. Hitler had previously had considerable success when he intervened in military affairs, but this time he blundered and ordered his forces not to retreat. Even after they had been surrounded they might have been able to break out, but Hitler refused to let them escape from the Stalingrad area. This turned defeat into catastrophe. About a quarter of a million men were lost, the Germans fell back, and the hope of reaching the oil of the Caucasus passed away.

The counter-attack begins

While the armies were struggling for the banks of the Volga, a British offensive began in North Africa. The new British commander in the Middle East, Alexander, took his time piling up superiority in material; at last the British war economy and the immense industrial power of the United States were to be applied to a military situation with no excuse for lack of success. Montgomery, the new commander of the Eighth Army, was one of the most cautious generals of the war; he remembered his days on the western front in the First World War. The battle of El Alamein started on 23 October with an artillery bombardment that would have gladdened the heart of Haig, and this was followed by a steady concentration of armour and eventually a tank battle on the grand scale. This sober approach was justified by its results: the northern end of the German line was broken, and the other forces in the line had to surrender because they were stranded in the desert. This time the pursuit across Libya was not interrupted: the desert army chased Rommel out of the arena that he had graced for so long and on 23 January Tripoli was captured. The battle in the desert, 1940–2, was for many British soldiers their happiest memory of the war. The soldiers of the Eighth Army who fought the desert campaigns remembered it as a struggle between professionals, with gentlemanly behaviour on both sides, no civilians to get in the way, and a victory that the British did not have to share with the Americans. Montgomery had his critics, but his soldiers admired him and were confident that he would see that they were better equipped and better prepared than their enemies.

In November British and American troops had landed on the Atlantic and on the Mediterranean coast of French North Africa. The Anglo-American military cooperation that began in North Africa ran harmoniously enough throughout the war for their armies to be able to combine their strength as well as forces of different nationalities had ever managed previously. Political problems gave a little more trouble in French North Africa and at later stages. The invading force accepted Admiral Darlan, an influential Vichy leader, as ruler of the region although he had been anti-British in the past and was regarded as dangerously close to being a Fascist. When he was, to the general relief, assassinated by a somewhat out-of-touch monarchist, the Americans wanted to deal with General Giraud rather than accept the more intransigent General de Gaulle as the French leader. This did Giraud little good, for de Gaulle had too much support and too strong a personality to be displaced, but it was a precursor of other political difficulties.

Churchill and Roosevelt met at Casablanca in Morocco in January, against the background of success in North Africa and even greater Russian success at Stalingrad. They declared that they would accept nothing short of an unconditional surrender. This decision has been criticized on the grounds that it made the Germans more ready to fight on when the war was clearly lost. It would have been difficult for anyone to snatch power from Hitler, even to negotiate peace; in any case Churchill and Roosevelt had to give the Soviet Union, which was bearing the weight of the struggle, a clear assurance that Britain and the United States would not make a separate peace. At the same time Churchill and Roosevelt agreed to increase the intensity of the one form of direct attack they could launch upon Germany, the strategic bombing offensive.

The landings in French North Africa and the pursuit across Libya after Alamein had gone so well that the Axis powers were almost forced out of the south side of the Mediterranean. But they brought reinforcements across the Mediterranean, rallied the desert army, and by February were established in Tunisia strongly enough to make a long siege-like operation necessary. When it was all over, in May, a quarter of a million Germans and Italians had to surrender for lack of transport back across the Mediterranean. There had been a division of opinion, with the Americans pressing for an invasion across the Channel as soon as possible and the British saying it would have to wait until

1944. If North Africa had been cleared without a struggle early in the year, and if a great many landing craft had been available, the choice of invading France might still have remained open, but the struggle in Tunisia made an invasion of France in 1943 impossible. Britain and America had to follow the policy described by Churchill as 'striking at the soft underbelly of the Axis', if they wanted to fight Germans anywhere in 1943.

In August they captured Sicily. Under the stress of this attack on Italian soil Mussolini's followers turned against him. A new government was formed and it began secret negotiations for an armistice. When troops landed on the mainland of Italy on 3 September, the Italian government announced that it had arranged an armistice and had changed sides. Neither of these dramatic events led to very much. The Germans promptly disarmed the Italian army and for the rest of the war treated Italy as an occupied country; the forces landed at the south end of Italy made slow progress because the series of mountain ranges splaying off the central line of the Apennines like ribs were very easy to defend. If the planners needed an anatomical analogy Churchill's remark was less apposite than Aneurin Bevan's question 'Is that the soft underbelly of the Axis? We are climbing up the backbone.'

In August Churchill and Roosevelt met again, this time in Quebec. Among other things they worked out arrangements for the use of atomic research. It was decided that British scientists would work on this research on a basis of equality wherever they could help, and that atomic weapons would be used only after the British and American governments had agreed about using them. The costs turned out to be very large. The Maud Committee, the body that had decided it was worth trying to make an atomic bomb, had suggested it might cost £5 million; the Manhattan Project, which finally made it, cost fifty or a hundred times as much. Possibly British scientists, accustomed to making do on less lavish resources, could have done the job for less, but as the American Treasury was paying the whole cost of development it had a strong interest in what was going on—especially as the Manhattan Project expenditure was kept secret until the end of the war—and wanted to secure whatever financial return there might be. It was agreed that the President of the United States should decide how much information of commercial value gained while making the bomb should be released to Britain at the end of the war. When this was settled the Project was ready to employ British scientists; in terms of mutual aid their services were of considerable use in the United States, and when the war ended they returned to Britain with a fund of knowledge about operating atomic installations.

The bombing offensive under Harris, which began in earnest with the 'thousand-bomber' raid on Cologne in May 1942, showed the limitations of bombing with conventional high explosive. Changes in Germany about this time make it particularly difficult to assess its effect. Until the winter of 1941 Hitler had quite reasonably expected the war against Russia to end as quickly as his other wars, and Germany did come close to complete success in the first few months. As a quick victory was expected, it seemed unnecessary to reduce the civilian standard of living in the way Britain had already done. By 1942 the Germans thought it was too late to transform their economy by building up new industries, but from then until 1945 Albert Speer, building on the organization left by Dr Todt, achieved a great deal, mainly by rationalizing production of the existing weapons. Military output rose steadily to a level that showed that in 1941 Germany had not been treating the war seriously. Any military shortages from which the Germans suffered in 1942 were entirely the result of their own overconfidence.

Because of this change the bomber offensive fell on an economy whose military sector was growing rapidly. Bombing had no noticeable effect on this development in 1942, partly because the weight of bombs dropped was very small by comparison with the closing months of the war. 'Area' bombing involved attacks on women and children which would once have been condemned as 'methods of barbarism', though this moral judgement may now be seen as sexist and ageist. The non-moral test of the effectiveness of the bomber offensive was to ask what else could have been done with the resources it absorbed. If less industrial capacity had been devoted to bombers, other aircraft might have been available for more immediately useful purposes: it was command of the air that enabled the Germans to capture Crete and enabled the Japanese to sink the *Prince of Wales* and the *Repulse* and subsequently to advance so quickly over Malaya and Burma. In February 1942 the German battleships *Scharnhorst* and *Gneisenau* were able to sail up the Channel from Brest to German waters: 'they were at sea for twelve hours, four of them in daylight, before they were discovered. And it was undoubtedly the failure of [British] air patrols which brought that about.'[10] Command of the air was most immediately useful in a battle zone, and concentration on long-range bombers was accompanied by a failure to ensure tactical superiority on occasions when it was vital.

The Battle of the Atlantic was linked to the bomber offensive. As in the First World War Britain's industries could keep going only if goods flowed uninterruptedly from North America. In addition an American army was brought across, provided with bases in southern England, and then equipped to invade Europe. Atlantic convoys did not suffer nearly as high a proportion of losses as convoys to Russia, and crews of ships torpedoed in the Atlantic had a better chance of survival than men in the icy waters of the Arctic Ocean, but it was still a desperate battle. In 1942 just over a thousand ships, totalling over 5 million tons, were sunk; at times in early 1943 things were even worse—in the first twenty days of March ninety-seven ships, totalling over half a million

---

10. S. W. Roskill, *The War at Sea* (1960), ii. 159. *Parliamentary Papers*, Cmd. 6775, makes it clear that Bomber Command was not suited to retaining control of the seas.

tons, were sunk.[11] In these months it was always possible that the link with the world outside Europe would be broken and rations would have to be cut or industrial production reduced. But in the first half of 1943 as many German submarines were sunk as in the whole of 1942, and the attack was blunted. Much more powerful submarines were being developed, which would have been a serious threat because they were faster and could take in air while under water through a snorkel, but they did not appear in combat until the war was almost over.

In the 1942–3 struggle the air force was not as useful as might have been hoped. Bombing the submarine bases did not help much; bombs were dropped off the target, or when they fell in the right place the submarine pens were too well protected to be much damaged. The aircraft of Coastal Command which swept the millions of square miles of the Atlantic achieved far more, spotting and sometimes bombing submarines and intercepting the flights of the German Condors which acted as convoy spotters for the submarines. But Coastal Command did not really have enough planes for the job, and could have used more if long-range patrol planes had been built instead of bombers. The bomber offensive caused its own supply problems; bringing oil to Britain was difficult, and aeroplanes flying deep into Germany consumed enormous quantities of aviation fuel. If the offensive had been suspended for lack of fuel, as sometimes seemed possible, it would have been the result of concentrating on attacks which could not produce immediate results and neglecting the problems of protecting the supply routes.

Air power was much more effective in the war against Japan. At first it was directed at specific objectives: in the summer of 1942 Japanese expansion was checked decisively in the battles of the Coral Sea and Midway. Carrier-based aeroplanes of the two fleets sought out the opposing carriers and endeavoured to sink them. The Americans were successful, and without air support the Japanese found it hard to advance any further. To some extent they had allowed for this in their strategy of gaining a wide screen of captured territory that would take a long time to reconquer and then waiting behind this screen until peace could be negotiated. The Americans responded by concentrating on a few selected islands, leaving most of them cut off and unable to obtain supplies after the Japanese had lost command of the sea and air. The Americans could choose which island in a group to land on and establish an airbase from which they could establish command of the air in the region. Advances of this sort could not have been carried out in Europe, but they did display a sensible use of air power.

The United States had decided at Casablanca to join in the bomber offensive in Europe. Their air force was designed for daytime bombing, and this offered some hope of hitting small but important targets such as the ball-

11. Roskill, *The War at Sea*, ii. 367 and iii, pt. 2, app. zz.

bearing factories at Schweinfurt which might have a direct effect on the German war effort. Daytime raids were made which inflicted some damage on the factories, but too many bombers were lost for the attacks to go on. To carry out daytime bombing without crippling losses, the bombers needed escorts of fighters, which involved producing a fighter which could fly long distances. Fighters like the British Spitfire, superbly designed for attacking bombers flying over England, had always been designed for home defence. The American Mustang (P-51), originally designed for the RAF, was adapted to accompany bombers to their targets and then, while they were making their attack, take on the defending fighters.[12] Partly because the RAF was already committed to night bombing before the Mustang came into production, it never showed much interest in the new aeroplane. It fitted the needs of American daytime bombing very well and after December 1943 German fighters had to penetrate a defensive screen in order to intercept the bombers. Once they were opposed in the air, the German fighters were steadily driven out of the sky.

This success was not due entirely to American skill. The limiting factor in the German economy was the supply of raw materials. When people in Britain compared their mobilization of labour with that of Germany and concluded that the British system was superior because British mobilization was even more complete, they were assuming that the two countries had the same problems. It would have been of little use for Speer to produce even larger numbers of tanks, guns, and aircraft if the German economy had run out of the petrol needed to move them about or the nitrogen needed to make explosives for them to fight with. As long as the sea routes remained open, Britain could import all the raw materials needed, and under Lend-Lease had no trouble about paying for them. On the other hand, though Germany naturally suffered from the shortages of skilled labour that affect all countries fighting modern war, and could not obtain much surplus raw materials or factory capacity from occupied Europe, a steady supply of forced labour could be dragged to German factories from the occupied countries. Hitler had ideological objections to German women working in factories and, in a grisly perversion of belief, he insisted that a considerable amount of the resources of the Reich should be devoted to the extermination of the Jews in Europe. This was a monstrous crime; it was also a wasteful blunder, and much of the concentration camp system weakened military production by depriving Speer of supplies of labour. Even so, running the Reich on more humane and rational lines would not have relieved the shortages that actually arose there. Lack of oil, and more particularly of aviation spirit, as much as the Mustang, crippled the German air force by making it impossible to give new pilots adequate training and at times forcing the air force to leave the sky open while

12. W. L. Craven and J. F. Gate, *The [US] Army Air Force in World War Two* (1955), 217–19.

it accumulated new stocks. The British and Americans could then bomb the synthetic oil refineries on which future supplies depended.

Harris rejected all suggestions that bombing should concentrate on German oil production. Later study has shown that oil was the weak point to attack; although Britain did not at first have the bomber strength to carry out the original Royal Air Force 'oil plan', it was the right basis for the aerial onslaught. Instead bombs fell wholesale on German cities. Many of them fell on or near steel foundries but, as the United States Strategic Bombing Survey pointed out after the war, a blast furnace is built rather like an air raid shelter and a steel foundry undergoes stresses and strains equal to heavy bombing during the normal processes of manufacture. German production went up in 1943 by over 50 per cent.

Towards the end of 1943 Churchill, Roosevelt, and Stalin met at Tehran to discuss the future conduct of the war. When dealing with Roosevelt, Churchill had taken it for granted that Britain and the United States were equals and that their relationship was closer than that of any of the other nations united against Germany. This was a sensible attitude, which gave Britain its best prospect of equality. Roosevelt accepted it with some reservations, but he did not intend to get into a position where Britain and the United States were automatically united against Russia. He shared a widespread American fear that Britain was going to use American help to increase the power of the British Empire; his own opinion was that the British Empire ought to relax its power and perhaps come to an end. In the negotiations for Lend-Lease the United States had listed conditions that were intended to end the system of Imperial Preference. Roosevelt pressed Churchill to grant independence to India, and when Churchill said he had not become His Majesty's first minister in order to preside over the dissolution of the British Empire his pronouncement was directed at Roosevelt as well as Hitler.

At Tehran Roosevelt was anxious to show Stalin that there was no English-speaking alliance against him. Churchill's desire to create such an alliance led Roosevelt and Stalin to draw together to avoid being outmanoeuvred by perfidious Albion. Neither Roosevelt nor Stalin believed that any country except his own was fit to rule an empire, and both of them spoke the language of anti-imperialism. As the cardinal fact of the military situation was the Russian army, which was driving back the best part of the German army, 1943 was not a good time to think of an alignment against Russia. Russia had only a slight numerical superiority at this stage, and Germany still held a good deal of Russian territory. Stalin's concern at Tehran was to make sure that there would be a Second Front, an Anglo-American landing in France which would divert a sizeable portion of the German army away from the east.

By the beginning of 1944 the invasion of France was in sight. The difficulties of the operation showed how hard it would have been for Hitler to attempt an invasion any time after the immediate shock of Dunkirk. An exploratory raid on Dieppe in 1942 had shown that the French ports on the Channel were strongly defended. Capturing a port in working order would be difficult; capturing a devastated port would be useless and landing supplies without a port would be almost impossible. The answer was to build the 'Mulberry harbour', an artificial port made of steel and reinforced concrete, which could be taken across the Channel and set up where it was needed. This gave the invading force great freedom of choice. An attack on Calais seemed the obvious route, because the sea journey was shorter than anywhere else and also because the Germans were about to start firing their V-1s, pilotless aeroplanes flown off a ramp and directed to London. The first one was launched about a week after the landing in France, and in September the first V-2 rockets were fired at London. Both of them carried about a ton of high explosive. The V-1 could be shot down or intercepted by the balloon barrage; the V-2 was harder to stop, though it caused less nervous strain because it arrived without warning. These new weapons were an expensive way to deliver high explosive because, unlike an ordinary aeroplane, they could be used only once but they were disturbing for Londoners, who thought the Blitz was over for good.[13] Too few V-1s and V-2s were fired to affect people's morale seriously but they destroyed a good deal of housing and reminded people in England that the war was not over yet.

Capturing the V-weapon bases and launching pads and halting the attack on London looked like an additional reason for landing near Calais, and General Eisenhower, the American commander of the combined invading force, reckoned that this reasoning would lead the Germans to concentrate their forces near Calais. Misinformation was manufactured to encourage them in this belief, and the attack was prepared for a section of the Normandy coast which was a little less heavily defended, although it did involve a longer Channel crossing. The preparations for D-Day included turning most of the south of England into a transit camp, transferring the weight of the aerial attack from strategic bombing to an onslaught against railways in France to cut the German lines of communication, and sealing Britain off from almost all contact with the outside world so that no word of the destination of the invasion should leak out. The whole expedition was nearly put off by gales that blew up at the beginning of June, but in the event they only convinced the Germans that no attack would come at that time. On 5 June Eisenhower took his decision, and the next day the invasion began. If it were driven back into the sea, launching another attack would be very hard. The war on land would virtually be left to the Germans and the Russians, with the British and Americans doing what they could in Italy.

---

13. Birkenhead, *The Prof in Two Worlds*, 258–61 and app. II. The V-2s were particularly expensive.

From D-Day to the end of the war

One limiting factor was the supply of landing craft. The Americans needed landing craft in the Pacific to fight the Japanese effectively, and in fact had more there than in Europe. A secondary attack on the south of France, which was carried out in August, also required landing craft. There were only just enough for the Normandy operations; the 1943 invasion proposed by the Americans would have been possible only if resources had been diverted from all other production. The beaches were held strongly despite all that had been done to mislead the Germans and cut their communications. Progress was slow, and on the American beaches casualties were heavy, partly through bad luck, partly because they had not provided as many specialized landing devices as the British. D-Day was a splendid opportunity to produce gadgets. Apart from the artificial harbours there were tanks for going through minefields, tanks for going over soft sand, tanks to act as ramps for other tanks to run up, and an underwater pipeline to pump oil under the Channel to France.

The Germans brought up reinforcements, and established a strong position around Caen at the eastern end of the invasion area. They were not able to block the western end as effectively and the Americans began to advance, slowly at first, towards Avranches and the border between Normandy and Brittany. When, in early August, the Americans broke the last counter-attack and forced their way into open country, there was no second line of defence for them to face. They swung round to the north-east, so that the powerful force facing the British at the east end of the invasion area was taken in the rear and surrounded at Falaise. By 21 August this force had surrendered, and it seemed for a time as though there was little left to do. German divisions in several parts of France were cut off with no line of retreat. Paris rose and liberated herself just before the advancing armies arrived, and the main German force had difficulty finding bridges across the Seine for its withdrawal. France was freed as rapidly as she had originally been overrun and was cleared of Germans by the end of September. But the pace could not be kept up. Cherbourg was the nearest port that was still in reasonable working order and the advance was running ahead of its supplies. A shortage of oil forced the leading formations to go slowly, and eventually brought them to a halt. The Germans had time to reorganize.

On 1 September Eisenhower decided that the invading forces were spread over too wide an area to be treated as a single strategic unit, and he took over command in France from Montgomery. At this point Montgomery suggested that one of the armies, equipped with all the transport it needed, should drive forward on a fairly narrow front, with the others following up slowly on its flank. He proposed that the British army, which held the northern flank, should advance swiftly towards Berlin and strike a decisive blow that would immediately end the war. Eisenhower's American generals were not in favour of a plan that gave the star role to Montgomery, and his talents had never seemed best suited to a war of movement. Although his attempt later in the month to penetrate deep into Holland by landing paratroops at the Arnhem bridges came close enough to success to suggest that he could work out plans for a bold strategy, his victories had been won by a judicious massing of force rather than by advances into the unknown. The American General Patton had more of the temperament needed for a single audacious attack; Eisenhower declined to undertake an advance on a narrow front, and ordered his armies to move forward together.

After the wartime alliance with Russia had dissolved, this decision was criticized on the grounds that an advance on a single front would have enabled Britain and the United States to impose a settlement of European frontiers that guarded their interests better than the arrangements finally reached in 1945. This view of 'how we won the war and lost the peace' rests on a misunderstanding of the situation in 1944. In September American anti-German feeling reached its peak with the formulation of the Morgenthau Plan, which would have stripped Germany of her heavy industry and turned her back into an agricultural economy. In October Churchill and Stalin discussed the post-war settlement of eastern Europe at Moscow. Churchill accepted that Russia's determination to dominate eastern Europe had not changed since the summer of 1939. Greece was placed in the British sphere of influence, Hungary and Yugoslavia were to be treated as areas in which both countries had an interest, and Romania and Bulgaria were to be controlled by Russia. The first test of the agreement came a couple of months later when Russia did not protest at British suppression of the Greek Communists. Eastern Europe could hardly have been partitioned on terms more favourable to Britain (which was assumed to be acting for the United States); when the agreement was made, Russian armies had already established themselves in much of the area that was being parcelled out. Britain and the United States would not have claimed they had 'won the war'; they knew how much of the victory had been gained by the Russian army. The plans for dividing Germany into occupation zones were being worked out during 1944, and probably no change in the military situation after September would have affected them.

The bombing offensive against Germany was resumed in the second half of 1944, and rose to its final intensity. A little under a megaton had been dropped before D-Day, and a little over a megaton, or more than half the total weight of bombs dropped on Germany, fell after D-day. An attack of this magnitude brought results; German war production fell steadily, though it never dropped back to the pre-1942 level. Obviously no economy benefits from suffering a one-megaton attack, but the question is whether the resources and energy devoted to bombing could have made a more direct contribution to defeating the German army in the field.

Inside his besieged Fortress Europa Hitler's reserves of oil and of military manpower were almost exhausted. He decided to gamble on a counter-attack. Just before Christmas the American section of the line near the Ardennes was pushed back some distance. The Germans had so little petrol by this stage that they relied on capturing adequate supplies for a breakthrough. They failed to do so, and had to fall back. Perhaps feeling confident that this attack would discourage any further pressure in the west, the Germans now switched more and more forces to the east. When the three leaders met at Yalta to discuss the closing stages of the war, the Russians were facing the stiffest opposition and could still claim to be playing the major part in the war.

At Yalta the leaders approved the plan for dividing Germany into zones of occupation that had been worked out, a scheme for a United Nations Organization was devised which recognized the facts of the situation and accepted the sovereignty of the great powers, and Russia agreed to join the war against Japan within three months of the end of the war against Germany. After the war it was suggested that Russia had not deserved to do so well at the conference, but public opinion in Britain and the United States would have been upset and puzzled at the idea of a breach in the alliance, and military opinion would not have encouraged it either. The east European successor states created at Versailles had been able to gain considerable freedom of action because Germany and Russia had been so weak, but in 1945 Russia was strong and Germany was being struck down. Yalta recognized this situation but there were already signs of trouble: the Soviet Union wanted to impose on Poland an exclusively pro-Russian government, but Britain was committed to the government in exile set up immediately after the German and Russian invasions in 1939. The Soviet Union had the stronger position, which it exploited as fully as possible.

By the end it was little more than Hitler's own will that kept the German people fighting; he had drummed his message of national defiance into his audiences for many years, and the spell was never quite broken. On 12 April Roosevelt died, and Hitler thought for a moment that the alliance might disintegrate. But by the end of the month the Russians were forcing their way into Berlin; in a last Wagnerian scene of multiple suicide in the Fuhrerbunker the driving force of the Third Reich was destroyed. Once Hitler was dead there was a little futile squabbling about the succession, but the German leaders saw no point in further resistance and the war in Europe ended on 8 May. The British and American armies had come further east than the agreed zones, and had to withdraw a little. The British held the northern flank throughout the advance and, partly because of this, north-western Germany became the British occupation zone. The last phases of the war had been relatively simple, with supplies abundant, reinforcements available if ever they were required, and a constant German shortage of everything their armies needed. Because no decisive weakness could be found and used to destroy the German position, resistance went on until the whole war effort collapsed at several points at once like the wonderful one-hoss shay.[14]

Churchill had insisted, during the later stages of planning the war in Europe, that Britain should take part in the war against Japan, which was expected to last for another eighteen months. This was a serious commitment, but essential if the British position in eastern Asia was to be re-established. After the shock of the initial defeats by Japan, the British wanted to avoid being seen as passive beneficiaries of American victories. In Burma British forces had been successful in very difficult country; in the summer of 1944 they had eventually won the long-drawn-out battle of Kohima, but Burma was not cleared of Japanese forces for another year, when Rangoon fell in May 1945; the British had overwhelming superiority in the air, which was vital for transport and for bringing up support when needed, as well as for tactical bombing, but the slow rate of advance showed how long a time it would have taken to reduce the Japanese Empire by destroying the Japanese armies.

In this stage of the war strategic bombing came much closer to playing a decisive role. Once the Americans had command of the air their bomber attacks on the islands of Japan steadily destroyed its cities and their industrial capacity. The Japanese industrial base was smaller than that of Germany, the area of the country was much smaller, and the weight of the attack was comparable to the bomber attack of the last nine months of the war against Germany, and by July the Japanese had begun to consider the possibility of surrender.

On 17 July the scientists in the New Mexico desert had exploded the first atomic bomb. It seems to have been taken for granted that the bomb would be used against Japan; nobody appears to have thought of trying to keep the whole thing secret although the Americans and the British wanted to tell the Russians as little as possible about it—Churchill considered locking up Niels Bohr, one of the world's greatest nuclear physicists, for security reasons.[15] The most important secret was simply that the bomb worked. All the rest was engineering; pro-Communist scientists saved the Russians some money by revealing the details of processes to the Soviet Union, but the British and American governments behaved as though the processes of making a bomb were some modern abracadabra that could be kept secret for ever. The governments imagined that the Russians would take an indefinitely long time to learn to make a bomb, but the scientists knew that it would take only about four years.

As nobody made a deliberate decision to keep the bomb secret by refraining from dropping it, all the arguments were concerned with the best way to use it.

14. The wonderful one-hoss shay 'went to pieces all at once; I All at once and nothing first' in O. W. Holmes's *The Deacon's Masterpiece*. Sound strategy tries to find one weak point and make it break down first.

15. Margaret Gowing, *Britain and Atomic Energy 1939–1949* (1964), 358.

If a demonstration test was announced in advance, but did not work, the Japanese would be more stubborn than ever. They were not people to give in lightly; their treatment of prisoners of war showed their poor opinion of people who surrendered rather than dying in battle. It may have been quite certain that Japan had lost, but then Germany had clearly lost the war some months before surrendering. A decision not to drop the bomb would have been hard to make, and hard to justify. The British government was consulted before the bomb was dropped, as was required by the Quebec Agreement, but it was not certain how seriously a refusal to give permission would have been taken. On 6 August the first atomic bomb was released, on Hiroshima; its impact was in the same range as an exceptionally heavy attack with conventional bombs—2,000 planes, each carrying a 10-ton bomb, which was the heaviest conventional bomb used in the war, would have had about the same explosive effect, though the incendiary effect would have been rather less. The Russians, who had been acting as negotiators and putting the Anglo-American terms to Japan, promptly entered the war, just three months after the end of the war with Germany. On the 9th another bomb was dropped, on Nagasaki. On the 10th the Japanese peace party prevailed in the Cabinet, and began arranging to bring the war to an end.

People in Britain, except for those directly concerned with the operations against Japan, had lost interest in the fighting. The war had not caused nearly as many casualties as the First World War. It was suggested that British soldiers would not have stood up to the long wearing struggle in the trenches, and it was part of British strategy to see that nothing like that happened again. Some sectors of the war were nevertheless extremely dangerous: out of 800 merchant navy ships that sailed to Archangel, fifty-eight were sunk on the way out and another twenty-seven on the way back; the Atlantic was not as perilous, but many good ships were lost; and Bomber Command used up men quickly—there is a grim note in the official history about the way the 'Dambusters' were selected for a precision raid from among those reaching the end of their second tour of duty 'since it was rare to survive two tours of operations'.[16] The airmen of Bomber Command were picked men, like the junior officers who died in the Flanders mud in the First War, and they died as bravely. But very few men in uniform were as exposed to danger as the soldiers of the First War, though civilians were much more involved than civilians in the earlier war. In 1940 and 1941 Britain might have been defeated and destroyed, and the whole country was involved in a great struggle, but there was a much longer period of fighting after the danger of defeat was over than there had been in the First World War. In 1918 the issue looked undecided only three or four months before Germany surrendered; the result of the Second World

---

16. Roskill, *The War at Sea*, iii, pt. 2, app. R; C. Webster and N. Frankland, *The Strategic Air Offensive against Germany* (1961), ii. 175.

War was predictable by mid-1943, but it took two years of serious fighting to end it. In those years Britain was losing her place as a dominant member of the alliance. Russia and the United States had much larger resources, and could wage war on a vaster scale. In 1940 England had saved herself by her exertions but there was no question of saving Europe by her example; it was not certain that she could save herself for long without assistance from the United States. The question might have become one of whether Germany could use Britain as the basis for building a wider empire. With this decline in the country's importance, and the loss of the drama of uncertainty about the result, the British were naturally more interested in thinking about what would happen after the war. From 1943 onwards the Army Bureau of Current Affairs had been telling soldiers to prepare for the new post-war world that they were fighting for. In the First World War people fought to get back to 1914; in the Second World War people were more enthusiastic about the country they saw developing during the war itself than in trying to get back to the 1930s. War propaganda had been almost entirely in terms of the brave new world to come, and little had been said about what had been happening in Hitler's Europe. Hitler's diplomacy had been a reversion to the morality of Bismarck, but in his treatment of Jews and east Europeans he went back much further, to the habits of Attila and Genghiz Khan. When the concentration camps were discovered, people at first thought of them in terms of Germany's economic collapse at the end of the war, or of individual sadism among the camp staff; the idea that it had been government policy to make corpses, much as other governments might make tanks or houses, took a little time to sink in. One aspect of the 1930s survived: the country was not very interested in the outside world, and at the end of the war felt that it had done enough for the world recently.

9

The domestic side of the war

1939–1945

Gingerly into war

The outbreak of war made little immediate difference in Britain. The government had been moving slowly towards a wartime system of organization, and the outbreak of war did not make it move much faster. It had arranged for children to be evacuated from towns when war broke out; one unforeseen result was that the comfortable classes in the countryside discovered that there were poor and ill-clothed children in England. They could have found this out quite easily by looking at the rural poor, who were very little better off than the children of the unemployed, though they may not have been verminous—one thing that made the comfortable classes realize the plight of the poor was the lice on the 'evacuees'.

The government's domestic policy rested on the principle that the economy was to be controlled, rather than entrusted to the free play of the market as in 1914, and run on more egalitarian lines than the German economy, which used a complicated system of priorities. This was laid down at the beginning of the war and remained unchanged until the end though it came to be applied more intensively. Control began with the Emergency Powers Act, passed as soon as the war began, which gave the government legal authority to do almost anything it thought was necessary for running the war effectively. The Home Secretary, for instance, could imprison without trial people whom he thought might be a danger to the State; these powers were used to arrest members of pro-Nazi and pro-German societies, and also to arrest refugees who had fled to Britain in the years before the war. A few refugees were German agents and some members of pro-German organizations had transferred their allegiance from Britain to Germany, but many of the arrests made no sense. They were an early sign that the country was ready to run the war as a democratic form of totalitarian state. It was accepted that everybody (except for the Independent Labour Party, and the Communists once they had accepted the Nazi–Soviet Pact) stood together and allowed the State unlimited power, just as in an orthodox totalitarian State. But it was also accepted that people had a right to complain and that Parliament had a right to challenge the government; there were regulations against spreading alarm and despondency, but they were amended to 'deliberately' lowering morale, and then fell out of use.

The blackout showed how democratic totalitarianism worked. The exaggerated idea of the effectiveness of bombing that led to the great evacuation at the beginning of the war was accompanied by a belief that the slightest chink of light at night was of immense assistance to German bombers, and so the Air Raid Precautions forces, assisted by crowds of local busybodies, pounced on every flicker that they saw. There is remarkably little evidence that careless lighting helped German bombers even at the peak of the night-bombing offensive in the winter of 1940–1, but deaths in road accidents went up by several thousands. The blackout probably helped national morale: a great many people felt that by taking care about lighting they were doing something for the war effort, and Chamberlain's government should have given people more opportunities to feel involved in their country's efforts.

At a more technical level Chamberlain's government laid down the lines on which the economy was to be organized. It decided that money was to be borrowed for the war at 3 per cent. Investors had to be convinced that the rate would never be allowed to slide upwards, and the market had to be controlled to prevent private borrowers from bidding against the government for money. People had to be prevented from moving their money out of the country, and a formal organization had to be provided for other countries whose money was based on sterling. From the beginning of the war the Sterling Area served to make sure that residents in sterling countries (the Commonwealth except Canada, and a number of closely connected states like Iraq) did not rush to buy dollars and deprive the British government of the money it was looking forward to borrowing.

The government realized that rationing would become necessary, though its preparations for this were not as far advanced as its arrangements for controlling the money market. Bacon, butter, and cheese were not rationed until January 1940, and meat was not rationed for another two months. On 3 April Chamberlain, in one of his best appointments, made Lord Woolton Minister of Food. The rationing system depended on supplying equal quantities of basic food for everybody, and there was less allocation of special allowances than in the more elaborate German system. The government felt committed to making sure that shops always had large enough supplies to meet the ration. This objective was attained almost all the time, but unrationed foods were in short enough supply to make housewives spend a great deal of time in queues waiting their turn for whatever they could buy off the ration. The queue became the symbol of wartime Britain, and its implicit values—fair shares, peaceful and patient waiting, and no advantages for the rich—were part of what the country was fighting for. The queues were so long because some people could afford to buy more than before the war. As the unemployed began to be reabsorbed into the economy, they were naturally better off, though this took some time to have an effect; early in 1940 there were still over a million people out of work. Very few skilled workers had been trained in the depression of the early 1930s. More people had been trained in the late 1930s, but they were men of just the right age to recruit for the army. A shortage of skilled workers was inevitable, and they could insist that their wages must rise to keep pace with any increase in the cost of living. The government may have been prepared to see a certain amount of inflation as a form of forced saving, but it realized that prices could go up indefinitely if wages were going to rise in step with them. In November 1939 the government decided to subsidize some food prices on a temporary basis to keep them steady, and for about a dozen years afterwards the government bought food directly from importers which it sold for less than it had paid, and it subsidized British farmers to produce as much as possible inside the country. Because prices were held down in this way wages rose less than they would otherwise have done, and the policy of subsidies also meant that people could afford to buy what was in the shops.

The organization of the domestic side of the war economy was accompanied by a steady increase in war production. The government expected a long war, and had no strategic plans for turning it into a short war. This meant keeping imports of war materials within bounds, establishing new factories, training workers, and building up machinery that would be producing at full capacity by 1943. In the long run this approach was justified; by 1943 a higher proportion of British resources was committed to war than any other country had ever achieved and British war production was eight and a half times the level set in the first three months of the war.[1] But to make this effective the country had to survive until production had reached its peak, and the 1939–40 programme certainly had not solved the bulk of its supply problems. Chamberlain's government had set out on the right road, but it was travelling very slowly.

The defeat in Norway showed a good many solid members of the community—including Conservative backbenchers—that the war was not proceeding as smoothly as they had thought. The difficulties of helping Norway on the other side of the North Sea may have been underestimated, but nobody could question Germany's success. On 7 May the Commons discussed the question, on the motion to adjourn for the Whitsun recess. There was a good deal of doubt and unhappiness among Conservatives, but no certainty that they would vote against the government. After the first day's debate the Labour Party decided to vote against the motion, despite the risk that this

---

1. Central Statistical Office, *Statistical Digest of the War* (1951), 139. This aggregate table is made up of the whole wide diversity of things used in modern war, bullets, tanks, radar sets, ships, and so on. But production reached a peak in a sufficient number of items in 1943 to show that this was not just a statistical curiosity.

would drive the uneasy Conservatives back to supporting Chamberlain. If the government majority remained unbroken, the Opposition would be accused of trying to gain a party advantage by dividing the House.

Several Conservatives had clearly been shaken when Amery, who had served in Baldwin's Cabinet, applied to the government the words with which Cromwell dismissed the Rump Parliament: 'You have sat here too long for any good you have been doing . . . in the name of God, go.' Chamberlain made the ill-judged remark 'I appeal to my friends', which left him open to the reply that the crisis was more important than friendship; Lloyd George demanded that Chamberlain should set the example of sacrifice by giving up the seals of office, and added a plea that Churchill should not allow himself to be made into an air raid shelter to protect his colleagues. When the House divided, about forty government supporters voted against the government and about sixty others abstained; the government majority, normally over 200, fell to eighty-one.

At first Chamberlain hoped to bring the Liberal and Labour Parties in to strengthen his government, but in case he could not win fresh support he summoned to his office on 9 May his two potential successors, Churchill and Halifax, and asked which of them it should be. Churchill had said he would serve under Halifax but—urged by friends beforehand—he remained silent when the question was put. There was a very long pause, and then Halifax accepted the situation and said Churchill should be Prime Minister. Chamberlain, the King, most Conservatives, and a section of the Labour Party would have preferred Halifax, but there was really no choice. Churchill could rule without Halifax; Halifax could be Prime Minister only if Churchill was at the head of a war committee, holding something like the position Lloyd George had wanted at the beginning of the December 1916 struggle for power. Some Conservatives had thought the Labour Party would reject Churchill because of his attitude in the General Strike and on India, but by 1939 the Labour Party had come round to regarding him as an enemy of the dictators and a man who would have liked to save the League. On 10 May the Labour Party announced that it was not prepared to serve under Chamberlain, but would serve under his successor. This settled Chamberlain's fate.

Churchill

Churchill's whole life seemed to have been dedicated to preparing him for this moment. Thirty years previously Sir Edward Grey had said that his activity of mind would disqualify him for any Cabinet post except that of Prime Minister. He had held almost all the important government offices, he knew more about war than any other British Prime Minister, and he possessed the eloquence to summon the people to a task which looked, for some months to come, increasingly difficult and almost hopeless. When he said 'Let us so bear ourselves that, though the British Empire and its Commonwealth last for a thousand years, men shall still say "This was their finest hour",[2] he had compressed the whole historical situation into one sentence. The country had on other occasions stood decisively against an attempt to bring the whole continent of Europe under the domination of a single power, but never before had the dominant power been as unrelievedly evil as Hitler's Reich, nor perhaps had any other power come so close to success. The strain was immense: the British Empire had been losing its central cohesion under the effect of nationalism, but British dominance within it was accepted until the great efforts of the Second World War sapped her strength. If its strength had to go, it could not have gone in a better cause than resistance in 1940.

The vulgar jingoism and petty spitefulness that had appeared at times in the First War was found much less often in the Second World War. But in the first nine months of the war there was an absence of enthusiasm and a feeling that the government was detached from the people and even from the war itself. Churchill changed all this; in a phrase put in his mouth in another context, he 'put some humanizing ginger' into the conduct of the war.[3] The country now had some idea what it was fighting for, and it knew the government was wholeheartedly committed to the war and at the same time understood what the people wanted.

In the debate on Norway a number of speakers had suggested that a small War Cabinet like Lloyd George's was needed. Churchill himself had doubts about this, but he set up a Cabinet of five: under his chairmanship Attlee and Greenwood represented the Labour Party and Halifax and Chamberlain represented the orthodox Conservatives. The Labour Party wanted a much more thoroughgoing purge of the supporters of Munich, but Churchill knew that opening up fresh divisions would not unite the country, and he had no intention of damaging his party in the way Lloyd George had damaged the Liberals. Because Chamberlain resisted the temptation to go away and sulk as Asquith had done, Churchill could hold the Conservatives together reasonably easily. Chamberlain had been overthrown in a more open way than Asquith, but he still had a majority of the Commons behind him and might have caused Churchill some embarrassment if he had appealed to the loyalty of his party. In fact he served with unbroken loyalty until the onset of cancer forced him to retire in October and led to his death a month later. Churchill then took up the leadership of the Conservative Party, partly because power would have been inconveniently divided if anybody else had been Conservative leader and partly because it strengthened his position in dealing with his Labour colleagues.

When Chamberlain retired, Labour representation in the War Cabinet was

2. Winston S. Churchill, *The Second World War* (1948–54), i. 597.
3. Beerbohm's cartoon, facing p. 306 in Randolph Churchill, *Winston S. Churchill* (1967), vol. ii.

strengthened by the promotion of Ernest Bevin. Churchill had brought Bevin, the General Secretary of the Transport and General Workers' Union, into the government as Minister of Labour, and he had quickly seen that Bevin was ideally suited for the job of helping run a war. Until 1940 the job of the Ministry of Labour was to make sure that strikes did not happen; Bevin interpreted his job as one in which he treated the entire population as a reservoir of manpower, some of which should flow into the armed forces, some into war production, and some into replacing workers who had moved from peacetime jobs into the war effort. At first it was suggested that he should use the widespread powers of compulsion given to him and compel people to go to jobs for which they were required. Bevin gave the logical response that the factories had not yet been built and there was no difficulty finding workers for the work to be done, but behind this lay his determination to avoid industrial conscription if possible and to place labour on the same footing as capital. Eventually he used industrial conscription to sort out a few residual problems, but long before that he had shown that workers and their trade unions were to be taken seriously as part of the community. This was something of a new departure: the government had negotiated with trade unions in the First World War, but Lloyd George's tricky habits in negotiation and the unions' conviction that a number of pledges had been broken, combined with the employers' refusal to deal with them as equals, had prevented negotiating habits from changing much. In the Second World War the government was again anxious that work should go ahead without interruption. Striking before going to arbitration was made illegal, and arbitration meant that employers had to accept unions. Bevin insisted that working conditions in factories should be made as tolerable as possible by providing canteens and personnel departments and by enforcing factory legislation; apart from the satisfaction of advancing causes that he had upheld throughout his union career, he knew that making the fullest possible use of available labour would need a high level of mobility, and if people were well treated at work mobility would be easier to achieve.

Bevin's great triumphs were still some way in the future, and in the summer of 1940 Lord Beaverbrook, who joined the War Cabinet at the same time as Bevin, had played the most prominent part in the war effort. The switch from the slow production of bombers to the hurried construction of squadrons of fighters, and his exploits in seizing men and material and diverting them to aircraft production, convinced everybody that here was a minister who got things done. It was no way to run a long-term war, because it put everybody else's production plans out of order, but in the summer of 1940 surviving the next few weeks of air fighting was all that mattered.

Churchill had come to power just as disaster began to descend. In his first five weeks of office he visited France several times to encourage the French government to resist, to take its fleet and leave for North Africa, and to merge

Britain and France into one nation. It was no use, and by late June the British knew that their country was the only one left in Europe to resist Hitler. By this time they felt distinctly more cheerful about the war; Churchill made many contributions to the war effort, but his most obvious contribution was that he clearly enjoyed what was going on, and the British people accepted this and even began to enjoy it too. Nazi philosophy valued war and struggle but the Germans did not enjoy the war, although they did not allow this to affect their morale. At least until exhaustion set in during the last year or two of fighting, the British found that the war released them from all sorts of constraints and provided them with challenges—opportunities to travel, change jobs, drop some of the habits of respectability, and to treat other people as equals. This exhilaration might not have survived large casualty figures but, in the event, people found the Second World War more fun than the First.

Churchill was the man to encourage this mood. He satisfied the need to feel that everybody was doing something worth while, and this was as important as making everybody feel that they were going to win. Very few people seem to have considered the possibility of defeat, and so it was fairly easy for Churchill to lay it down, without any widespread discussion, that the war would go on. People thought it was entirely reasonable for him to declare that his war aim was 'Victory—victory at all costs'. His behaviour on taking office, when 'he was conscious of a profound sense of relief' because affairs were in safe hands, was reminiscent of Chatham's conviction that he 'could save the country and nobody else could';[4] in the next few months he seemed more like the younger Pitt with his commitment to war without end and, as Bevan pointed out, with his oratorical triumphs followed by military defeats.[5] But the defeats were—granted the initial collapse in France—more or less inevitable. It was Churchill's task to make them bearable, and in this he was successful.

The 'spirit of Dunkirk' followed logically from what he had to say. The dominant feeling at the time of Dunkirk was that the country was a community, in which everybody had to stand or fall together. The British upper class may have believed that fighting would mean the end of its privileged position, but it had no doubt that its duty was to fight—and no other upper class in Europe showed the same simple patriotic readiness to resist Germany.[6] The working class had gone through two very grim decades after the glowing promises of the First World War, and some of the trouble had been caused by Churchill himself; it too had no doubt that in 1940 it had to fight for the country, and the men and women who worked seven days a week in their

4. Churchill, *The Second World War*, ii. 24 and i. 601. Churchill's speeches were designed for the House of Commons; however, his radio speeches (sometimes repetitions of what he had said in the House) were what really cheered the public up.

5. 'If speeches could win a war, then we have as good as won' (M. Foot, *Aneurin Bevan* (1962), i. 343).

6. H. Nicolson, *Diaries* (1966–8), ii. 23–4 and references given there.

factories in the summer of crisis, to turn out weapons to give the armies retrieved from Dunkirk a fair chance of resisting invaders, were also responding with an enthusiasm not seen elsewhere in Europe. The spirit of Dunkirk was sometimes invoked to deal with later crises but roused no comparable response, because no later crisis was as dangerous as Dunkirk and the summer of 1940. This spirit of community emerged around the time Churchill became Prime Minister and lasted more or less throughout the war. It would have been hard to keep up in peacetime because it rested too much on the acceptance of democratic totalitarianism to be an entirely comfortable basis for society. Undoubtedly it helped people to put up with the bombing of the winter of 1940–1, though less democratic systems of government turned out to be just as good at nerving Germans and Russians to put up with heavy wartime suffering.

Social demands of the war

The more prosperous classes were right to think that, at least for the duration of the war, they would have to pay for Britain's contribution. Real wages remained fairly steady, and there was not much transfer from working-class expenditure to the war effort. But the most spectacular gains were made by using machinery more efficiently and by developing the economy: war production took a steadily rising share of the national income as much because the national income rose as because civilian expenditure fell. There were social changes; fuller mobilization of workers meant fewer servants, who fell in numbers from 1.2 million to 0.5 million as women left for the factories. This decline was sharper than the fall during the First World War, and was more permanent. Money was extracted from the taxpayer in a more sophisticated way as the Treasury realized that it had to control the whole economy to keep it from succumbing to inflation. The 1941 budget was designed to adjust the financial situation to meet the demand for real resources, and was entitled to be considered the first budget which really accepted Keynes's ideas about the effect of government financial policy on the economy. Previous attempts to explain the impact of the budget in Keynesian terms had not been ready to consider the economy as a whole. In 1941 Sir Kingsley Wood took the items of government expenditure, showed what would be covered by existing taxes and by borrowing and what would be covered by foreign credits, and treated the difference as the gap that had to be filled up by taxation. Otherwise, he explained, it would be filled up by forced saving accompanied by inflation and rising prices. When the budget was seen in these terms, it was easier for the government to work out what it could do to expand the war effort and what attempts at expansion would be unrealistic because they would not correspond to any resources that existed. Once the United States had committed itself to providing unlimited credit for the purchase of raw materials and food, the limits on resources were relaxed. Nevertheless, on the financial side the Treasury had to raise taxes as much as possible, in order to keep the inflationary gap under control, and to help with this it issued tax credits to be paid after the war.

The graduated purchase tax introduced in 1940 assessed most items bought by the working class at the lower levels of tax. The really heavy incidence of purchase tax fell on the luxuries of the upper class, just as income tax combined with surtax raised the marginal rate on the highest incomes to 97.5p in the pound. Equality of sacrifice worked mainly by bringing everyone towards a uniform subsistence level, and as the working class was already quite close to this level, it had much less to lose. Wartime fiscal policy was egalitarian enough for any socialist: excess profits tax, levied on the extent to which profits rose above a peacetime base, went up to 100 per cent, so that people worried much less about war profiteers than in the First World War—some manufacturers could expand their businesses by building factories which would help them prepare for the post-war world, but their activities had none of the socially disruptive effects of the First World War profiteers. The less wealthy also benefited from the Rent Restriction Act, which froze rents at the 1939 level. Wartime economic policy transferred about 10 per cent of the national income from rent and dividends, which were usually received by the upper class, to wages and salaries, which went mainly to the middle and lower class.

Another innovation in taxation affected working-class incomes. Changes in income tax and the increase in money wages brought more wage-earners up to the level at which they had to pay income tax, though allowances and rebates meant that it was unusual for a manual worker to pay at the standard rate unless he was married and his wife was also at work. In September 1943 a scheme for Pay As You Earn was introduced, which made it easy to deduct tax from wages at the time they were paid by the employer.

Most of these financial measures with their generally egalitarian effect had been put into effect before it was apparent that political opinion was moving to the left. Movements of opinion were hard to detect in the opening stages of the war. Churchill was attacked in the House of Commons between early 1941 and late 1942, but his opponents had few political principles in common. About a couple of dozen Members were willing to vote against the government's conduct of military affairs, and a rather larger number thought it did no harm for the government to be kept on its toes. The simultaneous defeats in Greece and in the Libyan campaign were bound to lead to criticism; later on the fall of Tobruk caused alarm, and the loss of Singapore, with all its overtones of imperial dissolution, was the worst moment of the war for Churchill. His control of British war planning was so complete that he was the natural target for attack. Some critics said that he was trying to do too much, and suggested in particular that he should stop being Minister of Defence to give

himself enough time to supervise all the activities of the government. Churchill defended himself by saying that he was in charge and that he would decide
the structure of the government for as long as he was Prime Minister. As
Minister of Defence he had frequent discussions with the Chiefs of Staff; the
three Service Ministers became steadily less important and, after Eden moved
from the War Office to became Foreign Secretary when Halifax went to Washington as Ambassador in December 1940, they sank to the powerless position
of Kitchener after he had surrendered his control over strategy to Robertson
in the First World War. His discussions with the Chiefs of Staff enabled
Churchill to follow strategic developments; he provided a stream of military
suggestions and insisted on being given reasons when they were not accepted,
but did not override military decisions except when wider political reasons—
which usually meant diplomatic pressure—made it necessary. Lord Alanbrooke's *Diaries* show that Churchill could sometimes be very irritating when
pressing his suggestions on the Chiefs of Staff, but probably it did the Chiefs
of Staff no harm to be forced to think twice about the policies they had
adopted. Churchill was at first a link between the War Cabinet and the Chiefs
of Staff, but as the war went on the War Cabinet dropped further and further
out of sight. Though it had been a useful shock absorber when the war was
going badly, it became less relevant when all was going well. In the second half
of the war Churchill spent more and more time in conferences with the
American and Russian leaders, and the British Chiefs of Staff had to discuss
questions with the American Chiefs of Staff. The American military structure
was very like the British, but Roosevelt had no need to consult his Cabinet on
strategy and Churchill probably found this political arrangement attractive.
His relations with his generals were far better than Lloyd George's but, as he
had much more control over what they did, he had to take the responsibility
for it; he could not say in his memoirs, as Lloyd George had done, that he had
known better than his generals but they would not listen.

Military relations with the United States were inevitably closer than with
Russia and the social structure was affected by having so many American
servicemen in the United Kingdom during the two years before D-Day, but
people realized that the Russian army was bearing more of the strain of the
war than anybody else, which helped to move public opinion towards the left.
Churchill did not underestimate the great military effort of the Russians, but
he never doubted that Communists were dangerous people who wanted to
undermine the British Empire. The British Communist Party had denounced
the war that broke out in 1939 as an imperialist war, but when Russia was
dragged into it the party line was switched to approval of the war. Communists devoted their energies to helping the work of war production and are
sometimes given a lot of credit for checking strikes, though the increase in
production in the previous year shows that their contribution was not
indispensable. They encouraged the propaganda campaigns in 1942 and 1943

for an invasion of France to open a Second Front against Germany, but many amateur strategists, some enlisted under Lord Beaverbrook, also asked for an immediate attack across the Channel.

Japan's attack in the East endangered the British position in India. Although Congress had not been consulted about the declaration of war in 1939, Hitler's Germany was so racialist that Indians could hardly help supporting the British government against it. But no such considerations applied to the war with Japan: an Asian people was triumphing over European domination, and Congress supporters became much more ready than before to demand that the British should 'Quit India'. Sir Stafford Cripps, who had gained reflected glory for Russia's resistance from the accident of being the British ambassador in Moscow at the time of the German attack, was sent to India in the summer of 1942 to negotiate with the leaders of Congress on the basis of a promise of independence at the end of the war. Gandhi called the offer 'a post-dated cheque on a crashing bank'[7] and it was rejected; possibly it was already too late, but this looks like the last moment at which Congress could have negotiated independence for a united India. Civil disobedience began, and the government acted briskly to stop it; by the end of 1942 over 15,000 Indians were under arrest for political reasons. Because the Japanese offensive was checked and the military situation improved the British were able to hold its ground after the failure of Cripps's mission, but in 1943 the elements of British control were shaken by a famine in Bengal worse than anything seen earlier in the twentieth century. Over a million people died, and rioting broke out between Hindus and Muslims.

Looking forward to the post-war world

Independence for India followed logically enough from the British war aims of freedom and democracy, though Churchill believed that he and Roosevelt had avoided using terms that implied any weakening of the British Empire when they drew up the Atlantic Charter at their first meeting, before the United States entered the war. The British people had to wait until December 1942 and the publication of the Beveridge Report for a statement of war aims that meant much to them. In 1941 Greenwood, the deputy leader of the Labour Party, was demoted to the task of drawing up plans for the post-war world. He asked Sir William Beveridge to produce a plan for social welfare, and Beveridge produced a report that has shaped all subsequent British thinking about the issue.

The first principle was that everyone should make a single weekly payment to buy a stamp for a government insurance card to provide cover for all the setbacks that cause poverty. After the disasters of the 1930s provision for

---

7. This is the version given in *Annual Register of World Events for 1942*, 145.

people out of work was naturally Beveridge's first preoccupation; he estimated that on average about 8.5 per cent of the working population would be unemployed and he wanted them covered for an indefinite period, with no danger of the exhaustion of insurance benefits followed by reliance on poor relief that had caused the bitterness of the means test. The most original aspect of the Report was the proposal for a national health service to insure everyone for medical treatment. The pre-war system had insured wage-earners, but not their wives and families, and had left salary-earners to make their own insurance arrangements. Beveridge's plan also included the old-age, widows', and orphans' pension schemes set up in the 1920s, and proposed a family allowance for children because large families had been found in the surveys in the 1930s to be one of the causes of poverty. The finances of the Report were hard to work out, because wartime inflation was changing all the wage and price levels, but Beveridge suggested that some benefits should increase by stages, perhaps not reaching their final value until twenty years after the war ended. He also said that an agency would be needed to give assistance to people whose pensions had not yet reached the level needed for an adequate standard of living.

The Report was received with immense enthusiasm in Britain, in the United States, and in Commonwealth countries. The German government paid it the compliment of denouncing it as fraudulent. The response to the Report made it clear that one of the things for which ordinary people were fighting was economic security, and that they believed Beveridge opened the way to freedom from want. Against this background the government might have been expected to welcome the Report, if only because of its value as war propaganda. But the government was not eager to arrange a debate in the Commons, and when one was held Members had to insist very strenuously before they could obtain a third day for discussion. Churchill seems to have lost touch with the feeling of the country with this failure early in 1943 to understand the enthusiasm of the Commons and the people for the Beveridge Report; his parliamentary position was becoming unchallengeable as the Germans were obviously beginning to lose the war, but he was thinking only about the war and showed signs of forgetting what people were fighting for. In the debate the Tory knights from Croydon and from Kensington rose to say that their constituents did not think money should be spent on all these welfare schemes, though the debate also showed why it was said at the time that all Conservatives under 40 approved of the Report and all Conservatives over 40 disapproved of it. The Labour Party was wholeheartedly committed to the Report, and most of the Labour Members who did not hold office voted for an amendment pressing the government to act quickly upon the Report. During the debate the government accepted family allowances, and expressed general sympathy for the rest of the Report, but this came as rather a grudging concession. Beveridge's Report was not the only sign of interest in the post-war world. The Barlow Report in 1940 tried to find some way of enabling the community to get the benefit of increases in land values, and the Uthwatt Report in 1941 outlined a scheme for more attractive town planning. The Abercrombie proposals for the post-war rebuilding and development of London were welcomed by town planners and by people who believed it would solve traffic problems more or less for ever. The government began to have difficulty in reminding people that the war was still on, and was far from won. In 1943, when the Reports were appearing and were being discussed, the British war effort reached the limit: no more workers were available to expand the armed forces or the labour force in factories producing for military purposes. Bevin pushed his powers to their furthest point and conscripted women for some jobs, but this did lead to some suggestions that he was going almost too far. One slight weakness in the allocation of labour was that too many miners had been accepted for military service. Efforts were made to get them back from the army, but this was not enough. Some young men had to be ordered to go into coal-mining rather than the armed forces when they reached military age; the 'Bevin boys' did their best, and the immediate crisis was avoided, but it could be seen that all the country's resources were being stretched as far as they would go, and after 1943 the level of war production declined. Until the summer of 1944 the British military forces in Europe were larger than the American, but it was becoming clear that future weight of numbers would determine weight of influence. In 1943 the British government had to decide whether to gamble on the war ending in 1944, in which case the British war effort could go on unchecked, or prepare for a longer war and a restricted British contribution. In these calculations the supply of labour was the limiting factor. People were undoubtedly under heavy strain, which may explain why they thought about the post-war world so much. When the V-1s and V-2s came over in 1944, morale was not as good as it had been during the bombing of 1940 and 1941, even though it seemed fairly certain that the military advance through France and Belgium would soon end the V-raids; apart from the shock and disappointment of finding that the Germans still had ways of making life unpleasant, part of this weakness of morale may have been due to the difficulty of life in wartime Britain.

The general standard of living had been brought to something like that of a semi-skilled pre-war worker. Food rationing was handled with great understanding by Lord Woolton, who left the mark of his personality on the food policy of the whole war; in fact he was in charge only during the years of military crisis, and in November 1943 he left to become Minister of Reconstruction, but his successors remembered how he had run things. The Ministry of Food had to give housewives advice that would be accepted; the size of the rations went up and went down, but manipulating the ration system was not always practicable, and delicate guidance was needed—people were nudged towards buying carrots, which like other vegetables were never rationed, by being told that carrots would help them see in the blackout (which, to a very limited extent, was true). The Ministry composed recipes which looked as though they might be interesting, encouraged people to try stinging nettles as a substitute for spinach, and did its best to get them to put jam on bread and butter straight from the jar without putting it on the plate, where some of it was bound to be wasted. But although there was never a dull moment while Woolton was around, wartime food was not interesting. In a frequently quoted passage about the 1930s Orwell wrote that the unemployed wanted 'something a little bit "tasty"' without worrying too much about whether it was properly nutritious.[8] Wartime food was just the opposite: it was carefully balanced to give a healthy diet, but it was not tasty, partly because fat for frying—which was what the unemployed meant by 'tasty'—was in short supply). A neat blend of rationing and variety was applied to tinned food, almost all of which was sold on 'points', which meant that people could choose what tinned food they wanted (and could find in the shops) and pay for it with the designated number of points. Clothing was sold in the same way. Chocolate and sweets were sold on another set of points, labelled 'personal points' in the ration books to show that this was some sort of treat. Agricultural production was increased, as in the First World War. There was much less meat because land was ploughed up for corn which provided more food from the same area. Many people 'dug for victory' by growing vegetables on little allotments of their own. The health of the population improved, perhaps because almost everybody could afford a reasonable basic diet, and perhaps because the Ministry of Food took care that rations provided vitamins and calories that people would not have worried about for themselves. As the improvement in the nation's health included a drop in suicide figures, it is possible that people simply found life more interesting than in the years before the war.

The extension of rationing made British society still more egalitarian, and the points system encouraged this approach in a way; the points operated as an extra currency, issued to everybody on an equal footing. This egalitarian tendency may have encouraged one form of political protest in the last years of the war. The three major parties refrained from fighting by-elections and did not oppose the candidate put forward by the party that had previously held the seat. Just as in the First World War, this led to the appearance of independent candidates and to the emergence of a new minor party. But in the First War the newcomer had been Page Croft's National Party on the right; in the Second War it was the Common Wealth Party, led by Sir Richard Acland, an ex-Liberal, which campaigned mainly on the platform that nobody should have an income of over £1,000 a year. Some people voted Common Wealth because it gave them a chance to vote against the government, but its

---

8. G. Orwell, *The Road to Wigan Pier* (1937), 95.

serious political appeal was to the left wing of the Labour Party and to voters who thought wartime egalitarianism ought to be maintained in peacetime. It won a number of by-elections, and did well in others, to the fury of the Conservatives, who thought it was simply a shadow organization representing the Labour Party. The Labour leadership was not much happier about the prospect, foreseeing another round of struggle between the right and the left of the party. The political truce, kept up at a time when politics and the shaping of the post-war world were under discussion, inevitably left the work of shaping opinion about the future in unofficial hands. Beveridge campaigned on behalf of his Report. Victor Gollancz, the pre-war publisher of the Left Book Club, brought out more books attacking the Conservatives' record. *Guilty Men*, published in the summer of 1940, had blamed the government of Baldwin and MacDonald and Chamberlain for the plight of the men who had to be evacuated from the Dunkirk beaches, and *Tory MP* reminded everyone that some Conservatives had been in favour of a policy of friendship with Germany. J. B. Priestley spoke and wrote for a community in which everybody had a fair and equal chance. Bevan's magazine *Tribune* asked, in the words of Colonel Rainborough during the Civil War, 'whether the poorest he that is in England has not as great a right to live as the richest he', and clearly did not think the Coalition government—and perhaps not even the official leaders of the Labour Party—were concerned with the poorest he.[9]

Churchill and Eden, the two leading Conservatives, were primarily concerned with military and foreign affairs. The domestic side of the war effort was coordinated by Sir John Anderson, who was at one stage considered by Churchill to be the man to become Prime Minister if he and Eden were to be killed; as Lord President of the Council, Anderson acted as chairman of a committee which had central control of the war effort because it allocated supplies of labour, material, shipping space, and finance. Three Labour politicians, Attlee (Deputy Prime Minister), Morrison (Home Secretary), and Bevin (Minister of Labour), were probably the most important ministers concerned with domestic affairs under Anderson's direction, and they were ready to look for opportunities of carrying out changes during the war. But the rule of the Coalition was that no controversial legislation should be passed; the Ministry of Fuel clearly thought that nationalization would improve morale in the mines, but this was not acceptable to the Conservative Party. Bevin had a certain amount of difficulty with his Catering Wages Bill, which set up a wages board for the industry. Working conditions were bad, and pay was low or non-existent for some waiters who were expected to live on their tips. About a third of the Conservative Party voted against the Bill as an unnecessary extension of government activity, but Bevin was able to insist that it was essential for running the industry in wartime and so the government supported it.

9. V. Brome, *Aneurin Bevan* (1953), 135.

Nothing on a larger scale could be passed if one party was strongly opposed to it.

The 1944 Education Act was affected in a number of ways by concern about unity. It was the only really large-scale piece of legislation passed during the war, apart from legislation concerned with war powers, and it was meant to end all the old struggles. The 1944 Act is one of the very few Acts of Parliament to be known by the name of the Minister responsible, and 'the Butler Act' is a well-deserved compliment to its author. The Act took up the question of the age at which children could leave school where it had been left before the war, and gave the Minister power to raise the age of compulsory attendance to 15 and then to 16 when the expansion was thought feasible; it was understood that the first step would be taken almost immediately after the war. This extended education was to be secondary education for all. No more schools were to educate children at all ages, so all children would change schools at about 11; children took the scholarship for free places at grammar schools at that age, and it was accepted that an examination of this sort would still be used to assign children to secondary schools. Although the process of selection for secondary education became the leading issue in political discussion about education in the 1950s, it seems to have been taken for granted in the 1940s that things would go on as before except that more children would take part, and the point was hardly discussed in the debate on the Act. People had not really thought what would have to be changed if the country tried to educate every child to the level of a skilled worker.

The debate on the Second Reading showed how important religion still was in educational politics. Butler had made great efforts to bring together the three religious groups—Church of England, Free Church, and Roman Catholic—which any policy had to take into account. One point in the Act united all religious bodies in a mood of common approval: it laid down for the first time that each day at every school in the state system must start with an act of collective worship, though parents could ask for their children to be excused attendance if they chose. The rest of the religious question was purely a matter of finance, and Butler's grants to the Church of England and the Roman Catholics were generous enough to satisfy their official leaders. When the Bill came up for debate, some Roman Catholic Members were not satisfied, and wanted 100 per cent of the costs paid by the government. They obtained no more than the 50 per cent previously agreed in the Bill, but the argument over religion in education took up almost the entire debate. A few Labour Members did say how glad they were that children were to get more of a chance to be educated, but there was still an air of nineteenth-century idealism over the discussion—a few years later the argument would have concentrated on the importance of education for maximizing the gross national product rather than religion. The government was disturbed for a few days when an amendment laying down that women teachers were entitled to equal pay was added to the Bill. Churchill announced that he would not allow this and that the government would resign if the amendment was not reversed. The government got its way, with only a couple of dozen Labour Members voting against the removal of the amendment.

The Act was not the only sign of interest in education in the closing years of the war. The Fleming Committee suggested that the sharp class division between the public schools and the rest of the country should be reduced by giving at least 25 per cent of public-school places to children selected and paid for by the county councils. The scheme would have moved the public schools a little closer to the position of those grammar schools which did not enter fully into the scheme of the 1944 Act but accepted direct grants from the Ministry of Education and undertook to admit half their pupils on the basis of the recommendations of their county councils. The Fleming recommendation was not taken up, mainly because paying boarding-school fees for so many children would have cost a lot of money at a time when county councils foresaw much larger general expenditures on education. The ideal that education should be carried on in a gentlemanly way still remained: it was realized that universities would have to welcome students on their academic merits and pay less attention to money and social background than before the war but, when it was proposed that students on government scholarships should receive grants large enough to let them enjoy university life without any need to work for money in the summer or to repay the grant afterwards, the idea was accepted without much discussion.

The people and their government

Education did interest a lot of people at the time, but probably even more people were concerned about unemployment. In 1944 the government published a White Paper on the subject which represented a considerable step forward in official thinking. The White Paper's approach can be compared with Beveridge's book *Full Employment in a Free Society* to see which was the better guide to post-war policy: the White Paper committed the government to maintaining a high and stable level of employment, which presumably meant a lower level of unemployment than the 8.5 per cent assumed for the purposes of the Beveridge Report, but Beveridge's book, published just after the White Paper, asked for 'full employment', defined as 'always having more vacant jobs than unemployed men, not slightly fewer jobs'.[10] He admitted that this would leave a margin of frictional unemployment, but he said that government policy ought to make sure that there was no structural unemployment. The White Paper declared that a budget deficit to avoid unemployment was undesirable, but said national insurance contributions might be varied

10. W. H. Beveridge, *Full Employment in a Free Society* (1944), 18.

according to the state of the economy, so that if there was a danger of unemployment the insurance funds could run at a deficit and thus restore the level of demand in the economy. Beveridge said that this would be inadequate, would be administratively inconvenient, and might lead governments to try to cut down on benefits later on. He was wholeheartedly in favour of budget deficits as the way to restore demand, and suggested that drawing up a list of public works for future use, as recommended in the White Paper, amounted to saying that the government should neglect development work, however necessary, until it fitted conveniently into the state of the economy. Beveridge stated that the White Paper did no more than pretend to follow Keynes's principles. In this, and in other points, he may have been unfair to the White Paper; public works were recommended in the text of Keynes's *General Theory*, and it was not unreasonable to say that they should wait until the level of demand in the economy justified introducing them. But whatever there may have been to say for the White Paper, post-war practice followed Beveridge. Full employment, in his sense of the term, was regarded as one of the most important objects of economic policy; there was no attempt to draw up lists of public works in times of expansion which were put into effect in time of recession; and a budget deficit was seen as the most effective way of restoring demand to the economy. Beveridge cannot be said to have shaped employment policy in the same direct way as he shaped social welfare policy for the postwar world, because the influence of his book cannot be estimated as easily as the influence of his Report, but the great majority of the population seems to have agreed that unemployment was the main economic evil to be resisted.

At the end of 1944 the Labour Party took a clear step to the left. The leaders of the party realized that an election would soon be held, and intended to fight on a programme of retaining a good deal of the wartime government controls on the economy but not doing much to nationalize industry. The party conference was not satisfied with this, and asked for a programme of nationalization on the lines of the programmes drawn up in the 1930s, and this the party leaders accepted. The shadow of the end of the First World War still hung over the political scene, and its effect was increased by the first faint suggestions that some people wanted to get back to 'before the war'. Churchill considered that the Coalition government could go on after the war, and at one stage suggested that a referendum could be held to find out whether this was acceptable to the electorate. But the Labour Party disliked coalitions, and in any case the Coalition would have had more difficulty agreeing about policy if it had gone on after the war. The Labour half of the Coalition had no desire to get back to the days before the war; on the other hand Woolton, one of the greatest practitioners of 'war socialism', was quite certain that conditions in peacetime were so different that the country ought to return as far as possible to the free play of the market.[11] The democratic totalitarianism of the war

11. Lord Woolton, *Memoirs* (1959), 295, 304.

years was wearing thin by the time Germany surrendered, and left relatively little mark on British life.

The government spent a larger proportion of the national income than ever before, just as it had done in the First World War, and although the government's share fell after the war, it never sank to the pre-war level. The lesson that the government could run the economy without unemployment was learned again, and this time was not forgotten. But the government's relation to the people changed rather less: the spirit of intense national unity, combined with a willingness to allow the government a very free hand, did not survive the war for long.

Just before the war there had been some early attempts to examine the country's social habits, though Mass-Observation, the organization that carried out these inquiries, was not popular. During the war the government tried similar methods to find out what people were thinking and how their morale was standing up to the war: the nickname Cooper's Snoopers given to the inquirers for the Minister of Information indicates their unpopularity. No doubt a government which had to conduct a total war needed such methods, but clearly it was felt that the government ought not to concern itself so closely with what its subjects were doing. In 1940 the Gallup Poll began to ask people which party they would vote for, but nobody treated their findings seriously for some years. Before the war people had had a highly developed sense of keeping themselves to themselves; this was given up to some extent for the war, and when it did return after the war, it was less intense than in the past. Concern with respectability never returned to the height it had reached before the war, Before 1914 neither the upper class, nor the working class below the chapel-going 'aristocracy of labour', were concerned about being respectable, but between the wars this attitude of mind spread from the middle class to the whole country. It did not survive the war undamaged. Fighting a war is not a respectable activity, and on the underside of society there were people who ran a black market in food or other things in short supply. The black market was never very large, and people did not treat the war as an opportunity for a great display of dishonesty, but it did mark a turning point for some things: drinking and drunkenness, which were obvious signs of lack of respectability, had been going steadily downwards for over half a century, but after the war they began to rise again.[12] On the whole the largest changes

12. D. E. Butler and J. Freeman, *British Political Facts 1900–1960* (1963), 236 lists:

	Convictions for drunkenness	Barrels of beer drunk (m.)		Convictions for drunkenness	Barrels of beer drunk (m.)
1910	161,992	35	1940	44,699	27
1920	95,763	35	1950	45,533	26
1930	53,080	24	1960	65,170	27

which followed the war were changes in the way that individuals behaved rather than in the relations between them and the government. With the passage of time commercial polls and sample surveys were accepted as a reasonable way to find out what people were thinking, but an official government opinion poll would probably not have been well received. Willingness to be polled and surveyed was one small sign of people's willingness not to keep themselves to themselves so much; absence of enthusiasm for government surveys went with a feeling that, except in some moment of emergency, the government and the people were two separate things, and it might be just as well to keep them separate. People expected the government to be helpful, and had more ideas about what the government could do, but they did not propose to be drowned in a flood of gratitude.

One step was taken during the war towards carrying out the Beveridge Report: a Bill setting up family allowances of 25p per week for each child after the first was introduced in February 1945. Beveridge had originally suggested that allowances should be at the level of 40p per week, but the government had already said that it intended to provide free meals at school and give allowances at a rate lower than Beveridge had suggested. School meals had been provided on a much larger scale during the war than ever before, partly to enable mothers to go out and work in factories, and the government was quite ready to continue the scheme, particularly because it made sure that children got one cooked meal a day. Another piece of social legislation provided assistance for 'special', or depressed, areas to attract new factories because judicious planning of the location of industry was seen as a line of defence against the re-emergence of areas of high unemployment.

This Bill passed the Commons in the last days of the Coalition. As the war in Germany was clearly coming to an end, Churchill felt it was time to decide what would happen next. He wanted the Coalition to go on; his party and the Labour Party wanted an election fairly soon. While the war against Japan had still to be won, it was ten years since the last election, and people had never felt as much interest in the war against Japan as in the war against Germany. On 18 May Churchill asked the Labour Party to continue the Coalition government until the war against Japan had been brought to a successful conclusion, and he indicated that, if it did not agree to this, the coalition would be brought to an end and there would be an election in July. The Labour Party said on 20 May that it did not want to remain in the Coalition for long, though it asked for the election to be put off until October. Churchill did not accept this suggestion, and on 23 May the great ministry which had saved the country and had laid solid foundations for social reform was brought to an end. A 'caretaker' government was formed to run the country for the period until the election result was known. Except for Churchill and Eden, the 'caretaker' ministers were not a very inspiring group, and the contrast between them and the Labour alternative did not help the Conservatives as much as Churchill might have hoped.

Voting in the election took place on 5 July, but the ballot boxes were not opened until 26 July to allow time for soldiers' votes from all over the world to be brought back for counting. During the curious weeks of suspense in July Churchill led the British delegation to the Potsdam Conference, and Attlee came as an observer so that if he were to become Prime Minister he could pick up the threads of policy with as little difficulty as possible. Churchill seems to have been quite confident that the Conservatives would win, though in retro-spect it appears that they suffered from a number of crushing handicaps, some of them inflicted by Churchill himself, who was ill advised by Beaverbrook and Brendan Bracken and failed to understand how serious-minded the elect-orate had become.

To some extent the election was about Conservative pre-war policy. By this time everybody took it for granted that Chamberlain's foreign policy had been wrong-headed, and some people voted on this basis. The Conservatives were supposed to know about foreign policy, and had failed. Many more people must have voted against the pre-war unemployment; at the time voters accepted the idea that nobody could do much about unemployment, as had been seen in the 1935 election, but by 1945 people had come to expect full employment, and to blame the Conservatives for the lack of jobs. To set against these heavy disadvantages the Conservatives had Churchill. He toured the country, and enormous crowds came out to cheer him wherever he went. The people felt a debt of gratitude to him, and discharged it by the enthusiasm with which they welcomed him. Churchill thought that their cheering meant that they believed they ought to vote for him, but this did not follow at all—politics is not run on a basis of admiration for what is past, and political gratitude was long ago defined as a lively expectation of future favours.

Churchill did not convince people that he had any clear idea of what to do with the future. The BBC allowed ten broadcast talks by the major parties; Churchill did not have anything positive to say, so his remark that if the Labour Party was returned it would set up a Gestapo to run the country was given even more attention than it deserved. The public had never been quite sure how to take his free-flowing denunciations of Hitler and Mussolini dur-ing the war, which at times seemed a little undignified, but to suggest that Attlee and Bevin and Morrison were going to set up a Gestapo was silly enough to do him some harm; the Labour leaders were, in their different ways, not men to suffer fools gladly, but they were no more supporters of dictatorship than Churchill himself. They had the advantage, very rarely enjoyed by the Opposition at an election, of having been ministers in high repute until a few weeks previously; during the war they had established themselves as men who could be trusted, and presumably Churchill had trusted them. Churchill also did himself no good by getting into an argument about the constitution of the Labour Party. The party chairman, who holds the position for one year only, was the effervescent Professor Laski; during the election Laski reminded Attlee of his responsibilities to the party, and Churchill claimed that this proved that the Labour Party was dominated by its National Executive Committee, made up of men who had never been elected by the people. Again, nobody believed in this story of Attlee being a helpless puppet—Attlee may have been, as Churchill said later, a modest little man with a great deal to be modest about, but during the election Churchill seemed fated to pick out the points at which Attlee's armour was invulnerable.

In any case, the election was not to be settled by a popularity contest between the leaders, and Churchill's approach did not give the Conservatives much chance to say what they thought the country should be like after the war. In their brief references to the subject the Conservatives said they did accept the Beveridge Report, but from the nature of the two parties, they had to be more explicit than the Labour Party to persuade the electorate to believe them on this point. Instead they seemed content to treat the issue as one that all men of good will agreed about, so there was no need to discuss it in detail. But most observers believed that the electorate was in a serious mood, and would have put up with a great many detailed speeches on the subject. In 1918 people had thought the Germans were going to pay for everything; in 1945 nobody imagined that this would be possible, and it was all the more important to make sure that politicians intended to press ahead with the things they had promised, even if there were some financial obstacles. Because the Conservatives did not stress their determination to carry out reforms the electorate may have suspected that they would lay aside any schemes for social welfare which turned out to be hard to pay for.

As in 1918, the most important single domestic issue was housing. The stock of houses which had been just about adequate in 1939 had suffered losses from German bombing and from the natural passage of time, and new building during the war had sunk almost to nothing. The Labour Party could point to the great increases in arms production achieved during the war by government planning of the economy, and could say that a similar approach would solve the housing problem; the Conservatives had nothing distinctive to say in reply.

The issue on which there was the clearest difference between the parties was nationalization and, while there is no sign that it aroused enthusiasm for the Labour Party among the electorate at large, it did no harm: at least it showed that the Labour Party was anxious to get away from the bad old days of the years between the wars, and as the main industries on the nationalization list had been under state control during the war, people could see that private owners were not essential for running coal or the railways. Including nationalization in the programme probably raised the enthusiasm of the Labour organization, without provoking any corresponding enthusiasm to resist on the Conservative side.

	Votes	Seats	% of all votes cast
Conservative	9,988,306	213	39.6
Liberal	2,248,226	12	9.0
Labour	11,995,152	393	47.6
Other	854,294	22	2.8

When the ballot boxes were opened it was soon clear that the Labour Party had won. Conservatives said that it was because Labour men had stayed at home, working in factories, and built up their party organization in the trade unions while Conservatives were away fighting, but presumably they would have agreed with the Labour Party's request that the election should be delayed until October if they had thought this before the election. The army was in fact predominantly Labour, which was not surprising because men between 21 and 30 had leaned more to the Labour Party than most other age groups before the war, and organizations like the Army Bureau of Current Affairs had kept soldiers in touch with movements of opinion at home. Although Conservative organization may have suffered, there was really no need for such explanations; from 1942 or 1943 the Conservatives had had a number of warnings that they needed to adapt to a changed world, and the election showed that voters did not believe the warnings had been taken seriously enough.

10

The post-war world: dream and reality

1945–1949

___

Britain's place in the world

The Labour government came to office in a world that had changed much more than people realized. It had to adjust to the new world, and measures that were attributed to its socialist principles were often the result of external pressure. The most fundamental change was that America and Russia decided to take a full part in international affairs. If they had done this earlier, the affairs of Europe would have run on different lines; their willingness to intervene in 1945 meant that they were the two dominant powers in the world. Compared with the other countries of Europe, Britain's position might be envied and admired, and the country could be seen as the equal of America and Russia rather than of France and Germany. Maintaining this wartime position as one of the three dominant powers would obviously be an immense strain, but in 1945 nobody thought it impossible or doubted that it should be undertaken.

The task was even harder because the bonds of empire had loosened during the war. The problem of India had to be faced, and other, less immediate tensions had to be dealt with. Britain's changed position in international trade was bound to affect the commercial aspects of the Commonwealth. Compared with the external difficulties, the internal situation was relatively easy to understand: the middle class wanted to get back to the pre-war world of low taxes, servants, and an ordered society in which people knew their place and the working class wanted to keep the full employment, the adequate wages, and the prospect of increased social services that had opened up during the war. During the war the middle class had become poorer and the working class had become better off, but it was not clear whether this was to become permanent.

The United States government terminated the Lend-Lease agreement when the war with Japan came to an end, as had been provided in the legislation, and made no alternative provision for Britain's imports. This left only the briefest pause to adapt the economy to peacetime activity. The war with Japan had been expected to last some time and give a breathing space for converting the economy back to a peacetime basis, because Britain would not be as fully involved as in the war against Germany. The government decided that it had to negotiate a large loan from the United States to respond to the situation caused by the sudden end of the war with Japan. For the negotiations a short statement of the country's position was drawn up outlining the difficulties that it faced after the war. Foreign investments worth £1,118 million had been sold to pay for imports. 15.9 million tons of shipping, worth about £700 million, had been sunk. Damage to housing, caused by bombs and rockets, came to about £1,500 million. Machinery and equipment had not been repaired adequately during the war, and almost £900 million of depreciation had to be covered by new investment. Britain still had large foreign investments, yielding a return of about £170 million a year, but because armies in Egypt and India had been financed by loans raised on the spot, there were debts amounting to £3,355 million and, despite the low interest rates at the time, they would still cost about £75 million a year. Repaying the debts— sometimes called sterling balances, because they were the balances in favour of Britain's creditors—would obviously take a long time.

Before the war, when prices were lower, the United Kingdom had imported about £800 million a year, of which about half was covered by visible exports and the other half by receipts from shipping and by dividends from earlier investment. During the 1930s the balance of payments had been more or less neutral; the level of foreign investment ceased to rise. It was estimated that the country had to increase its exports to about 175 per cent of the pre-war volume to pay for what had previously been covered by invisible exports, and that this could be achieved in three or four years. To pay for imports during this period about £1,250 million would have to be borrowed.[1]

This sketch of the economic situation was masterly. Exports did reach 175 per cent of pre-war volume by 1950. Somewhat more was received from the United States than the 1945 estimate of what was needed, but this was due to inflation and some repayments to creditors owed sterling rather than a mistaken assessment of the trading position. In 1945 the American negotiators thought the British were being slightly pessimistic about their prospects, and they issued a loan for £1,100 million, of which something over £100 million was allocated to paying for Lend-Lease goods which had already started across the Atlantic and arrived after the ending of the agreement. Repayment did not start until 1951 and the true rate of interest on the loan was 1.6 per cent, low even by the standards of the time. The British negotiators had hoped at first for an interest-free loan or even a gift, and the government may have accepted some clauses with uncomfortable implications in order to keep the interest rate low. They agreed that holders of sterling outside the United Kingdom

---

1. *Parliamentary Papers*, Cmd. 6707.

could convert their money into dollars a year after the loan came into effect, and that Britain and America would not discriminate against each other in trade. This meant that the Ottawa system of Imperial Preference could not be expanded, for there were no other areas in which the two countries were likely to discriminate. The terms of the loan required the government to commit itself to maintaining a fixed exchange rate with the American dollar, which in turn was linked to gold, in accordance with the Bretton Woods Agreement worked out in 1944 to avert any return to the trade dislocation of the 1930s. There was some argument about how closely this linked the pound to gold. Nobody wanted the old inflexible link to gold, which was blamed for the unemployment of the 1930s; defenders of Bretton Woods pointed out that chronic unemployment was specifically laid down as one of the conditions that would justify devaluation against the American dollar, and argued as though exchange rates could change without much difficulty, but opponents of Bretton Woods (or of the American loan) pointed out that governments could not alter exchange rates by more than 10 per cent without a great deal of international consultation. They also pointed out the difficulty of setting a fixed rate just after the war. At the beginning of the war the exchange rate for the pound slid down to $4.03 to £1. This level was maintained during the war and accepted for post-war purposes, but it was improbable that the pound was worth as much in 1945 as in 1939.

The active and distinctive work of the Labour government was conducted with the pound at $4.03. The loan was spent faster than had been expected, mainly because prices rose rapidly all over the world just after the war. Converting to civilian life, making up for wartime neglect, and spending of involuntary wartime savings meant demand for both investment and consumption was strong, and this demand could not be met. Rising American prices reduced the purchasing power of the loan, and while it also reduced the eventual cost of repayment, this consolation was by its nature distant. Ministers had seen strong post-war demand in 1919 and 1920, and they were afraid that the unemployment and depression which followed it could easily return. The government's critics suggested that it should deflate the economy to stabilize prices, and undoubtedly rising prices reduced the popularity of the government. But as import prices were going up so rapidly, deflation might not have had much effect. The Conservative opposition at first seemed not to understand the need for exports, and said the government was paying too much attention to exports and not enough to the home market. Because Germany and Japan were too shattered by the war to compete, Britain had an excellent opportunity to secure new export markets. Pushed on by the government, exporters made great efforts and were successful at least for a time. It has been suggested that demand was so strong in these post-war years that they provided poor-quality goods and assumed—much as shopkeepers did during the years of scarcity—that the customer would put up with anything.

As a result, when the Germans and the Japanese returned to world markets, they did not find it too hard to win customers away from the British. There was another reason why the export drive began well, and faded later on. A great deal of British trade was still with commodity-producing countries, which were doing well in the late 1940s. People grumbled at the rising prices of imports, but the commodity-producing countries could buy large quantities of British exports in exchange: when the boom in commodity prices broke, British imports cost less, but export markets became weaker.

As the American loan began to run out, the Opposition shifted its ground and complained that too much was being spent on imports of tobacco, which absorbed 10 per cent of the loan, and films, which took about 4 per cent. The government knew that there were limits to the amount of austerity of life that it could ask of people, but in August 1947 it imposed a prohibitive duty on American films. Tobacco consumption had gone up considerably during the war and the tax on it was raised sharply, mainly for foreign exchange reasons. But the real drain on the loan was the convertibility clause: by the beginning of 1947 many countries selling to Britain were insisting on payment in convertible currency which could be turned into dollars, and in July, when all sterling outside the United Kingdom could be turned into dollars, the loan flowed out faster than ever. The loan was not intended to be spent on repaying the wartime sterling debts, but these debts were not always identifiable. As a trading currency sterling passed freely round the non-dollar world, and when the barrier between the sterling and dollar worlds came down, a certain amount of sterling debt was turned into dollars. In the loan negotiations it had been assumed, at least on the American side, that Britain would recover her commercial position as quickly as after the First World War. This had not happened: after five weeks of convertibility exchange controls had to be restored on 20 August, sterling ceased to be convertible, and the government looked for ways to cut spending.

Fortunately for Britain the American Secretary of State, George Marshall, had a few weeks previously suggested that the United States might provide financial aid to Europe. Ernest Bevin, as Foreign Secretary, had responded to the suggestion very quickly, and the Marshall Plan was set up to provide gifts, not loans, to help Europe recover from the war. The United Kingdom received about £700 million under the Plan. Marshall Aid caused some trouble because it seemed to give every American congressman power over British financial resources: they responded to any British suggestions that the country was recovering from the war satisfactorily by saying it was time to save their taxpayers' money by ending aid payments. By the time Marshall Aid began to arrive, the exchange value of the pound was under pressure, and this was intensified by a slight recession in the United States. For most of 1949 the government struggled to avoid devaluation. The balance of payments showed a steady deficit and every business that could keep out of sterling held its money in some other currency. Sir Stafford Cripps, the Chancellor of the Exchequer, asserted boldly that the country would not devalue, and the government seemed to treat the battle to hold the exchange rate as an affair of national honour rather than a question of economic management. By September the pressure was too great, and the pound was devalued to a level of $2.80. Most other currencies were devalued, in terms of dollars, at the same time; the operation was as much a general revision of the exchange rates laid down at the end of the war as an event in British history, but the British took it much more seriously than anybody else.

Cripps felt guilty because he had said there would be no devaluation; the government had been shown to be unable to control the financial situation; politicians felt that devaluation was discreditable and that the existing exchange rate was in some way bound up with national prestige. Devaluation really meant that it made no sense to try to return to the financial position of the 1930s; the fall was too great, and the dominance of the United States was too obvious. Politicians were sure devaluation would lead to electoral disaster, but the government gained ground in the opinion polls in the next few months. On the whole the economic effects were beneficial, but the step robbed the Labour government of some of its confidence and encouraged its opponents.

It also provided the government with a strong hint that the world really had changed since 1939 and that Britain would not be able to regain her pre-war position. When Attlee formed his government, he initially thought of making Bevin Chancellor of the Exchequer and Dalton Foreign Secretary. Among the people who advised him to change the two appointments round was George VI, and it has been suggested that it was wrong for the King to influence such decisions, or alternatively that he did not actually have any effect on the choice. Undoubtedly the King was only one among a number of people putting arguments to Attlee, but he certainly had a right to give advice, and it would be harsh to say that the Prime Minister ought never to take the monarch's advice. One reason for appointing Bevin was that he was thought likely to 'stand up to the Russians'. In the summer of 1945 the Americans were intent on withdrawing from Europe, and the Russians were intent on consolidating the fruits of victory. They were clearly determined to establish themselves in the countries assigned to them in wartime discussions, and in addition to set up a Polish government that would be subservient to them. This post-war acquisition of a sphere of influence was not morally elevated, but most of it rested on the Yalta Agreement, and in any case very little could be done about it. The opening months of the peace were embittered by British and American attempts to persuade the Russians that the three countries ought to decide their foreign policies by voting among themselves. The Russians, who foresaw that the United States and the United Kingdom would always vote together, were not in the least interested and went on building up a defensive belt on

Russia's western frontier. The Russians used some very undiplomatic language in this period, but they were never unkind enough to allude to the belt of states designed to put Russia in quarantine after the First World War by calling their east European satellites a cordon sanitaire.

If Anglo-American concerns had simply been about the Russian implementation of the Yalta Agreement, or even the establishment of police states, they might have had no consequences. The United States would not, and Britain could not, do anything about changes in eastern Europe, so their moralizing and Churchill's reference in August 1945 to an 'iron curtain' coming down over Europe might have led to nothing more than diplomatic irritation.[2] But behind the complaints about the way the Russians were behaving as conquerors lay a fear that they intended to advance further into Europe and acquire still more territory. Russian aloofness when the Communist Party was gaining control of China in the civil war in 1949, and during the Italian general election of 1948, in which the United States government took a keen and active interest, suggest that Stalin was more concerned to establish a strong defensive position in eastern Europe than to launch a grand assault to carry the revolution to western Europe, but acting on this analysis would obviously have been dangerous.

In 1946 the British government had troops in Germany, in Greece, in Persia, in India, in Egypt, in Palestine, and in the Far East. There was some concern in the United States that the war might turn out to have been fought to rebuild the British Empire, but this overseas activity had to be paid for in foreign exchange and the British balance of payments was too weak for it to go on for long. Occupying Germany was expensive; in the winter of 1945–6 the world was moving towards a disastrous wheat shortage, and bread rationing, which had been avoided throughout the war, had to be imposed in order to provide enough wheat to prevent famine in Germany and India. The country accepted this, like a good many other things in the past six years, but the strain was growing. Inside the Cabinet Dalton as Chancellor became almost Gladstonian in his enthusiasm for British withdrawal. Bevin resisted this and, as he was politically more powerful, was able to stretch British resources to the limit. Attlee said he was not directly concerned with foreign affairs, but this amounted to tacit support for Bevin. Attlee was not directly concerned with economic affairs either, and his thoughts (at least as recorded in *A Prime Minister Remembers*[3]) seem to have been directed to foreign policy rather than economic affairs. His laconic comments showed very little understanding of the economic problem.

Attlee and Bevin were not militarists or imperialists, but during their time

---

2. 16 Aug. 1945, *Commons Debates*, ccccxiii. 84.

3. Atlee devoted twice as much space to foreign affairs as to all domestic problems when reminiscing to Francis Williams (Francis Williams, *A Prime Minister Remembers: The War and Post-War Memoirs of the Rt Hon Earl Attlee* (1961)).

in office the country, which had spent so little on defence before 1939, spent much more of the national income on armaments than any other country in western Europe. Britain was more of a world power than any other European country after the war, but nobody asked if it was prudent to spend more money on military affairs than other countries of comparable strength and size. The government expected to play a decisive role in diplomacy and perhaps in a future war. The Conservatives supported higher military expenditure enthusiastically; they welcomed the National Service Bill in 1947, which imposed eighteen months of military service in peacetime and expressed regret at the loss of military power when the period was reduced to twelve months under pressure from the left wing of the Labour Party. This was not seen as an economic question, for the Labour left argued that Russia had no aggressive intentions and that conscription in peacetime was an unjustified restriction of liberty.

The government also felt the country had to enter the race for atomic weapons. This was announced as discreetly as possible: the Minister of Defence slipped it in as a subordinate clause when referring to a Defence White Paper which laid heavy stress on research in aviation and avoided any reference to atomic weapons. The remark passed quite unnoticed, and while the government frequently mentioned peaceful uses of atomic energy it said nothing more about atomic weapons.[4] The decision to enter this expensive activity was almost inevitable. The news that atomic bombs had been dropped on Japan was accompanied by predictions that atomic energy would provide almost unlimited electric power at cheap rates, and involvement in wartime development naturally led to a strong desire to go into the commercial side of atomic energy. In the months after the war the United States exploited the Quebec Agreement at least as fully as it was entitled to. The British government might have been content not to make its own bombs if it had been taken into the confidence of the United States, but Washington followed a policy of exclusion culminating in the passage of the McMahon Act, which prohibited any sharing of American information on atomic matters. Because the United Kingdom entered the field of independent atomic research as a reaction against this, British atomic weapons were always in a sense a diplomatic weapon against the United States, which might be used to trigger off a war or to provide other countries with knowledge about nuclear weapons. Attlee and Bevin, supported by Churchill, were convinced that the American alliance was the most important part of the British diplomatic position, but it was clear that America would not be a perfect ally from the British point of view. British politicians wanted to be treated as equals by the Americans, and the Americans were by this stage conscious that they were more prosperous and more powerful. At the same time the Americans were often unready to see the

---

4. 12 May 1948, *Commons Debates*, ccccl. 2117; *Parliamentary Papers*, Cmd. 7327, esp. p. 7.

difficulties of the British position, and expected complete British agreement with American policy.

Withdrawal from empire

This could be seen in the process of imperial withdrawal. The government made some useful and uncontroversial preparations to withdraw from West Africa in the not too distant future, but the issues that attracted attention were India and Palestine. Over India British and American policy was in agreement: Britain should leave as soon as was practicable. Churchill growled at the way the British Empire was clattering down, but it was impossible to think of fighting an imperial war to hold India. On the whole the Labour Party sympathized with the Hindus and the Congress Party, and the Conservatives preferred the Muslims. The government did not want to partition India and allow the Muslims a separate state, but by the end of the war their position was so strong, and their desire for partition so obvious, that it was very hard to resist. Wavell, the Viceroy at the end of the war, was not the man to bring the Indian politicians together. He was a taciturn man, well suited to the military requirements of his post, but not able to negotiate with political leaders once the war was over. At the end of 1946 the government replaced him with Mountbatten, a naval commander with royal connections, a well-developed political sense, and more sympathy for Congress than anyone of comparable prestige. At the same time the government announced that Britain would leave on 1 June 1948 whatever the situation might be. This checked American anti-imperialism, and confronted politicians in India with a more definite problem than before. Whether people realized it or not, the announcement of a deadline made partition inevitable. All that the Muslim League had to do was to sit still until the British departure; its power among the Muslims ensured that a united India could not be created without its consent. Mountbatten saw this quickly enough when he reached India in March 1947, and he also saw that the structure of government was dissolving. Civil servants were worried about their new masters, police forces were beginning to divide into Muslim and Hindu factions, rioting inspired by religious hatred was becoming more frequent, and it was possible that the army would begin to divide on religious lines. Mountbatten decided not only to accept partition but also to advance the date of independence. He hoped to reconcile the Congress leaders to partition by offering independence sooner than previously suggested, and he also foresaw difficulty in maintaining British authority for a whole year. The decision to accelerate independence caused many difficulties, and may have been responsible for a great deal of bloodshed, but it is also possible that British authority would have broken down before June 1948. In May the British Cabinet and the Indian leaders accepted partition and accelerated independence. Early in June Mountbatten announced that independence would come in August, and he set to work to draw boundary lines and divide up the assets of the Empire in India. Pakistan, two large areas of land separated by an even larger area of India, looked a most improbable country, and it was made even less plausible by ethnic and linguistic differences between the inhabitants of the eastern and the western sections. India was also an assemblage of different people, divided in language and united in religion only in the sense that Nehru's secularist socialism and Gandhi's syncretism—the hymn 'Abide with Me' was played at his funeral—had roots in a very sophisticated Hindu faith.

Independence came on 15 August. 'Long years ago', Nehru said at the celebrations, 'we made a tryst with destiny'; now India was going to meet her destiny and the greatest of all the movements for national independence had triumphed. From the imperial point of view the story had ended happily; Britain remained on good terms with both of the new countries and Mountbatten stayed on, the last Viceroy turning into the first Governor-General of independent India. Nehru became Prime Minister; Gandhi did not enter the government, but his political influence remained immense. But, while the British withdrew, the partition lines were crumbling; they had not been established long enough to enable Hindus and Muslims to adjust to the new situation. British control might have broken down if independence had not been granted so swiftly, but the massacres of the weeks after partition point to the heavy price paid for this abrupt departure. Muslims fled to Pakistan, Hindus to India; many of them never reached their destination. In the east a fragile peace was established, partly because of Gandhi's presence; on the western frontier fighting went on for weeks. The deaths ran into the hundreds of thousands. Nobody can be blamed for this collapse into butchery in the way that Hitler and Stalin can be blamed for taking their bloody decisions, but it was an unhappy way to end the Empire in India.

The Palestine Mandate came to an equally unsatisfactory end—in some ways it was worse, because the British government did not emerge on good terms with any of the contestants. In November 1917 the British government had declared in the Balfour Declaration that Palestine should become a national home for the Jewish people. As Palestine was inhabited mainly by Arabs, this sowed the seeds of trouble, though the harvest took some years to ripen. Britain secured the Palestine Mandate as part of her extensive gains in the Middle East in 1919. Jewish immigration flowed fairly slowly in the 1920s, but in the early 1930s British policy encouraged a more rapid rate of immigration, and after Hitler came to power in 1933 there was a flood of Jewish refugees. By 1936 the Arabs had become much more determined to resist the change than in earlier years. In 1922, 11 per cent of the population of Palestine was Jewish; by 1939 the figure had risen to 29 per cent. In 1939 the British government gave way to the increasingly desperate and violent Arab opposition by announcing strict limits on Jewish immigration.

The Labour 1945 election programme accepted the Zionist point of view, and the American government was also Zionist. Once in office Bevin became more and more impressed by the argument that making Palestine into an independent country for Jewish immigrants would mean dispossessing the Arab inhabitants and annoying Britain's Arab allies all over the Middle East. The oil of the Middle East had not yet become one of the dominant economic facts of the post-war world, but the Suez Canal and the remains of the Middle East hegemony established after the First World War were powerful reasons for Britain to want to avoid offending the Arabs. The United States pressed for 100,000 Jewish immigrants to be admitted, which would have gone a long way towards accepting the principle of letting in a virtually unrestricted flow of immigrants. The British government was not willing to admit the proposed 100,000 immigrants, and illegal immigration became an ever-increasing problem as boats were chartered to smuggle refugees into Palestine. Inside Palestine Jewish guerrilla forces took up arms against the British, and the country slid towards the condition of Ireland under the Black and Tans. British troops were kept under better control than they had been in Ireland, but Jewish 'terrorist' activity rapidly reduced British sympathy for Zionism. In America, and to some extent in other countries, there was a feeling of guilt for allowing the Jews to be massacred by Hitler; people in Britain knew that they had done their best to defeat Hitler, and were less ready to admit that Jewish displaced persons in the refugee camps of Europe had special claims to be allowed to go to a new country and settle it.

During the course of 1946 it became clear that no conceivable settlement would please either side in the struggle. Anti-Jewish feeling increased in Britain as a result of Jewish efforts to establish their position by force. The Arabs showed no readiness to make concessions to the Jewish desire to set up a state of their own and in fact felt that the British were pursuing an anti-Arab policy by allowing Jews in at all. In February 1947 the government referred the Palestine Mandate to the United Nations and invited it to settle the issue. In November the United Nations issued its plan for partitioning Palestine and setting up an independent state of Israel, and invited the United Kingdom to administer the plan. Britain declined to do so, and prepared to withdraw from Palestine. The Mandate came to an end in May 1948 and the newly created state of Israel was immediately attacked by the neighbouring Arab countries, but proved quite capable of defending itself. The Arabs tended to blame Britain and America for the creation of Israel, and the Israelis had no reason to feel grateful to Britain. This was one of the least successful disengagements from empire since Yorktown. The British tended to blame the United States, and in particular to exaggerate the influence of the Jewish section of the American electorate.

In other, less inflammable, areas problems were handled quite skilfully. Burma became independent, and left the Commonwealth in the belief that this made independence more complete. Ireland became a republic in April 1949, and left the Commonwealth. This was partly out of irritation that the British government did not end partition by handing Ulster over to Ireland, and in response Parliament passed an Act, when Ireland departed, declaring that partition would be ended only with the consent of the Parliament of Northern Ireland. Canada abolished the right of appeal to the Privy Council, and acquired the right to amend her own constitution except for the vital clauses defining federal and provincial powers; French Canadians felt it might be safer to keep the right to change this section far away in London instead of trusting it anywhere near Anglophone Canadians. Newfoundland, which had relapsed from its self-governing status and become a Crown Colony during the 1930s because of financial difficulties, voted in 1949 to join Canada. In 1950 a conference of Commonwealth Foreign Ministers at Colombo decided to set up a plan for mutual financial assistance, which provided the framework for aid for the newly independent Asian members.

A more important question for the continuance of the Commonwealth arose when India wanted to become a republic. In constitutional theory the Commonwealth was a unity because the King was the head of state of all the member nations and the Governors-General acted as his representatives. The Indian decision awakened some emotional opposition in Britain, but the important question was whether India wanted to remain a member of the Commonwealth. The Commonwealth Prime Ministers at the 1949 conference assured Nehru that remaining a member would not compromise India's independence of action and would provide her with useful diplomatic contacts. India became a republic and stayed in the Commonwealth; the King took up the new title of Head of the Commonwealth.

India's presence in the Commonwealth was among other things a source of steady pressure on Britain not to become too committed in the Cold War. During the period of tension between Russia and America in the 1950s the Commonwealth had to consider the feelings of India as a non-aligned country, and this helped to explain the moderating role that Britain and Canada tried to play. On the other hand, Pakistan aligned itself with the West some of the time, in the hope of receiving diplomatic support in its dispute with India over Kashmir.

The Cold War

Whatever the moderating effect of the Commonwealth, Britain stood on America's side against Russia. Marshall Aid had no specific political conditions, but the recipients were clearly under some sort of obligation to the United States. In February 1948 the Communist ministers in Czechoslovakia carried out a *coup d'état* and dragged the country into alliance with Russia. The coup showed that it was unwise to give Communists control of the police, but, just as British intervention in Greece was no proof of aggressive intentions in the Balkans, Russia's seizure of Czechoslovakia did not prove that Russian armies were going to advance to the west. Attlee believed that the United States did not take the threat of Russian aggression seriously until free access through East Germany to the American, British, and French sectors of Berlin was blocked in June 1948.[5] The United States and Britain flew in supplies for ten months until the Russians gave way and allowed free access again. The United States and Britain managed this crisis skilfully, and it encouraged the Western countries to work out the 1949 agreements that set up the North Atlantic Treaty Organization for an initial period of twenty years, which could be renewed; the signatories gave mutual guarantees of each other's territory in Europe, though not of their colonial possessions. The treaty contained provisions for economic cooperation, though in the event the nations of the alliance worked through the Organization for European Economic Cooperation when they wanted to coordinate their economic policies.

The government responded to the military needs of the alliance by starting a programme of rearmament and increasing the period of national service to eighteen months. This stretched the economy still further, but was not beyond the country's powers. The ideal of a united Europe had emerged as an important force on the other side of the Channel, but the government did not believe that the British really wanted to surrender any of their sovereignty to a European Parliament and showed practically no interest in the meetings of the Council of Europe at Strasbourg. The Opposition was more willing to take an interest; Churchill went to Strasbourg and was given the applause due to the greatest living European. He had spoken of Britain at the centre of three circles, the English-speaking world, the Commonwealth, and Europe. The post-war government continued to be America's closest ally, and paid considerable attention to changes in the Commonwealth, but the interest it took in Europe was that of an outsider.

A Conservative government would probably have followed a fairly similar foreign policy. An even more active foreign policy would have strained the economy too far, and it seems unlikely that the Conservatives would have been less active. Churchill said fierce things about the granting of independence to India, and possibly he would have involved Britain in an attempt—almost certainly hopeless—to resist the change. The Conservatives at times suggested that they would get on better than the socialists with the Americans. Congressmen did sometimes complain at paying for what they called the excesses of the Welfare State, but if the Conservatives had been in power the Americans would have complained about paying for the British Empire—if anything, relations went better because the Labour government understood why Americans were suspicious of it; Americans found British imperialists particularly

5. Williams, *A Prime Minister Remembers*, 172.

irritating because they never understood what American anti-imperialism was all about. At a more personal level, most people would think Churchill was a more attractive person than Attlee, but any British Prime Minister in the late 1940s needed to establish good relations with Truman and Nehru, and it is quite possible that Churchill would have failed disastrously with both of them. Attlee was ideally suited for getting on with them. Under Bevin the Foreign Office emerged from the obscurity into which it had fallen after Eden's resignation in 1938, but it was greatly helped by the good relations Attlee had with a number of heads of government.

Domestic policy of the Labour government

In domestic affairs the difference between government and Opposition was sharp—perhaps all the sharper because the Labour front bench seemed to Conservatives to be so reasonable and moderate on foreign policy. The Opposition saw the Parliamentary Labour Party as an uneasy alliance of sound men like Bevin and wild men like Bevan. On foreign policy Bevin and Attlee defied the left wing of their party; on domestic affairs, it was thought, they were dragged at the chariot wheels of the Labour left. This picture was not accurate. However much the left wing of the party felt that Bevin was playing the American or the Arab game, they had no doubt that he was a good socialist. The Labour Party was, by the normal standards of parties of the left, unusually united on domestic affairs. The great mass of legislation placed before the Commons helped to keep the Labour Party together.

The Labour government's legislation has been called a social revolution, but much of it was legislation against a counter-revolution. Many of the developments which became established in the 1940s had been foreshadowed in the First World War, and then been swept away after 1918. Governments in the 1920s wanted to get back to 'before the war' and, if they did not succeed in this impossible aim, at least they reduced the power of the trade unions, made sure that the State would not go very far in providing welfare services, and forced the government to retire from the central role in the economy which it had played during the war years. Between 1945 and 1951 the temporary developments of the Second World War were established as normal parts of English life. There was some reaction against this in the 1950s, but by then very few people really hoped or wanted to go back to 'before the war'. In 1945 there was a good deal of enthusiasm for a brave new world, and one of its most clearly defined features was simply that it should avoid the evils of the 1930s.

The most controversial legislation of the Labour government was the nationalization programme, but even here the political resistance was slight. The Conservatives did not find it easy to understand what had happened in the election, and were afraid that strenuous opposition would only make them more unpopular. The Bank of England was taken over with no trouble at all;

most capitalist countries already had state-run central banks, and Churchill fairly clearly thought there were good arguments for nationalization. In fact, there was so little debate that nobody asked what difference nationalization would make. If the Governor was always to be a banker with a banker's concern for the soundness and international standing of sterling, changing the way in which the Governor was chosen would change very little. A dominant Chancellor of the Exchequer could impose a policy on the Bank, as Cripps asserted when he said 'The Bank is my creature',[6] but then a Chancellor with a clear-cut policy might have imposed it on Norman between the wars. Keeping the airlines nationalized was even less controversial: nobody imagined a private company could run them without a subsidy, and if the government chose to run them itself nobody would object and the aircraft manufacturers would probably feel safer financially.

Nationalization of coal and the railways had been in Labour Party programmes for many years, the workers in the two industries were strongly in favour of the step, and the position of the owners had become very weak. Both industries had done badly between the wars, and had not been able to spend much money on development during the war. The railway lines and the rolling stock were worn down, the mines were running into difficult seams and needed new equipment. Both industries needed large-scale capital investment, but they were in decline and offered unattractive prospects to private industry. Fifteen or twenty years later both industries were sinking back into their interwar state of depression but until then coal-mining and rail transport were two of the most essential sectors of the economy. There was a good case for nationalizing these industries that owed nothing to the general case for socialism.

Yet the performance of these two industries did more than anything else to reduce enthusiasm for public ownership, and thus weakening the Labour government. Vesting day for the coal industry was 1 January 1947. The flag of the National Coal Board went up at the pitheads; the miners' long fight against the owners was over. But the first few months of 1947 were the coldest the country had had for over sixty years. The government asserted that only another 2 million tons of coal (or 1 per cent of total national production) were needed to avoid disaster, but the coal did not come; for a few weeks trains could not run, factories had to close, unemployment returned to the levels of the 1930s, and housewives found gas and electricity flowing at such low pressure that simple meals took hours to cook. Obviously the Coal Board could not have transformed the situation within six weeks of taking office, but equally obviously the public was looking for someone to blame and as a result

---

6. A. Shonfield, *British Economic Policy since the* War (1958), 213. But Shonfield went on: 'More to the point is the remark made to me subsequently by a Conservative politician with more exact knowledge of the inner workings of the institution: "Somebody may have to nationalise the Bank of England one of these days; the Socialists don't know how."'

it was hostile to the nationalized industry ever afterwards. Supporters of the free play of the market must have been amused by the way the Coal Board's attempts to keep down prices added to its troubles. Although coal prices had gone up faster than most during the war, the large unsatisfied demand after nationalization showed that they could certainly have been raised still further. Prices were kept down to check inflation and to provide assistance to British manufacturers, so demand rose all the higher; there were complaints that the coal miners were betraying the country, and there were also complaints that the Coal Board was not running at a profit. Small coal was sold at a high price which was used to subsidize the sales of large coal, and people complained that the mines produced too much small and dirty coal and not enough large clean lumps. The miners had enjoyed wage rises during the war which brought them back to something like their pre-1914 position as aristocrats of labour; it was not surprising, particularly when there was so little they could buy with their wages, that they took more time off than before. After the war workers wanted a five-day week, with no work on Saturday mornings; several industries conceded the point, and the Coal Board accepted it for the mines. But so great was the demand for coal that union leaders had to go round their men persuading them that their union and their government depended on them to give up their Saturday mornings. This was a fair enough account of the state of the balance of payments and the miners went back to a five-and-a-half day week, but there was an understandable increase in absenteeism and in unofficial strikes, and a sharp fall in the miners' initial feeling that the National Coal Board was on their side in a way the owners could never be.

On the railways the story was much the same. There had been complaints before the war about the way they ran, and they had been facing severe competition from road transport in almost every field of operation—the transport of heavy loads like coal was left to the railways, but everything else could be done by lorries, by cars, or by buses. The growth of the Transport Workers' Union and the decline of the National Union of Railwaymen reflected this change. During the war the petrol shortage and the need to move great quantities of troops and weapons round the country restored the position of the railways. The 1947 Transport Act took over everything that ran on wheels for profit, except for short-distance road haulage, lorries used by companies for their own products, and municipal bus companies, so the Transport Commission could think in terms of subsidizing rail traffic from road profits, but passengers noticed that trains ran late, were dirty, and sometimes were cancelled. The railways received no credit for the fact that fares had risen rather less than most other things, and any increase in fares drove customers away, which left the railways with no financial room for manoeuvre.

Coal and the railways gave the critics of nationalization plenty of opportunity to blame the principle of public ownership for the failures of these two industries to provide the service that people wanted. The weaknesses that had made nationalization necessary also made it certain that customers would be dissatisfied. Capital was provided for making up arrears of maintenance work, and probably nobody except the government could have done this. Coal production went up, though not as fast as had been hoped. Older miners were retiring and young men were hard to recruit. The government assured them that there would be no return to the 1930s and that this time coal-mining employment would be secure, but this was not enough to tempt people to go down the mines.

Electricity and gas were taken over in the course of 1948 with much less trouble. This was not a great change: gas and electricity were in many cases produced by municipal authorities and electricity was already integrated into a single system by the government-operated central grid. Town gas, produced by coking coal, was a declining industry and electricity required capital on a very large scale. In industries like this the case for nationalization was admitted to be strong. The Opposition attacked the failure of nationalization to produce any dramatic improvement in coal or the railways, but did not seem completely confident that private enterprise could run either of the public utility industries.

The steel industry generated the only intense struggle in Parliament over the principle of nationalization. Because there were disputes inside the government about the need for nationalization and about the form it should take, the Bill was not introduced early enough in the lifetime of the 1945 Parliament to pass the House of Commons in three successive sessions, but the government prepared the ground by introducing a Bill amending the 1911 Parliament Act in the 1947–8 session. This Bill reduced the length of the Lords' veto by a year and, as it was to apply from the date it was introduced into the Commons, the iron and steel nationalization Bill which was introduced in the 1948–9 session could be passed into law, despite the Lords, in the lifetime of the 1945 Parliament. The Lords had not previously done much to hinder the Labour legislative programme; Lord Beaverbrook had rallied some opposition against the American loan, but on most issues they had followed the leadership of Lord Salisbury and accepted Bills from the Commons without any drastic amendment. On the Iron and Steel Bill they took a more active line, as had been foreseen, but their main concern was to stop the Bill taking effect until after the general election which had to be held by 1950. The Bill took over the shares of the companies in the steel business and transferred them to a unifying central board, but the organizational structure of the industry was left unchanged. No doubt the board would have taken decisions when installing new plant that reflected some approach to central planning, but it was a form of public ownership which could very easily be reversed.

Many people saw the nationalization Acts as the distinctively socialist part of the government's programme. Some thought it ran the economy in a way that could be called socialist. The repeal of the 1927 Trade Disputes Act in 1946, one of the first pieces of legislation of the new Parliament, was welcomed by trade union leaders as a sign that they were not seen as revolutionaries. But in addition a great deal of legislation was based on wartime reports and recommendations. Much of it lay in the area of reforms to which the pre-1914 Liberal Party had been moving before it disintegrated into internecine struggles.

By 1949 it was accepted that Britain was a 'Welfare State'. The phrase was widely used, outside Britain as well as inside; the word 'welfare' confused North Americans, for whom it had overtones of the poor law, but inside Britain it was always used in tones of approval; Liberals and Conservatives pointed out that their parties had also played a part in building the Welfare State. The contribution of the Labour government was the 1946 National Insurance Act and the accompanying National Health Service Act, which was in fact the enactment of the Beveridge Report. There were one or two small changes; Beveridge's idea that old-age pensions should rise slowly for a period of twenty years was abandoned, and they began at a level high enough to mean men over 65 and women over 60 would not need to go to the National Assistance Board unless special circumstances arose. The scheme of a single unified payment for flat-rate benefits was intended to give everybody a right to a subsistence income without any means test. It also assured people of support in time of unemployment; although decades passed before unemployment returned to anything like the level of the 1920s and 1930s, the fear of it hung in the air for some years, and everybody was anxious to guard against it.

The distinctive feature of the British Welfare State was the health service, with its basic principle that no money was to be paid for anything to do with medicine. Hospitals were given grants by the government, and this almost eliminated the tiresome practice of flag days for collecting money from passers-by in the street. Some hospital governors complained that the voluntary principle was being removed, but this aroused very little response. False teeth, spectacles, and medical prescriptions were provided free of charge, and there was an immense immediate demand for them. Critics of the health service suggested that this was wasteful and that people were getting things they did not need. It is much more likely that these patients had not previously been able to afford them: working-class budgets of the 1930s allowed very little for medical expenses beyond the cost of insurance for medical consultation.

The serious resistance to the health service came from the doctors. The hospital consultants on the whole felt their interests had been looked after, and were glad to see the fund-raising side of hospital activity become less important. The general practitioners were less happy. The scheme asked them to set up practices of 1,000 to 3,000 patients each, for which the Ministry of Health paid them a basic fee and a capitation payment for each patient. Most doctors received a higher income under this arrangement than they had

earned previously, but they were afraid that the system might later be converted into a salaried service or that they might lose their right to remain in
private practice or that the Ministry of Health might dictate to them on
medical issues and tell them what drugs to use for particular diseases. The
dispute was ludicrously like that of 1911: on the one hand, a Welsh minister in
charge of the scheme, with a gift for organizing things smoothly and easily but
a taste for victory rather than conciliation in debate; on the other hand,
general practitioners uneasy about the future, led by medical politicians who
were much more intransigent than the doctors they led; the same votes, in
December 1946 and February 1948, to refuse to act inside the service; the same
realization that, whatever the votes might say, a doctors' strike was not practicable. Assurances were given on the detailed points in dispute; doctors were
allowed to keep private patients who could arrange to be treated outside the
service or be given a bed in a private hospital by paying for it. The National
Health Service started work on 5 July 1948.

Critics of the service attacked the amount of money spent on it. Some of
their points were understandable; the service was free to everybody from all
over the world, and this internationalism seemed overgenerous. Some of their
criticism simply ignored the steady rise in all prices, and argued as though the
health service could run on a fixed amount of cash. The politicians of the
1940s and 1950s tacitly agreed that the health service should receive a steady 4
per cent of the national income. More expensive and more effective drugs
such as penicillin and the antibiotics were coming into use, and in other
countries the proportion of national income devoted to medical expenses
went up. The National Health Service may have provided the same real
services at a lower cost than elsewhere, but reluctance to increase the share of
the national income spent on the service at a time when medical costs and
medical salaries were going up was likely to undermine the whole system in
the long run.

The pre-1939 foundations of the Welfare State were not always easy to trace,
but the 1948 Criminal Justice Act was clearly related to earlier discussions, for
it was based on a draft Bill that had been prepared before the war but not
discussed. The Act moved towards greater leniency for criminals; flogging was
virtually abolished, the probation service was extended, and an attempt was
made to reduce the danger that conviction and imprisonment for young
offenders would simply initiate them into the world of crime. The Opposition
in Parliament accepted this without too much discussion, but ferocious dele-
gates at Conservative Party conferences for some years afterwards would ask
for flogging to be brought back. An amendment to abolish capital punishment
was passed on a free vote in the Commons; as was the case throughout the
struggle over capital punishment in the next twenty years, the bulk of the
abolitionists were Labour MPs, the bulk of the retentionists were Conservative. When the Bill came to the House of Lords, the capital punishment

amendment was defeated, and the original Bill was then accepted. At this stage the bishops were strongly retentionist; probably the view of the bench of bishops changed more completely during the years of discussion than that of any other parliamentary group. Other changes in the law allowed citizens to sue the government as of right, instead of having to ask the government for permission to sue, and extended the system of legal aid to cover civil cases, with a considerable effect on the number of divorces.[7] Divorce would inevitably have become more frequent after the war: wartime marriages were sometimes hasty, some marriages broke down under the stress of wartime separation, and, more generally, the way people saw life and marriage had changed, but legal aid made it easier to act on these developments.

The old question of the land reappeared, though in a less controversial form than in the 1910s or the 1960s. The Agriculture Act of 1947 put the marketing boards and subsidies for farmers, which had been developing over the past ten or fifteen years and had grown so important during the war, into a permanent form. It allowed eventual dispossession of a farmer for bad husbandry, but in every other way it made the position gained by farmers during the war secure; it can be disputed whether the working class became better off during the war, but farmers undoubtedly did. The 1947 Act stabilized their gains, and it was said that only after the Act had been passed were they prosperous enough to pay their Conservative Party membership fees. Dalton, as Chancellor of the Exchequer, strengthened the National Trust and made it easy to give property of historical or artistic importance to the nation in lieu of death duties. In 1947 the Town and Country Planning Act attempted to deal with the old problem of increment in land values that Lloyd George and Snowden had tried to tackle. The Act declared that all future increment in land value caused by development was the property of the State, and set up a fund of £300 million to compensate landowners whose land might go up in price as a result of development, if this potential increase had not yet been realized.

Quite apart from this massive legislative programme, the Labour government had to run the country, and in the circumstances of 1945 the first task was to make the economy work efficiently on a peacetime basis. Dalton was convinced of the virtues of low interest rates. He had praised cheap money in his pre-war book on public finance, and when he took office he was determined to carry his policy into effect. For eighteen months or so he was fairly successful. The war had been financed with loans at 3 per cent; in 1946 Dalton issued irredeemable government bonds paying 2.5 per cent, the rate offered by Goschen in the 1890s. This could be managed only by allowing a larger and

7. David Butler and Gareth Butler, *British Political Facts 1900–2000* (2000) gives figures for divorces on p. 351. They rose from 8,000 in 1940 to 32,000 in 1950, a faster rate of growth than the climb from 62,000 in 1970 to 158,000 in 1980.

larger proportion of the government's debts to take the form of short-term obligations. Dalton was not particularly worried by this, because it built up a high level of demand, which was what he wanted. The cold weather and fuel crisis early in 1947 brought the extreme version of this policy to an end, but the nationalization compensation was paid in 3 per cent stock and the combination of a high level of demand and a very liquid government debt was maintained throughout the Labour government's period of office. Dalton's budgets began by reducing taxes because military expenditure was diminishing, but, while the general level of income tax went down, the level of supertax went up so that rich people were no better off. Dalton wanted to restore the death duties to something of their former importance. They had contributed about 10 per cent of the national revenue ever since the beginning of the century, but during the Second World War they had fallen to 3 per cent of national revenue. Dalton's increase of the rate of duty to a top rate of 80 per cent did for a short time raise its contribution. The improvement did not last long; property owners found increasingly ingenious ways of handing on their money before death and the yield of the duties slipped back to 3 per cent of total revenue.

Dalton's boisterous personality made people think he was deliberately following an inflationist policy. A remark he made about allotting money to help depressed areas 'with a song in his heart' was misapplied to suggest that he was spending money light-heartedly in all directions.[8] War savings provided a great deal of suppressed demand in the system, and he was only concerned that it should push the economy forward without worrying too much about its effect on prices, although his budgets were much less inflationary than those produced just after 1918. He knew that the country's foreign exchange position had to be protected. Probably he underestimated the dangers of convertibility, though he may simply have felt that it was an unavoidable condition of the American loan, which was generally recognized to be indispensable. After convertibility had to be abandoned in the summer of 1947, deflationary measures were prepared, and Dalton introduced a budget in the autumn. This had been done only once before in peacetime, in 1931, and the comparison underlined the fact that a real crisis existed. Dalton genially told a reporter just before going into the Commons that the budget increased purchase tax and profits tax; this was printed in the evening papers, and Dalton had to resign on account of his indiscretion.

His successor, Cripps, was more austere in personality, and had a more dominant position in the Cabinet. The contrast in personality led people to overemphasize the differences in policy. The Cabinet had shared Dalton's view that things were going well and the economy could be encouraged to move forward, and in 1947 he had been ready to increase taxes to improve the

8. H. Dalton, *Memoirs, 1945–1960* (1962), 110.

balance of payments. When Cripps came to the Treasury, the need for restraint was generally accepted. He did not remove excess demand from the economy completely, and to some extent he accepted the Daltonian approach of allowing high demand and relying on strict control of the supply side to restrain inflation. His 1948 budget increased the tax on tobacco to a height that was intended to reduce consumption and thus save foreign exchange. He also imposed a temporary surcharge on unearned income that rose to a maximum of £1.40 per pound received, which amounted to a capital levy of about 1 per cent of the underlying wealth. Cripps's puritanism of manner was ideally suited for the task of calling on people for self-sacrifice, and he obtained a considerable response. Manufacturers felt it was their duty to go into export markets. For about thirty months from early in 1948 trade union leaders persuaded their followers not to press for wage increases, and real wages fell a little. Nobody enjoyed this period, and the word 'austerity' clung to it and the Labour Party for some time to come; Cripps was not a man to make people enjoy things, but nobody could have made a struggle to maintain a sound balance of payments as exhilarating as 1940. Churchill found Cripps a satisfying target—'there, but for the grace of God, goes God' caught Cripps's sense of mission rather well. But while people made jokes about Cripps, they were the jokes that schoolboys made about a headmaster behind his back.[9]

Dalton had not kept up the full wartime rigour of the planning process, though items in short supply were controlled by allocation and licensing. Under Cripps more ambitious attempts at planning were made, but they were not successful: the forecasts and targets were not reached, or sometimes were exceeded in a way which disturbed the general pattern of the plan. As the years went by, the forecasts became less sweeping and planning lost its high prestige. Devaluation in 1949 released the economy from some overstrain, but, even if an economy could be fully planned by modern economic techniques, the resources available in the late 1940s were certainly not enough to run a planned economy in peacetime. Planning in war was relatively easy because the object was to reduce supplies for civilian consumption and produce a large but finite range of products for the fighting forces. In peacetime no overriding objective could be set in the way that higher arms production had been the wartime objective because the number of different things to produce was unlimited. Nevertheless, Cripps's policies did produce more exports, a more controlled increase in prices than had been seen earlier in the 1940s, and a relatively high rate of economic growth.

9. M. Sissons and P. French (eds.), *The Age of Austerity* (1961), 179.

Opposition to the Labour government

The Labour government, despite this long list of achievements, was increasingly unpopular with some sections of the public. This unpopularity was not primarily a matter of grumbling about rationing; undoubtedly people found rationing a tiresome restriction and queuing an annoying way to spend their time, but this was not the source of the deepest bitterness. Food rationing continued throughout the Labour government's tenure of office. The trivial concessions given by Ministers of Food at Christmas time—an ounce of butter extra, or the right to buy another twopence worth of meat—would have tested the patience of any population by reminding them of the possibility of plenty, and the fact that it was clearly not coming yet. Woolton had a gift for good public relations; his Labour successors had a gift for upsetting their public. Dr Summerskill may possibly have been correct when she said very few people could tell the difference between butter and margarine, but it gave the impression that she was not really interested in doing anything to help people indulge their preference for buying butter. Odd food, such as whale meat, and odd food with odder names, such as snoek, were offered to the public; and were rejected. Such things, it was felt, might be expected of a government dominated by the image of the vegetarian Cripps.

But annoying though all this was, there is little sign that it affected many votes. The strident emotions of the period were felt by the people who had voted Conservative in 1945 and felt, as Evelyn Waugh the novelist put it, that living under a socialist government was like living under an army of occupation. Insult was far from a one-sided matter: paladins of the left, like Bevan, who said the Tory party which imposed the Means Test was lower than vermin, or Shinwell, who said that the rest of the country apart from the working class wasn't worth a tinker's cuss, caused quite understandable alarm, and some people were even more upset when they were told that Sir Hartley Shawcross had said: 'We are the masters now.' Members of the middle class, whose political judgement had perhaps been dulled by the war, mistook Sir Hartley (who had been slightly misquoted) for the leader of a rebellious working class swarming forward to wipe out civilization in Britain.[10]

The opposition to the Labour government drew its strength from two rather different sources, which would have had some difficulty in working out a common policy if they had had to go into details. Many people simply wanted to get back to before the war. At one level this meant having servants again; they had left for other jobs to an even greater extent than in the First World War, and had shown much less sign of coming back. People spoke as if they had all gone off to factories, a comment that suggested that servants were generally underrated; conscientious and tidy girls, who could have got the

10. V. Brome, *Aneurin Bevan* (1953), 189; H. Hopkins, *The New Look* (1963), 154.

better jobs (and nobody ever complained about the servant problem without explaining that service in her house was one of the better jobs), went in for typing instead.[11] Members of the middle class who were really determined to get back to 'before the war' emigrated. At first they went to South Africa, and when the Nationalist Party defeated Smuts's pro-British government in 1948 they went to Kenya or Rhodesia instead. In any case Africa seemed to offer the prospect of servants, no income tax to speak of, and no rationing, and they shook the dust of Britain off their feet. This was a drastic answer, though to some extent it was only a resumption of the normal British habit of emigration, which had been in decline in the 1930s and during the war. Many people were worse off than they had been before the war, though their position did not deteriorate under the Labour government and their complaints about their financial problems were an assertion that the government ought to be doing something to restore their previous position.

The country's income distribution had not altered much in aggregate terms: before the war the top 10 per cent of the population had enjoyed 38 per cent of the national income (post-tax), and after the war the top 10 per cent enjoyed 30 per cent. The next 40 per cent had gained an extra 5 per cent of national income, and the rest had gained an extra 3 per cent. As the total national income was about the same in the years just after the war as in 1938, the top 10 per cent had lost almost a quarter of its income.[12] But discontent went deeper than this. Aggregate figures do not show how many people were worse off than before the war, because the people filling places in the top 10 or the top 50 per cent were not necessarily the people who had occupied these places before the war. Salaries in old-established occupations went up very little, and did not keep up with the rising cost of living or with the additional demands of the income tax. These people sometimes found they earned less than skilled manual workers or people in newly created middle-class jobs, and they resented the change as well as disliking the actual limitation of their resources. The middle class tended to assume that all manual workers should get less than anybody who worked in a bank or an office; the rapid increase in the pay for jobs like coal-mining during the 1940s contradicted this assumption and led to discontent.

The middle class had been overtaken by the laws of supply and demand. For about a century punctuality, literacy, and honesty with money had been in relatively short supply, and clerical salaries had reflected the fact. The demand for people to keep the books for firms and banks after industrialization had created a clerical middle class, but the qualities required were no longer in such short supply. The traditional middle-class occupations lost ground under Conservative as well as Labour governments, but the middle class did not see

11. Guy Routh, *Occupation and Pay in Great Britain 1906–60* (1965), 25 and 33.
12. Dudley Seers, *The Levelling of Incomes since 1938* (1951), 39.

the problem just after the war in that way: it assumed that the change was all the fault of socialism. *The Economist* put the view of this section of society concisely when it wrote that the middle class should have 'more than its numerical weight in British politics—instead of less, as at present'.[13]

People outside politics could afford to sound the trumpets for class warfare in this way, but the Opposition in Parliament had decided not to resist the Labour legislation with any great determination, lest worse befall. As a result, while some supporters of the Conservative Party were as rancorous as at any time in the century except for the height of the Ulster crisis, resistance in the Commons was less strenuous than in the years before 1914. Finding out whether the Labour government in fact neglected the middle class is more complicated. Under the wartime Coalition the working classes had greatly improved their relative position and no Labour government could attempt to reverse this change, which meant the middle class was bound to feel ill treated. The prices of items for living in a specifically middle-class way went up faster than the working-class cost-of-living index during the war but rose slower after the war and, apart from this slight relative gain, the middle classes did unexpectedly well out of the social welfare legislation of the Labour government.[14] A fair amount of this advantage came simply because they knew how to handle the machinery rather better than the working class, so they got all they were entitled to. But in addition the 1911 Insurance Act had been designed to help the manual worker and had assumed that non-manual workers could look after themselves; many salaried workers were better off as a result of the National Health Service, though this varied according to their previous arrangements. Probably the change of the 1940s that affected the social position of the middle class most sharply was the 1944 Education Act, but its effects were very far from uniform.

The Act carried into effect the proposals of the Hadow Report of 1926, which had discovered that children were divided into academically skilled, technically skilled, and practically minded groups. As this was in accordance with both Plato's theories and the existing organization of schools for education after 11, it was accepted without too much argument. The examination by which working-class students had won scholarships to grammar schools was brought up to date by including intelligence tests, and became the universal examination by which everybody was classified. At the same time fees for state secondary education were abolished. This development was initially a blessing for the middle classes, because their children went on to secondary education, usually costing a certain amount in fees. But one reason why the middle classes had paid fees was to make sure that their children did not go to the same schools as the mass of the population, so the abolition of fees brought

13. *The Economist*, 14 Feb. 1948, quoted in W. G. Runciman, *Relative Deprivation and Social Justice* (1966), 130.
14. Seers, *The Levelling of Incomes since 1938*, 11–14.

trouble; parents who had been able to guarantee a little social exclusiveness for their children by paying fees and sending them to a grammar school had now to deal with a world in which the grammar school was less exclusive than before and in which the examination results might consign their children to a secondary modern school. And there was never any doubt that this was not a happy fate. Educationists talked about parity of esteem, and the eleven-plus examination was said to assess children's aptitude, but everybody knew that the examination was just the old examination for grammar school scholarships, and that going to a secondary modern school was a sign of failure. Some of the more thinly populated counties of Wales and some Labour councils with strong views about equality established comprehensive secondary schools to which all the children of the area went without an examination. The middle class found even the limited egalitarianism of the eleven-plus examination, combined with abolition of fees, quite distasteful enough. Those who could afford it sent their children to private fee-paying schools, which led to a boom in public-school applications for entrance, and several new fee-paying schools were opened. Those who could not afford this way out were not likely to feel in any way reconciled to the Labour government.

Another line of attack on the government was launched by people who had no particular desire to get back to the past, but supported the free play of the market and untrammelled private enterprise. In theory they should have welcomed developments like higher pay for coal miners; miners and coal were in short supply, and high wages were presumably the best way to produce more. Demands for economic liberalism and private enterprise were made at both a theoretical and a practical level; the theoretical case was that British industry was being held back by controls and restrictions, and that everything would go much better if market considerations were allowed greater weight. This case is hard to prove. The British economy expanded rather faster under the Labour government's system of controls than it had done for any equally long peace-time period since 1873 at least, though this does not necessarily mean that the government was running the economy in the best possible way; the period of post-war reconstruction was exceptional, and committed supporters of the free market approach might say that the rate of growth fell in the 1950s, after the controls had been removed, because new and subtler problems had appeared that did not have to be faced in the late 1940s.

The relatively rapid expansion of the economy was in one sense the cause of the more practical complaints about Labour's conduct of the economy. Each individual business in the late 1940s could sell much more and increase its profits. The obstacle to this was the government: by restrictions on raw materials, by refusals to grant building licences when requested, and by insisting on detailed explanations why a proposed development was desirable, it stopped businesses from going ahead and doing their job of making and selling things. Douglas Jay, who asked people to believe that the man from

Whitehall knew best what should be done, presented the government's attitude in its most unattractive light. This did not go down well. People had had enough of Whitehall: they wanted to be free to manage, or even to mismanage, their own affairs. Well-meant attempts to help, such as the government's proposal of Industrial Development Councils for each industry, were rejected.

But although any single business, given a free hand, could have expanded very rapidly in the late 1940s, the government had to consider what would happen if all businesses expanded at the same time. In the existing state of more or less repressed demand, the natural result would have been a brisk inflation which would have been brought to a speedy end either by shortage of materials or by government deflation of the economy; this would have been a return to the events of 1919–21, and the government was determined not to have a slump like the one after the First World War. Imports were restricted, and were allocated by the government, but if this limitation on production had been removed, there was the question of finding labour. The government, in its attempts to plan the economy, sometimes referred to 'bottlenecks', by which it meant items that were in short supply and were holding up the efforts of other producers. Steel was one of the materials in short enough supply to be handled by allocation and this was a 'bottleneck', but the term could hardly be used to describe the fact that the whole of the labour force was employed and that in this sense there was a shortage of labour.

All the pre-war unemployed had found jobs, but this did not ease the situation as much as might have been expected. About a million fewer workers were unemployed in 1948 than in 1938, but the government was employing about 400,000 more people in the armed forces, which were twice as large as in the year before the war, and about 600,000 more in the Civil Service, which was about 75 per cent larger than just before the war. The Opposition said the civil service should be cut, and Labour backbenchers said the armed forces should be cut, but, until one or other of these steps was taken, employers had to manage with the existing labour force. In the 1930s it rose, taking employed and unemployed together, by about 10 per cent; in the 1940s it increased by about 3 per cent. There was not even the possibility of finding people anxious to leave declining trades, because no trades were declining. Agriculture had been placed on a sounder footing than before, and coal, textiles, and the railways, which contracted and lost workers to new industries in the 1950s, were all being encouraged in the late 1940s.

The government possessed some residual powers to direct labour, and could influence the flow through the Labour Exchanges, but this authority could not be used in a sweeping way. The controls and licences that limited the activity of businesses operated through prohibitions. Positive commands to 'make this' or 'sell that' could not go much beyond issuing certain licences, particularly for steel, on condition firms increased their exports. Positive commands to workers to go into particular jobs were equally hard to apply.

Even so, the overall shortage of labour would have held back some industries. Businesses in the 1930s had grown accustomed to a situation in which all the factors of production were readily available, but profits were hard to obtain, and they were now plunged into a different situation, in which profits were easy to obtain but the factors of production were in short supply. They wanted the best of both worlds, and blamed the government because this was not possible.

People who wanted businesses to enjoy the free play of the market and people who wanted to get back to the pre-war world might be united in their detestation of the government, but turning their feelings into coherent political action presented some problems. The Conservative Party had been badly shaken by the 1945 result, but applied itself to the work of reorganization with more resilience than most defeated parties. A good deal of its activity was really intended to ease the 'back to pre-war' section out of this frame of mind. Candidates' contributions to constituency funds were restricted, because some of the safest Conservative seats had gone to candidates simply because they could promise a thousand pounds a year to constituency funds. Policy documents like 'The Industrial Charter' set out to show reactionary party members and the general public that industrial workers had rights which must be respected. Lord Woolton launched a successful public appeal for £1 million, which freed the party from the fear of being controlled by a few wealthy contributors who might want honours or influence over policy, and it also showed the general public that the Conservative Party was not an immensely wealthy organization. The Central Office now became distinctly richer than Transport House, and acquired a talented staff, many of whom became promising new recruits to the Conservative parliamentary party in the 1950s. The Conservatives accepted the Welfare State, but they disagreed with some items of the Labour Party's social policy: they would not have taken so firm a line with the doctors over the health service, and at the time of the harsh 1946–7 winter they suggested that the government should put off requiring children to stay at school until 15, which was due to take place in September 1947. Nothing came of the suggestion, but the winter of 1947 was probably the moment at which the Conservatives began to feel they might win the next election.

They took more interest in local government elections than in the past. Voting in parliamentary by-elections showed none of the wide fluctuations seen in earlier and in later decades, and the government lost no seats even though from 1947 onwards the Conservatives were ahead in the opinion polls, which were beginning to be published regularly but were not yet taken seriously. The Opposition had to build up its confidence by gaining ground in municipal elections, and had several successes, of which the most conspicuous was in London in 1949, when it won as many seats as the Labour Party though the Labour Party retained control because it had a majority among the aldermen.

The Conservatives had strong newspaper support from the *Mail,* the *Express,* and the *Telegraph,* and they did very well at finding the small but significant points at which the government was vulnerable. The 'groundnuts' scheme provided an excellent target. The government opened up an area of East Africa for planting groundnuts to raise economic activity in the region and provide a supply of vegetable fat for Britain—the policy of aid to colonies and underdeveloped countries was only beginning to be established, and the government had to show that the scheme would benefit people in Britain as well as in East Africa. However commendable the principle of the scheme, the area chosen was unsuitable and the undertaking had to be closed down as an almost total loss. People were not yet accustomed to governments undertaking large-scale operations in peacetime on which large-scale losses might be suffered, and the government was attacked effectively on the issue—the memory of it sank so deep into the minds of enthusiastic Conservatives that almost twenty years later, in the 1964 election, a Conservative heckler shouted 'groundnuts' at the leader of the Labour Party.

The government was disturbed by newspaper attacks, and set up a Royal Commission to inquire into the state of the press. It is hard to see what this Commission was intended to do; the press was flourishing, and the papers that attacked the government were doing no more than their readers and their proprietors wanted. No doubt the government would have preferred newspapers to be run by calm and impartial editors who found that there was always a great deal to be said for what the government was doing, but this was not what readers wanted at the time. They wanted denunciation. Labour newspapers had a circulation that was much smaller than the Labour vote; the Liberal press was somewhat stronger than the Liberal vote.

The threat of novelty

There was a general mood of hostility to novelty that may have encouraged hostility to the innovations of the Labour government. The high level of interest in literature and the arts that had developed during the war fell away sharply. Opposition to novelty and resurgent hostility were strikingly demonstrated at the time of the Picasso–Matisse exhibition at the end of 1945. By this time Picasso was the world's leading painter, and it would have been hard to name anyone else who unquestionably stood above Matisse. Nevertheless, their exhibition was greeted with abuse which sounded exactly like the attacks on Roger Fry's Post-Impressionist exhibition in 1910. British artists were, at just about this time, emerging from the backwater into which they had slipped after the death of Turner. It was only after the war that painters like Sutherland and Bacon began to win an established position and, in particular, to be accepted on the continent of Europe—the award to Moore of the prize for non-Italian sculptors at the 1948 Venice Biennale was a recognition that at least one British artist was considered important outside the country. The enemies of Picasso and Matisse were not inspired by mere chauvinism: they disapproved of British art as well, and attempts by municipal authorities to improve their towns by putting up sculpture often provoked objections—it was clear that a large number of people thought statues should be portraits, of a strictly representational type, and the idea of statues as art was still not universally acceptable. When Reg Butler won a competition for *The Unknown Political Prisoner* with an entry in wire, there were complaints from people who clearly thought that marble or bronze were the only materials worthy of a sculptor.

None of this resistance to modern art was new. The enemies of novelty obviously wanted to get back to the days before the war when, they imagined, there was no modern art, and their resistance was the last determined stand against artistic novelty. By the 1950s it was much harder to protest publicly about something just because it was new, and enemies of innovation were no longer able to say 'I don't know much about art but I know what I like' without being laughed at. The war had for a time done something to elevate taste; whether this was through any real change or simply because the better writers and musicians were given facilities for publishing and performing that were not available to everybody is harder to say. It was during the war and particularly with the publication of *Four Quartets* that T. S. Eliot extended his reputation beyond the circle of the specialists and became nationally accepted as a leading poet. He went on to write verse plays, and for a short time, just after the war, the success of his *Cocktail Party* and plays of Christopher Fry like *The Lady's Not for Burning* led critics to think that the English theatre might be revived by verse drama with religious overtones. The rest of the theatre certainly needed something to make it more interesting, for it had firmly turned its back on all the changes since Ibsen and was devoting itself to 'well-made' plays in the tradition of Scribe and Sardou. The most talented of these commercial playwrights, Terence Rattigan, who later explicitly acknowledged his debt by writing a modernized version of Dumas's *La Dame aux caméllias*, exposed himself a little too frankly in the preface to his collected plays by announcing that he aimed to appeal to the taste of 'Aunt Edna', a (fictional) lady of great respectability and limited enthusiasm for new ideas. The confession did him no good, perhaps because it explained the situation too honestly for people to like it.

The theatre was firmly fixed as a minority entertainment, and an entertainment in which American musicals like *Oklahoma* and *Annie Get Your Gun* dominated the stage. In the years immediately after the war cinemas were doing wonderful business, and drew upon an almost universal audience. Cinemas primarily meant American films, and when the drain on currency led to the prohibitive duty imposed in 1947, the American companies made arrangements which let them take out $17 million a year of their profits, but required them to leave the remainder in Britain, where it could be used for making more films. The government tried to encourage British film-making by setting up a National Film Finance Corporation, drawn on mainly by Sir Alexander Korda's British Lion, and by laying down a quota: 45 per cent of films shown were to be British. The quota was too large for the existing Rank production companies to fill satisfactorily. They were afraid of controversial and contemporary subjects and took refuge in expensive historical productions. The film-making success of the late 1940s were the Ealing comedies produced by an independent company, which pleased everybody by showing English people to be kind-hearted, eccentric, and inefficient. Even at the height of the post-war cinema boom government encouragement was never very successful. Few people thought the BBC's resumption in 1946 of the television services that it had begun in a small way before the war would change the pattern of entertainment much.

The all-pervasive use of television was one feature of Orwell's nightmare of the future *Nineteen Eighty-Four*. Orwell was an anarchist with a considerable gift for saying things that dominant intellectual opinion would be saying in two or three years' time; he had fought in the Spanish Civil War, and had returned with a dislike for both Communists and Fascists. He said, rather misleadingly, that he was a supporter of the Labour Party. In the conditions of the 1940s socialism meant rationing and controls, and Orwell disliked this approach to life. In *Animal Farm* at the end of the war he had attacked the Communist rulers of Russia for betraying the ideals of the revolution; Orwell was deeply attached to the ideals of the revolution and his feeling of betrayal strengthened his dislike for the methods of Stalinism. But his book appealed to people who had no sympathy for the ideals of the Russian or any other revolution and argued that governments are all the same and there is no point in trying to change things. *Nineteen Eighty-Four*, his other really successful book, was also used to teach a lesson rather different from the one Orwell had in mind. The book rested on the assumption, for which Orwell himself had condemned James Burnham a few years earlier, that things would go much as they were at present, only worse. A perpetual state of war or preparation for war, in which governments would insist that the needs of the struggle demanded absolute obedience, accompanied by rationing and shortages, would go on for ever. The portrayal of the methods of 'thought-control' was particularly admired. In the diplomatic background of the story there was no sign that Orwell thought the capitalist powers in any way less bad than the Communist; the country in which Winston Smith was brainwashed had become Airstrip One of an American Empire. However, the book was treated as an attack on Russia and on the shortages in Britain at the time, and so it was regarded by most people as an attack upon the left. Orwell's picture of the future turned out to be inaccurate, and Huxley's *Brave New World* (1932), set in an almost uncontrollably affluent society, turned out to be a much better prediction of the future. But Orwell's book had much more effect in terms of politics; any supporter of the Labour government who heard that Orwell was a socialist must have asked to be saved from such friends. People wanted an attack on the way of life into which they seemed to be sinking in the 1940s, and Orwell provided it. He also seemed in *Animal Farm* to justify the Cold War, although a good deal of *Nineteen Eighty-Four* argues that living in the conditions of the Cold War would be dangerous to freedom.

Orwell did not look at the English middle class after the 1930s and, while he disliked the sort of people who gave *Animal Farm* and *Nineteen Eighty-Four* an enthusiastic welcome, he did not write about them. The opposition to the Labour government was at its most intense in the levels of society written about by Angus Wilson; some of the short stories in *The Wrong Set* and his novel *Hemlock and After* show how those who felt they were living under 'the army of occupation' were seen by an unsympathetic observer. Neither Wilson nor Orwell were innovators as authors, but after the 1930s innovation ceased to be so predominant a concern of writers. It was not necessarily a sign of failure of talent, but perhaps there were no literary giants of the sort that had flourished in the first three decades of the century. Writers seemed relatively content with the techniques at their disposal, and this could perhaps be said in a more general sense. Among artists and writers innovation had been fashionable for most of the period from the turn of the century to the 1940s. Even though the innovations had not always been followed up to any great extent, the process had left the artists and writers rather exhausted, and they now wanted a pause to reconsider their position, at just the time that their audience was preparing to accept novelty willingly.

11

The afterglow

1949–1956

The last years of the Labour government

The first results of devaluation seemed highly satisfactory. British trade figures improved rapidly, and there were suggestions that the rate chosen had taken too pessimistic a view of the economic prospects. The government was willing to let the economy run slightly more freely, while regulating the general level of demand and encouraging specific areas of expansion. In November 1948 and March 1949 Harold Wilson, the President of the Board of Trade, cancelled a large number of economic restrictions in 'bonfires of controls'. Clothes rationing ended in 1949, and the proportion of imports that came in under government bulk-purchasing schemes was steadily reduced. Planning was immensely difficult, and in any case there was no real reason why planning had to be part of socialism—it would, after all, be possible to have a society in which all industry had been nationalized and all the rewards of industry were shared out in a socialist manner, and yet the different nationalized industries used their economic bargaining power against each other.

While the Labour Party was not consciously moving in this direction, it was hard to see in the late 1940s where it intended to go next. Morrison wanted a policy that would appeal to the middle classes, but did not explain what positive proposals this policy would include. The left wing of the party wanted more nationalization, but, apart from making sure that the Steel Bill survived the Lords, they could not expect to arouse any enthusiasm over sugar, water, and cement, the next industries on the list to be taken over. It was hard to think of any of them as 'commanding heights of the economy'. Insurance was considered but, under pressure from the collectors employed by the companies and by the cooperative societies, this changed into a proposal for making all insurance companies into mutual companies with no shareholders, in which the policy-holders kept all the profits. This was not very exciting, but nobody had any better suggestions; Attlee, Bevin, Cripps, and Morrison had been in high office for about ten years and were showing signs of strain; Attlee never seems to have been very interested in ideas, and while Bevin was ready to take up new ideas, he was too autocratic to let other people discuss proposals he disliked. By 1950 the Labour Party was becalmed, though it is possible that a period of stability would have suited the mood of the electorate very well.

An election had to be held by July 1950. Cripps persuaded Attlee that any budget produced just before an election would look like an attempt to influence the vote, so the election was held in February. A slightly later election, at a pleasanter time of year when people had had a little longer to see that devaluation was working out rather well, would have been tactically wiser for the government. The 1950 election was held in a mood of looking back to the immediate past and also back to the 1930s. The Conservatives accepted the whole of the Welfare State but argued that the way forward must now be to set the people free to work out their own salvation, and reminded everyone how unpleasant the post-war years had been, with rationing, restrictions, drabness, and shortages in all directions. The Labour reply pointed to the complete and continued disappearance of the grinding unemployment of the 1930s, to the establishment of the Welfare State, and to the reorganization of British industry. To the complaints about rationing they replied with the slogan 'Fair Shares for All'.

This defence was fairly successful; despite the efforts of Woolton and the modernizers, the Conservatives attracted only 4 per cent more of the electorate than in 1945. The Liberals made a great effort, and put up 475 candidates, but so many of them lost their deposits that the chief effect was to make the party look silly. The Labour Party held on to almost all of its 1945 share of the vote, and might in normal circumstances have claimed that its level of popular support showed that its policy had been accepted. However, the electoral

	Votes	Seats	% of all votes cast
Conservative	12,502,567	298	43.5
Liberal	2,621,548	9	9.1
Labour	13,266,592	315	46.1
Other	381,964	3	1.3

system made the answer more complicated. The 1948 Representation of the People Act had helped the Labour Party by bringing plural voting to an end and by abolishing the twelve university seats and the business franchise, which affected about ten seats. On the other hand the redistribution of seats told against it: a large proportion of the Labour votes came from impregnable mining areas where they were in a sense wasted, but in 1945 this had been balanced by the over-representation of slum areas which were safe Labour seats with small electorates. The 1948 Act redistributed these seats out of existence, and so created the situation, which applied throughout the 1950s, that the two parties would win equal numbers of seats in the Commons if Labour polled 2 per cent more of the total vote than the Conservatives. In 1950 the Labour Party polled 2.6 per cent more, but it was also hampered by Communist opposition in marginal seats. The Communist Party never had as much effect on the electoral situation as in 1950; its intervention presented the Conservatives with up to four seats.

The government's effective majority of six left it ill placed for passing contentious legislation, but in fact it was more concerned to prepare to fight the next election by steps like ending petrol rationing. These preparations had to be laid aside in June when war broke out in Korea. Because the Soviet Union was boycotting meetings of the UN Security Council, the United States and its allies could pass a resolution enabling the United Nations to assist South Korea when it was invaded by North Korea. This seemed to be conclusive proof of the aggressive intentions of the Soviet Union, and it was the duty of the United States and its allies to resist. The British government promptly committed troops to the UN force. Throughout the war the American contribution was far larger than that of her allies and, although the British was the next largest, it was not really comparable; this led to misunderstandings because the British did not always realize how far the United States was committed or how far the Americans thought the war was the most important of the world's problems.

Apart from the direct cost of the British military contribution, the war also drove up prices of raw materials. Bulk purchasing had meant that the government always held, or was committed to holding, large stocks of commodities, but in 1950 the government was running down its stocks and private traders were confident they did not need such large stocks, or perhaps could not afford to hold them. Bulk purchasing had suited Britain's trading position in the 1940s very well. Long-term contracts made by a single purchaser on a rising market held back the rise as much as possible, and if individual purchasers had gone into the market they would probably have been played off against each other by the sellers. The Canadian wheat agreement of 1946, by which the British bought on favourable terms on the grounds that the price of wheat might suffer from a post-war slump, was so advantageous that the Canadian wheat board became less and less inclined to enter another agreement as the market price went up and up. When the Korean War was over, prices of food and raw materials slid steadily downwards, and in these new conditions individual purchasers buying on a relatively small scale were probably best placed to drive the price down quickly for British consumers.

The experience of the Korean War suggests that bulk purchasing was given up a year or two earlier than was wise. The reduction of stocks in 1950 led to a large balance-of-payments surplus, but stocks had to be replenished in 1951 at even higher prices, so the money ran out faster than it had come in. The large

1950 surplus seemed to show that the government had been right to give up Marshall Aid at the end of the year and say that the British economy could stand on its own feet. The experience of 1951 was a nasty reminder that the problems had not all been solved. The gloom was increased by predictions that the price of raw materials would go on rising and the terms of trade would steadily move against exporters of industrial goods, with more unpleasant results for Britain than for almost any other country. As it turned out, the Korean War price rise was the last stage in the advance of the 1940s, and it would have been much less severe if the United States had not undertaken an immense stockpiling programme as well as preparing for war. The programme stimulated producers of raw materials, but after the war they were left with new lines of production just as war demand was declining, the US stockpile hung over the market, and prices fell sharply.

Bulk purchase or no bulk purchase, the British could not do much about the increase in commodity prices. Wage stability, which had been maintained by co-operation between trade union leaders and the government since mid-1947, came to an end late in 1950. The balance of payments was bound to come under pressure as a result. The government had committed itself to a large rearmament programme. About 7 per cent of the national income was already being spent on armaments before the Korean War began, which was a high peacetime level by pre-1939 standards. In the first discussions of rearmament, in August 1950, the government undertook spending of £3,400 million over a three-year period which would raise the proportion to 10 per cent. Quite apart from a general fear of Russian aggression, European countries were afraid that the United States was going to become deeply involved in the war in Korea and the problems of the Far East and lose interest in Europe; American representatives at the negotiations reminded the various European countries about the dangers of a relapse into isolationism which, however unwelcome to President Truman's Administration, might be forced on it by the pressure of opinion. The argument was that European countries had to be ready to fight if they were to be helped to rearm. France, with a large Communist Party and a shaky currency, could not take the lead; Germany was still distrusted after the war. Britain was the only country which could show the American people that Europe was a worthwhile investment. At this stage the United States felt able to promise additional aid to help her European allies rearm.

Cooperation with the United States carried with it a certain amount of power to influence United States policy. The UN force pressed forward into North Korea and advanced towards the Chinese border, and when the Chinese moved to help the North Koreans, General MacArthur, the American commander of the UN force, suggested widening the war by bombing China. This alarmed people in Britain and in America's other European allies. Attlee flew to Washington early in December 1950 and put to Truman the arguments against widening the war. It is impossible to tell how important this was:

Truman implied in his memoirs that he had already decided what to do, but when reminiscing Attlee suggested that his own intervention was decisive. Truman went on to dismiss MacArthur and make it clear that the war was to be limited to the defence of South Korea. When the Chinese army threatened to engulf the UN forces, the European countries were once more asked to show that they were wholehearted in their desire to save themselves from Communist expansionism, and once more Britain was asked to play the leading role. In February 1951 the government said it would spend £4,700 million over the next three years, which came to 14 per cent of the national income.

The government that faced this new and heavy task looked rather different from the one that had gained so slender a majority in February 1950. Cripps had broken down under the strain, and had resigned in October, to be succeeded by Hugh Gaitskell, a professional economist who was disliked by both the Conservatives and the left wing of the Labour Party for his public school and academic background. By early 1951 Bevin was too ill to run the Foreign Office, and was succeeded by Morrison. The changes made the government slightly more middle-class, slightly less imaginative, and slightly more right-wing, and left Bevan feeling ignored because he had been given neither of these important posts. The Conservative opposition became fiercer, and tried to wear the government out by keeping the House of Commons sitting late at night.

Gaitskell approached the task of drawing up his budget for 1951 with great technical skill. Dalton and Cripps had taken a lot of excess demand out of the economy by running budget surpluses on current account, but they never convincingly explained the relationship between real resources and the money accounts of the budget. Gaitskell understood the relationship and, once the military commitments had been undertaken, his budget made the best possible attempt to provide the money without generating inflation inside the country. Prices had already begun to rise because import prices were going up so quickly, and the Chancellor declined to increase the food subsidies because this would have meant additional taxation; he had raised the standard rate of income tax by 2.5p to 47.5p in the pound and felt that this was as much as people would stand. He also limited government expenditure on the health service by imposing charges on prescriptions, on spectacles, and on false teeth. This angered Bevan, who resigned at the sight of his creation being put on a cash basis. In his resignation speech he referred not only to the health charges, but also to the possibility that the strain of rearmament would make it difficult for Western countries to continue to run their affairs democratically. Harold Wilson, who followed him out of the government, gave as his reason for resignation his fear that the new £4,700 million rearmament programme was going to be too much of a strain on the economy.

On the economic point at issue Wilson was right. The budget had managed to provide the financial conditions for a transfer of real resources, but in some areas the resources could not be moved quickly and in others—supply of raw materials, supply of skilled engineers, supply of plans to work on—they were simply not available. The American government, with its immensely superior purchasing power, had priced the other countries out of the market. Rearmament primarily affected a single sector of the economy, engineering and metalworking, and doubling the national expenditure on defence subjected this sector to intense strain. At the same time the extension of national service to a two-year period made the labour market less flexible because it reduced the number of young men available at the time of their lives when they would be readiest to move to new jobs.

The economy creaked and groaned under the pressure of the shift to military production and away from the export trades. The balance of payments could be improved a bit by cutting down on imports, but the country was not importing so many luxury goods that this could be done at all easily. A cut in imports meant a cut in food rations. From the summer of 1951 onwards the general balance-of-payments position was made worse by the other countries in the Sterling Area, who ran deficits on their trade. They were perfectly entitled to do this, but it made life harder for the British government, which, as banker for the whole Sterling Area, had to meet the deficits out of the Area's pool assets.

The government had not quite run out of ideas. Wage restraint was urged once more and, after appeals to companies to restrain dividend increases in the same way, legislation to freeze dividends was prepared, and measures were prepared for abolishing the practice of resale price maintenance, by which manufacturers and wholesalers prevented retailers from reducing prices. A further difficulty had arisen in the Middle East; at the end of April 1951 the government of Iran nationalized the oil refinery built at Abadan by the Anglo-Iranian Company, most of whose shares were owned by the British government. A government usually has a clear legal right to nationalize, as long as it pays compensation, but in 1933 the Iranian government had renounced the right to nationalize the refinery. Action based on the 1933 agreement would look like a return to imperialism for undisguised financial motives; inaction was felt to be humiliating, and the loss of the refinery meant that expensive Western hemisphere oil had to be imported instead. The Opposition taunted the government for its feebleness; it was suggested that the government was being weak-kneed in not sending troops to recapture the refinery, and Morrison, the Foreign Secretary, was in favour of military action. The Cabinet decided that sending out a force would be too dangerous, strategically and diplomatically, and might merely lead to the destruction of the refinery.

By November the government was practically exhausted. There was no sign that things would improve soon, and it was hard to control the Commons with a majority of six. An election would clear the air and, if it left the government in office, give an opportunity for repairing divisions in the party.

The Conservative Party continued to say it would set the people free, a line of approach designed to appeal to Liberals who had given up the struggle or had no candidate to vote for. It declared that a Conservative government would give people 'more red meat' as one of the incentives to work harder, which was undoubtedly attractive at a time when the meat ration was eightpence worth of meat a week per person. It also promised to build 300,000 houses in a year and to refrain from interfering with the Welfare State; Lord Woolton went so far as to say that the food subsidies would not be cut.[1] The Labour Party continued to stand on its record in office, but it could now point to Attlee's flight to Washington and ask 'Whose finger on the trigger?', to suggest that when a war was going on Churchill might be too impulsive to be really safe.

It is hard to tell how accurately the opinion polls of the day could measure public opinion. Surveys taken in the ten months before the election suggest that the Conservatives had a lead of about 9 per cent of the popular vote. Whether it was because the Labour Party made a great defensive effort, or because people at the last minute felt nervous about changing governments, or simply that the surveys had over-represented the prosperous classes, the Labour Party polled slightly more of the total vote than the Conservatives— not enough to outweigh the geographical advantage enjoyed by the Conservatives, but enough to remind the new government that it could not claim to have a strong mandate for its policies.

	Votes	Seats	% of all votes cast
Conservative	13,717,538	321	48.0
Liberal	730,556	6	2.5
Labour	13,948,605	295	48.8

Overseas policy under Churchill

Churchill as Prime Minister did not try to keep an eye on all departments. At first he attempted to run the government by appointing members of the House of Lords as 'overlords', each of whom would coordinate the work of a number of departments. This was never very effective, and power in domestic affairs tended to drift into the hands of Butler, the Chancellor of the Exchequer. Churchill did not have a high opinion of Butler, but as he was not very interested in economic affairs, he accepted the situation with a fairly good grace. His main interest was in foreign policy and defence, and even here he conserved his flagging energies by leaving to Eden as Foreign Secretary a good

1. Lord Woolton, *Memoirs* (1959), 367–9.

deal of freedom of action in the smaller issues which he regarded as specialized questions. Eden could deal with Egypt, Iran, and the Far East without
much intervention by the Prime Minister. Of these problems Iran was settled
without the British government doing much about it. The international oil
companies set up a blockade of Iranian oil, and their control of shipping and
the sales system enabled them to stop the Iranian government selling the oil it
had seized. Eventually a coup, supported by the US Central Intelligence
Agency, overthrew the Iranian Prime Minister, and a new arrangement for the
oil was worked out. As the new arrangement transferred part of the British
concession to American firms, the whole transaction left the British government feeling that it might find itself being extruded from the Middle East by
its American ally.

The desire of the Egyptian government to revoke the 1936 treaty which gave
the British the right to occupy bases in the Canal Zone had troubled the
Labour government's last months of office. Entangled as it was in Abadan, it
could not afford to look as if it was giving way. The new government had to
face the problem, which was complicated by the overthrow of King Farouk in
July 1952 and the emergence of a military government, first under General
Neguib and then under Colonel Nasser. For some months the British government held on to an increasingly awkward position, but in 1954 arrangements
were made for Sudan to become an independent country and for Britain to
withdraw from the Canal Zone, and the temporary occupation begun under
Gladstone in 1882 was at an end. The Canal still remained an international
waterway under the treaty of 1888, and the Suez Canal Company continued to
run it under the agreements made between 1854 and 1888.

The withdrawal was not popular with Conservatives, many of whom were
sensitive when taunted about their bellicosity over Abadan when in opposition in 1951. But in 1954 Eden's reputation rose to new heights because of his
handling of Indo-China and European rearmament. France had never fully
re-established her position in Indo-China after the war. A Communist-
inspired rebellion under Ho Chi Minh challenged the colonial government
and began to gain ground. The United States considered intervening on the
French side, but would do so only if Britain would help as well. The British
government did not think the French had much chance of holding on to
Indo-China, and certainly was not willing to join in the war. British influence
in Washington was exerted to strengthen the opposition to American
intervention.

The situation became easier when Mendès-France became premier of
France on a policy of ending the war. At the Geneva Conference in 1954 Eden
played a considerable part in persuading the representatives of the Communist powers to be content with rather less than they might have expected.
Negotiations were complicated because the United States refused to take part
in the conference; officially it stayed away to avoid meeting representatives of

the Chinese government, which it had not recognized, but in fact it seems to have thought that the conference would be a disaster for the Western powers and wanted to dissociate itself from the debacle. Eden and Mendès-France emerged with much better terms than the Americans had expected. The United States had anticipated that the whole of Indo-China would be dominated by the Viet Minh; when it discovered how much had been saved, it set about creating the South-East Asia Treaty Organization to defend the successor states of Laos, Cambodia, and South Vietnam against further Communist expansion.

This success strengthened Eden's position for his next diplomatic achievement. Very soon after the creation of the North Atlantic Treaty Organization (NATO) it was clear that the member nations were not providing all the forces they had promised. The United States began urging the other members to allow West German troops to be armed and added to the NATO forces in some way. European opinion was not enthusiastic: it felt that arming Germans would only provoke the Russians to become more hostile, and enough Europeans had lived under German occupation to have some sympathy with the Russians. At first it was suggested that a European Defence Community (EDC) should be set up to organize a supranational force in which the troops contributed by the member nations were so completely integrated that their own governments could not use them independently. The whole German contribution to NATO defence would be controlled by the EDC, and thus the German government would not acquire any forces of its own. The British government thought that this was a good arrangement, for other people. It explained that, whatever Churchill might have said at The Hague and Strasbourg while in opposition, it was not going to join organizations designed to create federal institutions for western Europe. It declined to join Euratom or the European Coal and Steel Community, and it declined to contribute its forces to the EDC. This made an EDC unattractive to France; a British offer of a permanent contribution of troops to the continent of Europe within the EDC would have provided as a counterweight to Germany, and German rearmament might then have been acceptable. But, as it stood, EDC looked like another way to create a dominant Germany in Europe. The French government was badly divided, and it left the issue of the EDC treaties to a free vote in the National Assembly. The opponents of EDC, who were more frightened of Germany than of Russia, prevailed.

American opinion was divided between withdrawal from European affairs and commitment to Germany without regard for France. In the United States France was in any case not regarded as important, and Churchill and some of his personal friends shared this view. Eden had disliked Churchill's European pronouncements in opposition and his pro-French views made him more concerned than other British or American politicians to avoid bringing about German rearmament in a way that was offensive to France. He proposed that

Britain should reassure France by promising to keep four divisions on the continent of Europe for the next fifty years, and by promising that these forces could be withdrawn only with the permission of the Western European Union countries.[2] This commitment caused trouble later; when Germany ceased being an occupied territory, she stopped paying for the British troops on her soil, and the four divisions became a steady drain of foreign exchange which led to uncomfortable pleas that someone should do something to help Britain pay for the commitment. But at the time the proposal worked. The British promise to stay on the Continent reassured France, and German rearmament went ahead. The British troops were not to be placed under a federal authority, and the idea of a supranational structure for European defence was not revived, but Europe's defensive position was stronger than before.

Whether because of the increase in European strength or because of the death of Stalin, the attitude of Russia had become more conciliatory. During the 1950 election campaign Churchill had launched the idea that heads of government should meet 'at the summit'. He had originally meant it as a way to stop a grave situation becoming worse, but he remained committed to the idea of a summit conference when conditions became easier. He knew that he had first to convince the United States government that it would be useful, and here he was fortunate that about twelve months after his return to office his wartime colleague General Eisenhower became President of the United States. The two men found themselves in curiously similar positions: they used their prestige to bring unprofitable foreign ventures to an end, in the Korean War and in the Suez Canal base, and they persuaded their political supporters to accept the expansion of social welfare carried out in both countries in the previous decade or two. Churchill hoped to revive the wartime association and gain a special role of influence at Washington, with which he intended to persuade the United States government to agree to a summit conference. Eisenhower was in general doubtful about its usefulness, but he was always ready to listen to arguments in its favour. In the summer of 1953 Churchill suffered a stroke; this was kept so secret that very few people realized how seriously ill he was.[3] He might have retired at this point if Anthony Eden, who was universally accepted as his obvious successor, had not been ill at the same time. Churchill revived his pressure for a conference when he returned to work in the autumn, and Stalin's successors, who were much more ready to play an active role in the world outside Russia than he had been, showed some willingness for a conference. Churchill had retired before it took place, but the meeting of Eisenhower, Eden, Faure, and Bulganin at Geneva in the summer of 1955 owed a good deal to his patience and enthusiasm. It did not lead to any lasting relaxation of tension, and relations between Russia and the West

2. Belgium, France, Germany, Italy, Luxembourg, the Netherlands, and the United Kingdom.
3. Lord Moran, *Winston Churchill. The Struggle for Survival* (1968), 431–501.

deteriorated soon afterwards. Diplomats drew the conclusion that it was wiser to start with preliminary negotiations before a summit conference, instead of leaving all the difficult questions to Foreign Ministers to discuss after the conference, but the idea of a summit conference was taken up again later in the 1950s.

The Conservatives had been pleased to find, when they came to office, that the Labour government had made a good deal of progress towards the construction of a British atomic bomb. If the new government wanted to go on claiming that Britain was for some purposes the equal of America and Russia, it had next to consider whether to make a British hydrogen bomb, and in 1954 Churchill announced that the government had decided to make it. There were protests from many of the people who would have protested if they had known an atomic bomb was being made in the late 1940s. So many of the reasons for making a British hydrogen bomb revolved around the idea of pressing the Americans into a closer partnership that they could not be discussed openly. The government did not imagine that the nuclear strength of Russia and America was so finely balanced that the British contribution would be decisive, but, if Anglo-American bombing plans had to be coordinated, there had to be military consultation between the two countries. The idea that possession of the bomb made Britain the equal of Russia and the United States looked reasonable enough in terms of military technology, because in the early 1950s nuclear bombs would have been dropped from aeroplanes just like the two 1945 bombs, and after rearming for the Korean War the British government had enough Valiants, Vulcans, and Victors in its V-bomber force to be able to launch bombing raids. American and Russian tests had shown that an H-bomb could be made, which had previously been thought unlikely by physicists as respected as Oppenheimer, and once it was known that it would work it was fairly easy to work out how to use an atomic bomb to trigger a fusion process.

Those who expected the H-bomb to place Britain on a footing of equality with America and Russia had not realized how the world had changed. When he had to convince his more imperialist followers that Suez was no longer useful, Churchill showed them how one H-bomb would devastate the whole Suez area: England was not much bigger than the Suez area, and was particularly vulnerable to hydrogen bombs. From a strategic point of view the bomb was a weapon that British governments would find very hard to use, but it was a consolation for those who thought the United States might withdraw from Europe, or ignore British interests in some other way, to reflect that Britain could exact a heavy price from anyone who attacked her, and could touch off a general war.

Churchill, for whom the Anglo-American alliance was the most important factor in diplomacy, was not the man to suggest this rather unfavourable view of the Americans, but anti-Americanism was more widespread in Britain than

anyone cared to say openly. It was spread so widely across the political spectrum that it could not be expressed as a policy, and the men of the centre
could continue to follow a pro-American line. People on the Conservative
right felt that the United States was always chipping away at the British
Empire, at British oil, and at British prestige; they often supported moves to
get back to 'before the war' in domestic policy, and they disliked the American
way of life, which they found vulgar and egalitarian and altogether too ready
to think the businessman more important than the gentleman. On the left,
some anti-Americanism was based on fears of what American influence
would do to British socialism, and some on sympathy for the Soviet Union.
Inside the government some ministers, while possibly sympathetic to some of
America's long-term aims, thought the Americans were not very competent at
running policy. People who felt like this might adopt Macmillan's philosophical view that they were 'Greeks in the American Empire' and must run it
'as the Greek slaves ran the operations of the Emperor Claudius',[4] or they
might share Eden's slightly too obvious feeling that the American Secretary of
State, John Foster Dulles, was an international disaster looking for a place to
happen. Partly because of the pressures of the situation, partly because
Churchill did not propose to lose touch with Eisenhower, these feelings did
not affect government policy much. Foreign policy was reasonably
successful—in one respect too successful: people were able to slip into the
habit of forgetting how much the world had changed in the last dozen years.

This view could survive in colonial as well as in foreign affairs. After the
rapid changes of the 1940s relatively little seemed to happen. In the Gold Coast
elections were held in 1951; as the Convention People's Party won a majority,
its leader, Dr Nkrumah, was released from prison, where he had been serving a
sentence for political offences, and was made Leader of Government Business
in the new legislature. In Nigeria developments were more complicated: the
country was divided into three regions, each with a political party of its own,
and the British government felt it ought to reconcile them before independence so that the country would not dissolve on regional lines. The British
government had a more direct interest in delay. The leaders of the northern
region opposed rapid moves to independence, because their region was short
of educated people. They were afraid that the two southern regions might be
able to establish themselves in a position of permanent dominance if it was
granted before the northern group had time to organize. As it would have an
electoral majority after independence, it was worth supporting for the sake of
good relations in the future. The people of Asante, the northern region of the
Gold Coast, were less educated and wanted the British to stay longer, but as
they were a minority there was not much point in supporting them and
offending the section that was bound to come to power after independence.

4. Anthony Sampson, *Macmillan* (1967), 61.

In West Africa it was fairly easy to accept independence as the objective of policy, because there were no white settlers and the large commercial companies could look after their own interests. Opinion in Britain certainly would not have allowed the communities of white settlers in Kenya and Rhodesia to be abandoned, and a section of British opinion would have opposed steps reducing their political power. In 1952 a revolt broke out in Kenya, organized by the Mau Mau movement, which blended Kikuyu tribalism and anti-colonialism in a mixture dominated by the former. Apart from questions of political control, the British settler monopoly of the Highlands, some of the best farming land in Kenya, was bound to lead to tension. British troops were sent to protect the settlers, and after a fairly difficult struggle in 1953 and 1954 the revolt was defeated. It had been crude and savage enough to convince British opinion that it had to be resisted, but British troops could not be used indefinitely to stop the majority in Kenya from getting political power peacefully, and Mau Mau had shown that the settlers, outnumbered a hundred to one, could not protect their own position.

In its last months of office the Labour government had raised the issue of federating the two Rhodesias and Nyasaland as a step towards independence. When the Conservatives came to power they decided to go ahead, and to ignore the opposition expressed by Africans consulted informally. The Central African Federation could bring together the mineral wealth of Northern Rhodesia, the large white population of Southern Rhodesia, and the overcrowded African population of Nyasaland. Its economic base would be strong enough to raise development loans, and in particular to finance the building of the Kariba Dam to provide supplies of electricity and of water for farmers and for miners on the Copperbelt in Northern Rhodesia. The new Federation was presented to the world as an exercise in partnership—a word that could be presented in Britain as a synonym for equality and could be explained to white inhabitants of the Federation as the partnership between horse and rider. The British government said it would appoint a Royal Commission to report on the progress of the Federation early in the 1960s.

In Malaya independence in the immediate future seemed much more possible. The British response to an attempt by Communist guerrillas to take the country was among the most intelligent counter-insurgency operations undertaken by any government in the period, but the task was easier than other countries. Almost all the Communists were Chinese, so the support of the Malayan section of the population could be enlisted by pursuing a conciliatory policy. The British made it clear that they did not expect to stay in Malaya for ever, and would grant independence once the Communists had been defeated. With a certain amount of goodwill gained in this way, it was possible to move the population into strategic villages that could be defended against infiltration, which cut the Communists off from their supporters in the countryside. The whole operation lasted from 1948 to 1957, but it was successful enough to convince the government that it knew how to handle Communist revolts; it could see that independence sometimes had to be granted to crush revolts, and this made it more ready to consider independence for other colonies.

Financial policy under Butler

This success in external policy rested on a fairly sound economic base. When Butler came to office, his first task as Chancellor of the Exchequer was to take further steps to deal with the balance-of-payments problem. To show that the government wanted to use monetary policy as one way to influence the economy, he raised the bank rate to 2.5 per cent from the 2 per cent at which it had been kept, except for a few weeks in September 1939, ever since 1932. But the main line of defence had to be physical controls: licences were required for imports, and were given with a sparing hand. This short-term reaction to a foreign exchange problem was almost the only occasion on which Butler adopted much the same policy as Gaitskell would have done, but a legendary figure called Mr Butskell was invented by *The Economist*, and denounced by the Labour left as the symbol of a supposed similarity of purpose.

Butler accepted the doctrine of setting the economy free, and followed it in an almost dogmatic way. The Conservative Party was behind him; experience of controls had convinced the modernizers that this was no way to run an economy, and those who wanted to get back to the past were certain that there had been no planning before the war. Those who could remember that in the 1930s there had been considerable enthusiasm for planning kept quiet, partly because the Conservative Party felt no desire to remind the public of its role then. Butler suggested letting the exchange value of the pound float freely with no support from the foreign exchange reserves, which would have been an extreme venture in setting the economy free. The proposal was discussed in February and in June 1952 but, largely because of Lord Cherwell's influence with Churchill, nothing came of it; Gaitskell took the opportunity later to say how sound he considered Cherwell's stand to have been.[5] Opponents of the scheme seem to have assumed that, although the foreign exchange reserves would not be used to defend the pound, the Bank of England would raise interest rates to support it. This would have taken the economy back to the late 1920s when high interest rates held back the development of the economy in order to defend the pound. If the pound had simply been left to fluctuate in terms of other currencies, people conducting trade in terms of sterling might have found the situation confusing but it would have removed the need for high interest rates.

The Conservative government took other steps to set the economy free

---

5. Lord Birkenhead, *The Prof in Two Worlds* (1961), 284–9.

between 1952 and the end of 1954. It reduced the allocating and licensing needed for building, it reduced income tax, it 'unblocked' the sterling debts and encouraged overseas investment, it ended restrictions on hire purchase sales and restrictions on the right to strike, and it ended rationing. Presumably a Labour government would have ended rationing and brought income tax down from the Korean War level as soon as it could, but it might well have moved more slowly than the Conservatives about the other measures, and it would have been much more worried by the rise in unemployment in 1952. The steps taken to defend the foreign exchange reserves caused a slight recession. The textile industry suffered most, as foreign competition began to be a serious threat, but other manufacturers realized that the recession would soon be over and, even though they could have run their factories for a time with fewer employees, they kept workers on in order to avoid the problem of finding new workers, which had been so difficult ever since 1939. The terms of trade improved when the economy recovered because the increase in import prices caused by the Korean War was short-lived, but prices for industrial exports did not fall, which meant more could be bought for the same amount of exports. This stroke of good fortune helped to relax some of the tensions in the economy.

Once the shock of Korea was over, the balance of payments began to show a steady surplus for the first time since before the war. The government stated that the country needed a surplus of between £300 million and £350 million a year to invest overseas and to pay off the sterling debts left over by the war. The current trade surplus, including invisible exports, ran at something like the £300 million a year that was needed, though military expenditure overseas, from Germany to Hong Kong, reduced it to about half the desired amount. The balance went to long-term investment overseas; Britain had returned to the conditions of the 1920s except that almost all the investment was in the Sterling Area or in Canada, and elsewhere it was restricted as severely as in the 1940s.

This desire for long-term investments helped international trade. If the surpluses had simply been accumulated year by year in Britain, the British reserves of gold would have gone up, but other countries would have found their reserves running down, which would have restricted trade. If the surpluses had been used to repay the wartime debts with sterling countries, international trade would have gone on, though not necessarily in a direction that suited Britain. The Labour government had 'blocked' the debts, which meant the creditors could draw their money only in the quantities and at the times that the British government allowed, and it preferred its creditors to draw money to buy British goods. In 1952 the debts were 'unblocked', so they could pass from one country to another and be used as money for international trading purposes. India and Egypt could now transfer their claims on London to other countries, and this helped to them keep going when their exports went down in price in the post-Korea slump in raw materials. Their assets in sterling were normally held as short-term bonds in London that could easily be cashed and turned into gold or dollars. It would do the holders of these sterling bonds no good if they all asked for gold or dollars at once, because the British gold and dollars were only about a quarter of the total debt. But if they did not want to wait for eventual repayment, they could use their sterling assets to pay for imports from other countries.

Sterling Area countries could borrow money in London, and in return were expected not to press for repayment of the wartime debts. When the debts passed on to countries which did not belong to the Sterling Area, they would have no special borrowing position in London to restrain them. The Chancellor of the Exchequer could reasonably and probably successfully ask Commonwealth Finance Ministers not to weaken the system by running up deficits with the outside world. The independent members of the Commonwealth habitually ran deficits with the outside world, partly financed by British investment. Most of the colonies ran surpluses with the rest of the world that were larger than their deficits in trade with Britain, so their assets in sterling increased steadily until independence. Independence was normally accompanied by a drive for domestic investment at home, so they spent their sterling assets, and these assets passed into the hands of countries outside the Sterling Area.

The government's financial figures depended on obtaining correct returns from everybody who had anything to do with foreign exchange. As this did not happen, the annual balance-of-payments statement always contained a large balancing item to make the sums add up properly. Estimating the level of overseas investment was also difficult, and became harder after 1945. In the nineteenth century and the early twentieth century a good deal of foreign investment took the form of sales of bonds by public subscription that could be traced. After the Second World War most investment was 'direct', with companies setting up subsidiaries in foreign countries and reinvesting the profits there, which was very hard to trace accurately.

Undoubtedly the largest single field of foreign investment in the post-war world was oil. Anglo-Iranian (later British Petroleum) and Shell (40 per cent British-owned) invested about as large a proportion of the national income as the railway companies in the mid-nineteenth century, but as most of it came from ploughing back profits and depreciation reserves, it was hard to measure the net investment. This concentration of investment on oil matched the increase in British consumption, which rose about 30 per cent a year from 2 million tons a year just after the war to 28 million tons a year nine years later. Consumption rose all over the world, and was met mainly by a sharp increase in Middle East production. Oil there was much cheaper than in the traditional areas such as the United States, and profits were accordingly high. The oil companies, and the governments that stood behind them, asserted that the low level of public services provided in the Middle East meant that the companies had to spend money on activities that would be undertaken by governments elsewhere.

Emerging from austerity

Because of this foreign investment, which was so much larger than in the 1930s and 1940s, Britain's reserves of foreign currency were vulnerable whenever the holders of assets denominated in sterling became worried about the safety of their money, and these crises of confidence were all the more likely because it was hard to get an up-to-date statement of the balance of payments. Heavy foreign investment also restricted the amount of resources available for domestic investment. Under the Labour government the level of non-housing investment had been high, but housing was neglected. Bevan, the Minister responsible, was preoccupied with setting up the health service and had to ask for large sums of money from the Exchequer for it. It was Labour policy that housing should mainly be built by local councils for letting to the less prosperous at subsidized rents and, as Bevan was not in a strong position to ask the Exchequer to lend money to local councils, building was held back to about 200,000 houses a year. This reduced the mobility of labour and forced many people to live in uncomfortable and inadequate homes.

Undoubtedly it was impossible to do everything at once, but Churchill argued in 1950 that the government had got its priorities wrong. He condemned the ambitious school-building programme and asked for 'bedrooms before schoolrooms'.[6] The 1950 Conservative conference asked for 300,000 houses a year, and the party leadership accepted this figure. Macmillan was made Minister of Housing in 1951 with the task of building the 300,000 houses. By 1953 the target had been reached and the performance was sustained in 1954. The housing problem was nearer to being under control than at any time since 1939.

This concentration on house-building, combined with the relaxation of the system of building licences and the repeal of the 1947 Act giving development rights to the government, launched a property boom. New office blocks were built, houses which could be changed from controlled to uncontrolled tenancies produced large profits, and the price of land went up. The property boom was only one area where the relaxation of controls on the economy allowed assets to be bought for less than their market value; many of the mergers and takeovers of the 1950s were financial operations by which assets were bought cheaply rather than industrial operations to make firms more efficient. The increase in building was at first matched by a decline in other forms of

---

6. 6 Nov. 1950, *Commons Debates*, ccclxxx. 705. Churchill was taking up a remark made earlier in the debate by a Labour backbencher.

investment inside Britain. Non-building investment, after allowing for rising prices, did not get back to the 1951 level until 1955. A higher rate of overall British investment, at home and abroad, would fairly certainly have led to inflationary pressure or an adverse balance of payments.

Complacency about the achievements of the post-war government was not restricted to matters of investment, nor confined to one party alone. Life after the war had been so much less comfortable than expected that everybody took it for granted that investment and the social services had been making tremendous strides. The Welfare State, it was felt, had been built and would stand to be the admiration of the world, and several European countries did feel they should follow Britain in extending their social services. They spent fairly lavishly to provide for old-age pensions, family allowances, and other cash benefits, though in general they set up their health services without fighting their doctors. By the 1950s, according to the 1955 Guillebaud Report, Britain was keeping the proportion of the national income spent on health services unchanged, when many other prosperous countries were spending more and more on health. Because the Labour Party was quite certain that there was nothing to improve about the Welfare State it had built, and the Conservatives thought that welfare benefits were almost too luxurious, there was a truce in discussions of social services, and in the same way a great many people were convinced that the level of investment in the late 1940s was so high that nothing more needed to be done.

Defence expenditure, it was conceded, was too high. The £4,700 million programme was abandoned, and expenditure began to fall back from the 12 or 13 per cent of the national income that it had reached in 1951–2. Defence and the social services were receiving less of the national income, investment was not increasing very much and less of the national income went to pay for any given amount of imports, because the terms of trade were improving. As a result there was more money to spend on consumer goods. The national income, after remaining stable in 1952, went up steadily for the next three years. Although production and average income had reached pre-war levels by 1948 or 1949, good production figures until the mid-1950s were often referred to as 'post-war peaks', with a misleading suggestion that pre-war peaks had been even higher.

The treatment of trade unions showed how completely the supporters of 'setting the people free' had triumphed over the 'back to before the war' group in forming Conservative policy. Sir Walter Monckton was appointed Minister of Labour and fairly clearly was told to maintain good relations between the government and the unions. The repeal of the Trade Disputes Act was left undisturbed. The right to strike was accepted and the 1940s system of compulsory arbitration was wound up. During the 1940s trade unions had won the right to be consulted on questions that affected them, and it was accepted that Royal Commissions on most issues had to contain a trade unionist;

businessmen and trade unionists usually got equal representation on committees concerned with economic issues, an arrangement that would have surprised business leaders in most countries outside Scandinavia.

Most of the excess demand had been squeezed out of the economy by the time of the Korean War and, as prices of imports rapidly fell back to the 1950 level, there was no longer much demand inflation. But real wages had not increased since 1947, and pressure for wage increases built up. The unions' successes were resented by people who felt the government was being too soft with the working classes. Annual wage increases, given voluntarily or under the threat of a strike, seemed to have become normal. As the money value of the increases was more than the real increase in production, this encouraged a cost-inflation in which prices rose slightly more slowly than money wages. In a world of philosophers this might have been accepted as one of the disadvantages of setting the people free. In the Britain of the early 1950s it was regarded as shocking that the unions should use their recently recovered freedom.

The government avoided taking an anti-Communist line on strikes, though the discussion was embittered by the belief of the press and many non-specialist commentators that the strikes and the pressure for increases in pay were all the result of Communist infiltration. Communists had gained positions of influence in trade unions and it was sometimes said they used these positions to mislead workers into asking for more money to sabotage the economy. This was not very helpful: the idea that only a desire to sabotage the economy could lead people to ask for more money was an excessively non-materialist way of looking at life. Trade unionists found Communist leadership attractive when they wanted a militant policy on wages, but negotiations were much more peaceful in the 1950s than they were after the great reduction of Communist influence in the 1960s. About as many days were lost owing to strikes in the depressed 1930s as in the full employment in the 1950s. Strikes cost many more working days in the 1920s; though they never cost as many days as the common cold.

The 1952 budget had to reduce demand in order to deal with the Korean War balance-of-payments problems. The cuts in food subsidies probably made trade unions a little more willing to ask for pay increases, but because of the improvement in the terms of trade prices did not go up. In 1953 the food subsidies were again reduced, and at the same time the standard rate of income tax was cut by 2.5p. This was a step away from the sharp increases in direct taxation and deliberate government action to hold down prices of the 1940s, which had benefited the poor at the expense of the rich. 'Setting the people free' clearly included reducing the process of redistributing income, and the end of food subsidies meant that people would pay a market price for what they wanted and the government would not guide them into spending their money on food.

Some people saw the ending of rationing as another great struggle between socialism and capitalism; some Conservatives spoke as though the Labour Party positively enjoyed running the rationing system, and some members of the Labour Party said that ending rationing would lead to economic disaster; and some people even saw the reopening of the London commodity markets in these terms of high principle. For a time it seemed as though sterling crises had been a problem of post-war recovery. Convertibility in 1947, devaluation in 1949, and Korea in 1951 had brought a summer crisis every other year, but there was no sterling crisis in 1953. The 1953 budget gave investment allowances for firms spending money on new equipment, and this checked the drop in non-housing investment and helped to encourage the 'investment boom' of 1954 and 1955. Butler was so pleased by its success that he said in 1954 that, at the current rate of progress, people in Britain could double their standard of living in the next twenty-five years.[7]

This prediction of a rate of growth of just under 3 per cent a year, which was distinctly smaller than the rate of growth between 1945 and the Korean War, was regarded as bold, and even as wild and impracticable. Partly because living conditions were so miserable, and partly because most of the growth went to defence, social services, and the less consumer-oriented forms of investment, nobody had realized how quickly the economy was recovering immediately after the war. Butler predicted a rate of growth that was lower than that of the late 1940s for a number of reasons. The American loan and Marshall Aid had allowed the Labour government to run a large deficit on its balance of payments. Just after the war there was a great hunger for goods; the United States had goods to sell, but the world shortage of dollars made it hard for customers to buy. By 'blocking' sterling the Labour government had created a slightly artificial market in countries that held sterling and could not do anything with it except buy British goods.

Germany and Japan had come back to world export trade early in the 1950s; it was bad luck for British exporters that they returned during the Korean War, when Britain was unusually ill placed for resisting new competitors. As competition increased, foreign customers who had been ready to buy anything in the late 1940s became more selective. They had often been sold goods they would buy only in a sellers' market, and some of them were sceptical about British goods by the early 1950s. Although the improvement in the terms of trade made the balance-of-payments position easier, the countries that produced the raw materials that were going down in price became less prosperous and less able to buy British goods, for which they had previously been a good market.

No sections of the economy had been declining in the late 1940s, but by the time Butler made his prediction it was already clear that cotton textiles had returned to their long-term decline. Just after the war, with Japanese

7. *The Annual Register of World Events for 1954*, 45, called it 'a daring forecast'.

competition temporarily eliminated and India still mainly concerned with domestic demand, this was not so obvious. By the 1950s this competition, paying lower wages and equipped with newly installed machinery, was driving Lancashire out of the business it had dominated for almost two centuries. In 1906 Britain sold cotton goods all over the world, and the cotton industry was devoted to Free Trade. By 1955 Britain was a net importer of cotton goods, and Lancashire was demanding Protection. The change was inevitable, but it was a nasty shock for the economy. No other industries were in quite the same position, though coal and the railways might slip back to the problems of the 1920s and 1930s.

The Conservatives accepted the general principle of nationalization of some industries and never tried to privatize coal or the railways, possibly because it was most unlikely that any purchasers could have been found. The election programme had promised privatization of steel and of road transport: steel was sold off successfully, on a basis that gave a preference to the original owners; and only one company, Richard Thomas & Baldwin, could not be disposed of. Relatively few of the previous owners wanted to get back into road haulage, and in the end British Railways was left with a distinctly larger share of the trade than the government had intended.

By early 1955 the investment boom, and the accompanying increase in consumption, had gone so far that Butler decided that expansion would have to be held back. Two increases in the bank rate followed in quick succession, and restrictions were reimposed on hire purchase sales by laying down requirements about the size of deposits. The more doctrinaire supporters of the free play of the market disliked even this slight intervention in the economy, but on the whole they could feel that freedom had worked, and perhaps had worked all the better because the Conservatives had made so little attempt to get back to 'before the war'.

The government showed in other ways, such as not reviving parliamentary seats for the universities, that it was determined to give no hint of putting the clock back. The most striking example of readiness to ignore the traditionalist wing of the Conservative Party came in the struggle over commercial, or independent, television. The television service of the BBC had started again in 1946, but it was a small section of the Corporation's work. Radio stood at the peak of its influence; during the war the BBC's introductory 'This is London calling' had been the voice of truth and of hope to a captive continent, and it owed that position to its refusal to transmit anything that sounded like propaganda—or, the sophisticated would say, to its realization that good propaganda rests on a reputation for truthfulness. Its success in the war confirmed all the Reithian principles about setting high and elevating standards. At the time television was being revived, the Corporation was much more interested in another minority service it was launching—the Third Programme, designed specially for people who wanted modern poetry, classical music, and discussion of scholarly issues. The small audience for television could and did grow; the audience for the Third Programme did not expand, partly because the Programme steadily raised its standards. It did useful things, such as encouraging Dylan Thomas, the last poet to be both popular and taken seriously by other poets, but the Third Programme absorbed too much of the energy of the Corporation and led it to neglect television or at least treat it as subordinate to radio.

The combination of this neglect with the spirit of Reith meant that BBC television was dull and limited. It may have suited the years of austerity, but after that it was extremely vulnerable. By the time of the 1951 election a group of people with considerable influence inside the Conservative Party organization was ready with suggestions for an alternative television system run on a profit-making basis. They captured the Cabinet and got their plan accepted. It was of course opposed by the Labour Party, who believed in the BBC and had no desire to see another medium of communication run by people who would be likely to oppose any sort of socialism. The more significant division came inside the Conservative Party, where a considerable number of the traditionalists resisted the scheme. In the House of Lords the government had some difficulty rallying support and defending its television proposals.

It was denounced for being like the American system, and the opponents of the proposal made it clear that they believed 'American' and 'vulgar' meant the same thing. Technically the British and American arrangements differed: advertisers in the United States supported individual programmes by advertising on them, and could force a change of programme by withdrawing their support if they felt they were not getting a large enough audience. In Britain the organizing companies produced the programmes shown, and the advertisers simply bought minutes of time in which to present an advertising message. The news programmes were produced by a separate company, Independent Television News, and were supplied to all the organizing companies. These provisions reduced the power of the advertisers over the producing companies, but the difference was not all that significant.

The introduction of commercial television was a poor reward for the newspapers' support for the Conservatives when they were in opposition. When it was launched late in 1955, the advertisers waited to see how large an audience they were being offered, and for about a year the producing companies ran up debts. The audience proved to be reasonably large and the advertisers began to buy time, and the troubles of the producing companies were over. Advertisers became more selective about the newspapers in which they bought space, concentrating on the papers with the largest circulations, which provided more customers per pound spent. Other newspapers lost ground financially as a result, and all newspapers lost some of their authority. By the end of the war almost everybody in the country saw a newspaper, a scale of circulation that had never existed before and seems unlikely to exist anywhere ever again. The

Express, the paper for the people who felt they were getting ahead, and the *Mirror*, the paper for the working class, had sales of over 4 million each. The *Express* probably helped the modernizers against the traditionalists inside the Conservative Party, but it did not affect people's political views much. The *Mirror* seems to have increased the Labour vote in 1945 and in 1951. Newspapers had a hint of the pulpit about them and, while the *Mirror* and the *Express* were more successful than their rivals at popularizing and secularizing this approach, there was always a note of earnest exhortation that suited the serious-minded 1940s. Television had a hint of the university lecture about it, and while Independent Television was more successful than the BBC at popularizing and intellectualizing this approach, the cool, not completely committed, and slightly cynical approach of the lecturer suited the mood of the 1950s. No doubt television would have been popular at any time, but its characteristic approach suited the spirit of the age particularly well. Newspapers had been something that people talked about; in the 1950s they talked about television programmes instead. Television also captured the universal audience that had watched films in the 1940s. The British film industry contracted sharply, as its audience diminished. Television, and in particular commercial television, had a good effect on mass communication. BBC television became distinctly livelier as the Corporation realized that it would have to interest an audience if it was to have any effect on it. British films also became more interesting, and began to attract audiences in other countries.

The traditionalists had been right to think that commercial television would do them no good. It promoted a view of society which was much more like a marketplace than the orderly system of deference to one's betters which they had hoped to see re-established, and it challenged the idea that some affairs of state were too important to be discussed in public, which had been one of the strengths of the system of deference. The supporters of the marketplace could feel more confident that their view of the world would be accepted. But although opposition to the values of the marketplace and opposition to American influence did not affect government policy much, they were still strong in the country, and have to be remembered when considering the political situation at this time.

The 1955 general election

When it lost in 1951, the Labour Party seemed well placed to recover. It had polled more votes than the Conservatives, it had a front bench of ex-ministers who were known to the public, and it had a government with a weak majority in front of it. But nothing went as might have been expected. The party had carried out all the measures about which people felt widespread enthusiasm, and it had no new ideas to unite it. The price of its leaders' intellectual sterility was paid during the 1950s when the party quarrelled over old issues.

Quite early in the new Parliament it was clear that Bevan and his followers had been right to say the rearmament programme was too large. This might have enabled him to return to a position within the leadership of the party, but a fresh issue had arisen; German rearmament, in one form or another, was accepted by the party leadership but Bevan opposed it. He believed that rearmament would alarm the Russians, and would commit the West to trying to solve issues by military means. He was confident that the answer to Communism was to find a social system that was economically and culturally more attractive than it. Militarism, he argued with a hint of Orwell's *Nineteen Eighty-Four*, led to McCarthyism—the hunt for anyone with disturbing or subversive ideas which was going on in the United States at the time. And some of the driving force behind Bevanism came from the belief that the United States was not a satisfactory type of society and that Britain should take care not to develop in the same way. Anti-German feeling entered into it, and Bevan's position was also strengthened by the fact that there was no real hatred of Russia in Britain. In emotional terms people were balanced between Russia and America: the United States attracted much more positive liking, but it often aroused strong irritation, and this irritation found its most overt political expression in the Bevanite struggle.

Bevan was better placed to fight against the party leadership than almost any other rebel. In 1952 six out of the seven seats on the Labour Party's National Executive Committee that were filled by the votes of the local constituency parties were won by Bevanites, which led the Bevanites to claim that the leadership controlled the party only by lobbying a small group of leaders of large trade unions. In 1954, when German rearmament was debated at the party conference, the opponents of rearmament polled about 75 per cent of the votes of the constituency parties. The leadership's majority at the conference was small enough and sufficiently dependent on trade union strength to show that, if the constituency party votes reflected the views of the unpaid party workers, the Labour Party machine was going to be disorganized at the next election.

Bevan had too few supporters among Labour Members of Parliament to threaten Attlee's position but too many for the party leadership to be able to crush him. Attlee supported the American alliance, and believed in a bipartisan foreign policy; Bevan thought a bipartisan policy took control of foreign affairs out of the hands of the people and gave it to the supporters of special interests. Attlee was not strongly opposed to Bevan: Morrison, as the exponent of the policy of a Labour Party which could appeal to the lower middle class, and Gaitskell, as the victim of Bevan's attacks in 1951, were the chief spokesmen for the anti-Bevanite party leadership. As deputy leader and because of his years of service in organizing the party, Morrison had a good claim to succeed Attlee. On the other hand, Bevan and Gaitskell would be stronger candidates if the party wanted a young leader.

At the beginning of 1955 Churchill decided to retire, and in April he did at long last hand over power to Eden. The long wait, and the perpetual subordination to a man with whom he was not on very close terms, had done Eden no good. But he entered on a satisfactory inheritance: he could reasonably call an election almost immediately, and then he could rule as his own master. For the election he had splendid prospects, with success in housing, the end of rationing, his own diplomatic prestige, a divided Opposition that had produced no new ideas, and Butler's budget. Although he had thought earlier in the year that the country might be heading for balance-of-payments difficulties, the Chancellor of the Exchequer felt he could cut income tax by another 2.5p. The government asked for a general election; public interest was lower than it had been for some time past, and there was a distinct drop in the number of votes cast.

	Votes	Seats	% of all votes cast
Conservative	13,286,569	344	49.7
Liberal	702,405	6	2.7
Labour	12,404,970	277	46.4

The Conservative majority was now large enough to give the government political freedom of action, but economic circumstances tied it down. During the summer the disadvantages of investing abroad rather than building up the reserves became clear. There was a balance-of-payments deficit which, although not large, was enough to make many holders of sterling feel they would be safer if they sold their holdings. Butler convinced the September meeting of the International Monetary Fund that Britain was not going to adopt a floating exchange rate, which would have led to a sharp fall in the value of sterling, but foreign confidence in the British economy had still to be restored. Deflationary measures to reduce the pressure on resources caused by the investment boom were the obvious step. In October a second budget was introduced in which all rates of purchase tax were increased by one-fifth, and in addition it was imposed on a number of household goods such as saucepans which had been exempt. About as much extra revenue was raised as had been by the reductions in income tax in the spring: taken together, the two budgets transferred some of the weight of taxation from the rich to the poor and, while there might be a case for openly adjusting taxation in this direction, the way in which it was done led economists to say, 'The only rational explanation of the reduction in income-tax is that it was an exclusively political move made with an eye on the forthcoming general election.'[8]

8. G. D. N. Worswick and P. H. Ady, *The British Economy 1950–1959* (1962), 34.

Butler's prestige fell when the boom had to be stopped. He became Lord Privy Seal and was replaced at the Treasury by Macmillan; in the party the modernizers and businessmen began to lose ground, and the people who wanted to get back to 'before the war' made their opinions heard more loudly than they had done for some time. They may have felt this was electorally safer once the 1955 election was won, and they were also encouraged by the signs that Butler's power was declining and that modern Conservatism was in retreat. The government's share of the vote dropped sharply in a by-election in the normally safe Conservative seat of Tonbridge. Conservative newspapers suggested that the Prime Minister was not firmly in command of the situation, and within six months of the election Eden thought it necessary to deny that he was thinking of resigning.

The impatience with Eden was not easy to justify; the balance of payments was improving and he could hardly be blamed for the deterioration in relations between Russia and the West. But the more traditionally minded of the Conservatives felt that it was time to reassert old values. They had not ventured to criticize Churchill, but they wanted to see policies that restored the position of the traditional middle classes and revived the strength of Britain's imperial position. The middle class, taken as a whole, had in fact been gaining ground relative to the working class throughout the early 1950s, and Butler's two 1955 budgets had reinforced the tendency of salaries to increase faster than wages. But the middle classes could not be treated as a single unit. The rising level of average salaries reflected the appearance of new and rather well-paid salaried jobs rather than an increase in the incomes of the traditional middle class. Airline pilots, programme directors for television, and market research consultants helped to create a prosperous middle class holding jobs that often had not existed before the war, but this was no consolation for solicitors, clergymen, or middle-class gentlefolk living on income from investments, often in gilt-edged stock, on which the income had lost much of its purchasing power in the steady rise in prices since 1939. The assumption that a manual job should not pay as well as a non-manual job was not very reasonable, because there had always been a fair amount of overlapping between skilled workers and clerks or small shopkeepers, but the middle class complained as though the high wages obtained by miners in the late 1940s or by car workers in the 1950s were some infringement of a preordained order of society. The declining section of the middle class blamed the working class, and also blamed the government for not resisting the working class. The government could hardly convince them that really they had lost ground to members of other sections of the middle class, but a government that tried to reinstate all members of the middle class in their pre-war position, as they fondly remembered it, was going to have a difficult job on its hands.

The confused state of the Conservatives was presumably some consolation for Attlee when he retired from the leadership of the Labour Party in

November 1955. He had been chosen as the man who divided the party least, and had run it on that basis, and he knew that many members of the party would oppose anything that looked like a return to the personal dominance exercised by MacDonald. Attlee was never a commanding figure in the party at large, though he kept his Cabinet firmly under control when he was Prime Minister. His form of leadership, which left it to other people to put forward ideas, followed the same lines as Asquith's or Baldwin's, and did not involve constant intervention in the manner of Lloyd George or Neville Chamberlain. For his successor the Parliamentary Labour Party elected Gaitskell, who polled more votes than Morrison and Bevan put together; Attlee had indicated one of Gaitskell's claims by saying the party needed to be led by someone born in the twentieth century. As a man who was interested in ideas Gaitskell could be expected to give his party something new to talk about, but it was far from certain that the country at that moment wanted—whatever it needed—a leader who had been born in the twentieth century.

Early in 1956 the success of the play *Look Back in Anger* threw a curious light on British attitudes. Artistically and intellectually it was the first of a number of plays that revived the moribund London theatre and was also the first of a series of attacks on the way British life was developing. In 1956 the note in the play which seemed to catch people's political feelings was the hero's complaint 'people of our generation aren't able to die for good causes any more. We had all that done for us, in the thirties and the forties, when we were still kids. There aren't any good brave causes left.' On the other hand, there was an older man's note of nostalgia:

The England I remembered was the one I left in 1914, and I was happy to go on remembering it that way. . . . Those long cool evenings in the [Indian] hills, everything purple and golden. Your mother and I were so happy then. It seemed as if we had everything we could ever want. I think the last day the sun shone was when that dirty little train steamed out of that crowded suffocating Indian station, and the battalion band playing for all it was worth.[9]

Britain had reached a position where it could set up a Welfare State running with capitalist efficiency, like West Germany, or a Welfare State running with experimental and socialist overtones, like Sweden; the emotions awakened by Osborne's play did not belong to the real world. But the country turned away from the choice, and decided that the future prospects were too unexciting to be faced willingly. This attitude could do no good in the long run; it was particularly dangerous that it was in the ascendant when the problem of Suez arose.

9. J. Osborne, *Look Back in Anger* (1960), 66 and 84; first performed May 1956.

The Suez crisis of 1956

In July 1956 the American government decided that it was not willing to help the Egyptian government to build a dam at Aswan on the Nile for irrigation and hydroelectricity, perhaps because opposition in Congress to foreign aid in general was unexpectedly strong, or perhaps because President Nasser of Egypt was regarded as too ready to negotiate with Russia. As a result the British government also withdrew its offer to help pay the costs of the dam. Nasser decided to get money for the dam by nationalizing the Suez Canal Company, paying compensation at the market price of the shares. His right to do so was much clearer than the right of Iran to nationalize the Abadan oil refinery, for Egypt had not renounced the right to nationalize. Nevertheless, British opinion regarded Nasser's action as a blow that had to be parried. The Canal had been the route to India; it was still the route to Australia; it was the route for the growing imports of oil. Besides, the Canal Company had always charged low passage rates, and Nasser would presumably increase them to pay for the dam.

When the Commons debated the issue on 2 August, Eden uncompromisingly denied that Nasser had any right to act as he had. Gaitskell said in reply that Egypt had done nothing to Britain that would justify the use of force, but he also compared Nasser with Hitler and Mussolini. These were dangerous names to use; they encouraged people to think that the nationalization of the Canal was something like the occupation of the Rhineland in 1936, and the implication was that it should be resisted. The French government was concerned because the Canal Company was a French company, and in addition it wanted to see Nasser crushed because it believed he was the main support of the uprising that had broken out in Algeria in 1954 and that overthrowing him might end the revolt. So British and French military planners began assembling forces for the operation known as Musketeer, which involved landing a force in Egypt and occupying the Canal (and presumably overthrowing Nasser, though this was not so clear). The force was mainly British, the commanders were British, and the bombers needed to knock out the Egyptian air force were almost all British.

A conference of twenty-two countries with an interest in the Canal was held in August, and eighteen of the nations agreed that the Canal ought to be internationalized: the governments whose subjects used the Canal would set up a committee to take the place of the Canal Company and run the Canal, and make sure that it was kept open in accordance with the treaty of 1888. The Canal Company ordered all its pilots to leave their jobs; it was widely believed in Britain and France that the Egyptians were not technically capable of running the Canal or finding new pilots, but the Egyptian government proved it could run the Canal, and new pilots were recruited quite easily. Egypt also declined to accept the internationalization proposed by the eighteen nations in London, and by early September the initial shock of nationalization was dying and the use of force was becoming less acceptable to world opinion; the British and French governments were left feeling that they were not getting anywhere.

At this stage Eden still wanted to keep in touch with the United States. When Dulles suggested a Suez Canal Users' Association (SCUA), Eden agreed to discuss it, though he made it clear that he welcomed it mainly as a way to keep the United States in touch with Britain and France, and he seems to have thought that if Egypt would not recognize the authority of the SCUA, the United States would help to impose it upon Nasser by force. Dulles had no intention of allowing this to happen; while he said Nasser must be made to 'disgorge', he stated that the United States did not intend to shoot its way through the Canal, and later on he said that 'there were no teeth in the plan'.[10] But Eden had been interested in it only because he had thought it had teeth.

From early August the French government had been supplying military equipment to Israel, with some suggestion of cooperation against Nasser. Israel could defend its own frontiers against Egypt, but an advance forward across the Sinai desert would require command of the air. France could not provide this, so in mid-October (or perhaps earlier) the French government suggested to Eden that the Musketeer plan (which had been kept at a few weeks' readiness) should be adapted to synchronize with an Israeli advance against Egypt. For Israel the attack on the Egyptian air force was what mattered; the fact that an Anglo-French force would also be attacking Egypt was gratifying but less important. For France, the more people who attacked Nasser the merrier. The British government thought an outbreak of fighting caused by an Israeli attack would let it claim that it was only going into the struggle to separate the combatants. Cooperation with Israel was contrary to the whole line of British policy since at least 1948. The United Kingdom had tried to keep on good terms with the Arab countries, partly because of the growing importance of oil, partly because the Middle East had been a British sphere of influence since the First World War and there was a risk that Russia might begin to take an interest in it. Sentimental supporters of the Arabs saw them as splendid desert horsemen having nothing in common with the corrupt or downtrodden Egyptians: this view seems to have gained some support in London, though Egypt was for Arabs the country to which they looked in many ways for guidance and leadership.

By mid-October the British and Egyptian Foreign Secretaries had worked out six principles on which the Canal could be run. The Egyptians accepted that SCUA, teeth or no teeth, was a body with a legitimate interest in the level of tolls. France was not in the least eager for the success of these negotiations, but failed to frustrate them. Eden declined to show any interest in the Foreign

10. H. Thomas, *The Suez Affair* (1967), 94.

Secretary's negotiations, and instead took him on a number of more or less well-concealed visits to French ministers in the second half of October. The timing of the plan seems to have been decided by the British belief that the United States would not take any steps hostile to Israel before the American presidential election in November. This calculation exaggerated the importance of the Jewish vote in New York; financial support from the Jewish community may have been important to Truman in the months before the 1948 election but no Republican candidate expected to get Jewish money or votes in any great numbers, whatever foreign policy he followed.

On 29 October Israel attacked Egypt. On the 30th Britain and France called on both sides to withdraw to positions ten miles from the Canal and allow British and French troops to come in and occupy the Canal. Israel could occupy almost the whole Sinai peninsula; Egypt had to give up Sinai and the Canal. Egypt did not accept this ultimatum, and Musketeer was put into operation. At the same time Britain and France vetoed a Security Council resolution asking for all nations to refrain from using force in the Middle East. On the 31st the bombing of Egyptian airfields began, and the invasion fleet set sail. But as it had to come all the way from Malta—Cyprus was a useful air base, but had no harbours large enough for an expedition on this scale—it could not reach Port Said, at the north end of the Canal, until 6 November. Once the Egyptian air force was paralysed there was not much for Britain and France to do. Israeli forces advanced through the Sinai peninsula, and arrived at about the ten-mile line, but there was little comfort elsewhere for the government. The Egyptians sank forty-seven blockships in the Canal.[11] Eisenhower made it clear, in an angry telephone conversation with Eden, that he disapproved of the British action and would do his best to stop it. The Opposition objected so strenuously and violently to government policy that one sitting of the House had to be suspended for tempers to calm down. At the United Nations the General Assembly voted by sixty-four to five (the United Kingdom, France, Israel, Australia, and New Zealand) that there should be a ceasefire: when Israeli forces reached the ten-mile line they were ready to accept the ceasefire, which left Britain and France more stranded than ever. The invasion fleet was still on its way from Malta, and it could hardly come ashore to keep the peace if both sides had already accepted the UN ceasefire. On 5 November paratroops were dropped near Port Said, and on the 6th the fleet arrived. Port Said was taken later in the day, and troops set off on the hundred miles to Suez, at the south end of the Canal.

But before they had got very far they heard that Britain and France had accepted the ceasefire. To some extent the pressure of the United Nations and of the Opposition in Parliament had weakened the government's position;

11. Ibid. 130.

two resignations by junior ministers, the knowledge that a dozen Conservative Members were about to present a formal protest, and the possibility that dissatisfied Cabinet ministers like Macleod or Monckton might resign meant that the government could no longer be completely sure of its own survival; pressure on the gold reserves, which had had to meet sales of £100 million of sterling, and the knowledge that oil would be in short supply and could only be obtained from the United States, all combined to convince the British government that the operation would have to stop. In Paris the franc was steady; the government had no doubts about its parliamentary support and was not particularly concerned about the United Nations. The British decision to stop came as a most unwelcome surprise, but as the expedition was completely integrated and was under British command the French had to accept the decision. The military operations had been successful—only twenty-one British soldiers were killed in the whole undertaking—but the political situation made this success useless.

Eden's health was already poor, and it has been suggested that the medical treatment he received had affected his judgement. At this point he had to go to Jamaica to rest. While he was away, the government, temporarily led by Butler, was forced step by step to withdraw from Egypt and to leave the task of peacekeeping to the UN Emergency Force, and the work of clearing the Canal to Egypt and the UN. The popularity of the government in the country seems to have been almost unaffected by the whole performance: a fairly vocal section of middle-class opinion which had supported the Conservatives turned to the Labour Party, but the opinion polls at the time suggested that a slightly larger section of pro-Labour working-class opinion felt that the operation had been justified. The government's attempts to explain what it had been doing were not impressive: at first it said it had intervened to separate the combatants; then it congratulated itself on bringing the UN Emergency Force into existence, which, as Healey commented from the Labour side during the debate, was rather as though Al Capone expected to be thanked for bringing about improvements in the Chicago police force; and then it said it had found stacks of Russian arms in Egypt, which showed that a Communist plot was afoot. In reality the discovery only showed that Nasser took weapons from both sides in the Cold War; he had larger stocks of British arms. The French government acknowledged straightforwardly that it had cooperated with Israel, but the British government stuck to its story that it had not even known that Israel was going to attack Egypt. This showed the real weakness of the British government's policy over Suez: it knew that what it was doing—going back into Egypt to recover control of the Canal—could not be defended in public but nevertheless it went ahead. As nobody outside the country believed its story anyway, it gained the discredit of being dishonest as well as imperialist. Britain's allies in the Middle East, particularly Nuri es-Said in Iraq, were weakened by the episode, and Nasser was greatly strengthened; he repudiated the terms of the compromise for the Canal worked out in mid-October, and kept control of it in Egyptian hands.

While the Suez operations did not affect the feelings of the general public much, they did affect people closer to the centre of politics. Some Conservatives thought the operation might have succeeded if the Labour Party had not protested so loudly; it is most unlikely that Labour's fierce opposition really made much difference, and the Labour Party had no particular reason to approve of a policy about which it had never been consulted. Gaitskell aroused a more direct and personal bitterness, partly because in a broadcast he asked Conservatives to overthrow Eden and, in effect, to set up someone like Butler as a sort of Ramsay MacDonald in reverse, and partly because people thought that in August he had encouraged a forceful response. To make things worse, his attitude seemed to be pro-American; Bevan was less vehement in his condemnation of the operations and, while it was good tactics for the Conservatives to play on any division there might be between Gaitskell and Bevan, it probably was true that Bevan disliked the way the United States had come to assert control over British policy. Part of the Conservative reaction was a series of protests: by those who felt the United States was working to destroy the British Empire. A resolution was brought forward condemning the American attitude by about 120 Conservative backbenchers who were presumably not made any less hostile to the United States by the Labour Party's general willingness to welcome American anti-imperialism.

Suez embittered the Labour Party as well. It indicated that the Conservative Party had not given up its past policies as much as had appeared during the early 1950s. Suez seemed to be a piece of imperialism and deception which, although it had not succeeded, had been presented to the public in an untruthful way that concealed the size of the defeat. The result was that the Opposition remained constantly suspicious of the government. Consultation between government and Opposition was not essential for the conduct of foreign policy, as had been seen at the outbreak of the Boer War and the two World Wars, but some degree of trust was needed. The general public was not normally told what was going on, but from the early 1920s, when Baldwin and MacDonald established fairly friendly relations, until 1956, Prime Ministers and leaders of the Opposition were almost always on close enough terms to discuss things in an amiable way. After 1956 this was no longer the case; the doubt and bitterness remained at the highest levels in Britain long after it had been forgotten by everybody else except the Arabs, who felt that Britain was still imperialist at heart.

12

They 'never had it so good'

1957–1961

Rebuilding after Suez

Eden's position did not survive the Suez failure. He came back from Jamaica and tried to carry on, but his colleagues were uneasy about going on with a leader who had caused so much trouble, and the recurring fever that had attacked him from time to time in the past three years forced him to resign. His career was like that of Neville Chamberlain's in its masterful ascent to the premiership followed by excessive activity in office and then a dramatic loss of power. His departure eased the shock of Suez for the country. Butler had been building up his claim to lead the party for years and people outside the centre of power thought he would succeed Eden, but he had not given the impression of being totally committed to Suez and he was blamed for the decision to withdraw taken while he was acting Prime Minister. People with long memories remembered that he had helped to defend Munich and appeasement. Macmillan was understood to have been an eager supporter of Suez; back-bench MPs did not know that it was his insistence that he could not defend the exchange value of the pound any longer that had been the final blow that brought the whole operation to a stop. Opinion in the Conservative Party was assessed by private consultations and not by a vote of the parliamentary party, but there is no reason to doubt that Macmillan was the man the Conservatives wanted.

Between 1924 and 1939 Macmillan had disagreed with the party leadership on domestic policy, where he thought much more could be done to reduce unemployment, and on foreign policy, where he thought Hitler should be resisted. By 1956 these views were party orthodoxy, and in any case Macmillan did not look unorthodox; he gave a well-cultivated impression of an Edwardian gentleman of leisure with a great fondness for the past and its customs. The Conservative backbenchers may easily have thought that Macmillan was less favourable to change than Butler, though on this they were probably wrong. Macmillan thought people ought to have served in the armed forces when the need arose. He had been badly wounded in the First World War; he had a poor opinion of Gaitskell, who had been a civil servant during the Second World War. Like Macmillan, Gaitskell was a very intelligent, rather shy man with no fear of originality or independence of thought. Apart from the natural party difference that Gaitskell believed in equality and Macmillan thought people should be able to amass and hold their own fortunes, there was a personal difference between them: Gaitskell was a man of rigid principle who thought Macmillan was a crook, and Macmillan was a man of flexible techniques who thought Gaitskell was a prig.

Macmillan was clearly the best man to lead the Conservatives in the circumstances of 1957. He threaded his way skilfully through many difficulties; he looked more impressive on other, later occasions, but perhaps he never again solved problems as dextrously as in his first eighteen months as Prime Minister. He saw the alliance with the United States as Britain's principal diplomatic concern. Like Churchill he had known Eisenhower during the war, and he was able to build a close political relationship upon this personal friendship. Macmillan thought Britain should never take important steps in foreign affairs without the approval of the United States. This meant cutting the country off from France, but the position of the French government seemed unimpressive as it plunged further into the problem of holding Algeria.

The Conservative Party was in an anti-American mood, so Britain had to be seen to have a position of her own. The British H-bomb was on the point of completion, and Macmillan ordered it to be tested. Shortly afterwards Duncan Sandys, the Minister of Defence—the seventh since 1951—announced that National Service would come to an end, on the grounds that greater reliance on nuclear weapons would let the United Kingdom reduce its forces equipped with conventional weapons. This doctrine became less fashionable later on, when people argued that conventional strength was needed for fighting at anything below the nuclear level, but at the time Sandys's approach was very attractive for political and financial reasons. After switching to reliance on nuclear weapons the government not only ended conscription but also claimed it was justified in withdrawing troops from Germany despite the 1954 agreements: it argued that the general strength of Europe was increased by the existence of a British nuclear force close at hand. This was a fairly clear statement that the British bomb was built in case the United States was in some circumstances unwilling to commit its nuclear forces to the defence of Europe, but European opinion was not won over by the thought of a British bomb to back up the American bomb, and reckoned that the troops were being withdrawn from Germany because they cost more foreign exchange than expected. The Sandys strategy had obvious attractions for anyone who thought too much was being spent on defence. In 1953 expenditure reached a peacetime peak of just over £1,500 million—over 12 per cent of the national income. Spending was held at this level in cash terms, and as prices went upwards steadily it declined in real terms. Dependence on nuclear bombs, which were relatively cheap to make once the initial plant had been built, helped the government to keep defence spending steady, and thus bring down the proportion of national income devoted to defence quite considerably. And such was the importance attached to possessing the H-bomb that only a small minority pointed out that in fact military spending was being cut.

The newly formed government took a more conciliatory attitude than its predecessor over Cyprus. The Greek majority wanted Enosis, or union with Greece; the Turkish two-ninths of the population disliked the idea. Archbishop Makarios, the effective leader of the community because Greek bishops are elected by their flocks, supported the demand and when its more violent supporters turned to guerrilla activity he did not denounce their attacks on British troops. Most Conservatives valued Turkey's friendship more than that of Greece and felt that British rule might as well continue because it had kept the problem under control so far. Partition was rejected on the grounds that it was hard to find a region in the island where the Turks were in a comfortable majority. Eden's government arrested the Archbishop and sent him to the Seychelles; Macmillan's government released him, and fairly certainly wanted to get out of the island, but its backbenchers had no such desire and Lord Salisbury resigned from the Cabinet when the Archbishop was released. A change of Governors from Lord Harding to Sir Hugh Foot in December 1957 opened the way to negotiations. Decolonization in Ghana and Malaya went ahead with less controversy; both countries became independent in 1957, and both of them followed the Indian example and remained members of the Commonwealth. The numerical balance in conferences of Commonwealth Prime Ministers was moving towards the underdeveloped countries, and this in turn encouraged the British government to think harder about the economic aspects of Commonwealth relations.

Just after the July 1957 Commonwealth Prime Ministers' conference John Diefenbaker, the recently elected Conservative Prime Minister of Canada, declared that his country should take another 15 per cent of its imports from the United Kingdom and reduce imports from the United States accordingly. He seems not to have thought how this could be done, but the British government had to respond. In September Thorneycroft, who had succeeded Macmillan at the Exchequer, put forward a proposal for a free trade area between Canada and the United Kingdom which would eliminate tariff barriers between the two countries and allow British manufacturers to sell more in Canada than before, and thus carry out Diefenbaker's suggestion. The 1947 General Agreement on Tariffs and Trade (GATT) permitted a free trade area, though it did not allow preferences based on reductions in duties along the lines of the 1932 Ottawa Agreements, but the Canadian government had no appetite for a customs union and the idea was dropped.

The British government had wanted to explore the Canadian suggestion quickly because of its effect on European trade negotiations. In March 1957

France, West Germany, Italy, the Netherlands, Belgium, and Luxembourg had signed the Treaty of Rome and formed a economic community, a form of customs union in which the members have no tariffs between one another and also have a uniform tariff against all other countries' products. A uniform tariff implied a unified policy for agriculture and taxation, and the Treaty indicated that the community was going to develop into an ever closer union. Its tariff proposals meant that if the United Kingdom joined the Community it would have to end Commonwealth preferences and support British farmers by customs duties that would raise the price of food to the purchaser rather than the existing system of subsidies paid by the taxpayer. The government saw the advantages of the wider industrial market that would be opened up by abolishing tariff barriers and proposed that the whole of western Europe should form a free trade area, with no customs duties on manufactured products, but with all the members free to set their own tariffs on imports from outside the Area. This would have been in accordance with the GATT, would allow the six-nation Economic Community to maintain its unified system, and would also allow the United Kingdom to import food cheaply and continue to give preferences to Commonwealth countries. The proposal was discussed for about two years after the signing of the Treaty of Rome, but eventually it was rejected by the French government, which felt that Britain had found an ingenious arrangement for getting the best of both worlds, and in particular for reducing the benefits of the Community for French agriculture.

In the first half of 1957 Britain's international credit seemed to be recovering in both a political and an economic sense from the shock of Suez. The political recovery went on and Macmillan set out to find ways to reduce the tension between Russia and the NATO countries. The economic task was harder. The money in short-term bonds which had left London at the time of Suez returned in the spring and, while Thorneycroft's budget maintained the check on investment and domestic spending that had been in effect since Butler's second 1955 budget, he could by July speak with some confidence about expansion of the economy. He was then the victim of misfortune: the French franc had been kept steady in international terms since 1949, but prices had been going up fast enough to undermine its value. In August it was in effect devalued, bankers thought that other currencies might change their values, and the short-term money that had come in during the spring left again. The Chancellor of the Exchequer had to face a crisis of confidence and responded by raising the bank rate to 7 per cent to make London more attractive for short-term money, the normal way to deal with this problem.

At the same time he carried his efforts to restrain the economy to extreme lengths. People who wanted to get back to 'before the war' came closer to dominating domestic policy than at any time since 1939. Price stability was taken as the government's main objective, closely linked with maintenance of the exchange value of sterling at $2.80. The Opposition agreed that maintaining sterling should be a paramount objective, partly to avoid being seen as the party of devaluation but also because it believed the 1949 devaluation had caused the set-back in the 1950 election, and had perhaps led to the increase in prices which had helped cause defeat in 1951. This bipartisan acceptance of maintaining the current value of sterling was in sharp contrast to Butler's readiness to think of going on to a floating rate but, once accepted, the new attitude became firmly established.

In order to restrain the economy investment was reduced in the nationalized industries, where spending was directly under government control, and lending by banks or hire purchase firms was again discouraged. The Opposition argued that this would increase unemployment and that, if the economy was planned properly, useful investment could be carried out and the value of the pound could be maintained. This did not suit the mood of the government at all; many of its supporters had felt that Churchill, Butler, and Monckton had been too soft on the trade unions in the early 1950s, and that the time had now come to hold them in check. Thorneycroft was an early supporter of the idea that, if the amount of money in circulation was strictly limited, wages could not rise faster than production: if some workers got a wage increase, there would simply be less money for everybody else unless enough goods had been produced to meet the wage increase. At a less sophisticated level it was natural enough that Lord Hailsham, who had been one of the leaders of Conservative anti-Americanism just after Suez, should by the end of the year be one of the men most vocal in saying that trade unions were betraying the country: Suez and the worsening of industrial relations were symptoms of a feeling that the post-war world was less pleasant than had been thought. Naturally enough strikes increased, though they did not rise above the relatively low levels of the years immediately after the General Strike.

Keeping the purchasing power of money stable mattered most to the people, mainly outside industry, whose incomes were more or less fixed. But the other industrial countries were also concerned to keep prices steady, and the rapid rise in French prices in the 1950s was seen as an awful warning. The United States and Britain placed more emphasis than France on stable prices, but all three countries spent comparable proportions of their national income on defence. The United States economy in the 1950s was if anything even more sluggish than the British was becoming after 1955. Only in Germany, where defence expenditures were low, was price stability reconciled with economic growth.

International comparisons of this sort were becoming more common, not so much out of a greater willingness to look at the outside world as because more figures were available. Macmillan as Chancellor had said accurately enough that economic forecasting based on the figures available was rather like looking up trains in last year's railway timetable, but statistics were becoming available and those issued by the Organization for European

Economic Co-operation[1] enabled British politicians to select appropriate items for comparing their country's performance with others. The Labour Party complained that Britain was devoting less of the national income to new investment than most European countries, that economic growth at least since 1955 was slower, and that it was likely to continue to be slower under the Thorneycroft policy. The economists who advised Thorneycroft, whose views were best expressed by Robbins and Paish, tended to be more interested in the problems of keeping prices stable than of growth, and were also enthusiastic about maintaining a high level of investment overseas. After discussing the way that in the late 1940s the United Kingdom had in effect borrowed from the United States to invest in Commonwealth countries, Paish went on: 'It is probably a pity that means could not have been found to continue the process, for the United Kingdom has all the qualifications for a successful exporter of capital—specialized institutions, financial connections, long experience: all the qualifications, that is, except one, the availability of adequate resources to invest.'[2] The City of London went on investing abroad, adequate resources or not, which helped to explain why the reserves were vulnerable to fluctuations like those of August and September 1957, and the need to remain on good terms with countries in the Sterling Area made it hard to think of reducing overseas investment.

While Thorneycroft's advisers were concerned with checking inflation after Keynesian methods had removed the restraints of large-scale unemployment, many economists were turning to the post-Keynesian question of getting the economy to grow as fast as possible. To the regret of the left wing the 1957 Labour Party conference in effect gave up considering further nationalization and began to commit itself to economic growth as an objective. In the years after 1951 the party had not found any industries as obviously suitable for nationalization as coal and the railways had been in the past, partly because other industries were harder to define as single units to be taken over. The programme referred to the 500 powerful companies which dominated the economy, and implied that they would be nationalized if they 'failed the nation', but this was really no more than an additional means to control the economy as a whole. Planning, combined with a more expansive economic policy than the Conservatives', would mean that there would be more for everybody.

This change of tack was not the most fiercely contested part of the 1957 conference agenda. The Labour Party had to face the question of the British attitude to the hydrogen bomb, and the result dismayed the left wing of the party. Most people who thought that the country should act according to

---

1. Several functions of the OEEC, including that of issuing figures, were later taken over by the Organization for Economic Cooperation and Development.

2. F. W. Paish, *Studies in an Inflationary Economy* (1962), 158.

higher moral standards than other nations said it should give up its stock of hydrogen bombs, and claimed that this would have a great effect on world opinion. The left wing had hoped that Bevan would put forward this argument, but he declared that Britain needed the bomb to be an important country, and asked the conference 'not to send the British Foreign Secretary naked into the conference chamber'. The supporters of moral force might have foreseen this; their alliance with Bevan from 1951 to 1955 had rested on a common belief that the United States was not behaving in a moral way, but in 1957 the moralizers wanted to have an effect on the United States by example, while Bevan wanted to keep the British H-bomb because he knew that it was, among other things, an anti-American bargaining counter.

Both sides took it for granted that Britain was a great power, less important than the United States and the Soviet Union, but still to be compared with them rather than with any other country when forming policy. A few students of strategy pointed out that Britain was not a great power, and that British possession of the bomb made several countries which thought themselves equally important want to have nuclear weapons also—as Crossman put it, 'the right to distrust the Americans cannot remain a British monopoly'.[3] Views of this sort were not popular, especially when accompanied as in Crossman's case by a suggestion that conscription might be needed to keep the army at an adequate level.

If people had fully understood the implications of the success of the Soviet Union and, just a few weeks later, of the United States in launching intercontinental ballistic missiles, they would have seen that the British position was being eroded. While the United States and the Soviet Union depended on aeroplanes to deliver the H-bomb, Britain was technologically on equal terms with them, though her air force was smaller. But a rocket attack, which could not be fended off, was altogether more dangerous, especially if it was accompanied by an improved rocket defence against aeroplanes. Keeping up a nuclear force cost relatively little, but building up a rocket delivery system would be much more expensive. Attempts were made to develop British rockets, but they cost too much to be politically practicable. The public found it hard to understand how high the cost of new weapons would be, and did not realize that many of them had to be scrapped before they came into production. The United Kingdom did not have the resources needed for this expensive form of competition. The cancellation of a weapon in the United States was an inconvenience; the cancellation of Blue Streak in 1960 had implications that might have changed the whole structure of British foreign policy.

The high cost of nuclear involvement was one argument for British withdrawal from it, but most of the campaign for renunciation of nuclear weapons

---

3. 27 Feb. 1958; *Commons Debates*, dlxxxiii, 634.

was based on moral arguments and assumed that Britain ought to continue to exercise considerable influence in the world. The Campaign for Nuclear Disarmament, which asked for unilateral British disarmament, owed some of its success in attracting support because it was filling a vacuum. Nothing in the politics of the early 1950s had inspired enthusiasm, and its emergence was one of the first signs that people were taking a new interest in political change after a period of tranquil apathy. In this way the Campaign had an effect on the wider world; the marches and demonstrations it organized and the interest taken in civil disobedience by some of its members foreshadowed the methods used by politically active people in several other countries for years to come. The organizing strength of the Campaign came mainly from the left wing of the Labour Party, so that it inherited most of the force of Bevanism. Its appeal was distinctly wider than that, because it seemed to be the pressure group through which people could express a general desire for peace. The Campaign caused problems inside the Labour Party, but it also indicated to Macmillan that he should do something about the world situation.

The ascendancy of Macmillan

In 1957 there was little enough that he could do. He had first to hold his government together. He was a more skilful debater than the leader of the Opposition, and could occasionally play off the Labour left against him. Conservatives MPs, many of whom felt that it could not have been right both to go to Suez and to leave so ignominiously, recovered their composure. They survived the strain of passing a Rent Act that, for more expensive property, ended the limitations on rent imposed by the 1939 Act and, in some cases, the 1915 Act. The government said it would loosen up the housing market, provide landlords with a rate of return that would enable them to carry out repairs, and might even lead people to resume building houses for rent; the Labour Party said it would lead to evictions and widespread rent increases. Very little came of these predictions: the government amended the Act to restrain evictions; rents did not rise sharply because much of the country had no acute shortage of houses, and London rents had been going up for some time. Repairs continued to be neglected, the government went on looking for ways of persuading landlords to stop their houses turning into slums; and nobody built houses for rent. Small-scale landlords, who in the past had bought a house or two to let, now had more opportunities to invest their money in shares or in building societies, and these forms of investment were more convenient than owning a house. Before the First World War large-scale developers built for rent because few people bought houses, but they greatly preferred to turn their money over quickly by building to sell and by the 1950s many more people could afford to buy a house on a mortgage. On the other hand, new houses could not be built cheaply enough for low-paid workers to rent them, so they had to rely on subsidized council building to provide cheap houses. The Rent Act did not change any of this, and outside London made very little difference. But putting it through the Commons had been a hard battle, in which the Conservatives were afraid they might become unpopular. When it was over, and government popularity emerged relatively undamaged, they felt much more confident.

By the time of the 1957 Conservative conference party morale was higher than at any time since the 1955 election. Lord Hailsham was the hero of the occasion, as the man who had stated most forthrightly the feelings of the party on such issues as the United States and the trade unions. While the party traditionalists were happy, unemployment had by the winter reached a higher level than at any time since the war, and production was no higher than in 1955. Macmillan began to shift his ground a little, and to remind people that he had been Member for Stockton between the wars and was determined not to let unemployment return. The Chancellor of the Exchequer was less ready to change and, to limit the amount of money in circulation, he said that budget estimates must not exceed those of the previous year. As prices had crept forward during the year despite all his efforts, this would reduce the real value of government spending. When the issue arose, Macmillan decided that estimates could go £50 million over the rate for the previous year. He then accepted the resignations of the Chancellor and the two Secretaries to the Treasury, dismissed this as 'a little local difficulty', and set off on a tour of the Commonwealth to India and Australia. The tour greatly increased his confidence; as he remarked in Australia, 'at home you always have to be a politician, but when you are abroad you almost feel yourself a statesman'.[4] The tour may have taken some of the fine edge off his instinct for noticing danger ahead, which had been very strong since he became Prime Minister, but he undoubtedly returned with a public reputation that was more impressive than before.

Thorneycroft's resignation made it politically difficult to produce an expansionist budget in 1958. The ex-Chancellor had been regarded as the defender of the stable price index, and the government could not endanger its reputation in this area. On the other hand, there had been a good deal of investment since 1955 with no extra production to show for it. Expanding the economy was the natural response and, at a time of unemployment and idle industrial plant, would not necessarily lead to increased prices. As taxes could not be altered, the government relaxed credit. The bank rate was brought down quite quickly from 7 to 4 per cent. Hire purchase restrictions were made less and less severe. Banks were encouraged to lend, and set about encouraging people to borrow. After the 1958 budget companies were no longer charged a higher rate on their profits if they paid them to shareholders as dividends, and

4. Anthony Sampson, *Macmillan: A Study in Ambiguity* (1967), 138.

even if this merely recognized that companies were paying out more of their profits than in the early 1950s, it did encourage further distribution of dividends. The Stock Exchange boom that followed helped to put shareholders in a good mood. The government successfully resisted a strike by London bus drivers, which established its reputation for firmness and discouraged other strikes. At the same time levels of consumption began to rise quite rapidly. Import prices, which had gone up for a short period after Suez, fell once more. Production rose from the low level to which it had fallen by the end of 1957. By the end of 1958 Macmillan and his new Chancellor, Heathcote Amory, had almost moved back to the position of Butler in the early 1950s when he was setting the economy free and watching prosperity rise.

When Macmillan succeeded Butler at the Exchequer in 1955, his place at the Foreign Office had been given to Selwyn Lloyd, which was generally taken as a sign that Eden proposed to retain a good deal of control over foreign affairs. Macmillan kept Lloyd when he became Prime Minister, partly to avoid any suggestion that the Suez operation had been a mistake and partly to maintain Eden's dominance of foreign policy. Early in 1958 the Russian leaders began asking for another summit conference. Macmillan was immediately certain that this would be useful, but the United States and Germany opposed the idea and nothing came of it.

In July there was a revolt in Iraq; the pro-British King Faisal and his chief minister, Nuri es-Said, were killed by the mob and an unstable regime under General Kassem took over. This change was really a delayed result of Suez, but the United States was already worried by the civil war that was imminent in Lebanon so American troops went there and British troops were flown to Jordan, which drew what might have been just a normal change of government in the Middle East into the struggle of the great powers. The Russians again suggested a summit meeting, this time associated with the United Nations, and the British agreed. There was no enthusiasm in Washington, and the Russians quickly changed their policy and asked for an emergency session of the General Assembly. American and British intervention in the Middle East was accepted rather than approved, but the Russians gained nothing by their change of approach.

By the end of 1958 representatives of America, Russia, and Britain were talking in Geneva about ways to end the testing of nuclear weapons, a topic which grew more important as evidence accumulated that tests in the atmosphere produced radioactive fall-out which might reach dangerous levels, and at a loftier diplomatic level Macmillan was trying to persuade the Western leaders that a summit conference could not do any harm and might have a good effect. Doubters pointed out that Eisenhower was not in good health and would not shine in dealing with a hostile debater because his talents had always lain in conciliation and in winning over people who wanted to be won over, and added that Western public opinion would be so eager for progress if a conference were held that Western negotiators might have to consent to bad agreements rather than reach no agreement at all.

Khrushchev threatened to give East Germany full control over Berlin to force the Western powers to go back on their refusal to recognize the government of East Germany or face a crisis about the position of Berlin. In February Macmillan visited Moscow to see if he could persuade Khrushchev to take a more conciliatory line to make it easier for the Western leaders to meet him. Khrushchev was unhelpful at first, and early in the visit he had a diplomatic toothache to avoid meeting Macmillan. But the discussions became distinctly more friendly as the week went on, and by the time they ended Macmillan felt he had gained enough ground to put the arguments for a summit in Paris, Bonn, and Washington. Thus he emerged as the active man of the alliance, dragging the other countries behind him to the summit. When he became Prime Minister he had been mocked as 'Supermac' and as 'Macwonder'; by the spring of 1959 his supporters were able to feel that these titles were simply an accurate assessment of his position. The shock to British prestige caused by Suez was almost forgotten, and the country seemed as dominant a power as at any time in the 1950s.

By 1959 the economy stood on the edge of a great leap forward. Macmillan said in July 1957 that people 'have never had it so good', a phrase that was to become altogether more closely linked with him than he intended.[5] At the time it was said, it may not have been accurate; production in 1958 was no higher than in 1955, and the three years of credit freeze had done more to hold back the economy than to maintain a stable level of prices. But the economy suddenly expanded between September 1958, when industrial production was at the 1955 level (105 per cent of the 1954 level), and December 1959, when production was 117 per cent of the 1954 level. Macmillan's slogan dominated politics and everyday life. Partly because the expansion was started by making credit easier to come by, and partly because of a change in people's wants, a great deal of the expansion was devoted to buying 'consumer durables'. Most families had a washing machine, which was particularly popular in the north, about one family in three had a refrigerator, which was particularly popular in the south, and about one family in three owned a car. Well over half the population had at least one of these consumer durables by the end of the 1950s, and much of this had come during Macmillan's years of power. In 1955, 40 per cent of homes owned a television set; by 1959 the figure had risen to 70 per cent. Prosperity concentrated on a few specific products, and it was also limited geographically. The metalworking, engineering, car-producing region that stretched from London to a little beyond Birmingham was transformed in the late 1950s in much the way that industrial England had moved, over a hundred years earlier, from the 'hungry forties' to the peaceful comfort of the

---

5. Anthony Sampson, *Macmillan* (1967), 158–9.

skilled craftsmen who came to London to admire the Great Exhibition of 1851. Older industrial regions, particularly Lancashire and Scotland, did not share in the 1958–60 boom. When the Chancellor of the Exchequer prepared his 1959 budget, more people were unemployed than earlier in the 1950s and overall production was not going up very much, despite the gratifying increase in the consumer durables trades. He determined to stimulate the economy by budgeting for a large deficit, and in the mood of the day the deficit had to be produced more by reductions in taxation than by any increase in government spending.

The major item of the budget was a reduction by 3.75p to 38.5p of the standard rate of income tax. The lower rates of income tax were also reduced, the tax on beer was cut, and post-war credits on income tax paid during the war were repaid faster, but the budget stood or fell by the cut on income tax. The economy continued to grow rapidly, though the cut in taxes did more good to the regions that were already prosperous than to the rest of the country. Opposing the budget was not easy; Labour Members claimed to have met many drinkers in their constituencies who would have preferred old-age pensioners to have the benefit of the revenue devoted to reducing the price of beer, but the government was not impressed.

The summer was warm and dry. Eisenhower paid a visit to Britain and appeared with Macmillan on television. Their conversation was not particularly profound, but it did show that the Prime Minister was on the best of terms with the President of the United States. By the autumn Macmillan felt that opinion polls showing a fairly comfortable Conservative lead meant that it was time for a general election. In the first week or two of the campaign the Labour Party appeared to be catching up. The Labour programme paid little attention to nationalization, and not much more to planning and reorganizing the economy, but it did lay considerable emphasis on increasing government spending to improve the social services. In the previous few years the Opposition had been particularly ready to argue for old-age pensioners, and this helped to persuade voters that the Labour Party was the one to choose if they wanted better social welfare programmes.

The Labour rally seems to have died away from the day that Gaitskell said his party's social programme could be paid for without any increase in income tax, which raised more doubts than it settled. He argued quite correctly that, if economic growth went on at the pace of the previous twelve months, the increases could be paid for easily. People may not have believed that growth would go on, or they may have wanted to know what Gaitskell would do if he had to choose between social welfare and tax stability: in any case they were not favourably impressed by his statement, and the Labour Party began to fall back. In the election the government received only tepid support from some newspapers that were normally Conservative, and other papers went over to the Labour side. They changed mainly out of dissatisfaction with the government's conduct of colonial policy: Suez had lost the government a fair amount of support in intellectual circles and, although a settlement in Cyprus had been reached early in 1959 by which the Turkish minority was given some guarantees inside an independent country, there had been incidents when the troops maintaining law and order had been strained beyond endurance. It had also become known that some Mau Mau prisoners who had been reported to have died as a result of drinking contaminated water had in fact been beaten to death. In Nyasaland the administration had responded to demonstrations in February and March 1959 in favour of independence with a set of measures that the Devlin Report subsequently described as a 'police state'. The government declined to accept the Report, and this was mentioned disapprovingly by the press but, although this may have reduced the size of the Conservative victory, it did no more.

	Votes	Seats	% of all votes cast
Conservative	13,749,830	365	49.4
Liberal	1,638,571	6	5.9
Labour	12,215,538	258	43.8

A cartoon after the election showed the Prime Minister sitting back and saying 'well, gentlemen, I think we all fought a good fight' to the 'colleagues' who had made victory possible—a motor car, a television set, a vacuum cleaner, and so on.[6] Some commentators spoke as if the Labour Party had gone down for ever. It became fashionable to say that a government in power could now manipulate the economy to produce a boom when it wanted, and could find from the opinion polls when the time was ripe for a dissolution to minimize the risk of defeat. This ignored the fact that, once people believed the government could improve the economic situation, they would blame it for not producing improvements faster or for not producing the type of improvements that were needed.

Social change in the late 1950s

Voters might very well support the government because they felt well off, but more ambitious commentators suggested that the country had in some way become more middle-class. They did not really explain what is involved in becoming middle-class. The Conservatives share of the total vote was higher in 1924 and in 1935 than in 1959, but the middle class, on any possible defin-ition, was obviously smaller between the wars than later on; changes in the

6. D. E. Butler and R. Rose, *The British General Election of 1959* (1960), 201.

Conservative vote could not be directly linked to any increase in the size of the middle class. Undoubtedly more people had acquired possessions but it is not clear that valuing possessions is a particularly middle-class habit. The stories of the munitions workers in the First World War hurrying out to spend their high earnings on pianos and fur coats suggest that people in the working classes had always liked buying things if only they had the money.

Employees had not become strikingly better off in the twentieth century. Their post-tax incomes would buy about 80 per cent more in 1958–9 than in 1911–12—the sharp rise in taxation conceals some of the improvement in people's position, because the money taken in taxes is returned in state-provided services.[7] These services are not directly linked to income; social services depend a great deal on size of family, and the benefits of roads and of defence are very hard to allocate. One worker in a thousand earned £2,632 after tax.

Levels of income after tax and changes 1911–12 and 1958–9

Employees (tenth)	Upper limit of income 1958–9 (£)	As percentage of 1911–12 income
Bottom tenth	205	190
2nd	270	165
3rd	327	176
4th	405	191
5th (median)	470	194
6th	537	191
7th	601	183
8th	685	173
Top tenth	821	170

Source: Routh, *Occupations and Pay in Great Britain 1906–60*, 55.

These changes brought the middle third of the earning population rather closer to the top third, and improved the position of the people right down at the bottom, but the lowest 30 per cent—the poor, according to the definitions of Booth and Rowntree—had fallen behind the central third, though state-provided services probably did something to reduce the gap. These figures suggest that a single-income family in the late 1950s would not get very far in buying consumer durables; the average skilled worker earning about £800 a year (before tax and national insurance payments) was not very likely to buy a new car costing £400 or £500. Workers in exceptional trades, with a good deal of overtime, or men with families who were just beginning to earn money but

7. G. Routh, *Occupations and Pay in Great Britain 1906–60* (1965), 88. Note that less than half the working population earn more than the average skilled worker.

had not yet left home, might find they could afford such things, but the normal basis for working-class prosperity was the two-income family; with fewer children, wives could spend more of their lives in paid work.

For some time about half the British population has said it is working-class and half has said it is middle-class. For at least as long as sociologists have been asking people what class they think they belong to a quarter or a third of the manual working class has called itself middle-class, and this did not affect the political situation as it developed in the 1950s. On the sort of classifications accepted by sociologists, such as the division into manual and non-manual workers, not much more than a third of the population could be called middle-class in the 1960s. Neither the self-assessment figures nor the sociologists' assessment changed very much in the late 1950s. Non-manual workers made up 20 per cent of the working population in 1911 and 31.5 per cent in 1959, but among men the figure rose only from 22 per cent to 28 per cent. Among women the figure rose from 16.75 per cent to 40 per cent, but almost all of this change was accounted for by a decline of 1.25 million in the number of women in private domestic service (counted as manual work) and an increase of 1.1 million in the number of secretaries. This change was unlikely to make much political difference because servants tended to sympathize with the interests of their employers and voted accordingly, and the occupational shift among women was otherwise no greater than among men.[8]

Some forms of behaviour were seen as working-class rather than middle-class. In the economic field going on strike was a working-class activity. The industrial history of the late 1950s does not suggest that people were behaving in a more middle-class way than in the early 1950s. In the spring of 1958 London bus workers went on strike to try to maintain a position that was declining relative to other workers, but this was unsuccessful, and they continued to lose ground. The new aristocracy of labour were the motor car workers and the electrical workers; the electrical workers pursued an aggressive policy partly because the Communist-dominated union leadership believed in a fighting policy, but there is little evidence that this was the reason why the membership turned against the leadership. The car industry was represented by a very different union, with the result that industrial policy was handled by shop stewards who took rather a primitive approach to industrial relations. Their attitude looked sophisticated and effete compared with that of some managers; the British Motor Corporation dismissed 6,000 men without notice one morning in June 1956, and for some time afterwards enjoyed the sort of labour relations that ensured that few of their workers were going to think themselves middle-class.

Middle-class respectability had always included a feeling of respect for the police and a feeling that the police were on the side of solid citizens. This

---

8. Routh, *Occupations and Pay*, esp. pp. 4–87 and 43–9.

friendly relationship was weakened by the problem of motoring offences; drivers who had broken the law often asked why the police were not away catching criminals, and showed little sign of realizing that motoring offences endangered far more lives than anything done by the criminal classes. As motoring offences increased more rapidly than almost any other sort of crime, the opportunities for friction rose quickly. One of the hardest duties of the police has always been that of 'keeping an eye' on shady activities that cannot be completely suppressed. In the mid-1950s the authorities had tried to enforce the laws against homosexual conduct more rigorously than in the previous few years. The campaign had not really had the support of public opinion and, as it used policemen as agents provocateurs, it reduced public sympathy for the police force. Two changes in other areas of the law showed that the government felt the police were under too much strain because of the way they had to use their discretion. Prostitutes had always in effect been allowed to solicit in public, subject to occasional arrest and a trivial fine; in 1959 the fine was made much larger by the Street Offences Act to show that they were not to solicit in public, though they could continue their trade in other ways. The Betting and Gaming Act passed by the government shortly after its re-election also relieved the police force from some invidious duties and illustrated the decline of respectability. Cash betting was illegal and cash bookmakers were in the same position as prostitutes; sometimes they were arrested and fined, but most of the time the police simply 'kept an eye' on them. The new Act allowed bookmakers to take cash bets in licensed betting shops, and it also allowed people to set up casinos for gambling. The gambling provisions of the new law turned out to be much less well drafted than the provisions for betting and there was steady pressure for stricter legislation.

In the late 1950s there was a good deal of earnest social criticism in the theatre. Osborne's *Look Back in Anger* was followed by *The Entertainer*, which again reflected the attitude that present-day England was in a dreadful mess, that there was something to be said for the old Edwardian stability though it was no longer recoverable, and that nobody had satisfying answers for the future. For a few years plays with a committed attitude were fashionable; they were praised for their realism, and condemned for bringing in the kitchen sink and the discomforts of lower-class life too often. Translations of most of Brecht's work were put on, and his political attitude of admiration-tempered-by-doubt for the working classes was also to be seen in writers like Wesker. For perhaps five years political commitment went with a willingness to write plays that were meant to shock Rattigan's Aunt Edna; Sheila Delaney wrote *A Taste of Honey* because she saw one of Rattigan's plays and felt sure she could do better. The two trends diverged in the early 1960s; writers concerned with social criticism turned to direct political satire while playwrights became less concerned about social criticism though their range of choice of plot, of subject matter, and of language remained much wider than they had been before 1956.

American plays and musicals had dominated the London stage in the late 1940s and early 1950s; the revival of the theatre after *Look Back in Anger* reduced this dominance and then led to a series of London productions appearing successfully on Broadway. In non-theatrical social criticism American influence became very noticeable in the late 1950s. *The Affluent Society*, *The Organization Man*, and *The Power Elite* were all written about the United States, but they were widely read by people who were afraid that Britain was going to follow the United States. Galbraith's contrast between 'private affluence and public squalor' returned to an analysis that had been neglected in the Britain of the 1950s;[9] the idea that people were being deprived of individuality by commercial and industrial organization aroused some response; and there were fairly widespread fears that the insidious influence of an inner ring, denounced by political journalists as 'the Establishment', was preventing the public from exercising full political freedom. Among social critics the strongest influence was that of people working on the borderland between literary criticism and sociology; Raymond Williams's *Culture and Society* and Richard Hoggart's *The Uses of Literacy* argued that once upon a time there had been a rough but wholesome unity about English society but that this had now been broken down and commercialized. Almost all of this school of writing agreed in denouncing the middle class, and in particular the new commercial middle class that had done well in trade, and most of them took a favourable view of the working class and attributed to it the virtues of warmth of heart, solidarity with neighbours and workmates, and distrust of the thrusting individual who tramples his way to success. John Braine's *Room at the Top* (1957), a novel about a Yorkshire accountant who throws over his true love to marry a wool magnate's daughter, cannot have owed its high sales among the London intelligentsia entirely to the hero's exciting sex life.

The writers of the period saw themselves as supporters of the left, though their enthusiasm for the certainties of the past meant that really they were opposed to the modern world and would probably be against any government that came to terms with contemporary problems. Just after the 1959 election the Labour Party presented no encouraging alternative to the government. Gaitskell was generally thought to have done quite well in the election, but as soon as it was over he moved further to the right than was practicable for a man who lacked the prestige of victory. Members of the right wing of the party, who wanted to improve society by fairly small-scale changes at strategically chosen points, said that nationalization was no longer an important issue; members of the left wing, who said that reform required sweeping

---

9. Galbraith's famous phrase was his translation of Sallust's 'Privatim opulentia publicae egestas', which R. H. Tawney quoted in the original in his *Equality* (1931), 116.

changes, insisted that the 1918 commitment to nationalization should be retained in the party constitution.

During the election the party's official defence policy had been to set up a non-nuclear club: the United Kingdom would give up nuclear weapons, and all potential manufacturers of nuclear weapons, which at that time primarily meant France, would promise not to make them. This formula held the party together during the election, but afterwards the Campaign for Nuclear Disarmament rallied its forces and the 1960 party conference passed a resolution in favour of unilateral British renunciation of nuclear weapons. Gaitskell was highly praised for the speech he made at the time, in which he said he would fight and fight and fight again to preserve the Labour Party, and he subsequently made it clear that he would remain leader and would not accept the decision of the conference. Wilson opposed him for the leadership of the parliamentary party and said the party leadership and the conference majority ought to work out a compromise; Gaitskell won by 166 votes to eighty-one, a margin of victory that might not have survived another defeat at a party conference. Although Gaitskell's friends were able to win over enough trade unions in 1961 to reverse the previous decision, the Labour Party spent most of the first two years after the election in internal struggle.

Fortunately for the Labour Party, the Liberal Party had not been able to gain as much from its divisions as might have been expected. The Liberal Party in the 1950s had been on the left in foreign policy and on the right in domestic policy, it had opposed Suez strongly, but it had voted in favour of the 1957 budget with its remissions of surtax and encouragement to overseas investment. It had been even more strongly opposed to planning in the 1950s than the Conservatives, and complained of such surviving vestiges of planning as the Capital Issues Committee. Between 1955 and 1959 it had done well in some by-elections, but most of its best performances came in areas of Conservative strength, and many of its votes seem to have come from people who wanted the government to be still more active in combating inflation. In the 1959 election it gained slightly more votes from the Conservatives than from the Labour Party.[10] The new leader, Jo Grimond, chosen in 1956, knew that a party in opposition has to oppose the government, and saw that just after the 1959 election the Labour Party was the most likely source of Liberal votes, but he could not find a way to divide the Labour leadership from its trade union supporters. The Liberal Party was committed to nuclear disarmament, and it could hope to win over intellectual members of the Labour Party who were not devoted to socialism, but this was not really enough to establish it as the party of the left. Its policies left it unable to profit from the weak condition of the left in 1960.

10. Butler and Rose, *The British General Election of 1959*, 195.

Problems after the triumph

Macmillan showed no intention of resting on his laurels in 1959. He had moved so adroitly from the Thorneycroft policy of restraint to the Heathcote Amory policy of expansion that nobody worried about the change. Before the election he had let the market take its course in economic affairs, but after the election government grants were used to induce car and steel firms to go to regions that were not prospering, and political considerations were allowed to lead to an economically irrational division of the plants. He undertook no changes in colonial policy before the election, but the appointment of liberal-minded Macleod as Secretary for the Colonies immediately after the election showed that a new approach was to be adopted. In the course of three years Macleod took decisive steps that ended the British Empire in Africa.

Nigeria was proceeding to independence on a basis of universal suffrage that would give power to the pro-British and traditional rulers of the northern region. Tanganyika presented even fewer internal problems because the Tanganyika African National Union dominated the politics of the country so completely that there was no risk of internal division. In Uganda it was not easy to find a form of constitution into which Buganda, the largest of the tribal kingdoms, could be fitted. Pro-Buganda feeling in Britain prevented the government from setting up a unitary state in Uganda. But these difficulties were slight compared with those of the countries in which there was a white settler community.

Kenya was the easiest white settler problem. The Africans were divided along familiar lines: the Kenya African National Union (KANU), representing the Kikuyu and the Luo, the two largest and best-educated tribes, wanted independence quickly under a government with as few restrictions on its powers as possible; and the Kenya African Democratic Union (KADU), representing the minority tribes, wanted a federal system with decentralized powers. As in Nigeria, in Ghana, and in Cyprus the less powerful group in the community adopted a pro-British attitude and asked for independence to be delayed. Communal electoral rolls, to make sure that all groups were represented, had been used in India before independence, and were in use in the Central African Federation for the same purpose, and in Kenya they enabled Africans, Europeans, who were given more seats than their numbers justified, and Asians, who were about as numerous as Europeans, to be represented in the legislative council. The 1960 constitution gave the African members a majority in the Assembly, but the Governor retained the powers of the executive, and used them to keep the obvious African leader, Jomo Kenyatta, in detention on the grounds that he had been involved in the Mau Mau rebellion and was still politically dangerous. As a result KANU refused to form a government in 1961 after the first election under the new constitution. KADU was less sympathetic to Kenyatta, a Kikuyu, but after forming a government it found the pressure of African opinion for the release of Kenyatta so great that it had to join the chorus. The Governor refused to grant the request, describing Kenyatta as a 'leader to darkness and death'. As soon as there was an African majority in the Assembly white farmers and Conservative back-benchers suggested that the British government should be ready to buy out settlers. The government declined to have anything to do with the suggestion, partly because it would encourage Africans to make life difficult for the settlers, who would then move out and leave their land for the Africans. The small settler community owned so much of the best land that the issue was bound to cause tension, but by 1962 the British government was committed to setting up an independent multiracial country in which the African majority would have political power but a great deal of economic power would be retained by a relatively wealthy white minority.

The Central African Federation presented even more complicated problems. The three component parts, Nyasaland and the two Rhodesias, each had about the same number of Africans, with sharply differing numbers of white inhabitants. In Nyasaland the powers of the Governor could be transferred to an African government with as little trouble as in Ghana though it would not be sovereign, because it would still be part of the Federation, which controlled major financial issues and relations with the outside world. The British government recognized that the police measures of 1959 had not been wise, and Macleod began establishing an African government, which was made easier because there was an obvious African leader, Hastings Banda, available to become Chief Minister at the appropriate moment. In Northern Rhodesia the economic power and superior education of the white population was seen as offsetting the numerical superiority of the Africans, and Macleod devoted considerable ingenuity to devising an electoral system in which Members who had secured an adequate quota of both African and white votes would hold the balance of power in the Assembly. In Southern Rhodesia the white population was clearly dominant, and all that could be done for the Africans was to make sure that they held some seats in the Assembly and to establish a Board to review legislation and veto Bills that worsened the position of the Africans.

Apart from these subsidiary difficulties, the British government had to arrange the review of the progress of the Federation that it had promised to hold in the 1960s. Members of the Monckton Commission wanted their review to have unrestricted terms of reference, including the power to recommend the dissolution of the Federation, while the Prime Minister of the Federation, Sir Roy Welensky, was anxious to make sure that they had to accept the general assumption that the Federation would go on. The British government displayed great tactical ingenuity in persuading Welensky that the Commission could not recommend the break-up of the Federation, while convincing the Commissioners that if they found the Federation had no prospect of success they could say so. The Liberal and Labour Parties declined to be represented on the Commission because they felt too many of its members were likely to ignore African hostility to the Federation, which probably made the Commission more acceptable to the government of the Federation.

Macmillan could never forget the problem of the Federation in the early 1960s but he had wider issues before him. The summit conference for which he had worked so hard the previous year finally took place in May 1960, but the atmosphere of friendship and diminished tension had been wearing thin. When an American U-2 aeroplane, used for flying over Russia and photographing the country, was shot down, the Russian government denounced American espionage in terms which suggested the conference was unlikely to succeed. Khrushchev asked for an apology from Eisenhower when the conference began, and, when he did not receive one, declined to take part in any discussions.

British policy for the previous two years had tended towards a position which might be described as 'neutral on the Western side'. This made Commonwealth relations easier, because almost all the new members stood uncommitted between Russia and America, and it also suited commercial partnership with the members of the European Free Trade Association (EFTA), set up after the failure of the attempt to include all western Europe in a free trade area. The members of EFTA agreed to eliminate their tariff barriers against one another though maintaining their tariffs against other people unchanged. They regarded the association as provisional, because they hoped to reach agreement with the European Economic Community (EEC). On the other hand, two of them, Sweden and Switzerland, stood outside NATO and were 'neutral on the Western side' by choice, the 1955 treaty, which led to the withdrawal of the Russian army of occupation required Austria to remain neutral, Norway and Denmark were not enthusiastic members of NATO, and Portugal was a little distant from direct confrontation. If Britain went on standing slightly detached from NATO, EFTA would suit her political position very well. The failure of the summit conference strengthened the purely political arguments in favour of membership of the EEC.

Macmillan's position was slightly shaken by the failure of the summit, and a little later his relations with other Commonwealth leaders deteriorated. On a tour of Africa early in 1960 he warned his listeners in a speech to the South African Parliament that a 'wind of change' was sweeping over Africa and made it clear that the United Kingdom would not fight against the wind by supporting apartheid. Later in the year South Africa decided in a plebiscite to become a republic, and asked to be accepted at the Prime Ministers' conferences on the same basis as before. Other members of the Commonwealth, from India onwards, had been accepted in this way when they became republics, but several members were glad to have an opportunity to say they found the apartheid policy objectionable. Only Britain, Australia, and New Zealand supported South Africa at the Prime Ministers' conference in March 1961 and

South Africa withdrew before any formal decision was taken. Macmillan's attempts to help South Africa were not generally well received, and his failure suggested that Britain was now only one among equals.

In international terms his position was at its most glittering in the 1960 session of the United Nations General Assembly. Khrushchev and a number of other heads of governments came to the opening debate, and Khrushchev's opening speech was aggressive enough to dismay the West and to attract newly independent countries. President Eisenhower did not go to the United Nations but Macmillan's speech the following week was sufficiently calm, imperturbable, and forceful to make him appear as the leader of the West. When Khrushchev interrupted him, Macmillan said 'I'll take that in translation'—not a very good joke, but at the time people were so frightened of the Russian leader that anyone who stood up to him was regarded as a heroic figure.

This aspect of Macmillan's ascendancy inevitably ended with the election, later in the year, of John Kennedy as President of the United States. Kennedy felt quite capable of handling diplomatic affairs on his own, and showed more enthusiasm for individual meetings with Khrushchev than for summits for four countries. His personal relations with Macmillan were good, and he clearly found the Prime Minister the most sympathetic of the heads of government he met. But this was not the same as Eisenhower's assumption, based only partly on wartime memories, that the United States should regard Britain as a closer ally than any other friendly country. Although Kennedy's personal tastes, and those of many people in his administration, may have been more Anglophile than those of Eisenhower or of Dulles, American policy after 1960 was rather less ready to accept the idea of a 'special relationship' between Britain and the United States, partly because the Democratic Party contained many Anglophobes and partly because a 'special relationship' might irritate America's other allies.

The British government had other troubles. The 1959 boom began to slow down in 1960; there was not much unused capacity available, and unemployment had been reduced so sharply that it was hard to find extra workers for new development. Once the increase in production began, it was so swift that there was little time to adjust to it. Items in short supply remained in short supply because nobody had time to work out what would be needed next. Shortages of capacity drove imports up, and exports moved up less quickly. The 1958 balance of trade surplus of £455 million, well above the annual target laid down at the beginning of the 1950s, dwindled away to a deficit by 1960 and, as investment overseas went on, the deficit on the balance of payments was even larger. Government expenditure went up faster than any other form of overseas spending, as aid to underdeveloped countries increased, the cost of keeping troops in Germany in accordance with the 1954 agreements went up, and spending on keeping troops in tropical areas like Kenya, Borneo, and the

Persian Gulf rose. Aid to underdeveloped countries, quite apart from its humanitarian aspects, made them into better customers for British trade, and most of the troops overseas were in areas where there were British investments. The question was whether these long-term advantages could be afforded in the short run.

While government expenditure overseas was going up so fast, all government spending was increasing inconveniently quickly. Throughout the 1950s the Conservatives had been proud of reducing the proportion of the national income spent by the government. Most of the reduction was the result of restricting spending on defence to the £1,500 million to £1,600 million level; using interest rates to control the economy meant that the proportion spent on interest on the National Debt remained steady, and the ending of food subsidies reduced spending on social welfare.

By the early 1960s this attitude was becoming harder to maintain. Defence costs began to go up steadily because soldiers' pay had to be increased to attract volunteers after the end of conscription, weapons were growing more complicated, and the stability of costs in the 1950s had involved cutting down on innovation. The air force still used the V-bombers of the 1953–5 period, and replacements never got very far off the drawing board. When Blue Streak had to be abandoned in 1960 because it was costing far more than expected, the details of the Sandys strategy of relying on a nuclear deterrent had to be re-examined. The deterrent strategy made better sense if it relied on a British rocket, but building a rocket to reach targets in Russia cost so much that the diplomatic advantages could not justify the cost. The government decided to save money by buying an American rocket, and chose the Skybolt, which was being designed to be launched from an aeroplane at a target on the ground hundreds of miles away; the Opposition claimed that this complicated device would not work.

Government spending went up in non-military areas. The road system had to be improved because cars on the road had increased in the 1950s, and people preferred road haulage rather than transport by train. Building motorways and tidying and straightening less important roads was just starting in 1958, but as motorways ceased to be exotic harbingers of the future and became normal items of government spending they turned out to be very expensive, costing a pound or two per square foot of road surface, and the accompanying bridges over the Forth and the Bristol Avon were also expensive. Roads were a necessary investment but were not seen as a social service. Education was no doubt a social service but by the early 1960s it was also seen as an investment. For many years the United Kingdom had paid less attention to technological education than Germany, the United States, and the Soviet Union, but during the 1950s the government realized it had to be taken more seriously and set up colleges of advanced technology. Perhaps because secondary education was now taken for granted or because post-war changes implied that everybody who could benefit from a university education should have one, more and more candidates for university admission were coming forward, and by the late 1950s it was clear that turning them away by raising the number of 'A' level passes required would mean the universities were rejecting talented students. The government set up eight new universities and encouraged the older ones to expand, but the emphasis on science, which had been encouraged in the 1950s, could not be maintained, because the students who were coming forward in increasing numbers were more interested in the social sciences; sociology, which offered students some hope of curing the problems of society, was particularly popular.

Only a relatively small proportion of the population went to colleges of technology or to universities, old or new, and high expenditure on this sector was regarded as an investment, as could be seen in the complaints about the 'brain drain', or emigration from Britain of highly educated people, especially scientists and doctors, to the richer English-speaking countries.[11] Emigration had resumed after 1945 and, while it never reached the levels of the 1860s or the decade before 1914, it was higher than between 1918 and 1939. By 1962 the departure of the highly educated was being deplored; in the past they had not been missed, but in a more education-conscious world it was realized that their departure might handicap scientific and medical activity inside the country. It was suggested that facilities for research rather than higher pay drew people overseas, but emigrants from the highly educated section of society had been going abroad, for money or for a change of scene, long before Australia, Canada, and the United States offered better facilities for research than Britain.

While the Conservative Party was inclined to see education as an investment in economic development, the Labour Party thought about it as a social service and also as an instrument of social engineering. The social service approach led to pressure for classes of no more than forty in primary schools and no more than thirty in secondary schools, which could be accepted in principle by everybody, although the expense was considerable and the government was perhaps rather less willing to spend money on schools than on higher education. The clash of principle came over the organization of secondary schools. By 1959 the Labour Party was committed to support of comprehensive education in secondary schools partly because it believed class distinctions would be reduced if children went to the same schools instead of being separated from one another at 11, and partly because the eleven-plus examination was not a good predictor of future achievement. About 10 or 20 per cent of children were placed in schools which their subsequent records

11. Between 1900 and 1965 sixty-four scientists from the United States, forty-five from the United Kingdom, and forty-three from Germany were awarded Nobel Prizes in physics, chemistry, or medicine. In the following thirty years the comparable figures were 101, twenty-five, and thirteen.

suggested were unsuitable and, as most of the others could have been placed without much difficulty, the examination did not seem to be doing much, though other ways of placing children in secondary schools were even less effective. Assigning children on the basis of teachers' reports on their prospects undoubtedly made sure that primary education was not dominated by preparation for the examination, but teachers' recommendations were not particularly accurate predictors and sometimes leaned towards the better-dressed and better-spoken children. Predicting children's development at the age of 11 seemed too difficult a task.

The idealistic and the technical arguments against separation at 11 were strongly supported by the wishes of the parents. Middle-class parents had been pleased to find that the eleven-plus examination usually assigned their children to grammar schools, and other parents were so pleased that their children were receiving secondary education that they did not worry much about its quality. The 1944 Education Act said nothing about the organization of secondary education, and at first people accepted secondary modern schools without too much question. Possibly this would have gone on if they had received the same financing and the same quality of teachers as the grammar schools. But slowly people realized that the eleven-plus examination was the gateway to a system of education in which a quarter of the children were being educated on better terms than the rest. Using an examination of dubious predictive powers as a prelude to an unequal pattern of education was likely to be heavily criticized once the majority began to be interested in their children's secondary education. During the 1950s parents became more anxious about the examination results, and made their children worried as well. Conservative Ministers of Education had used their power to stop county councils setting up comprehensive systems, but in the early 1960s the Ministry was beginning to give up its commitment to the eleven-plus examination. This was not easy. A large number of the more devoted Conservatives were supporters of the grammar schools, and in the 1959 election the Conservatives had probably benefited from their support of the grammar schools because it rallied their followers. A switch to comprehensive education after the election would dishearten loyal Conservatives and might not conciliate parents who had recently discovered the disadvantages of the eleven-plus examination and thought of the Labour Party as the party committed to abolishing it.

Pressures for a new approach

By 1961 the government had noticed the growing pressure for a higher level of public expenditure on education and on other things. Plans began to be made for increasing spending; commissions and committees examined various aspects of education. The 1961 budget had to meet these rising costs, and was designed also to provide some incentives for the more prosperous classes. The surtax allowances were increased so that taxpayers with earned income did not have to pay it until their incomes were about £5,000 a year. A little earlier the Minister of Health had decided that higher spending on the health service should be met by raising the charge on prescriptions, and this combination of reducing surtax payments and increasing prescription charges infuriated the Labour Party, though it still seemed too disunited to threaten the government's position. The budget also gave the Chancellor power to increase or diminish customs and excise duties and purchase tax by one-tenth of the existing rate.

This power was very soon needed. The 1960 balance-of-payments deficit worried holders of sterling, and the 1961 figures looked no better. This was very different from the 1957 speculative attack. The Chancellor of the Exchequer had plenty of time to prepare ways to restrain the economy. He revived most of the measures used to check demand between 1955 and 1958: the bank rate was raised to 7 per cent, banks were told to restrict credit, government spending was cut, and the Chancellor exercised his newly acquired power to vary indirect taxes. Companies were asked not to increase dividends and a 'pay pause' was proclaimed. The government did not intervene in the economy to the extent of forbidding private employers to give wage increases, but it did announce that government employees would not receive increases.

This transformation from surtax cuts in April to the emergency measures of July left the Opposition at once hopeful and suspicious. The course of events looked altogether too like 1957: the crisis and restrictive measures would no doubt be followed by the whistling-up of an election boom. These suspicions were not confined to the Opposition; the government's position in the opinion polls dropped sharply, and the reputation of the Prime Minister declined even more abruptly. Britain's international prestige fell at the same time, with suggestions that the country was becoming 'the sick man of Europe' and had lost its power to control events. All that had happened was that the implications of the events of the 1950s, which had been obscured by Britain's relationship with the United States, were now becoming clear. It could now be seen that Britain was not a power in the same class as Russia and America although slightly weaker than either, and ought to be seen as a country of the same level of importance as France. People spoke of the change in apocalyptic terms that made sense only if several other countries had suddenly turned out to be more important than Britain. One test for a great power is the capacity to influence events a long way from its own territory, and this test showed that Britain was distinctly less powerful than twenty or even ten years previously. Some of the sense of decline in the early 1960s was an accurate, though belated, realization of this fact, but part of it was an unreflecting acceptance of the antithesis that 'England cannot afford to be little. She must be what she is, or nothing.'[12] She was not a nation of the rank of Russia or America, therefore she was nothing. This readiness to believe the worst was reinforced by people in other English-speaking countries, many of whom had been brought up to think of England as the real centre of the world stage. At the time of Suez both Nixon, the American Vice-President, and St Laurent, the Canadian Prime Minister, had spoken as though it was only at this crisis that they had realized Britain and France no longer dominated the world, and it took other people rather longer to realize the situation.

This exaggerated feeling that Britain had collapsed was not the best background for the government's announcement that it had changed its mind and wanted to join the EEC. The announcement came within a week of the crisis measures of July, and the government looked as if it had decided that the country's economic position was hopeless and could only be salvaged by the EEC. Macmillan mentioned other considerations in his speech. He referred to de Gaulle's statement that he looked forward to a *Europe des patries* as a sign that the members of the EEC were not committed to setting up a federation in which countries would lose their identity. This remark illustrated one of his problems throughout the negotiations for British entry. In the Conservative Party, and in the country as a whole, there was considerable suspicion at the idea of a federation, and no precise commitment to it. A considerable but vague enthusiasm for Europe arose, especially among the intellectual classes. It was fashionable to think of the English-speaking countries as coarse and materialistic, and to dwell on the pleasures of continental holidays and the more relaxed European attitude to wine and irregular hours. This mood may have helped the government to win support for its proposal, which was otherwise supported almost entirely on economic grounds; nobody was willing to say that it would be desirable to surrender British sovereignty to a European authority. This was no doubt welcome to de Gaulle, but it made the supporters of European federation among the members of the EEC a little less enthusiastic than they might otherwise have been about the British application.

Before announcing the decision to apply, the government sent ministers round the countries of the Commonwealth and got responses that were at best non-committal and at worst expressed 'grave concern', the diplomat's phrase for 'violent objection'. The British negotiators had also to remember their commitments to the EFTA, and they had to bear in mind the fact that unconditional acceptance of the Treaty of Rome meant a different form of assistance for agricultural prices. Farmers were afraid they would receive less, and other people were afraid the price of food would go up.

Both major parties were divided on the issue. In the Labour Party the

12. Originally said by Huskisson in 1828, and quoted approvingly in *Cambridge History of the British Empire* (1940), ii, 414.

divisions were fairly clear-cut, because the Labour Party was something of a coalition between people who would have been happy with a Liberal Party that had persevered in the path of social reform that it had seemed to be following in 1885 and 1909, and people who wanted a more rigorous approach to equality and government intervention in the economy; with exceptions on both sides, most of the right wing supported British entry and most of the left wing was opposed to it. The party's official policy was to wait and see how negotiations went, and Gaitskell held firmly to this position for fifteen months. In the Labour Party it was fairly easy to find people who had taken the left wing attitude on every issue since 1945 and earlier. No doubt a caricature Conservative right-winger would have opposed the American loan in 1945, voted against leaving Egypt in 1954, and been in favour of Suez, would have supported hanging and flogging, opposed changing the laws on homosexuality, and would then have objected to Britain joining the EEC, but it was hard to find individuals who had committed themselves to all of these causes. While Conservative opponents of British entry had no existing organization to call on, they soon rallied and an opposition group had been formed by the time the government decided to begin negotiations. The argument went on at several levels for the next eighteen months. Most of the press supported British entry, but Lord Beaverbrook's papers were determinedly opposed, and the *Daily Express* in particular was conducted as a campaigning newspaper. Opinion polls indicated that almost all the time there was a narrow majority in favour of the application being made, but the number of people answering 'Don't know' was large enough to be decisive if it came down on one side or the other. Informed opinion was at first fairly strongly in favour of British entry, but this feeling came to a peak shortly after the decision to apply, held firm, and then dwindled a little.

The negotiations themselves were a matter of extraordinary complexity. Heath, who had been the Conservative Chief Whip, conducted them with great skill; in addition to conducting the discussions in Brussels he had to work out the implications of tariff levels with industrial leaders, keep up some minimal contact with Commonwealth and EFTA opinion, and avoid giving any impression that the country was making imprudent concessions. Convincing the EEC members that the government was eager to join while not seeming to people in Britain to be yielding too much was very hard; critics in the Labour Party said that he was 'negotiating on his knees'.[13] The major attraction of entry was that manufacturers would have a much larger market and could obtain economies of scale because customs barriers would be removed. The danger was that British manufacturers might not be able to adjust to the new conditions, or might find the EEC common tariff drove up the cost of imports enough to raise the general level of prices. The interests of

13. N. Beloff, *The General Says No* (1963), 143.

the Commonwealth would be guarded and a rise in costs might be avoided if a long list of items could be imported free of duty. Canadian aluminium, Indian tea, and New Zealand butter might all be protected in this way, just as former French colonies had been given a special trading position under the Treaty of Rome.

The government badly needed to succeed in the negotiations. Shifts of opinion in the early 1960s suggested that, despite the election result, the ideas put forward by the Labour Party in 1959 had prevailed with the public. People wanted more government spending for public services like roads and universities and for welfare services like old-age pensions. Unless this was to mean higher taxation, which was unlikely to be popular, the economy would have to grow faster, and Gaitskell's reliance during the election on economic growth became generally accepted. Between 1959 and 1961 the government had tried to run the economy in the relaxed and uncontrolled way that had been so successful between 1951 and 1955. By 1961 the attempt was clearly not working. A return to planning was becoming fashionable. Macmillan, who had used the slogan 'Conservative freedom works' in 1959, recalled that in his youth he had been a supporter of planning and began changing the emphasis of government activity. The 'pay pause' imposed in 1961 was not the best introduction for this change. Public sympathy for teachers was growing and people began to feel that nurses ought to be paid as much as typists; however, as the pay pause applied only to employees paid for by the government, their claims were likely to be held back. The Minister of Education showed this by rejecting recommendations by the officially recognized Burnham Committee for a salary increase for teachers.

The government tried to reduce the deficits on the expenditure of the nationalized industries. In the late 1950s more industries were declining as cotton had declined five years earlier. Coal and the railways were sliding back to their pre-1939 condition after a revival of prosperity in the 1940s. By 1955 coal surpluses were beginning to pile up because of competition from steadily increasing imports of oil. Suez and the closing of the Canal interrupted these imports, and for a time coal was reprieved, though the government responded to the closing of the Canal by pressing ahead with nuclear power stations, which worsened the long-term prospects for coal. When the Canal was reopened, the oil flowed again, and coal fell back once more. Many pits were bound to run at a loss and were piling up coal which could not be sold. Ten years after the government had been trying to persuade people to take coal-mining jobs because coal was so vital, it was trying to persuade them to leave. Cotton had contracted slowly, with loud protests and with few arrangements for redeployment or for retraining. The coal industry was managed rather better: pits were closed with much less fuss than might have been expected, some miners from these pits went to the rich coalfields of the east Midlands and others were retrained for new jobs. Coal was protected by a duty against oil, but cotton had been protected by tariffs and quotas against the products of underdeveloped countries.

Shrinking the railways was in some ways like shrinking the coal mines; the organization was large enough to do the job by stages and to attempt to fit men into new jobs. But the financial accounts for the railways were far more difficult to work out. It was not too hard to tell whether a pit was paying its way, and to decide that the pits that were losing most money were the ones to close. For railways it was necessary to find out what each section of track cost, how much traffic it carried, and how much traffic other lines would lose if it were closed down. The Beeching Report, a complex exercise in cost accounting, perhaps suited the spirit of the 1950s rather than the early 1960s. It suggested that about one-third of all railway track in the country should be closed down, but the government realized that closing lines had social costs which had to be considered before taking action; reducing expenditure on the railways might cut towns and villages off from the world and, if the inhabitants moved away to begin new lives, money would have to be spent on new houses and schools.

Concern about the 'quality of life' was stronger in the early 1960s than in the 1950s. This led to readiness to see more public support for the arts, and to resistance to commercial enterprises which threatened the beauty of the countryside or the amenities of town life. Supporters of the 1962 Commonwealth Immigration Act no doubt saw it as another piece of resistance to change that might have led to rapid economic growth at the expense of quality of life. Citizens from Commonwealth countries had always been allowed to enter the United Kingdom freely, but relatively few of them did so before the 1950s, and citizens from the pre-war Commonwealth countries attracted no attention if they visited the country or returned home. In the 1950s a flow of West Indians, Indians, and Pakistanis began to come to Britain. From the economist's point of view the country seemed to have found a fund of labour to draw on in the way West Germany drew on Italy and Turkey, or Italy drew on its underemployed agricultural labour. This development was not welcomed by the people who found themselves living near the immigrants. Occasionally it was suggested that immigrants took low wages and undercut the market rate, and it was sometimes said that they were violent and noisy. While some of them were bachelors earning much more than before, and behaving as might be expected, most of them were quiet people with fairly strict ideas about family life. The hostility to them came largely from a simple feeling that black people were undesirable, just as Irish Catholics had been thought undesirable in the nineteenth century and European aliens had aroused hostility earlier in the twentieth century. The shortage of housing made matters worse; the immigrants were blamed for it, and then were blamed for living in slums. The Immigration Bill was welcomed by public opinion although it was condemned by the Labour Party and by a good deal of the Conservative press. It allowed immigrants to come if they had certain skills, or if they had relations in the country, or if they had jobs waiting for them. Liberally minded people opposed the Bill, partly on grounds of humane feeling and partly to promote economic growth, but some of these humane and tolerant people did not understand that other people who were relatively uneducated and unaccustomed to novelty were suffering real problems and were likely to blame immigrants who came into the country and lived near them.

13

The overstrained economy

1961–1967

Conservatism in a serious mood

The deflationary measures of July 1961, and the subsequent unemployment, caused more uneasiness and hostility than the previous slowdown in 1955–7. People had come to expect something better than periodic expansion and restraint. In their earlier clashes Macmillan had done well at dismissing Gaitskell as a man who took things too seriously. But nonchalance could go too far; when Macmillan wrote 'exporting is fun' in the draft of a speech in 1960 designed to encourage traders, it seemed to fit his approach so exactly that it was printed almost as though he had said it. He had thought better of it and never said the phrase, but reporters used it from the text given out in advance. Politicians were now expected to be serious and to take problems seriously, and Macmillan was suspected of losing touch with reality. In the debate on the deflationary measures, Wilson gave up almost completely the jokes and quips that had made his economic speeches in the 1950s one of the more entertaining parts of the Commons routine. Instead he was earnest; he referred to the spirit of Dunkirk; he realized that politicians were expected to show a sense of purpose.

The government took the first step towards Conservative planning by establishing the National Economic Development Council (NEDC) to produce indicative plans by consulting the various industries to see what they could do. This resembled the French approach, though the French planning authority (the Commissariat du Plan) had considerably greater powers than the NEDC to control the flow of credit and direct the large nationalized sector of the economy. The Commissariat intervened at selected points in industry; the arguments about planning in Britain took it for granted that the government should let each industry (operating through its Economic Development Council) work out its own problems, so there would be no direct government intervention in an industry or a particular sector of the economy. The NEDC suggested that a rate of economic growth of 4 per cent a year ought to be reached, and no politicians thinking about growth dared be seen suggesting anything less.

Selwyn Lloyd, as Chancellor of the Exchequer, thought growth should wait. His pay pause, in which all wage increases were discouraged, was unlikely to survive once production started going up. When the pay pause came to an end, after provoking a great deal of trade union activity among white-collar workers, he proposed a 'guiding light' for wage increases of 2.5 per cent, which presumably was his estimate of the sustainable rate of growth. Because people wanted public expenditure to increase, and felt their personal consumption should go up as well, restraining demand attracted mounting hostility. Government and Opposition were more conscious than ever that the next election would be a judgement on their policy, and studied opinion surveys even more closely than in the 1950s. Polls and by-elections left it uncertain whether the Labour Party or the Liberal Party was benefiting more from the government's obvious unpopularity. The Conservatives could hope that the negotiations at Brussels would succeed, or that Khrushchev would become more friendly, or that the economy could soon be encouraged to expand, but meanwhile they could only wait.

The 1962 budget reflected the new serious-mindedness, and a hostility to people who made money easily: it taxed capital gains made from owning shares for less than six months, or owning land for less than three years. The tax on profits from land was only to be expected: owners of land were benefiting from the increasing demand for houses and factories. In the London area, which was expanding steadily across south-east England, more and more of the cost of a house was for the land on which it was built. All sorts of people wanted to come to London, from teenagers who knew that it was the place where things happened to managing directors who wanted a smart company address close to the source of finance. People already in London wanted more space. The dingy offices of the past were condemned as ill lit, inconvenient, and out of date; shiny and conspicuous new office blocks, of varying degrees of ugliness, were put up and attracted commuters into London from further and further afield. The less prosperous parts of the country fell behind. Even in 1959, when the boom had been running at its fastest, Lancashire and Scotland had not felt the government was doing much for them; the north-east had been less restive, but its economic position was also weak.

Macmillan wanted to present his government to the world as youthful and modernizing. He also wanted to encourage economic growth as soon as possible, and felt Lloyd might be too cautious about this. As the by-elections returned gloomier results, the Prime Minister's political plans became bolder and in July seven Cabinet ministers out of twenty-one were dismissed in what came to be known as the Night of the Long Knives. Some commentators who were fascinated by this sweeping exercise of power spoke of the Prime Minister as a presidential figure, by which they meant that his power was unchecked by his Cabinet or his party, but this assumed that Macmillan could make the changes without any damage to himself. The reaction of his party was not favourable; his backbenchers made it fairly clear that they thought he had been too drastic, and Nigel Birch, one of the parliamentary secretaries who had resigned with Thorneycroft in 1958, said that Macmillan was altogether too fond of dropping Chancellors of the Exchequer when they tried to restrain demand. Lloyd had his loyal supporters; the taxation of short-term capital gains had annoyed some Conservatives but many others felt that he had stuck to difficult jobs for his party, had tried to fight inflation, and deserved better treatment.

Macmillan was much the oldest member of the new Cabinet and looked out of touch with the seriousness that was becoming more accepted in politics and with the enthusiasm for youth that was growing up in the country at large. Despite his support for planning in the 1930s, he seemed temperamentally unsuited to run a policy of planning.[1] A few days after his Cabinet changes he announced that the government was setting up a National Incomes Commission to direct the course of wages and salaries, but, because he made the announcement in a speech winding up a Commons debate, it inevitably looked as though it had been designed to extricate him from trouble over the ministerial changes and criticism of the slow growth of the economy. The trade unions declined to have anything to do with the Commission and, while trade unions were not popular at the time, their refusal to treat it seriously did not attract criticism. Planning required either a government which commanded enough prestige to force its will upon people or a system in which people could be confident that they would be treated fairly. After the ministerial changes Macmillan did not possess either claim to authority.

Entry to the European Economic Community (EEC) was still one of his hopes for the future. Arguments about planning and rates of growth concentrated on quantitative estimates of effects, and the discussion of entry to the EEC might have been expected to involve supporters of entry estimating how much it would increase growth and opponents producing rival calculations. But nothing so rational took place. In October the Labour Party in effect committed itself against entry when Gaitskell laid down conditions which clearly could not be obtained although everybody said they were desirable. In his speech, which was directed to the mainly anti-entry left wing of the party, he appealed to 'a thousand years of history' rather than to 'nicely calculated less and more'. The following month, at the Conservative conference, Butler replied by leaving the thousand years of history to the Labour Party and claiming 'For us, the future'. The Labour left felt some sympathy for the anti-American Conservatives who made up a considerable section of the anti-entry minority, but the government was firmly in command of its party and seemed well-placed to campaign at the next election as the party that brought the United Kingdom into Europe.

1. His views were best expressed in *The Middle Way* (1938).

On the whole the Conservatives had had good luck throughout their dozen years of office: declining import prices, friendly people in power in Washington, no need to produce expensive new weapons which would drive up the arms bill, and a fair degree of success in convincing people that their standard of living was increasing as fast as it could. The twelve months from the Conservative Party conference of October 1962 were a long tale of disaster; some misfortunes were the natural result of the policy the Conservatives had followed, and some were sheer bad luck. In November a world crisis broke out because the Soviet Union had been establishing missile bases in Cuba. President Kennedy handled the situation very skilfully, setting up a blockade of the island until the Russian government agreed to withdraw the missiles. Fortunately for the world, the problem was resolved without any fighting, but the British government's prestige suffered because the issue seemed to have been settled without Britain taking any part in it.

In December the American government announced that it was going to scrap the Skybolt missile on which British hopes of remaining a major nuclear power had rested. The reaction showed how nuclear weapons were valued as a way to retain influence over the United States. A large number of Conservative backbenchers signed a motion which read as though they thought the American government had made Skybolt go wrong, and when Macmillan met Kennedy he said that a decision that left the country without effective nuclear weapons would probably convince the Conservative Party that the alliance with the United States had been a mistake. It would sweep Macmillan away and replace him with an anti-American government. The President accepted this argument, and allowed Britain to acquire American Polaris submarines that could be used without any consultation with other countries in the event of 'a supreme national emergency'.

France was offered an opportunity to obtain Polaris submarines on similar terms. This had not been discussed with de Gaulle, and he was not interested; he saw the Polaris agreement as proof that Britain was ultimately more concerned about relations with the United States than with Europe. There were already signs of difficulty in the Brussels negotiations, because the European representatives were growing less willing to make concessions and were beginning to ask Britain to adopt the EEC method of supporting farmers by tariffs without any prolonged transition period, which meant prices would probably go up sharply almost immediately after entry. In the middle of January de Gaulle made it clear that he thought the negotiations should be broken off. As they went on, he formally declared on 29 January that France would have nothing more to do with the application. Macmillan insisted that the negotiations would certainly have been successful and that only de Gaulle's veto could have stopped them. Several difficult points in fact remained to be negotiated, unless Britain was ready to sign the Treaty of Rome without amendment, but de Gaulle's concern about the political unity of the

'Anglo-Saxons', as he called the Americans and the British, was obviously the immediate reason for the failure of the talks.

The failure of Skybolt exposed the dangers of the government's desire to have effective nuclear weapons without paying for them, and the failure of the Brussels negotiations showed how hard it was to be America's closest ally and a member of the EEC at the same time. But the government was simply unlucky that the winter of 1962–3 was about as severe as that of 1946–7. The steps taken in 1961 to restore the balance of payments were driving unemployment up, but it would have risen less if the bad weather had not held up transport and interfered with building. In the worst month 878,000 people were out of work.

The government had claimed the credit for the 1959 boom, and now it was blamed for economic weakness. At the same time it was running into more complex and less rational criticism. Television programmes satirizing the government became popular; the most celebrated of them, *That was the Week That Was*, helped to show that the BBC could be quite as lively as commercial television, but the government must have wished it could control its state broadcasting system as stringently as other governments. *Private Eye*, the well-informed and sometimes accurate magazine of the satirists, rapidly achieved a circulation quite as large as that of other weekly magazines like the *Spectator* and *New Statesman* and went on to become an old-established feature of London cultural life. Satire was popular in theatres and in nightclubs in the early 1960s; there was a certain amount of general social comment, but one satirical theme was that the government had been in office too long and had lost the respect of the people. The satirists probably won most approval among people who took a steady interest in public affairs, but at the same time the government was unpopular among people who were not very interested in politics, probably because the economy was doing so badly.

The hostility of people who were interested in politics was partly due to economic weakness, but was also caused by a feeling that the country no longer had a national purpose. This sentiment also existed outside Britain. Late in 1962 Acheson, an American ex-Secretary of State who was relatively pro-British, invited the United Kingdom to retire from the nuclear arms race, saying that the United States could deal with the Soviet Union and the British contribution amounted to only 2 per cent of American firepower. This suggested that he did not accept the function of Britain's nuclear force in providing diplomatic leverage on the United States as well as military leverage against the Soviet Union. He caused much more anger by saying 'Britain has lost an Empire and has not yet found a role.' But this comment seemed justified; people were slowly realizing that their country was no longer a great power, but they found it hard to decide what to do about the change.[2]

2. See *The Times*, 6 Dec. 1962 and following days, to find out how much Acheson had upset people.

British dominance had depended as much on the readiness of other countries to imitate British ways of doing things as on direct military power; other countries now seemed to see Britain as a lesson in what not to do and, even if some of this was due to the elegance and journalistic skill with which British commentators outlined what was wrong, the country's influence was sinking towards that of other countries of the second rank. British politicians had always taken it for granted that their country was important; on the left they talked about moral influence and eschewed the emphasis placed on empire by the right, but both groups assumed that Britain was going to influence other people. In the discussion over entry to the EEC, the few people who calculated its impact in economic terms were probably not concerned about the effect on the country's status, but the people who saw it as a political question argued whether influence was best exerted in Europe or in the Commonwealth. Left-wing opponents of entry thought of the Commonwealth in terms of the new members who had become independent since the war, and right-wing opponents thought of the old members from before the war, but both groups thought the Commonwealth was the right place to exert influence. Supporters of British entry suggested, often clumsily, that Britain would dominate the community politically. A few months earlier Macmillan had told the Commonwealth Prime Ministers' conference that Britain was as free to decide her own policy as any other member. This was reasonable enough, and certainly the suggestions made by people who wanted the Commonwealth to draw closer together were not practical politics; the other members did not want closer unity, and had not done so for a very long time. But Britain's decisions were going to affect the trading prospects of most other members and they naturally wanted to influence those decisions. By going ahead with the application to join the Community, the British government alarmed other Commonwealth governments. When the application was rejected, the British government could not turn back to the Commonwealth, and the countries of the European Free Trade Area felt that it had not paid enough attention to the problems of EFTA during the negotiations.

After the failure at Brussels

The government had the difficult task of restoring its international prestige, its reputation among people who took an interest in politics, and its popularity with the electorate. Rapid economic development would probably solve these problems, and the government had begun to unfreeze the economy even before de Gaulle's rejection. Purchase tax was reduced, with a particularly large cut in the rate on motor cars, the lower levels of income tax were rearranged in a way that gave substantial and fairly equal reliefs for all income taxpayers, and Schedule A of the income tax was abolished, which meant owner-occupiers were no longer taxed on the notional value of the rent that they could obtain if they let their houses instead of living in them. Abolition made owning a house to live in even more attractive than before, especially as the interest on mortgages, which naturally had been tax-deductible in the days of Schedule A, remained deductible and provided cheap financing for a safe and prudent form of investment which began to show signs of very gratifying appreciation.

These relaxations came only fifteen to eighteen months after the restrictive measures of July 1961, so the period of restraint was much shorter than in the late 1950s. There was correspondingly less time to establish a secure balance of payments position. It was argued that 'the reserves are there to be spent' and Maudling, the Chancellor of the Exchequer, argued that, as the balance of payments showed a surplus over the long run, the reserves could cover a deficit in the first year or two while growth was being speeded up and be replenished once faster growth had been established.[3] The reserves of gold and dollars had fluctuated around £1,000 million ever since 1945, and even in 1947, the worst year after the war, the deficit on the current account was only £318 million, so the reserves looked large enough to cover the deficit of a bad year.

While growth was to be speeded up, the increase in national wealth was not to be devoted entirely to larger private spending. Enoch Powell as Minister of Health obtained enough money to carry out more hospital development than for many years past, and he made the spending habits of the National Health Service more efficient. Building roads and putting up bridges across the river estuaries were beginning to cost large sums, but they were also beginning to make travel and transport easier than in the past. Because of the increase in the birth rate immediately after the war there were more children of school age, a change—nicknamed the 'bulge'—which had been foreseen. But in the 1960s many more children stayed at school after 15, a 'trend' that had not been fully foreseen, and schools had great difficulty in meeting the demands on them.

In January 1963 Hugh Gaitskell died after a very short illness. His political position, and his reputation among the electorate, had been becoming steadily stronger during the previous year, partly because of the government's troubles over the cancellation of Skybolt and the imminent collapse of the European Community negotiations. Labour MPs wanted above everything else a leader cool enough and ruthless enough to deal with Macmillan and see that the government did not recover as it had done in 1958 and 1959. They chose Harold Wilson as leader, despite his record of opposition to the majority of the parliamentary party and even though they had voted for George Brown, his principal opponent for the leadership, when the two men had contested the deputy leadership of the party a few months earlier. Wilson soon showed he was the man for the job. His first speeches as leader showed that he wanted

3. 3 Apr. 1963, *Commons Debates*, dclxxv. 471.

to restore British prestige by making the country more modern. This approach made him look a little like President Kennedy, whose political approach was greatly admired in Britain, and it set him in sharp contrast to Macmillan; too much of the Prime Minister's reputation had been staked on the Community negotiations, and after the rejection people were less inclined to take him seriously.

The government had been troubled by a number of Russian espionage successes. Unfairly but inevitably it was only when spies were caught that the public realized anything was wrong, but cases like those of Blake and the Krogers in 1961 damaged the prestige of the government. Early in 1963 the government struck back at the press, which had assumed altogether too readily that a former Civil Lord of the Admiralty had been closely connected with another spy, Vassall. Two journalists were sent to prison for contempt of court when they refused to reveal the source of their stories.

This probably made the press more willing to attack the government. It was known that there had been some sort of connection between the Minister of War, John Profumo, and Christine Keeler, a woman of about half his age. Hints and innuendoes linking them were published and were obliquely referred to in the House of Commons, and Macmillan delegated the task of examining Profumo's position to a group of ministers, after which Profumo made a statement to the House of Commons. He declared that he had not abused his ministerial position and that there had been 'no impropriety whatsoever in my acquaintanceship with Miss Keeler'. The first point was fairly certainly true, the second was not. When this was revealed a few weeks later and Macmillan's conduct of the case was debated in Parliament on 17 June, Wilson avoided any references to private morals, and stuck to the risk to security raised by the fact that the girl had been having an affair with a Russian diplomat called Ivanov at the time she was associating with Profumo. In the Commons the main point of discussion was whether Macmillan had behaved reasonably; the Prime Minister maintained that he had acted honourably and had been deceived, and his critics argued that he had taken the matter altogether too lightly and had failed in his duty to coordinate the security services. This view was not confined to the Opposition benches; twenty-seven Conservatives abstained and Birch improved the occasion by quoting Browning's line 'let him never come back to us'. There were rumblings and discussions, but Macmillan said on television that he hoped to lead his party at the next election and his party accepted the argument that, although his reputation for good sense had suffered badly, it would look like a confession of something worse if he retired.

Outside Parliament the discussion ranged more widely. It was accepted that, as he had made an untruthful statement in the Commons, Profumo had to go. Ten years earlier everybody would have said that the mere fact of his associating with Christine Keeler showed that he was unfit for public office. In the 1960s feelings were less clear-cut. During his denunciation of the Prime Minister Birch, asked 'What are whores about?', but this dividing line had been becoming blurred. Women were distinctly less careful of their reputation for chastity than at the beginning of the century, and probably were less careful of their chastity as well. The trial in 1960 for obscene publication in which a jury decided that D. H. Lawrence's *Lady Chatterley's Lover* could be published unexpurgated was probably the public event which best represented this change; conflicting attitudes clashed very explicitly, and not merely in literary terms—it was regarded as anachronistic in more ways than one when the prosecuting counsel asked the jury, 'Would you want your servants to read this book?' The verdict that the book was not obscene reflected the advance of a more relaxed attitude.

By the time of the party conference in the autumn Macmillan's control over the Conservatives seemed more or less re-established. But just as the conference was beginning, he had to have a prostate operation. If he had been high in public and party favour, as Churchill had been at the time of his stroke ten years earlier, he might have retained his position, but in the circumstances he had to resign. At the conference there was a good deal of support for Lord Hailsham as his successor, several Cabinet ministers wanted Butler, and many Conservative MPs preferred Maudling. Macmillan arranged a complicated system of consultation to discover a successor acceptable to all sections of the party, and the name produced by this method was that of Lord Home, who had been Foreign Secretary since 1960. Hailsham and Home were candidates only by a curious piece of timing. When Lord Stansgate died in 1960, his heir, the Labour MP Wedgwood Benn, refused to accept his title, and stood again at the by-election after he had been declared to be a peer. The size of his majority, and the tone of public comment, showed strong support for letting people renounce peerages they had inherited, and Macmillan, who in 1958 had had legislation passed to allow life peerages as well as the traditional hereditary peerages, had no objection to reform of the House of Lords. The new Act allowed anyone succeeding to a peerage to give it up, and also gave anyone who had already succeeded to a title twelve months to renounce his peerage. Hailsham announced, at the party conference, that he would renounce his title, and Home agreed to give up his title and become plain Sir Alec Douglas-Home KT if he were chosen party leader.

The emergence of Douglas-Home caused considerable surprise. While Macmillan said Douglas-Home had strong support in all sections of the party, his supporters kept quiet and his opponents made it clear that they thought the choice was a mistake. Douglas-Home was seen as out of touch with the modern world and unable to adapt himself to the work of modernization. This criticism, justified or not, did not take account of the problems inside the Conservative Party. Douglas-Home's supporters thought that he would be able to repeat Macmillan's success in restoring the morale of the party and, after that, winning the support of the electorate. Butler or Maudling might be more effective for winning votes but, if they failed to rally the party behind them, they would have no organization to help them convince the electorate. This was plausible enough, but Douglas-Home had no radical background like Macmillan and was unlikely to establish himself by debating successes in the Commons.

The way he was chosen did the Conservatives no good. The Labour MPs had elected Wilson leader of the Labour Party, a straightforward procedure everybody could understand; Douglas-Home had been presented as Prime Minister after consultations that were never meant to be understood by the public. Being elected gives a leader legitimacy in the modern world; emerging as the result of consultations is not a process that commands general respect. Some of the complaints about the selection process simply implied that an Old Etonian conspiracy had gathered together to impose Douglas-Home on a party and a country that did not want him, but there was also a feeling that Prime Ministers should be seen to be chosen fairly. Douglas-Home had a slight setback in forming his Cabinet: two of the modernizers, Macleod and Powell, declined to serve under him, and it was believed that if Butler had declined to serve, Douglas-Home would have had to give up trying to form a Cabinet.

As Prime Minister he had to follow the policy launched by Macmillan and Maudling of trying to expand the economy as fast as possible and regain popular support by showing that prosperity had returned. The rate of economic growth was improving rapidly, and all that mattered was to avoid disturbing it. A possible deficit in the balance of foreign trade seemed to be the only immediate threat to growth, and the doctrine of drawing on the reserves meant that it was to be ignored. As declining prosperity had caused a good deal of the government's loss of popularity, industrial revival began to restore its position. During his last months in office Macmillan had played, as Kennedy wrote, an 'indispensable role in bringing about the limitation of nuclear testing':[4] Russia, the United States, and the United Kingdom signed a treaty giving up testing nuclear weapons above ground in order to curtail the fallout of radioactive material. The countries which had hydrogen bombs were ready to step back from the expense of an arms race, and the negotiations reflected credit on the British government. Countries like China and France, which wanted to make hydrogen bombs of their own, saw the treaty as a manoeuvre to stop them challenging the position of the countries that already had hydrogen bombs, but the world in general regarded it as a victory for sanity.

The government lost some prestige because Britain's rate of economic growth between 1959 and 1963 rose much less than that of countries in western

4. Anthony Sampson, *Macmillan* (1967), app.

Europe, and their incomes per head overtook that of people in Britain. In 1958 the British domestic product per head of £360 a year was lower than in the United States, Canada, Sweden, Australia, Switzerland, or New Zealand, but this might be seen as simply the natural result of Britain's involvement in two destructive wars. By 1963 British domestic product of £495 a head had been overtaken by France and Germany, with incomes of about £510 a head.[5] Foreigners looking at Britain, and people inside the country who found these international comparisons important, drew the conclusion that Britain was losing ground, and the more sensational commentators spoke as though the country was growing poorer when all that was happening was that other nations were growing rich faster.

The fine statistical comparisons needed for these judgements were unlikely to mean very much to ordinary people in Britain. They went in increasing numbers to the continent of Europe for their holidays, but the inhabitants of holiday resorts have never been particularly prosperous so British visitors were not likely to appreciate the real wealth of the countries they visited. They already knew they could become somewhat better off by emigrating to Canada or Australia, and people did go and often settled down very happily. But things were not too bad in Britain; so far as can be measured, after allowing for increases in prices, British incomes per head during the period of Conservative rule since 1951 increased faster than incomes in Canada or the United States. Few complaints about the rate of growth had been heard in those countries until 1960, and there was no reason why people in Britain should have been more critical.

The government plunged into modernization and planning with the fervour of converts anxious to avoid roasting at the stake. Both political parties accepted the goal of 4 per cent growth suggested by the NEDC, and the government published an estimate of future government spending which showed that commitments already undertaken would make public spending grow at the 4 per cent rate. The government would have to increase its share of the national income, or reduce some item of spending that was already established, or drive the rate of growth up beyond 4 per cent if it wanted to undertake any further spending in the next four or five years. On one occasion during the summer of 1964 Callaghan, the Labour 'shadow' Chancellor of the Exchequer, did say that a 5 or 6 per cent rate of growth would be necessary; Wilson said that he believed the whole Labour programme could be carried out without any permanent increase in taxes but an increase in taxes would be imposed if necessary.

The period of waiting for the election was unusually long. After a period of teasing people that did nothing to help his reputation for taking serious things

---

5. *UN Statistical Yearbook for 1966*, table 7A. The French figure for 1958 was distorted by inflation, soon to be followed by devaluation.

seriously, Douglas-Home announced that the election would be held in October, the last moment that was legally permissible. This would allow him as long as possible to rally his party and allow reflation to do its work. But reflation was running too fast for comfort; in his 1964 budget Maudling increased taxes on tobacco and alcohol in order to reduce personal spending. He seems to have wanted to hold the election in the spring, because he was worried about the balance of payments and did not want to have the excitement of an election disturbing the difficult months of late summer. Douglas-Home felt that he needed more time to meet the members of his party and build up their enthusiasm. He seems to have reckoned that, as he was not likely to out-debate Wilson, he would not spend much time in the House of Commons and would concentrate on touring the constituencies when he was not attending to his administrative duties.

Because the election was delayed to the last possible moment, problems piled up. The government continued to insist that the reserves would see the country through any difficulties about the balance of payments, but Malaysia, Rhodesia, and the aircraft industry were harder to ignore. The Colonial Office had decided, when dealing with British possessions in Borneo, that federation was as usual the answer; in 1963 Malaya, the city of Singapore, and the colonies in Borneo were fitted into a federation christened Malaysia, in which it was hoped that Malays and Chinese would be evenly enough balanced to settle down and live together. The government of Indonesia, which had been looking forward to absorbing the Borneo colonies when the British left, protested against this and moved towards a 'confrontation' by a series of guerrilla raids into the British part of Borneo. The new Malaysian federation had to resist Indonesian pressure, and it was uncomfortably aware that when Indonesia had applied pressure to the last Dutch colonies in the East Indies, the United States had supported the Indonesian claim. The British government seems to have begun negotiating by early 1964 to give tacit support to the United States in Vietnam provided it ceased supporting the Indonesian government.

When the Monckton Commission reported on the Central African Federation, it said that the constituent states should be allowed to disaffiliate if they wanted to. Nyasaland and Northern Rhodesia chose to become separate states, and the Federation was dismantled. These two colonies could proceed fairly easily towards independence based on 'one man, one vote'. Southern Rhodesia was a different story; the white minority was numerous enough and sufficiently well organized to be able to assert its strength, and the African leadership was divided and less talented than in most of the other colonies that had moved towards independence. It would have been very hard for the British government to force a large-scale enfranchisement of Africans on the Southern Rhodesian electorate. On the other hand, giving independence to the white Rhodesian minority, which might have been acceptable in 1950, was not possible in 1964 because opinions had developed and so many new

African states had become independent. At a conference of Commonwealth Prime Ministers in the summer of 1964 the British government managed to avoid committing itself one way or the other; it could point out the difficulties of making a choice just before the general election, and some of the visiting Prime Ministers probably felt that, as Douglas-Home would not grant independence to a white minority government, it was safer to wait for the election of a Labour government which might be more sympathetic to the African majority before asking for any other decisions.

The difficulties of the aircraft industry were caused by the problem of maintaining a British nuclear striking force which was fully independent because all its equipment was British-made. The Nassau Agreement to acquire Polaris submarines was a step away from independence, but the Royal Air Force still had high hopes for its TSR-2 aeroplane. A surprisingly large part of the country's entire research budget went into the aircraft industry, and one or two fairly small-scale incidents showed that the government did not have effective control over the way the industry spent money on defence contracts. The government was trapped by the general failure to understand that large-scale developments in modern conditions sometimes fail and have to be written off. It had already had to write off several projects, and it did not want to cancel any more just before the election, especially if the cancellations made a British-built nuclear weapons system seem impossible.

At last the election came, at the end of a warm summer which was believed to have helped the government's chances a little. During the campaign opinion polls showed that the two large parties had very much the same level of support. The Labour Party concentrated on domestic issues, stressing the inadequacy of welfare payments, the unsatisfactory effects of selection for secondary education, the rising cost of land and the high untaxed profits made from it, and the general need for modernization by planning the economy. The Conservatives pointed out that the Labour proposals would cost a great deal of money, and reminded people that steps towards modernization had been taken in the last few years and the economy had grown quite quickly since 1962. Douglas-Home himself dwelt on the nuclear deterrent and the need for Britain to remain an important country; although the electorate was not very interested in the nuclear deterrent, his approach served to remind people that the Conservatives had years of experience of handling foreign policy problems.

The election gave the Labour Party a majority, but it was the smallest majority any party had ever had without being dependent on cooperation with a minor group. Before the election the Liberals had said that if they held the balance in the new Parliament, they would use it to turn the Conservatives out. So many decisions had been deferred until after the election that a government without a majority would have faced an even more difficult position than the minority governments of 1924 and 1929.

	Votes	Seats	% of all votes cast
Conservative	11,981,047	303	43.3
Liberal	3,101,106	9	11.2
Labour	12,205,812	317	44.1

The new government and the economic position (1964)

The Labour government took one fundamental decision in its first days of office: it decided not to devalue the pound. Devaluation would be a drastic cure for a balance-of-payments deficit, reducing the demand for imports by making them more expensive and at the same time increasing the profit margin that manufacturers could expect from goods sold abroad. On the other hand, prices would go up, resources would have to shift from domestic consumption towards exports, and profits would increase at the expense of real wages. In addition there was a clear, even if not very rational, belief that devaluation meant national humiliation. Understandably the government decided to try to cure the deficit by less drastic methods.

Initial Treasury reports suggested that the overseas deficit for the year would be about £800 million. Revised figures showed that the deficit on the current account was £358 million, slightly more than the disastrous 1947 record. The impact of overseas investment revealed the weakness in the theory that 'the reserves are there to be spent'. The net outflow of capital for investment during the year was about as large as the deficit on the current account, and together the two items came to about three-quarters of the entire reserves. Foreigners who held money in London on a short-term basis were naturally alarmed at the weakness of the reserves, and decided that their wealth would be safer somewhere else. As the short-term liabilities amounted to four times the reserves, they could not be repaid without external help if they were presented for payment.

Taking one year with another, British exports, including dividends and other invisible items, covered the cost of imports. The total outflow was alarmingly high because of the tendency to invest so much money overseas, and the situation was made even more uncomfortable by the large short-term holdings. But the new government believed that if it devalued it would be letting the heavy flow of investment drive the pound to an artificially low level and it rejected this course just as it rejected a policy of deflation which would have imposed an artificially high rate of interest and low rate of economic activity in order to support the outflow of investment.

It was one thing to hold these views, and another to make them effective. By November the holders of short-term debt were showing signs of concern. The position of the balance of payments was alarming enough in itself and their fears were probably increased by the preview of the budget presented by Callaghan, the newly appointed Chancellor of the Exchequer. Holders of sterling who had been frightened by the small deficit under Butler and the moderate deficit under Lloyd were most unlikely to remain calm after the enormous Maudling deficit. The preview of Callaghan's budget may have brought the crisis closer because its proposals were believed, probably incorrectly, to be inflationary. Benefits for most of the national insurance schemes were raised, income tax for the 6.5 million people who paid at the standard rate was increased to help cover the cost, and the government cancelled the TSR-2 aeroplane, which meant that by the 1970s the country would no longer have a British-built nuclear weapons system. At the same time it announced that the system of company taxation would be changed. Previously company profits were taxed at a relatively high rate but dividends were paid without being taxed a second time; under the new system companies would pay corporation tax, at a lower rate than before, but dividends would be treated as untaxed income and be subject to income tax. All capital gains, and not just short-term gains, were to be taxed. These last two changes were no more than a move towards the American system of taxation, but some people regarded them as a prelude to an attack on property.

The government was fairly well placed for raising international loans to meet the drain on the reserves caused by the withdrawal of short-term funds. The United States had fairly similar balance-of-payments difficulties caused by an outflow of investment money which exceeded her trading surplus; if the pound was devalued the dollar would come under heavier pressure and the American government would in its turn have to choose between deflation and devaluation. The British government hesitated over increasing the bank rate, and might have kept it lower if it had acted sooner, but with powerful American support the Bank of England borrowed $3,000 million in short-term loans. The government tried to deal with the balance-of-payments deficit by reducing its own overseas expenditure and by encouraging companies trading abroad to bring their profits back to the United Kingdom instead of keeping them overseas. It also imposed a 15 per cent surcharge on imports except food and raw materials. This step annoyed many other countries and particularly the other members of the EFTA, and its effect was bound to be slow. The deficit was too large to be ended quickly, and the short-term holders of sterling would be uneasy for as long as it lasted. So much world trade was financed in sterling, so many financial institutions had interests in sterling and so many individuals could find ways to take a position against sterling in which they would benefit from a devaluation that it was not possible to think of meeting all the demands for sterling simply by using the reserves. The private resources of the individuals and companies who were convinced that sterling must fall might still be too much for all the official resources of the central bankers, the Western governments, and the International Monetary Fund.

It was soon clear that the public blamed the Conservatives for leaving the balance-of-payments deficit, and the government hoped to be in the happy position of being able to take the credit for pleasant things it did, and blame the previous government for unpleasant things. This could not go on for long; the government was blamed for giving ministers and MPs an immediate salary increase while delaying the payment of increased national insurance benefits for four or five months. The Labour Party lost a seat at a by-election and looked as if it might find itself at the mercy of the Liberals after all.

Wilson as Prime Minister was determined to govern as though he had a majority, and he took it for granted that the country wanted a government which acted decisively. He possessed the gift of presenting himself as a man who understood the problems and would work full-time at solving them; the detached and amateur approach sometimes adopted by Macmillan and Douglas-Home was not in fashion, and Wilson expressed the mood of the times. This did not necessarily mean that his decisions were right, because he had to deal with a short-run financial crisis, solve the problems of Rhodesia and Malaysia, and prepare for the election which was expected from month to month. The long-term planning which the Labour Party had stressed in opposition was less relevant than a simple ability to adjust policy to circumstances.

Malaysia was relatively easy: reinforcements were sent to patrol the frontier with Indonesia in Borneo, and the government made sure that there was no United States support for Indonesia. President Johnson was re-elected later in 1964 on a platform of social reform and opposition to the aggressive ideas on foreign policy put forward by his opponent, Senator Goldwater. All the signs suggested that the American and British governments could get on very well together. They had to cooperate in order to avoid increasing the strain on their foreign exchange positions, and it seemed reasonable for the British government to continue to give Johnson a free hand in Vietnam in exchange for a free hand in Indonesia. Malaysia remained unshaken by pressure from the Indonesian government, which eventually crumbled under the strain of keeping up the confrontation. After a period of confusion, in which the Communists tried to gain a monopoly of power and were massacred, a military government was set up which recognized that confrontation was doing Indonesia no good.

Rhodesia was an altogether harder problem. Smith, the Rhodesian Prime Minister, had probably hoped that if re-elected the Conservatives would be more sympathetic to the white Rhodesians than they had been before the election. Some of his followers thought in terms of a unilateral declaration of independence as soon as the Labour government was elected. Wilson briskly and fiercely warned the Rhodesians against any such step; whether because of

this, or because they wanted to make further preparations, they opened negotiations with the British government. Wilson's warnings seemed to have dealt
with the crisis, and the Conservatives were badly divided about the way to
handle the problem. The general result was to improve the Labour Party's
position for the immediate future.

The government's plans for economic change were directed to goals in the
relatively distant future. Its first objective was a 'prices and incomes policy'
based on persuading industrial management and the trade unions to accept a
Prices and Incomes Board which could regulate increases more effectively
than the National Incomes Commission because it rested on mutual agreement. Within the relative economic tranquillity that the Board was intended
to provide, the industrial managers would offer estimates of the way their
businesses would develop over the next five years, and when these estimates
were brought together and harmonized into a consistent scheme by economists' analysis, a National Plan would emerge. Industrialists would benefit by
knowing with more certainty than in the past how much expansion they could
expect in other sectors of the economy. This information would let them plan
for a higher rate of growth, which meant everybody was better off.

George Brown, as minister for economic affairs, was fairly successful in the
first stages of this programme. The managers and the trade unions duly
declared they intended to cooperate in the work of the Prices and Incomes
Board. His Department could begin collecting estimates to be worked
together into the National Plan. The Board began well, and showed signs of
becoming an authority that could examine aspects of economic activity effectively. By interpreting rather widely its responsibility to look into price levels, it
examined the ways in which banks treated customers, manufacturers of
detergents ran their advertising campaigns, and architects fixed their fees, and
it made recommendations for improvement. It believed that on issues of
wages policy it should act rather like the Swedish central authority and lay
down fairly binding suggestions for pay increases.

The Department of Economic Affairs, like the French Commissariat du
Plan, was meant not just to collect estimates but also to induce the manufacturers to set their estimates as high as possible. The National Plan had to
record the present position accurately, but it also had to push people into
making greater efforts in the future than they would otherwise have done. The
Plan acquired its own momentum and it did push people forward, helped by
the emphasis that had been placed on a rate of growth of 4 per cent a year.
When the Plan eventually appeared, it was fairly clear that it was more a
matter of aspiration than of practical economics. The planners most visibly
disregarded the constraints on growth when considering the supply of labour.
They accepted a target of expanding the national income by 25 per cent by
1970, which meant a rate of growth of just under 4 per cent, but their figures
showed that to do this about 200,000 more workers were needed than seemed

likely to be available. The prices and incomes policy was intended to check the tendency to inflation that had persisted in the economy ever since Beveridge's definition of full employment—more vacant jobs than workers to fill them—had been tacitly accepted, but no incomes policy could prevent a rise in wages if there was a steady demand for 200,000 more workers than could be found. Employers would have to bid against each other, by offering higher wages or fringe benefits, to get enough workers to play their part in the Plan. The National Plan was likely to reproduce the very high level of demand that had existed under the 1945–51 Labour government, without the stringent physical controls that had been available just after the war. The government had in 1964 forbidden further office development in London, but it was ready to operate most of the economy with very little compulsion. This may have reassured economists that government decree would not divert resources into the wrong channels, but it left open the possibility that a shortage of labour would lead to large wage increases.

More workers could easily be found: Commonwealth citizens from the West Indies, India, and Pakistan were ready and eager to come. The question of Commonwealth immigration had been lurking below the surface during the election, and the results suggest that the Labour Party lost three or four seats on the issue in areas where immigrants had arrived and local conditions were unpleasant enough to make the voters want to blame somebody. Poor housing in Smethwick or Slough was not the fault of the immigrants, but the inhabitants thought differently and were influenced by the slogan 'If you want a nigger neighbour, vote Labour'.

Dissatisfaction over immigration rose after the election. Some Conservatives suggested that their party ought to take a more determined stand against immigration than it had done in the Commonwealth Immigration Act, and the government decided that the existing arrangements allowed too much immigration. It issued a White Paper showing how it would interpret the Act in future, laying down a decidedly more restrictive policy, at least so far as entry to the country was concerned. The White Paper also suggested ways in which the immigrants might be cared for more effectively once they were inside the country, and legislation against discrimination in public places was passed. Some people argued that legislation was not the best way to deal with the problem, but other countries faced with the same situation had fallen back on legislation after first believing that there must be less formal ways of acting.

The White Paper stated that no more than 8,500 Commonwealth immigrants, of whom 1,000 would be from Malta, were to be allowed work permits every year. All questions about freedom of movement and Commonwealth solidarity apart, this closed one of the ways in which the labour shortage revealed in the National Plan might have been made up. Rapid economic growth has often been accompanied by rapid increase of the working population; Britain had no underemployed rural population to draw into the economy, as there was in the countries of Europe that had been thriving since the war, but workers from the underdeveloped parts of the Commonwealth might have enabled the economy to grow as intended. Nobody opposed immigration as a conscious choice between growth and keeping Britain white, but this was the effect of the policy in the White Paper.

The rate of growth caused little worry in the first year or two of the Labour government. The economy slowed down in 1964 but was still moving ahead confidently. Profits had already risen sharply; in 1965 wage-earners claimed their share. Wage increases were well above increases in the national income, so wages gained a larger share of the national income, mainly at the expense of profits. The government did not resist this process, partly perhaps because it felt that wages ought to receive a larger share of the national income, and partly because it wanted to conciliate the trade unions in order to get them to accept the authority of the Prices and Incomes Board once it was operating. The government also remembered that it would have to hold an election to avoid being strangled by its narrow majority.

The government stressed its determination to nationalize the steel industry. Nationalization was certainly one way to concentrate the industry into the smaller number of larger units that would enable it to compete with the vast integrated plants that had recently been set up in other countries, but the White Paper laying down principles for steel nationalization was seen more as a gesture to convince the left wing of the Labour Party that the government had not forgotten its manifesto commitments. Its majority was not large enough to think of passing a Bill before the next election. Even the White Paper led to trouble for the government because two Labour Members could not support it, which could have cost the government its majority in a division.

The 1965 budget, with its new system of company taxation and capital gains taxation, was complicated but it did not apply new principles to the objectives—as opposed to the technique—of raising revenue. A comparison with the days before the 1909 budget, with its substantial provisions for new spending on battleships and on old-age pensions, shows how government activity had changed. In 1908 the government raised about £130 million, £52 million from taxes on income and capital, such as income tax, surtax, and death duties, and £75 million from taxes on spending, such as the customs and excise duties on alcohol and tobacco. This came to about 7 per cent of the national income of £1,875 million. By 1965 taxes on income and capital had risen to £5,998 million and taxes on spending, which had risen less quickly, yielded £3,766 million. As the national income had risen to £32,339 million, the revenue amounted to 30 per cent of the total. This seventeenfold increase in national income does not mean that the country was that much better off: the population had risen by 25 per cent and the price indexes had gone up sevenfold. Price indexes are the best obtainable measure of inflation, but they have their problems: they combine many different items, some of which (like candles) were used less and less and some of which (like refrigerators) were used more and more. The cheapest motor cars cost less, in cash terms, in 1965 than in 1908 and they consumed less petrol to the kilometre. Food prices had gone up to somewhat more than seven times the 1908 level. House prices, on the average, had risen about seven times, but this average included sharp rises in the south-east and slower increases elsewhere. High taxes pushed alcohol and tobacco prices up to far more than seven times the 1908 level. Early in the century high duties were imposed on alcohol to promote temperance; by the 1960s high duties on tobacco, first imposed to reduce imports, were imposed to discourage smoking because it was dangerous to people's health.[6]

The 1965 budget was so complicated that it took up a great deal of the parliamentary year. The Conservatives fought it with considerable technical skill, though this may not have done them any good. Inevitably they emerged looking as if they thought capital gains ought not to be taxed. Furthermore, they took up so much time that the government was not pressed to bring forward items of its programme like the nationalization of steel which the Liberals might dislike so much that they would join the Conservatives in a determined attempt to overthrow the government. By the time it reached the summer recess the government was exhausted, but it had avoided disaster. The Conservatives were less satisfied. After the 1964 election Douglas-Home had arranged for future leaders of the Conservative Party to be elected by the parliamentary party. He was uneasily aware that he was not the leader to convince people that his party was really up-to-date, and that he was not a debater to crush Wilson in the House of Commons. When opinion polls consistently showed that the public preferred Wilson to Douglas-Home, Conservative Members became convinced that a change of leader was essential, without asking if anybody else could do better. Douglas-Home resigned in August, and the parliamentary party chose Heath, the hero of the European Community negotiations, as his successor. They seem to have thought Heath would precisely match Wilson's qualities, would defeat him in debate, would force him into making mistakes, and would deal a swift knockout blow. Whether the leader of the opposition ought to resemble his Opponent or not—possibly Maudling's unhurried approach would have been an effective contrast to Wilson—Heath did not possess quite the qualities he had been credited with. When he had the better case, he could drive the fact home, but he lacked the debater's gift of making his case look a little better than it was. In some ways his approach to politics was rather like that of Gaitskell; he liked working out policies for himself and applying them to new situations. But this

---

6. These figures are taken from various tables in London and Cambridge Economic Service, *The British Economy: Key Statistics, 1900–1966*.

was a long way from the powerful infighter poised to deliver the decisive thrust that the Conservatives had thought they were choosing.

People spoke as if the choice of Heath as Conservative leader was a great step in the democratization of politics, and it was sometimes pointed out that both party leaders came from grammar schools, as though this showed that the way to the top was now open to talent with no regard to birth. Their social origins were not really very different from those of Asquith and Law, the two party leaders in 1914. Their parents had incomes a little above the national average; neither of them owed anything to inherited wealth or to family connections, but neither of them rose from as low in the social scale as Lloyd George or MacDonald. Wilson and Heath had been at their grammar schools before the 1944 Education Act, they came from an educational background confined to less than 10 per cent of the population, and they had gone on to Oxford.

Social attitudes and external problems

As a result of the 1944 Act, grammar school places were available for about 30 per cent of children going to secondary schools. Comprehensive schools were part of the Labour programme, and could be effectively encouraged without legislation. Conservative Ministers of Education had used their powers to prevent Labour local education authorities from setting up comprehensive schools; the Labour Minister used his powers to require all local education authorities to submit plans for reorganizing education in a way that would eliminate selection at 11 plus. This was the most complete assertion of central authority in education that had ever taken place, though it was only the logical conclusion of previous changes. A few local authorities tried to resist by submitting plans that did not eliminate selection, but had to yield to ministerial insistence. On the other hand, local authorities that changed almost all of their schools over to a comprehensive system, but retained a few distinguished grammar schools, found that their proposals were acceptable.

Local authorities also undertook an expansion of their housing programmes. Between 1956 and 1963 building barely maintained the level of 300,000 new houses a year reached in the early 1950s, and this contributed to the increase in house prices in the early 1960s. In 1964 and 1965 about 30 per cent more houses were built, about half of them by municipal councils, who were still the only people building houses to rent.

In 1965 Parliament abolished capital punishment for murder. The issue had become a symbol of the division between people who took a libertarian view of society and people who were afraid social discipline might break down with disastrous consequences. In the 1950s the Conservative government had offered a compromise by making murder under certain circumstances a non-capital crime, to be punished by a long term of imprisonment, but the issue was not going to be ended by any compromise. Opponents of capital punishment regarded it as intolerable that any executions at all should take place; supporters of capital punishment sometimes used arguments that would have justified its use in a great many crimes apart from murder.

The division did not run very precisely along party lines, and the party leaders were happy to say that the Whips should not issue instructions to Members on this sort of question. As most Labour Members of Parliament opposed the death penalty, and most Conservatives wanted to keep it, abolition was unlikely to be carried in a House of Commons with a Conservative majority. Most working-class voters opposed the change, but did not seem to be influenced by the issue at general elections. The most determined supporters of the death penalty were enthusiastic Conservatives, and one or two Conservative abolitionist Members had some difficulty with their local party organizations because of their views. Labour Party enthusiasts tended to be enthusiastic abolitionists, and in their minds this particular cause was one of a wide spectrum of issues concerned with personal liberty and colonial independence. Sidney Silverman, the very skilful parliamentarian who organized the abolitionists, was also one of the leaders of the Movement for Colonial Freedom, which agitated for Britain's withdrawal from her colonial possessions.

The nineteenth-century liberal tradition had not disappeared, but the political parties continued to be divided primarily on economic issues. The Labour Party supported greater equality helped by state action, and on the whole it had inherited Mill's belief in giving people a wide range of freedom in issues where their actions did not affect other people; the Conservative Party stood for greater individual freedom to prosper in a less controlled economic system, but it was more likely to say that certain moral principles ought to be expressed in legislation on crime even if it did mean restricting people's freedom of action. At the beginning of the century the moral attitudes of the unenfranchised people at the bottom of the social scale were less restrictive than those of the classes concerned about respectability who made up the great bulk of the electorate. By the 1930s the ideal of respectability was accepted throughout society, but by the 1960s it was much less universally accepted and some sections of the middle class, especially around London, were consciously uninhibited and regarded freedom from restraint as a good thing for its own sake.

The greater freedom, or laxer sense of social discipline, showed itself in fashions and styles. In the serious arts British writers and performers had taken an honourable place from the beginning of the century and earlier. The English style in acting had grown less formal and less exhibitionist as taste turned away from the bravura displays of Irving and Tree, but Olivier and Gielgud were accepted as examples for actors in any country in the world. By the 1940s ballet companies had appeared, where none had existed thirty years before, that could tour all over the world. Composers like Elgar and Vaughan Williams were perhaps too purely British to have much appeal to the world outside, but Britten had won an international reputation. Interest in music had increased, and had become more discriminating; the brilliant criticism of Shaw in the 1890s and the complaints of Elgar may have given too poor an impression of British musical performance at the beginning of the century, but it does seem also that, helped by the BBC, standards of performance rose considerably and public interest in classical music had certainly increased and became better informed and more wide-ranging. Although it was much easier for people to listen to music at home at the end of the period than at the beginning, because of the developments of radio and of records and tapes, audiences had increased, and the number of orchestras had also gone up.

But while Britain after the Second World War was no longer an importer of culture, the country was still an importer of fashions and styles. English textiles and English tailors might make the English gentleman the best-dressed man in the world, but then one of the features of a gentleman's clothes is that they are never quite up to date. English outdoor clothes for older women were admired, but they were also expected not to be too exciting. English clothes were the clothes of a ruling class. And so it was all the more surprising that, in an ironic echo of her position in other fields at the beginning of the century, England in the mid-1960s set the fashions for the young and provided stars for popular entertainment. It was not quite what Macmillan had meant when he said the British must be Greeks in a world in which the Americans were the Romans, but the Greeks had been entertainers for the Roman Empire and it looked for a moment as though the English were going to take up the same role by providing popular singing groups such as the Beatles and women's fashions for the young such as the miniskirt. People who worried about the country's status in the world were serious-minded men and women who wanted the country to be influential in some more dignified way, and the young people who set the new fashions were much less interested in questions of global prestige. They had grown up in a country which was not in fact a great power, and they probably did not expect it to behave like one. Life would have been easier for political leaders if fewer people had felt that the world's problems, wherever they might be, were problems that the British government should solve. But while people realized that British power was less than in the past, there were still pressures for the country to take an interest in faraway places.

The Labour government was very pleased with its good relations with the American government. Even while Macmillan was Prime Minister the Democratic administration in Washington had been ready to receive potential Labour ministers, and after Macmillan resigned it had been fairly clear that a change of government was expected and would be welcome. Home was not as strongly pro-American as Churchill and Macmillan had been; the Labour leaders recognized that being received in Washington helped their electoral prospects. They did not object to suggestions of continued British involvement in Asian affairs, often expressed in the phrase 'East of Suez'; they were quite willing to support the United States to the extent of guaranteeing the former British possessions around the Indian Ocean. The defence of Malaysia went satisfactorily, which suggested that the policy of retaining a post-imperial role might not be unattractive. The United States was glad to have another Western power cooperating in East Aria to reduce the expense and possible odium of operating there. From the British point of view the cost was an unwelcome aspect of the case, and once the left wing of the Labour Party realized what its government was committing itself to, protests began to be heard. These protests became louder when it was realized that the 'East of Suez' policy committed Britain to some degree of acceptance of the American policy in Vietnam. During 1965 the American involvement there increased. Wilson plunged into attempts to mediate, in order to check the expansion of the war and the embarrassment that it might cause him. A delegation to try to end the fighting was set up at a conference of Commonwealth Prime Ministers. It did not achieve anything, but it did extricate the British government from an awkward situation. Most of the Prime Ministers at the conference felt that American policy was becoming imperialist, and although the British government was ready to let the United States see that it was under pressure to move towards the non-aligned position of the majority of the Commonwealth countries, it was committed to allowing the American government a free hand on the issue. A policy of inactivity, punctuated by attempts to mediate, suited the British position better than anything else.

There was pressure for British policy towards Rhodesia to become more active. The negotiations with Smith and his government made little progress; Smith's supporters were becoming impatient, and on 10 November his government declared Rhodesia independent. The British government had said in previous negotiations that it would not use force to subdue a revolt, but that it would employ all possible trade sanctions to cripple the Rhodesian economy. The decision not to use force was probably unavoidable: moving troops into central Africa would have been uncomfortably reminiscent of the Boer War, for the white Rhodesians were about as numerous as the Boers had been, and were well equipped for resistance.[7] An airborne invasion immediately after the unilateral declaration of independence might have brought the white Rhodesians back to their allegiance, but resistance, followed by the deaths of Rhodesians, would have made it even harder to reach a stable and permanent settlement. People with sensationalized memories of the events at the Curragh in 1914 even suggested that the army might have refused to obey orders to subdue the revolt. This was most unlikely, but if British troops had had to

---

7. The technical problems of using force were discussed in *The Economist*, 17 Dec. 1966, 1222.

fight white Rhodesians, the British government could not have relied on the support of the Opposition or of the electorate. Wilson did say that the United Kingdom would intervene if law and order broke down in Rhodesia, and this might have been a hint to African resistance movements to attack the rebel government and provide a basis for British intervention. But the African political movements were not strong; part of the reason why the position of the white Rhodesians had gone unchallenged was that the Africans had no leader who could unite his countrymen behind him in the same way as in most other African countries under British rule. Wilson had visited Rhodesia during the negotiations before the declaration of independence and it was said he had been disturbed to find how limited was the supply of talent among the African leaders.

Other countries were full of enthusiasm for the idea of a British expedition-ary force to subdue the rebels, and some Commonwealth leaders suggested that on past occasions, when dealing with rebels who were not white, much more drastic action had been taken. But there were no parallels; no previous British government since 1776 had been faced by a rebel colonial government with an officially organized army of its own. Economic sanctions seemed much less likely to cause trouble than an attempt at armed invasion. The weakest part of the Rhodesian economy was its reliance on imports of oil; the next weakest was its dependence on tobacco exports to cover most of its import bill. Restrictions on imports of oil looked for a short time like an effective weapon, but after supplies began to come in through South Africa it was clear that the British government would have to rely on the slow effects of making it impossible for the Rhodesians to sell their tobacco or else come to terms with the rebel government. The best that the British government could hope for was an arrangement that would leave the white Rhodesians in com-mand of the situation for the foreseeable future but guarantee the position of the Africans as a group that could acquire political power with the passage of time, and the white Rhodesians showed no great desire to accept this limita-tion on their freedom of action.

The British government spent more of its time worrying about economic issues than about these problems of external policy. The deficit on the balance of payments was considerably lower in 1965 than in 1964, and new regulations, which for the first time restricted investment in prosperous Sterling Area countries, reduced the amount of capital sent out of the country and lessened the strain on the reserves. But people were still uneasy about holding sterling, and the resources of the world's official banking institutions were put under great strain when there was another run on it in the summer of 1965.[8] The

8. *The Economist*, 23 July 1966, 364 (just after the deflationary measures) gave figures suggesting that in 1956 the average outcome of the balance of payments was a surplus of £50m. a year, and by 1965 it was a deficit of £50m. a year.

United Kingdom had to repay these short-term loans, which amounted to over 1 per cent of the gross national product, over the next five years; the loans were mainly banking transactions, which meant that they would be repaid not out of a British trading surplus but by rebuilding the short-term reserves of the London money market, but this only meant that the British economic position would be as vulnerable to short-term shifts of opinion in the international financial community as it had been for most of the period since the First World War.

Most other governments took an ambivalent attitude to the United Kingdom's problems; they wanted the debts repaid, but the economies of a number of countries were slowing down at the same time and deflationary measures in Britain would make life harder elsewhere. If the British government was prepared to take the risk that an uncontrollable monetary crisis would force it to devalue, several other governments were prepared to help it avoid deflating and reducing its imports.

Cuts in government spending were recommended from various directions. The Governor of the Bank of England said in public that they were desirable; criticizing the government in public was not the normal British interpretation of his position, though central bankers frequently did so in other countries, but Lord Cromer had organized so much of the international short-term credit needed by the government that he could not be rebuked, though he was not reappointed when his term of office came to an end. Some Conservatives led by Powell turned against the idea of an 'East of Suez' policy; they said that the United Kingdom was a European country and should not try to revive the ghosts of empire by spending a lot of money on distant defence positions. The government was alarmed by the rate of increase in defence spending in the early 1960s, and set up a review of spending which fixed financial limits for defence and then set out to fit the policy into the money available. The Navy suffered more than the other services; it was not allowed an expensive aircraft carrier which it had hoped for, and Mayhew, the Minister for the Navy, resigned early in 1966. He had adopted the complicated but not illogical

	Annual averages for		
	1954–7	1958–61	1962–5
Current account	97	44	−86
Capital	−152	−138	−209
Total (including balancing item)	24	−9	−258

The heavy weight of the capital account payments is obvious; if the country had given up either foreign investment or government spending on defence and foreign aid, the accounts would have balanced. However, the Bank of International Settlements did say, in 1968, that the pound was overvalued by the 1960s.

position that the 'East of Suez' policy was on general grounds not desirable but that, if the Cabinet insisted on it, enough money should be spent to make it effective; he resigned when the government neither decided to give up the policy nor showed any willingness to pay for it. The long-run implication of the refusal to pay for the aircraft carrier was that the country could not afford the 'East of Suez' policy.

Heath, as leader of the Opposition, had his own suggestions for reducing government expenditure. Opposition parties habitually complain about waste-fulness, and past experience suggests that these complaints impress the elector-ate only when it already thinks the government is running things inefficiently. There was no sign of this sort of discontent in 1966, and the Conservative attack was not successful. The other aspects of Heath's attack on government spend-ing were more interesting. He abandoned the enthusiasm for government planning that had been accepted by both major parties for some years previ-ously, and praised the free play of the market. He also said that the expense of social welfare was rising too fast, and that payments should be restricted to people who could show, after an examination of their financial position, that they needed help. It was not clear whether he meant that the whole social insurance system which had been built up from the 1911 Act onwards should be replaced or only that items like family allowances which were not financed out of insurance contributions should be put on a means test basis.

Commentators at the time spoke of a struggle for the 'middle ground' in politics, but this was not what Heath was doing. In the early 1960s both political parties seemed ready to accept a mixed economy, in which most industry was privately owned, and in which the government acted as a plan-ning agent which influenced individual business decisions but did not impose direct controls on them. It looked as if the political parties would no longer dispute the relationship between the organization of the economy and the government. Heath stepped away from the 'middle ground', but he was not able to win support for the move. When the election came, in March 1966, the Conservatives had little chance of success. Wilson looked like a natural ruler, Heath looked like a civil servant, and it was unfortunate for his party that when he wanted to say it would be prepared to take unpopular decisions he said it would be ruthless, which gave the impression that it might not consider the damage caused to people by its decisions. Wilson spoke of taking tough decisions, which gave a rather more favourable impression of a man who realized that some measures might lead to discomfort.

The government seemed to know its business; part of its satisfactory repu-tation was due to relatively small-scale operations, such as the increase in money given to the arts, which remained small even though distinctly larger than before, and the tidying and rationalizing of arrangements for aid to underdeveloped countries. In a preview of the budget shortly before the election the Chancellor of the Exchequer said he would not increase taxes noticeably, but would tax forms of gambling that had previously been exempt. The election was not exciting, and became steadily less exciting as it became clear that the government was going to be re-elected.

	Votes	Seats	% of all votes cast
Conservative	11,418,433	253	41.9
Liberal	2,327,533	12	8.6
Labour	13,064,941	363	47.9

Labour on its own

Ever since the flaws had begun to appear in Macmillan's armour in 1961 or 1962, the country had constantly been expecting a general election, and many people added to this a belief that a Labour government would set everything right. To Wilson's left were supporters who expected a lavish flow of public expenditure unchecked by worries about the balance of payments; to his right were supporters who thought that the new government would run the capitalist system more efficiently than the Conservatives had done. These hopes had survived while Labour had a majority of only three, but they were in the long run likely to be disappointed; at the very least, the government could not satisfy all of its supporters.

This should have restrained the people who talked about the Conservative defeat in much the same exaggerated terms as had been used to discuss the Labour defeat in 1959. The Liberal Party had developed a new approach for the 1960s and it faced a serious problem after the 1966 election. Under Grimond the Liberals had moved to the left on domestic issues and claimed that, as the Labour Party could not provide an effective challenge to the Conservatives, people who wanted to end Conservative rule should vote Liberal. In the 1964–6 Parliament the Liberals voted with the government a good deal of the time; this was not a comfortable role for a party in opposition, but at least they could speak as if their support was vital for the survival of the Labour government. The 1966 election left no obvious political role for them to play.

The budget contained the promised tax on gambling, and also a tax on employment: in effect employees were divided into three categories, and employers had to pay a tax, receive a bonus, or remain in a neutral position, according to whether their employees were considered to be productive or not. The basis of division was rather old-fashioned: producers of goods were considered productive and earned a bonus, while producers of services were considered unproductive and were taxed. The differentiation among employees led to confusion, which obscured the fact that the tax was likely to be fairly deflationary in the long run, and sharply deflationary at first because the tax was paid some time before employers received bonuses for workers considered 'productive'.

The Department of Economic Affairs brought forward legislation to give it statutory powers to delay wage increases while they were discussed by the Prices and Incomes Board, which would try to protect the national interest by deciding what pay increases were possible in jobs where wages were fixed by union negotiation. The powers given to the Board were too sweeping for the Minister of Technology, Frank Cousins, previously the leader of the largest of the trade unions, and he resigned rather than remain in a government that deprived his union members of the right to reach settlements on the basis of conditions within the industry.

While Parliament was working over the early stages of this Bill, a new financial crisis was developing. Some people blamed a seamen's strike in the late spring, and some people blamed the continuing balance of payments deficit which, despite the improvement in 1965, still showed no signs of getting back into surplus in 1966. As the period of summer weakness for sterling came on, more and more money moved out of the country, and by July the government had to consider, as so many British governments had done previously, what was to be done about the pound. Several Cabinet ministers wanted to devalue and run a policy of growth unworried by the value of the pound, in much the way that the French had done in the 1950s. But although the Prime Minister admitted that it might be necessary to consider floating the pound if the economy ran too slowly, he successfully led the resistance to devaluing in this crisis.[9]

This decision left no alternative to deflation. The international monetary authorities were almost at the end of their resources, and were beginning to question whether the United Kingdom was a sound risk. The main novelty in the deflationary measures was that the Prices and Incomes Bill was amended drastically, to make dividend increases illegal for twelve months, to make wage increases illegal for six months and legal only under special circumstances for the next six, and to restrict price increases for a similar period. The cost side of inflation was thus to be stopped by law, while demand was reduced by the traditional measures of reducing government expenditure and restricting investment and credit for business expansion. Four per cent growth lay dead; opinion fell back on the more modest 3 per cent growth indicated by Butler in 1954. The National Plan was unlikely to recover its prestige and re-emerge as a path to economic growth if external pressures could overthrow all its calculations. The Labour government had to show whether it could be more successful than the Conservatives at managing the painful process of deflation and looking after the economy at a time of rising unemployment.

9. R. H. S. Crossman, *Diaries of a Cabinet Minister*, i (1975), 576–7.

The Prime Minister was probably resigned to the fact that the Labour Party was not monolithic and would never be completely without quarrels, and that after his return to deflation the left wing of the party would once more say that only a policy of socialism would make steady economic progress possible. The Labour leadership faced this problem calmly. A couple of dozen MPs on the left of the party regularly abstained or voted against the government on issues concerned with the operation of the Prices and Incomes Act. Wilson was stung into saying that dogs are allowed to bite once but if they bite too often their licences are revoked, but most of the time the party leaders ignored the rebels in a more dignified way and did not threaten them with the sanctions of party discipline.

The rebels soon had a larger issue on which to fight. There had been hints, after the election, that the government was thinking again about the EEC, but there had been no suggestion before July that Gaitskell's strict conditions were to be relaxed. Access to a larger market appealed to people searching for a way to increase British exports and, although countries in the Commonwealth did not want the United Kingdom to enter the Community, they could not provide an alternative solution for her economic problems. George Brown, who had been a firm supporter of the earlier attempt to enter the Community, became Foreign Secretary a few weeks after the deflationary measures were introduced. He was regarded as the most dynamic man in the Cabinet; he had offered his resignation in July because his hopes that the Department of Economic Affairs could bring about a rapid economic expansion were clearly going to be frustrated, and an attempt to enter the Community offered scope to his talents. The government was already convinced that British industry should be consolidated into larger units: the corporation tax, the nationalization of the steel industry, and the proposed creation of the Industrial Reorganization Corporation all pointed in the same direction. Entry to the Community followed logically from this line of thought. When the government announced in November that it was going to apply again for membership, the left-wing Labour and right-wing Conservative opponents appeared once more, but they commanded less support than in the past.

Because opposition to the policy was weaker the government could commit itself to Europe more fully than its predecessor had done. Wilson and Brown went to visit the capitals of the six Community countries. At times the importance of France's position was overstated—Wilson wanted to minimize the obstacles to entry, the other European opponents of British entry wanted de Gaulle to take the responsibility for rejecting it, and de Gaulle was very willing to take the central role—but it was true that the Paris discussions were the most important. The French President gave Wilson and Brown very little comfort; their task became even less hopeful when Dr Kiesinger, the German Chancellor, made it clear that while he would prefer to see the United Kingdom inside the Community he regarded the alliance with France as one of the foundations of German policy and would not oppose de Gaulle over the issue of British entry.

At home the government now had the votes to renationalize the steel industry. The heart had gone out of the struggle; at the fiercest moments, around 1950, steel really had been vital for controlling the economy, but by the mid-1960s it was suffering from overproduction and surplus capacity; nationalization would come just in time for the government to supervise the contraction of another industry that had passed its prime. Parliament spent more time and energy on legislation that recognized people's changed attitudes to government and to private morality. The Conservatives usually thought the great twentieth-century increase in the power of the government was a consequence of the two world wars and of socialism which might fade away under a long period of Conservative rule. The Labour Party thought the problem was more deep-seated and proposed, as a first step to deal with it, the creation of a Parliamentary Commissioner (popularly known as an Ombudsman, after the Scandinavian official on whom his role was modelled) who could investigate the confidential files of the Civil Service when it was suspected that there had been an abuse in the administration of power, and could issue reports about what emerged.

The Bill creating the office of Parliamentary Commissioner was brought forward by the government. Private Members introduced two Bills, also inspired by J. S. Mill's type of liberalism, to legalize homosexual acts between consenting adults and to allow abortion when it was justified on medical, psychological, or social grounds. These Bills were handled in the way the Bill abolishing capital punishment had been handled in the previous Parliament: the government did not officially support them, and issued no party whip, but it allowed enough parliamentary time to make sure that attempts to 'talk them out' were not successful. Outside Parliament the changes seem to have been welcomed by public opinion; surveys showed majorities in favour of both pieces of legislation, and the opponents of change seemed either to be apologetic about their position or to be unreasonable—the advocates of a libertarian approach now held the calm, commanding, central position which in the past had been held by the supporters of a restrictive morality.

The majorities for the two Acts came from the Labour Party, and the Acts may have consoled government supporters who were unhappy about other aspects of its policy. Approval of American intervention in Vietnam, even though it was not accompanied by tangible assistance, and government restriction of wage increases were not what they expected from a Labour government. Hints, even more obscure than those of Heath during the election, that the social services were going to be placed on a selective basis caused dismay. When the deflationary measures launched in July 1966 began to take effect, discontent became more widespread; they could work only by creating unemployment, and the idea of a Labour government creating unemployment naturally alienated its supporters. In the 1967 local government elections, dominated as usual almost entirely by voters' feelings about the central government, the Labour Party did badly.

A response of more long-term significance came from Wales and Scotland. Curing inflation and balance-of-payments difficulties by means of deflation had always hurt stagnant regions more than prosperous regions; deflation in London and the Midlands meant less overtime, but in Scotland, Wales, and the north-east of England it meant that unemployment rose to the level suffered by London in the 1930s. In 1962 the Conservatives had been worried enough by the effect of deflation on the north-east of England to appoint Lord Hailsham as a minister with special responsibility for the region. In 1966 deflation coincided with an increase in nationalist feeling in Wales and Scotland.

Welsh and Scottish nationalist movements had been in existence for a good many years, but they had done so badly in elections, including the 1966 parliamentary election, that nobody took them seriously. But very soon after the 1966 election Plaid Cymru (Welsh nationalists) won a by-election, which gave them their first seat in the House of Commons. In the months that followed they and the Scottish Nationalists did unexpectedly well. The government seemed uncertain whether they were transient phenomena that would pass away when deflation was ended, or real forces to be countered by devolution of power from Westminster to a regional authority. While the nationalists did well, the Liberals made no progress. Signs of a Liberal revival had often been seen between elections in the previous dozen years. In 1967 the conditions seemed particularly favourable: regionalism and devolution were causes the Liberals had championed, and they had always retained some strength in Scotland and Wales. Grimond had shifted the party's emphasis to the left, which might have been expected to attract people who were no longer satisfied with the Labour Party. But in England it was the Conservatives, and in Wales and Scotland the nationalists, who benefited from the government's unpopularity.

Inevitably there were limits to the policy of deflation. The government did not like a policy that worked by causing unemployment, and its dislike for its own policy made for faulty execution: good trade figures were greeted as a sign that British imports and exports were on the right track, and bad figures were waved aside as the result of short-term influences. This did not convince private traders and they became less and less willing to hold sterling. Until some moment in the late summer steady deflation might have maintained the existing exchange rate, though the government might not have had the electoral fortitude to impose such severe deflation and might not have been wise to try. By September or October it was too late. Everybody expected that sterling would be devalued as a result of the Community negotiations, either to adjust the British economy to the strains of entry or as a result of the breakdown of negotiations, and nobody wanted to be caught holding sterling when it happened.

A dock strike, which distorted the figures of imports and exports, was the final straw. Wilson said, quite accurately, that the monthly balance-of-payments figures for September and October were not typical. But nobody was interested: the best that could be done, as every holder of sterling hurried to buy other currencies from the Bank of England, was to arrange that the devaluation of 18 November should be a modest 14 per cent (from \$2.80 to \$2.40 to the pound), small enough not to lead to competitive devaluations by other major trading countries. The public was understandably enraged: the government had said that it was vital to avoid devaluation, had struggled to avoid devaluation, and had now devalued. De Gaulle within a couple of weeks declared that the United Kingdom was not ready to enter the Common Market and brought the negotiations to an end. When ministers looked at the problems of transferring resources to the task of exporting, they decided that the 'East of Suez' role was too expensive to maintain; troop withdrawals were hastened, and there was a further and almost final contraction of British imperial power, ironically to an accompaniment of requests from Malaysia, Singapore, and Australia that the British should stay. 'East of Suez' had been the basis of the relationship between Britain and the United States for the previous three or four years; the British withdrawal meant an end to post-imperial discussions of ways to maintain the ghost of an empire in the East.

Devaluation was followed by a ministerial change: Callaghan, the Chancellor of the Exchequer, and Jenkins, the Home Secretary, exchanged posts. By comparison with many of the Cabinet reshuffles that had become a feature of political life in the previous thirty years it was small, but it was significant. Callaghan had carried out a strenuous programme of altering the tax system and had convinced everyone of his determination to defend the sterling exchange rate, but had not been as successful at understanding the subtleties of the international monetary system; Jenkins did not impose deflationary taxation quickly enough after devaluation, but seemed more at ease with international problems. As Home Secretary he had been a convinced supporter of liberal legislation, Callaghan was distinctly less committed to change of this sort, and, although a Private Member's Bill to make divorce easier was passed soon after, this seemed to complete the current agenda for libertarian reform. This may be overstating the differences in the attitudes of the two ministers. Under Jenkins the requirements for conviction had changed from the traditional unanimous verdict of guilty from all twelve jurors to the acceptance of guilty verdicts given by a majority of ten to two, which was seen by keen advocates of civil liberties as a blow to an old-established safeguard. On the other hand, it was under Callaghan that the question of the death penalty was taken up a little earlier than had originally been required, and in

1969 the five-year suspension period was made permanent. There was fairly certainly a feeling that libertarian reform had gone as far as the public wanted: the government felt confident that it need not take any action upon the report of the Wootton Commission, which had suggested some steps towards the legalization of cannabis, or respond to an Arts Council report suggesting the ending of all censorship. Libertarians could see scope for new advances, but their failure to make any progress does suggest a general feeling that it was time for reassessment rather than fresh reforms or the reimposition of old standards.

Once Jenkins was fully established at the Exchequer, he set about convincing ministers that devaluation would be effective only if it was accompanied by deflation, or prices would rise by the amount of the currency depreciation and there would be no additional goods to supply to export markets. The housing programme, which had been pushed ahead very rapidly under Crossman in the first years of the Labour government, was cut very substantially. Between 1964 and 1967, 1,650,000 homes had been begun; between 1968 and 1971 only 1,400,000 were begun. In the period of rapid growth a good many flats had been built in tower blocks, which were found far from satisfactory, and in a few cases were not even safe. The need for new housing had been real enough, and had been met, but there was general relief that it was possible to slacken the pace and to transfer resources to other things, though most of the drop in house-building disappeared into the maw of the need for a sound budget and a balance-of-payments surplus rather than into alternative types of expenditure. Apart from the cuts in government spending, tax increases in the 1968 budget reduced demand by about £900 million, and Jenkins warned people that it would be followed by 'two years of hard slog'. At the time, the Parliamentary Labour Party welcomed the budget, mainly because it taxed investment income at above 100 per cent and thus amounted to a form of capital levy. But in a wider context the budget could be seen as the end of one more attempt to push the economy forward by driving up demand without too much thought about the effect of this financial policy upon real resources.

14

Cracking under the strain

1968–1976

The last years of the Labour government

For three or four years nobody realized how deflationary a policy Jenkins had initiated. Some of its effects were obscured by the way devaluation increases import prices immediately, which makes the balance of payments even worse for a few months, before those higher prices reduce the demand for imports, and lower export prices improve prospects for overseas sales. For some months the balance of payments remained in deficit, and fears grew that the devaluation had not gone far enough. In much the same way, deflation takes time to work its way through the system, and in 1968 people were only feeling the effects of the deflationary measures taken earlier to try to maintain the old exchange value of the pound. Government spending was kept down fairly effectively, taxes were increased again in November, and the new exchange rate was defended effectively when international confidence moved away from the dollar and towards the Deutschmark.

Those who managed to keep their jobs did not suffer any decline in living standards during the deflation, though the only workers whose real wages were allowed to go up were those who could claim that their larger-than-average wage increases would be matched by future increases in productivity. Much of the cost of deflation was met by a further drop in industrial profits, whose share of the national income had been falling for some time; the process accelerated in the late 1960s and led naturally enough to a decline in investment, which was perhaps made worse by the approach the Prices and Incomes Board took to return on investment. This passed more or less unnoticed; attention was fixed on the other victims of deflation, the unemployed, who in 1965 at the peak of demand generated by Maudling were just over 1 per cent of the working population, and were 2 per cent at the time Jenkins relaxed his stringent policy in 1970.

This increase in unemployment was intolerable for Labour supporters, who spoke as if the 1930s had returned; the government's popularity, measured by opinion polls, or at by-elections or municipal elections, sank very low, and the dissatisfaction of party members with their government threatened to become a deeper-rooted problem. Some of the wide fluctuations in public opinion in the 1960s and 1970s were due to normal discontent with the government, perhaps expressed more violently in opinion polls because people knew they influenced the government. But some of it went deeper: considerable hostility to authority flourished at the same time as a dangerous overestimation of what a government could achieve. The two attitudes were logically connected: if governments can provide a Golden Age—and earlier in the 1960s they had been ready to suggest that they could—then a government which failed to provide a Golden Age was clearly neglecting its duty for corrupt or malevolent reasons. In the late 1960s ordinary people who disliked the government simply became supporters of the Conservative Party. But people working for newspapers and broadcasting, who saw themselves as a creative minority, were committed enough to opposition to conventional ideas to find this alternative unacceptable. They wanted to attack the government for not being left-wing enough. Some of this opposition had roots in the new approach to Marxism that had begun after events in 1956 had shown how far the Stalinist version had gone wrong. This line of thought had some serious intellectual content, and it gained considerable influence in the Labour Party in the early 1970s. Another type of left-wing feeling, some of whose features were caught with brutal accuracy in the American phrase 'radical chic', rested much more on a belief that progress ought to shock the bourgeoisie. In the late 1960s the bourgeoisie seemed to have become immune to shock, whether because it was too frightened or else too pleased by the new libertarian attitudes—Leonard Woolf's comment that people in the 1960s could not realize how restricted life had been at the beginning of the century did imply that everybody would welcome the disappearance of these restrictions. Resistance to this mood of change came as much from the working class as anywhere else. Opposition to racial discrimination brought together several strands of opinion in this mood: the desire for equality, the desire for fair treatment, the desire to make moral judgements without qualifications or reservations, and the desire to hit at the sort of patriotism which said that the British were different from everyone else and probably better as well. When Enoch Powell put himself at the head of the opposition to immigration by a speech in April 1968 which hinted that rivers of blood would flow if it was not stopped, his attitude was considered shocking by every public commentator, and was obviously welcomed by much of the rest of the population. Powell and Heath parted company over the speech, but neither Heath nor anyone else could resist the mood on which Powell was playing; only about a month before his speech the government had gone back on previous commitments and had announced that Asians of Indian descent who were being expelled from Kenya would not be allowed automatically into Britain even though they held United Kingdom passports. The argument about immigration showed the relative powerlessness of broadcasting and the press to change people's minds on something they took seriously; the public was ready to say that immigrants inside the country should be treated fairly, but it was convinced that immigration had gone too far, and denunciation by those who saw themselves as leaders of opinion did little more than build up Powell as an independent political force in the country.

The 'radicalism of the communicators' was more effective in other directions. Its frequently expressed approval of the young (given added point by the fact that an unusually large proportion of the population was between 15 and 25) had a lot to do with the decision to reduce the voting age from 21 to 18 in 1969. Concern about the rights of women led to legislation requiring employers to move towards equal pay for women. In a slightly more wide-ranging way this attitude carried with it a feeling of contempt for businessmen and for politicians. Some journalists qualified their contempt for businessmen by admiring those who built up fortunes by swift and dramatic coups in which they bought or sold companies or selected the right shares to buy, but even these writers clearly regarded building up a firm by saving and reinvesting as dull and unimportant. Further to the left, opinion was even less tolerant; when Heath in 1973 referred to some exploits of adroit businessmen in avoiding tax as 'the unacceptable face of capitalism', the phrase was taken up and repeated as though he had intended it to apply to the whole of capitalism, which was certainly not what he meant.

Perhaps it was surprising that his remark attracted so much attention, for it was not a period in which politicians received much respect. Allowing for the demands of caricature, a good deal of the public mood was caught by the cartoons of Gerald Scarfe, who drew in a style of brilliant distortion which made it impossible for him to speak well of anyone. His work showed a hatred of all men holding authority that enabled him to hold up a mirror to his times, and the current of self-hatred that ran so close to the surface also matched an important part of his readers' feelings. Politicians were blamed for not bringing peace, prosperity, and happiness, even though they probably had at this time less power—because of the weakness of the British economy and the relative decline in Britain's international position—to bring peace and prosperity than they had had earlier in the century. Blaming them for this did no good, and made people happier only in the shortest of short runs.

A civil war in Nigeria illustrated several of these features of British life, including a hostility to the British Empire which might have made sense during the struggle for colonial freedom but, after decolonization had taken place so quickly and so amicably, felt rather as though people needed something to hate. The Ibo tribe waged a hard-fought civil war for a couple of years in an attempt to set up an independent nation of Biafra in the eastern region of the country. The British government, like almost all other governments, supported Nigerian unity, and was the target for a sincere, non-partisan, and ill-informed attack as a result. The supporters of Biafra said that genocide—the extermination of the whole Ibo people—was being carried out, and that the British government could and should stop it. The Nigerian government in fact conducted the civil war in a way that showed it realized that it would have to govern the Ibos after it won the war. How much influence the British government could have wielded is not clear; certainly Wilson argued in his memoirs that pressing the Nigerian government too hard would have done no good and would have reduced British influence in West Africa, because several members of the Nigerian government wanted to wage war more ruthlessly and could have got Russian support for such a policy. It was a great relief for the government when the war ended suddenly in January 1970 and peace was restored to a united Nigeria in a calm that stopped the vicarious breast-beating in Britain.

By then the government was past the worst of its troubles. In the first few months after devaluation it showed signs of breaking up. Lord Longford resigned over the delay in raising the school-leaving age. In March 1968 Brown resigned, and in July Gunter resigned; neither of them mentioned any specific point of disagreement, but both of them said the way Wilson ran his government was intolerable. Less exalted members of the Labour Party were troubled by the apparent lack of activity. Much of the 1968 parliamentary session was taken up by a immensely complex Transport Bill concerned entirely with the administrative side of transport. The simple problem of transport was that while everybody said that railways were a splendid thing, fewer and fewer people used them, and the proportion of traffic that went by road increased year by year. This could not easily be cured by legislation, but the government seemed to have nothing to offer in any other area, and certainly the Prime Minister realized that his position had suffered and could not be restored by any immediate show of activity. Before the 1967 devaluation, about half-way through his tenure of office, he had been eager to hurry off on foreign visits and in particular had tried to help to end the war in Vietnam; after devaluation he travelled less, and this withdrawal from doing anything very visible was at its most complete in 1968.

The amount of time spent in early 1969 on an attempt to reform the House of Lords strengthened the impression that the government had no policy to solve more immediate problems. The Lords had occasionally held up one or two small items of Labour legislation or orders in council, but this aroused very little public interest. As Leader of the House of Commons Crossman had made some progress in working out an agreed measure of reform with the Conservatives which would have changed the House of Lords into an assembly of nominated members chosen by the party leaders in a way that would normally give the government of the day a majority. A Bill based on these preliminary discussions was brought forward and was resisted by the Labour left, who did not want to do anything that might give the Lords a better claim to a political role, and by Conservatives who felt that a nominated majority would destroy all that was valuable in the old House of Lords. The opponents of the Bill could agree in resisting it, if in very little else, and so time-consuming were their speeches and so low the prestige of the government that the Bill had to be abandoned.

This was one of the first signs that the House of Commons was emerging from a quarter of a century of domination by the central organizations of the two major parties. Since 1945 governments could expect, much more confidently than in earlier generations, that they would get their legislation passed by the Commons; after 1969 governments could not be quite so sure about it. The House of Commons may have felt some of the loss of respect for authority that was widespread at the time, but in any case it became less predictable and this set the stage for the defeat of an attempt to amend trade union law later in the year.

A Royal Commission on trade union law (usually called after its chairman, Lord Donovan) had reported the previous year, and the majority had concluded that really nothing need be done. It pointed out that important bargaining took place at plant level rather than in the more widely publicized nationwide negotiations, but its only conclusion was that formal power should follow real power. Its lack of concern about the number of strikes was taken as a sign of complacency, and advocates of reform underlined the fact that three-quarters of the days lost in strikes went in unofficial disputes— more politely called plant bargaining by the Commission majority—and suggested that these strikes were more disruptive than official strikes. In the 1950s many of the unofficial strikes had been in the coal mines, and had no immediate effect on the rest of the economy and could be accepted as the result of the long history of bad industrial relations in coal-mining. The unofficial strikes of the 1960s in car manufacturing, the docks, and shipbuilding put a lot of other people out of work because lack of supplies closed the production processes. The number of days lost per thousand workers might be less than in the United States or Japan, but it was argued that the clear-cut and official strikes in those countries disrupted production much less. Despite this, the general tranquillity which had settled on industrial relations in the 1930s had gone on after the Second World War; in the years just after the General Strike it was still quite common to lose over 6 million days in strikes in a year, but after 1932 this level had been reached only once, in 1957. If the Donovan Report recommended letting sleeping dogs lie, at least the dogs did seem to be sleeping very soundly.

But sterner counsels prevailed; in April the government promised legislation to allow it to impose settlements in some inter-union disputes and to tell workers who had gone on unofficial strike to return to work for twenty-eight days. The accompanying provisions to make it easier to secure union recognition did not reduce trade union hostility to the prospect of fines for ignoring instructions to go back to work. British unions had been struggling for a hundred years to stop the courts having any jurisdiction over strike activity; and British firms were not liable to be fined for what they did in strikes. Unofficial strikes might be hampering production, but too many Labour MPs were committed to the trade union movement by belief, by upbringing, and by the nature of their political support for the Labour government to deal with the problem. It could not muster the votes to send the Bill to a committee for detailed discussion, so it would have to be debated in sittings of the whole House. Its Labour opponents could obstruct it and the Conservatives could put forward proposals for much more drastic legislation at a time when the government would be ill placed to defend the unions.

A satisfactory compromise might have been worked out if union leaders had been as powerful as the public imagined. Attempts to draw up a prices and incomes policy earlier in the 1960s had assumed that the Trades Union Congress (TUC) and the Federation of British Industry (FBI) later the Confederation of British Industry, (CBI) could tell their members what to do. Whatever the position of firms, trade unions had very little power to stop their members going on unofficial strike. In June the government accepted a TUC promise to try to stop unofficial strikes and gave up trying to force its Bill through Parliament. This retreat did no good. Unofficial strikes went on, although Vic Feather, the General Secretary of the TUC, hurried round trying to arbitrate disputes. Partly because the incomes policy was relaxed at the end of 1969 disputes became more common, and the number of days lost rose quite sharply. During the 1970 general election the Prime Minister had to help to get negotiations started in a newspaper strike when he needed time to campaign. Political leaders were taking on a difficult task when they tried to give collective bargaining a greater weight of authority at a time when it was hard to put new constraints on anyone's freedom of action. Increasing violence and black rioting in the United States, the 1968 riots and general strike which nearly overthrew the Fifth Republic, and the beginnings of political terrorism in Germany all show that the problem of authority was nothing unique to Britain, but this meant that trying to overcome trade unions' long-standing desire to keep the law out of collective bargaining was more likely than ever to meet resistance.

The readiness to challenge established authority which had spread so widely in the 1960s produced its most dramatic effects, so far as the United Kingdom was concerned, in Northern Ireland. The Protestant two-thirds of the population of Northern Ireland were so committed to remaining united with Britain, and the Catholic one-third so committed to joining the Irish Free State (after 1949, the Republic), that all politics focused on this single issue in a way that meant the Unionists could never lose and the Nationalists could never win an election. The majority had reinforced its position by a system of plural voting, of gerrymandered constituencies, and of allocation of jobs in local government and of welfare benefits—especially housing—that made it unlikely that the Catholic minority could play its full part politically or that the system would change into one of class politics in which poor Protestants and poor Catholics could unite to improve their economic position within the United Kingdom.

Late in the 1960s peaceful demonstrations for rights which everyone in Great Britain took for granted, like equal representation and equal chances for applicants for social benefits, did unite fair-minded Protestants with the Catholic minority. The violent response of the unbending Protestants gained for the civil rights campaign just the sort of sympathy that had been won for blacks by a similar strategy of non-violence in the American South. But history in Ireland was not on the side of non-violence. In February 1969 Terence O'Neill held an election specifically to strengthen his hand against his own right wing. He and his moderate supporters in the Unionist majority did not do well, and in April he had to retire in favour of James Chichester-Clark, who was expected to reassure the right. Even so, attacks on the Catholic areas by the more violent Unionists reached a point where the British government sent troops to Northern Ireland in the summer to protect the minority. The government could now put more pressure on the Unionists at Stormont to end the sort of discrimination that had been exposed in the Cameron Report on conditions in Northern Ireland. A good deal of progress was made in this direction, but the troops did have to work with the Northern Ireland government, and as time passed they sometimes looked a little like an instrument of the Unionists. The Catholic minority had usually seen its best hope of improvement in uniting the whole island of Ireland in one country, and the violent supporters of this policy, the Irish Republican Army (IRA), announced that they would defend the minority against the Protestants and, they claimed, against the British soldiers as defenders of the status quo.

This argument could be presented more plausibly after the change of government in June 1970. The Unionist MPs at Westminster were members of the Conservative Party, and the government had to pay some attention to their requests for a slackening of the pace of reform. Suspected troublemakers were arrested and interned without trial. Maudling, who as Home Secretary was responsible for Northern Ireland, thought these Irish problems were among the less interesting and important of his many duties, and it is only fair to say that at this point Northern Ireland needed a minister with no other responsibilities. In any case, the situation got worse. Between 1968 and 1970 thirty-nine people had been killed in skirmishes and isolated assaults; in 1971, 173 people were killed. At the same time Catholics in Protestant areas and Protestants in Catholic areas were threatened and attacked often enough to make them move house, so districts became more and more completely homogeneous. The minority moved more completely to the belief that ending partition was the only answer, but, while steps towards equality were too slow to conciliate the Catholics, they came fast enough to disturb and worry the Unionists. In 1971 Chichester-Clark in turn became a victim of the iron law that reforming Unionists offend their own right-wingers, and his place was taken by Brian Faulkner, who had at times objected to the pace of reform, though not so assertively that he was unacceptable to the British government.

In 1972 the whole system of government seemed to be breaking down. On 30 January thirteen opponents of the union with Britain were killed in the streets of Londonderry by British troops; the argument over whether they were peaceful demonstrators or a screen for an IRA attack went on for decades, but clearly such things could happen only when the country was approaching civil war. Two months later the British Parliament suspended the system set up in 1920: the Stormont Parliament was closed down and William Whitelaw was appointed minister responsible solely for Northern Ireland affairs. No immediate improvement followed; the toll of deaths rose to 467 in 1972, the process of increased separation of the two communities went grimly forward, and there were signs that the IRA proposed to widen the conflict by exploding bombs in Britain.

The initial step of sending in troops had been seen as useful and necessary, and Callaghan, as Home Secretary, handled the situation well. He went to Northern Ireland and showed every sign of feeling at home there, and he applied pressure for change at a rate which produced some effect without breaking up the Unionist government. The spirit of opposition to authority that was so active in Britain inevitably expressed itself in hostility to maintenance of the union; the fact that two-thirds of the Northern Irish population were determined to keep the union intact was ignored on the left and stressed on the right, which led to the comment that a right-winger wanted majority rule in Ulster but not in Rhodesia, while a left-winger wanted precisely the opposite.

The reputation of the Labour government was helped by its handling of the early months of the crisis, and from the middle of 1969 it made up some lost ground. Investment in North Sea gas started to show results as the new supplies began to displace gas made from coal. In the early 1960s coal production at a little over 190 million tons a year was about the same as in the late 1940s, but by 1970 the figure had fallen by about a quarter to a little over 140 million tons. New hopes for the country, and fresh problems for the coal industry, arose when significant quantities of oil were found in the North Sea in 1968 and 1969. Lord Robens, the chairman of the Coal Board, directed the policy of closing coal pits and finding new jobs for the miners with notable skill, but it was still a difficult operation and wages in this declining occupation almost inevitably fell behind those in more prosperous industries.

The policy of devaluation and deflation, and concentration on the balance of payments at all costs, began to show results. Heath had consistently failed to win people's approval even when Wilson appeared most discredited, and it looked as if the Conservatives had owed their commanding position in 1967 and 1968 to the government's unpopularity and to the fact that much less of the protest vote went to minor parties than in the 1957–8 and 1962–3 periods of comparable Conservative unpopularity. As the balance of payments began to move towards a surplus, the government seemed to have got something right at last, and its position improved. The unemployment figures stopped going up, workers felt they were getting some tangible reward for the long freeze when the prices and incomes legislation was for all practical purposes ended late in 1969, and a flood of successful wage claims swept in. The change of mood which followed was natural enough, but it had been so completely taken for granted that the Labour government was doomed that everybody was astonished at the recovery. The Conservative leaders held a private conference at Selsdon Park with mixed results. They gained support for their proposals to limit the power of trade unions and defend law and order against the relaxed standards of the 1960s, but people were uneasy about their support for the free play of the market, and reducing government intervention in the economy sounded like cuts in the social services.

Taxes were reduced by about £220 million in the 1970 budget, but the remission looked so slight when the government had all the room for manoeuvre provided by a budget surplus of about £3 billion and a balance-of-payments surplus of £1 billion that it was taken as a sign that there would be no election in the immediate future. But as the opinion polls moved to show a Labour lead, with some confirmation from the party's reasonably good performance in the municipal elections, it was natural for Wilson to think of an election. Asking for a dissolution used to be a formal Cabinet decision but is now understood to be the responsibility of the Prime Minister alone. Prime Ministers sometimes take a good deal of advice before acting, and Wilson took pains to see that the Cabinet and most of the parliamentary party agreed with his decision before announcing that there would be an election on 18 June. By the last few days before the announcement the Labour Party was so convinced that it would win that Wilson could quite justifiably write in his memoirs, 'Had I decided against a June election I would have been adjudged certifiable'.[1]

The surveys and municipal elections showed only that, after lagging behind for years, the government had become more popular than the Opposition for one or two months, but at the time all the politicians except Heath thought Labour would hold most of its seats. What it would do with its majority was far from clear. A Bill to provide workers with pensions linked to their earnings was almost the only piece of legislation Labour had to offer. Wilson put his claim for re-election by saying that the balance-of-payments surplus showed that Labour could govern more competently than the Conservatives. As he was not going to say anything specific, he campaigned by visiting committee

---

1. Harold Wilson, *The Labour Government 1964–1970* (1971), 781.

rooms, saying a few confident sentences for television, and radiating a general conviction that all was well. Like any Leader of the Opposition, Heath had to say things were going badly, and he dwelt on the steady rise in prices, which he claimed a thrifty and efficient Conservative government would hold in check. On election night everybody was just getting ready to say he had again fought a sober and uninspiring campaign when the first results came in and at once showed that the Conservatives would have a modest but perfectly adequate majority.

	Votes	Seats	% of all votes cast
Conservative	13,145,123	330	46.4
Liberal	2,117,033	6	7.5
Labour	12,178,295	287	43.0
All others	906,345	7	3.2

The hints of a nationalist movement in Scotland and Wales faded away. Labour regained the seats lost to the Scottish and the Welsh nationalists in by-elections, though the Scottish Nationalists won a seat in the Western Isles. The two major parties between them received about eight-ninths of the total votes cast, which meant that as many voters as in the 1960s, though not quite as many as in the 1950s, found one or other major party was politically satisfactory.

Heath in control

The result was regarded very much as Heath's own victory; he had remained confident when everyone round him believed the gloomy tale of the opinion polls, which probably confirmed his inclination not to listen very hard to his colleagues' views in future. His own deepest commitment was to Europe, and here he could get off to a quick start because the Labour government had begun preparing a new application after de Gaulle resigned in 1969. His successor, President Pompidou, might not have inherited all of his prestige, but it was soon clear that he was in a position to veto the application if he chose. It was not until May 1971 that Pompidou made it known, after a long private discussion with Heath, that he was satisfied about Britain's European credentials. This probably meant he had been convinced that Heath believed that entering the EEC was something valuable that should be pursued for its own sake and not just used as part of a plan for repairing the British economy or building up Britain's political standing. Heath may well have been the only British politician who could have persuaded the President that he was in earnest about this, and he probably went on to show that what he wanted was a close association of countries, not a single superstate into which Britain and France and the rest would merge and disappear.

Once Pompidou had given his approval, the Brussels negotiations went ahead quickly. The British negotiators knew they had to accept the Treaty of Rome if they were to be taken seriously, and that, whatever might have been attempted in 1962, the best they could now do was to obtain transitional arrangements to soften and delay the shock of entry. In particular they accepted the general principle of the Common Agricultural Policy that the six original members had worked out in the mid-1960s. The Commission kept farm incomes up by imposing tariffs on food from outside the Community and buying produce from inside the Community at prices high enough to give farmers a fair standard of living, even when this meant paying considerably more than world prices. This policy almost unavoidably produced surpluses of food which had to be stored or sold at a reduced price with the help of subsidies from EEC taxpayers, because nobody else would buy it at the prices paid by the Commission. When touring Europe to make his application in 1967, Wilson had told the member of the Commission responsible for agriculture that this would cost the British balance of payments $760 million—then £270 million—a year if it was not modified. This figure, like the implied increase in food prices, may have been overstated, but it indicates one aspect of the struggle over the EEC which was so important a part of British politics between 1971 and 1975.

These questions of food prices helped to reduce the willingness to negotiate which the Labour Party had shown when in office, though Labour supporters of entry said a Labour government might have found the terms Heath negotiated at Brussels entirely satisfactory. When the Commons debated the general principle of entry in October 1971, Wilson announced that a Labour government would renegotiate the terms or leave the Community. While both major parties were divided on the issue, Labour supporters of entry were more numerous than the Conservative opponents; in a free vote after the October debate, the government's White Paper was welcomed by 356 votes to 244, thirty-nine Conservatives voting against it and sixty-nine Labour MPs for it, which suggested that the government could carry the enabling legislation to give effect to the treaty through the Commons without difficulty. In reality Labour supporters of entry could approve the general principle on a free vote but could hardly ignore the party whips on a steady succession of small issues, so opponents of entry could hope to defeat the government on some issue on which the Labour Party was united and some Conservatives voted with it, and at the very least force Heath to return to the negotiating table. This strategy would have been almost certain to succeed if the government had had to put forward the whole treaty in its Bill. Even the relatively short Bill that it submitted took up the great bulk of the 1972 session. Because the minorities within the two major parties placed the question of Europe on something like the same level of importance as party loyalty, the voting was unpredictable enough to bring a tension into the conflict that had not been known since the great nineteenth-century battles of 1866–7 and 1886. On Second Reading the majority was only eight, on the Common Agricultural Policy it was down to five, and on movements of capital within the Community it fell to four. A more flexible man than Heath would have faltered, or tried to find a compromise where none was to be found. He stuck to his position, the Bill moved into calmer waters, and at last passed Third Reading on 13 July by 301 votes to 284.

Early in 1972 the idea of a referendum came into the discussion. The three other countries negotiating for entry at the same time as Britain arranged to hold referendums—Denmark and Ireland voted in favour of entry, Norway voted against—and Pompidou held a referendum to find whether the French were in favour of the enlargement of the EEC. While a referendum was a thoroughly European device, it could not be dismissed as something unheard of in the British constitution, because ten days after Pompidou announced the French referendum the British government proposed that referendums should be held periodically in Northern Ireland to reassure Unionists that nobody would try to push them into the Republic against their wishes. From a wider point of view a referendum seemed in accordance with the ideas of greater popular participation in government which had gained ground in the later 1960s. A week after Pompidou announced the French referendum, the National Executive Committee of the Labour Party committed the party to a referendum on membership of the EEC.

Britain became a member of the EEC, under the transitional arrangements worked out at Brussels, at the beginning of 1973. By that time the pressure of the 1972 session and the desire to get membership off to a good start had combined with the government's concern about its normal mid-term unpopularity to make Heath take drastic action to put more vitality into the economy. The Conservatives were never as unpopular as the Labour government in the late 1960s, and Heath always received a fair amount of support from intellectual leaders of opinion because of his position on Europe. Among most people who earned their living by handling ideas and concepts—except among economists, who were relatively evenly divided on its merits—the idea of entering the Community was becoming the accepted orthodoxy. The Labour Party was blamed for changing its mind after accepting entry from 1966 to 1970, and the general attitude expressed in public was that the Conservatives ought to be supported because of their position on Europe.

While this strengthened their position, the Conservatives could not have faced an election in 1971 or 1972 with any confidence. Their economic policy was based on so complete a misinterpretation of what was happening in the economy that it threatened to undermine the government, and they might have thought about their trade union policy more carefully if they had realized how much resistance it was going to encounter. A Conservative government is naturally likely to feel that its Labour predecessor has been imposing excessively heavy taxes and indulging in over-lavish government spending, and Heath's ministers could hardly have helped starting with this idea in June 1970. The campaign encouraged them to believe that the main problem in the economy was the high level of inflation and the shaky nature of the balance-of-payments surplus of the last months of the 1960s. Heath's attacks on rising prices had been well received, and an unexpected deficit in the May trade figures encouraged the idea that the economy was being pushed quite fast enough.

Conservative strategy probably suffered because of the death, within a month of taking office, of Iain Macleod, the Chancellor of the Exchequer. His successor, Anthony Barber, was more interested in reorganizing the system of taxation than most Chancellors. The two innovations made by Asquith in 1907 had never been fully fitted into the rest of the income tax system: Barber wanted to integrate the old standard rate of income tax and the separately administered tax called surtax on higher incomes, which began at £5,000 a year in 1971, into a single income tax rising by steps; and he also wanted to end the calculation of earned income relief, by which taxpayers paid only on a major fraction—seven-ninths in 1971—of earned income which did not come from interest, rent, or dividends, and replace it with a lower nominal rate of income tax with a special investment surcharge on interest, rent, and dividends. Party policy committed him to getting rid of the existing selective employment tax, and his need for revenue, together with the rules of the EEC, led him to set up a value added tax in its place. This tax was designed to be entirely neutral except that it could be remitted in the case of exports; processors and manufacturers and wholesalers and retailers all paid a tax at the same rate upon the amount by which the article had increased in cost ('value added') between their buying it and their selling it to the next person in the chain. The tax was complicated to set up and to administer, and involved everyone except the final customer in an elaborate relationship with the tax authorities. The net effect on revenue and on demand of these tax changes was not meant to be substantial, but they naturally took up a great deal of Barber's attention.

This left him too little time to analyse the economic situation and appreciate how much the Labour government had reduced the level of demand in the economy. He also failed to notice the way his colleagues' attitude to government spending changed as they carried out the policies to which they were committed. His announcement in the autumn of 1970 that there would be a number of cuts in government spending, and that income tax would be reduced by 2.5p, was clearly in accordance with party principle and the view that the government was spending and taxing too much. People still thought the economy was running at a high level of demand, and tax cuts were expected to make businessmen more enterprising in their approach. The non-interventionist frame of mind which had led the Conservatives to oppose prices and incomes policies in the late 1960s was made clear when John Davies, the Minister for Trade and Industry, declared that it was not the government's intention to help 'lame ducks', as he called industries that needed subsidies if they were to survive.

By the end of 1970 the weakness of this analysis was clear. The balance-of-payments surplus was perfectly soundly based, but unemployment, stationary in late 1969, was once more rising alarmingly rapidly and was reaching levels that had not been seen in the post-war period. By the time the government realized what was happening it looked as if a million people would soon be out of work, while the 1971 balance-of-payments surplus was so large that the government seemed to be free from this habitual constraint on its freedom of action. Early in 1971 Davies had to confront a very prominent lame duck: the famous car and aero-engine firm of Rolls-Royce had set out to develop a new aero-engine without fully estimating the costs, by 1970 it was having difficulty raising money to continue the programme, and by February 1971 it was bankrupt. Losing this old-established firm with its well-deserved reputation for very high-quality production would have been a heavy blow to national pride at any time; to make matters worse, the new engine was intended for aeroplanes produced by the American firm of Lockheed, and if Rolls-Royce stopped work it would drag Lockheed down with it. The American economy was in the same listless condition as the British, and the US government was in no mood to have its unemployment made worse by British opposition to government intervention. Within days of Rolls-Royce's announcement of bankruptcy, American pressure and British pride had forced the government to rescue it. The firm was nationalized, the motor car section was sold back to private ownership, and the aero-engine side went on under government ownership. This was embarrassing, but at least it was over quickly. In June Upper Clyde Shipyards, which had been put together by the Labour government with lavish subsidies as part of the policy of intervention and concentration, went bankrupt. The workers responded by taking over the shipyard and announcing that they would go on working with the materials already available. By occupying the shipyard they prevented any reorganization that depended on selling off the assets and by going on working they made it much harder for anyone to talk about lazy workers going on strike. Partly for these reasons and partly for fear of a revival of Scottish nationalism if unemployment spread on the Clyde, the government found itself forced into a policy of intervention to save the shipyard from closing.

Rolls-Royce and Upper Clyde Shipyards were conspicuous departures from the principle of non-intervention, but they did not cost very much money. Much larger increases in government spending took place in health, education, and local government. The 1970 election platform recommended keeping expenditure down and leaving the public with a larger portion of their earnings in the form of disposable income, but in practice these ministries spent money as lavishly as any peacetime British government, perhaps mainly out of a feeling that the government should be generous in order to raise the level of demand and reduce unemployment. In the last year of Labour government public spending had been equal to 50 per cent of the national income; by 1972 this figure had risen to 52 per cent.

For centuries local government organization consisted of making towns of sufficient importance into boroughs and leaving the rest of the country organized in counties, which naturally were rural in emphasis. This made a good deal of sense when towns wanted a distinctly higher level of services in paving, lighting, and water supply than the surrounding countryside did, and when religious differences between urban Free Churchmen and the rural Church of England meant that they saw no prospect of agreement on educational questions. But by the second half of the twentieth century these problems mattered much less; the Churches' only concern about educational politics was the percentage of the costs of their schools that the government would pay, while large towns and their hinterlands had to work together much more than at the beginning of the century on questions like overspill housing from cities, the impact of road transport, and the location of places of work for suburban commuters. In 1969 a Royal Commission under Lord Redcliffe-Maud had recommended a very sweeping change of local government, and most of its suggestions were accepted. The most striking proposal was that half a dozen large 'conurbation' authorities should be created which would administer a whole heavily urbanized region like Merseyside or South Yorkshire. Other regional authorities were set up to run the affairs of large cities and the countryside round them; the new county of Avon, for instance, included Bristol and its rural hinterland. The Report also suggested reducing elected authorities from something over a thousand to something over a hundred by eliminating the smallest authorities, the urban district and rural district councils.

Reducing the number of authorities looked like a simplification of local government, but this was true only in the sense that there would be fewer elected councillors. The amount of work to be done by councils remained unchanged, and in one area it increased significantly. The Seebohm Commission had just proposed increasing the number of social workers and improving their qualifications and pay. This precisely fitted developments in the universities; more students had been graduating, and the expanding profession of social work, like the traditional profession of teaching, fitted the prevailing attitude of repugnance to commercial or industrial careers. Spending on social work rose sharply in percentage terms, but a much larger total increase was caused by following the practice of the most open-handed authority when amalgamating several of them. The financial problems caused by consolidating the staff after reducing the number of authorities was made much worse by councillors' readiness to imagine that they were skilled land developers who could undertake ambitious, not to say speculative, schemes of new commercial building. Some of these schemes had corrupt overtones; in the early 1970s the bankruptcy of John Poulson's architectural firm revealed that for some years he had been manipulating the decisions of a number of Scottish and north of England councils by bribing administrative and elected officials. Other cases of municipal corruption, of which perhaps the most widely ramifying was in South Wales, came to light at about the same time. Enough of them were in old-established Labour strongholds to suggest that the root of the trouble was councillors with entrenched power who welcomed development and could be persuaded to help it along for relatively small amounts of money.

Spending on education also increased, though not for such dubious reasons. Probably the most important development during Margaret Thatcher's three and a half years as Minister was the fulfilment of the Labour policy of comprehensive education; in 1970 less than a third of secondary schoolchildren were in comprehensive schools, and by 1974 the figure was over two-thirds. It might seem much less important that her response, when Barber demanded economies in his first few months of office, was to stop supplying free milk to primary schoolchildren irrespective of parental income, but milk and a means test were emotional matters; putting the two together made her look like an ogre and made it harder for her to resist other pressures for spending. Some of the money went to improve education for the youngest children, and the long-awaited raising of the school leaving age to 16, which was due to come in 1973, led to growing pressure to provide more teachers. A really powerful minister might have resisted this and shown that a great many children were already staying for an extra year and that the population of school age was about to drop as a result of the decline in the birth rate in the 1960s; instead, as popular pressure built up, there was a dramatic and unjustified increase in the number of recruits for the teaching profession encouraged to enter the training colleges, though by the time they emerged the need for additional teachers had vanished.

In something of the same spirit of generous government spending, the administration of health and social services was changed. Sir Keith Joseph later came, like Thatcher, to be regarded as an opponent of high expenditure and bureaucratic control, but in his 1972 reorganization of the health service he showed the readiness to spend money and to increase the proportion of civil servants to doctors, nurses, and other health staff which in theory he disliked. He did not desert his principles just because he had become a minister, but he realized that these administrative changes, on which reductions in government spending would depend, were being carried out at a time when the rising tide of unemployment held out alarming prospects for the Conservatives' popularity and their EEC policy. Despite periodic increases the insurance benefits set up by the legislation of the late 1940s had never been high enough to avoid making a large number of claimants dependent on national assistance or, as it was later called, supplementary benefit. Insurance benefits came as a matter of right; supplementary benefit was means-tested. Joseph tried to reduce the discretionary element, and the attendant bitterness, by setting up a family income supplement scheme to provide a minimum entitlement for each family, though this entitlement could not be kept high enough to avoid the need for supplementary benefit without undermining all the insurance schemes, and rising unemployment naturally pushed more people into needing supplementary benefit.

Unemployment fairly certainly strengthened resistance to Conservative trade union policy. The Industrial Relations Act of 1971 fulfilled their election commitment to restrain the power of the unions, and went considerably further towards the North American attitude to trade unions that was implied in the Labour 1969 Bill. Unions had to register if they were to go on enjoying the special legal status they had acquired over the years; ballots before strikes could be imposed if the government thought it appropriate, and so could delays of up to sixty days before strikes began, with fines (and the implication of prison if the fines were not paid) for workers who did not obey the law. Unions, whether registered or not, could also be fined, but this was less likely to cause trouble because it did not imply imprisonment. This put rather more power over their members into the hands of the union leaders, a gift they had no desire to receive. British trade unionists believed American unions accepted this system of registration and control by the courts because in return the law made employers recognize them as legitimate bargainers; British unions were proud that they had won a comparable position without any help from the law. Trade unionists shared the widespread belief that the government could intervene to manipulate the economy in any way it chose, and the rapid rise in unemployment while the Industrial Relations Bill was going through Parliament encouraged the belief that the government wanted to weaken the working class by creating a pool of unemployed workers while turning the unions into part of the employers' apparatus for obtaining adequate and disciplined labour.

It is most unlikely that the government had such grandiose ideas, but the blend of Marxist and conspiracy theories so widespread at the time did encourage unions to resist more fiercely than they might otherwise have done. The TUC resolved that member unions should formally remove themselves from the government's register, and it suspended the membership of those which refused to do so. One-day strikes were held to protest against the Act, and the Engineers' Union incurred several large fines because its members were particularly apt to become involved in offences against the Act. The Act did nothing to improve industrial relations, and may have made them worse. Between 1970 and 1974 almost as many days were lost in strikes as in the five years of labour unrest before 1914, and one government was discredited and replaced by another which seemed alarmingly dependent on the trade unions. But this cannot all be attributed to the Act: in 1970 days lost had already risen to 10 million, and the increase to 13.5 million days lost in 1971 must have owed something to pressure for wage increases. Unions did not usually demand wage increases so aggressively when unemployment was going up, but prices did not usually keep rising so fast in a recession. Despite a Confederation of British Industry undertaking in July to keep price increases down to 5 per cent, and a government commitment to keep down prices in the nationalized industries by subsidizing their losses, prices went up by about 9 per cent in 1971 and money wages went up by about 10 per cent.

Out of control

In 1971 the government realized that the economy was suffering from severe deflation. Taxes were reduced, in two steps, by about £500 million, or about 1 per cent of the national income. Bank credit was relaxed, and so were the government and Bank of England directives which ever since 1939 had advised banks that certain types of borrowers, such as exporters or house builders, were to be given priority and other types of borrowers, such as dealers in property, were to be avoided as far as possible. The clearing banks—reduced by this stage to four large and seven or eight smaller houses—cooperated with one another in observing these rules and in making sure that none of them suffered as a result of doing so. Early in 1971 Barber announced in the White Paper *Competition and Credit Control* that the banks should compete with each other, and should compete simply by lending money to good risks without asking whether they were in priority categories or not. It was only after the supply of broad money (M3) had increased about 84 per cent in three years that cynics said arrangements had been made for competition but not for credit control.

The change was meant to stimulate development and to allow the businessmen who were taking the risks to decide what were the best opportunities for expansion. But, while new money can be put into circulation at the stroke of a pen, it takes time for industrial managers to carry out investment in new factories or machines. Economic conditions between 1968 and 1971 had not encouraged investment, and it took several months for industrialists to alter course. Meanwhile the banks had to lend the new money coming into their hands, and they had no official restraints on lending policy. They lent to people who wanted to buy existing assets, and as a result the price of shares on the Stock Exchange and the price of houses went up very impressively: houses in the London area doubled in price between mid-1971 and mid-1972, and it was noticed that the share index reached a peak just as unemployment touched 1 million early in 1972. This was the way the theory of the free market said expansion usually started; and in 1973 and again in 1974 the proportion of the national income devoted to investment did go up. But the government was in no mood to wait for this, and in his 1972 budget the Chancellor reduced taxes by over £1 billion. Unemployment fell so soon after this that it could not have been caused by the monetary effects of the budget, though no doubt the changes were good for confidence. Wages went up very fast, rising in money terms by something like 18 per cent and, as the rise in prices slackened slightly, in real terms by something over 10 per cent.

This was of course too good to last, but the economy was at the happy stage of the economic cycle where real wages and investment can increase at the same time; optimists always attribute this to bringing unused resources and unemployed workers back into the system, and pessimists say that it always causes a deterioration in the balance of payments, which in 1972 showed neither surplus nor deficit. Economic expansion was probably helped by the government's announcement that it would not be tied to defending a fixed rate of exchange, which meant that it regretted the cooperative attitude it had taken in the currency disturbances of 1971. Since 1945 the industrialized nations had run in slightly different trade cycles, so they were never all expanding or all contracting at the same time. By 1970 these cycles had moved much closer together, and nearly all the industrialized nations were in a recession at the same time. In August 1971 President Nixon announced that the United States would no longer buy gold from central banks at a fixed rate of $35 an ounce. For some years the United States had been having difficulty in maintaining the Bretton Woods system with its fixed dollar price for gold, but the announcement caught the world without any immediately acceptable system to replace it. Nixon's step showed what had been at stake in the British government's long defence of the exchange rate, for after the 1967 devaluation other rates had changed too often for the system to survive. The Bretton Woods system could only work if nations were willing to subject their own economies to some inconvenience in order to keep it going.

When an attempt was made, at the Smithsonian Institution in Washington at the end of 1971, to establish a new range of fixed exchange rates, the British government was persuaded to accept a rate of $2.60 to the pound, or 8 per cent above the 1967–71 level. Germany and Japan moved their currencies up further against the US dollar, but their trading position in the post-war world had been strong enough to justify the step. Britain's performance did not justify moving above the 1967–71 level; the government's abandonment of the fixed rate recognized this and also recognized that the Smithsonian system was not likely to last long. This was accepted early in 1973 and the world moved to a system of floating rates very like that of the 1930s, though governments realized that they had to cooperate more than they had done before 1939. Discussion in

Britain still concentrated on the pound–dollar exchange rate, but the 'Smith-sonian depreciation', giving the pound's value in terms of the currencies of all important trading countries, was a better indicator of the position, and it showed that the pound went down by about 10 per cent in 1972.

When Nixon cut the link between gold and the dollar, he also established a prices and incomes policy which ran quite satisfactorily for about two years. It was at the peak of its success, and Nixon was on the verge of an overwhelming victory in the presidential election, in the autumn of 1972. By then Heath wanted to do something similar, but at first he felt inhibited by his party's opposition to the Labour government's prices and incomes policy. Several members of his party felt deeply committed to avoiding the sort of direct intervention needed to run a prices and incomes policy. When he held discussions with the TUC and the CBI, the TUC came very close to saying that the government must adopt the policy of the Labour Party, including repeal of the Industrial Relations Act; and in November Heath switched to a policy very like Nixon's. During a three-month freeze no increases would be allowed, and then, after a Pay Board and a Prices Commission had been set up, maximum increases of £1 a week plus 4 per cent of existing wages would be permitted.

This 'U-turn' was reasonably popular. The Labour Party was losing ground, perhaps because of its internal divisions over the EEC, perhaps because Labour policy was moving to the left with the adoption of a policy of 'a fundamental and irreversible shift in the balance of power and wealth'. The increasing number and intensity of strikes must have hurt the Labour Party as well. In 1972 the number of days lost in strikes rose to 24 million. About half of this was lost in a national coal strike early in the year in which the miners reacted against the deterioration in their position in the 1960s. They won a good deal of popular support, and they were able to make their strike effective unusually quickly by picketing power stations. The government had to give way, a great many other unions followed where the miners had led, and they looked like the motive power driving prices up. For whatever reason, the Labour lead in opinion polls became less impressive in 1973 than it had been in 1971 and 1972, though the polls, and some striking by-election results, suggested that voters had gone Liberal rather than Conservative.

The bills for the unsustainably fast expansion of 1972 were beginning to arrive, by no means all from inside Britain. Several central banks relaxed their monetary policies between mid-1971 and early 1973 to an extent that suggested they had taken seriously *The Economist*'s offhand comment, offered a fort-night after Nixon cut the link with gold, that 'Finance ministers . . . should welcome the freedom of not having to look over their shoulders all the time at their balances of payments and to be able [*sic*] to pursue economic goals which should be much more vote-gaining.' All over the world people responded by rushing to buy anything that seemed safer than cash. In Britain, or at least in London, the feature of this international urge to spend that attracted most attention was the boom in pictures and other works of art, which enriched the art dealers and must later have left many of the purchasers aware that they had bought things in which they were not really interested at prices which were not maintained for more than a few months. The price of property went up steadily; easy credit encouraged dealers to buy blocks of flats and sell them to the individual occupiers or to acquire pieces of land which they could develop and sell at a much higher price if they got planning permission. Barber did little to restrain this: he called his 1973 budget 'neutral', by which he meant that taxes were not changed and the public sector would again have to borrow about £2 billion. While money remained readily available, interest rates rose: the rates on long-term government bonds went up to 12 per cent in 1973 and industrial firms had to pay even more, which made fixed investment difficult, though dealers in shares or property expected to make their profit so quickly that the cost of borrowing would not affect them much. The relaxing of credit control had encouraged the development of new 'secondary' banks which borrowed at high rates and lent at even higher, without maintaining the large reserves or the nationwide branch system of the clearing banks. Their flexibility in handling money and their optimism about the future made them the natural source of funds for traders who expected to turn their money over in a short time.

For several years the price asked for British exports had gone up slightly faster than the price of imports. In 1973 this was dramatically reversed; a great many raw materials from wheat to copper and from sugar to gold (freedom from its links to the dollar left it free to move like any other commodity) went up in price. Membership of the EEC insulated Britain from some of these problems of sharply fluctuating food prices, but still the pressure threatened to cut into the standard of living. With this fear the government put forward its plan for the 1973–4 phase of its incomes policy: an ill-defined increase of a little over 7 per cent would be allowed in any case, and if the cost of living went up more than 7 per cent it would be taken to have passed a 'threshold' after which a wage increase of 40p would be allowed, and each further 1 per cent increase in prices would allow another 40p in wages. This meant that real pre-tax wages increased with each threshold that was passed for everyone earning the average wage or less. No doubt the authors of this scheme felt quite sure that price increases would be below 7 per cent and just wanted to assure wage-earners that the existing standard of living was a fixed point from which they would not fall. This looked reasonable because living standards had not slipped back, except for workers who became unemployed, at any time since the Second World War, but consumption had never risen so much faster than production as it had in 1972. The consumer boom had come earlier in the cycle than in 1958–60 (the most comparable consumer boom), and people would need quite as much good fortune as in the 1950s if they were to keep what they had just gained.

As in the 1950s, television was the striking novelty in the boom—this time, colour television. The number of licences for colour sets more or less doubled every year from 1970 to 1974, rising from 200,000 in 1969, when it was still regarded as an unreliable toy that ate up television revenue for the sake of a minority interest, to 5.5 million in 1974, when it dominated the scene. Although most of the sets in use were still monochrome, no television producer thought in black and white, and nobody objected to the idea of buying colour sets in the way people had objected on intellectual grounds to buying television sets at all in the 1950s. The growth of colour television coincided with a sharp drop in film-making in Britain. Spending on film production dropped to about a third of the level of the late 1960s, and a fair amount of what was made came from firms closely linked to television. American money had financed the boom of the 1960s, and American money was leaving, possibly to concentrate on very expensive productions in the United States, possibly because Britain no longer provided the mixture of glitter and social conflict that had been the basis for films made in Britain in the 1960s. There was certainly no diminution in the number of talented people available; though there were so few opportunities in film-making, the television companies were able to recruit very successful teams for production in serial form of adaptations of books like *The Forsyte Saga* and Trollope's six parliamentary novels, or for long illustrated lecture series like Lord Clark's *Civilisation*. For actors in these series it was possible to draw on a great range of talent in the theatre, though here a curious and not entirely welcome division was appearing. The government had committed itself to supporting the theatre, and by the early 1970s two successful national companies, the Royal Shakespeare Company and the National Theatre—still based on the Old Vic theatre—were doing well. The trouble was that they were doing so well that the commercial theatres had some difficulty in competing in the realm of serious drama and seemed willing to avoid the challenge by returning to triviality. Undoubtedly this was what a lot of people wanted, and the two-level theatre, of subsidized serious work and commercial triviality, might be the best that anyone could do. Certainly theatres flourished, and, just as the sale of television shows was one sort of export, the British theatre was one of the attractions which by the mid-1970s had gone a long way towards turning tourism into a positive item in the balance of payments.

None of this, pleasant though it was, could meet the drain on the balance of payments of the flood of imports for the boom. The government said that it was going all out for growth. Whether this approach could ever have worked is doubtful, but must for ever remain unknown because the government's position was destroyed by two problems concerned with fuel. The miners had at the time been reasonably satisfied by the 1972 settlement, but after eighteen months of rising prices and generous wage settlements they had lost most of the ground they had gained. The government recognized this, and offered allowances for shift working in its pay rules for 1973–4 which would let the miners receive increases well above the average. The Coal Board offered the whole increase at once; the miners assumed that, as in normal bargaining, there was more to come. In November they decided, just after events in the Middle East had improved their bargaining position, to stop the overtime working on which British mines depended for their normal level of production.

By 1974 Britain imported about 2 million barrels of oil a day. This immense increase in consumption, which had cut away the position of coal-mining and had not even been much affected by the development of the natural gas in the North Sea, owed a great deal to the unchanged or even reduced prices that had been asked in the 1950s and 1960s. By the beginning of the 1960s the countries from which the oil came were so annoyed by the way they got no better prices for their exports while import prices went up that they formed the Organization of Petroleum Exporting Countries (OPEC), and pushed up oil prices like most commodity prices in the early 1970s. When another war broke out between Israel and Egypt in October 1973, the Arab oil-producing countries imposed a partial embargo on oil for the West, and the members of OPEC found that they could raise oil prices sharply and successfully. By the end of the year the price had increased by about $8 a barrel, which meant that Britain's oil bill would go up by £2.5 billion a year. While this strengthened the miners' position, the government was afraid that mining productivity would not go up even if there was a large wage increase, and it decided to resist the miners. Their successful strike in 1972 was thought to have encouraged the great wave of inflation, and the government believed that other unions would not accept the miners as a special case and would press forward with claims to match anything the miners were awarded. In December, when the ban on overtime was beginning to affect stocks of coal, the government announced reductions in spending calculated to lower demand by over £1 billion, and special measures to reduce fuel consumption, of which the most startling was that factories would be supplied with power for only three days a week, and would have to make the best working arrangements they could. The three-day week worked better than might have been expected, production fell by only about 20 per cent, and it looked as if the stocks of coal might last through the winter. By mid-January the government announced that a four-day week might be practicable. But the miners were determined to get their pay increase; they took a ballot among their members which produced an 80 per cent vote in favour of a strike. Ministers had already been discussing holding a general election; the prospect of a miners' strike, which would probably have meant a two-day week, made an election inevitable.

The Conservatives felt the prospects were good, and the Labour Party was decidedly worried: it was true that the miners were probably more respected, because of the unpleasantness and danger of their job, than any other workers, but strikes and trade unions were not popular causes to defend. As unemployment returned to roughly the 1970 level and was falling fast, and as real wages were still going up, the economy seemed to be doing well, and the miners and the Labour Party might be accused of ruining it. On the other hand, the Conservative claim that the election was about who governs Britain did not have much effect. The government suffered because of rising prices and also because of a feeling that it had been so abrasive that it had brought questions about its authority upon itself. The Labour Party had its own answer to the problems of rising prices and the place of trade unions in ruling the country; the party leadership and the union leadership said they would agree on a 'social contract' (sometimes referred to as a 'social compact') which meant that the Labour Party would carry out certain reforms and the unions would be responsible about wage claims. So little of this had been worked out by the time of the election that people could only have voted for it in a spirit of trust in their leaders. Trust was clearly in short supply, and the major parties were going to suffer for this. In Northern Ireland the intransigent Unionists successfully challenged the Unionists who worked with the Conservatives. Scottish Nationalists, who in 1969 had suffered when the Treasury published a hypothetical 'Scottish budget' to show that Scotland could not afford independence, could now say firmly that all their plans for the country were possible because the oil in the North Sea was in the territory that would belong to an independent Scotland. And the Liberals, who in 1959 and in 1964 had seen a substantial bridgehead in public opinion shrivel and fade away as the election came closer, now had a chance to fight while discontent with the major parties was still rising to a peak. The Labour Party benefited from one of the few interventions by a private citizen that has changed votes in a recent election; Enoch Powell announced that he would vote Labour because its policy of trying to amend the conditions of British membership of the EEC and then submitting the results to the people held out the prospect of escape from the continental entanglements into which Heath had led the country. Powell's position as a leader of opinion owed so much to his attacks on immigration that the Labour Party cannot have been completely happy about his support, but it would have been impossible, and imprudent as well, to repudiate it.

Nevertheless, the opinion polls showed that the Conservatives would get slightly more votes than the Labour Party; and this forecast turned out to be correct. What could not be predicted was that the Labour Party won four more seats than the Conservatives. It has been argued that this was the result of tactical voting by supporters of the Labour Party who voted Liberal or Nationalist in seats that Labour could not win, in order to keep the Conservatives out. The estimate is that this cost Labour 350,000 votes, but cost the Conservatives three seats.[2] This result may not have been caused by such

2. M. Steed, in app. to D. E. Butler and D. Kavanagh, *The British General Election of February 1974* (1974), 328.

conscious calculation, for one would have thought that such sophisticated supporters of the Labour Party would have declared their views to opinion pollsters. Perhaps Labour voters in hopeless seats were a little shaken by the unpopularity of trade unions among their neighbours and took the less controversial course of voting for a third party.

	Votes	Seats	% of all votes cast
Conservative	11,868,906	296	37.8
Liberal	6,063,470	14	19.3
Labour	11,639,243	301	37.1
Scottish Nationalist	632,032	7	2.0
Plaid Cymru	171,364	2	0.5
United Ulster Unionist	366,703	11	1.2
Others	598,444	4	1.9

Heath tried negotiating with the Liberals to put together a coalition, but the Liberals pointed out that a Liberal–Conservative alliance would fall short of a majority, and that the Labour Party could count on enough votes from Plaid Cymru and the Independents and from the determination of the United Ulster Unionists to vote against what they regarded as the anti-unionist approach of the Conservatives to mean that even a theoretically possible alliance of Conservatives, Liberals, and Scottish Nationalists was most unlikely to be able to survive. The Scottish Nationalists had done well, running far ahead of the Liberals in Scotland (Conservatives 21 seats with 32.9 per cent of the vote; Liberals 3 with 7.9 per cent; Labour 40 with 36.6 per cent; SNP 7 with 21.9 per cent). The Liberals were understandably disappointed that they had won very few seats because their support was spread thinly but evenly all across the country. Liberal activists saw themselves as being on the left and would not have wanted to support a Conservative government; Liberal voters were more likely to have reflected the general feeling that Heath had had his chance at sharpening issues and putting them aggressively and that it was now time for something more emollient.

One step at a time

And so Harold Wilson became Prime Minister again, somewhat to his surprise. He could have been forgiven for feeling that becoming Prime Minister in 1974 was much less pleasant than it had been in 1970 or even 1964. A settlement had to be found to get the miners back to work as soon as possible. The balance-of-payments deficit was reaching levels that dwarfed previous crises; in 1973 it had been about £1.5 billion, and the increased price of oil would probably raise it to about £4 billion even if nothing else went wrong. As prices went up, they reached the points at which the thresholds caused a succession of automatic wage increases. A government with Labour's 1966 majority and a Prime Minister with all of Wilson's 1964 prestige would have found the position difficult, but in 1974 there was no majority and it had become fashionable to sneer at Wilson, ostensibly because he had accepted his party's change of front over the EEC and perhaps in reality because so many people were disappointed by what had happened to the dreams of the 1960s.

Many people were also disappointed by what happened to the dreams of the 1970s. Investors on the Stock Exchange became nervous and began selling; prices fell heavily from 1973 onwards until eventually in December 1974 the *Financial Times* index, launched in 1935 at 100, had fallen back to its 1958 level of 150. As building society interest rates rose to 11 per cent, house prices stopped going up; office blocks and land for development, which had been handled in some of the wilder deals financed at higher rates, became almost impossible to sell. Secondary banks involved in these activities found that, whatever their future prospects, such assets were no use at all as security for short-term loans. Between 1973 and late 1975 the Bank of England and the large clearing banks had to provide money embarrassingly often to keep these energetic and unsound banks from going bankrupt and destroying the London money market; if the secondary banks had tried to realize the security for their loans in one great wave of liquidation, it would have driven prices so low that even the soundest institutions would have suffered. While the collapse of the secondary banks was handled without catastrophe, it tied up the resources of the clearing banks so that they would have had difficulty providing credit for new investment if there had been any demand for it. But because so large a budget deficit had to be financed and because money had to be drawn in from overseas to cover the balance-of-payments deficit, the government had to pay up to 17 per cent on long-dated bonds. Other interest rates were so high that those with any choice in the matter stayed away from banks, borrowed nothing, and repaid old debts.

In opposition Healey had promised to bring 'howls of anguish' from the rich. The budget he produced almost immediately after becoming Chancellor of the Exchequer, with its increase in income tax from 30p to 33p and other changes, was designed to honour his pledge. In the months that followed Healey treated the increase in the price of oil as deflationary because it withdrew money from circulation by transferring it to the members of OPEC faster than they could spend it or lend it. However sound the analysis, the United Kingdom was not a very persuasive advocate of reflation because it already had a serious deficit. While other industrial countries saw rising prices as the immediate problem, Healey undertook a policy of reflation in Britain, and switched from tax increases to tax cuts; in July he lowered value added tax from 10 to 8 per cent and after the October election he reduced corporation tax by over £1 billion. Simply because the raw materials which they held to use in their work had gone up in price many companies had been showing large profits, which would do nothing for them in the long run because they would have to restock at the new high prices, but in the short run brought crushing tax bills. Reducing corporation tax looked paradoxical in the middle of an inflation which fed on itself as prices went through successive thresholds and wages rose to match, but the companies were clearly in trouble. For a few weeks in 1974 it looked as if firms might fall into government ownership simply by going bankrupt, but the government knew it did not have the administrative talent or structure available to run existing companies, and could not offer other jobs to the people working in them. By the autumn it was clear that the government would have to save the private sector, and that unemployment would in any case return to the level of early 1972.

Although the government could survive for some months without a parliamentary majority, there would have to be another election soon. Public opinion found the absence of a majority disconcerting, and this helped to make it fashionable to say Britain was becoming ungovernable. Although prices rose more slowly in the summer of 1974 so that inflation was not as pressing a problem as it had been earlier in the year and was to be again in 1975, nobody was convinced when Healey implied that prices were under control, and it was even suggested that they might go up at rates traditionally associated with South America. The triumph of the trade unions undoubtedly alarmed some people: Heath might have been making unnecessary trouble over the dispute with the miners, but still it was worrying to think that trade unions might acquire a power of veto over the government.

The Irish situation did nothing to reassure people. Heath could see that fear of being united with the rest of the island had turned the Protestant majority into a monolithic block, and he hoped to assuage this fear by announcing in 1972 that there would be periodic referendums on partition. A new Assembly was to be created with powers distinctly more limited than those of the old Stormont Parliament, and the British government would allow these powers to be exercised only by a power-sharing Northern Ireland government that represented both communities. A referendum was held in March 1973, and a predictably large proportion of the electorate voted to retain the union with Britain. Opponents of the union advised their supporters to abstain and were able to make this advice effective. The elections for the new Assembly in June produced as much support for power-sharing between the two communities as anyone could have expected; three substantial parties emerged, the Social Democratic and Labour Party (SDLP) representing the Catholic minority, a number of intransigent Unionist groups (of which Ian Paisley's Democratic Unionist Party proved the most durable), that came together as the United Ulster Unionist Coalition, and a more flexible Unionist group under Faulkner's leadership. Any two of these parties could command a majority, and a Faulkner-SDLP coalition would represent both communities. The violence of the fighting was slightly reduced in 1973; 251 people were killed, a little more than half as many as in 1972. Nobody in Britain thought things had improved, because the IRA opened a new offensive by exploding bombs in Birmingham, London, and Aldershot. It may have taken this step because the counter-insurgency methods of the British army were beginning to have some effect, but the new departure certainly made people in Britain more aware of the problem in Ireland and more pessimistic about it.

Whitelaw's skill and diplomacy in months of negotiation as minister responsible for Northern Ireland brought the Faulkner Unionists and the SDLP together, despite the natural concern of the Faulknerites that they would be rejected by their supporters for being too conciliatory and the equally natural concern of the SDLP that they would be shot by the IRA for the same offence. By December 1973 the two groups were ready to work together in a 'power-sharing' executive, and Whitelaw became Secretary of State for Employment, in the hope that the skill in conciliation he had shown in Ireland would work as well in Britain. Politicians in the power-sharing executive were sorry to see him go; they knew their slightly artificial basis for cooperation needed all the help it could get. The United Kingdom election in February put the executive under new pressures before it was able to bear them. The United Ulster Unionist Coalition, who had little more than a third of the seats in the Assembly, polled just over half the votes cast in the general election and, partly because the power-sharers were far from being united enough to put forward a single set of candidates, won eleven of the twelve Northern Ireland seats. This was a harsh warning to the Faulknerites that their support was disappearing, but they stuck to the work of the executive, while asking that it should move slowly and in particular should not lay too much emphasis on proposals for cooperation with the Republic of Ireland or for the speedy release of prisoners who had been interned without trial under suspicion of belonging to one of the para-military terrorist organizations. The SDLP thought the Labour government would be more sympathetic to their point of view and would press the Faulknerites to move faster. This might eventually have broken the power-sharing executive up, but in May the Ulster Workers' Committee, a loyalist group with no visible links to the United Unionists at Westminster, launched a political general strike against the executive. In its first days this seems to have been a minority movement which relied on intimidation to keep people away from work, but when Wilson announced his disapproval of the strike and was ill advised enough to call the people of Ulster 'spongers' (because they benefited from the system of progressive taxation and welfare measures that transferred money from Britain to Northern Ireland), the strike won general support among the Protestant majority. The Faulknerites resigned from the executive because their position had become impossible, and Northern Ireland settled down to twenty years of direct rule from London.

Elections to a Northern Ireland constitutional convention in 1975, in which the Unionists won about 60 per cent of the seats under a system of proportional representation, showed that the Faulknerites were correct in their fears. A good deal of the discrimination of Ulster's first fifty years had been eliminated, but the two communities were as far apart as ever and the province's understandable reputation for instability and violence meant that it was unlikely to get the investment it needed to reach any modest level of prosperity. As about as many people were killed in 1974 and 1975 as in 1973, it was hard to see any improvement in the situation. But by 1976 there were signs that the peace of exhaustion was settling on the problem. Supporters of drastic change were losing hope, and the army's counter-intelligence system was penetrating the IRA.

The army had to take an interest in politics in Northern Ireland. Officers seem to have speculated about the army's role in a way that led to rumours in the summer of 1974 that they were discussing when it might be appropriate to intervene in British politics. Parts of the intelligence services seem to have decided that it was already time to do so. Events elsewhere were not entirely reassuring: a group of army officers was ruling Portugal at the time, there were hints of an army coup in Italy, and the colonels who had been ruling Greece for the past half-dozen years were at their least reasonable. But such ideas would have found no audience in Britain if the notion had not grown up that the country was out of control.

The 'social contract' announced in June was less reassuring than had been hoped. The government gave up trying to restrain wage increases by law, repealed the Industrial Relations Act, increased old-age pensions and other benefits, subsidized food prices, placed restrictions on rent increases, and allowed the nationalized industries to run up deficits. In return the union leaders said they would not ask for wage increases more than once a year and would keep the increases down to something like the rise in the cost of living. Even if they had possessed effective control over their members, keeping real wages undiminished was going to impose a heavy burden on the economy when the increase in oil prices was reducing the real national income and state-financed benefits were going up so much. These benefits were referred to as the 'social wage', but most of the 'social wage' went to people who were old or ill or otherwise outside the main stream of wage bargaining. People at work paid for it rather than benefiting from it; by the 1970s workers earning the average industrial wage paid income tax at the standard rate on two-fifths of their income, and Healey's tax increases cut painfully into their take-home pay. Workers set out to recover the lost ground, and their union leaders could not do much to stop them.

Wilson prudently held another election in October before he had to do something about this strain on the economy. Nobody felt comfortable with so fragile a government, though it seemed unlikely that a new election would provide anyone with an overwhelming majority. The Conservatives tried to respond to this by suggesting a government of national unity, but it was never at all clear what substance there was to this phrase. The Labour Party could claim that it had taken over at a time of crisis and stopped things getting worse. It had done enough in its eight months in office to show how different it was from the Labour government of the 1960s, even though the men at the top in 1974 were much the same as the men who had been at the top in 1970, apart from Michael Foot, who entered the government as a sort of living pledge that the wishes of the trade unions would be remembered. Distinctly fewer votes were cast in October, only partly because the electoral register was eight months older. Opinion polls suggested that the Labour Party would win a clear majority, though not many people were convinced by this. Perhaps inspired by what had happened in February, some supporters of other parties seem to have voted tactically by combining to support the candidate most likely to keep Labour out.[3]

Unless all the parties in opposition agreed that they wanted an election, Wilson's position was secure; a string of by-election defeats might bring down his government by convincing the opposition parties that all of them would gain by having an election. They were very unlikely to believe that some different combination ought to rule the country without an election. The Liberals fell back slightly, and Liberal activists felt unkindly treated by fate and the electoral system when they won so few seats for so many votes. But people who vote Liberal once and then move on to another party—who are very

	Votes	Seats	% of all votes cast
Conservative	10,464,817	276	35.8
Liberal	5,346,754	13	18.3
Labour	11,457,079	319	39.2
Scottish Nationalist	839,617	11	2.8
Plaid Cymru	166,321	3	0.6
United Ulster Unionist	407,778	10	1.4
Others	508,040	3	1.7

3. M. Steed, in app. to D. E. Butler and D. Kavanagh, *The British General Election of October 1974* (1975), 294.

different from the activists—give an impression of voting Liberal as a holding action while they decide what to do next, and they might have been quite unworried by the party's lack of success. No doubt other parties receive some essentially negative votes, but they seem to draw a decidedly larger proportion of their total strength from people who steadily vote Labour or Conservative election after election.

The 1974 elections forced people to ask which sort of support the Scottish Nationalists attracted. They continued to advance, winning slightly more votes in Scotland than the Conservatives (SNP 11 seats with 30.4 per cent of the vote; Conservatives 16 with 24.7 per cent; Liberals 3 with 8.3 per cent; Labour 41 with 36.9 per cent). The subsequent collapse of the Scottish Conservatives made it unlikely that the SNP could win a majority of the seats in Scotland on a minority vote. Until about 1972 and the growth of the conviction that 'It's Scottish oil', the Scottish Nationalists had not really been doing better than Plaid Cymru. In 1974 the problems of Plaid Cymru became apparent; it did well in the small Welsh-speaking section of rural western Wales and was clearly to be taken seriously there but in the densely populated industrial areas of Wales it made no progress. Scottish nationalism had no such division to face, partly because it faced no linguistic difficulties. Gaelic had declined so much that saying a few ritual words in it aroused none of the fears about compulsory bilingualism that alarmed the large group of Welshmen who could speak nothing but English. But while Scottish nationalism could appeal to all regions of Scotland, it was not clear whether it got votes as a protest against the effects of unsatisfactory government policies or because there had been a real change of consciousness in Scotland. Apart from the picturesque and thinly populated Highlands, Scotland was roughly divided into a declining west and a prosperous east, and this was going to be accentuated by North Sea oil. Glasgow and the area round it, now grouped into the region of Strathclyde, in which something like half the population of Scotland lived, had grown to worldwide importance on coal, iron, and shipbuilding during the Industrial Revolution. The Labour Party was naturally strong in this region, and went on polling enough of the vote there to mean that the Scottish Nationalists, whose strength was spread more evenly across the country, were unlikely to win many seats in Strathclyde unless the people of the region lost their faith that the Labour Party could do something about unemployment. The decline of the basic industries meant that the region faced serious difficulties even if it could attract new types of work, while the east coast had fewer declining industries to impede its progress and had been doing reasonably well before the development of oil began. Although some of the platforms for drilling and pumping the oil came from Clyde shipyards, most of its effect was to be seen on the east coast and in particular in Aberdeen.

The oil lay in areas of the North Sea that, because of the waves and the weather, presented more difficulties than the development of gas had done. In the early years much of the technical skill and the equipment was provided by Americans who had had experience of developments off the Texas and Louisiana shores. But British firms adapted to the needs of this new industry quite quickly, and a good many problems would have looked less formidable if the rest of the British economy had been as bold and as flexible as the oil sector. Oil was a very large undertaking: it was estimated that in a dozen years between 1972 and 1985 about £25 billion, or about one-quarter of the national income for a year, would have been invested in it. The costs went up sharply because oil-drilling equipment was in great demand after the OPEC price increases, but North Sea oil was relatively expensive to produce, and would not have been a practicable area for investment before the price increases. Once the price of a 35-gallon barrel of oil from the Middle East had been pushed up to $12, about $1 was assigned to capital and production costs and the rest went to the host government. Capital and production costs in the North Sea amount to about $6, and the British government—after considerable argument and some evidence that in the early 1970s the oil companies got very favourable terms—took the other $6, which indicated an annual revenue of over £3 billion for the British, or alternatively the Scottish, government.

While Scotland's uneasiness had to be taken seriously (and Wales would expect some recognition if Scotland's position changed), it could not receive immediate attention. The government's slender majority forced it to take problems one at a time, and in October 1974 the major problem in sight was the EEC. Renegotiation had begun soon after the February election and it was soon clear that, while the Treaty of Rome would not be rewritten, the government could hope for changes that would let it fulfil its promise to win concessions and then submit them to the electorate for approval. With a thin majority and an economy showing signs of slipping out of control, holding yet another general election would be rather like the 1807 election described by Sidney Smith as 'building a brick wall for the express purpose of dashing out their brains against it'. The Labour Party was divided between what would later be known as Euro-sceptics and Euro-fanatics, while the Conservatives could present a relatively united front on the issue. So a referendum had obvious advantages for the government. Those who were afraid a popular vote might endanger Britain's membership talked about the duty of the government to make up its mind on the question, and the sovereignty of Parliament. Supporters of a referendum asked for popular participation in the serious, almost irreversible decision to be taken. If they had been very outspoken they might have added that the doctrine of unchallenged parliamentary sovereignty rested on a basis of unquestioned respect in the minds of the people which Parliament no longer commanded. However unwelcome this might have been at Westminster, it was probably one reason why the referendum—dismissed in the past with relatively little difficulty—became accepted as an addition to the British way of running politics.

A referendum helped the Labour Party by reducing to a minimum the discussion about what the renegotiations had achieved. In a general election the Conservatives would have argued that the negotiations had not produced any substantial improvement on the 1971 terms, and Labour supporters of entry would have had to reply that they had done very well at the expense of the other EEC countries. Food prices and the effect of membership on the balance of payments were the main issues to be discussed in the renegotiation; no British politician would endanger the whole process by demanding better terms for New Zealand's butter or Mauritius's sugar, though naturally opponents of membership raised such points, and they also asked what would happen to British sovereignty. People who were afraid that the British government would lose control over questions it had previously been legally entitled to settle for itself (which may be taken as a definition of the slightly abstract phrase 'loss of sovereignty') were relieved that European Monetary Union—the most immediately tangible issue that raised the question of sovereignty—with exchange rates fixed immutably, perhaps secured by a common European currency, had receded into the background under the stress of floating exchange rates. The negotiators could hardly take up the undoubted fact that some people simply disliked the idea of close association with foreigners. On food prices they had to accept the initial political agreement of the 1950s that tariffs would be used to support EEC farmers, who were not likely to give up this protection. The British got fairly generous treatment in successive decisions about the exchange rate at which the pound should be translated into other EEC currencies, which kept the cost of food lower than it would have been if Britain had been buying from other EEC countries at the current exchange rate. This left the question of the balance of payments: the British income per head was perceptibly below the Community average, but because trade outside the EEC was an important part of Britain's national income the United Kingdom would pay a large amount to Community funds through the common tariff, which would then go to small and subsidized farmers in France and Germany. The renegotiators were more successful here, and as long as Britain's income per head was no more than 85 per cent of the Community average (which looked like being the case for an indefinite time to come) the British Exchequer would not have to pay the full amount that would have been due under the existing arrangements.

This was not a very exciting concession to bring back, even when accompanied by other gains of similar complexity. The government might have found this mildly embarrassing in an election if Heath had been able to compare it with his own policy. The referendum solved this problem; and in February 1975 Heath lost his position as Leader of the Opposition. The party's revised rules obliged leaders to stand for re-election and he was challenged by Margaret Thatcher. In the first round she received eleven votes more than Heath, who then withdrew, and in the second round she received a clear majority of the votes cast. Her success in the first round was partly a vote of no confidence in Heath, who was blamed for holding the February election and for losing two elections in a year, but it could also be seen as a vote for the principles Heath had put forward before becoming Prime Minister. Thatcher and Heath came from similar backgrounds: families with small businesses but no independent means, and for both of them success at Oxford was the stepping stone to wider prospects. In 1970 their views on policy seemed very similar: lower taxes, less government activity, and more opportunities for businessmen to make money by taking risks. Heath had come to support very wide-ranging government intervention, and felt some hostility to business-men because they did not invest as enthusiastically and patriotically as he had hoped. Some of Thatcher's supporters felt she could revive the principles that the party had accepted in the late 1960s. Sir Keith Joseph, for whose opinions she clearly had great respect, caught public attention if not public approval with a series of speeches in favour of a more disciplined way of life and the ideology of the free market. Unkind commentators did note that Thatcher and Joseph had presided over some of the largest increases in departmental spending during Heath's premiership, even if these increases were dwarfed by what happened under the Labour government. The government apparently felt that, because it had to concentrate on the EEC negotiations, it could not do anything to check the increases in prices, which were rising at about 26 per cent a year by mid-1975, or in wages, which were going up by about 35 per cent a year. Supporters of membership in the government took the risk of letting the economy run on its alarming course in order to parry any attempts by opponents of EEC membership to blame the Community if there was any sharp drop in living standards. The referendum itself passed off with much less damage to the constitution than its opponents had predicted. Wilson reserved his own judgement until the spring of 1975, and then declared that, all things considered, he thought the new terms were acceptable. The Labour Party announced its opposition to membership, but it was nothing new for Wilson to find that he and the party were not quite in step, and the EEC debate avoided the bitterness of the arguments about deflation and unemployment in the late 1960s. Ministers who opposed the terms were allowed to 'agree to differ' (like the Liberals in the 1930s) in speeches outside, but not inside, the Commons. The government devised a simple question for the ballot, sent a statement of the cases for and against entry to every voter, and provided £125,000 for each side, though they could raise unlimited amounts from their supporters as well: the pro-Europeans received lavish support from a wide range of companies and individuals, and the opponents got much smaller sums from individuals and trade unions. Despite this imbalance, the general debate seemed reasonably evenly matched; the sup-porters of entry had men like Wilson and Heath and Jenkins to make solid speeches to reassure the voters, and the opponents had orators like Foot and

Powell and the unexpectedly successful Peter Shore to rouse people to a feeling of the value of British independence and the possible disadvantages of the EEC. Opinion polls had for some time shown that, while views about membership were volatile and fairly evenly divided, there was considerably more support for 'membership if recommended by the government' than simply for 'membership', and the size of the majority for membership may confirm this. Distinctly fewer votes were cast in the referendum than in any recent general election, which may show the effect of canvassing by political parties on elections; and on 5 June the supporters of entry won by 17,378,581 votes to 8,470,073. The long debate about EEC membership had ended by treating the issue with all the serious consideration it deserved, even if the details of the debate had sometimes been hard to follow.

A government which had got through such a struggle, and had managed to avoid shattering a clearly divided party, might have hoped for a pause to rest. It had instead to face the problems of rising prices and rising unemployment that had been ignored during the EEC debate. In fifteen months public spending had gone up by about 40 per cent and risen to a level equal to almost 60 per cent of the national income, as a result of increased benefits paid to enable social services to keep up with inflation, wage increases to maintain civil servants' real income, and an increase in the number of civil servants. Nobody, except the civil servants taken on in this period, was in real terms better off as a result, but the economy was distorted in an attempt to avoid, or at least delay, the fall in living standards that seemed inevitable after the overspending of the early 1970s and the worsening in the terms of trade, seen most conspicuously in the rise in oil prices. In 1975 those who lost their jobs carried the burden, but the distortion of the economy could be seen in two ways. The exchange value of the pound had slipped very little since the summer of 1973, despite the increase in the balance-of-payments deficit, simply because the OPEC countries did not want to put too much money into the United States and found London the only other convenient place to deposit it. Lending it to Britain had the additional advantage of maintaining the level of demand for their oil. By mid-1975 they were beginning to feel uneasy about keeping their money in sterling and, as they moved into other currencies, the pound fell from a 'Smithsonian devaluation' of 24 per cent to a level 30 per cent below where it had been four years earlier.

At the same time inflation inside the country was beginning to alarm everyone, including trade unionists, who could see that price increases were eating up all their wage increases. Trade unions agreed to a voluntary policy, with no legal sanctions to back it up, of letting everyone earning less than £8,500 a year (a considerable income when MPs received only £5,750 a year) have one increase of no more than £6 a week in the next year. The scheme worked reasonably well; at the end of twelve months prices were rising at about two-thirds the level of mid-1975 and a further year of voluntary pay restraint was then accepted. Even these steps did not noticeably hold back the increase in unemployment, which rose above the 1 million level and seemed likely to stay above it for several years to come. Voluntary wage restraint did not give private industry a rate of return that encouraged investment, and when the government created a National Enterprise Board (NEB) to carry out public investment in new industries, it soon found itself saving old firms from collapse. The large family-owned electronics firm of Ferranti had to be bought up to avert closure. British Leyland, the largest car firm in the country, was insolvent; the NEB was put in charge, and later almost had to take over the American-owned firm of Rootes, though Chrysler was persuaded to keep its subsidiary in production by a grant of £162 million.

Those earning over £8,500 a year were still a small minority; at just about the time the pay policy was being worked out, a Royal Commission led by Lord Diamond presented a report which had a good deal of information about the prosperous part of society. The 10 per cent of the population with the highest incomes earned £2,857 a year or more, and received 27 per cent of all the income earned by individuals, though after tax this was reduced to 23 per cent. The highest-paid 1 per cent received 6 per cent of the total, a decline from 8.4 per cent in 1959 and 11.2 per cent in 1949. Wealth was less evenly distributed: the richest 10 per cent owned £10,500 or more, and held 67 per cent of all personal wealth; the richest 1 per cent, each of whom owned £44,000 or more, held 28 per cent of all personal wealth; it was noted that in 1913 this group alone had owned 69 per cent of all personal wealth. The Report tended to ignore the claims on wealth held by individuals in the form of pension rights, although these rights, whether in the form of an old-age pension or of schemes linked to employment, were a type of wealth that had grown very quickly during the twentieth century. *The Times* commented that owning an unmortgaged house was enough to put one in the wealthiest 10 per cent, and teased the Labour Party by pointing out that while this was very pleasant for the half of the population who lived in houses they owned (mortgaged or unmortgaged), the other half could join them in relative prosperity only if they too had a chance to buy their homes.[4]

This was a reminder that over 30 per cent of the population lived in houses or flats rented from municipal authorities, most of whom saw themselves as benevolent landlords and had no desire to sell off their housing stock. The government was preparing to increase the activity of the municipalities as landlords by its Community Land Act. Such large speculative profits in land had been made by those who were shrewd enough to get out by mid-1973 that the new Act provided that a piece of land to be developed should be sold to the municipality at its value for its existing use, and might then be bought back at the price appropriate for the proposed new use. This appeared to solve

4. *The Times*, 31 July 1975.

the problem of capturing the unearned increase in the value of land which had puzzled Lloyd George and Snowden and the Labour government of 1945, but it involved laying on municipalities the duty of intervening in a great multitude of transactions, and they turned out to be unable to act at the speed required for building development to proceed.

Some of the problems facing Wilson in the 1960s had gone on into the 1970s. Rhodesia was still independent, unreconciled, and unrecognized. Under the Conservatives Douglas-Home and Smith had worked out a scheme to make Rhodesia legally independent and guarantee the position of the African majority; before the government put it into effect a commission under Lord Pearce was asked to survey African opinion, and the commission was convinced by the mobilization of opinion under the leadership of Bishop Muzorewa that the proposals were not acceptable, so they were laid aside. The important change in the situation was the withdrawal of Portugal from her African colonies. In 1975 Angola and Mozambique were about to emerge as independent states which would serve as bases for guerrilla attacks on Rhodesia and the way was open for the problem, which had drifted on for ten years of negotiation in which the British government never had power to make its views effective, to be settled by force of arms.

As the pay policy worked its way through the winter into the spring of 1976, the headlines were devoted to the difficulties of the unlucky Liberal leader Jeremy Thorpe, who was about to lose his position because of allegations of a homosexual affair over a dozen years previously. On 16 March Harold Wilson announced that he intended to retire because he had reached the age of 60. During the uncertainty of choosing a successor the pound dropped by about 5 per cent against all other currencies; this may have been partly due to the further troubles of British Leyland, but by this stage the currency was so weak that, whenever attention turned to Britain, holders of sterling responded by getting rid of it. The parliamentary party responded rather more calmly, and on 5 April James Callaghan was chosen as Wilson's successor on the third ballot.

It would be unkind to Wilson, or perhaps an underestimate of his quality, to say that his virtues—optimism in adversity, loyalty to his social origins, unwillingness to give pain to his supporters—could not by themselves solve the problems which faced him and the country during his long period of office. His weaknesses were by no means peculiar to him; it was partly the coincidence of name that led to the suggestion that 1957–76 was the period of the two Harolds, Macmillan and Wilson, but what they had in common was not likely to do the country good. Almost unavoidably they overestimated Britain's position in the world; anyone born before the First World War or emerging into politics in the years of Churchill's world-ranging greatness was likely to start with an idea of Britain as a power equal to any other. Both men of course realized that this was no longer the case, but they had not worked out any way to meet the situation, and the degree of reliance that both of them placed on the American alliance in the 1960s was no longer realistic. Both of them were very clever men, and at times behaved as if they thought cleverness would be enough to carry the nation forward, which encouraged other people to think in the same way. An obvious example lay in the area of economic policy. In the years of the two Harolds no British politician would have called himself anything other than a Keynesian, but what they meant was that a budget deficit would solve all the problems of economic policy. Keynes may really have been more interested in encouraging investment and in lowering the real wages of those in work so that it would be economically possible to take on new workers.[5] Those who thought Keynesianism meant budget deficits behaved as though they had found an intellectual trick which produced a policy which was both easy and effective. Macmillan once almost committed himself to saying 'exporting is fun'; he and a good many other people seemed to think investing was fun rather than a risky and difficult process. Obviously Britain's problems were not simply an intellectual misunderstanding of what Keynes meant, or even a failure to invest in new machinery. The Britain of 1906 had still been practising a good many of what could be called the Victorian virtues; and its financial strength and political prestige owed a good deal to those virtues. As the twentieth century went on, those virtues came increasingly to be regarded as old-fashioned; and no doubt they were dull and constricting.

On the basis of those virtues, Britain had by the beginning of the century established a system of government in which power was used responsibly by a small group of specialized politicians who depended on an electorate that included a steadily widening range of the whole population. This pattern of government had achieved many things, including the acquisition of a vast overseas empire with relatively little difficulty or resistance. In the first half of the new century the system had been changed into one of universal suffrage with a party structure that gave the organized working class at least as large a share of power as it possessed in any other country. The government had set up the framework of a welfare system that endeavoured to recognize the needs of many previously neglected sections of society, and had taken substantial steps towards dissolving the Empire peacefully and amicably. In the third quarter of the century things had gone much less well. It would be hard to say how much of the change was due to the fact that Britain had been living on the accumulated reserves, moral and financial, of the nineteenth century, how much to the damage of the two world wars, and how much to mismanagement in the decades after the Second World War; but Britain was making relatively little impact on the minds of people outside the country, and inside the country decline and decay had come almost to be taken for granted. The

5. J. M. Keynes, *The General Theory of Employment, Interest and Money* (1936), 14 and 30.

decline was perfectly real, but it was sometimes overstated. Britain could not be ranked with the United States or the Soviet Union, as had been imagined in 1945, but it made equally little sense for people to talk as if it had ceased to rank among the nine or ten most important countries. The immediate question was whether the country should be led in a common-sense sort of way that accepted the decline as irreversible and tried to make the best of it, or whether relics of the past that had outlived their usefulness could be cleared away without dividing the country too much for new developments to go ahead.

15

'The end of an old song'[1]

1976–1985

Labour on a tightrope

James Callaghan's qualities fitted him to fill the post of Prime Minister entirely adequately. Unlike Wilson and Macmillan, he never appeared overwhelmed with pleasure at his own cleverness; he was able to work better with other people than Wilson and Heath had done; and he conveyed the impression that common sense was the most important quality in politics and that he possessed it. He was determined to hang on to power, without necessarily doing very much with it, which was as much as the Labour Party could hope for. As the party had been led by Oxford graduates for the past forty years, it felt mildly relieved that he had never been to a university and had stronger links with the trade union movement than any Labour leader of the first rank since union leaders ceased going into the House of Commons in the late 1940s. At the time the public felt no desire for burning conviction in politics, so his inability to project it was no handicap. In the final round of the leadership contest Callaghan defeated Foot by 176 votes to 137; Foot's personal qualities inspired affection and as Secretary of State for Employment he had gained a good deal of support among trade unionists, so while the size of his vote reflected the advance of the left he had support elsewhere in the party and could have defeated anyone who was not skilfully placed in the centre of the party.

Labour's election manifesto in 1974 had committed the party to working closely with the unions and refraining from imposing an incomes policy by law. The 1975 acceptance of a maximum increase in pay of £6 a week was, at least nominally, a voluntary step on the part of the unions. They may have reckoned that, election commitment or no election commitment, an incomes policy would be imposed by law unless they helped to take steps to deal with prices rising by 3 per cent a month; but this remained unsaid. Legislation was passed to hold down prices and dividends, but wage restraint was left to the

1. James, Lord Seafield, on signing the Act of Union of 1707.

union leaders' awareness of the dangers of an economic crisis. The social contract had already produced legislation to protect the job security of the employed and increased welfare benefits. Union leaders went on to press for some of the more controversial items of the 1974 programme, of which the nationalization of shipbuilding and the control of loading and unloading operations in the docks caused the government most trouble in 1976. The government's majority in the Commons was fragile enough for the Conservatives to hope that, if they delayed things long enough, death, retirement, or defection might destroy it. A clause to protect dockers from losing their jobs as a result of the containerization of ships' cargoes was defeated by Labour abstentions, and on another occasion the government was saved from defeat only because a Labour MP cast his vote when he was supposed to be 'paired'. By the end of the 1975–6 session it was clear that no further legislation could be passed simply by the votes of the Labour Party and those nationalists from Wales and Northern Ireland who habitually voted with it.

In his 1976 budget Healey had undertaken to reduce income tax if the trade unions extended their voluntary agreement to fix maximum wage increases for another year. This was denounced as surrendering control of government policy to the unions, but at the time it seemed to be the only way to run the country. In earlier decades Healey's proposals would have meant little to the unions, for manual workers rarely had to pay income tax before 1939, and up to the 1960s they usually paid only at the lower rates charged on the first few hundred pounds of taxable income. But inflation had driven incomes up much faster than the threshold for starting to pay at the standard rate had been changed, and successive Chancellors had tried to help the less well-off by eliminating all tax at the lower rates rather than widen the band of income that paid at a reduced rate, so more and more trade unionists were paying substantial amounts of income tax by the 1970s and they found the government's proposals attractive.

These negotiations with the unions, which condemned MPs to voting for budget proposals in principle without knowing what figures would eventually be filled in, led to an agreement that no pay increases should exceed 5 per cent. But discussions had moved too slowly to reassure overseas creditors about the large balance of payments deficit. The increase in oil prices and the ill-fated attempt to cope with the deflationary effect of that increase by expansion, when most countries wanted to combat rising prices rather than prevent declining production, had left Britain with much larger debts by 1976 than ever before. Other countries had held about £4 billion of short-term sterling debt for the twenty-five years after 1945, but this rose to about £12 billion in the 1970s. The government was in much the same position as Wilson's government in July 1966, although all the figures were much larger. In June Healey raised a short-term loan of $5 billion in order to have time to produce deflationary measures in July, but his proposals turned out to be inadequate.

By October the flow of money out of London had become a torrent. The oil-exporting countries, which had supplied Britain with oil on credit for a couple of years, began to be afraid that they would never be paid: in 1975 and 1976 they moved about £2 billion of their money elsewhere. The pound lost 23 per cent of its international trading value in the twelve months up to October 1976 and fell to $1.52.[2] After brief and brisk negotiations with the International Monetary Fund (IMF) a loan of £2.3 billion was arranged; reductions in the government's borrowing requirements to cut the supply of money were severe enough to have convinced the bankers of 1931 that here was a Labour government which knew when it had no room for manoeuvre. Tied down by the IMF agreement and the need to conciliate the unions, with no reliable majority in the Commons, the government seemed doomed to a short and far from merry life.

Behind the shift from negotiating with the unions about pay policy to general restraint lay a debate between supporters of two conflicting interpretations of the views of Keynes. Advocates of budget deficits to stimulate demand were criticized for neglecting the impact on the economy of increasing the amount of money in circulation. Concern with financing the borrowing of the government and other public institutions such as the nationalized industries—all summed up as the Public Sector Borrowing Requirement—without putting too much new money in circulation had a lot in common with the version of Keynesianism to be found in Kingsley Wood's 1941 budget and Gaitskell's 1951 budget. Healey's imposition of 'cash limits' on departmental spending in 1975 had been a step towards accepting the doctrine of monetarism that the amount of money in circulation was important. It had reversed the acceptance in 1962 of the Plowden Report, which had suggested that, once a programme for public spending had been adopted, changes in prices should not affect it—if prices went up, the spending department should be given money to go ahead as before. 'Cash limits', and the drift of taxpayers into higher ranges of income tax as the result of inflation, looked like bringing the economy under the control advocated by the monetarists. In July 1976 the government again showed its belief that 'money matters' by declaring that the Borrowing Requirement should be held down to £9 billion a year. When this was not enough to restore confidence and a further appeal for a loan had to be made, the IMF asked that limits on the amount of money in circulation should take account of the balance of payments as well. The official end of reliance on stimulative deficits was signalled by Callaghan's speech to the 1976 Labour conference in which he condemned the idea that 'you could just spend your way out of a recession and increase employment by cutting taxes and boosting spending. . . . that option no longer exists. . . . it worked by injecting

2. Trade-weighted indexes of currency values can be worked out. The difficulty is that when a currency changes value the relative value of the trade of its country also changes, so that the index loses much of its reliability with the passage of time.

inflation into the economy. And each time that happened the average level of unemployment has risen. Higher inflation followed by higher unemployment. That is the history of the past twenty years.'

The accuracy of this account of the 1950s and 1960s was debatable—Callaghan, like several other Chancellors, had spent as much time cutting spending as increasing it—but the shift in policy that he was proclaiming was perhaps as important as the wartime acceptance of Keynesianism, and certainly more important than anything said about growth and planning around 1960. For most of the next decade the Borrowing Requirement was kept at about the £11 billion level reached in 1976 and because gross national product increased considerably in money terms as prices went up, the Borrowing Requirement became a smaller and smaller fraction of the national income. This was not the Gladstonian policy of balancing each budget, or the relatively austere Keynesianism of the post-war years when Chancellors held borrowing down to a very low level, but it was less disturbing than the rapidly increasing deficits of the early 1970s. Deficits on this scale seemed to swamp the economy rather than stimulate it; industrial production was only 1 or 2 per cent more in 1977 than in 1970, despite the shift from a balanced budget to an £11 billion deficit. Some commentators said that this showed that the long expansion since the war had been caused by cheap oil or was simply the upswing of the long cycle described by Kondratieff, and they usually added that this meant economic progress would be harder in the decades ahead. The change of policy might deal with some of these problems, but it was not going to be popular. Real wages stopped going up in the first year of incomes policy and fell by 7 per cent in the second year, while unemployment rose towards 6 per cent.

When the Conservatives closed in for the kill, they found the government was not as defenceless as it looked. It ignored some defeats in the Commons, and it put together shifting alliances with the smaller parties. For some months it drew support from the Scottish and Welsh nationalists when it brought forward the issue of devolution. The case for devolution was that neglect at Westminster had led the Scots and Welsh to think of independence, and that if they had assemblies of their own to look after questions that concerned them directly they would be satisfied and would stop making demands that would break up the United Kingdom. This involved the risk that local institutions might not solve the problems of these relatively poor parts of Britain and would then be used by the nationalists as bases for a march towards independence. The more confident among the English, who thought concessions to the nationalists unnecessary, and the less confident among the Scots and Welsh, who thought devolution would open the floodgates to something they considered destructive, were natural allies in opposing it. Home Rule for Ireland, and the system of government of Northern Ireland that flowed directly from it, had been sweeping measures of devolution, though the British government in 1972 had shown that it was nothing more than devolution by taking back the powers given to Northern Ireland in 1920. Late in 1976 the proposals for Scotland and Wales were put forward together in the Devolution Bill, though the two countries were not to be put on an equal footing. The Bill did not give the Edinburgh assembly the powers over police and justice which had allowed the Northern Ireland government so much freedom of action, but it did offer the Scots legislative powers over education and health, housing, and local government that were wide enough to make the Bill quite attractive to people who simply wanted to look after their own local affairs in the way proponents of devolution had hoped. Overseeing the devolved powers held by the Secretary of State for Wales held very little attraction for anyone; the assembly in Cardiff looked like another sort of county council perched on the top of the municipal pyramid. The nationalists said the Bill gave no recognition to the national aspirations of their countries, and that shortcomings like the denial of revenue-raising powers to the assemblies meant that it provided no stable base for autonomy short of independence.

Even so, they supported the Bill because it was better than anything they could get from the Conservatives, who had withdrawn from their previous willingness to consider devolution. Nationalist support enabled the government to survive. Labour MPs, and in particular some Labour MPs from Scotland and from the north of England, were uneasy about the dangers of a disunited kingdom, the restraints imposed upon government activity by any dispersal of powers, and the risk of competition among sections of the country to attract industrial capital. Some of them became determined enemies of devolution and many others were anxious for fuller discussion of it. The government did not get a majority for imposing a closure on proceedings in February 1977, and the opponents of the Bill settled down for an infinitely protracted debate. The government now had no reliable majority, because the nationalists had no really solid reason for supporting it.

If an early election meant disaster for the Labour Party, the Liberals were quite as badly placed; and the Liberal leader could see other reasons for cooperation. The departure of Thorpe in an atmosphere of deepening scandal had been a heavy blow to the Liberals. They had rallied rather successfully by holding a leadership election on the basis of one party member, one vote. The winner, David Steel, a lowland Scot who had made his name by taking the Abortion Bill through Parliament in the 1960s, stood somewhat to the left of Thorpe. He knew that working with either major party would annoy some Liberals who worried about their independence, or would have preferred to work with the other major party, but he reckoned that he could get his MPs to cooperate with the Labour Party, if only to put off an election. He wanted his party to have some experience of how government worked, and thought it would benefit from being seen in a more serious role than in the recent past. He may also have hoped that closer contacts with Liberals would open the way to party realignment if the right wing of the Labour Party found the pressure from the Labour left too intense. The Liberals could promise steady support to the government for some months because no legislation was coming forward that would cause them any difficulty. They would have found it hard to vote for anything like the nationalization of shipbuilding (though the measure had come just in time to save private yards from ruin in the decline of world trade) or for other steps to strengthen the powers of the central government. But after the 1975–6 session very little business of this sort remained on the Labour agenda. The Liberals would have disliked being asked to support a Royal Commission report in favour of workers' control in industry, administered through the trade unions, but it was never put forward in Parliament, mainly because employers were fervent in opposing it and the unions were not very interested. The state of the parliamentary timetable let Steel tell his party that cooperation with the Labour Party involved no concessions to socialism, while Callaghan could tell his supporters that cooperation to avoid electoral disaster did not involve any sacrifice of principle. In March 1977 the two parties arranged what became known as 'the Lib–Lab pact'.

The devolution legislation that dominated the Commons during the lifetime of the Lib–Lab pact suited both parties. Nobody could say that it was not important, so the Labour leadership could resist pressure from the left for measures that might alarm the Liberals by pointing to vital legislation already before the House, and the Liberals could reflect that they had supported devolution long before the Labour Party. The Conservatives had to remember that opposition to the Bill might lose them even more votes in Scotland and Wales while merely boring people in England. So, after the 1976–7 Bill had been talked to death, it was revived for the next session in the form of separate Bills for Scotland and Wales, which included the referendum in the two countries conceded the previous year. Further amendments were passed which required the measures to secure not only a simple majority in the referendum but also the support of 40 per cent of the electorate. As no government since 1935 had gained so much support in winning a general election (though the Labour Party was supported by 40.01 per cent of the electorate while losing the 1951 election), this was a formidable obstacle. There were very few other changes to the legislation; the two votes were to be held on 1 March 1979, which gave the voters a little longer to forget the drop in real wages and perhaps come back to the Labour Party. People in England felt no enthusiasm for what was called 'the break-up of the United Kingdom', but they were unworried by the change.

The Labour left objected strongly to the general tendency of government policy. Early in the 1970s it thought it had got the party pledged to government action to increase equality, and welcomed the steps in this direction taken in 1974 and 1975: but it saw the financial crisis forcing Callaghan to give up equality much as Wilson had abandoned growth in 1966 and 1967. Deflation naturally increased unemployment: ever since the end of the war 2 per cent of the labour force out of work had been taken as a danger point, and the left lost its faith in Wilson partly because unemployment rose above this level in the late 1960s. Things had become worse under Heath, but even he had been afraid of letting unemployment reach the 1 million figure and had undertaken his U-turn in 1972 to end the deflation. But the Labour government, even though it included representatives of the left like Foot and Benn, let unemployment rise to 1.4 million. The left believed that import controls and direction of the use of capital would solve the balance-of-payments problem without the limits on trade union activity needed for an incomes policy or reduction in real wages or deflation; it was distressed by the government's readiness to draw back from the interventionism of the immediate past. The Civil Service shrank in numbers; government spending did little more than keep pace with inflation; municipalities built fewer houses than in the mid-1970s because the central government reduced their grants; and when the government acquired some additional shares in British Petroleum as one result of the financial collapse of 1974, it quickly sold them off at a profit. The feeling of betrayal prompted by all this was not very different from the hostility felt about MacDonald in the 1930s. Because they thought the party's values were being abandoned party enthusiasts became convinced that the only way to control the party leadership was to change the party constitution. In 1978 the leadership had the power and prestige of office, and could hold this pressure back. If the leadership lost the prestige of government before the memory of Callaghan's deflation had faded away, the internal opposition would return to the attack and would be difficult to resist.

After the overthrow of Heath the Conservatives had repudiated the policies he adopted in the second half of his premiership, and had returned to the policy of withdrawing from intervention in the economy and limiting trade union power that he had accepted for the first half of his premiership. So the Labour left and the Conservatives could agree in opposing incomes policy, if on nothing else, and the Conservatives hoped to defeat the government by getting the left to vote with them. But while the left voted against the government as often as was safe, it knew it would not be forgiven if it brought about an election in which Labour was defeated.

Rising unemployment and falling real wages made it hard to negotiate a third year of incomes policy, but Healey got the unions to agree that wage increases should not exceed 10 per cent in return for another 1p reduction in income tax. This was interpreted flexibly enough for most of the previous year's drop in real wages to be regained, and the government recovered some of its lost popularity. To defend the 10 per cent limit the government resisted a demand for a larger increase from the firemen's union, taking the risk that if there were a catastrophic fire both government and firemen would be blamed for their obstinacy. Troops were moved to fire duty, to save lives rather than property; no disastrous fire put pressure on the government to give way; and the eventual settlement left the pay policy intact and discouraged other unions from attacking it.

The government's hopes for something better than constant negotiations with the unions were based upon North Sea oil, which by 1978 was beginning to flow in quantities large enough to affect the whole economy. Britain moved quickly away from dependence on imported oil, which improved the balance of payments, and the oil companies started making large payments to the Exchequer once they had recovered their investment, which soon came to about 4 per cent of the government's total revenue.

Britain was at the same time moving away from reliance on imports for food. Farmers were the most clear-cut beneficiaries of Britain's entry to the European Community, because the Common Agricultural Policy helped them at least as much as it helped farmers in the rest of the Community and they responded by increasing production. At the time of entry Britain grew 49.2 per cent of her food and by the end of the 1970s this figure had risen to 59.3 per cent. (Some crops, from tea to oranges, are not grown in Britain, and the supply of temperate zone foods rose from 61.2 per cent to 73.9 per cent.) Britain's share of world trade continued to diminish; some of this was a sign of industrial decline, but it also represented a shift of resources towards self-sufficiency, based on investment in oil and in agriculture.

By the summer of 1978 the government could hope for some reward for the years of restraint. The Liberals ended the Lib–Lab pact politely enough to show that, while they wanted to fight the next election as a separate party, they hoped it could be revived afterwards. As the nationalists would not endanger the government before the referendums, it could hold on until the following March; but by August it looked as if Callaghan would announce an election at the Trades Union Congress in September. At the same time the government asked the TUC, in no very conciliatory way, for a fourth year of incomes policy; no cuts in income tax were offered, and a maximum pay increase of 5 per cent was suggested. It was reasonable to say that real wages could not go up as fast as in the previous twelve months, but the TUC felt unable to accept this ultimatum. The day after the proposal was rejected the Prime Minister announced there would be no autumn election. A renewed incomes policy would have been a strong election plank, but without it he had to choose between holding an election immediately after failing to reach agreement with the TUC or facing unrestricted wage demands. Later on he was blamed for not holding an autumn election, but the real trouble was that he had not prepared a plan to deal with the fact that no incomes policy had ever lasted for a fourth year. A flood of wage claims like those of 1963–4, 1969–70, and 1975 was only to be expected in 1978–9. The government tried to use its powers over prices and investment to stop private companies giving large wage increases, but by the end of the year the public sector had become the main area of discontent. The

Ford motor workers started the rush by winning a 17 per cent pay increase in a strike immediately after the end of the incomes policy, and the strike of the lorry drivers caused more widespread difficulty and dislocation of industrial production than any other dispute, but what caught the public eye was the visible effect of the strike of the dustmen (at a hygienically cold time of winter), the first-ever strike by nurses, and the macabre problems caused by the strike of the Liverpool gravediggers. In the private sector overtime and allowances for expenses had probably been used to give workers a bit more than the pay policy allowed; Professor Clegg, whose work as director of research for the Donovan Commission had won him the approval of trade union leaders, was appointed as a commissioner to compare public sector pay with that of the private sector. It was said afterwards that Clegg leaned to the side of the workers, but at the time the Conservatives agreed to bring his recommendations into effect if they won the election.

At the beginning of what became known as the 'winter of discontent', Callaghan had upset people by suggesting that Britain's troubles were much smaller than those of other countries (soon paraphrased as 'What crisis?'), but it was also felt that the Conservatives were too extreme in their approach to trade unions and to political issues in general. The wave of strikes which drove the number of days lost in 1979 up to 29.5 million, and the aggressive picketing with which some of them were conducted, led the public to welcome Conservative proposals to enlarge the police force and reduce the legal immunities of trade unions. The government decided to put the election off until October, the last possible moment, and hope that the summer would restore everyone's good humour, but this strategy was destroyed by the March referendums. In Scotland 33 per cent of the electorate voted for devolution and 31 per cent against it; as devolution had not gained the support of 40 per cent of the electorate the legislation lapsed. The Nationalists asserted that the government ought to produce a new piece of legislation, but the opinion polls suggested they had lost a good deal of support. Skilful debating by anti-devolutionists like Tam Dalyell had brought out previously unnoticed difficulties in the proposals, but some Scots seem to have supported devolution more to show London that they wanted attention paid to their problems than because they were committed to the policy.

The Welsh referendum was a one-sided rejection of the proposals: 12 per cent of the electorate voted for devolution and 47 per cent against. In Scotland the Labour Party had campaigned for devolution but many organizations in the Labour Party in Wales opposed it; the Scottish Nationalists had not been particularly hostile to the Labour Party, so it was easy enough for the Labour Party to work with them, but Plaid Cymru had won support by campaigning against Labour governments and against Labour municipal corruption. The dominant figure in the debate was Neil Kinnock, descended from a Scottish mining family which had moved to Wales, who became prominent in a group of Labour MPs organizing opposition to the proposals. The assembly at Cardiff was an easy target because it looked like another form of the municipal government with all its failings which Plaid Cymru had denounced so effectively. Some Scots were afraid that their assembly might be dominated by Strathclyde, made up of Glasgow and the surrounding region, which might spend too much of the revenue on its local problems of poverty, and relations with Westminster could also cause problems. But the proposals for Scotland won some support from people who valued devolution for its own sake while the proposals for Wales gained very little support except from nationalists, who saw them as a step towards what they really wanted. In elections later in 1979 and in 1983 the vote for Plaid Cymru fell much less far from its peak in the early 1970s than the Scottish Nationalist vote, which suggested that for a time Scottish nationalism had attracted the whole country, while Welsh nationalism had a permanent appeal for a cultural and linguistic minority which was strongest in Gwynedd, and in the 1970s had gained support elsewhere.

The dispute about Welsh television in 1980 showed that national sentiment could reawaken easily, and illustrated the ambiguity of attitudes to the Welsh-language. All parties promised to set up a Welsh language television channel in the 1979 election, but after the election the government considered reinterpreting the pledge in a way that was widely thought to be a betrayal. The protest at this in Wales went far beyond Plaid Cymru and the speakers of Welsh; even allowing for those who wanted Welsh to be kept off the three existing channels, it was clear that many of the non-Welsh-speaking Welsh valued the language as a sign of cultural distinctiveness and would oppose unfair treatment for it. The government prudently gave way; the Welsh-language channel was set up, but inevitably attracted only a small number of viewers.

By then a new government was in office, after an election precipitated by the nationalist question but not otherwise affected by it. Because the Scottish Nationalists believed the government should have enacted devolution after the referendum and the Liberals wanted to prove their independence, the government lost a motion of no confidence on 28 March by 311 votes to 310, and for the first time since 1924 an election was held at a time chosen by the Commons rather than the Prime Minister. The Labour Party had no time to recover from the damage done by the winter of discontent; Callaghan's personal popularity as an advocate of moderation did not outweigh memories of the 1976 deflation, the steady rise in prices, and the recent strikes. Some converts from Labour—an ex-editor of the *New Statesman*, a couple of Harold Wilson's peers, and so on—supported the Conservatives and, while their collective weight was undoubtedly less than that of Powell's support for Labour in 1974, their appearance reminded people that the Labour Party was no longer able to recruit from other parties as it had done in the past. The desire for further cuts in income tax was widespread, and this could only damage the

Labour Party, which was seen as the party of high taxes. The Labour left had some success in having the tax threshold linked to rises in the cost of living. The Liberals wanted a shift from direct to indirect taxes, which would have surprised their Free Trade forefathers, and the Conservatives wanted to reduce all rates of tax. They promised that government spending would be cut, and talked as if this was just a matter of ending government extravagance by dismissing superfluous civil servants. Change on the scale that they implied clearly meant abolishing some government activities. In less than twenty years government spending had advanced from 33 per cent of the national income to 41 per cent, and reversing this would require a drastic reappraisal of the role of the State.

For two or three generations the dividing line between manual and non-manual workers (sometimes called the line between the middle class and the working class) had been the best guide to voting habits. Labour's original electoral base was being eroded because manual workers were becoming a smaller proportion of the workforce, but it was winning more non-manual support than in the past. Governments spent more, and a good deal of it went to pay non-manual workers who might go on strike against their central or municipal government employers but were likely to vote Labour because they had every reason to want the State to spend more. Schoolteachers and social workers were understood to belong to the middle class, but by the 1970s they had some interests in common with the traditional unionized working class and no longer paid so much attention to ideas about the respectability and social prestige of their jobs. While this non-manual group was providing recruits to Labour, the Conservatives were attracting some manual workers by promising lower taxes, a better chance to work their way forward, and, in particular, the opportunity to buy their own homes. Self-employed manual workers were very likely to respond to this and by 1979 were voting in very much the same way as the general run of non-manual workers. Owner-occupiers had always tended to vote Conservative; by 1979 this was affecting working-class voting and the Conservatives' proposal to sell council houses to sitting tenants was, like other steps towards a property-owning democracy, a measure that would increase the number of electors who leaned towards the Conservatives. Even though substantial numbers of council tenants wanted to buy their homes, the general reputation of council housing was low, and this probably intensified the widespread feeling that governments could not run publicly owned sectors of the economy efficiently. It may also be guessed that Labour suffered because some of its supporters sneered at owner-occupiers.

The weakening of the line between manual and non-manual workers and the emergence of new lines of division did not mean that no important issues remained to be settled. The line between collectivist and individualist values remained much the same as it had been most of the century, but workers were no longer so sure on which side of the line their jobs placed them.

	Votes	Seats	% of all votes cast
Conservative	13,697,690	339	43.9
Liberal	4,313,811	11	13.8
Labour	11,523,148	269	36.9
Scottish Nationalist	504,259	2	1.6
Plaid Cymru	132,544	2	0.4
Unionists in Ulster	410,419	10	1.3
Others	630,107	2	2.0

The Conservatives gained fewer seats than might have been expected from their substantial lead over the Labour Party in votes. They gained votes in roughly equal numbers from the Liberals and from Labour, but, while the Liberals lost what they had gained when both major parties were unpopular in the 1970s, Labour held on, helped by its constantly renewed supply of under-populated inner-city seats, where the destruction of slums and the desire for more living space thinned out the population of its strongholds. Its weakness was shown more clearly in the first direct election for the European Parliament, held a few weeks later, in which the Conservatives won sixty seats and the Labour Party won seventeen, leaving two for Unionists in Northern Ireland and one each for nationalists in Scotland and in Northern Ireland.

Labour and Conservatives on a tightrope

Thatcher was a politician of strong and simple opinions. If Callaghan had embodied common sense, Thatcher added conviction to common sense. What she said about reducing the role of government, stopping prices going up, and enabling everybody to become better off by individual effort sounded very attractive after fifteen or eighteen years of eager government intervention. During those years people felt they had become better off only when they had escaped from government control for short bursts of prosperity. Occasionally they shook off restraints like incomes policy, but they rather expected restrictions to return after a year or two of growth too rapid to be sustained accompanied by price increases that became more and more alarming. Intervention seemed to lead to slow growth, rising unemployment, and a steady decline in prosperity relative to other nations. Non-intervention might offer something different.

Thatcher's control of her government was not complete. Supporters of her views, which could be seen as the attitudes of the middle class on the way up, were balanced in the Cabinet by advocates of a tradition of looking after those lower in the social scale, upheld mainly by those who already had a well-established position. So a dispute about Conservative principles might erupt, though the new government had to start by tackling the large amount of unfinished business left by the Labour government.

Effective force for change in Rhodesia was unleashed only when Portugal gave up its colonies in Angola and Mozambique in 1975. Once guerrilla forces could operate from bases in Mozambique on Rhodesia's north and east borders, they could drive the South African government to press Smith to establish a moderate African government like that of Malawi. Smith accepted this and by 1978 he had brought a number of African leaders, of whom Bishop Muzorewa was the most conspicuous, into a delicately balanced coalition of blacks and whites. This government was denounced as a façade for continued white rule, and the general election it held under universal suffrage, with various guarantees for the position of the whites, in April 1979 was not quite like the election going on in Britain at the same time. The main question was whether the government could get a high enough turnout to show that the guerrillas could not make African voters boycott the election. The 64 per cent turnout showed that the government had quite a strong position: and when Muzorewa went on to become Prime Minister of the awkwardly named Zimbabwe-Rhodesia, Thatcher's first impulse was to recognize his government.

Recognition would probably have been accepted. The other members of the European Community had never been very concerned about the issue and the Muzorewa government had enough support in Congress to make it hard for the American government to oppose the move. But the Foreign Secretary, Lord Carrington, persuaded Thatcher to try to reconcile the guerrillas with Muzorewa's government, to reduce the risk that they would fight on and that other African governments would say the whites were still in control. If the guerrillas took part in an impartially administered election, the winner of the election would hold unquestioned authority. All sides accepted this policy; Lord Soames went to Zimbabwe-Rhodesia as a combination of a proconsul and an election returning officer, and in the 1980 election the parties led by the guerrillas won decisively and then presided over the emergence of Zimbabwe as an independent state. The election result was not what Thatcher wanted, but the British could at least feel that they had ended a problem that had caused them more diplomatic difficulty than anything else in the whole process of decolonization. But the length of the dispute, and the high moral tone in which well-wishers had given advice to Britain, had encouraged a feeling that the Commonwealth might deserve 'tepid applause' but was interested mainly in influencing British policy towards Rhodesia and, later on, towards South Africa.[3]

3. *The Economist,* 10 Oct. 1981 and 3 Dec. 1983.

At least it cost very little. The Conservatives came to office just as the high cost of membership of the European Community was becoming inescapable. The transition period in which Britain was shielded from the impact of the Common Agricultural Policy (CAP) ran out in 1978, and in the weeks before the election it became known officially that the concessions gained in the 1974–5 renegotiations would save Britain only about £350 million of the £1 billion to £1.5 billion due to be paid out annually. Labour ministers would never have found it easy to ask for further renegotiations, but Thatcher had no record of hostility to the Community to live down, nor any perfervid statements in favour of it to disavow. Like most people in Britain, she accepted the Community as a not especially welcome part of the background of political life but saw no reason why it should be a drain on Britain's financial resources. The other members of the Community agreed it was anomalous for Britain to be a large net contributor with a lower per capita income than six of the nine members, but were less ready to give Britain permanent guarantees against losses that presumably had been foreseen at the moment of entry. Year-by-year rebates were granted, and the refunds of the early 1980s reduced the net payments to about £500 million. Some Community countries argued that Britain's energy resources solved all her problems, which implied that coal and oil were assets more permanent than agriculture or industry. Opponents of Britain's claims could also hope that British agriculture would expand until its CAP benefits balanced Britain's other contributions to Community funds, but the rate of growth of British agriculture slowed in the early 1980s, perhaps because farmers could see that the CAP was being criticized and that other claims on funds would increase as the less prosperous countries of southern Europe (of which Greece in 1981 was the first) joined the Community. Opposition to the CAP could not be taken too far; in 1982 the convention that unanimity was needed for important decisions was ignored, and the other nine members increased the farm budget despite Britain's opposition. But Thatcher's strategy of stating a sweetly reasonable case with great determination eventually had its effect, and at Fontainebleau in 1984 an agreement was reached that gave a fairly permanent guarantee that Britain's net payments would only be about half the level they would otherwise have been.

In Northern Ireland the prospect of a settlement lay even further in the future. Perhaps the assassination of Lord Mountbatten while on holiday in the Republic of Ireland in 1979 showed that the IRA was having difficulty penetrating the defences that had gone up in Northern Ireland, and the fall in the number of deaths in 1980 was a more positively encouraging sign. Towards the end of the year members of Sinn Fein set out to show their refusal to accept British rule by going on hunger strike in prison. As forcible feeding of hunger strikers had recently been ended, they were free to choose whether to live or die, which gave them an opportunity to emulate the famous Lord Mayor of Cork who starved himself to death in an English prison in 1920. In 1981 ten

IRA members (including one, Bobby Sands, who had been elected to Parliament while in prison) did starve themselves to death. The government stood unmoved and made it clear that unrelenting self-sacrifice by a minority would not be allowed to break up the United Kingdom. In August the hunger strikers gave up; tension had naturally been increased and the number of deaths rose slightly, but it never returned to the levels seen in the 1970s. Proposals for political change became no more than the background to restoring tranquillity by transferring responsibility to the reorganized Royal Ulster Constabulary and drawing back from military operations, in the hope that this might improve relations with the Republic of Ireland and erode the IRA bases of operation north and south of the border.

While the EEC contributions and the emergence of Zimbabwe were handled at least as successfully as any problems faced by British governments in the preceding ten or fifteen years, the real challenge faced and even welcomed by the new government was the wave of pay increases far larger than could be matched by the sluggish growth of production of an economy that had been doing badly for years. By the time of the election the winter of discontent was affecting prices: under incomes policy price increases had fallen from a level of 27 per cent between mid-1974 and mid-1975 to only 8 per cent between mid-1977 and mid-1978, but by early 1979 they were going up faster. If the Labour government regretted being forced into an election before people could forget the strikes, at least it did not have to face the bill for them. That fell to the new Chancellor of the Exchequer, Sir Geoffrey Howe, but his budget in June 1979 dealt with questions of taxation and left the problems of prices until later.

His budget brought the standard rate of income tax of 33p in the pound back to the 1970–4 level of 30p. The highest rate of tax was reduced from 83p to 60p, with corresponding cuts in other rates of surtax. (The investment surcharge stayed at 15p: those who paid at the top marginal rate of 98p rather than use the methods of tax avoidance, from life insurance to National Savings certificates, provided by the government, would now pay at 75p.) To pay for these tax cuts the rates of value added tax were made uniform at a new, sharply increased rate of 15 per cent. Those who accepted the theory that inflation is driven forward by the size of the budget deficit would have expected the long-term effects of these changes upon prices to be neutral, and Howe laid down a medium-term financial strategy along the lines Healey had followed since 1976: the Public Sector Borrowing Requirement would not exceed £8 billion a year, and the supply of money would be tightly controlled. Whatever the effects in years to come, the increases in value added tax pushed prices up at once and made everyone feel they would go on rising. The small minority who paid the higher rates of income tax were rather better off, and the great majority who paid at the standard rate or did not pay at all were slightly worse off, but reductions in income tax were seen as a long-overdue relaxation of the fiscal burden and increases in value added tax were treated as another rise in the cost of living, to be counteracted by pay increases.

The implications of the new government's idea of its role in the economy took some time to sink in. Governments had shifted regularly from expansionist to deflationary policies, but it was taken for granted that really they preferred spending money; circumstances might make them slow down, but they would spend more when times changed. Thatcher and Howe thought a government should prefer reducing taxes to spending money, so that it took as little of the national income as possible. The public was probably not surprised to see spending cuts once again after enjoying the delights of anarchy when the incomes policy collapsed, but it had not realized that this policy would be maintained and that ministers had few inhibitions about increasing unemployment to cut costs because they believed that some jobs were of so little use that the workers might as well be turned out to look for something more useful to do. The new government had its own commitments to higher spending. Its acceptance of Clegg's proposals for increasing Civil Service pay would cost at least £300 million a year. In opposition it had vociferously approved of the programme for a 3 per cent real increase in defence spending that the members of the NATO alliance had undertaken in 1977. A smaller item, a promise to spend more money on the police force, was intended to give substance to the claim that the Conservatives cared about law and order, with the implication that their opponents did not.

The phrase 'law and order' linked two issues. After the 1920s indictable criminal offences had risen year by year, unaffected by changes of government or by the steady expansion of the police force. Sometimes it was suggested that a bigger police force just led to better reporting of crime, or that victims had become more sensitive and reported crimes they would have ignored in the past, but most people believed that crime was increasing and that a larger police force would hold it in check. Calls for law and order were also prompted by an increase in what would once have been called 'riotous assembly'. Picketing in strikes, taking part in political demonstrations, and watching football matches do not necessarily have much in common, but by the late 1970s all of them were carried out in a much more violent way than for many years past. The images of strikers fighting the police at Saltley, of political enthusiasts of the extreme left and right fighting each other whenever the police would let them, and of supporters of association football clubs treating matches as an excuse for battles with supporters of the other side (leading up to a riot in 1985 at Brussels in which Liverpool supporters fought with Italian spectators, thirty-eight of whom were killed, which led to an international ban upon all matches with English clubs) left a general impression of violence that made the majority support more rigorous policing, which in turn led a minority to speak as if these changes were laying the foundations of a police state.

Concern about law and order was matched by concern about prices, which went up by 12 per cent in 1979 and by 18 per cent in 1980; the government hoped that spending cuts would control the effects of pre-election light-heartedness but gave no sign of more direct intervention. Unemployment had declined very little during the financial relaxation of the Labour government's last months in office and never fell below 5 per cent, so it was no surprise that it soon went back above 6 per cent when public spending was cut. The Opposition protested, but its complaints carried less weight because people could remember that so many jobs had been lost between 1974 and 1977.

Changes in the age distribution of the population and in the shape of the economy made unemployment harder to reduce. Between the 1971 and the 1981 censuses the section of the population aged between 15 and 65 rose by just under a million, moving from 63 per cent to 64.5 per cent of the total. The rise in the birth rate had reached a peak in the mid-1960s, so in 1981, 2,727,947 people aged from 15 to 17 were about to enter the labour market, compared with 2,239,760 people in this age group in 1971; and it was argued that these young people were paid such high wages, compared with what was paid to established workers, that they could not find jobs easily. As in the 1920s and 1930s the proportion of the population that was looking for work was rising rapidly, but between the wars the problem was reduced by the convention that married women ought not to bring a second income to their family when other families had no earnings. By the 1970s this attitude was out of date; women demanded greater freedom, including freedom to compete for jobs. Women would probably have become a larger part of the labour force even if attitudes had not changed. Jobs were disappearing in steel, in coal-mining, in shipbuilding, and in car-making, which had always been more or less closed to women, while the posts for typists, clerks, and receptionists offered in the expanding sectors of the economy had come to be seen as jobs for women. So it was hard to say whether women looked for jobs because they felt liberated, or felt liberated because it was easier to find jobs than in the past. Young people entering the labour market might have no preconceptions that some jobs were for men and some were for women, but they still had to contend with the inability of the market to handle a flood of new workers, although clearly this was not going to last long because the birth rate of the early 1980s was only about two-thirds of what it had been at the 1960s peak. Workers looking for a job found their problems intensified by the legislation of the mid-1970s which tried to improve workers' conditions by requiring fairly generous payments linked to years of service for those who lost their jobs (or were 'declared redundant'). This cushioned the pain of losing a job, but it also made employers much more careful about taking on new workers because they had to think about the costs of laying them off if the economy slowed down.

While more workers were looking for jobs and changes in the law discouraged the creation of new jobs, sharp changes in the financial background made employment harder to expand. Sterling sank lower in the mid-1970s and then rose higher at the beginning of the 1980s than the country's economic prospects justified. Oil prices early in 1979 seemed to be moving up gently from $12 a barrel, but the economic advantage of North Sea oil was immensely increased when the Shah of Iran was overthrown by a religious revolution in the course of which his country's oil production was sharply reduced. Prompt action by OPEC pushed prices up to $33 a barrel by the end of 1980. Any bank or currency dealer trying to put money where it would benefit from increases in the price of oil would naturally think of sterling as the most convenient of the petro-currencies: the readily tradeable National Debt provided a vast range of opportunities for investing this money. (Everybody felt sure the price of oil could only move upwards, but theoreticians noted that other man-oeuvres could be carried out in sterling if the oil price fell—facilities for dealing in Arabian riyals or Venezuelan bolivars were distinctly limited, but there were well-tested facilities for selling sterling short.) As money poured into sterling, its value rose to a peak of just over $2.40 late in 1980. The government's efforts to resist price increases by allowing interest rates to go up provided another reason for keeping short-term funds in London By late 1979 the minimum lending rate was 17 per cent and twelve months later it was still at 16 per cent. The effects were much the same as Montagu Norman's policy of holding the bank rate at 7 per cent in 1920: employers dismissed workers as fast as they could in order to reduce their overdrafts, and banks received large inflows of money that could not prudently be used for long-term investment in Britain.

The abrupt rise in the value of the pound hampered trade, and the government applied its free market principles to the problem. The exchange controls imposed at the beginning of the Second World War were dismantled. During those forty years life insurance had expanded substantially and pension plans had turned from a rare and ill-understood privilege into a benefit taken for granted in any salaried post, enjoyed by all workers in nationalized industries and coming to be expected by wage-earners elsewhere. Partly because people earned enough to be able to save, and partly because life insurance and retirement pensions were the most tax-efficient way to do so, City of London institutions had built up large investment funds. The exchange controls had limited the amount they could invest overseas, so, when the controls were removed, they set about balancing their portfolios on a world-wide basis. The beneficiaries of the funds probably got better pensions as a result, and some of the impact of short-term money flowing into London was neutralized by the substantial sums that went overseas for investment. The outward flow never took as much of the national income as the outflow in the years before 1914, but funds invested overseas, which came to about £12.5 billion when exchange controls were removed, had risen to £70 billion five years later. Money flowed into Britain as well, earning a higher immediate rate of return than the money going out, but on balance about £35 billion to £40 billion went out of the country which might have been used to finance the expansion of new industries in Britain, although the pound might have risen to heights that impeded exports even more if the money had not gone overseas.

The government seemed unmoved by this, and expressed its view of the situation by referring to the need for 'real jobs'. Even allowing for the low level of capital investment for each worker, British workers were less productive than those in most industrialized countries. Ministers were worried by the large numbers of people employed by central and local governments and in particular by the conditions of the nationalized industries, which made losses that the Exchequer had to meet. The Labour government had given a clear-headed manager, Michael Edwardes, a fairly free hand to cut losses at the car manufacturer British Leyland even if it reduced employment. This was a large step away from a policy which, when Labour came to office, looked like a desire to preserve all existing jobs no matter what the cost. The Conservatives followed a similar policy; an aggressive businessman, Ian MacGregor, was brought back from the United States to cut the steel industry's losses, which he did by paying steelworkers generously to give up their jobs, and then closing the more irredeemably unprofitable steelworks. The new school of managers sharply reduced the long-term drain on the Exchequer of the nationalized industries; at first losses were higher than before, but most of this money was spent to reduce costs in the future. The policy involved a considerable loss of jobs, but its defenders said that the point of having a steel industry or a motor industry was to provide steel or cars at reasonable prices rather than maintain jobs at great expense in industries that were bound to contract.

Some nationalized industries, such as North Sea oil and gas or the telecommunications section that emerged as a separate organization when the Post Office was divided in two, were likely to be profitable, and ministers became more and more enthusiastic about selling these industries to private investors. The Labour government's sale of British Petroleum shares in 1977 was one example of privatization, but the success of the government's election promise to let council tenants buy their homes was much more important. The opportunity was accepted eagerly, perhaps because sitting tenants were given large discounts, or because owning property was attractive, or because municipal landlords imposed irritating regulations. About three-quarters of a million homes were sold in six years, at an average price of around £8,000. Labour councils denounced this in terms that suggested that council houses were let solely to people on the verge of destitution, and that all tenants who bought their homes were incipient members of the exploitative bourgeoisie. The position of councils in the housing market was under pressure from another direction: the blocks of flats they had put up quickly in the 1960s turned out to be so unsatisfactory that by the 1980s councils faced bills for repairs and restoration considerably larger than all the proceeds of the sale of houses.

Steps towards denationalization, now usually called privatization, fitted government policy in several ways. If privatized industries made losses, that was their own concern: shares in the aircraft firms nationalized in 1976 under the name of British Aerospace were sold to the public and the government could then insist that the firm had to be run simply to make a profit. Proceeds from sales could be counted as a reduction in the borrowing requirement; more British Petroleum shares and a part of the government's North Sea holdings were sold as a way to avoid borrowing more money. The industries nationalized in the 1940s would not be so easy to sell, and the government spent heavily to keep the coal and steel industries going, but it hoped to reduce the activity of the state and to avoid industrial conflict with its own employees in the future. The state employed considerably more people in its non-commercial activities and these activities cost a good deal, not all of it under the direct control of the central government. Ministers hoped that they could show enough Gladstonian firmness to reduce the Civil Service salary bill, and they also wanted to attack the rate support grant system under which the central government paid for about 60 per cent of municipal activity, which cost about £11 billion in 1979–80. The government began by reducing the percentage paid and the activities it had to support, and went on to give the Secretary of State power to fix a maximum rate. Labour councils wanted to keep up a high level of municipal services and some of them seemed intent on setting up 'socialism in one borough'; the central government did not want to spend its money supporting this, but the pattern of reliance on central funds was so complex that the government could not simply tell councils to spend what they liked and pay for all of it out of their own rates. And so the Conservatives imposed limits on municipal autonomy which had the effect of increasing rather than diminishing the power of the central government.

Early in the 1979 Parliament Labour MPs amused themselves by shouting 'U-turn' when the government seemed to be moderating its policies, with the implication that it was about to change course as Heath had done late in 1972. This probably embarrassed the ministers who did want moderation, and it helped Thatcher to rally her supporters behind her slogan 'There is no alternative'. Government policy was not changed: nationalized industries were trimmed, limits were placed on government spending, interest rates stayed high, and the Opposition naturally said that the rising unemployment of the 1980s was a direct result. The phrase 'real jobs' had some validity, in the sense that productivity went up among those who still had jobs, but the policy left resources of both capital and labour unused. When the rate of inflation began to fall and the level of unemployment went on rising, previous post-war governments had changed course and behaved in the way Callaghan had condemned in 1976. The Conservatives stuck to their policy, and Howe's deflationary budget in 1981 provoked howls of anguish on every side. In the course of 1981 Thatcher dismissed three or four ministers who showed some support for reflation, and provided new terms for the old debate by calling them 'wet', whereupon the two sides of the struggle in the party came to be called 'wets' and 'drys'. The 'drys' held all the important posts for economic matters; the 'wets' built up a group of ex-ministers and dissatisfied ministers waiting for a chance to overthrow the Prime Minister.

These disputes were almost driven out of the headlines by the more spectacular quarrels in the Labour Party. Its members ignored the fact that in 1979 the Conservatives had been further ahead of their opponents in terms of share of the popular vote than any party had been since the Labour victory of 1945, and they behaved as if waiting for Conservative mistakes would be quite sufficient to recover the lost votes. The left claimed that the leadership's neglect of socialist principle had caused the defeat, and pressed on with its plans to make the leadership accountable to the party enthusiasts. In 1979 the attack advanced successfully on two fronts: the rules were changed to require all Labour MPs to submit themselves to their constituency organizations after each election (with the implication that anyone who had not followed the line preferred by the enthusiasts would be replaced); and pressure mounted to have the party leader chosen by a conference representing party members rather than the parliamentary party. The drive to change the constitution was skilfully organized and was given energy by the sense of betrayal aroused by the defeated government (exacerbated by the way some unwelcome Conservative moves were presented for debating purposes as simply the logical result of steps taken by the Labour government). In June 1980 it was agreed that a new method of choosing the leader would soon be adopted. In October Callaghan resigned, allowing the parliamentary party to choose a leader before the new constitution came into effect. This was believed to be meant to give Denis Healey as good a chance of winning as possible, but the MPs chose Foot as party leader by a margin of ten votes over Healey. Early in 1981 a special conference created an electoral college for future elections in which the trade unions would have 40 per cent of the votes, the constituency parties 30 per cent, and the parliamentary party 30 per cent. The left expected to have a large majority in the constituency section and support from strong minorities in the other sections, a calculation borne out by the election for the deputy leadership later in the year: Healey beat Benn by the narrowest of margins, and owed his slender majority to the fact that some left-wing MPs abstained out of personal distrust of Benn.

Who dares wins

The Labour Party had moved to the left in policy as well as in terms of constitution and leadership. Its programme of heavier taxes, of extension of government power by nationalization and planning agreements, and of withdrawal from the European Community established the policies that the Labour left thought had been abandoned in the 1960s and betrayed in the 1970s. The right wing was dismayed to see what the party had become. Roy Jenkins, the reforming Home Secretary and hard-hitting Chancellor of the Exchequer of the 1960s, had become President of the Commission of the European Community; he made it clear that when he came back to the United Kingdom he would work to realign the centre and the left. Three of Callaghan's Cabinet ministers, who in 1980 had fought to place the choice of party leader in the hands of the party members as in the Liberal Party, joined Jenkins after their defeat at the 1981 special conference, and in March the four of them launched the Social Democratic Party, which quickly attracted a couple of dozen Labour backbench MPs. The new party had close links with the Liberals: its creators were deeply committed to the European Community, which the Liberals had supported since the 1950s, while very few of the Labour MPs who worried about the party's shift to the left but were uneasy about membership of the Community joined the new party. The Social Democrats also found common ground with the Liberals in a desire to 'break the mould' of British politics; the phrase implied that the political dominance of the two major parties should be brought to an end, probably by adopting a system of proportional representation that would make it hard for any single party to win a parliamentary majority. Most governments would then have to be coalitions of the European type, where parties in the centre of the spectrum can expect to be welcomed as partners in successive governments.

Because the two major parties had been moving away from the centre, people who wanted a policy of moderation and compromise felt that there was no party to represent them. The Alliance, as the joint efforts of the Liberals and Social Democrats soon came to be called, implied that 'breaking the mould' would get people back to the politics of consensus that were attributed to the legendary Mr Butskell of the 1950s. Forced to choose between a government committed to economic theories associated with higher unemployment and an Opposition that seemed to want to get back to a siege economy, voters naturally welcomed a less brutal approach. The Conservatives seemed to be going back to the 1930s and the Labour Party appeared to embrace the less enjoyable aspects of the 1940s, so the Alliance looked more humane and up to date. And in a series of by-elections after the Social Democrats' secession from the Labour Party the Alliance won a number of seats that had previously been held securely by one or other major party, and did well enough elsewhere to have won over 400 seats if an election had been held in 1981.

The Alliance was greatly helped by the interest that the media were bound to take in anything new, perhaps reinforced by the personal approval felt for it by many journalists and broadcasters. But when politicians in the major parties spoke of the Alliance as the creation of the media, they revealed that they did not realize how unpopular they had become. Some of this was due to trivial causes, such as the broadcasting of Commons proceedings that showed how raucously the MPs behaved, and some of it to a record of twenty years in which politicians had failed to produce effective policies. The Alliance looked like an answer to the demand for an effective government.

The volatility of public feeling and the inability of politicians to do anything about it (and perhaps the capacity of the mass media to encourage developments without necessarily understanding them) was shown in a very different way in the summer of 1981. Discontent might be widespread, but drafting new programmes for the Social Democrats was rather a specialized response to it. Tension between the police and young people had been increasing for some years, encouraged by the development of 'riotous assembly'. Tension between the police and recent Asian and West Indian immigrants had also been growing as their newly created communities tried to work out their relations with their neighbours and got less help in this from the police than they had hoped for. Youths of West Indian descent in Brixton in south London became more and more convinced that the police were discriminating against them on racial grounds; the police and many people around Brixton became sure that it was a less safe place than the rest of the country. In April heavy police patrolling of the district led to riots that looked like a struggle for control of the streets; tranquillity was restored after a week or so, and the subsequent inquiry concluded that the police had a hard job in a difficult area but that heavy patrolling had not been a sensible way to manage things. Well before the Scarman Report appeared, riots broke out in late June and early July in a number of cities in England, most notably in Liverpool. Some people said that racial tension had spread to other parts of the country, but the riots were much more obviously directed against the police, whom black and white fought together, than against one race or another. Opponents of the government's economic policy said the riots were the result of unemployment, but outside Brixton the riots took place in the early evening often enough to suggest that the rioters came home from work or school, had tea, changed into thicker boots, and went out to look for excitement. If frustration with the narrowness of life and its prospects helped to cause the riots, which would explain why people from the West Indies rioted more than anyone else, it was understandable that the mood of excitement on the streets died away in July as the country prepared to celebrate the wedding of the Prince of Wales and Lady Diana Spencer.

The royal family had survived relatively undamaged in the decline of confidence in British institutions in the previous twenty or thirty years. The

Queen's Silver Jubilee in 1977 had provided the public with an opportunity to enjoy itself when political and economic affairs gave no reason for feeling happy; the royal wedding in 1981 gave everyone something to remember (and greatly helped sales and rentals of the newly developed video cassette recorder in the process). The sophisticated sneered at the fairytale princess and at the way the ceremony was designed as a spectacle for television, but this showed no understanding of the forces that keep nations together. The symbolism of royal ceremonies in previous centuries had been intended to impress the participants, who were the most important people in the country. By the twentieth century these ceremonies had to be designed for the entire country to watch, and the country welcomed the pageantry and the glitter in a more united spirit than could be expected on any other occasion. The outbursts of national feeling provoked by sporting events were unstable and could be destructive. The Churches still had a hold on the attention of the faithful, but had almost entirely lost their capacity for making ordinary people feel that they belonged to a community. Foreign visitors undoubtedly still felt that the unarmed police were wonderful, but critics inside the country said they were racist, or unable to catch criminals, or apt to become a political force at the disposal of the government. The police were in any case being issued with firearms more frequently, which led to other problems: the injury and even the death of citizens as a result of police mishandling of their weapons was the immediate cause of a new outbreak of riots in Brixton, in Liverpool, and in other disturbed parts of large cities in the autumn of 1985. The armed services retained a good deal of public respect, shown in an indirect way when left-wing politicians preceded their speeches asking for cuts in arms spending by saying that they did not want to criticize the armed forces. The rescue by the Special Air Service of hostages held in the Iranian Embassy in 1980 was a skilful and acrobatic feat, achieved with a level of approval that showed people wanted Britain to have a chance to assert herself. The withdrawal from empire and entry into the European Community looked like steps, however sensible, that had been taken because Britain was too weak to do anything else. Some members of the royal family still served as a stabilizing force in national life, but marriage break-ups and other signs of strain suggested that marrying into the royal family was much easier than living happily ever after. The end of the Prince of Wales's marriage led on to events as dramatic as some earlier royal marital problems. The limits placed on constitutional monarchy meant that even in the best of circumstances it could not go beyond maintaining stability.

People who wanted politicians to provide the energy to bringing about change had to contemplate a paradoxical pair of party leaders. Foot's principles were those of an interventionist socialist who believed the State could run society, but he could never convince people that his government would be competent enough to do this, and his friends said that his instincts leaned towards an anarchist version of socialism. Thatcher clearly possessed the dynamism and probably the efficiency to carry out an interventionist policy but was firmly committed to a non-interventionist role for the State. She was said to be divisive and so, at a deeper level than her opponents understood, she was. For almost a century one of the forces holding British society together was what Beatrice Webb called 'a new consciousness of sin among men of intellect and men of property'. The dislocation of urbanization and industrialization had caught the attention of the rich in the 1880s, and the troubles of the 1920s and 1930s, not fully understood until the 1940s, had made an important section of the rich accept the case for reform, which in turn had greatly helped the setting up of the Welfare State and probably eased the process of decolonization. Most Conservative leaders from Disraeli onwards had allowed this sentiment considerable importance in forming their policies, and several leaders of the Labour Party had accepted the same assumptions.

By the 1970s this approach was breaking down. The Labour left repudiated it as paternalist, and Thatcher's supporters in the Conservative Party were free from the notion that society owed a debt to the poor which had been accepted for a generation or two. 'Thatcherism' meant rather more than balancing the budget and cutting government spending; its attraction and also its divisiveness lay in an appeal to individual effort and a promise that those who made the effort would get what they wanted. This might not be a doctrine for the majority of the country, but it was hard to see any other doctrine that could win a majority. The dominant wing of the Labour Party asked for equality but set out to build up a majority by convincing individuals that each one of them belonged to a disadvantaged minority that the Labour Party was going to look after. As each minority claim looked like a claim for special treatment, no common policy was going to convince them that they had a common interest. The desire for paternalist reform still survived; but its supporters were divided between the right wing of the Labour Party, the Alliance, and the anti-Thatcherite wing of the Conservative Party, which clearly placed its hopes in pushing her out. The new guilt-free Conservatives had a considerable appeal to British nationalism, with its own divisive features. Thatcher said in 1978 that she understood why people felt they were being swamped by immigrants. This did little to make immigrants feel welcome, but the small amount of public support gained in the 1970s by the National Front, a fringe political party that depended entirely on its opposition to immigration and immigrants, faded away once the more worried members of the white community felt that the government understood their anxiety.

Fortunately for the government, Zimbabwe was the only problem of decolonization in which common sense required it to withdraw unconditionally. Thus its reputation for asserting Britain's position was compromised less than that of almost every post-war government. In four colonies the population wanted to stay under British rule because the alternative was to be absorbed by a neighbouring state, and the government wanted to defend the position of each of them as far as was possible. Opinion in Gibraltar had been tested in 1967, when the government of the colony held a referendum in which forty-four people voted for union with Spain, 580 had not voted, and 12,138 had voted to remain a British colony. General Franco was then ruling Spain, and a vote held twelve or fifteen years later, when a constitutional monarchy had been set up, would probably have been less overwhelming. It would obviously be some time before developments in Spain, the reopening of the frontier, and the possible effects of common membership of the European Community altered the views of the inhabitants of the Rock. While Gibraltar could hardly become independent, British Honduras could manage well enough as an independent state if it did not feel threatened by Guatemala's claim to a great deal of her territory. British diplomats spent some years persuading other countries that British Honduras had a right to self-determination, and in 1981 it emerged as an independent state under the name of Belize, with about 2,000 British soldiers still stationed there to protect the border.

The 1,800 inhabitants of the Falklands Islands were numerically less signifi-cant than the population of Gibraltar, let alone Belize. The islands had been disputed between Britain and Spain in the late eighteenth century, and Argen-tina stood as the successor to the Spanish claim. The descendants of the people from Britain who had settled the islands in the 1830s showed no inter-est in relations with Argentina. By 1982 the military government ruling Argen-tina was so unpopular that it needed a success of some sort; a negotiated transfer of the islands might meet their needs, but the islanders' friends in the House of Commons had blocked previous attempts by the Foreign Office to find a formula for a transfer. The government of Argentina decided that seizure by force would show its power more effectively, and on 2 April Argen-tina seized the Falkland Islands, 600 or 700 kilometres east of her coastline, and also South Georgia, another 1,200 kilometres further east. The British government sent a task force off to sail 13,000 kilometres to the south, and began negotiating about the islands. With a great deal of goodwill and some concern about the feelings of the islanders, two governments with full free-dom of action might have settled the question peacefully; but Argentina had raised the stakes so far and so fast that it was hard to avoid humiliation for one side or the other. The rulers of Argentina could not agree among themselves on concessions to offer the British, and the British government had to win some concessions for the islanders if it was to concede eventual control over the islands. Popular opinion in Britain thought the campaign was justified and the popular press picked up this sentiment exuberantly and vulgarly. Intel-lectual opinion was uneasy about fighting for the islanders, and in some cases was rather obviously afraid that victory would be a triumph for Thatcher. People who had never before condemned the principle of fighting against a military dictatorship expressed lurid fears about the feasibility of the operation: on 25 April the *Sunday Times* said that 'a mass invasion could be achieved only at horrendous losses' and spoke of the only courses open to the British being 'as things stand, unthinkable'.

South Georgia was recaptured later on the 25th without any British casualties, and the expedition turned west to the Falklands. On 2 May a British submarine sank an Argentinian heavy cruiser, the *General Belgrano*. Subsequent investigation of the sinking of the *Belgrano* showed that the Defence Minister had not been able to keep up with the information coming to the naval authorities through the Northwood signals system from the Fleet in the South Atlantic; the government asserted that the need for secrecy about intelligence operations, including the question of which countries supplied information, meant that nothing could be said about the problem. At the time it was simply seen as the next step towards landing troops. To avoid the Argentinian forces in Port Stanley at the easternmost tip of the islands, the British went ashore in the sound between the two large islands of the archipelago, far enough west for the Argentinian air force, at the limit of its flying range, to launch a series of determined attacks on the landing area. Between 21 and 25 May the British lost four ships but the Argentinians lost too many planes to be able to continue the attack. After the landing was completed, the British advanced across the difficult terrain of East Falkland until Port Stanley was surrounded. Cut off from help and facing a well-trained, well-equipped force about three-fifths the size of their own, the Argentinian troops surrendered on 14 June. The military government fell, but the elected government that took its place showed no desire for negotiations that might have transferred the islands to Argentina in fifty or sixty years' time and the British government was certainly not going to think of moving any faster.

The campaign satisfied everyone in Britain who hoped the country would assert itself, and also pleased those who wanted it to act efficiently and effectively. The popularity of the government and of the Prime Minister rose sharply; she had committed herself totally to the campaign, and its success ended any idea that the Conservatives who wanted the government to concentrate on reducing unemployment would be able to dislodge her. The Alliance approved of the campaign and confined itself to making suggestions for improving the government's policy. Once the expedition had succeeded, the government was bound to benefit, especially as British casualties—255 servicemen and civilians killed—were accepted as a price low enough to be justified by victory, and the opposition to the use of force that gained acceptance inside the Labour Party could be seen as support in time of war for a government Labour had condemned on moral grounds in time of peace.

In 1983 the government turned in a businesslike way to clarify the position of Hong Kong. Britain held most of the territory of the small, densely populated, and prosperous colony under a ninety-nine-year lease ending in 1997. The Chinese government was eclectic enough in its communism to want to preserve the thriving business community; the British government was much more concerned to provide a long period in which business could go ahead as usual in the whole territory than to keep the original fragment of territory that had been ceded in freehold in 1842. In 1984 they were able to agree that the whole colony would revert to China in 1997 under a form of government that would let it keep its own commercial and capitalist way of life for at least fifty years after the transfer. The population would undoubtedly have preferred to stay under British rule or at least be given the right to emigrate to Britain. The British government felt that, as its lease was running out and its military strength in the region was non-existent, it had done the best it could to look after the interests of the people of the colony and stay on good terms with China.

This settlement came after a general election in which the government had won a success that surprised nobody. Unemployment had reached 12 per cent during the Falklands campaign; it went on rising, though much more slowly, in the next couple of years, and passed the 3 million level which (with a smaller working population) was never reached in the 1930s, but even in economic policy the government could claim one substantial success. In 1981 prices had gone up by 12 per cent, which was very close to the average rate of increase in the dozen years after 1970, but in 1982 the increase was only 7 per cent and it soon fell to 5 per cent. This was still much higher than the rate of increase in the 1950s and 1960s, and the Labour Party argued that the relative stability of prices was not worth the cost in unemployment, but after the 1970s people no longer believed that rising prices really did cure unemployment or improve the standard of living. The government won popular approval by carrying out its election promise to reduce inflation; governments had been so unsuccessful in the recent past that people were glad to have a leader with a clear policy that was put into effect.

In the exciting days of 1981 the Alliance had attracted not only the people who shared its point of view but also those who simply wanted a government that could get things done properly. Most of this group moved to support the Conservatives in 1982, though the Alliance remained in a much stronger position than that of the Liberals for the past forty years. The Labour Party showed how weak it was by insisting that it was too soon to have an election. In the autumn of 1982 memories of the Falklands might have distorted an election, but even in June 1983 the Labour Party was still complaining that the government was holding a 'cut and run' election before the proper time, which suggested that it would have been hard to find a date for the election that really suited the Opposition.

Labour's fears were justified. The Alliance improved its position in the weeks before polling day, but probably even the gloomiest Labour organizers did not expect their party's share of the total vote to be lower than at any election since 1918. Foot said the opinion polls must be wrong because large and enthusiastic audiences came to his meetings, but this only suggested he did not understand the strategy to which he was committed. A policy had been adopted to arouse enthusiasm on the left, and the enthusiasts were then meant to win support for it among the rest of the electorate. The opinion polls simply showed that the enthusiasts had failed. Labour supporters cherished the hope that voters would rise up against unemployment, but the issue did not have this effect; the great majority of workers stayed in work and their real wages stayed above the general level reached under the Labour government, while the improvement in 1978 and 1979 was dismissed as something that could not be sustained. Total income fell in the early 1980s and 1.5 million people lost their jobs, but this fall in living standards was felt almost exclusively by those who lost their jobs. Maintaining the unemployed absorbed all the money saved by cutting government spending and a good deal of North Sea oil revenue as well, so it was certainly true that all taxpayers were worse off than they would have been if employment had not fallen and production had gone up accordingly. Unemployment caused serious anxiety only when people were afraid it might spread to them; the government did badly in seats where unemployment was high (which were usually safe Labour seats already), but the issue mattered much less once unemployment stopped going up.

In aggregate terms it might look as if in 1983 the Alliance had taken about 8 per cent of the total 1979 vote from Labour and about 1.5 per cent from the Conservatives. It seems fairly certain that many Labour voters went over to the Conservatives, though it is hard to say if they were dissatisfied with their old party or attracted by their new one, and the Alliance undoubtedly won votes from Conservatives, presumably with 'wet' leanings, as well as from Labour.

	Votes	Seats	% of all votes cast
Conservative	13,012,602	397	42.4
Liberal–Social Democratic Alliance	7,780,587	23	25.4
Labour	8,457,124	209	27.6
Scottish Nationalist	331,975	2	1.1
Plaid Cymru	125,309	2	0.4
Unionists in Ulster	436,696	15	1.4
Others	526,612	2	1.7

The seats won bore very little relation to the votes cast: the Alliance polled nearly as many votes as the Labour Party but won only a few more seats than the Unionists in Ulster with their tiny fraction of the total vote. Politicians in the Alliance naturally felt that this strengthened their case for proportional representation (though their voters showed little sign of sharing their feelings) but could reflect that they had advanced all across the country and had come second in 332 seats, while the Labour vote had fallen to a quarter of the electorate, heavily concentrated in South Wales, the less prosperous parts of the industrial north of England, and much of industrial Scotland.

During the election Francis Pym, one of the 'wets' in the Cabinet, suggested that too large a majority might have disadvantages. This sounded like encouraging people to vote against the government and he was dismissed immediately after the election, but there was some sense to his remark. The Conservatives had the support of a large section of the nation and no other party had the strength to challenge it, but they had gained more seats than the Labour Party in 1945 with a decidedly smaller share of the vote, so perhaps seventy of their seats would be impossible to hold if a single dominant party re-emerged on the left or if their opponents reached an agreement to share seats as they had done in 1906. So a large group of Conservative MPs would find it unusually hard to respond calmly when their government faced the unpopularity that often occurs a couple of years after an election.

Foot resigned as leader of the Opposition at once. He had been almost as unsuccessful in leading his party as Arthur Balfour; he had been swept into the leadership by the bitterness aroused by the 1974–9 government and he had watched the right secede and the left impose an unpopular programme on the party without being able to prevent it or provide any new ideas for the party. His successor, Neil Kinnock, was elected under the 1981 rules which were meant to secure the position of the left, but he soon made it clear that his attachment to the left was qualified by a recognition of its great capacity for annoying people. Kinnock had gained part of his support because he had refused office in the government of the 1970s and most of it because of his power as an orator, but it looked as if he would have to rely on Thatcher's weaknesses and his own capacity to appear reasonable rather than on his party's positive qualities to win back some of the lost supporters.

The government attack on the collectivist state

After the election the Conservatives intensified the attack on public ownership. During the 1979–83 Parliament £1.4 billion of publicly owned enterprises had been sold off; in the first fifteen months of the new Parliament £1.7 billion were sold. Well over half of this came from the sale of oil shares and most of the rest from Jaguar cars and Cable and Wireless. No other sales produced over £100 million and the industries nationalized by the 1945 Labour government remained untouched. These sales were dwarfed by the sale of British Telecom in November 1984. It was clearly intended to match the sale of council houses in the 1979–83 Parliament: at a sale price of £4 billion it would realize a comparable sum of money and, if the sale of council houses was meant to produce a property-owning democracy, the sale of British Telecom was intended to produce a share-conscious electorate. The issuers were very successful at persuading a large number of people to buy and hold the shares, and over a million purchasers became owners of shares for the first time in their lives. The shares went to so large a premium that the Labour Party said that national assets were being sold for well below their true value and declared that they would buy the shares back compulsorily at the issue price, but the sale was so successful that only very brave politicians would have stuck to that pledge. Whatever the value of the shares the publicly owned telephone system had been so notorious for inefficiency and perverse technical ingenuity that very few people questioned the terms of the privatization. The zeal shown in the early decades of the Labour Party for nationalizing inefficient and declining industries had led the party into a trap: public ownership probably reduced the dislocation that accompanies the decline of an industry, but the nationalized industries were so unsuccessful that public ownership had no chance of becoming popular. Earlier in the century public ownership had given the Labour Party a distinctive issue with which to win its position on the left, but by the 1980s nationalization was a backward-looking vote-loser.

Coal had been one of the first industries considered for public ownership, and was one of the first to be nationalized after 1945. For the next dozen years it had been essential for British fuel supply, and then it had been run down peacefully and harmoniously in the 1960s as oil replaced coal. Between 1970 and 1984 the price of oil rose fifteenfold, and Britain became the world's fifth largest oil producer, which made it hard to plan a future for coal. All fuel became more valuable, but the miners won pay increases to make up for the decline in their real wages in the 1960s, so coal never became very profitable. Energy from coal and from oil were sold at about the same price, but, as about two-thirds of the oil price went to the Treasury in tax, only a deep concern that Britain's oil supplies might turn out to be a transient North Sea bubble would lead the government to support coal mines which paid no tax and lost money on their operations.

At first the National Union of Mineworkers (NUM) and the Conservative government circled each other warily. The government gave up one plan to close uneconomic pits; the miners declined to support their executive when it asked them to vote for a national strike. After the 1983 election the government contemplated the six months' supply of unsold coal that had piled up and moved MacGregor from the steel industry, where he had reduced the work-force by a half and cut capacity by rather less, to the coal industry in order to make it less unprofitable.

Arthur Scargill, the newly elected president of the NUM, welcomed the opportunity for a fight. He had gained prominence in the union by organizing the 'flying pickets' who went to power stations in the strikes of the 1970s to stop coal being delivered, and by his role in the pickets' fight against the police at the Saltley coke depot in 1972. He firmly believed that the 1973–4 strike had brought down the Heath government, though other people thought that the miners' contribution had really been to precipitate an election, which Labour won by looking more reasonable than Heath. By 1984 the NUM leadership wanted a strike, but it was not clear if they simply wanted to stop all pit closures or hoped to reverse the result of the 1983 election as well. As they were not sure that they could win a vote for a national strike, they called for each region to go on strike: this could be done with no ballot, though it was rather bold to ask prosperous regions to go on strike without a ballot to preserve other men's jobs. In the 1960s miners had been ready to give up their jobs because they could find employment elsewhere; by the 1980s the problem of finding work for young men was so great that one of Scargill's strongest cards was his appeal to preserve jobs for 'your children's children'.

The productive Nottinghamshire region was not willing to go on strike without a national ballot, and the NUM organized its 'flying pickets', bringing miners from Scargill's own Yorkshire region to try to stop the Nottinghamshire miners from working. In 1973 strikers could picket wherever they chose, and breaches of the peace by pickets were often ignored, but 'flying pickets' became so unpopular after the 1979 strikes that the law was changed to confine picketing to the strikers' own place of work. The Coal Board and the government wanted to avoid making the miners look like victims of special legislation, which might have rallied the trade union movement around them. They did not use the new law during the coal strike, even though it turned out to be far more violent than British strikes had been in the past seventy years. The police forces of the country had been becoming integrated into a national force, and the strike accelerated the process. Police reinforcements were brought from other counties to enable working miners to get through the massed lines of pickets; the pitched battles that followed would have been unthinkable a generation earlier, and may have owed as much to the habit of 'riotous assembly' learned elsewhere as to the needs of the occasion. The police were able to get working miners through the pickets without using force on a scale that alienated the public, and by the autumn the Energy Minister felt it was safe to say that the supply of electricity would be maintained throughout the winter; imports of fuel, the existing stocks of coal, and the flow of coal from Nottinghamshire had made the strikers' objectives unattainable.

The strike involved over 100,000 men for a year, and had wider ramifications than even the largest purely industrial dispute. Some people welcomed it as an attack on the government, and the 'radicalism of the communicators' may have led the miners to overestimate the pressure of public opinion on the government. The columnist who wrote in the *Guardian* on 7 August 'I hope he [Mr Scargill] will, as he must, make Mrs Thatcher crawl', was expressing the view of an articulate minority; when Thatcher called the miners 'the enemy within', with a hint that they were a bit like the Argentinians, she was probably going further than her supporters really wanted.

At the 1984 Trades Union Congress and Labour Party conference the miners and the left were able to push the unions and the party into expressing a degree of support for the miners which it was always clear would not be translated into action, and into a condemnation of the police which would do the party no good. For a moment in October it looked as if the union representing the pit deputies responsible for safety had found a way to a settlement, but the NUM continued to insist that no pit should close simply because it made heavy losses, and the opportunity passed away. Harold Macmillan (recently created Earl of Stockton as part of an attempt to revive the practice of creating hereditary peerages) compared the miners with the soldiers at Passchendaele, which expressed the respect many people felt for their determination and endurance, and also conveyed a hint about their leadership and its capacity for choosing sensible object-ives. After the negotiations with the pit deputies the strike began to crum-ble, with about a thousand men returning to work every week, some because their resources were completely exhausted and some because they had lost their faith in their leaders. After electricity supplies had flowed uninterrupted throughout a cold winter, the miners were on the brink of abandoning their leaders when the leadership announced at the beginning of March 1985 that, although the strike had not been settled, everybody should return to work. As the government had foreseen, a great many miners took the rather generous redundancy terms available for those who were ready to give up their jobs, and other trade unions followed a less militant policy after the great strike, which gave employers a freer hand to restructure British industry.

Public support for the government, indicated by its standing in opinion polls and its success in the 1984 European elections, in which it won forty-five seats to Labour's thirty-two, diminished after the strike. Probably some people had said they would vote Conservative simply to support the government against a Labour Party that looked like a subsidiary of the NUM. Once this threat was removed, people could consider the faults of the government and the attractions of its opponents in the way that is normal in the lull between election campaigns. The Alliance insisted that reasonableness and three-party politics were the answer, and was able to show their electoral effectiveness in by-elections and in county council elections. Kinnock demonstrated his independence of his supporters on the left by an attack on them which reminded people of the Gaitskell of 1961 by its eloquence and ferocity. Some familiar problems returned, and helped to reduce the popularity of the gov-ernment. Partly because of the strain placed on the markets by the issue of British Telecom shares, but mainly because of the immense strength of the

American dollar, the pound had sunk on the foreign exchange markets. Ministers had in their non-interventionist way encouraged it to drift lower to help exports, but early in 1985 signs of a crisis could be seen; although the pound was higher in terms of the lira and the French franc, and even a little higher in terms of the mark than it had been at its weakest moment in 1976, the government was forced to raise interest rates sharply for fear that the pound should fall to one dollar. The measures taken to defend the currency were not severe, but they showed that the exchange rate could still cause trouble.

The government faced some difficulties over municipal reorganization. Conservatives disliked the Greater London Council and the other metropolitan counties created for the conurbations after the 1969 Redcliffe–Maud Report, and in 1983 set out to abolish them. This was an understandable response to their lavish spending, and perhaps a natural way for Conservatives to react against bodies which lay far enough to the left for some people to call them the 'loony Labour left', but the government had to create non-elected bodies to undertake some services they performed which could not easily be transferred to the boroughs within the conurbations. The Labour leader of the GLC, Ken Livingstone, ran a skilful publicity campaign to defend his council, and a large number of Conservative backbenchers, including some of Thatcher's enemies among the ex-ministers, voted against the government when the proposals were first put forward, the House of Lords did its best to provide the successor bodies with enough powers to make it possible to revive them as elected bodies in the future, and Labour councils undertook resistance by non-cooperation, but the legislation became law more or less as intended.

The episode showed how ready the government was to tackle existing institutions and how much less ready it was to think about constructive measures to replace them. Undoubtedly there was much to attack; twentieth-century Britain had shown very little of the ruthlessness of the Victorians in attacking abuses, so the ground was cluttered with relics that had lived too long. Thatcher's inclination was to sweep them away and take it for granted that a free and unencumbered market would provide any replacements that were really needed. The coal dispute illustrated this approach: because the market and geological good fortune provided a fuel that was cheaper and cleaner than coal, the right thing to do was to close down the unprofitable parts of the coal industry and let the oil industry develop the resources of the North Sea so that taxpayers and consumers of coal could get as much revenue and as cheap a supply of energy as possible. A keen eye for questions of profit and loss would reveal plenty of industries that had been overtaken by change which were kept going at a level of activity that penalized everybody else and gave people in the industry a purely temporary respite from change. Some gloomy people said British industry was so accustomed to being directed and supported by the State that it would not respond to opportunities that would have been welcomed elsewhere: in 1981 and 1982 the United States was clearing away obsolete economic interests in much the same way as Britain, but in the United States new jobs were soon created to replace those that had been lost, while Britain simply endured a high level of long-term unemployment. Those who believed in the free market replied that, after a long period of interventionist government, businessmen needed time to become used to creating new lines of work, and all that could be said was that if they took too long a reaction would arise that demanded an end to unemployment, no matter what the cost in loss of efficiency.

The wider question was to find how far people could rely on the activity of the marketplace. The dispute over large municipalities illustrated the problem: it was easy to show their weaknesses, but not so easy to show that anything which took their place would be cheaper, and very hard to show that new institutions would be more responsive to public opinion. The structure of payments which lay at the administrative heart of the State was also subjected to analysis, though the course of the debate suggested that the system had grown too large for the politicians to be able to make it comprehensible. The original idea of the 1940s was that all the causes of poverty should be relieved by payments made as a matter of right, usually on the basis of the recipient's contribution to the national insurance scheme. It was always accepted that some extra payments would have to be made in difficult cases, and as time passed this transformed the whole system. The original plan had paid little attention to the financial problems of large families, and the family allowances set up in 1945 fell far behind rising prices. In the 1950s and 1960s schemes were developed, some at central and some at local government level, to help large families with low incomes to maintain a decent standard of living; most of them ignored the concentration upon payments as a matter of right laid down in the 1940s and depended on an examination of the family's income to make sure that it really was poor. In 1970 this approach was given more formal expression in the Family Income Supplementation Act, which provided funds for families that applied for help and could show that their income fell below set limits.

Because these schemes for large families were related to income, the assistance provided was bound to diminish or taper off as income increased. By the 1970s quite poor families were paying income tax at the standard rate. As schemes for income supplementation were based on gross income, it was entirely possible for a worker earning a below-average wage to find that an increase in pay led not only to higher income tax and national insurance contributions but also to such a decline in the level of various means-tested benefits that the family was actually worse off. Much more common than these extreme and paradoxical cases was the general problem of low-paid workers in an income band where income tax and the tapering of benefits between them meant that 80 to 90 per cent of any increase in gross pay was taken away.[4]

The Labour government of the late 1970s paid little attention to the growth of the poverty trap, as this band of income became known. Inflation made the problem harder to understand: as prices rose, all the figures involved were changed, so that an income of £30 a week, firmly lodged within the poverty trap in the early 1970s, was far below it in the late 1970s, although in practice a worker earning £40 a week in the early 1970s was probably getting £60 a week by the late 1970s and thus remained inside the trap. Changes of rates of benefit altered the shape of the trap, and this made it look as if the number of people involved ought to diminish. At the same time the government was setting up a State Earnings Related Pension Scheme (SERPS), to make universal the benefits provided by Civil Service or company pension plans; the problem was complicated and had been holding the attention of politicians for at least fifteen years, so the difficulties of the poverty trap had to wait until pensions had been settled.

The Conservatives were so concerned to keep government spending down, in the face of sharp increases in the cost of unemployment benefit, that they did very little about the problem for some years. In 1985 the government explored the possibility of ending the SERPS, out of concern that the scheme had underestimated the ratio of pensioners to workers likely to be found in the twenty-first century and placed an unrealistic burden on the latter. At the same time it set out to make the payment of benefits outside the national insurance scheme more rational. By moving towards paying family benefits on the basis of net income, allowing for the impact of income tax and the tapering of other benefits, they could eliminate the paradoxical situations in which pay rises made workers worse off. For most victims in the poverty trap, administrative good sense was not enough: unless the government was ready to say that people at the bottom of the scale should become worse off the return to payments linked to income either meant that people within the poverty trap would go on losing most of every pay increase gained, or else a great deal of revenue would have to be devoted to making the position of people at the top end of the poverty trap so much better that they had a substantial differential over people at the bottom end of the trap.

This may have been the most intractable problem of finance to face the government, but defence and the arts also presented difficulties. In both cases it was claimed that their requirements could not be judged on financial standards alone, and also that their costs normally rose faster than the general cost of living. The claims of defence had been pressed on politicians throughout

---

4. *The Economist*, 24 July 1975, 60–1, explained the operation of 'the poverty trap' very clearly. At that time people at various points in the income band from £1,500 to £2,400, depending on family circumstances and the grants and rebates that could be claimed, might find that an increase in earnings did them no good.

the century: the figures had risen two-hundredfold since 1906, although the rise in its share of the national income, which had gone up from 3 per cent in 1906 to 5 per cent by the time war broke out in 1914, had subsequently fluctuated around that figure in times of peace and took no larger a share of the national income in the 1980s than in 1914. The demand for very high levels of spending on single weapons had led to changes: the development of the Dreadnought, with its impact on the budget and on diplomacy, indicated the shape of things to come, but no pre-1945 government could have expected to see its successors in the 1980s wondering whether to commit a sum equal to a full year's spending on defence to buying the Trident submarine and nuclear missile system from the United States. Such a purchase, even if the cost was spread over a decade, was likely to lead to awkward reductions in all other defence spending; but the alternative was to withdraw from the struggle to maintain a nuclear force under British control that had been accepted by successive governments for forty years.

If questions of defence spending had been annoying governments for centuries, spending on the arts was a more recent problem. Apart from a few Civil List pensions, the central government spent practically nothing on the arts before the Second World War. Even after 1945 it spent rather less of its revenue on the arts than most governments of comparable wealth, but in the 1960s the principle was beginning to win acceptance, and in the 1970s it could be argued that spending on the arts produced a cash return by encouraging tourists to come to Britain. But this expenditure (like so much of the tourist activity involved) was London-centred: national theatre and opera companies turned out to be a service for Londoners first, with the rest of the country a distant second. It was unfortunate for everyone that the Arts Council became aware of this, and decided to put it right, at just the moment that the government was deciding that spending on the arts would have to suffer along with everything else in the struggle to keep down spending. Lobbyists set out to convince the government that saving a few million pounds in this way would be more trouble than it was worth—it seemed unlikely that Benvenuto Cellini and Sir Peter Hall of the National Theatre had been uniquely ill treated by their patrons, but the plangency of their protests had a great deal in common. The government also found itself being pressed to help with another revival of the British film industry, based this time in part on the increasingly sophisticated techniques developed in television and in part on a willingness to treat the twentieth century (or at least significant moments in twentieth-century Britain) as history to be interpreted through the camera; and the government responded to this pressure in a way that suggested it did not possess the subtlety and insight needed for encouraging artistic development.

The government's supporters would reply that anyone who wants to scythe through thick undergrowth had to lay subtlety aside or get nothing done, and that the first need was to catch up with the work of clearing the ground that had been neglected for forty years. The Labour Party had so many vested interests to defend in the trade unions, among workers in local or central government, and in all the other institutions which had passed unexamined for decades, that its approach seemed simply to ask what changes the government was making, and then say they ought to be stopped. The Alliance looked too kind to destroy old-fashioned institutions that ought to be replaced and perhaps too removed from the practical world to devise anything to take their place. This left Thatcherism in uneasy possession of the field, as a partial acceptance of the idea that the country would run better if it got rid of some self-made obstacles to progress.

If people from before 1914 had seen the direction indicated for change they might not have been pleased, but the confidence in progress implicit in Thatcherism would have been more familiar to them than the overconfidence alternating with a gloomy acceptance of decline that had underlain British attitudes for quarter of a century. The new mood might be philistine, and it might ignore the desire to help the weak at the expense of the strong, but it could not be dismissed or consigned to a backwater. It was better suited for clearing things away than for building them up, but the British had for some time been trying to build things up without clearing away what was useless. Rebuilding after the clearance might be a task for someone else: the removal of rubbish in the early 1980s was a good preparation for a fresh start.

16

Withering away

1985–1992

The role of government

The question whether the government ought to do more than clear away old-fashioned restrictions and restraints was given vivid expression in a dispute which broke out over the Westland Helicopter firm late in 1985. The firm's capital base was so weak that it needed a partner; Brittan, the Secretary of State for Trade and Industry, with the active support of the Prime Minister and the acquiescence of the Cabinet, gave his approval to a proposal that an American company should take Westland over. The Secretary of State for Defence, Heseltine, wanted time to look for alternatives, and pressed the Cabinet to encourage a group of firms from the continent of Europe to support Westland. Brittan's view prevailed and Heseltine resigned, but during the dispute it became clear that Brittan had privately given to the press a government document critical of Heseltine's methods. In a Commons debate about whether Brittan had done this on his own account or with the encouragement of the Prime Minister, she was able to convince her supporters that she was not to blame. Brittan resigned over the leak, but Thatcher clearly did not disapprove of him and a few years later she appointed him as one of the two British Community Commissioners at Brussels, where he became responsible for trade policy. Behind the fuss over proper behaviour lay the question whether the government should simply make sure that market forces operated without restriction (in what was becoming known as the 'Anglo-American' approach to economic organization), or should intervene to guide its development (in what was taken to be a more 'European' manner); Heseltine's continued presence on the back benches made it likely to remain important.

The memories of the great coal strike were dying away when another long and symbolic strike raised some similar questions. The printers who worked for London newspapers had gained a special position in the early nineteenth century because they were manual workers who had to be able to read, and they had developed great skill in setting type from handwritten copy at high speed. After the Second World War their position came to depend on union power and an absence of workshop discipline which enabled them to benefit from lightning strikes that threatened production. The proprietors realized that nothing is quite so hard to sell as a large pile of yesterday's newspapers, and often made concessions which ate up their profits. But improvements in the printers' conditions of work were undermining their monopoly; they began to set from typed copy and, once journalists typed their copy electronically, it could be printed without being reset. The proprietor of *The Times*, Lord Thomson, came from Toronto, where electronic setting had been introduced in the 1960s after a long strike which had decided the issue for North America, and he tried to introduce the new technique in 1978. The printers resisted the change and, after a strike lasting just under a year, he gave up his attempt to change printing methods and soon afterwards sold his London newspapers to Rupert Murdoch, an Australian from an old newspaper-owning family.

The government was eager to see redevelopment of the docklands area—the old East End of London—and approved ambitious plans for it. By the end of the 1980s progress had reached a point where more public money was needed for infrastructure than the government was ready to provide and development was checked until a new Underground line had been built, but in the mid-1980s there had been widespread approval when Murdoch began building a printing plant at Wapping and said he was going to launch a new newspaper there. Perhaps this really had been his original intention, but his preparations enabled him to respond to a print union strike at his existing newspapers early in 1986 by dismissing the entire staff and moving production of all his papers to the docklands. The machinery there was run by the Electricians' Union, which accepted an agreement not to call strikes in return for being recognized as the only union with which managers would negotiate, and most of the journalists followed Murdoch's summons to the new plant and typed their articles directly for printing. The displaced printers stood outside the plant and tried their best to turn picketing into a siege operation by throwing stones and other missiles at the buses used to bring the journalists and electrical workers to the premises. The government saw this as another contest between law and order and the enemies of progress, and police support for people going to work at the Wapping plant was strong and effective.

Printers on other newspapers could see that electronic typesetting was bound to come, and they settled for the best terms they could negotiate. Newspaper publishing became much more profitable as the proprietors benefited from the long-delayed modernization of the production process. New papers set out to serve various parts of the market: the *Independent* was launched in 1986 for the more restrained of those who were to become known as young upwardly mobile professionals, a phrase with the acronym 'yuppies', and the *Sunday Sport* was designed for the traditional entertainments of men in the working class. And yet the press did not regain its pre-television position of dominance; sales never got back to where they were in the 1950s, and newspapers found they could no longer rely on representatives of the general public, empanelled as juries, to take their side. Newspapers taken to court in libel actions had previously seen judges as their enemies and had felt confident that juries would be on their side. This was no longer the case; judges might suggest that damages for people aggrieved by what the newspapers had printed about them should be moderate, but in the 1980s the wife of a mass murderer, a bankrupt MP who had turned himself into a popular novelist, and a youthful television star all received very large damages. Understandably the newspapers pointed out that in the United States they could with impunity have accused Sonia Sutcliffe of cashing in on misfortune, Jeffrey Archer of visiting prostitutes, or Jason Donovan being hypocritical about being homosexual, but there was no sign that the public would have welcomed the importation of this aspect of the American way of life. Newspapers were very welcome as entertainment, but even the broadsheet papers were not taken too seriously as sources of moral authority, and the public would clearly have liked all of them to be punished if they became a nuisance.

The government would not have welcomed American freedom of speech: it spent a good deal of money, and a certain amount of its credibility, on attempts to stop a former counter-espionage agent, Peter Wright, publishing memoirs which alleged that parts of the secret services had been out of control in the mid-1970s when it had been fashionable to believe that the country was ungovernable. No American government would have imagined that the publication of *Spycatcher* could have been stopped. But in other ways the government was strongly committed to the United States. Possibly the decision in favour of an American firm in the Westland case and the cancellation, a little later, of the Nimrod observation aeroplane and the purchase of the AWACS aeroplane from an American firm in its place meant only that, at least in defence purchases, the United States offered the best deals in the market. Thatcher's own commitment to the American connection was shown at its fullest in British support and provision of flight facilities for an American bombing raid on Libya in April 1986 to try to restrain its ruler Colonel Qaddafi, who was believed to be a worldwide supporter of terrorist organizations, including the IRA, and of various groups that attacked airports and aeroplanes. She also found that she and President Reagan were in complete agreement in wanting to remove all barriers to world trade.

Europe

Greater freedom for trade and related services was the aspect of the Single European Act, approved by the governments of the Community early in 1986 and ratified by its parliaments in the course of the year, which attracted the British government. The Act—an Act in the diplomatic sense rather than legislation at Westminster—was written in terms designed to free the Community countries from obstructions to trade and to freedom of movement for people and for capital. The Act also allowed more decisions on technical issues at Brussels to be taken by qualified majorities rather than requiring unanimous acceptance by member states and, as it was hard to divide policy questions from their technical aspects, issues became more likely to be settled by majority voting. This move towards greater European integration was inspired by a spirit of 'federalism', in the sense of a belief that a central Community government ought to have sovereign power over a wide range of issues, even though the governments of the nation-states that made up the Community would still have sovereignty on other issues. The idea of a division of sovereignty was so unfamiliar in Britain—though it was a commonplace in several other English-speaking countries—that it was discussed in terms that only increased people's confusion. Supporters of closer European integration talked as if the fact that the Royal Navy no longer ruled the seven seas and Britain no longer grew all her own food meant that she had already lost her sovereignty, while opponents of integration talked as if the Commissioners in Brussels were about to carry out a Cromwellian *coup d'état* and destroy the Westminster Parliament. They could also point to improved facilities for invasion from the Continent; in 1987 an agreement was reached to build the Channel Tunnel, which had been discussed for more than a hundred years, and work went ahead well enough for French and British engineers to meet under the Channel in 1990. It was all more expensive than had been expected, and the investors were left wondering if they would ever get their money back. Their fears must have been increased by the attitude of British Rail, which took no part in developing the Tunnel and seemed unwilling to make any improvement in its services in south-eastern England to help to provide faster travel between Britain and France.

Most of the other countries of the Community were already cooperating in running the exchange rate mechanism (ERM), set up in 1979 to provide something like a complex regional version of the Bretton Woods system. Because no single currency dominated the market in the way that gold and the US dollar had done in the 1940s, each member state undertook to keep the exchange values of its currency from moving too far above the lowest-valued or below the highest-valued currencies, though it still had the right to make a fundamental change in its exchange rate if the existing value was inappropriate. It could be argued that Britain had been prudent to stay out of this arrangement as it moved from the troubles of the 1970s to the exhilaration of being a petro-currency in the early 1980s, but by 1985 Lawson, the Chancellor of the Exchequer, was suggesting that membership might have a useful steadying effect on the currency and the economy. The Prime Minister replied very firmly that the time for this step had not yet come.

By 1986 the price of oil was falling and OPEC was weakening, mainly because Saudi Arabia was growing tired of cutting its output when none of the other members of OPEC was ready to make similar sacrifices to keep the cartel going. The British, like other non-OPEC producers, believed that the stimulus to the world economy of cheaper oil would be more useful than an artificially high price for producers and for everyone else, and resisted attempts to support the price. During its last defence of the administered price Arabia briefly produced less oil than Britain, though of course this stopped as soon as Arabia ended its quixotic struggle. Whatever the benefits of lower oil prices, expensive oil had given Britain its favourable balance-of-payments situation in the early 1980s and provided a base for overseas investment. Although vulnerable to distractions like the miners' strike, the exchange value of the pound had been driven so high in the early 1980s that it would have been hard to maintain it at the fixed rate required for ERM membership. Sterling's value came under strain in 1986 when the oil price fell, and the system of floating rates allowed this to be handled without too much disturbance by letting the pound sink in value. The balance of payments went back into deficit, though Lawson reflected that improved world credit markets made it easy to finance a deficit; and he might have added that Britain's deficit—even though increased by additional overseas investment—looked very small by the side of the eastern European and Latin American debts that had caused banks so much trouble earlier in the 1980s.

The British economy benefited from the expansion of the world economy after some problems in the early 1980s, and at times in the mid-1980s grew faster than most other industrialized economies. Revenue flowed in freely; taxes could be cut and in 1988–9 and 1989–90 the government had a surplus with which to repay debt. Most of this surplus came from the privatization of nationalized industries, but in 1989–90 there was even a small balance of regular revenue over expenditure. Perhaps the economy had all the more room to grow because it had been held back by the high interest rates and high exchange rates of the early 1980s, and in any case growth was not accompanied by development that might have provided more secure jobs for the future. The economic expansion of 1985 to 1989 rested upon a widespread willingness to incur new debt, some of it for personal consumption and some of it for financial operations that did not always lead to the investment needed if the debt was to be repaid. Bank lending went up by about one-third in the twelve months before the general election of June 1987. Old-established rules about lending money were relaxed; young people buying a house for the first time could get a mortgage for the whole price of the house and the lawyers' fees for the transaction as well, which meant they were able to borrow more than 100 per cent of the house's value.

Economic stimulants like these helped to give the government an expectedly easy victory in the election. In England it held on balance almost as many seats as in its 1983 triumph, though it lost half the seats it had held in Scotland

and Wales. Almost all these seats went to Labour, so Kinnock succeeded in his primary aim of making sure that Labour was well ahead of the Alliance of the Liberals and the Social Democratic Party (SDP) and so would be the only real challenger to the government in the next election. The Labour Party had given up the belief in widespread intervention throughout the economy that had damaged it so badly in 1983, but its defence policy still left it unable to say what it would do if the Soviet Union became aggressive. The Alliance seemed to have lost popularity in the months just before the election, but during the campaign it gained support, apparently mainly from Labour.

	Votes	Seats	% of all votes cast
Conservative	13,736,337	375	42.2
Liberal–Social Democratic Alliance	7,341,152	22	22.6
Labour	10,029,944	229	30.8
Scottish Nationalist	416,873	3	1.3
Plaid Cymru	123,589	3	0.4
Unionists in Ulster	400,430	13	1.2
SDLP	154,107	3	0.5
Others	327,134	2	1.0

During the election David Owen and David Steel had tried to appear together as joint leaders of the two Alliance parties. Owen's ability to give instantaneous and effective replies to interviewers' questions had made him look the more important of the two, but Steel transformed the position as soon as the election was over by calling for a merger between the Liberals and the Social Democrats. Most Social Democrats welcomed the proposal and the merger was confirmed by a ballot of the party. Owen and two other SDP MPs (out of five) opposed the idea and set off for the political wilderness; unification made slow progress in 1988 and was accepted at the beginning of 1989 only after enough hesitation and bitterness to make it hard for Steel to stand for the leadership of the new party, at first called the Social and Liberal Democratic Party and later the Liberal Democratic Party. As a small sliver of the old Liberal Party remained independent of the merger, the new name had its uses, though most people thought of the merged party simply as the Liberals.

When Paddy Ashdown was elected leader of the Liberal Democrats in the spring of 1989, his party seemed to have ended the problems of having two heads at the cost of removing itself to the political sidelines. In the 1989 election for the European Parliament the 36 per cent turnout was slightly higher than the 32 per cent turnout in 1979 and in 1984. The Conservatives' covert opposition to the Community in the campaign must have puzzled voters who remembered the government's support of the Single European Act, though their fall to only 34 per cent of the vote may have indicated wider dissatisfaction. The Labour Party's 40 per cent of the vote did not suggest that it had fully gained the confidence of the electorate, and the Liberal Democrats might have hoped to benefit because neither of the larger parties was doing well. But they got only 6 per cent of the vote; in England the Green Party did far better than ever before, with nearly 15 per cent of the vote, though it did somewhat less well in Scotland and Wales, where the nationalist parties also gained ground. Concern about the environment was increasing, helped by disasters like the explosion at the Soviet nuclear generating station at Chernobyl, and by reports that the thinning of the ozone layer of the upper atmosphere was likely to cause dangers from solar radiation, but the Green Party's complete failure to do equally well in later elections suggests that it did well in 1989 because the public was dissatisfied with the two major parties and was less ready to cast a protest vote for the Liberals than on most such occasions since the 1950s.

Discontent

In their 1987 manifesto the Conservatives promised to abolish 'the rates', the flat-rate tax on the assessed value of houses and other building and landed property that for centuries had been the main source of the revenue that local governments had raised for themselves. The central government had assisted the local authorities with grants from central funds to cover things like the reduction of municipal revenue caused by the 'derating' of industry in the 1920s, or to enable them to perform new duties in education or in housing. The less prosperous householders had their rates paid by the government, and it was reckoned that as a result only 18 million of the 35 million voters were ratepayers, of whom 6 million had their rates paid in whole or in part by the social services. The government argued that too many people benefited from a high level of local government spending while being able to leave paying the bills to the rate-paying minority and the Exchequer. Certainly the rates were unpopular; income tax was for most people a slightly tiresome matter of having payments deducted from their pay before they ever saw it, but the rates involved making payments more directly.

Thatcher was aware of their unpopularity and had begun talking about abolishing them when in opposition in the 1970s. The impulse to action came in Scotland, where the basic valuations of property, on which the rate was assessed, came up for revision every five years (in England and Wales reassessment was infrequent, and people took the rates as a fixed imposition upon the price of a house). The unpopularity of the new valuations appeared to ease the way to the changes the Conservatives had promised in the 1987 election, though the reassessment was really one of those changes where those who gain are ready to see it as a simple matter of justice without showing any gratitude for it, while those who lose are loud in their protests. The government did not see that any change in the system might provoke just the same response. It pointed to the injustice of charging the home of a single elderly pensioner just as much in rates as the home of a family in which adult sons and daughters were making demands on local services and were beginning to earn enough money to help pay for them, and it asserted that everybody made roughly the same demands on local services. Acting on this assumption it set up a 'community charge', to be levied at the same rate per head upon all adult residents in a municipality. Some remissions were made for poor residents, and cash transfers from central government to municipal governments were arranged in a way that was meant to ensure that municipalities would all levy about the same level of community charge if they were all equally frugal and efficient. The best-known precedent for a flat-rate tax per head, the poll tax in the reign of Richard II, was not encouraging; it had led to the Peasants' Revolt of 1381, and the demonstrations, refusals to pay, and riots that greeted the new poll tax in Scotland in 1989 and in England and Wales in 1990 indicated that the extreme left had for once picked up a popular cause on which to base extra-parliamentary agitation against the government. The central government reorganized its system of grants to municipalities and increased the amount paid to them in a series of attempts to keep down the bills that 'charge-payers' had to meet, but households of two 'charge-payers' still found they were paying more than they had done in the days of the rates, unless they were living in properties of such magnificence that there was no popular support for reducing their tax burden. It was estimated that hundreds of thousands of people kept their names off the electoral register to avoid being seen as prospective 'charge-payers'. This manoeuvre cast some doubt on surveys of opinion that claimed people were ready to pay higher taxes in order to have better public services, but did underline the tax's unpopularity.

The community charge might been better received if it could have been introduced just after the election, when there were no doubts about the prosperity of the economy. On 19 October 1987 prices fell suddenly and dramatically on stock exchanges all over the world, losing in a few hours as much of their value as they had done in months of decline on previous occasions, but central banks poured out additional funds to stabilize the system and share prices recovered so quickly that people felt confident that trouble was not going to spread outside the financial markets. In Britain the Chancellor radiated his confidence that he was the main architect of expansion, that growth would go on indefinitely, and that government borrowing to finance budget deficits was a thing of the past. Nigel Lawson's 1988 budget ignored the possibility that the fall of the stock market was a warning that the economy had already been stimulated enough in the months before the election. Instead it transformed the income tax system: income between £2,600 (for a taxpayer with no dependants) and £21,900 a year was to be taxed at 25 per cent, everything above that was to be taxed at 40 per cent, and the graduated severity of the surtax was removed. Most English-speaking countries were making similar changes at the same time, with the same implication that sharp tax increases could not easily be used to restrain the economy in future and that the idea of the past seventy or eighty years that voters would accept high rates of marginal tax in order to achieve greater equality had lost its credibility. The budget contained a gesture to old-established morality. Originally all the mortgage interest paid for buying a home could be deducted from income for tax purposes, partly because the home was subject to Schedule A taxation and partly because nobody saw it as a rapidly appreciating investment. The end of Schedule A in 1962 and the subsequent rapid increase in house prices had led in 1974 to a new rule that an owner could deduct only the interest on the first £25,000 (increased to £30,000 in 1983) from income. But these limits had been intended for a world in which houses and flats were bought by married couples, or occasionally by single individuals. If a working couple who were not married bought a home, each of the partners could deduct the interest on £30,000. The 1988 budget laid down that after 31 August one property meant one deduction. This gave people (as long as they stayed unmarried) five months to buy a home and establish a mortgage under the old system of the double deduction, and the prospect encouraged a frenzy of forming more or less temporary alliances to purchase, a rush to borrow, and an extraordinary increase in house prices, which rose by just under 25 per cent (from an average price of £44,000 to £54,000) in 1988. This could not last; prices fell slightly in 1989, partly because of the ending of the exemption, and those who had formed temporary residential partnerships to benefit from rising prices now found that they were stuck together for longer than they had expected.

By this time the state of the economy could not be ignored. Imports were too high to be contemplated with detachment and the Chancellor searched for some way to keep the economy under control, but there clearly was no way to do it painlessly. Higher taxes and even faster repayment of government debt might have been tried in the past, but higher taxes were regarded as unthinkable when the budget was already showing a surplus and the more melodramatic City commentators were predicting a shortage of British government bonds. Higher interest rates would control domestic inflation and check the increase in credit that had driven it forward, but would also push the pound higher, which would make imports more attractive and cause exporters even more difficulty in finding markets.

In the later 1980s the expansion of the economy became a matter of social as well as normal financial interest. Caryl Churchill's play *Serious Money* opened in 1987 and won more audience support from the yuppies who were being drawn into the expanding financial service sector of the economy than the author had perhaps hoped. A satire on the City of London, undoubtedly intended as a vicious attack on the iniquity of capitalism, was welcomed by its self-confident acolytes (who were not accustomed to receiving theatrical attention) as jolly good fun. Takeovers of one company by another provided much the same focal point for excitement as in earlier booms and, as in earlier booms, led to a concentration upon financial operations which drew people's attention away from industrial development. The increased importance of institutions like banks, investment and unit trusts, pension funds, and insurance companies was shown in the way that company employees—people working for Guinness and for the Westminster Bank attracted attention in the courts—took part in undesirable trading practices which previously would have been expected only of private individuals trading for their own accounts. This really only attracted attention at the end of the 1980s, when expansion had been brought to a painful stop. Between 1986 and 1989 the yuppies were lords of the ascendant and some of them may have imagined—like the unfortunate hero of Tom Wolfe's novel about similar developments in New York—that they were masters of the universe.

Some aspects of City organization changed dramatically; the Stock Exchange had been criticized for running a set of interlocking cartels rather than a really open trading market, and it agreed to carry out a transformation that became known—with a not entirely modest bow to cosmology—as 'the big bang'. The new system started on 27 October 1986. The Exchange was no longer divided into brokers who took orders from the general public and jobbers who tried to bring these orders to buy and sell into balance. Instead bigger firms were created to take the orders and make the market, dealing mainly in large orders for the financial institutions which dominated the market. The exchange changed its name to the International Stock Exchange to underline the point that it wanted to be a global trading centre cooperating on a worldwide basis with Tokyo (nine time zones ahead of London) and New York (five time zones behind London). This worked quite well, and London kept its position as a place where large orders could be carried out quickly and settled promptly.

While big firms were needed for a market in which institutions dealt in large blocks and owned a steadily increasing proportion of all shares, they were also useful for handling the vast number of transactions, involving very small individual purchases, that went with the increase in shareholding linked to privatization. The sales of publicly owned industries went ahead reasonably successfully, though with disputes that had their paradoxical side. Privatization of the telephone system had been popular because people thought that government management had produced a system that did not work properly, and the only committed opposition to the privatization of gas in 1986 had come from the management of the industry. British Airways had been turned into a very profitable business in the course of a reorganization specifically intended to lead up to the 1987 privatization, and British Steel was sold to the public without difficulty in 1988. But in the debate about the 1989 privatization of water supply the opponents of the proposal put their case by dwelling upon the problems and inefficiencies of the existing system. They argued in effect that private firms could not put right the problems bequeathed by decades of public management, and they gained some support; the measure went ahead, but it encountered much more doubt and resistance than the other sales, and Scotland was able to retain its existing public system. The distribution of electricity and the non-nuclear electric generating systems were privatized in 1990, but opponents of nuclear energy found to their astonished delight that the City of London shared their scepticism about nuclear-powered generating stations. The electricity they produced was not particularly cheap, but what really made them unsaleable was the impossibility of saying what would be the cost of cleaning up and closing down the stations at the end of their useful life.

As the contraction of credit began to have its effect and interest rates rose steadily throughout 1989 and then stayed at a high level in 1990, the economy slowed down, and financial scandals emerged, as often happens at this stage of the trade cycle. The scandals at the end of the 1980s did suggest that the new forms of regulation that had accompanied changes in the City's financial organization had not been very successful at protecting investors. Uninformed investors were defrauded by the Barlow Clowes firm or lost money they entrusted to the Levitt Group. Lloyd's, the famous privately organized insurance business, had blossomed as a patron of modern architecture when its new stainless steel building (with piping and ductwork hung down the outside of it) was opened in 1986 in a mood of confident expansion. Rich and well-connected investors put their money into providing financial backing for insurers—on whose advice it was hard to be certain—and invested it in some cases in the high-return, very high-risk insurance which bears the burden when great catastrophes consume all of the protection provided by the less ambitious underwriters and lead their victims to call on the heroic syndicates that deal in London Market Excess of Loss insurance. When hurricanes, asbestosis insurance policies written decades earlier, and devastating fires on North Sea oil rigs left them facing ruin, the investors asked who had got them into this mess, and it was not easy to find any creditable answer.

The business failure which caused most widespread disquiet was that of Robert Maxwell, who overstretched himself in the printing, publishing, and communications field, and fell off his luxurious yacht at a time when it was clear his accounts could never be made to balance. It then became clear that for several months he had kept his various firms going by taking money out of their pension funds to support the price of shares that he had used to secure loans, and that some of the £400 million he had used in this way was irrecoverably lost. Pension funds, offering most people in steady employment a prospect of retirement on something more substantial than the old-age pension and less arduous than rigorous personal saving, were a product of the world after 1945. Even in the 1970s a Royal Commission had been unwilling to treat money in these funds as a form of personal wealth, and yet people had come to take it for granted that they would receive their pension. The victims of funds run by Maxwell's companies faced a drastic loss of future income, and political parties committed themselves to making these funds more secure in the future.

The uneasiness to be seen at the end of the 1980s was not a simple matter of financial misadventure. The role of the public services was more open to question than before; there was an argument about whether this was due to the financial stringency of Thatcher's premiership—illustrated by changes like the decision of the Royal Shakespeare Company not to use its London base in the Barbican regularly—but some of it was a matter of incompetence. The problems of British Rail, with trains that were unable to cope with snow on the track and later were held up by autumn leaves, may have lightened the hearts of everyone except those who had to travel by train. London Transport's advertising campaign to improve the behaviour of its passengers (in the hope that some of this would rub off on its staff) may have had the same effect, but it was not going to bring back to life the thirty-one people burned to death in a fire at King's Cross caused by poor maintenance. The central government knew that people thought British education was not providing a moral basis for living and also was not producing a trained workforce for a modern economy; it set out to give schools power to run their own affairs on a grant-maintained basis, which was intended in the long run to lead to the disappearance of local education authorities and leave the schools dealing directly with the central government and the national curriculum which it had imposed. In health arrangements it gave doctors and hospitals the opportunity to handle for themselves the money provided by the Treasury; this change too would take power away from local authorities, and it would diminish the day-to-day power of intervention of the Ministry of Health. Both changes were described as reducing the power of the State and increasing the power of ordinary citizens, but they were also likely to reduce the power of local municipal authorities in a way that would leave schools and teachers, doctors and hospitals, and all who needed their services, more directly dependent—at the very least in terms of financial support—upon the central government. By a coincidence of terminology, some of the government's more determined opponents at the end of the 1980s organized a Charter 88 to ask for restraints on its executive power, and a couple of years later the government offered Citizen's Charters to meet the same issue of uneasiness about the exercise of government power by people who wielded that power more for their own convenience as producers than in order to make life easier for the general public as consumers.

While these changes showed some willingness to shake up the administrative systems that had grown up in the previous half-century, it was harder to see what was being done to prevent miscarriages of justice for which the police were responsible. Early in the 1990s it became clear that eighteen people had received very long prison sentences for crimes connected with the IRA bombing campaign of the mid-1970s which they had not committed. During the bombing campaign the police had been under great pressure to show results, and the Minister responsible had not been able to concentrate on this aspect of his work, but it was still dismaying to see the judges were determined to resist any reopening of the cases, perhaps because they thought social stability would suffer if anyone was allowed to discover that the courts sometimes made mistakes, perhaps because they could not believe that the police had presented intentionally misleading evidence. No doubt the IRA benefited from the reversal of the convictions, but the propaganda advantage which it gained rested on the fact that nobody outside the police and judicial system thought that imprisoning innocent people could be justified. Many other cases began to emerge, with no question of IRA involvement, in which the police had improved upon the available evidence for the purpose of getting quick convictions rather than establishing the truth.

Most of the more serious cases of injustice involved victims of Irish or other immigrant descent, and some of them raised serious questions about police treatment of such people, but this problem had become much more complicated than any simple matter of racial unfairness. In the 1950s and 1960s immigration had been seen in terms of West Indians who wanted to fit into the British way of life without suffering from discrimination based on the colour of their skin, and by the 1980s they seemed to be doing well enough at the superficial level of success in sport and popular entertainment. But immigrants from India, Pakistan, and Bangladesh did not intend to fit into the way of life of the majority of the population so easily. They were relatively likely to want to go into business for themselves; when the Bank of Credit and Commerce International was made bankrupt by the fraudulent activity of its organizers in the Gulf, many immigrant businessmen in Britain suffered because they had opened accounts with it in the belief that it was more sympathetic to their needs than the established British banks. Business apart, people from the Indian subcontinent had a culture of their own which at some points was hard to reconcile with British culture. There were arguments about education, and in particular about the way girls should be educated. In 1988 Salman Rushdie, a novelist from a Muslim background who had won a high reputation in intellectual circles, published *The Satanic Verses*, a book which made fun of the prophet Muhammad. Nineteenth-century Christians would have been irritated if Jesus Christ had been treated in the same way, but in the twentieth century they had come to put up with such things patiently. In Iran the respected leader of the Shi'ite Muslims said *The Satanic Verses* was blasphemous and Rushdie should be killed. The response to this decree showed that Muslims in Britain had not been assimilated into the wider community and that Muslims throughout the world did not like the way that secular values were gaining ground. Translators of the book were murdered; Rushdie went into hiding; intellectuals who had spent their lives stressing their tolerance had to explain that assassinating authors was one of the things they could not tolerate. But many Muslims in Britain were annoyed by toler-ance for blasphemy, and a few of them would not have been sorry to see Rushdie dead. Islam, like many religions, had begun in days when neither tolerance nor the equality of women commanded much support; these old-established aspects of the faith (which might be called fundamentalist) were hard to accommodate in late twentieth-century Britain, and raised questions about the clash of cultures which were more complicated than the straightforward, if insoluble, problems of racism.

After Thatcher

Lawson continued to put the case for entering the ERM, and Thatcher grew worried enough by this to recall a former economic adviser, Sir Alan Walters, whom she trusted to provide her with the arguments against membership. In October 1989 Lawson resigned in protest against the development of parallel economic policies, one based on Number 10 and one on Number 11 Downing Street. His departure did not make as much impression as it would have done in the months after his post-election budget, but it increased the uneasiness among Conservative supporters that had been indicated in the European elec-tion. Sir Anthony Meyer stood against the Prime Minister for the party leader-ship in the new session of Parliament to give MPs an opportunity to show if they were worried about high interest rates, the poll tax, and the risk that her combative attitude to the Community was losing friends. Thatcher won the support of over 80 per cent of the Conservative MPs, easily meeting the requirement that on the first ballot a successful candidate needed the support of a majority of the MPs, and a lead of 15 per cent over the runner-up to demonstrate a commanding position.

In the summer of 1990 Thatcher committed the country very firmly to support United Nations military action to rescue Kuwait, which had just been annexed by Iraq. Kuwait had been loosely connected with the British Empire in India, and British forces had gone to protect it when Iraq had threatened it in 1961, shortly after becoming independent. This imperial echo probably influenced opinion much less than the shock of seeing a small and harmless (if oil-rich) country wiped off the map by a bellicose neighbour; the policy of UN intervention went unchallenged during the months of preparation for battle and, when it led to swift and decisive military success, some people argued in favour of further intervention in Iraq, although this would in practice never have been accepted by Iraq's neighbours. But by then Thatcher was no longer in office to enjoy the triumph, and instead it brought some relief to the first awkward moments in office of her successor.

Lawson's departure weakened Thatcher's power to resist ministerial pressure to join the ERM, particularly when it was advocated as a step to reassure foreign investors that the exchange rate would remain unchanged, thus opening the way to reductions in interest rates. Her new Chancellor of the Exchequer, John Major, had shown a calm willingness to use high interest rates to damp down the economy, and by 1990 this was bringing on a recession. Although several other industrialized countries suffered as well, none of them suffered for as long as Britain; output went down, month by month, for almost two years. The south-east of England, which had increased in prosperity faster than the rest of the country for seventy years, was most severely affected, perhaps because so much of the expansion of the later 1980s had been based on borrowing, and borrowing was easier in the south-east than anywhere else. In the 1920s high interest rates had been specifically intended to restore the pre-war ratios between gold, the pound, and the US dollar, even at a high price in unemployment. No comparably clear goal underlay the deflation at the end of the 1980s, but it too ran the risk of driving the pound up to a damagingly high exchange rate. Entry to the ERM early in October 1990 was accompanied by a welcome cut in interest rates, but the tight money policy had already forced the pound up, and economists predicted that maintaining the value of the pound at DM2.95 for ERM purposes might be difficult. The step did not improve relations between Britain and the other members of the Community as much as had been hoped; later in October a meeting of the Council of heads of state and governments decided that the Community ought to move towards establishing a single currency. The British had not been told that this important issue would be discussed, and Thatcher responded by declaring her hostility to the onward march of centralization. The firmness, almost fierceness, with which she declared her opposition to closer European cooperation alarmed Sir Geoffrey Howe, who by now held virtually meaningless office as Deputy Prime Minister. He resigned, and declared in his resignation speech that ministers had put up with Thatcher's little ways too long and too patiently. This encouraged Heseltine to offer himself as a candidate for the leadership. He did differ from Thatcher on Europe, but backbenchers were much more likely to be attracted by the fact that he had consistently warned that the poll tax would be a vote-loser.

On the first ballot Thatcher just failed to get the 15 per cent lead that would have ruled out a second ballot. When her ministers told her that she would probably lose to Heseltine in the next ballot, she retired, partly to avoid humiliation and partly to steer the succession to someone she preferred.

Major had already made a favourable impression on his party by his capacity
to be at the same time polite and firm, but Thatcher's support, based on his
lack of firm commitment to European integration and his readiness to reduce
government intervention and spending, was certainly one of the reasons why
he got almost as many votes in the second ballot as his two opponents, Heseltine and Hurd, the Foreign Secretary, put together. They withdrew rather than
force a third ballot. Thatcher had fallen in unusual circumstances: a respected
minister had resigned on the issue of relations with the European Community, backbenchers were worried about the separate issue of the poll tax,
and a dynamic former minister who had opposed the Prime Minister on both
issues was ready to challenge her. While nothing exactly like this would happen again, the fact that a Prime Minister could be overthrown undoubtedly
changed the way in which difficult situations would be approached in future.

Thatcher's overthrow may have shown that her party was, as in 1922, afraid
of a 'dynamic force', but nobody thought the changes associated with her
could be reversed. Economists could argue that tax reduction had gone too far,
but nobody expected to return to the idea of equality of income through fiscal
machinery. Trade unions were much less powerful than they had been in the
1970s, and had lost over a quarter of their membership, partly because of
Conservative legislation, partly because of the shift from an industrial to a
service-based economy. Privatization had been successful enough to banish
the idea of renationalization from political discussion. No political leader can
have much effect on what happens in other countries, but the overthrow of
communism as a political system in eastern Europe at the end of the 1980s
might have been followed by attempts to maintain government-owned enterprises if Thatcher had not provided an example of a different way to run
things. As an anti-interventionist, she had naturally done nothing to encourage feminists who wanted an active government to advance their agenda for
change, but her presence at the top of the political system changed a great
many preconceptions about what were normal things for women to do. At an
even more intangible level, she had done a lot to ensure that Britain was less
likely to be seen as 'the sick man of Europe' in the 1980s than in the 1970s.

Major had become Prime Minister after only eleven years in Parliament, a
very short parliamentary career by previous standards. His main Cabinet
change was to appoint Heseltine as Secretary for the Environment to get rid of
the poll tax as quickly as possible. The council tax which replaced it was
simply a new version of the rates, with a more flexible system of valuation that
might let taxation keep up with changes in relative prices, but its great advantage was that any change would be seen as an improvement on the poll tax. By
this time the recession was biting deeply; Major, who had a gift for neat if not
always discreet phrasing that went rather surprisingly with his public image of
a grey, unassertive man, had declared as Chancellor, 'If it's not hurting, it's not
working'; and as Prime Minister he found the policy of restraint was leading

to bankruptcies and a rising level of unemployment that made an early election very unlikely.

In December 1991 the Maastricht summit of the European Community searched for ways to increase the role of the Community; most of the twelve existing members may have hoped that this would permanently settle the framework of its activity before new members from Scandinavia or post-Communist eastern Europe were admitted. The British government was strongly in favour of including new members, but there were suspicions that it saw this partly as a way of balancing the influence of Germany, which had been greatly increased in 1990 by the ending of the 1945 division of the country, and partly as a way of making it harder to reach agreement on steps towards the 'ever closer union' which was accepted as Community policy. And Britain kept away from involvement in closer union in two important issues discussed at Maastricht. Under the ERM member governments could still alter the exchange rate of their currencies, but at Maastricht it was proposed that in 1999 the currencies of all participating Community members should be locked together and denominated in terms of a Single European Currency, and that in 2002 coins and banknotes in this new currency, which subsequently became known as the euro, should replace all existing currency. After this, a country would have to withdraw from the system and reinvent a currency of its own if it wanted to change the relationship of its own wages and prices to those of other Community countries, or else have no more autonomy in monetary issues than an Australian state or a Canadian province. In much the same spirit of Community interventionism, a 'social chapter' had been drawn up to establish uniform working conditions throughout the Community. Major had said that he wanted to place Britain 'at the heart of Europe', though probably he simply wanted to avoid the disagreements with other members of the Community that had marked Thatcher's premiership. But he could not repudiate Thatcher without annoying a large number of his own supporters, and in any case he was not enthusiastic about interventionism. The other governments of the Community pledged themselves—in some cases without much analysis of the problems of running a single currency—to monetary union and the 'social chapter'; Britain reserved its position on both issues politely and in a way that allowed it to work with the Community in future without any dramatic change of approach.

When the 1992 election was at last announced, the Conservatives had clearly failed to mesh the business cycle with the electoral cycle, and had to face the prospect of steadily rising unemployment, returning to the worst levels of the early 1980s, without visible signs of economic recovery. The new Chancellor of the Exchequer, Norman Lamont, found the strain of keeping cheerful a little too much for him, and entertained the nation by reporting 'green shoots' of growth when nobody else could see anything of the sort. The Labour Party was fortunate that it had given up almost all of its plans for strict government direction of the economy before the collapse of the Communist system in eastern Europe and the Soviet Union between 1989 and 1991 had revealed how astonishingly unsuccessful central planning had been. It still hoped for government cooperation with industry in working out new lines of development, but its most definite commitments were to raise old-age pensions and child benefits and to increase income tax and national insurance contributions from the better-paid to finance them. Probably most voters would have responded to the proposed higher rate of tax on incomes above £40,000 a year with equanimity, but an increase in national insurance contributions which would affect everybody working a forty-hour week who earned over £10 an hour gave the Conservatives a chance to attack the Labour Party as unregenerate supporters of high taxation. In 1987 Labour had said that only people who earned over £500 a week would be worse off under its tax proposals; in 1992 it was preparing to cast its net rather more widely. At times the argument over tax levels looked like the only issue in the campaign. The Conservatives had little to offer except unfinished business from Thatcher's period; the Labour Party was sufficiently alarmed by successive defeats to want to look receptive to the new way of doing things, but was not able to show that it had really adjusted to what was going on. The Liberals managed a substantial recovery from the low level to which they had fallen when uneasiness about the merger with the Social Democrats had badly undermined their position. Although his party did less well in 1992 than in 1983 or 1987, any assessment of Ashdown's performance had to acknowledge that he became leader at a difficult time.

	Votes	Seats	% of all votes cast
Conservative	14,092,235	336	41.9
Liberal–Social Democratic Alliance	6,002,809	20	17.8
Labour	11,562,717	271	34.4
Scottish Nationalist	629,555	3	1.9
Plaid Cymru	154,390	4	0.5
Unionists in Ulster	415,412	13	1.2
SDLP	184,445	4	0.5
Others	576,835	—	1.7

The opinion polls—which in nearly every election since 1945 had offered a helpful guide to the way voters felt—had throughout the campaign indicated that the Labour Party was doing better than the Conservatives, and it had been generally expected that no party would have a majority. Naturally the polling agencies said that voters had been converted to Conservatism at the last moment, although, as the opinion polls underestimated Conservative strength up to the end of the campaign, they might have been underestimating it in the months before the election. Those who believed that voters turned away from Labour late in the campaign attributed the change to reminders that Labour had put forward a shadow budget just before the election which involved increases in income tax, or to the overconfidence shown by Kinnock and others in at a party rally in the last week of the campaign, or to Major's refusal to give up and his fortitude in getting on to a soapbox and coming more directly in contact with voters than most politicians. The hundreds of thousands of potential voters believed to have kept themselves off the register in order to escape the poll tax were mentioned, and it was suggested that voters had consistently lied to the pollsters because they thought it sounded moral and proper to say they wanted higher taxes and increased social spending, although they had no intention of voting for so self-denying a policy. The reputation of the opinion polls also suffered because polls in Scotland a little before the election seemed to show very strong support for Scottish independence, but in the election the Conservatives regained ground lost in 1987. Although the vote for the Scottish National Party was higher than it had been since 1974, it did less well than the pre-election polls had indicated and lost some seats gained at by-elections, returning to Westminster with fewer MPs than Plaid Cymru, which continued to advance in the handful of seats in which there was a substantial number of Welsh-speaking voters. In Ireland the IRA's adoption of parliamentary politics seemed to have been rebuffed when Protestant voters supported the more pacific SDLP and defeated the only Sinn Fein MP. It had been hoped in 1985 that involving the Irish Republic officially in the political institutions of Northern Ireland would reduce Catholic alienation and encourage police cooperation across the border, but this had not yet happened; political violence still went on, with no sign that it was shaking people's old-established political allegiances.

In the four British general elections between 1979 and 1992 the Conservative share of the total vote looked steady and solid, confronted by a non-Conservative vote that moved sharply away from Labour in 1983 and then drifted back slowly. Ingenious ideas for Labour and Liberal cooperation were sometimes heard; they took it for granted that all non-Conservative votes were anti-Conservative votes, even though the Conservatives seem to have benefited in 1992 from using the argument that a vote for the Liberals could lead to a Labour government. Labour won more seats in 1992 than would have been expected from its share of the vote; perhaps it concentrated its resources skilfully in winnable areas, but it also benefited from its strength in seats that were losing voters as people moved out of cramped cities into the expanding suburban hinterland.

Kinnock, understandably disappointed at the result and conscious that he could hardly lead his party into a third election, resigned as quickly as Foot had done in 1983. John Smith was chosen within three months of the election as leader of the party with virtually no opposition by an electoral college, which underlined the fact that the trade unions were still of great importance in the Labour Party. He was Scottish, and some critics asked if a leader from a region where Labour still held most of the seats could modify its approach to the parts of the country where it had been doing badly in recent decades in a way that would appeal to the prosperous working- and middle-class voters who felt that Labour had little to offer them. In the early 1960s Wilson had made the Labour Party look relevant to people who had done well in the Conservative prosperity of the 1950s, but the Labour Party had found the process disconcerting enough not to be ready to choose 'another Harold Wilson'. Smith was chosen in the belief that he could combine acceptance of the need for change with an acknowledgement of the importance of the old values of the party.

The Conservatives, while still committed to business and privatization as they had been under Thatcher, modified that position slightly. They wanted to look committed to Europe but had difficulty in maintaining much sympathy for the interventionist approach which dominated thinking in Brussels, and occasionally looked hostile to it. The government responded very cautiously to Denmark's rejection of the Maastricht Treaty in a referendum in the summer of 1992, which delayed the unanimous consent needed to make the treaty come into effect, but it must have noticed the widespread pleasure expressed in the country at this defeat for the expanding power of Brussels. A few weeks later the British financial authorities suffered a serious setback over the ERM; membership had tied the pound to the Deutschmark at a time when Germany needed high interest rates to deal with the inflationary impact of reunification, and the Deutschmark led the pound and the other European currencies to a level in terms of non-Community currencies that made exporting much more difficult. At the same time the pound was bound to be weak compared with the rest of the Community if it did not accept the high level of German interest rates. Faced by the problem of high unemployment as well, the government tried to maintain the value of the currency in the ERM simply by using the foreign exchange reserves, and this turned out to be inadequate. In mid-September Britain was forced to leave the ERM and declined to express any readiness to return to it. Its new value, about 15 per cent lower than before, was more sustainable, but the failure did nothing for the government's prestige or its reputation for Community spirit. Just after the election the transfer of Heseltine—one of the few politicians of recent decades to prosper after resignation in the way that was normal in the nineteenth century—to the ministry in charge of trade and industry suggested that the government would encourage some coordination of economic development. But Heseltine was Thatcherite enough to want to press on with the contraction of coal-mining, and this was so unpopular at a time of high unemployment (and his precipitate methods were so unsound in law) that he had to retreat in confusion.

After this it was unlikely that he could persuade the Prime Minister to give up his opposition to the idea of active government intervention and his preference for leaving people alone to manage their own affairs. Major had said that he hoped to see the country 'at ease with itself'. This was a substantial objective, and one with which it was hard to disagree, but the way he proposed to achieve it showed how considerable a change had come over the beliefs of successful politicians, of the thinkers who supported them, and of the voters who gave them power. For most of the twentieth century the basic idea in British political life, expressed in phrases like 'the Welfare State', had been that government intervention was the best way of looking after the needs of economic development, of taking care of people who were temporarily or permanently in need of help, and of making sure that society felt united enough to handle its problems. In the 1980s this idea had been challenged; at the beginning of the 1990s it did not have enough dynamic force behind it to provide effective opposition to political leaders who wanted to see this sort of intervention by the State withering away.

17

Search for a new way

1992–2001

The end of Conservative dominance

A few months after it was re-elected the government's popularity fell very sharply and it never recovered. The collapse of the policy of joining the exchange rate mechanism (ERM) was a visible sign of economic weakness, which dismayed the government's supporters, and the Labour Party was able in 1992 and in 1994 to choose new leaders who seemed able to solve the problems caused in the 1980s by its internal division and its failure to reassure voters that the party was reasonable and moderate. The timing of this dramatic and fairly long-term shift of opinion was rather surprising. Major's government must have thought it was lucky to be re-elected after the events of the first eighteen months of his premiership. Economic growth, which had been so satisfactory in the late 1980s, came to a stop and went into reverse. By the time Thatcher was forced from office unemployment had fallen to just over 1.5 million, not much more than it had been when she became Prime Minister, but it rose in the next two years rather faster than it had done in her first two years in power, and by early 1993 it was once more over the 3 million level. Real incomes per head were lower in 1992 than in 1988. These changes probably hurt Conservative supporters more than the recession of the early 1980s. Under Thatcher unemployment had hit workers in regions and industries that normally supported the Labour Party, but the misery of the early 1990s was spread over parts of the country that earlier on had suffered very little. For a time the great move to home ownership worked against the government; people who lost their jobs had difficulty in keeping up their mortgage payments, and they were particularly vulnerable if they had bought their homes with the very low downpayments made possible by the lavish lending practices of the late 1980s. House prices fell in cash terms, and people with large mortgages slipped into 'negative equity', where the value of their houses was not enough to repay the mortgages. They could not sell their houses and move, and were often saved from the threat of foreclosure only by the fact that lenders could not find purchasers for repossessed houses. Compared with the million or more people in negative equity, the tens of thousands of investors who had put their money into providing financial backing for insurers at Lloyd's looked like a relatively privileged group, but the idea that such solid members of society could be ruined was bound to weaken people's faith in the government.

All of these setbacks had been eating at the economy before the election. The simple idea that voters reward or punish governments according to the performance of the economy had made it natural to think Labour would win, and Major's success in getting re-elected at such a difficult moment made him expect that his party would be grateful to him and that the electorate would vote for him even more readily if he held an election at a time of greater prosperity. Neither expectation was fulfilled. When he set out to present the legislation required by the Maastricht Agreement to Parliament, Major found that a group in his party was deeply hostile, and it gained in strength as he put off holding the decisive vote. The government was defeated a couple of times in 1993 by the readiness of dedicated Conservative opponents of Maastricht to vote with the Opposition; and it had to resort to motions of confidence to sustain its position.

Voters behaved as if they had in some way been tricked into voting Conservative in 1992. In strictly fiscal terms this was understandable. While Major was preparing for the election, government spending had been allowed to go up in a way that had not been seen since the early 1970s. After the election this spending was held back, or paid for by increased taxes, and the Opposition claimed that there were twenty-four tax increases in the opening months of the new Parliament. The government replied that the pre-election spending had been intended to soften the downturn in the economy, and the post-election tax increases were meant to avert the danger of inflation. And on the latter point the government was more successful than anyone could have predicted. Past experience suggested that the sharp drop in the external value of the pound after leaving the ERM would naturally drive up the prices of all imports, and that the rising budget deficit caused by the recession and by pre-election spending would bring back the inflation of the 1980s or even of the 1970s. The growth of the deficit meant that the National Debt, which had risen over the centuries to £100 billion early in Thatcher's premiership and had doubled by the time she left office, had more than doubled during Major's premiership and exceeded £400 billion by 1997. This might have been expected to drive prices up sharply, but in the event they went up more slowly, even after the recession was over, than they had done since the 1960s. Long-term optimists hoped that the world was returning to a period of prosperity like that predicted for the third quarter of the century by Kondratieff in the early 1930s. At the same time industrial relations became more peaceful than at any time earlier in the century. From 1991 to 1995 fewer days were lost in strikes than in any comparable years of the 1930s, or in the crisis of 1940. Some of this was due to the severity of the recession, and some of it to diminished fear of rising prices, but there had been recession and even falling prices in earlier years of industrial strife in the century. It looks as if the move from large bodies of workers characteristic of an industrial economy to the smaller, more disparate groups to be found in an economy based on services had helped to reduce employees' reliance on strike action.

The economic stability of the 1990s was not enough to save the Conservatives. Some of their success in the 1980s had been due to the weakness of the Opposition. Michael Foot had clearly been out of touch with the voters, and Neil Kinnock had had to steer a difficult course, tacking between left-wing enthusiasts and an electorate which was uneasy about extreme views but found Thatcher's principles much more acceptable than those of the Labour left. When Kinnock resigned after losing in 1992, the emergence of John Smith as leader virtually without opposition had saved the Labour Party from having to choose between the old and the new, and in any case it was able to watch the Conservatives setting out on the road to self-destruction.

Several ministers had left Thatcher's government because of disputes about policy, but it had remained relatively free of scandal, and until the 1992 election Major's government had continued to escape trouble. After the election the government was battered by a wide range of difficulties that became known as 'sleaze', an ill-defined word that covered financial and sexual activities of politicians that might not be criminal but certainly were condemned in terms of immense moral disapproval by the media. Some of the problems had started during Thatcher's government. Ministers in departments concerned with defence and with trade had encouraged Matrix Churchill, manufacturers of highly engineered products that could be used to build up military capability, to export to Iraq and to provide the British intelligence services with information while doing so. When Matrix Churchill was charged by another department with exporting arms illegally, Major's government stretched its legal powers to the limit to try to prevent ministers from revealing what had really been going on. Alan Clark, who merely told the truth in court, and Michael Heseltine, who resisted the attempts to stop him explaining what had happened, looked like heroes by comparison with the ordinary run of their colleagues. When the judicial report on Matrix Churchill was eventually debated in 1996, the government survived by a margin of one vote.

This was an issue that affected the honour of the whole government. Most of the problems of 'sleaze' were simpler questions of bad behaviour by individual politicians. At first it was a matter of ministers who had been imprudent about their financial connections, but later in 1993 Major said that political discussion must 'get back to basics'. He meant that it should concentrate on keeping down inflation and encourage a sense of personal responsibility, probably in the hope that the Conservatives would give up their internal disputes about relations with the European Union and return to issues of domestic policy on which they were united against the Labour Party, but newspapers chose to interpret his words as something like Thatcher's earlier appeal to Victorian values and treated the phrase as a licence to explore the private lives of Conservative backbenchers. Half a dozen domestic scandals were brought out into the open in the first few weeks of 1994; it was hard to imagine that they were very relevant to the government's capacity to run the country, but they certainly helped to underline the idea of Conservative incompetence and of the need for a change. MPs who misused their political position to take money for asking parliamentary questions were obviously doing something wrong, and an MP who used a nominee to buy himself a council house for investment purposes was going to undermine voters' faith in his party even though he was not committing a specifically parliamentary offence. Fifteen Conservatives had to resign official positions between 1992 and 1997, and more scandals (including the imprisonment for perjury, in entirely separate cases, of Jonathan Aitken, a former Cabinet minister, and Jeffrey Archer, a former deputy chairman of the party) remained to be revealed after the 1997 election.

Major was determined to complete the work of privatization. He knew his party would be united on the issue, and he could always hope that the Labour left would oppose it in a way that embarrassed the Labour leadership. The main policy decisions were taken under Thatcher, but of the roughly £60 billion raised by privatization, about £25 billion came to the Treasury during Thatcher's premiership and over £35 billion during Major's term of office. Compared with the great treasure chests, like British Telecom, which was sold by stages for about £15 billion, electricity shares, which produced just a little less, and British Gas, which yielded about £6 billion, coal and the railways were by this time financially trivial. But they were the two great symbols of the 1945 Labour government's nationalization programme, and they were the only industries left to privatize. Coal rapidly lost its importance in the 1990s; production had fallen relatively little as a result of the 1984–5 coal strike, but it dropped to about half its previous level during Major's premiership, mainly because natural gas was used much more extensively for generating electricity, and employment in the industry declined still further. What was left of the industry was sold to private owners for about £1 billion.

The railways had somewhat better long-term prospects as passenger journeys increased in the 1980s and 1990s, but they were still running at a loss and the government realized that it would have to provide subsidies for the initial years of privatization, in the hope that the railways would be self-supporting in the foreseeable future. To get things moving quickly the Railtrack section of British Rail was sold as a separate corporation responsible for keeping the track and signalling systems in good order. The government went on to divide the country up into a couple of dozen regions and invited firms to bid to become train operating companies working with as low a subsidy as they thought practicable to run a region for a fixed time period. This proposal came late enough in the lifetime of the Parliament to mean that the Opposition could have delayed it fatally, but the Labour leadership saw no real point in doing anything of the sort. It was happier to think that the railway system would soon cease to be a drain on public funds of a type that cast discredit on public ownership.

Church and secular service

In the early 1990s the Church of England received an unusual amount of public attention as it debated the role of priesthood and the position of women. It had lost much of its old position, but that position had been so dominant that it had still to be seen as a great institution in decline, against a background of a fall in religious observance which was as rapid in the last decades of the century as at any time. It was estimated that at the end of the 1970s about 5.4 million people attended religious services in a week, and by the end of the 1990s this figure had fallen to 3.7 million, and that within this total Anglican attendance had fallen from 1.67 million to just under 1 million. Even at the end of the century over half the population of England had been baptized into the Church of England, but this proportion was falling fast enough to indicate a sharp drop in new baptisms in the last quarter of the century. The Church continued to maintain about 11,000 clergy, with a steadily increasing number of lay administrators. David Hare's play *Racing Demon*, which appeared in 1990, was schematic, melodramatic, and probably schismatic, but it gave a good account of the trials of clergy, who were uncomfortably aware that they were slipping into putting what the early Christians called 'serving tables' (and is now called social work) ahead of prayer and preaching, and that their Christian faith, under the pressures of modernizing theology and a changing non-religious world, was developing in a way that could not easily be explained to the laity. Church schools were popular, perhaps because parents thought religion encouraged moral standards, perhaps because they were believed to provide better background conditions for study. Obviously immigration brought more people of non-Christian religious beliefs to Britain, as well as bringing people from the West Indies of strong Protestant beliefs, but it was hard to say how many of these people felt anything more than the mild attachment to the religion into which they had been born which was felt by many people baptized into the Church of England. The worldwide stresses within Islam had their effects in Britain, and might cut Muslims off from the rest of society. In the middle of the century marriage in church was still the normal thing: half of all weddings took place in Church of England churches and only about 30 per cent of weddings took place in registry offices. By the end of the century most weddings were non-religious, probably helped by changes in regulations that allowed them to be held almost anywhere that the participants wanted. But among religious weddings Church of England ceremonies had declined only from 70 per cent to 66 per cent of the total. Obviously the fervent religious faith of the years before 1914 was rarely to be found, and would in some circles have been seen as in very poor taste, but the Church of England was enough of a national institution in a social if not in a directly religious sense to be unlikely to be allowed to manage its internal affairs without a good deal of advice from outside.

Plenty of outside advice accompanied the long-running campaign to ordain women as members of its clergy. Many of the non-religious laity saw it simply as a question about feminism and the rights of women, and the arguments that mattered to the Church probably meant very little to people like this. A change of this importance had to pass through the three divisions of the Church's General Synod—bishops, other clergy, and laity—and then go forward to Parliament, which had undertaken to pass or reject legislation from the Synod as quickly as possible. The Synod voted in favour late in 1992, and it was accepted by Parliament late in 1993. The debate about the change had been more intense among the clergy than among either bishops or laity and, although some of the opposition to the change came from Low Church clergy who interpreted the relevant passages of Scripture in a strict sense, much more attention was paid to the High Church opposition, which concentrated on the nature of priesthood. This was partly due to the glamour and glitter of its ceremonial, partly to its strength in and around London, and partly to the option open to High Church clergy of converting to Roman Catholicism. The Pope made it very clear that the Church he led was not going to accept women priests, and this encouraged an inflow of converts dissatisfied with the change in the Church of England. The Roman Catholic Church displayed its open-mindedness by accepting over a hundred married Church of England clergy as priests. The Church of England made financial provision for clergymen who felt they could not continue to work in a church that ordained women priests, which alleviated some of the bitterness, but did nothing to ease the Church's financial position. The Church had originally thought that, as priests never cease to be priests, their livings should be freeholds which they could lose only if they committed certain offences, so they never retired and simply handed over more and more of their work to curates in old age. This was less and less possible by the late twentieth century, and pensions became a serious issue of Church finance. In the mid-1980s about 60 per cent of the Church's central endowment income of £100 million went to supporting regular clerical stipends and about 20 per cent went to pensions. By 2000 about £90 million of the Church's central endowment income of £160 million was devoted to paying for pensions for retired clergy and only about £20 million was devoted to supporting clerical stipends, so Church of England clergy moved towards the position of all other ministers of religion by becoming more dependent on the financial support of their congregations. Rich congregations responded well enough, but this shift of financial resources was clearly going to make it hard to keep up parishes in poor areas. The Church Commissioners, who manage the endowment, were showing some signs of suffering under administrative pressure, and were spending rather less on supporting parish clergy than they were spending on bishops and their cathedrals.

The cathedrals and several other churches were a financial burden that was not directly connected with the religious role of the Church of England. It owned most of the ecclesiastical buildings in the country, including the overwhelming majority of the buildings of historical and artistic interest. Attractive though the buildings were, they had to be repaired and maintained at considerable expense; and their popularity with tourists increased the expense. The tradition of the Church had been to keep its buildings open at any time for people to pray; as people became more ready to rob churches, this became impracticable, but charging admission was another matter and it caused Church authorities some distress. Some tourists who thought the government paid for an Established Church through taxation (as in some continental countries) did not see why some churches asked them to pay for admission, or at least hinted at payment very strongly, but most of them accepted that this was part of the British heritage they had come to see. British governments sometimes wished that people would come to see the country's more recent achievements, but tourists rarely responded to this. Modern Britain was not very different from other modern countries, though some overseas visitors did say it was a little shabbier, a little less clean, and perhaps generally a little less up to date than their home countries. But its past was distinctive, glamorous, and easy to present to visitors from abroad or to natives of the islands. Cathedrals and churches were only a small part of the heritage to be preserved and shown to the country and the world. When the 1945 government strengthened the National Trust to safeguard country houses and other things it thought might be destroyed when its high death duties broke up family fortunes, it had no idea that it was investing in British tourism. Fifty years later many of the fortunes survived, but their visible possessions were powerful attractions for visitors.

The marketing of heritage could be satirized easily enough. In Julian Barnes's *England, England* a coarse and vulgar tycoon sets out to turn the Isle of Wight into a microcosm in which one can enjoy every bit of the heritage from Buckingham Palace to the Brontë cottage within a short bus ride. Not quite as implausible as people would have thought a hundred years ago, but the novel's coda is a little less straightforward: perhaps it is a mildly ironic reminder of the way that so much of the devotion to heritage began with the idea of a Golden Age before 1914, but on the other hand it may be Barnes's own proclamation that he believes in that Golden Age. Some critics complained that this emphasis on heritage as a tool to attract tourists was turning Britain into a theme park and that the idea of the Golden Age in the past was falsifying the picture by concentrating on the grace and elegance of life enjoyed by the upper class at the expense of the rest of society. A few coal mines that were reopened for tourists, Owen's New Lanark Mills, Iron-Bridge in Shropshire, and a few other buildings saved from the Industrial Revolution did not outweigh the massed ranks of hundreds of country houses. But in earlier generations the nation's past had been celebrated explicitly by historians in their writing; such an approach was by the late twentieth century thought to be unprofessional, and a readiness to judge the nation's past by an appeal to anachronistic moral standards was considered much more unbiased. Perhaps the country houses helped to keep the balance even.

While the heritage itself was an important side of British history, the interest taken in tourism was a sign of the shift to an economy based on services as the country earned some of what were called its invisible exports from people who came to see it, and as people who had more time and money to spend on leisure were ready to travel as part of their way of spending it. Critics taking a wider view sometimes felt they had delivered a crushing blow to the idea that a service economy could replace the old-established industrial economy by saying (plausibly enough), 'We can't live by taking in each other's washing.' This was true only in the sense that the industrial economy could not have survived by everybody buying cotton yarn from each other. There is an obvious limit to anyone's desire for cotton yarn, and a slightly less obvious limit to people's desire for food. By the end of the 1950s people had got over wartime shortages and did not increase the amount of food they ate, while their consumption of both soft and alcoholic drink went up very steadily. But while the amount eaten did not increase, the amount spent on it certainly increased. At a simple level people saved themselves time by giving up shelling peas at home and instead having them taken out of their pods and put in plastic bags and frozen in factories, and at a more elaborate level they had their *rognons de veau* prepared in the right burgundy and served from under a silver dome. All of this extra work and expense could be seen as part of the service economy.

Those who regretted the elimination of coal-mining as a source of mass employment, or believed that a national steel industry was as essential in 1990 as in 1940, complained about de-industrialization and sometimes talked as if earning a living by the sweat of one's brow was a welcome choice instead of originally being a punishment. All the signs were that the people who moved from industry to service regarded the change as an improvement. Operations were now controlled by computer programs written in the service sector to enable industry to go about its work more safely and more efficiently than before. The film *The Full Monty* was a fairy story about men changing from steelworkers to Chippendales, but nobody really thought that men could or should go back to the old labour-intensive way of making steel and, despite all the problems of the 1970s and 1980s, the flow of labour from industry to services was handled more smoothly than the transition from heavy industry to lighter industries between the wars.

The City of London had for centuries been the great example of a service sector with an important role in an industrial economy. As services grew in importance, and financial services employed more and more people in the British economy, it was to be expected that the City would become more important, but in the 1990s parts of it went through a change that was sometimes called Wimbledonization. The All-England Lawn Tennis and Croquet Club put on one of the most important and possibly the most attractive of the events in the international tennis season at Wimbledon, and everybody always said how well arranged things were. After the 1930s English players rarely enjoyed much success in the tournament, but nobody denied that local workers rolled the lawns very nicely. Obviously the City was not dominated by foreign performers to the same extent, and invisible exports linked to its operations still provided £25 billion of the national income in the late 1990s, but for some types of financial activity London seemed to be becoming the playing field on which American, Dutch, French, German, and Swiss firms enriched themselves and their London employees. At least seven British-owned merchant banks, some of them weakened by the speculative enthusiasm of the late 1980s, passed from British to overseas hands; English nationalists might also have mentioned Scottish purchases of the National Westminster Bank and of the Halifax Bank, which had recently been converted into a bank from a very successful building society. This could be seen as just part of globalization in which purchases made by British firms from British Petroleum to Vodafone caused equal disquiet in the United States and Germany. Concern about British economic development was obviously much less than it had been twenty years earlier, and some of it just rested on a feeling that people should not be enjoying themselves so much. Speculative enthusiasm caused trouble again at the beginning of the new century; it was perhaps just the price that had to be paid for the 'animal spirits' that seemed to be the best way to drive the machine forward.

As people became better off, they had larger disposable incomes, which they spent on services rather than industrial products. The new product which served as the emblem of the expansion of the 1990s was the modern telephone, a simple arrangement of wires and plastic which placed the user at the centre of a web of activities as a mobile phone or as the way into the internet. The potential for activity could be overestimated: dot.com companies fondly believed that a vast range of things could be sold over the internet, and discovered that people could not so easily be drawn away from the simple pleasures of going shopping. But the old industrial economy was clearly not going to be revived.

The financial development of sport showed the changes brought about by rising incomes and increased concentration on leisure. Professional sport developed at the end of the nineteenth century as entertainment for a mass working-class audience, and professional players earned much the same rates of pay as they would have received as skilled craftsmen. British football players were bound to this sort of payment until 1961, though they could already see that players in South America and on the continent of Europe could do much better. The mass crowds of the first half of the century dwindled in the 1950s; men found a lot of other things to do on Saturday afternoon, and watching football became a minority activity for rougher and rougher crowds. Television slowly opened the way to higher pay for players, and the failures of crowd control in the 1980s led to a clear-cut decision that watching football in person was to become expensive and restrained, because spectators were to be seated instead of standing to watch and were to pay prices for tickets which soon cost about as much as theatre tickets, while most people would watch it at home. At the same time competition among television stations gave the leading clubs financial opportunities unimagined in the past, though they very soon had to share their wealth with players who could move much more freely among clubs all over the world and expected to be paid at the same rates as other entertainers with worldwide markets. No other sport had quite the same market—by 1998 the World Cup for football came closer than anything known previously to dividing the human race into two equal halves, those who watched it on television and those who did not—but rugby football, motor racing, tennis, golf, and even cricket did well out of television and the public desire for something to watch. British enthusiasm for sport, or least for watching and supporting teams, had one odd feature: the teams and the players were so unsuccessful. In the first half of the twentieth century Britain was 'the country that taught the world to play', and teams from Britain (usually competing as England or Scotland or Wales or Ireland) were successful. England won the World Cup in 1966, and England supporters looked back to this success for decades, but it was the last effort of the old school rather than a sign that England had adapted to the new way of doing things.

A change could be seen in the way gambling was carried on. The football pools had for seventy years been the simple weekly entertainment which gave people a very slight chance of transforming their whole lives and provided enough smaller prizes to encourage people to take part. In November 1994 the government launched a National Lottery that offered even larger top prizes, and it displaced the pools to a considerable extent. If anything, spending the proceeds was what caused difficulty for the government. Critics had objected that the Lottery was a way to raise ordinary revenue without imposing taxes, and the government had replied that the proceeds would be spent on providing permanent benefits, mainly connected with the arts, and would not be used to take the place of money that ought to have come from general government revenue. The managers of the funds could provide money for buildings (or for other capital goods, such as equipment for brass bands or for cricket teams) but not for the regular subsidies to help cover running costs, which was what local organizers really wanted. In its last years Major's government started what became the largest single venture built with Lottery money, a modern equivalent of the Great Exhibition of 1851 at Greenwich to commemorate the year 2000, which was taken to be the beginning of the new millennium. Early progress was limited enough to mean that the incoming Labour government could have cancelled it in mid-1997 with discreet references to thrift and prudence, but it went ahead and hundreds of millions of Lottery money were spent on it. The Millennium Dome itself was a simple, reasonably elegant, and reasonably inexpensive way of covering a large floor area with a building that was not meant to last. But it was harder to decide what to put in it. The post-war Labour government had held a Festival of Britain in the centenary year of the Great Exhibition which had looked to the past by having a Dome of Discovery as one central feature, celebrating advances in knowledge. Neither scientific progress nor past achievements seemed suitable themes around which to organize the Millennium Dome; writers explained at length why the Dome was a failure, and they often said that nobody had found a theme for it, but they spent less time exploring the problem of finding a theme. Two pieces of public art may provide a microcosm of what was involved. Survey evidence suggested that the British public was more proud of the armed forces than of anything else about the country, but when the question arose of filling a vacant plinth below Nelson's column in Trafalgar Square it was clear that no self-respecting artist would offer anything connected with the theme of military glory already established there. A witty response to the challenge of the empty space was provided by Rachel Whitehead, who installed an upside-down replica of the plinth in transparent plastic. The British Library placed in its grounds a statue based on Blake's profoundly anti-intellectual picture of Newton the diabolical geometrician; however satisfactory as a statue, it was entirely out of keeping with the idea of a library. Elegant and lively critical art was easy to find, but the absence of any positive mood of creation and celebration might have warned the organizers of the Dome that finding exhibits attractive enough to draw visitors to their building would be harder than they realized.

The losses of the Dome were charged to the Lottery, but the public was beginning to feel that the line between Lottery revenue and ordinary revenue was too artificial to be maintained. The Labour government reinforced this attitude by making Lottery money available for projects in education, health, and urban renewal; it had been easy to say that there was never enough money for the arts, but it was not so easy to see how projects in these areas could deserve Lottery money but not be appropriate for government support out of regular revenue. Commentators suggested that Major would have preferred more of the money to go to sport and his wife would have liked to see more of it go to opera. He followed sport enthusiastically, and made no secret of it. It was true that it could do his popularity no harm, but his devotion was genuine enough; when he had to announce in 1997 that his political career had come to an end, the next thing he did was to go to the Oval to watch cricket. His successful opponent, Tony Blair, was well known to play rough-and-ready football with some of his political colleagues, which helped present them as active players of the people's game.

New Labour

John Smith had already had one heart attack, and his death in May 1994 was not unpredictable. It led the Labour Party to make a more clear-cut decision about its future direction. The choice of Blair, with about four-sevenths of the votes in the electoral college, against two-sevenths for the trade unionist John Prescott and one-seventh for Smith's deputy leader, Margaret Beckett, was an adequate but not overwhelming commitment to decisive change. Blair and his closest supporters had a 'project' which involved something like a return to 1906, with a commitment to social reform and to devolution of the powers of the central government, friendliness rather than hostility to businessmen who were expected to run the economy more effectively, and no interest whatsoever in public ownership. This was sometimes put in terms of a Third Way that was neither socialism nor capitalism, but it emerged rather more like capitalism shorn of some of its Thatcherite aggressiveness. The 'project' also involved discussions with some Liberal leaders about ending the division between the two parties that had developed early in the century, but this might have been only a manoeuvre on Blair's part to build up good relations with the Liberals in case he did not win a solid majority at the next election and needed to bring the Lib–Lab alliance of the 1970s back to life. Blair's eagerness to put his party on a new course was expressed most obviously in his constant references to 'New Labour', with a strong indication of the weaknesses of 'old Labour'. He brought this into the realm of policy by arranging to amend Clause IV of the party constitution to remove more or less all reference to public ownership. Nothing but the grim experience of four successive defeats, including the intense disappointment of having victory snatched away when it seemed to be within their grasp in 1992, would have made traditional Labour supporters put up with this.

Under the impact of departure from the ERM, negative equity, 'sleaze', and its other setbacks after the 1992 election, the government's popularity had sunk very low, but this had happened before. Thatcher's governments had always gone through periods of unpopularity, and had been 10 per cent behind Labour in the opinion polls a year before she was re-elected in 1987. Governments after 1945 normally went through a period of unpopularity between elections, almost always partly due to a period of economic instability, but more often than not they recovered and were re-elected. Major had waited the full five years between elections before dissolving in 1992, and it always looked very likely that he would do the same thing again, with the great advantage that this time he was holding office during a time of economic recovery and prosperity. Even if in hindsight the problems of the Conservatives in the mid-1990s look insoluble, very few of their opponents would in 1994 have imagined it was safe to leave the government to defeat itself. As leader of the Opposition for three years Blair had to hold on to a large lead in the opinion polls and make sure that nobody thought of returning to the Conservatives, and in this he was completely successful.

He possessed a type of eloquence which made it easy for him to present small practical steps in the direction of improvement as great expressions of the nobility of the human spirit. This was more satisfactory for voters, who are practical people who like their leaders to have some ideals but want them to be reasonable, than for commentators and political activists, who prefer something grander. Blair and his colleagues in the 'project' were sure that tax increases were unpopular, and were not at all certain that promises of large increases in social services could outweigh the damage done by the fear of tax increases. So their election preparations pointed to modest, quantifiable improvements in social services, such as cutting down the number of people who had to wait a year for routine operations under the Health Service, balanced by a promise that there would be no increase in income tax.

As political parties after 1945 undertook a strategy of semi-permanent national campaigning based on opinion-polling, they assumed at first that each party had a large block of committed supporters and then needed to win a small block of centre-minded 'floating voters' who liked part of one party's programme and saw advantages in the other programme as well. This view of the situation may have been accurate in the 1950s. When the Conservatives assessed the situation after their defeat in 1966, they found evidence that the blocks of committed voters were smaller than had been thought and that a great many people were ready to vote 'instrumentally' for the party they thought would produce direct benefits for them. In particular they found that people in the section of the electorate defined for advertising purposes as C2 (or skilled working class in the language of sociologists) were very instrumental in their approach, and that many of them lived in marginal seats. Thatcher took this approach very seriously and made a concentrated effort to win these voters over, recruiting the *Sun* to attract them to vote Conservative with some appeal to patriotism and a good deal of emphasis on becoming better off but no attempts to play on any 'deference voting' that might have been found in the working class.

Blair's pre-election campaign took this to its logical conclusion and rested on the idea that no section of the electorate should be written off as irreconcilable. Obviously the Labour Party was not going to win even a large minority of the business community to its side, but it could certainly do better in this section than in the past, and any visible success in winning this sort of support would reconcile people who liked parts of the Labour programme but were concerned that the party wanted to quarrel with an important part of the economic structure. Blair and his close associates were sometimes criticized for being too ready to please businessmen, and were sometimes assumed simply to be trying to raise campaign funds for election and pre-election spending that was very hard to finance out of ordinary Labour resources. No doubt some of this was true; Blair's promise to the Trades Union Congress that he would give them 'fairness, not favours' may have made trade unionists reflect that this would be better than the treatment they had had from the Conservatives, but it was not going to make them contribute much more than before. Blair needed a good deal of financial support for modern campaigning, though in office Labour legislated to keep election-year spending by the central offices down to only £15 million; but he also wanted to show that his party was attractive to a very diverse range of the public, and for this he set out to make his party much more acceptable to the press than ever before. The success of this operation no doubt owed a lot to the public relations skills of the Labour headquarters at Millbank, but it also fed on the Labour Party's demonstrable popularity. Neither newspapers nor television organizations want to quarrel with people who are going to hold power; Blair was able to make sure that he was treated better by the media than Foot or Kinnock had been, and to bring the *Sun* back to the Labour sympathies that it had given up in favour of Thatcher.

While Blair was laying the foundations of power in a modern state, Major was unable to regain any of the support he had lost. The opponents of the Maastricht Treaty in the Conservative Party rallied to make quite sure that he took no further steps towards the European Union (as it became known in 1993). He was unlikely to accept the 'social chapter', but it was well known that two of his most important ministers, Heseltine and Clarke, were in favour of closer relations with Europe and would have liked the United Kingdom to agree to adopt the euro in 1999 at the same time as other EU countries. The question could be debated at a great many different levels, but as the months went by the arguments for 'keeping the pound', for avoiding involvement with an exchange rate policy that would have to try to suit the needs of a dozen different countries at once, and for retaining control over economic policy in London prevailed over the attractions of not having to change money when going to the Continent, of not having any exchange rate risks when trading with nearby neighbours, and of being part of a monetary unit that could challenge the dollar. Conservative MPs moved to a Euro-sceptic position; Conservative organizers and activists became even more committed in the same direction, and chose candidates for the next election accordingly. By the summer of 1995 the Conservative Party was almost paralysed by rumours that Major was to be opposed for the leadership, with the implication that he might be thrown out as Thatcher had been in 1990, or at least that a 'stalking-horse' candidate would stand to test his weakness, as had happened in 1989. Major took the initiative and resigned to bring about a leadership contest at a time that suited him. He was opposed by John Redwood, a very junior Cabinet minister who had begun his career as an exceedingly 'dry' exponent of privatization policy, had become strongly opposed to increasing the country's involvement in the European Union, and on other issues could be seen as right-wing. It was a sign of the shift in Conservative sentiment that Major, who in 1990 had been seen as the most right-wing and Euro-sceptic of the leadership candidates, could now expect the support of the left wing of his party. In terms of simple votes cast Major defeated Redwood by a comfortable 218 votes to eighty-nine; if the votes of twenty-two MPs who abstained or were absent are counted against him, he had the support of just under two-thirds of his MPs.

Opposition to closer involvement in Europe came from another direction a few months later. Sir James Goldsmith announced that he would support candidates committed simply to demanding that a referendum should be held before the country adopted the euro, and he made it clear that he would finance the Referendum Party with £10 million or some other minor fraction of his immense annual income. This alarmed the Conservative leadership, who foresaw a considerable loss of seats if their vote was split, and in the spring of 1996 they announced that they would hold a referendum before carrying out any decision to adopt the euro, and the Labour Party took the same approach. Probably most of the leaders of both major parties were relieved by this; it was hard to see how votes were to be won on the issue, and yet it was important enough in the minds of some political enthusiasts to open up the danger of a party split or a desertion to the other side. The promise of a referendum would let parties contest a general election without taking up a dangerous position on this divisive question.

Accepting the referendum did not end the stalemate inside the Conservative Party, or alter the balance of opinion in the electorate; the Referendum Party went on with its preparations to oppose any MPs who were not fully committed to the principle of the referendum. The economy continued to advance very comfortably, but, whether because voters remembered how unpleasant the beginning of the 1990s had been, or because they felt the economy was doing well only because it was being dragged forward by the even more successful performance of the United States, or because they were determined to have a change of government, the Labour lead in the opinion polls declined very little as the last possible day for the election drew closer. By the dissolution Blair and Major were the only politicians in the country who were in doubt about the result; Major thought he could keep the loss of seats within bounds by the personal campaigning that was thought to have turned the scales in 1992, and Blair remained nervous that some moment of triumphalism would repel the voters as Kinnock was believed to have done in 1992. In the event the Labour Party received the largest share of the popular vote that any party had gained in any election since the break-up of the two-party electoral monopoly at the beginning of the 1970s, and the Labour major-ity in Parliament was the largest that any government had had since 1935.

This large majority had two direct effects. Before the election the Labour and Liberal Parties had worked out a programme for joint action, with devolution and reform of the House of Lords as the main legislative items. During the election there had clearly been tactical voting by Liberal and Labour supporters determined to unseat the Conservatives and ready to vote for what would normally have been their second choice in order to do so. Once he had his immense majority Blair could perfectly realistically tell his potential allies that he could not arrange a coalition with them, because his party could not see any need for it. Labour backbenchers would have opposed a coalition with the Liberals bitterly, and Labour frontbenchers would have felt that their career prospects were being blighted for the sake of an unneces-sary alliance. The Liberals had moved from being a minority party which could reasonably complain of being under-represented to a solid third party whose share of the vote had gone down slightly. They had done well at a time of Conservative weakness, which suggested that they were a party with a left-of-centre leadership that was very well suited for attracting right-of-centre voters. They gained their new seats from the Conservatives, so naturally they were in areas of above-average prosperity in the south and more particularly the south-west of England, with an area of noticeable strength in south-west London, and they were not able to build on their existing strength in Scotland. In 1906 the Liberals had been able to accept the Labour Representation Com-mittee as allies partly because their attack was going to be on Conservative seats; in 1997 the much more informal relationship between Labour and the Liberals was helped by the fact that the Liberals were an alternative choice for Conservatives rather than an obstacle to Labour success.

The performance of the Referendum Party showed what enthusiasm and a great deal of money could do to establish at very short notice a nationwide set of candidates. Estimates of its impact on the result depend on assumptions about where its votes came from. The leadership was undoubtedly made up of dissatisfied Conservatives, and after the election they argued that most of its 800,000 votes would have gone to the Conservatives, and claimed that it helped to defeat over a dozen pro-European Conservatives. The evidence of opinion polls indicates that it attracted a wider range of support from various political parties and that only about half of its votes came from Conservatives, which meant that its intervention affected half a dozen seats at most.

	Votes	Seats	% of all votes cast
Conservative	9,600,940	165	30.7
Liberal Democrat	5,242,947	46	16.8
Labour	13,517,911	419	43.2
Referendum	811,827	0	2.6
Scottish Nationalist	622,260	6	2.0
Plaid Cymru	161,030	4	0.5
Ulster Unionist	258,159	10	0.8
SDLP	190,814	3	0.6
Democratic Unionist	107,348	2	0.3
Sinn Fein	106,921	2	0.3
UK Unionist	12,817	1	—
Others	549,874	1	1.7

Labour in office: devolution

The Labour victory aroused great enthusiasm in the spirit of the slogan 'Things can only get better'. Some of it was simply a long-pent-up feeling that 'It's time for a change', which was all the stronger for those who felt the Conservatives ought to have gone out of office in 1992. This sentiment was not going to cause the new government any problems, but some people were ready to believe that despite the modesty of its election promises the government was going to carry out sweeping changes or at least that it ought to carry out sweeping changes. The size of the majority obtained for a moderate pro-gramme made people talk as if it was a majority for a different and more radical programme, and of course nobody can say what would have happened if a different Labour Party, untroubled by its successive defeats from 1979 onwards, had offered a radical programme. The Labour leadership set out to follow a very prudent financial policy in its first years in office, partly because it was bound by election promises to accept Conservative spending estimates for the immediate future and keep income tax unchanged, partly because it wanted the economic recovery to bring the deficit under control. It was uncomfortably aware that in 1964 and in 1974 newly elected Labour govern-ments had tried to carry out ambitious election promises very quickly, and had spent most of their time in office wrestling with economic problems that had probably been made worse by the post-election dash to spend. The 1997–2001 Labour government had some claim to be the first government since 1955 to have had no balance-of-payments crisis and no sudden pressure on the financial brakes. This may have been a matter of luck and continued expan-sion in the United States, but it was clearly welcome.

The new government may have been inhibited by its lack of experience, but obviously it was not going to allow any self-doubt to become visible. Despite the gulf caused by eighteen years in opposition, there was none of the searching for ministers with experience that had been seen in 1924 and in 1964. Ten or eleven people who had held government posts in the 1970s came back to office under Blair, but none of them were given positions of great importance and they were not included simply because they had been in office before. This absence of concern about the mystique of experience in office could also be seen in the contest for the Conservative leadership a few weeks later. Major resigned promptly, and five candidates to take his place came forward. The successful candidate, William Hague, was the youngest of them and the one with least ministerial experience, as he had been in the Cabinet for less than two years. He owed his success at least in part to the depth of concern about European issues among Conservatives and his own relatively middle-of-the-road position on the question. Clarke, who had been Chancellor of the Exchequer since 1993, was conspicuously in favour of adoption of the euro, and three candidates divided the hardline anti-euro vote. Hague was mildly opposed to the euro; he would probably have won Clarke's supporters over if they had had to choose between him and any of the other three. His subsequent difficulties as leader may have pointed to the disadvantages of letting a single political issue dominate the process and of choosing a leader without much experience, but it is fair to say that anyone facing Blair and his enormous majority would have had a hard task in making much of an impression.

The August peace of the holidays was suddenly turned into something tense and even dangerous by the death in a car crash of the Princess of Wales. The brilliant marriage of sixteen years earlier had broken down; the Prince of Wales had chosen a bride ideally suited to bring glamour and a capacity to show human sympathy to a royal family that needed to renew its links with its people, but he had failed to sustain the marriage, probably because he was all along much more deeply attached to Mrs Camilla Parker Bowles, who in terms of age and interest in rural life would have been a better wife for him. The Princess did not respond with the patient dignity shown in such a position by earlier royal brides like Queen Alexandra. She had never felt the royal family had supported her or appreciated her capacity for getting in touch with ordinary people, and she felt she had been brought in simply to provide a son and heir. She set out to build a position that was royal but independent of the royal family by leading a glamorous social life and at the same time maintaining a steady round of well-chosen charitable activities, of which her visiting of AIDS patients and her campaign against landmines probably made most impression. When it was realized that separation was doing nobody any good, the Prince and Princess proceeded to a divorce in 1996; it was easy enough to drive her out of the royal family, but she was able to maintain her royal position, shown by the fact that she was able to keep the title of Princess of

Wales. Nobody was very worried by her relationships with a number of men, but her hapless ex-husband's attachment to a divorced woman was taken in an altogether more solemn way, partly because he would have had to face the official opposition of the Church of England to the marriage of divorced people if he remarried, and partly because the Princess was such fun and he was not. In the summer of 1997 she travelled round France with Dodi al-Fayed, the son of the owner of Harrods, and it was with him that she was killed. The public response could hardly have been foreseen, but it was deep and intense: people went into the modern equivalent of public mourning, and enormous numbers of bunches of flowers were left outside her palace as marks of affection and respect. The royal family responded quite differently; for them she was an intruder who had brought the Prince little happiness and had disturbed the royal pattern of existence in many unwelcome ways. The Prime Minister had to explain the facts of the situation to them; his phrase 'she was the people's princess' summed up people's belief that her combination of enjoying herself and being helpful to others was the way that royalty ought to behave. The royal family managed to make it quite clear that they did not want to break their family holiday at Balmoral (some way west of Aberdeen) for a funeral service, but the public would have been outraged by anything less than a funeral service in Westminster Abbey attended by the royal family. Even during the service itself they were subjected to a philippic by the Princess of Wales's brother, and the applause that greeted it was a reminder of how much public approval they had lost by the way relations with the Princess had gone.

The new government faced a deepening divide between town and country. Major's government had taken steps to control legal possession of firearms. As this was handled by the police, it did very little to reduce possession of firearms by criminals and instead the police moved towards becoming a force armed with guns, but on the whole the measure was popular enough in towns. It was much less welcome in the countryside, but the annoyance was a mere shadow of that caused by the desire of Labour backbenchers to make fox-hunting illegal. Once Labour was in office, the government was torn between its desire to avoid offending the rural interest, which organized itself in the Countryside Alliance, and its sympathy with its backbenchers. Private Members' Bills were brought forward but, even though large majorities in the Commons supported them, they did not get on to the Statute Book while ministers were concerned about the rural minority. In 2001 an outbreak of foot-and-mouth disease among sheep and cattle caused bitterness that was probably even greater. The government consulted the farmers' lobby group, the National Farmers' Union, which was in favour of killing infected animals and all others that had been in contact with them, though the government's scientific adviser did recommend vaccination as long as it was acceptable to farmers. The government wanted a general election in May but delayed it until

June because of the epidemic; many farmers remained unplacated and blamed the government for all their troubles. Ministers were irritated, and spoke of reducing the system of subsidies and of ending the arrangement by which farmers did not insure against foot-and-mouth disease and were compensated directly by the government for animals slaughtered. These difficult relations made it very hard for farmers and government to work out together a response to enlargement of the European Union, which was about to admit a number of food-exporting countries in eastern Europe which would place a great strain on the intervention price system of the Common Agricultural Policy.

The government's desire for tranquillity in financial affairs after the 1997 election encouraged it to act boldly elsewhere. Labour Chancellors were always at least as cautious as their Conservative counterparts, but their supporters were much more eager for active government than the Conservatives and would be impatient if they had nothing to do. In the 1960s the energies of Labour MPs were absorbed in changing the law to fit what came to be seen as a sexual revolution; the government's strategy for the 1990s involved a number of constitutional changes in the way the United Kingdom was governed, and it could hope that they would occupy the backbenchers' time and energy. Callaghan's government in the 1970s had tried to set up devolved governments for Scotland and, with lesser powers, for Wales; and Blair's government returned to the issue. The idea of a Scots Parliament won wide approval and it was accepted by a three-to-one majority in a referendum in September 1997. About 62 per cent of the electorate voted, so this time devolution would have overcome the relatively exacting 40 per cent approval level that had been required for the 1979 vote. This may have been meant to set the Welsh a good example when they voted a week later, but enthusiasm for the Assembly was so mild that the margin of approval was only 0.6 per cent in a turnout so low that under 26 per cent of the electorate had voted for the proposal. The legislation for Scotland set up an effective Parliament with a good deal of autonomy in domestic affairs, and it had enough fiscal freedom of action, secured by a second question in the referendum, to be able to make its autonomy effective. The legislation for Wales transferred powers from county councils to a central authority in Cardiff rather than reducing the power of the government in London over Wales. Plaid Cymru underlined its desire for linguistic autonomy and its lack of interest in independence by supporting the legislation rather than asserting that Wales ought to have the same powers and rights as Scotland.

Most of the seats in the Scottish Parliament and the Welsh Assembly were contested in the traditional first-past-the-post system, but a substantial minority were distributed in proportion to the total votes cast. This partial acknowledgement of proportional representation had the double advantage of making it much less likely that the Scottish Nationalists or Plaid Cymru could secure a parliamentary majority based on a minority of the votes cast, and also of showing the Liberals that the Labour Party had not forgotten its willingness to discuss proportional representation with them when in opposition. Nobody was surprised when the elections of May 1999 produced a Scottish Parliament in which a Labour–Liberal coalition emerged as the natural government, but people had expected Labour to win a clear-cut majority in Wales, and thought Plaid Cymru would not advance much beyond the half-dozen constituencies in the Westminster Parliament where most of the voters can speak Welsh.

Labour's failure to win a clear-cut majority in Wales was attributed by some people to resentment at London interference in the choice of leader. Scotland and Wales looked like producing Labour majorities for the foreseeable future, but the central government made enough of an effort to see that leaders of the new governments were acceptable in Westminster to suggest that, whatever the constitutional changes, the Labour leadership intended to exert a form of democratic centralist control over them. The London government and local opinion in Scotland had agreed that Donald Dewar was the obvious choice as First Minister, but for Wales the Westminster leadership pushed forward Alan Michael as First Secretary (or chief minister) despite all the signs that local opinion preferred Rhodri Morgan. The leadership got its way when the Assembly met in July 1999, but Michael had to give way to Morgan eight months later. This conflict in Wales was of specialized interest, but it did make people watch what happened in London more carefully than they might otherwise have done.

In 1998 the government had held a referendum which gave it authority to re-create some part of the central municipal government for the Greater London region which the Conservatives had destroyed in 1986 by giving all its powers to the constituent boroughs. The boroughs were to keep most of these powers, but for the first time all the voters of the region were to elect a mayor for London who would be assisted by a small regional council. It looked as if the most important, and certainly the hardest, task of the new mayor and corporation would be that of getting transport in London to flow freely. Ken Livingstone, the Labour hero of the resistance to Thatcher's destruction of the Greater London Council, had become a Member of Parliament but was eager to stand for Mayor; Blair saw him as the sort of left-winger who had made it so hard for Labour to be elected in the 1980s. It was reasonable enough for Blair to encourage other Labour candidates for the post to come forward, but he devised an electoral college to choose who should run that was so obviously loaded against Livingstone that he gained enough sympathy to be able to stand as an independent on his previous record against candidates of the three national parties. In May 2000 he was elected Mayor and the official Labour candidate came third. An issue of principle soon arose; restoring the London Underground to the high quality of performance and comfort of the

1950s was going to need a lot of money, but the central government was sufficiently concerned about balancing the budget to prefer to finance change by a public–private financial initiative. Livingstone's opposition to this may have been ideological, but the government's accountants reported on the plan unfavourably enough to suggest that the Mayor had a strong practical case as well.

The central government had no comparable disagreements with the Scottish and Welsh legislatures; the Scottish Parliament abolished fees for university students, but this was just the sort of regional variation that devolution was designed to encourage. It created alternative centres of power, but it was true that for most of the twentieth century municipal government had provided alternative centres of power only in the very crude sense that people simply voted for or against whichever government was in office at Westminster. Voters who took this one-dimensional approach were likely to get the municipal governments they deserved. Devolution might go the same way, but Blair showed some signs of learning that one of its advantages was to let voters choose one broad approach at the national level and then modify it at the regional level, even when they voted for the same party all the time. Livingstone clearly owed some of his success to Londoners' desire to show that the Blair way was not the only way to do things. Commentators talked as though devolution meant the end of the United Kingdom, but the United Kingdom had never had a uniform administration for the whole country in the way that France and Spain had often done; Scotland had kept its own legal and religious arrangements after the 1707 Union, at a time when these were very important aspects of politics, and Wales had acquired a few elements of autonomy without the United Kingdom disintegrating.

The pre-election discussions with the Liberals had covered reform of the Lords as well as devolution, and late in 1998 the government brought forward a Bill to remove the hereditary peers from the House (though not depriving them of their titles or social status). The legislation looked forward to a second stage of reform, but for the time being it would leave a House consisting entirely of people appointed as life peers. Hague wanted more popular involvement in such things; he was arranging for Conservative leadership contests to be conducted by letting Conservative MPs put forward two names to be submitted to a vote of the entire party membership, and he wanted the new House of Lords to be elected, though on a different system from the House of Commons. The Conservative leadership in the Lords, under Lord Cranbourne, was more concerned about saving some portion of the hereditary principle. It convinced the government that the hereditary peers would have no reason to observe the existing political conventions if they were going to lose all their political powers and that they might use their legal right to reject all non-financial legislation until the legislation removing them had finally been passed under the Parliament Act. Losing one or two sessions of legislation would be a serious matter, and the government amended its Bill to allow ninety hereditary peers elected on party lines (as well as the Earl Marshal and the Lord Great Chamberlain) to sit until further reform of the Lords was carried out. Cranbourne probably reflected that the promise of further reform contained in the 1911 Parliament Act had taken eighty-seven years to fulfil, and he might have had some faint hope that his ninety hereditary peers would survive for a comparable length of time. Hague was furious that his efforts to present the Conservative Party as the party of popular election had been sabotaged by Cranbourne's manoeuvres.

The Conservatives had not welcomed devolution, and had provided much of the organization for the opposition to Welsh devolution, but in Irish affairs they had laid some foundations for constitutional change on which Blair felt able to build. At the end of 1993 Major and Reynolds, the Fianna Fail Prime Minister of Ireland, had signed the Downing Street Declaration, which acknowledged that the United Kingdom was not maintaining its position in Northern Ireland for any financial or other material interest and was willing to withdraw if the majority of the population of Northern Ireland wanted it to do so, and that the consent of the people of Northern Ireland was the only proper way to carry out changes there. The Declaration acknowledged the fact that the Irish government would take an active interest in the affairs of Northern Ireland, but only at the political and diplomatic level (and the Irish government might have added that it would expect the demographic balance in Northern Ireland to continue to move slowly in the nationalist direction). With the Irish dimension accepted in this way, the British government and also the Social Democratic and Labour Party (SDLP) set out to bring the leaders of Sinn Fein into political discussion on the basis that the IRA would give up its campaign to drive the British out by force of arms.

The negotiations were complicated by Sinn Fein's reminders that it did not control the IRA; while nobody could tell just what the balance of power was, both Sinn Fein and its IRA partners were deeply divided about giving up what they called the armed struggle, and supporters of a policy of peaceful advance had to bear in mind that their colleagues might shoot them if they appeared too peace-loving, or might break away and set up new and more intransigent organizations. In August 1994 the IRA announced a ceasefire which would let politicians start negotiating about the future of Northern Ireland, and led to a reduction in violence: deaths had been over 100 a year until 1982, and then had fluctuated between fifty and 100 a year, with some signs that Protestant paramilitaries were becoming better equipped for combat by the 1990s, but after 1994 the death rate was lower. Later in the year progress was delayed when his party forced Reynolds out of office and his successor, Bertie Ahern, almost immediately lost power to Fine Gael under John Bruton, but the negotiations had acquired some momentum, helped by a visit from the US President, William Clinton. When the IRA brought the truce to an end early in 1996 by a campaign of bombs in Britain, it was uncertain whether this was because the hard men were reasserting themselves or because the strategists reckoned that there would soon be a Labour government at Westminster which would be more sympathetic to the nationalists than the Conservatives had been. Fianna Fail, which probably had more freedom to manoeuvre because it had the reputation of being less likely to seek good relations with Britain than Fine Gael, returned to office just a few weeks after the Labour government was elected. A few weeks later a second IRA ceasefire was announced and political negotiations could begin.

The British government had not understood how much the involvement of the Irish government had changed the situation. Mo Mowlam, the Labour Secretary of State for Northern Ireland, was sympathetic to the nationalist cause, and seemed not to realize that the main task of the British government was to retain the confidence of the Ulster Unionists and encourage them to negotiate, while the Irish government played a similar role on the nationalist side. To counterbalance the impression that Mowlam had given, the Prime Minister declared that he was a unionist; in British terms, this was perfectly true, but he was not in Northern Irish terms firmly committed to the union, and the Unionists were irritated when they realized the difference. It was reasonably clear that the only way to run political business in Northern Ireland was to return to the power-sharing of fifteen years previously, with a Unionist First Minister leading the majority in the Assembly supported by an SDLP Deputy First Minister so that both sides would have a veto over any important changes. By Good Friday 1998 both sides had accepted this arrangement as part of a more wide-ranging agreement. The Irish Republic undertook to give up the claim to Northern Ireland enshrined in its constitution, Sinn Fein said it would make arrangements for decommissioning the IRA's stores of arms during the course of the development of the other provisions of the Good Friday Agreement, and the British government gave assurances to the Unionists that these undertakings to decommission arms would be enforced. The Agreement was submitted to referendums in the Irish Republic and in Northern Ireland. In the Republic it was accepted by a large majority with very little trouble. In Northern Ireland it passed by 71 per cent to 29 per cent, a very adequate majority under most circumstances but one that raised difficulties for the leadership of the Ulster Unionist Party. The relatively extreme Democratic Unionist Party claimed that all of the 29 per cent in the minority were Unionists and that a small majority of all Unionists were opposed to the agreement. This made no immediate difference. David Trimble had gained the leadership of the Ulster Unionists as a strong defender of Unionist rights, and as long as he controlled his own party he could maintain his position as the Unionist First Minister. By the end of the year direct rule by Britain had ended, the Assembly and its Executive were settling down to run the province, and people expressed relief that things were working out so well.

While the great reduction in violence was very welcome, and Northern Ireland was able to invite investment from the outside world more plausibly than had been the case for many years, some large issues remain unsettled. The Unionists wanted to see Sinn Fein become a political party like any other, rather than the political wing of a guerrilla army; Sinn Fein argued that any simple handing-over of arms to the British government would be a declaration that it had lost the war. Blair could see that Unionist distrust of Mowlam was part of the difficulty, and he replaced her with Mandelson, who could present himself as a man who had no preconceptions about Northern Ireland and simply wanted to make the Good Friday Agreement work. But this was not enough to save Trimble from the pressures on him; by 2000 it was fairly clear that only the internal divisions among the Unionists enabled him to hold them to a pro-agreement position. With 40 per cent of the Unionists supporting Ian Paisley's Democratic Unionists, Trimble could hold on to the 60 per cent of Unionists who voted Ulster Unionists as long as about one-third of the whole Unionist community supported him. This fragile arrangement pointed towards the grim lesson of history that leaders of the Northern Ireland Unionists gain their position by intransigence, and lose it by being too ready to work with the British government, which normally took it for granted that it had an inexhaustible supply of Unionist leaders who wanted to follow a conciliatory policy. The effects of refusal to compromise could also be seen on the nationalist side; Sinn Fein successfully avoided all arguments and appeals to give up its weapons, and in the 2001 general election its policy of resistance was rewarded. The Sinn Fein and the Democratic Unionist vote increased, the SDLP more or less held its ground, and the Ulster Unionist vote went down.

Labour in office: economic and social questions

Blair and his Chancellor of the Exchequer, Gordon Brown, probably felt that, if other things were entirely equal, better relations with the European Union and adoption of the euro were desirable, but it became clearer and clearer that half a dozen other things, including being re-elected in four or five years' time, meant much more to them. Everyone with strong feelings, favourable or unfavourable, about relations with the European Union was bound to think that everybody else was equally interested. Blair's determination to be as friendly as possible when he went to meetings of the Council of Ministers was such a contrast to the attitude of his two immediate predecessors that it was widely believed that he was enthusiastic about the policy of 'ever closer union' and, more specifically, that he wanted to adopt the euro. Brown's first policy decision after taking office was to let the Bank of England run its own interest rate policy in future in a way that kept inflation at 2.5 per cent, subject to a requirement to explain what had happened if price increases were to go as much as 1 per cent above or below the target. At the same time the Bank's informal powers of supervising what went on in the City were transferred to official regulators, a change that was accepted readily enough, because the Bank had not done well in handling setbacks like the collapse of Baring Brothers early in 1995.

This autonomy for the Bank reassured people in business and finance that the new government was not going to be highly interventionist. It also shielded the government from blame if interest rates went up—it was simply the Bank's cautious policy, and no fault of the government. And interest rates did go up, perhaps because the previous government had been holding interest rates lower than they should have been after running up the large deficit, perhaps because any governor of a central bank will push rates higher than even the least politically minded Chancellor of the Exchequer. In terms of both politics and economics the decision was sensible, but it meant that the government could not have an interest rate policy or an exchange rate policy specifically designed to bring about closer relations with the European Union. The government's view was that, if a policy that made sense on other grounds was compatible with moves towards the euro, it should be followed, but the euro was not to be allowed to dominate British policy. Brown underlined this by outlining five tests to be applied before adoption that would in a pragmatic way ensure that it would be advantageous to Britain, and he may have felt that his attitude was justified by the inconveniences caused to a number of European countries by a euro-based policy in the next few years.

Relations with the European Union, dominated by economic issues, probably took up more ministerial time and attention than all other issues of foreign policy, but European affairs extended beyond the boundaries of the EU. Major had gone on from involvement in the successful Gulf War to a more complicated and less satisfactory commitment to resolving the problems of Bosnia in the mid-1990s. The difficulties caused by the disintegration of Yugoslavia went on until the end of the decade; in 1999 NATO decided that the Serbian government's treatment of the Albanians in its southernmost province of Kosovo was intolerable, and it set out to force Serbia to acknowledge their rights. This was achieved almost entirely by bombing from the air, but it was clear that prolonged Serbian resistance would have made intervention on the ground necessary and that British troops would have been available for any operations of this sort. In 2000 smaller British forces were deployed to place some limits on the devastation of civil war in Sierra Leone, and the local population appeared ready to welcome a more complete assertion of British authority in the former colony. This background of intervention lay behind the very active British response to the suicide attacks launched on targets in the United States by dedicated Muslim zealots in September 2001. Apart from lesser damage, this onslaught destroyed the two great towers of the World

Trade Center in Manhattan with a loss of about 4,000 lives. People in Britain responded in a way that showed the closeness of the ties with the United States that had grown up; Blair was calm, eloquent, and determined in responding to the crisis; when investigation indicated that the attack had been organized by a group directed by Osama bin Laden, a fanatically committed Muslim, from a base in Afghanistan, British troops were organized to help the United States strike back at the authors of this devastation. Despite the obvious obstacles faced by any advance on Afghanistan, the American and British forces quickly defeated the Afghan regime and set up a broader-based government. It was disturbing to find that some Muslims in Britain felt that their first loyalty was to their co-religionists in Afghanistan and that some of them went there to resist the Western forces. In Northern Ireland the effects were more beneficial; the refusal of the IRA to decommission its stores of arms had been driving Trimble to step back from the power-sharing government in order to retain his leadership of the Unionists, but the attack on the World Trade Center led American supporters of the IRA to tell it that any further delay in decommissioning would be found inexplicable and intolerable. In late October the IRA began decommissioning, and it looked much more possible that the power-sharing government could begin to operate as had been intended in the Good Friday Agreement.

By this point the euro was about to emerge as a circulating currency, with notes and coins that became legal tender on 1 January 2001, after a two-year transition period when it had existed only as a unit of account. When it was launched in 1999 the pound had very nearly returned to the value of DM2.95 which had been unsustainably high in 1992. The euro was initially worth $1.18US and was if anything expected to rise in value; instead it dropped sharply, losing about 30 per cent of its value in terms of the dollar in the course of the next two years. This was greeted in Britain with a good deal of *schadenfreude* which was by no means confined to full-time Euro-sceptics. In terms of economic strategy it was hardly surprising if the process of convergence among the eleven currencies that merged into the euro had led by 1999 to an inappropriate exchange rate, and presumably it was sensible to correct this sooner rather than later. Part of the fall was attributed to poor management by the European Central Bank but this did not alter the fact that adoption of the euro at a correspondingly high value for the pound would expose the British economy to a more permanent form of the problems caused by the overvalued pound of the 1920s. From the point of view of sterling, a value for the pound which might have been a little too high for comfort when the euro was launched was wildly unsuitable a couple of years later after the euro had fallen so far. The Conservatives' policy commitment that they would not try to adopt the euro in the lifetime of the coming Parliament served to place them in a slightly more Euro-sceptic position than Brown's five tests; the intensity of politicians' ideological convictions on the issue could be seen in the way that some said the euro should never be adopted while others spoke simply about adopting it without explaining what steps, such as ending the Bank of England's freedom to set interest rates, should be taken to bring the value of the pound to a level which made this reasonable.

The Chancellor of the Exchequer began planning domestic spending by allocating money to departments for three years, which allowed ministers a little freedom to plan ahead in a way that had not been possible previously, and gave them a chance to work out policies that would serve as the foundation for requests for increases at the end of the three-year period. It also carried on the process of reassuring people that the Labour government was devoted to financial prudence and gave the Chancellor a breathing space to cope with the deficit and the Debt. While most Labour supporters were resigned to the fact that public ownership could not be revived in the foreseeable future, and regarded the constitutional reforms as reasonable steps to deal with problems of no great concern to England, they were certain that a Labour government would devote itself to improving the Welfare State after years of neglect, unwillingness to spend money on it, and ministerial contempt. Some ministers, when they looked at the condition of their departments, went on to express much the same ministerial contempt as the Conservatives. The Chief Inspector of Schools was generally taken to be speaking for the Secretary of State when he criticized the poor quality of teachers and the Secretary of State for Health did not raise morale in his Department.

Social benefits are subdivided between transfer payments and services provided. In theory transfer payments are a simple matter of giving money to those who need it; in practice there is never enough money, and it cannot be confined to those who need it without means-testing more efficient and more intrusive than any government would dare undertake. Brown was fairly successful at increasing revenue by what came to be called 'stealth taxes' which did not conflict with the income tax pledge and had little visible effect on people's incomes. His reduction of the tax exemption given to pension funds would make occupational pensions less valuable in future, but the impact of this reduction was up to forty years away and meant very little to the recipients. Privatized gas, water, and electricity firms which had been particularly profitable paid a 'windfall tax', whose proceeds were used for a 'New Deal' to improve the training and job-finding facilities available for young people who were out of work. This was a matter of making intelligent use of the decline in unemployment to make sure that people coming into the labour market were treated sensibly. A minimum wage was established for the first time; at £3.60 an hour it was low enough to be unlikely to price anyone out of the labour market, but it provided a safety net to make sure that other benefits were not used to drive wages down. It protected the position of recipients of the working families tax credit, which was designed to make sure that income tax would not be collected from people below the poverty line. The Minimum Income Guarantee was arranged to make sure that all old-age pensioners received at least £90 a week. All of this was done relatively thriftily; when Frank Field at the Department of Social Security devised a scheme for improved national insurance and social security at a net cost to the Treasury of £8 billion, he soon felt obliged to resign.

While the cash transfer side of reform of social benefits was handled with some dexterity, this was probably the easier side of the problem and certainly the one that could be effected more quickly. The Labour government knew before it came to office that neither the health nor the education aspects of the Welfare State were running as they should. Undoubtedly some of the trouble was that the Conservatives had wanted to save money on services which almost unavoidably cost more and more; with an ageing population, and medical science finding new and more expensive ways to keep people alive and healthy, the National Health Service was bound to cost more. Other countries had been more ready to recognize this. The British tended to look at the American system of private medicine, note that it cost a much larger share of the national income than the NHS and did not produce a noticeably healthier country, and conclude that they were getting good value for money from their service. But from the 1950s onwards several countries on the continent of Europe were spending more of their national income on medicine than Britain and were getting good value for their money by having more doctors in proportion to population and longer life expectancy. The NHS had been launched at a time when queuing was accepted as an after-effect of the war, and waiting lists became established as a natural part of British medicine. The Labour government had made an election commitment to reduce waiting lists for surgery because it was clear-cut and easily visible, but in the winter of 1999–2000 it realized that this was not the issue that most concerned people. So many patients with influenza wanted hospital beds that the system was overwhelmed; economizing by closing hospitals and reducing the number of beds from 194,000 to 103,000 in the course of the 1990s had left the NHS with no reserve of beds to handle an emergency. Blair announced, without much sign of consultation with his colleagues, that the financial resources of the NHS would be increased by 1 per cent of the national income. Even this would not bring British spending up to the general western European proportion of national income, but there were limits to how much new money could be spent (except by simply increasing the pay of existing medical staff). Training new doctors was a matter of years, and reorganizing hospitals could take almost as long. Blair was lucky that the plight of the NHS was not brought out fully until just after the 2001 general election, when the European Court gave a judgment that citizens of the European Union were entitled to go to other medical systems in the Union if their own country's service was delaying too long in attending to their needs and Britain looked like becoming a large-scale importer of medical services, but enough had been seen early in 2000 to make people uneasy about what was going on. Very few people really thought that the Conservatives could establish any control over the situation, and even fewer wanted to expand private medical services to a point where ordinary people were dependent on them, so the Labour Party was not in electoral danger. But the crisis diminished people's belief in the government; it slipped from being a golden hope for the future into being the least unsatisfactory choice available.

Major's government had ended an argument that had been going on ever since the expansion of higher education in the early 1960s. The status of the universities had been unquestioned, but their growth had been matched by that of the polytechnics, which had often begun as technical colleges or institutions at other levels that clearly did not have an unquestioned status. In 1992 thirty-nine polytechnics were made into universities, almost doubling the forty-seven existing universities. This solved the problem of 'parity of esteem', without necessarily changing the effectiveness of the education provided. At the same time the system of external assessment of universities was made more stringent. When Blair's government approached the issue of higher and further education, and said that it wanted 50 per cent of 18-year-old students to go on to universities or colleges of further education, it was far from clear that universities still had enough flexibility to respond to this ambitious policy. The government was well aware that education in schools was not satisfactory, but it did not ask how this would affect attempts to provide education for a very large intake at 18. For some years after 1945 government policy had aimed at providing very high-level education for a fairly small minority at school and university level. In the world of fiction this approach retained its hold on the imagination; in the late 1990s one of the great publishing successes in the English-speaking world was a revival of the boarding-school story: J. K. Rowling sold 100 million copies of her five *Harry Potter* books set in a school where a great deal of arcane knowledge had to be acquired, teachers were respected, and students could grow up and develop their virtues without having parents getting in the way. Fiction this might be, but it did suggest that equality was not the only thing to be considered in an adequate education policy. In the 1960s university expansion and the adoption of comprehensive education had been intended to open education to larger numbers of people. Doubts were constantly expressed about the quality of this education, partly out of a feeling that the least successful third of those at secondary schools were getting very little benefit from their time at school, partly out of a fear that standards were being inflated. Brown's readiness to accept the Conservative spending plans until 1999 had left schools with very little room for manoeuvre, and by the time of the 2001 election it looked as if quite a lot of money would have to be spent on education just to keep up the supply of teachers without finding very much opportunity for improvement.

Health and education were obviously areas for which the government was responsible, but it also found it was expected to do something about the problems of transport. The privatized railways operated less successfully than any other privatized industry; nobody would have dreamed of asking the government to return to running telephones or electricity, but soon after privatization it was clear that public involvement in railways was going to go on for some time. Railtrack's problems probably went back to under-investment and sudden cancellations of programmes under public ownership, but the privatized company failed to convince the financial institutions that it was capable of handling the large amounts of capital that it was going to need over the years. A serious accident at Hatfield showed just how poor the condition of the track really was, but this was attributed much more to recent penny-pinching by the company than to earlier neglect by British Rail. Shortly after the 2001 election Railtrack proved unable to raise the capital needed to maintain and improve the system, and the government set out to create a non-profit organization, which looked very like a return to public ownership. This left the train operating companies uncertain that they could get an adequate return from investment in modern rolling stock. Before nationalization track and rolling stock had been owned by the same company (as happens in most countries); under the system of divided ownership people could say that the government should act as the coordinating body to bring the two together, but there was little evidence that it had worked out any policy for doing so.

By the time of the 2001 election the government had to base its claim to re-election on the smoothness with which it had run the economy and kept tax rates and interest rates low, and the plea that it had identified what had to be done for the delivery of improvements in government services and would go on to satisfy demand in these areas in its second term. Its popularity according to opinion polls and by-election results had remained unshaken even in the weeks before the June 1999 election for the European Parliament. In this election the Conservatives had done better than Labour; voters who are look-ing for a chance to vote on general grounds against the government usually give warnings of it on other occasions, so this vote looked rather more like a rehearsal for taking a detached attitude to the European Union than hostility to the government. As Hague had not managed to build up a position of his own, he naturally tried to make something of opposition to the euro in the general election; while the voters were always likely to feel that social services mattered more, opposition to closer involvement in Europe had brought the Conservatives success in 1999, and any concentration on welfare issues was seen as apt to help the Labour Party because it was generally trusted to deal with such things. But European issues aroused very little interest; people knew that nothing decisive could happen before a referendum was held, and this allowed them to concentrate on things of more immediate interest. Hague also tried to bring forward crime and the question of asylum seekers, which attracted a good deal of attention after the election but probably would not have been seen as important enough to affect many votes.

	Votes	Seats	% of all votes cast
Conservative	8,357,292	166	31.7
Liberal Democrat	4,816,137	52	18.3
Labour	10,740,648	413	40.7
Scottish Nationalist	464,314	5	1.7
Plaid Cymru	195,893	4	0.7
Ulster Unionist	216,869	6	0.8
SDLP	192,965	3	0.7
Democratic Unionist	181,999	5	0.6
Sinn Fein	175,932	4	0.6
Others	1,026,481	1	3.8

The Conservatives gained a slightly larger share of the total vote than in 1997, but it did them surprisingly little good. Labour retained almost all the seats won in 1997, mainly because its policies had a reassuring effect in places where it had made unexpected gains. When Labour increased its majorities in Warwick or in Wimbledon in 2001, it did not do so by appealing to its trad-itional supporters, and results like this were more to be seen as the justifica-tion of Blair's idea that no section of the electorate should be written off as irreconcilable. The Conservatives were still divided but they did not have the weight of 'It's time for a change' running against them, and Labour did not have the charm of novelty about it that it had built up in 1997. Labour's majority in 1997 had been larger than that of any government since 1945 and its majority was only very slightly reduced in 2001. The popularity of the 1997–2001 Labour government, shaken only briefly by complaints about rising pet-rol prices in the summer of 2000, suggests that unambitious policies, avoiding any moves towards increasing public ownership but showing an active con-cern about improving public services, preferably without increasing taxation, had fitted the mood of the day. Avoiding inflation and balance-of-payments crises was no doubt helpful as well, but keeping away from these difficulties is not yet within a government's power to command. The steady decline of the stock market in 2000 and 2001, just after some predictions that prices were bound to go up for ever, underlined how hard it is to be sure that an economic problem has been overcome.

The other important aspect of the election campaign was the sharp drop in turnout. Over 80 per cent of the electorate voted in 1950 and 1951 and turnout in all elections from then until 1997 had fluctuated between 70 and 80 per cent. In 2001 under 60 per cent voted, a lower level of participation than anything seen since the very confused circumstances of 1918. This had not been foreseen, and it was not easy to explain. Opinion polls may have convinced everybody that the result was such a foregone conclusion that it was not worth voting, and their predictions of the parties' share of the vote were accurate enough to indicate that it was not a matter of abstention by disgruntled supporters of any one party. The media had complained about the skilful public relations campaign managed by the Labour Party's spin-doctors, and some voters—moved by pity for journalists confronted by the novel problem of politicians who did not tell them the whole truth—may have decided that it was not worth voting. It had become fashionable to lament the government's unambitious approach: nobody could be excited by thinking that Blair was going to build the New Jerusalem or that he was going to lead the socialist hordes to the final overthrow of the British way of life, and Hague did not even possess Blair's eloquence about the modest steps forward he was ready to take. The decline of the Churches had fortunately led to no decline in the level of national sanctimoniousness, but as irony had become the fashion the media felt they should sneer rather than pontificate. This was bound to encourage a feeling that nothing very worth while was going on in politics— the point was made very clear just after the election when prominent members of the British National Party were interviewed by some of the BBC's leading sneerers, who interviewed these exponents of racist policies in a more restrained and respectful way than they treated politicians from parties of more obvious importance. The assumption that political activity was important and could make a difference had been part of the way life was lived in Britain from early in the nineteenth century. Northern Ireland was seen, understandably from some points of view, as a more politicized society than the rest of the United Kingdom, but in most recent elections voting there had not reached the 70 per cent level established in Britain. In 2001 the turnout in Northern Ireland was much the same as in other elections there, which suggests an unchanged level of interest in politics. The drop in turnout in Britain was sharp enough to indicate a distinct loss of interest in the political process.

Hague had made virtually no progress in reducing the immense Labour majority and promptly resigned in the way that was coming to be accepted as appropriate for defeated leaders. The Conservative MPs had to put forward two names for the party membership to choose from; they passed over the more middle-of-the-road candidates and nominated Kenneth Clarke, who had had a long ministerial career and was respected as a successful debater but was seen as too enthusiastic an advocate of the euro to be really welcome to tradition-minded Conservatives, and Iain Duncan Smith, who had no ministerial experience and did not yet possess the practised skill to modify an existing policy without rousing controversy but was committed to opposition to the euro in a way that indicated the depth of his Conservatism. Duncan

Smith won by 155,933 votes to 100,864; for Clarke to lose to a man with so few claims to the leadership suggested very deep hostility to the euro and indicated a depth of division inside the Conservative Party that might hamper it at the next general election.

Undoubtedly there was popular opposition to the euro, which ran from highly sophisticated analysis to a belief that changing to the euro would set off an inflation like the one associated with the move to decimal currency in the early 1970s. Blair expressed confidence that if the government were sure that adoption of the euro would be good for the country, he and his ministers would be able to win a referendum on the issue. Certainly the old relationship between people and government had been one in which the government led and the people followed, and some of the opposition to the euro had been expressed in terms which suggested that people who were perfectly sincere in disliking the idea of the change were a little uneasy about the idea of resisting it if it was recommended by respected political leaders.

At the beginning of the twentieth century rule by an elite was accepted and worked reasonably satisfactorily. It could not survive unchanged under universal suffrage, particularly when political parties were becoming committed to producing large social change. In the middle of the twentieth century, with a government that introduced the Welfare State, it really did look as if political parties might become the agents for a secular transformation of society. But this never happened again, and the political parties lost the claim to be leading society to an altogether better world that they might briefly have had. The voters did not need the politicians nearly as much as the politicians needed the voters; if the voters left the politicians to run things with no great sign of public interest, as had inevitably happened in the eighteenth century, it would represent the loss of an important dimension in the way people had lived for two hundred years. But the politicians might respond, in the words of a Roman politician to the voters whose enthusiasm he had failed to rouse, 'There is a world elsewhere.'

A note on statistical evidence

Very few figures are as definite and conclusive as they look. For instance, the occupational background of MPs has been analysed in two different ways: J. A. Thomas in *The House of Commons 1832–1901* (1939) and *The House of Commons 1906–1911* (1958) records each major economic activity of the MPs he is studying, and on the average each MP turns up twice in his lists. J. F. S. Ross in *Parliamentary Representation* (1943) and *Elections and Electors* (1955) assigns each MP to one fixed category or another. Which is better? Both approaches have their advantages, which means that neither of them gives a conclusive answer.

Economic statistics are sometimes even less definite than political. The movement of real wages provides an example: indexes of prices and of money wages are only a rough approximation, and an index of real wages obtained by dividing one into the other is even rougher. Comparing A. L. Bowley, *Wages and Incomes in the United Kingdom since 1880* (1937), 94–5, with W. Ashworth, *An Economic History of England, 1870–1939* (1960), which speaks of national income rising and real wages remaining unchanged, or with S. Pollard, *Development of the British Economy* (1962), 24, which speaks of a slow rise in national income per head, a fall in real wages, and a distinct fall in the proportion of national income paid in wages, shows that economic figures are very slippery. The figures for the balance of payments are liable not to be conclusive; Harold Macmillan complained in the 1950s that the government was not able to establish accurate balance-of-payments figures for its own use, but nobody is sure that the problem has been solved in succeeding decades—certainly the problems of the late 1980s were not properly foreseen.

The components of a cost-of-living index change so much with the passage of time that they are always hard to compare, and it is particularly difficult in periods when prices change rapidly. The consumer price index, designed to measure the working-class standard of living, somewhat more than doubled from 1914 to 1920, and then went down again. The retail price index, designed for everyone except the richest 4 per cent, doubled from 1939 to 1951, rose more gradually in the 1950s and 1960s, and rose eightfold from 1967 to 1992, so the prices of the components of this index have risen fifty-five- or sixtyfold since before 1914. But the components are never fully comparable over such a long period of time: letters cost forty or sixty times what they did in 1906, but far more people have telephones now and some people communicate free on the internet. Average wages rose slightly faster in all subdivisions of the period, so there were no declines in real wages for more than a year or two at a time. Relative living standards changed a great deal, and the 'rich 4 per cent' of the population obviously come from very different backgrounds from those of any comparable group in 1906.

Studying change is made a little harder by changes in the currency. British coinage had for centuries been based on the pound of silver divided into twenty shillings, which were subdivided into twelve pence (in Latin, *libra, solidi,* and *denarii,* hence £ s. d.). In 1971 it was changed to a decimal coinage, keeping the pound at its existing value and subdividing it into 100 pennies. This came in the early stages of a great increase in prices; it has been suggested that the change increased inflation by making people ignore the value of money, but the physical details of the change were handled well enough.

Another almost simultaneous change makes income tax figures harder to follow. The broad indicator always used for income tax is the 'standard rate', which is the marginal rate for a large majority of those who pay the tax. It has always been expressed in pennies (or shillings) in the pound; until 1914 it moved up or down 1d. (0.42p) in a budget, for most of the century it moved 3d. (1.25p) or 6d. (2.5p) at a time, and since 1971 it has moved by 1p (2.4d.) at a time. Taxpayers used to pay on only a major fraction of earned income that did not come from interest, rent, or dividends. By 1973 they paid on only seven-ninths of their income. In 1973 this changed so that an investment surcharge was paid on interest, rent, and dividends, and the declared standard rate was the full marginal rate paid by most taxpayers. After all of this, 30p is the same standard rate as 7s. 9d. in the 1960s, and 25p is about the same as 4s. 6d. in the pound in the 1920s and 1930s.

Bibliography

General

No list of reading matter about the twentieth century can be more than an inadequate precis of Keith Robbins's *Bibliography of British History 1914–1989* (1996), with H. J. Hanham's *Bibliography of British History 1851–1914* (1976) for the early years. The mass of valuable and even indispensable books grows faster than anyone can read. The government is the main source of primary material: it publishes Blue Books and White Papers in a steady stream that grows wider and wider as the State undertakes responsibility in an increasing number of areas of life. It has also produced official histories of the two world wars, and it has published documents on foreign policy which, while primarily related to the outbreak of the two world wars, provides a reasonably complete account of British policy from 1898 to 1939. Government documents, such as Cabinet minutes and departmental papers, are now open for investigation down to the 1970s under the rule that almost all documents are made public after thirty years.

The parliamentary debates (Hansard) are fuller and even more accurate in the twentieth century than they had been previously. Reports in the nineteenth-century *Times* were often good enough to be the basis for Hansard; *The Times* continues to be a useful source, but it is no longer so commanding an authority; it has often been denounced for managing the news during the 1930s, but while this criticism is justified, we ought to remember that the reason we know so much about it is that *The Times* explained what it had done in its own *History of 'The Times'*. Other newspapers have managed the news, but a confessional history of the *Daily Express* or the *Daily Mirror* has not yet appeared. Even the *Daily Telegraph* (firmly right-wing) and the *Guardian* (moderately left-wing) have not offered any comparable history, though they are the two newspapers that rank next to *The Times* in usefulness. With the decline in importance of the monthly and quarterly magazines, which played so large a role in the shaping of nineteenth-century opinion, some of their importance may have passed to the serious weekly magazines—*The Economist*, the *Spectator*, and the *New Statesman*—but more of their general influence has gone to the heavy Sunday newspapers, the *Observer*, the *Sunday Times*, and the *Sunday Telegraph*. Finding out what influences the bulk of the population has never been easy; obviously a much larger proportion of the population spends far more of its time watching television at the present day than spent its time listening to sermons and reading devotional literature at the beginning of the century, but assessing the effects of this change is very difficult. And finding historical records of this sort of influence is also difficult.

Relatively few authors are rash enough to write books that try to cover much more than half of the century. Robbins himself wrote *The Eclipse of a Great Power: Modern Britain 1870–1992* (1994 edn.); A. F. Havighurst's *Twentieth-Century Britain* (1985 edn.) is a good clear account; and Walter Arnstein's *Britain, Yesterday and Today: 1830 to the Present* (1996 edn.) has perhaps escaped its author's Victorian antecedents. Some very interesting books deal with parts of the first half of the century (books on the second half of the century often start in 1945, and will be mentioned at that point). C. L. Mowat's *Britain between the Wars* (1955) is perhaps the best of these; it covers only twenty of the years under discussion, but within its chosen time span it is very thorough and very well informed. A. J. P. Taylor's *English History 1914–1945* (1965) covers a somewhat longer period, in a lively and stimulating way; however, it is less reliable. W. N. Medlicott's *Contemporary England 1914–1964* (1967) leaned somewhat too heavily to the diplomatic side, and in particular devotes a great deal of space to the diplomacy of the 1930s. A. J. Seaman's *Post-Victorian Britain 1902–1951* (1966) is a good book on a rather less ambitious scale, with a heavy concentration on the Second World War—the account given is enlightening but is out of proportion with the rest of the book.

Private authors have cooperated to produce very substantial works of reference. The *Annual Register of World Events* opens with a survey of British affairs which has broadened from its original record of parliamentary events and covers a great range of other activities from art and economics to law and religion. For economics at a more scholarly level, the *Abstract of British Historical Statistics* (1962) by B. R. Mitchell and Phyllis Deane, brought closer to the present day in B. R. Mitchell, *British Historical Statistics* (1990 edn.), covers a wide range of records. Biographical information for people safely dead can be found in the *Dictionary of National Biography* and its volumes of supplements which are about to be replaced by a second edition organized by the late Colin Matthew (some people are happily not in the *New DNB* because they are alive and in *Who's Who*). For political events and personalities, David Butler and Gareth Butler, *British Political Facts 1900–2000* (2000) is much the most convenient single source; it also contains a useful range of social and economic statistics. David Butler has also been the sustaining force behind the Nuffield election studies; after R. B. McCallum launched the genre by writing about the election of 1945 and H. G. Nicholas covered the 1950 election, Butler has written accounts of each of the fourteen subsequent elections, working with Dennis Kavanagh for the last eight books.

Some long-range interpretations of politics may be mentioned. The second half of John Mackintosh's *The British Cabinet* (1968 edn.) is devoted to the twentieth century, and *Conservative Century* (1990), edited by A. Seldon and S. Ball, deals with the dominant force in party politics. *Political Change in Britain* (1974 edn.), by David Butler and Donald Stokes, treats age groups as a political force more seriously than any other general study. R. T. McKenzie's *British Political Parties* was very well received when it first appeared in 1955, partly because its argument that the real structures of the Labour Party and the Conservative Party were really very similar, was well suited to the mood of British politics at the time. In response Samuel H. Beer's *Modern British Politics* (1965) tried with some success to show that the two parties have real differences of attitude, but they are not quite the differences that appear in the party programmes. W. G. Runciman's *Relative Deprivation and Social Justice* (1966) is a curious mixture of social survey, ethical speculation, and attempt to interpret twentieth-century history. The three volumes of *The Cambridge Social History of Britain, 1750–1950*, edited by F. M. L. Thompson (1990), are not subdivided chronologically, but the twentieth-century sections of several chapters are useful. R. C. O. Matthews *et al.*, *British Economic Growth 1856–1973* (1982) provides a wide range of information and debate, and David Cannadine relates the troubles of the fortunate in *The Decline and Fall of the British Aristocracy* (1990).

In the nineteenth century official biographers published lives in several volumes that contained masses of letters and other papers, though they provided very little reference to other material. The *Life of Winston S. Churchill*, two volumes by Randolph Churchill and six volumes by Martin Gilbert (1966–88) with fourteen companion volumes of documents, began in this way, though some endnotes were provided in later volumes. (Gilbert distilled his work into a one-volume *Life* in 1991.) Multi-volume *Lives* of Lloyd George by John Grigg (1973, 1978, 1985) and by Bentley Gilbert (1987, 1992) are moving forward and both of them have reached the beginning of his war premiership. But multi-volume lives were dying out before the Second World War. Robert Blake's distinguished *The Unknown Prime Minister:*

Andrew Bonar Law (1955) indicates the modern approach: a large book, with plenty of supporting material, but also a substantial array of footnotes to point readers to material, including private papers, that is much more freely available than in the past (R. J. Q. Adams's *Bonar Law* (1999) may throw a different light on his subject, but it is the same sort of one-volume life). David Marquand's *Ramsay MacDonald* (1977) is another good example of the modern manner, even if it forces several messages for the present-day upon its readers. Lives of other politicians, mainly in the modern mode, are noted in the chapters for which they are relevant.

One change since Victorian times is the informal amendment to the privy counsellor's oath that requires politicians to publish their memoirs: they no longer have independent means, they all believe they have a book in them that the public will buy, they want to defend themselves from colleagues who have told their own stories, and they are no longer as inhibited about revealing their private motives or the conduct of government as they used to be. In the early stages of this development Asquith's *Memories and Reflections* (1928) were a pretty clear example of a book written for money by a man who did not really want to take the public into his confidence, but the books that Lloyd George and Churchill wrote about the First and the Second World Wars were (however welcome the money) written to vindicate their policies and denounce their opponents. Lord Avon wrote to defend his policies; Macmillan wrote his *Memoirs* to please himself in six volumes (1966–73), and devoted his social energies to making sure that Alistair Horne's *Macmillan* (2 vols., 1988–9) would also please him. It is hard to understand why Attlee wrote *As it Happened* (1954). There are of course interesting autobiographies and impressive biographies of people apart from prime ministers; Dalton wrote three volumes of *Memoirs* (1953–62) out of an inability to restrain himself, and they are accordingly amusing and informative. Alan Bullock, *Ernest Bevin* (3 vols., 1960–3) and Robert Skidelsky's *John Maynard Keynes* (3 vols., 1983–2000) are important contributions to the general history of the century. Harold Nicolson's *George V* (1952) is full of useful material on the crises of the reign, pleasant to read, and not too courtier-like. The official lives of Edward VII (P. Magnus, 1964) and George VI (J. Wheeler Bennett, 1958) are less distinguished (and Magnus suggests that Edward was not really in touch with politics), but they contain a good deal of interesting information from the royal archives.

Economic affairs were not really accepted as part of history or politics at the beginning of the twentieth century, and analysis tended to be specialized and dull; some life was put into it by the Tariff Reform arguments, and later by the writings of Keynes (*The Economic Consequences of the Peace* (1919); *The Economic Consequences of Mr. Churchill* (1925)), but there are not many easy contemporary books about economic events for the pre-1945 period of the type that became much more common after 1945. There are some useful economic histories: Sir John Clapham's *Economic History of Modern Britain* (1952) provides a solid account of events in the earlier decades of the century, and W. Ashworth, *Economic History of England 1870–1939* (1960) provides a more modern approach. There is rather more in S. Pollard's *Development of the British Economy 1914–1980* (1983 edn.), and there is a commentary on some developments in A. Y. Youngson's *Britain's Economic Growth 1920–1966* (1968), though this book assumes a fair grasp of the economic situation in its readers. A. T. Peacock and J. Wiseman, *The Growth of Public Expenditure in the United Kingdom* (1961) is full of useful information about government spending, which they show had begun rising steadily and consistently (at constant prices per head of population) some time before the beginning of the period. M. Bowley's *Housing and the State 1919–1944* (1945) is a very useful study of one of the most important sectors of the economy. John Burnett, *A History of the Cost of Living* (1969) is a useful introduction to a problem which became more pressing in subsequent decades. A set of three books by B. S. Rowntree serves to show that things do get better: over the course of half a century he surveyed the condition of the working class and the poor in York on three different occasions, and published *Poverty* (1901), *Poverty and Progress* (1941), and *Poverty and the Welfare State* (1951) a few years after each of these surveys, and his *English Life and Leisure* (1951) should be added to the list.

The obvious place to begin looking at Commonwealth affairs is *The Oxford History of the British Empire: The Twentieth Century* (1999), edited by Judith Brown and Roger Louis. The British Documents on the End of Empire Project has brought out several volumes on developments under successive British governments. K. C. Wheare's *The Constitutional Structure of the Commonwealth* (1960) almost inevitably is heavily involved in legal forms; A. P. Thornton's *The Imperial Idea and its Enemies* (1959) is a useful corrective to this sort of approach, because it is concerned with power and thoughts about power to the exclusion of forms and precedents. J. A. Hobson's *Imperialism* (1902), which argued that imperial expansion was not only profitable but also of considerable importance to the whole British economy, was influential in its day but its arguments came to be seen as old-fashioned. They have recently been revived by Lance E. Davis and Robert A. Huttenback in *Mammon and the Pursuit of Empire* (1986) and by P. J. Cain and A. G. Hopkins in *British Imperialism* (1993). There are some interesting biographies: W. K. Hancock's *Smuts* (1962–8) is a well-controlled account of a complicated but well-controlled man. S. Gopal, *Jawaharlal Nehru* (3 vols., 1975) is very close to the events it describes, but is still useful. Judith Brown, *Gandhi: Prisoner of Hope* (1989) shows how much of Indian politics revolved round the idea of using Gandhi's influence to achieve un-Gandhian goals.

Chapter 1

Two substantial books which have provided foundations for study of the period are R. C. K. Ensor, *England 1870–1914* (1936) and E. Halevy, *The Rule of Democracy*, pt. 1 (1934). Peter Rowland, *The Last Liberal Governments*, pt. 1 (1968), covers a wide range of material in a traditional way. S. Nowell Smith, *Edwardian England 1901–1914* (1964) is a collection of essays by different authors on politics and social life, some of them very useful. Alan Sykes's *Tariff Reform in British Politics 1903–13* (1979) leads on to the election of 1906 and the two elections of 1910, covered in A. K. Russell's *Liberal Landslide* (1973) and Neal Blewett's *The Peers, the Parties and the People* (1972). The official biographies of the leading statesmen, J. A. Spender's *Life of Campbell-Bannerman* (1923) and Spender and C. Asquith's life of *Asquith* (1932), are a bit ponderous. Spender was a little more relaxed in his autobiography, *Life, Literature and Politics* (1927). There are more modern lives of both prime ministers, J. Wilson, *C-B* (1973) by John Wilson and *Asquith* by Roy Jenkins (1964), which is very good for 1906–16; after that it tails off a little. His daughter, Lady Asquith, recorded her memories of the pre-1914 Liberals in *Winston Churchill as I Knew Him* (1965). The long-delayed last volumes of *Joseph Chamberlain*, by J. Amery, appeared in 1969. Apart from the multi-volume lives mentioned earlier, there is a rather thin life of *Lloyd George* (1951) by Tom Jones and bigger ones by Frank Owen, *Tempestuous Journey* (1954) and by P. Rowland (1976). S. H. Zebel's *Balfour: A Political Biography* (1973) is more solid than the other lives. W. Stewart's *Keir Hardie* (1921) is still useful, though Kenneth Morgan's *Keir Hardie* (1975) draws on a much wider range of information. On individual topics, G. W. Monger, *The End of Isolation* (1963) discusses British foreign policy from 1900 to 1907; B. Semmel's *Imperialism and Social Reform* (1960) is a fairly firmly anti-imperialist account of social reformers like Chamberlain and Milner; A. L. Levine, *Industrial Retardation in Britain 1880–1914* (1967) indicates some economic problems; A. M. Gollin in '*The Observer*' and *J. L. Garvin*

(1958) gets a long way into the mechanics of running a political party; and Austen Chamberlain's *Politics from the Inside* (1936) is also very informative. For a wider perspective, M. Bruce, *The Coming of the Welfare State* (1961) takes the years before 1914 as the central point in his story; and Beatrice Webb gives details of what went on in the Poor Law Commission in *Our Partnership* (1948). O. Sitwell, in the earlier volumes of *Left Hand, Right Hand* and V. Sackville West in *The Edwardians* (1936) give accounts of the upper layers of society.

Chapter 2

Historians do not agree whether this was a period of repose and tranquillity or one of strife and incipient anarchy. For the first view, see Roy Jenkins, *Asquith* (1964) or any of a number of memoirs, such as C. Hassall's *Rupert Brooke* (1964); on the other side there is E. Halevy's *The Rule of Democracy*, pt. 2 (1952) or, for a more extreme version, G. Dangerfield's seductively written *Strange Death of Liberal England* (1936). Rowland's *The Last Liberal Governments*, pt. 2 (1971) is more agnostic. On the Conservative side, apart from the lives of Bonar law already mentioned, there are A. M. Gollin, *Proconsul in Politics* (1964), David Dutton *Austen Chamberlain: Gentleman in Politics* (1985), and John Kendle, *Walter Long, Ireland and the Union 1905–1920* (1992). The suffragists, in Dame Millicent Fawcett's *Women's Suffrage* (1912) and *The Women's Victory* (1920), and the suffragettes, in Dame Christabel Pankhurst's *Unshackled* (1959), left accounts of the struggle. A. Rosen's *Rise Up, Women* (1974) is a more modern account. M. Hyde, *Carson* (1953) and F. S. L. Lyons, *John Dillon* (1971) present the two men who came closest to greatness in the pre-1914 Irish struggle.

Chapter 3

The military side of the war was covered in several dozen volumes of Official Histories of the War, published steadily between 1920 and 1948. The work of the government in domestic policy when faced with wartime problems was covered in less overwhelming detail in a series of volumes produced by the Carnegie Endowment. On a more manageable scale, C. R. F. Cruttwell's *History of the Great War* (1936) is a good one-volume account of military operations, told from a standpoint somewhat critical of British commanders and their strategy. Trevor Wilson's *The Myriad Faces of War* (1988) and John Keegan's *The First World War* (1998) take a more wide-ranging approach. The politicians' attitude to strategy is discussed in G. Guinn's *Politics and Strategy* (1966). Liddell Hart's *The Real War* (1930) is more determinedly critical of everybody. Lloyd George's six volumes of *War Memoirs* (1933–6) also denounce the generals, though he was at pains to expose the follies of his civilian colleagues as well, dealing especially brusquely with those of the Asquithian Liberals. It is said that Churchill wrote five volumes of autobiography and the publisher made him disguise it as a history of the world war, *The World Crisis* (1923–9), because it was less egocentric than the other memoirs. Haig has been defended by Duff Cooper (1936) and by John Terraine (1963), though without complete success; Robertson by himself (1926) and by Victor Bonham-Carter (1963), again not completely successfully. Arthur Marwick's *The Deluge* (1965) is a very useful account of economic developments and social change inside England while the war was on. David Mitchell's *Women on the Warpath* (1967) is journalistic and sometimes clumsy, but it does cover one aspect of change quite interestingly. The political intrigues of the period took up a good deal of Beaverbrook's *Politicians and the War* (1928) and *Men and Power* (1956), in Addison's *Four and a Half Years* (1934), and are summed up in John Turner, *Politics and the Great War* (New Haven, 1992). Trevor Wilson's

Downfall of the Liberal Party (1966) begins in 1916, and follows the problems of the Asquithians down to 1930.

Chapter 4

When Lloyd George wrote *The Truth about the Peace Treaties* (1938), he knew that defending his role meant fighting Keynes's denunciation of 'the Carthaginian Peace' in *The Economic Consequences of the Peace* (1919). Lloyd George did not succeed, and lesser debaters have done no better. There is an excellent account of the negotiations, Margaret MacMillan, *Peacemakers* (2001), though Harold Nicolson had the advantage of personal knowledge when he wrote *Peacemaking 1919* (1933). R. B. McCallum's *Public Opinion and the Last Peace* (1944) is a helpful reminder of the limits on Lloyd George's freedom of action. A. C. Pigou's *Aspects of British Economic History 1918–25* (1947) shows some signs of the fact that it was written to indicate possible hazards in the economic situation immediately after the Second World War. Beaverbrook's *The Decline and Fall of Lloyd George* (1963) concentrates almost exclusively on the quarrels within the Cabinet, without really explaining why the Conservative backbenchers were becoming restive. S. Salvidge's *Salvidge of Liverpool* (1934) and Gerald Macmillan's *Honours for Sale* (1954) indicate some of the reasons for discontent, though not discussing the advance of the Labour party; books like G. D. H. Cole's *History of the Labour Party since 1914* (1947) and Catherine Ann Cline's *Recruits to Labour* (1963) present some of this side of the case, and more can be found from Maurice Cowling's *The Impact of Labour 1920–1924* (1971), concentrating on political leaders, and from R. McKibbin, *The Evolution of the Labour Party 1910–1924* (1974) on the party machine. N. Mansergh's *The Irish Question 1840–1921* (1965) is perhaps a little too much of a commentary without facts; E. Strauss's *Irish Nationalism and British Democracy* (1951) too inclined to stress economic factors. D. Gwynn's *History of Partition* (1950) is a fairly reasonable statement of what went on. Lord Birkenhead's *F. E.* (1965) shows almost too much filial piety, but deals with a man of great influence in the period. Two useful books on foreign policy begin at about the end of the war: F. S. Northedge, *The Troubled Giant* (1966) goes to 1939; W. N. Medlicott's *British Foreign Policy since Versailles* (1968) is mainly about the inter-war years with some extra chapters tacked on. Kenneth Morgan and Michael Kinnear deal with Lloyd George's post-1918 government and its end in *Consensus and Disunity* (1979) and *The Fall of Lloyd George* (1973).

Chapter 5

The major problem of the period is considered in W. R. Garside's *British Unemployment 1919–1939* (1990). The problems of the Liberals are considered in Michael Bentley's *The Liberal Mind 1914–1929* (1977) and are set in their context in Chris Cook's *The Age of Alignment* (1975). The rise of the Labour Party inspired R. W. Lyman's *The First Labour Government* (1957), R. K. Middlemas's none too sympathetic account of one base of Labour strength in *The Clydesiders* (1965), and E. G. Dowse's rather less coherent but much more friendly account of the Independent Labour Party in *Left in the Centre* (1966). The odd events at the end of the Labour government's tenure of office are made rather clearer by *The Zinovieff Letter* (1967) by L. Chester, S. Fay, and H. Young. Almost all of the section on the BBC is drawn from A. Briggs, *The Birth of Broadcasting* (1961). W. H. Crook's *The General Strike* (1931) approaches the topic from the industrial relations point of view; Julian Symons's *The General Strike* (1957) gives more of the social history, though it does not go back as far in time. Harold Nicolson's *George V (1952)* is helpful and entertaining about the

Labour government. Marquand's *MacDonald* (1977) is good; M. A. Hamilton's *Arthur Henderson* (1938) is useful but makes Henderson a little too good to be true; Snowden's *Autobiography* (1934) is not as informative as its often bitter tone might lead one to expect and, because the Snowdens threw their papers out once it was finished, books like Keith Laybourne's *Philip Snowden* (1988) are at a serious disadvantage. J. R. Clynes's *Memoirs* (1937) reveal a lot about the attitudes of a Labour leader, but not so much about the events in which he took part. Beatrice Webb's *Diaries 1924–1932* (1956) find fault with everyone except Sidney. Baldwin still needs a definitive biography: G. M. Young's *Stanley Baldwin* (1952), an official life, attacked the subject of the biography so vehemently that it provoked a defence, A. W. Baldwin's *My Father: The True Story* (1955), which makes some good points about the 1930s. *Baldwin* (1969), by R. K. Middlemas and J. Barnes, was heavy rather than conclusive. P. Williamson, *Stanley Baldwin* (1999) is more of an interesting intellectual history than a fully rounded life.

Chapter 6

David Dilks's *Neville Chamberlain* (1984) takes his life up to 1929, after which readers may have to fall back on Keith Feiling's *The Life of Neville Chamberlain* (1946). The years of the Baldwin government have not been well served, which may reflect the fact that not much happened. The 1929–31 Labour government lived through a more exciting period, and P. Williamson, *National Crisis and National Government* (1992) provides more detail than ever about it. R. Skidelsky's *Politicians and the Slump* (1967) is critical of the government, and points towards his later *Oswald Mosley* (1975) and *John Maynard Keynes* (3 vols., 1983–2000). R. Bassett's *1931* (1958) is a determined defence of MacDonald and his policies, which analyses the various accounts of the weeks of the change from a Labour to a National government, and finds discrepancies in almost everyone's story. R. Graves and A. Hodges, *The Long Week-end 1918–1939* (1940) is one of the best—though not the most serious—accounts of social life. Duff Cooper's *Old Men Forget* (1953), though useful mainly for the 1930s, begins to become informative during this period. On the Labour side Hugh Dalton's *Memoirs*, vol. i to 1931 (1953) is informative and irrepressibly cheerful about the 1929–31 government. The Macmillan Report and the May Report deserve some attention: they are almost the only reports to have had a direct effect on political and economic events.

Chapter 7

The 1930s is one of the most discussed and disputed decades of the century, with supporters of a firm foreign policy, or of Keynesian economics, or enemies of a Conservative government using the events to prove their respective cases, and being resisted in their efforts. The opening chapters of Churchill's *The Second World War* (1948) or J. Wheeler-Bennett's *Munich* (1966 edn.) or L. B. Namier's *Diplomatic Prelude* (1947) put the case against appeasement in terms that are a little more vehement than a professional historian might be expected to use. The attack is supported by Lord Avon (Anthony Eden) in *Facing the Dictators* (1962) and in Dalton's second volume of *Memoirs* (1957). Accordingly some shock and horror were expressed when A. J. P. Taylor argued in *The Origins of the Second World War* (1961) that Hitler had merely pursued the normal approach of traditional diplomacy in the late 1930s. Maurice Cowling accepted something of this as the background to his *The Impact of Hitler* (1975); more recently D. C. Watt explained in massive detail *How War Came* (1989). Feiling's *Chamberlain* has not been replaced and is still useful; Halifax has been defended by Birkenhead in his book of that name (1967); and Hoare published a good self-justification, *Nine Troubled Years* (1954). Tom Jones's *A Diary with Letters* (1951) was written from an appeaser's point of view, but does not help his side's case. On the other hand, R. Bassett's *Democracy and Foreign Policy* (1952) is a good defence of the National government's policy in Manchuria. Attitudes to the Spanish Civil War were analysed in a less committed, and less exciting, way by K. W. Watkins in *Britain Divided* (1963). There is an interesting contemporary study of one manifestation of feeling, *The Peace Ballot* (1935) by A. Livingston and M. Johnson. A more deeply committed book about an ugly part of the 1930s, George Orwell's *The Road to Wigan Pier* (1937) is a shout of protest about unemployment without any way out; H. W. Richardson argued, in *Economic Recovery in Britain 1932–1939* (1967), that things were not so bad during the slump. Malcolm Muggeridge's *The Thirties* (1940) is an impressionistic book by a comedian who would like to write tragedy if only he had a point of view—it is the source-book for some of the jokes in A. J. P. Taylor's *English History*. Colin Cross's *The Fascists in Britain* (1961) probably tells us as much as anyone needs to know about this subject. Harold Nicolson's *Diary*, vol. i (1966) is a great achievement in self-revelation, and is also a useful historical source. Much the same can be said of Sir Henry Channon's diary, *Chips* (1967), and it is even more entertaining.

Chapter 8

Writing about military events is dominated by the Official History of the War, military series, edited by Sir James Butler. A variety of different topics are handled, in one to four volumes; the series is informative and far from uncritical of the British performance. Churchill's *Second World War* (6 vols., 1948–54) is also very helpful, and is much easier to read—Churchill made considerable use of government papers, though his account is naturally Churchill-centred. Chester Wilmot's *The Struggle for Europe* (1959) is a good example of the 'how we won the war and lost the peace' school—the phrase is printed on the cover of this edition. Lord Alanbrooke's diaries were edited by Arthur Bryant into *The Turn of the Tide* (1957) and *Triumph in the West* (1959)—it has been suggested that he wrote his diary late at night, when he was too exhausted to see the difficulties of the day in perspective. C. Barnett's *The Desert Generals* (1960) argues that Churchill and Montgomery, the popular heroes, did less than was believed and that Wavell and Auchinleck were underestimated. J. F. C. Fuller's *The Second World War* (1949) is an attempt to repeat Liddell Hart by arguing that Germany could have been crushed with a lot less effort by the application of strategic principles rather than 'ironmongery', typified by the bombing offensive. The official history of the bombing offensive by C. Webster and N. Frankland (1961) certainly seems to be going rather further than the evidence would allow when it claims that the bombing offensive was 'decisive', which presumably means that Germany would have defeated America and Russia if it had not been for Bomber Command. There are also extensive American military histories, which show that the war against Germany was conducted on fairly amicable terms of equality with England.

Chapter 9

The Official History of the War, civil series, edited by Sir Keith Hancock, has volumes on a great variety of topics, but they are less of a unity than the military series volumes. Churchill was not as interested in domestic developments as in strategy and foreign policy and his epic is not so useful here. *John Anderson* (1962), by J. Wheeler-Bennett, is quite a useful book about the man who was at the centre of domestic planning, but inevitably it can give only limited space to the war years in a one-volume biography and it does not go into much detail. The Beveridge Report (1942) is an important summary of social thought and proposals. N. Longmate, *How We Lived Then* (1971) is a lively account of life at home; Paul Addison, *The Road to 1945* (1975) is useful on political developments; and Angus Calder's *The People's War* (1969) puts a staunch socialist case well. A. Bullock's *Ernest Bevin*, vol. ii (1966) covers the work of the Minister of Labour in even more detail than the subject will stand. Sentiment around the end of the war can be explored in the novels of J. B. Priestley, though they do lean rather further in an optimistic, egalitarian, and left-wing direction than some people would have liked. Evelyn Waugh's *Sword of Honour* (1965, drawn from three earlier novels about Guy Crouchback) survives very well, but it is written from a much more anti-Russian point of view than was common during the war (once the war was over, of course, sentiment turned against Russia as quickly as it turned against France in 1918). The general election of 1945 was the first to be described in a Nuffield election study, by W. B. MacCallum and A. Readman (1946).

Chapter 10

Two very good histories of the Labour government, *Labour in Power* by Kenneth Morgan and *The Labour Government* by Henry Pelling, came out in 1984; Peter Hennessy, *Never Again* (1992) takes a good deal of knowledge for granted. There are substantial biographies of Attlee by Kenneth Harris (1982), of Bevin by Alan Bullock (vol. iii, 1983), of Dalton by Ben Pimlott (1985), and of Morrison by B. Donoughue and G. W. Jones (1973). The last volume of Dalton's memoirs (1962) and the autobiography of Herbert Morrison are helpful; Attlee's are not. M. Sissons and P. French (eds.), *The Age of Austerity* (1961) is a collection of essays on various aspects of life under the Labour government; it is very useful for giving the atmosphere of the period, though it is by its nature not directly concerned to give facts. J. Marlowe's *The Seat of Pilate* (1959) explains how the British government found itself in so unpleasant a position in Palestine by the end of the Mandate; M. Edwardes, *The Last Years of British India* (1963) provides the background for independence and partition, and P. Moon, *Divide and Quit* (1961) is a good account of the difficulties and disasters of partition at one of the crisis points. Nationalization has been studied by W. A. Robson in *Nationalised Industry and Public Ownership* (1960), which is moderately favourable, and by R. Kelf-Cohen in *Nationalisation in Britain* (1958), which is rather more immoderately unfavourable. The historical background of the programme of nationalization is outlined in E. Barry O'Brien's *Nationalisation in British Politics* (1966). The year 1945 serves as a starting point for a number of useful books: Kenneth Morgan's *The People's Peace* (1990) is an excellent one-volume account of the post-war world down to the high tide of Thatcherism; David Childs, *Britain since 1945* (5th edn. 2001) gives a simpler but manageable account. Alec Cairncross's *The British Economy since 1945: Economic Policy and Performance 1945–1990* (1992) is the most comprehensive of the economic histories that start then, but G. D. N. Worswick and P. H. Ady, *The British Economy 1945–50* (1952) is a good account written close to the event, though J. C. R. Dow's *The Management of the British Economy 1945–60* (1964) may be more accurate, and is certainly more technical. Chris Wringley has edited contributions on *British Trade Unions 1945–1995* (1997) which adopt the same starting point.

Chapter 11

The early 1950s have been reasonably well covered: Joan Mitchell's *Crisis in Britain 1951* (1963) is a mildly pro-Bevanite account of the economic problems of the Labour government during its last year of office; and G. D. N. Worswick and P. H. Ady have produced a sequel to their volumes on the 1940s, *The British Economy 1951–1959* (1962)—the authors lean a little to the Labour side, so that the more critical attitude taken to the government in the 1950s may reflect an opinion held on grounds that are not confined to economics. Anthony Seldon's account of the sometimes neglected 1951–5 government, *Churchill's Indian Summer* (1981), is rather stolid but deserves attention. A. Shonfield's *British Economic Policy since the War* (1958) is really more directly concerned with the early 1950s than with the Labour government. Leslie Hunter's *The Road to Brighton Pier* (1959) attracted a considerable amount of attention when it first appeared because it was, by the standards of the time, frank to the point of indiscretion about the internal problems of the Labour Party in opposition during the period of conflict over the personality and policy of Aneurin Bevan. Frankness has become more common: Anthony Nutting's *No End of a Lesson* (1967) and Hugh Thomas's *The Suez Affair* (1967) present the facts of the Suez story with very few inhibitions; Lord Avon's *Full Circle* (1960) is understandably less informative about Suez, but it does contain a good deal that is useful about his work as Churchill's Foreign Secretary. Richard Lamb, *The Failure of the Eden Government* (1987) is worth a glance. Lord Moran's *Churchill: The Struggle for Survival* (1966) is very interesting about Churchill's personality, and is informative about the period when Churchill was incapacitated by his stroke. Churchill's ministers were readier to write memoirs than their predecessors: R. A. Butler's *The Art of the Possible* (1971) (elegantly supplemented by Anthony Howard's *R. A. B.* (1987)) is probably the best of them, but Woolton's *Memoirs* (1959) is informative about the position of a slightly confused minister, who was more in touch with public opinion than with his colleagues, and much the same can be said about Lord Hill's *Both Sides of the Hill* (1964), though Woolton never felt quite as humble as Hill about sitting at the same Cabinet table as all the upper-class ministers of the Churchill government.

Chapter 12

As public life became more open, well-informed if sometimes journalistic books were published which supplement information from the press, parliamentary debates, and Blue Books. Nora Beloff's *The General Says No (1963)* is a useful study of the Common Market negotiations, with a tendency to plunge off the deep end and compare the Labour Party with the Nazi Party or suggest that de Gaulle was insane. Anthony Sampson's more urbane *Anatomy of Britain* (1962), an amiable eulogy of all the important people he could interview, and his *Macmillan: A Study in Ambiguity* (1967) present rather a bland picture of the world in which almost everything is for the best; apart from Macmillan's memoirs mentioned earlier, Lord Kilmuir's *Memoirs* (1964) show that things were not always as smooth in the Cabinet, F. W. Paish's *Studies in an Inflationary Economy* (1963) explain the inconveniences of a policy of full employment (without necessarily proving the author's case for an increase in unemployment), and Sir Roy Welensky's *Welensky's 4000 Days* (1965) is a sharp reminder of just how difficult the problem of the Central African Federation had become and how nearly it slipped over into armed conflict well before the unilateral declaration of independence in 1965. A large number of books urging reforms, such as Michael Shanks's *The Stagnant Society* (1961) and Samuel Brittan's *The Treasury under the Tories* (1964) do contain a fair amount of information which is very useful after it has been disentangled from the surrounding exhortations.

Chapter 13

The spreading flood of paperback books made it easier to get some idea of what was going on in England, though whether it was the right idea was harder to tell. Clive Irving's *Scandal '63* (1963) gave a good instant history of the Profumo affair; Randolph Churchill's *The Struggle for the Tory Leadership* (1964) was another, clearly based on information provided by Harold Macmillan after his retirement—the book was reviewed in a hostile manner by Iain Macleod in the *Spectator* for 17 January 1964. There is a not particularly distinguished life of the winner, John Dickie's *The Reluctant Commoner* (1964). One problem of the 1960s is covered in Paul Foot's *Immigration and Race in British Politics* (1965). Arthur Marwick's *The Sixties* (1998) is a comparative study of four Western countries, but has some British material. The problems of the Labour government in economic affairs were described at the time in William Davis's *Three Years' Hard Labour* (1968), which brought the story up to the 1967 devaluation. George Brown writes well enough to make one wish he had said more in his *In My Way* (1971).

Chapter 14

Lovers of political history and political gossip were glad to see Harold Wilson's *The Labour Government 1964–1970* (1971) and the memoirs of his secretary, Marcia Williams, *Inside No. 10* (1972) and the subsequent opportunity to compare them with R. H. S. Crossman's informative and self-revealing *Diaries of a Cabinet Minister* (3 vols., 1975–7). Ben Pimlott and Philip Ziegler published substantial and readable lives of Wilson in 1992 and in 1993, shortly before his death. For his second spell in office these books are paralleled by Wilson's *Final Term: The Labour Government 1974–6* (1979), by Joe Haines, *The Corridors of Power* (1979), and by Barbara Castle, *The Castle Diaries 1974–76* (1980). D. E. Butler covered *The 1975 Referendum* (1976) with Uwe Kitzinger, whose *Diplomacy and Persuasion* (1974) had already described the EEC struggles of the early 1970s. The parliamentary aspect of the struggle can also be followed in Philip Norton's *Dissension in the House of Commons* (1975). Economic policy of successive governments since 1964 is studied with fairly impartial disapproval in M. Stewart, *The Jekyll and Hyde Years* (1977); and *The Labour Government's Economic Record 1964–1970* (1972), edited by W. Beckerman, gives a more detailed account of the first half of that period; *Britain's Economic Performance* (1980), edited by R. Caves and L. Krause, is concerned with the 1970s. The Conservative side is not so well documented; among other things, Heath has produced an apologia, *The Course of my Life* (1998), but took so long about it that it has to compete with John Campbell, *Edward Heath* (1993), and N. Fisher has some interesting things to say in his *Iain Macleod* (1975) and *The Tory Leadership* (1977). The nationalist crises have not inspired definitive studies, but the background can be studied in H. J. Hanham, *Scottish Nationalism* (1969), M. Wallace, *Northern Ireland* (1970), Richard Rose, *Governing without Consensus* (1971), Sabine Wichert, *Northern Ireland since 1945* (1991), and Alan Butt Philip, *The Welsh Question* (1975).

Chapter 15

Some political developments in the period attracted the attention of well-informed journalists. *The Pact* (1978), by Alistair Michie and Simon Hoggart, gives a sympathetic account of the period of Liberal–Labour cooperation during a period of weakening party discipline outlined in Philip Norton, *Dissension in the House of Commons 1974–9* (1980). *The Battle for the Labour Party* (1981), by D. Kogan and M. Kogan, acknowledges the skill with which the left pressed forward in the Labour Party, but is not otherwise sympathetic. The response to this movement away from the centre can be seen in I. Crewe and A. King, *SDP* (1995). Peter Wilsher's *Strike* (1985) is a good narrative of the coal strike. Political scientists have analysed samples of opinion in great detail to trace the changes of the 1970s; perhaps B. Sarivik and I. Crewe, in *Decade of Dealignment* (1983), have their feet planted more solidly on the ground than David Robertson in *Class and the British Electorate* (1984). Tam Dalyell's *Devolution: The End of Britain* (1977) put the case against devolution with a force that may have helped decide the result. Susan Crosland's *Tony Crosland* (1982) is always entertaining, and reminds us what a loss his early death was. John Campbell's *Roy Jenkins* (1984) is useful if perhaps less critical about his subject than Roy Jenkins in his autobiography *A Life at the Centre* (1991), and Joel Barnett's *Inside the Treasury* (1982) is informative about politicians and economies. James Callaghan wrote a fairly sober autobiography, *Time and Chance* (1987), and Kenneth Morgan's *Callaghan* (1997) is no more exciting. The most acute of the crises of the period is covered very informatively in Kathleen Burk and Alec Cairncross, 'Goodbye Great Britain': The 1976 IMF Crisis* (1992). The zenith of union influence and its subsequent decline are mapped in R. K. Middlemas's *Industry, Unions and Government* (1983). Perspectives change with time: Tom Sheriff's *A Deindustrialised Britain?* (1979) gave the impression that things could hardly go worse than they had under Labour, though Martin Holmes's *The Labour Government 1974–1979* (1985) found a certain amount to say in favour of the Labour government. Alan Townsend's *The Impact of Recession* (1983) suggested that they had gone on getting worse, but Jock Bruce-Gardyne gives a rather more favourable account of *Mrs Thatcher's First Administration* (1984). Margaret Thatcher, *The Downing Street Years* (1993) is obviously indispensable. Her *The Path to Power* (1995) is less important.

Chapter 16

By now almost all the politicians who have held Cabinet office obey the new convention of ministerial responsibility which requires them to publish a volume of memoirs about the experience; of the books that have appeared so far, Nigel Lawson's *The View from No. 11* (1992) will have to be taken seriously by historians of the period. M. Leapman's *Kinnock* (1987) gives some account of the man who was learning how to face Thatcher, only to be the victim of the Conservatives' change of leadership and shift of attitude outlined in Dennis Kavanagh and Anthony Seldon, *The Major Effect* (1994). Thatcher's fall is covered neatly and informatively in Alan Watkins's *A Conservative Coup* (1987); a useful but hostile interim biography, *One of Us* (1990 edn.), by Hugo Young, will no doubt be replaced by something better balanced. Peter Jenkins's *Mrs Thatcher's Revolution* (1988) is strongly committed to the view that there really was a great change in the 1980s; Peter Riddell, *The Thatcher Decade* (1989) and Dennis Kavanagh, *Thatcherism and British Politics* (1990 edn.) are ready enough to accept that she dominated British politics but are not so sure where that gets one. Some people certainly thought it led, with a great deal of fuss, to disaster; Edgar Wilson, *A Very British Miracle* (1992) will serve to expound this point of view, which can also be found in *Tony Benn: The Benn Diaries* (1995), edited by Ruth Winstone, worth mentioning not just for its own sake but also to remind readers of the volumes of diaries, covering the second half of the century, which he has been publishing over the years. As well as the Nuffield studies there are some interesting essays in a volume edited by A. S. King, *Britain at the Polls* (1992).

Chapter 17

Anthony Seldon was quick off the mark and completed his *Major* (1997) four months after the 1997 election. Major devoted his enforced leisure to *The Autobiography* (1999). Hywel Williams, *Guilty Men* (1998) is trivial, malicious, sometimes very funny, and sometimes informative about the problems of the Conservatives. Will Hutton's *The State we're In* (1995) is sometimes portentous about the country's problems, but it was taken very seriously at the time. A compromise between social reform and capitalism was outlined by Tony Blair in his *The Third Way* (1998) and this was elaborated by Anthony Giddens, the scholar behind it, in his *The Third Way and its Critics* (2000). John Rentoul brought his earlier life up to date in *Tony Blair: Prime Minister* (2001). Seldon organized another team for *The Blair Effect* (2001), a more sober account than the one given in Andrew Rawnsley, *Servants of the People* (2001). Paddy Ashdown published *The Ashdown Diaries* (2 vols., 2000, 2001)—undoubtedly revealing, but is it telling us something about Blair or about Ashdown? Polly Toynbee and David Walker, *Did Things Get Better?* (2001) is a straightforwardly pro-Labour account of Blair's government, but it brings together a good deal of information in a manageable form.

Maps, charts, tables

Map 1 The British Isles

Map 2 The British Empire 1919

Map 3 The Commonwealth 2001

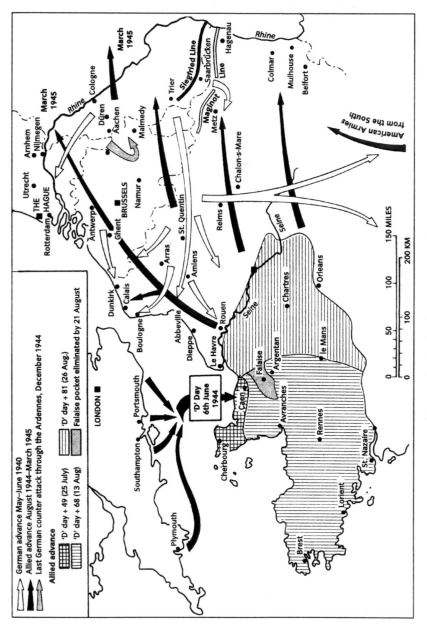

Map 4 The Battle of France 1940 and 1944

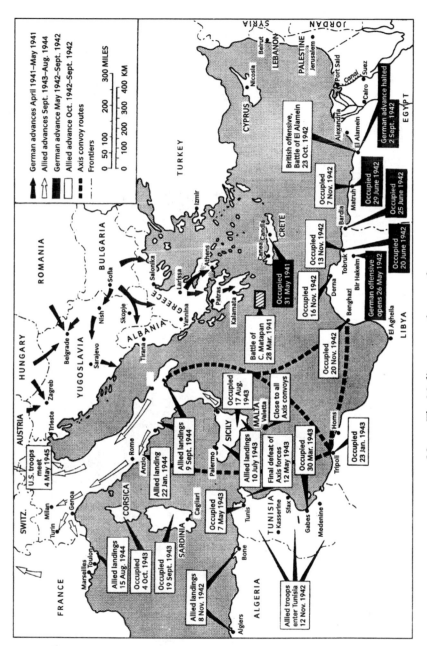

Map 5 The Mediterranean theatre of war 1940–1945

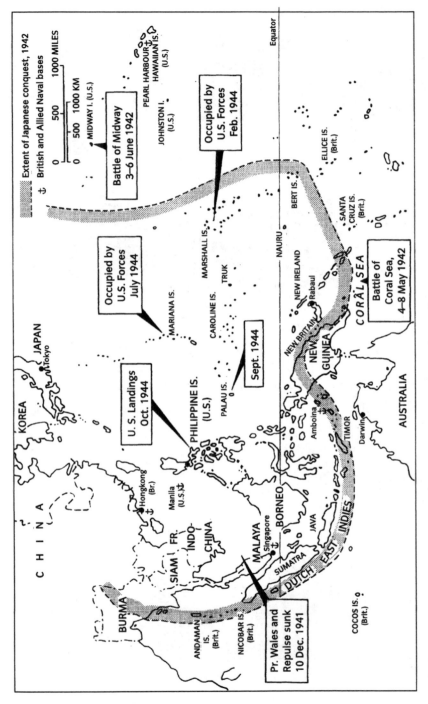

Map 6 The War in the Pacific 1941–1945

Extent of Japanese conquest, 1942
⚓ British and Allied Naval bases

0   500   1000 KM
0   500   1000 MILES

Battle of Midway
3–6 June 1942

MIDWAY I. (U.S.)

PEARL HARBOUR⚓
HAWAIIAN IS.
(U.S.)

JOHNSTON I.
(U.S.)

Occupied by
U.S. Forces
Feb. 1944

ELLICE IS.
(Brit.)

BERT IS.

SANTA
CRUZ IS.
(Brit.)

MARSHALL IS.

TRUK

CAROLINE IS.

NAURU

Occupied by
U.S. Forces
July 1944

MARIANA IS.

Sept. 1944

PALAU IS.

Battle of
Coral Sea,
4–8 May 1942

CORAL SEA

NEW IRELAND
Rabaul

NEW BRITAIN

NEW
GUINEA

JAPAN
Tokyo

KOREA

CHINA

U.S. Landings
Oct. 1944

PHILIPPINE IS.
(U.S.)

Hongkong
(Br.)

Manila (U.S.)⚓

BURMA

SIAM FR.
INDO-
CHINA

MALAYA
Singapore⚓

BORNEO

SUMATRA

JAVA

DUTCH EAST INDIES

Amboina
TIMOR

Darwin

AUSTRALIA

ANDAMAN
IS.
(Brit.)

NICOBAR IS.
(Brit.)

Pr. Wales and
Repulse sunk
10 Dec. 1941

COCOS IS.
(Brit.)

Equator

Map 7 The Palestine Mandate and after

Legend (within map):

- —·—· 1919 frontiers
- — — — 1921 division of mandate territory
- ··—··— 1941 division of Syria
- ········ U.N. resolution for partition of Palestine in 1947
- ——— frontiers of Israel in 1949
- occupied by Israel in 1967
  The territories are, from west to east:
  1. The Gaza Strip
  2. The West Bank
  3. The Golan Heights
- occupied by Israel in 1967–82

Transjordan: British mandate 1921–48 (also boundaries of Jordan after 1967)
Palestine: British mandate 1921–48
Syria: French mandate 1919–41
LEBANON: independent state since 1944
SYRIA: independent state since 1944
JORDAN: boundaries 1949–67
ISRAEL: boundaries since 1949

Map labels: Syria, LEBANON, SYRIA, JORDAN, Palestine, ISRAEL, Transjordan, EGYPT, ARABIA

N

0 25 50 miles
0 40 80 km

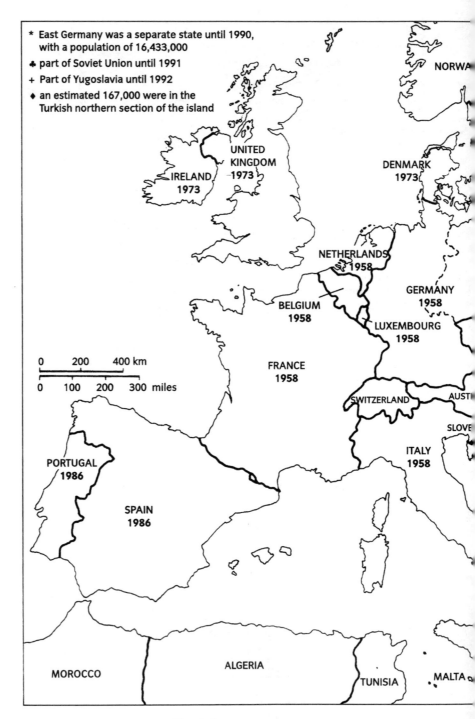

* East Germany was a separate state until 1990, with a population of 16,433,000
♣ part of Soviet Union until 1991
+ Part of Yugoslavia until 1992
♦ an estimated 167,000 were in the Turkish northern section of the island

NORWA

UNITED
KINGDOM
1973

IRELAND
1973

DENMARK
1973

NETHERLANDS
1958

GERMANY
1958

BELGIUM
1958

LUXEMBOURG
1958

FRANCE
1958

0   200   400 km

0   100   200   300 miles

SWITZERLAND   AUST

SLOVE

ITALY
1958

PORTUGAL
1986

SPAIN
1986

MOROCCO

ALGERIA

TUNISIA

MALTA

Map 8 Europe 1950–1992

FINLAND

WEDEN

ESTONIA

RUSSIA

LATVIA

LITHUANIA

to Russia

BELARUS

POLAND

ECH
UBLIC

UKRAINE

SLOVAKIA

HUNGARY

MOLDOVA

ROATIA

ROMANIA

BOSNIA-
IERZEGOVINA

SERBIA

MONTENEGRO

BULGARIA

MACEDONIA

TURKEY

ALBANIA

GREECE
1981

TURKEY

CYPRUS

Populations (in 000's)	
Albania	3,250
Austria	7,812
♣ Belarus	10,260
Belgium	9,978
+ Bosnia-Herzegovina	4,364
Bulgaria	8,980
+ Croatia	4,760
♦ Cyprus	650
Czech Republic	10,364
Denmark	5,146
♣ Estonia	1,582
Finland	4,998
France	56,440
★ Germany	79,112
Greece	10,269
Hungary	10,355
Ireland	3,523
Italy	57,746
♣ Latvia	2,681
♣ Lithuania	3,728
Luxembourg	384
+ Macedonia	2,033
Malta	352
Moldova	4,350
+ Montenegro	615
Netherlands	15,064
Norway	4,249
Poland	38,183
Portugal	10,525
Romania	23,190
♣ Russia	148.543
+ Serbia	9,791
+ Slovakia	5,310
Slovenia	1,962
Spain	39,321
Sweden	8,644
Switzerland	6,750
Turkey	56,473
♣ Ukraine	51,944
United Kingdom	57,410

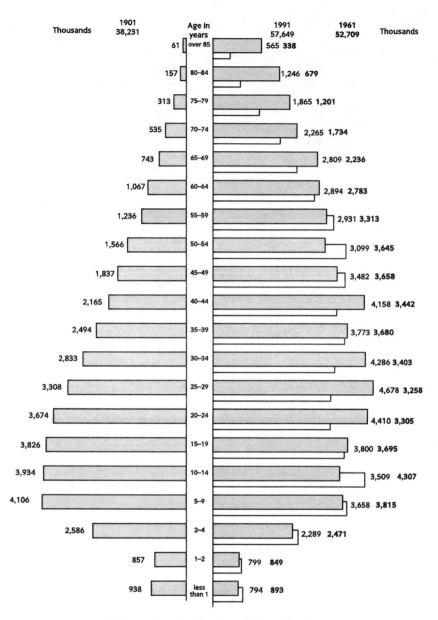

Chart 1 Age distribution of the population

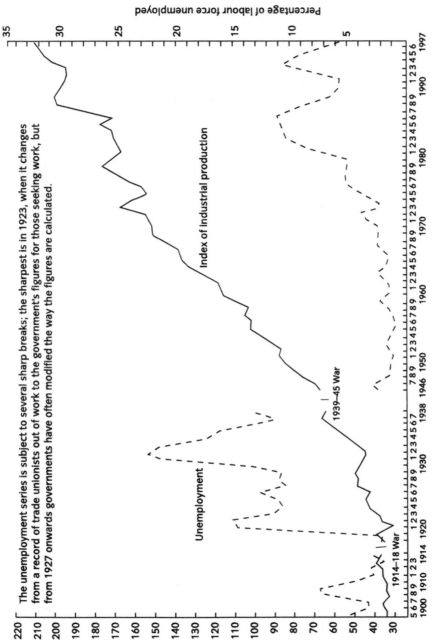

The unemployment series is subject to several sharp breaks; the sharpest is in 1923, when it changes from a record of trade unionists out of work to the government's figures for those seeking work, but from 1927 onwards governments have often modified the way the figures are calculated.

Chart 2 Unemployment and Industrial production

525

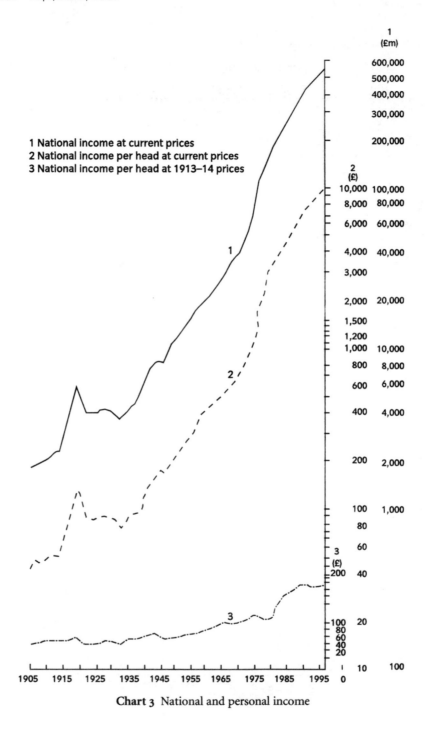

1
(£m)

1 National income at current prices
2 National income per head at current prices
3 National income per head at 1913–14 prices

2
(£)

3
(£)

Chart 3 National and personal income

Table 1 Cost of living

(This table is used to deflate current prices back to 1913–14 prices in the previous chart. Like any such series it faces obvious difficulties in comparing prices over a seventy-year period in which the things people buy have changed a great deal and prices have changed very sharply. This is made all the harder by the way the figures at the end of the table look very large compared with those at the beginning.)

Year	Value	Year	Value
1906	94	1952	395
1907	97	1953	402
1908	92	1954	409
1909	92	1955	422
1910	96	1956	441
1911	97	1957	453
1912	101	1958	466
1913	101	1959	469
1914	99	1960	474
1915	122	1961	490
1916	145	1962	511
1917	174	1963	521
1918	201	1964	538
1919	213	1965	564
1920	250	1966	586
1921	237	1967	600
1922	203	1968	629
1923	204	1969	663
1924	190	1970	705
1925	190	1971	771
1926	190	1972	826
1927	184	1973	902
1928	184	1974	1046
1929	180	1975	1300
1930	178	1976	1560
1931	169	1977	1856
1932	169	1978	1987
1933	162	1979	2227
1934	162	1980	2495
1935	162	1981	2706
1936	164	1982	2940
1937	169	1983	3076
1938	172	1984	3233
1939	177	1985	3396
1940	202	1986	3583
1941	222	1987	3723
1942	236	1988	3846
1943	243	1989	4133
1944	250	1990	4499
1945	255	1991	4848
1946	283	1992	5288
1947	302	1993	5371
1948	326	1994	5501
1949	334	1995	5694
1950	345	1996	5830
1951	372	1997	5986

Table 2 Government expenditure

(a) *Government expenditure by function, 1900–1967*

(Percentages of G.N.P. and total (i.e. central and local) government expenditure at current prices. £m.)

	1900	1910	1920	1928	1938	1950	1955	1967–8
Administration								
GNP	0.8	1.0	1.2	1.1	1.1	1.5	1.1	1.2
Expenditure	5.9	8.1	4.5	4.5	3.8	3.9	3.0	2.2
National Debt								
GNP	1.0	0.9	5.4	6.7	4.0	4.4	4.2	5.5
Expenditure	7.0	7.4	20.4	27.9	13.4	11.2	11.5	10.0
Law and order								
GNP	0.5	0.6	0.5	0.7	0.7	0.7	0.7	1.6
Expenditure	3.5	4.7	2.1	2.8	2.4	1.7	1.9	2.9
Overseas services								
GNP	0.1	0.1	. .	. .	0.1	1.5	0.5	0.9
Expenditure	0.4	0.4	0.2	0.1	0.2	3.9	1.3	1.7
Military and defence								
GNP	6.9	3.5	8.6	2.8	8.9	7.2	9.6	7.0
Expenditure	48.0	27.3	32.6	11.4	29.8	18.5	26.1	12.7
Social Services								
GNP	2.6	4.2	6.8	9.6	11.3	18.0	16.3	24.9
Expenditure	18.0	32.8	25.9	39.7	37.6	46.1	44.6	45.2
Economic services								
GNP	1.9	1.8	3.3	2.6	2.9	4.9	3.2	12.9
Expenditure	13.0	13.9	12.8	10.7	9.5	12.6	8.6	21.6
Environmental services								
GNP	0.6	0.7	0.4	0.7	1.0	0.8	1.1	2.0
Expenditure	4.3	5.3	1.6	2.9	3.2	2.1	3.0	3.7
All services								
GNP	14.4	12.7	26.2	24.2	30.0	39.0	36.6	55.2
Expenditure	100	100	100	100	100	100	100	100

Sources: (1900–55): Peacock and Wiseman, p. 86: (1967–8): *Public Expenditure: A New Presentation* (Cmnd. 4017).

(b) *Central government spending, 1980–1998*

	1980	1984	1997–8
Social Security (NI benefits)	14,405	21,514	43,391
To local authorities (current)	13,201	19,921	29,566
Defence	11,327	16,845	20,910
Health	11,228	15,413	43,561
Grants to personal sector	9,966	17,728	45,431
Debt	8,713	14,416	21,605
Other final consumption	7,290	9,600	12,479
Subsidies	4,299	4,803	1,618
Capital transfers	2,305	2,984	2,932
Grants abroad	1,823	2,128	2,549
Fixed capital	1,758	2,776	3,457
Revenue	80,287	119,288	240,288
Total spending	86,315	128,902	242,614
Spending as % of national income	50.6	54.0	54.6

Source: CSO *Financial Statistics*, March 1985. The proportion of national income spent by central government in 1975 was, by this measure, 58%.

Table 3 Production and output

Output of individual industries, 1907–1997 (£ million)

	1907 Gross output	1907 Net output	1935 Gross output	1935 Net output	1973 Gross output	1973 Net output	1983 Gross output	1983 Net output	1989 Gross output	1989 Net output	1997 Gross output	1997 Gross value added
Food, drink, and tobacco	283	87	665	203	11,975	3,493	37,425	8,958	55,029	13,268	76,355.6	19,616.4
Chemicals and allied industries	90	27	206	89	7,673	2,693	18,397	5,456	33,014	11,394	46,359.1	14,802.0
Metal manufacture	147	45	245	88	5,601	1,823	8,507	3,498	14,340	5,776	41,867.9	15,580.0
Engineering and allied industries	..	..	710	357	22,721	10,572	57,295	23,470	106,528	49,898	150,871.9	47,670.6
Textiles, leather, and clothing	458	187	656	249	6,143	2,631	10,275	3,852	16,263	6,250	20,451.9	7,899.6
Other manufactures	..	..	413	237	10,884	5,591	73,507	22,994	124,854	40,548	92,271.6	50,869.9
Mining and quarrying	134	115	167	136	1,439	1,022	4,958	3,326	3,700	2,030	5,461.5	2,440.1
Construction	..	..	295	150	12,531	5,337	29,264	16,284	66,268	20,426	87,731.2	29,461.6
Electricity and water }	51	32	181	128	3,836	2,043	37,883	12,974	46,386	15,418	46,259.9	16,824.9
Gas, oil and natural gas }							18,603	16,268	10,224	7,300	23,831.4	12,089.6

Sources: Annual Abstract of Statistics. This makes very little mention of oil production, but its value in 1983 was about £14bn.

Table 4 Employment in industries, 1871–1997 (millions of persons)

	Agriculture forestry, fishing	Mining and energy	Manufactures	Construction	Trade	Transport	Public and professional services	Domestic service (after 1979 financial services)	Total occupied population
1871	1.8	0.6	3.9	0.8	1.6	0.7	0.7	1.8	12.0
1881	1.7	0.6	4.2	0.9	1.9	0.9	0.8	2.0	13.1
1891	1.6	0.8	4.8	0.9	2.3	1.1	1.0	2.3	14.7
1901	1.5	0.9	5.5	1.3	2.3	1.3	1.3	2.3	16.7
1911	1.6	1.2	6.2	1.2	2.5	1.5	1.5	2.6	18.6
1921	1.4	1.5	6.9	0.8	2.6	1.4	2.1	1.3	19.3
1931	1.3	1.2	7.2	1.1	3.3	1.4	2.3	1.6	21.1
1951	1.1	0.9	8.8	1.4	3.2	1.7	3.3	0.5	22.6
1961	0.9	0.7	8.9	1.6	3.4	1.8	4.0	..	22.8
1971	0.4	0.4	8.1	1.3	2.6	2.0	5.7	..	24.4
1979	0.4	0.3	7.3	1.3	4.3	1.5	6.2	1.7	23.2
1983	0.4	0.3	5.6	1.0	4.2	1.3	6.2	1.8	21.1
1990	0.3	1.15	4.5	1.1	4.7	1.3	6.6	2.7	22.2
1997	0.3	0.4	4.1	1.1	4.3	1.3	7.5	4.3	23.2

Sources: Deane and Cole, p. 143; Key Statistics p. 9.

Table 5 Trade unions and strikes

	Total no. of members of trade unions (000s)	Working days lost (000s)		Total no. of members of trade unions (000s)	Working days lost 9000s)
1906	1,997	3,019	1952	9,535	1,792
1907	2,210	2,148	1953	9,583	2,184
1908	2,513	10,785	1954	9,523	2,457
1909	2,485	2,687	1955	9,556	3,781
1910	2,477	9,867	1956	9,726	2,083
1911	2,565	10,155	1957	9,762	8,412
1912	3,139	40,890	1958	9,813	3,462
1913	3,416	9,804	1959	9,626	5,270
1914	4,135	9,878	1960	9,610	3,024
1915	4,145	2,953	1961	9,821	3,046
1916	4,359	2,446	1962	9,883	5,795
1917	4,644	5,647	1963	9,872	1,755
1918	5,499	5,875	1964	9,917	2,524
1919	6,533	34,969	1965	10,068	2,925
1920	7,926	26,568	1966	10,180	2,398
1921	8,348	85,872	1967	10,034	2,783
1922	6,633	19,850	1968	10,036	4,719
1923	5,625	10,672	1969	10,307	6,925
1924	5,429	8,424	1970	11,000	10.908
1925	5,544	7,952	1971	11,128	13,551
1926	5,506	162,233	1972	11,353	23,909
1927	5,219	1,174	1973	11,449	7,197
1928	4,919	1,388	1974	11,756	14,750
1929	4,866	8,287	1975	11,950	5,957
1930	5,858	4,399	1976	12,286	3,284
1931	4,842	6,983	1977	12,846	9,985
1932	4,642	6,488	1978	13,112	9,306
1933	4,444	1,072	1979	13,289	29,474
1934	4,392	959	1980	12,952	11,964
1935	4,590	1,955	1981	12,162	4,266
1936	4,867	1,829	1982	11,694	5,313
1937	5,295	3,413	1983	11,593	3,754
1938	5,842	1,334	1984	11,236	27,135
1939	6,053	1,356	1985	10,994	6,402
1940	6,298	940	1986	10,821	1,920
1941	6,613	1,079	1987	10,539	3,546
1942	7,165	1,303	1988	10,475	3,702
1943	7,867	1,785	1989	10,376	4,128
1944	8,174	2,194	1990	10,158	1,903
1945	8,087	2,835	1991	9,967	761
1946	8,775	2,158	1992	9,585	528
1947	8,803	2,433	1993	9,048	649
1948	9,145	1,944	1994	8,700	278
1949	9,319	1,807	1995	8,278	415
1950	9,274	1,389	1996	8,089	1,303
1951	9,289	1,694	1997	6,577	235

These figures are taken from D. E. Butler and G. Butler *British Political Facts, 1900–2000* (London, 2000); I am grateful to David Butler for giving me permission to reprint them and for supplying me with more recent figures.

Table 6 The volume and direction of trade (£ million and percentages)

		1910		1930		1950		1975		1983		1990		1997	
Total imports		*678.3*	*100*	*919.5*	*100*	*2,602.9*	*100*	*24,037*	*100*	*65,963*	*100*	*126,165*	*100*	*188,595*	*100*
Commonwealth	E.C.	144.8	21.3	292.8	31.8	937.0	36.0	8,686	36.1	30,098	45.6	65,984	52.3	101,041	53.5+
Western Europe	Other Western Europe	299.7	33.9	223.9	24.3	630.6	24.2	3,518	14.6	10,444	15.9	15,716	12.5	11,343	6.0
Eastern Europe	North America	3.3	0.5	25.7	2.8	40.3	1.5	3,203	13.3	9,027	13.7	16,750	13.3	28,066	14.9
Russia	Other OECD	43.6	6.4	29.2	3.2	34.2	1.3	1,784	7.4	5,159	9.8	8,284	6.6	15,170	8.0
Middle East	OPEC	21.5	3.2	25.4	2.8	112.3	4.3	3,324	13.8	2,824	4.3	2,972	2.4	3,971	2.1
Far East	E. Europe and Russia	15.0	2.2	23.5	2.6	38.5	1.5	741	3.0	1,533	2.3	1,797	1.4	2,776	1.4+
North and Central America	Rest of World	151.7	22.4	196.9	21.4	450.9	17.3	2,665	11.1	6,786	10.3	13,882	11.0	26,228	13.9
South America		59.7	8.8	66.2	7.2	190.5	7.3								
Other areas		..	1.3	..	3.9	..	6.6								
Total exports and re-exports		*522.0*	*100*	*523.3*	*100*	*2,255.0*	*100*	*19,761*	*100*	*60,534*	*100*	*103,911*	*100*	*172,512*	*100*
Commonwealth	E.C.	136.8	26.2	226.6	41.8	935.7	41.5	6,349	32.1	26,513	43.8	55,081	53.0	96,120	55.7
Western Europe	Other Western Europe	185.2	35.5	146.8	27.6	595.1	26.4	3,268	16.5	7,517	12.4	9,038	8.7	7,994	4.6
Eastern Europe	North America	2.6	0.5	14.1	2.6	23.7	1.1	2,319	11.7	9,342	15.4	14,972	14.4	23,947	13.8
Russia	Other OECD	21.2	4.1	22.6	4.2	14.2	0.6	1,890	9.6	3,133	5.2	4,716	4.5	10,769	6.2
Middle East	OPEC	9.6	1.8	17.7	3.3	115.3	5.1	2,280	11.5	6,122	10.1	5,574	5.4	9,786	5.6
Far East	E. Europe and Russia	24.6	4.7	12.0	2.3	32.6	1.4	680	3.4	1,112	1.8	1,479	1.4	2,679	1.5
North and Central America	Rest of World	93.0	17.8	57.3	10.8	279.6	12.4	2,934	14.8	6,661	11.0	12,197	11.7	21,217	12.3
South America		48.2	9.2	31.9	6.0	130.2	5.8								
Other areas		..	0.2	..	8.6	..	5.7								

Commonwealth = all except Canada (i.e. all in Sterling Area).

Western Europe = Finland, Sweden, Norway, Iceland, Denmark, Germany, Netherlands, Belgium, Luxembourg, France, Switzerland, Portugal, Spain, Italy, Greece, Austria, Turkey.

Eastern Europe = Poland, Hungary, Czechoslovakia, Albania, Bulgaria, Romania.

Middle East = Egypt, Syria, Lebanon, Arabia, Muscat and Oman, Iraq, Iran, Afghanistan, Israel, Jordan.

Far East = Siam, China, Korea, Taiwan, Japan, Portuguese India, Sumatra, Java, Dutch Borneo and other Dutch possessions, Burma.

Source: Statistical Abstracts; E. C. A. Mission.

Table 7 The balance of payments (£ million)

	Imports	Domestic exports	Re-exports	Net overseas investment earning[1]	Net invisible trade	Overall balance on current account
1900	523.1	291.2	63.2	103.6	109.1	37.9
1910	678.3	430.4	103.8	170.0	146.7	167.3
1920	1,932.6	1,334.5	222.8	200.0	395.0	252.0
1930	1,044.0	570.8	86.8	220.0	194.0	25.0
1937	1,027.8	521.4	75.1	210.0	176.0	−144.0
1950	2,608.2	2,171.3	84.8	237.0	357.0	221.0
1965	5,071	4,848		435	215	− 110.0
1975	21,972	18,768		949	1,695	−1,673.0
1983	61,341	60,625		2,831	3,632	2,916
1990	120,713	102,038		4,029	4,295	−14,380
1997	183,590	171,798		11,097	19,823	6,303

Source: Mitchell and Deane; *Annual Abstract; Key Statistics*
[1] This figure is taken after allowing for investment income paid to foreign corporations and individuals.

Table 8 Overseas investment

	Accumulated balance (£m)[1]	Investment income (£m)
1906	2,745	134
1910	3,351	170
1930	3,725	209
1937	3,754	198
1946	2,329	110
1956	6–7,000	660
1964	10,000	800
1979	12,500	1,100
1983	55,565	2,831
1984	70,000	5,000
1990	29,570	4,028
1997	102,604	11,097

Sources: Imlah, *Economic Elements in the 'Pax Britannica'*: E.C.A. Mission; Schonfield, *British Economic Policy since the War*: 1965 Budget speech; *Annual Abstract of Statistics.*

[1] There are of course debts and foreign investments in England to be set against these assets. In 1964 foreign investment in England was about £4,000m., the sterling balances amounted to £3,100m., and the government had other debts of £1,300m. and assets (not counted above) of about £1,000m. The 1983 and 1990 figures are net.

Index